The centrality of Milton to the study of English literature often obscures the intense debates that rage about his ideological allegiances. The reception and interpretation of Milton's texts consistently present him as either a Christian republican or a committed individualist, a radical, heretical free-thinker, or a traditional absolutist. In *Milton's Warring Angels*, William Kolbrener provides a critical account of the reception and interpretation of Milton's texts. He argues that the governing scheme of Milton criticism, the opposition of "satanic" and "angelic" readings, derives from a historiographical tradition rooted in the Enlightenment. The Enlightenment antithesis between reason and authority, Kolbrener argues, has generated a set of interpretive approaches that inevitably end up violating the meaning of Milton's texts. Kolbrener shows how Milton articulates his thought in lexicons which are never fully assimilable to paradigms of modernity drawn from the Enlightenment. Instead, Milton's prose and poetry mediate between apparently contradictory positions; they join without ever reconciling the satanic and the angelic. By showing how Milton has for centuries resisted tendentious appropriations and reductive readings, Kolbrener explains the continuing critical fascination with this most enigmatic of writers.

MILTON'S WARRING ANGELS

Frontispiece to *Milton's Paradise Lost*, ed. Richard Bentley, D. D.
(London: Jacob Tonson, 1732)

MILTON'S WARRING ANGELS

A study of critical engagements

WILLIAM KOLBRENER

Bar-Ilan University

CAMBRIDGE
UNIVERSITY PRESS

Published by the Press Syndicate of the University of Cambridge
The Pitt Building, Trumpington Street, Cambridge CB2 1RP
40 West 20th Street, New York, NY 10011-4211, USA
10 Stamford Road, Oakleigh, Melbourne 3166, Australia

First published 1997

Printed in the United Kingdom at the University Press, Cambridge

A catalogue record for this book is avialable from the British Library

Library of Congress cataloguing in publication data
Kolbrener, William.
Milton's warring angels: a study of critical engagements /
William Kolbrener.
p.   cm.
Includes bibliographical references and index.
ISBN 0 521 58104 4 (hardback)
1. Milton, John, 1608–1674 – criticism and interpretation – History.
2. Milton, John, 1608–1674 – Political and social views.
3. Christian poetry, English – History and criticism.   4. Milton,
John, 1608–1674. De Doctrina Christiana.   5. Milton, John,
1608–1674 – Religion.   1. Title.
PR3588.K65   1997
821'.4 – dc20
96–23377
CIP

ISBN 0 521 58104 4 hardback

VN

For my parents

Contents

Acknowledgments

I am grateful to the Woodrow Wilson Foundation and the Lady Davis Fellowship Trust for supporting the early stages of the research for this book. Though these institutional debts are great, they are far out-weighed by my debts to colleagues and teachers. Many have responded to parts of this work: I am especially grateful to Vince Blasi, Sanford Budick, Kathy Eden, Margaret Ferguson, Harold Fisch, Jean Howard, Murray Roston, James Shapiro, Maria DeSantis, Victoria Silver, Dan Vitkus, John Whitman, Joseph Wittreich, and Richard Wohlman. I must also thank Francine Horowitz who helped me overcome many of the challenges of doing research in Israel.

Janel Mueller trusted my "newer voice" and included my paper on *Areopagitica* for a General Session on Milton at the MLA Convention in 1990; this book largely grew out of that initial scholarly engagement. David Norbrook helped me – also in the early stages – to conceive the general contours of this study; he was also indispensable in sharpening the arguments of chapter 1. Marshall Grossman and J. G. A. Pocock provided much needed criticism of chapter 6; while Paula Loscocco's insights enabled me to refine the arguments of chapter 7. I must also express my gratitude to Stanley Fish who has remained a generous teacher and colleague, even when I have engaged critically with his work.

There are three scholars, however, to whom I owe a special debt of gratitude: Edward Tayler taught me – among *many* other things – the virtues of *reading*, while Jeffrey Perl continues to provide a model of scholarly discipline and integrity which I can only hope to emulate. David Scott Kastan (a Miltonist if ever there was one) continually astounds me with both his generosity and his learning; without his encouragement and guidance, this book simply would not have been written.

Finally, to my wife Leslie, *eishes chayil*, and to my parents – to whom this book is dedicated – the extent of my debts can hardly be expressed, never fully requited.

An earlier version of chapter 2, " 'Plainly Partial': The Liberal *Areopagitica*" appeared in *English Literary History* (1993), and is reprinted with permission of the Johns Hopkins University Press; chapter 6 includes material from a *Common Knowledge* article, " 'In a Narrow and to Him a Dark Chamber': Milton Unabridged" (1996). The frontispiece, from Richard Bentley's 1732 edition of *Paradise Lost* (London: Jacob Tonson), is reproduced from the General Collections of the Rare Book and Manuscript Library at Columbia University.

Introduction

> He was in fact ... of *both* parties.[1]
>
> Christopher Hill

On the frontispiece to Richard Bentley's 1732 edition of *Paradise Lost*, beneath the engraving of the young John Milton, stands the Latin epigram, *Nascuntur Poetae, non fiunt* – "poets are born, not made." Notwithstanding this epigrammatic pronouncement (which echoes throughout Bentley's *Paradise Lost*), Bentley's text – with its audacious emendations meant to "correct" Milton's text – bears witness that the author "Milton" has been continually "made" and re-made in history. Indeed, as Bentley's contemporary Lewis Theobald observed, Bentley's Milton wrote in the manner that Bentley thought he "ought to have."[2]

In the following study, Bentley's *Paradise Lost* not only serves to prove Hans-Georg Gadamer's assertion that literary interpretation is "a productive activity," but to help establish a particular pattern and dynamic to the reception and interpretation of John Milton's texts.[3] To be sure, this is to follow a dominant mode in modern Milton scholarship in which, from Thorpe's *Milton Criticism* of 1951 to Tennenhouse and Armstrong's recent *Imaginary Puritan*, the presence of earlier Miltons – the products of previous interpretive undertakings – have pushed critics in the direction of historiography.[4] The primary historiographical trope of this study is a simple one: that of Milton's "warring angels" – or more particularly, that of angelic and satanic "camps" of critics. This bifurcation among readers of Milton – who have constructed opposing, if not contradictory images of the poet – has long been evident: "Nothing is more obvious in modern Miltonic studies," A. S. P. Woodhouse observed in 1949, "than the emergence of two schools, one of which is so

I

much impressed by Milton's heresies as to lose sight of his fundamental Christianity, while the other, in not unnatural reaction, insists on the traditional character of the poet's religion."[5]

The confrontation between opposing sets of critics (the military metaphor remains apt) continues to this day – though political categories have in many cases supplanted older theological ones. One of the primary aims of this study is to begin to focus a question posed by Steven Marcus and Charles Taylor in relation to Milton: "How and under what conditions do figures of cultural significance acquire dichotomous images?"[6] The answer begins, I will suggest, in what opposing critics, in fact, *agree upon*: that Milton must conform to either the requisites of satanic heresy *or* angelic orthodoxy. To put it in this way is perhaps only to re-state the question, though it emphasizes that *dispute* has become – and remains – a primary mode of expression for Milton scholars. To explain the power of the trope of dispute in Milton's reception (in an attempt at a more direct answer to the question of Marcus and Taylor) leads to the second historiographical trope of this study – that of "Whig history."

The resilience of opposed readings of Milton – which have had a variety of historical manifestations – presupposes an agreement about the forms and *telos* of history. In its baldest form, the Whig or Enlightenment narrative goes something like this: modernity – reasonable, liberal, and democratic – emerges from out of, indeed in opposition to, a feudal, traditional, if not authoritarian middle ages. By means of the narrative implicit in what Gadamer has called the "conquest of mythos by logos," the subject asserts its independence from authority, transcendence (with other forms of authority) fades, matter becomes independent from spirit, and sacred discourses give way to profane.[7] In each of these implicit narratives, a new, and related, opposition emerges. Thus Enlightenment historiography and its privileged opposition of "mythos and logos" leads to several corollary antitheses – those between freedom and authority, immanence and transcendence, God and creation, the secular and profane.

Yet where Herbert Butterfield, in 1930, saw in the history of his contemporaries the representation of the "whole course of centuries upon what is really a directing principle of progress," today the literary historian's narratives of Whig optimism have transformed into entropic accounts – no less Whig – of decline.[8] That is, the paradigm of the Whig historian is no longer, as it was for Butterfield, the scholar who is "Protestant, progressive, and whig, and the very model of the 19th-century gentleman."[9] Thus, Whig optimism – though thriving in the rhetoric of the so-called post-ideological world – has given way, in academic discourses, to a more sober Whig pessimism, which nonetheless preserves the rudiments (the dichotomies) upon which historical *telos* is preserved. For whether historiographical periodizations optimistically embrace the present for its triumph over a darkened feudal (or ideological) past, or turn (in despair at the disjunctions of modern life) towards a utopian past or future, the historical narratives that result all presuppose, as part of their historiographical equipment, the dualistic lexicons of angels and devils – Milton's warring camps of critics.

Where angels and devils disagree on which side of the dualisms to emphasize, they agree powerfully – implicitly – upon the abstract antitheses. Although Milton studies have been recently complicated by more nuanced understandings of Milton's place in early modernity, Enlightenment versions of history – and their attendent dichotomies – still provide the backdrop for much in contemporary Milton criticism. Thus, notwithstanding the ways in which historians such as Quentin Skinner, J. G. A. Pocock, and Blair Worden have complicated our understanding of the historiography of early modernity in England (not to mention the ways in which these views have come to influence the work of Miltonists as diverse as Thomas Corns, Nigel Smith, and Annabel Patterson), many literary critics have continued to embrace an outmoded set of historiographical suppositions with a remarkable tenacity.

Indeed, though the literary academy is quick – and right – to point to the rhetoricity and contingency of all narrative constructs, literary critics often continue to adopt (and at times unreflectively) an historiographical narrative that presupposes the birth of modernity and the modern individual in the seventeenth century. Although Butterfield's *Whig Interpretation of History* warned against the moralizing triumphalism of Whig history, many literary critics persist in abiding by historiographical narratives that alternatively extol or deplore – but assume as given – the emergence of the modern individual in the seventeenth century.

Assuming different variations of this narrative, satanic and angelic camps proffer their own alternative images of Milton – pitting, for example, the *bourgeois* individual against the puritan absolutist. Which is to say that devils and angels agree on the terms of war, but line up on different sides of the battlefield. Stanley Fish, for example, the most notable of contemporary angelic critics, constructs an "absolutist" Milton in direct competition with the "liberal" Milton of a previous generation; while Christopher Kendrick, in the most powerful contemporary variation of the satanic argument, transmutes Milton from a liberal to a bourgeois, re-fitting the satanic Milton according to the requisites of post-Marxism. Indeed, an implicit argument of this study is that Fish's angelic reading of Milton – once dominant in the field – sets the terms for a variety of contemporary satanic readings of Milton.[10] This latest set of tensions between Fish and a new generation of neo-Marxist critics realizes a paradigm initiated in the late seventeenth century – where versions of the radical Milton and versions of the orthodox Milton continually vie to supplant one another. Though, to be sure, not every critic will fit neatly into the category of either "devil" or "angel," the distinction – as this study will suggest – sheds light on the dynamics and tendencies of Milton's reception, from the end of the seventeenth century up until the present.

If "devils and angels" and Whig history are the closely related – if not inter-connected – analytical tropes of this study, then *mediation* is its primary interpretive trope. Which is to emphasize at the outset that if the reader believes this to be *merely* a reception history, she is wrong. The "engagements" of the subtitle of this work refer to those of Milton's critics, as well as Milton's own. Following Fredric Jameson's 1981 essay, this study takes seriously the suggestion that Miltonists need to be aware of "that 'vanishing mediator'" in Milton's texts which Jameson describes as "the religious instance." In Jameson's analysis, the relationship between private and public spheres, the realms of "belief" and "politics," can only be understood through the "concrete mediation" between these spheres: that is, religion.[11] The tri-partite form of this study, with the opening section on politics, the closing section on poetics, and a long middle section on Milton's theology, is meant to echo, in formal terms, Jameson's important emphasis. This strategy aims not only to foreground the importance of the religious tract, *De Doctrina Christiana*, in Milton's corpus, but it also attempts to emphasize the confluence between Milton's politics, theology, and poetics.[12] Further, the term "mediation" is meant to suggest that the assumption of the existence of a *bourgeois* public sphere separate from the private sphere, as well as the version of history upon which this separation is founded (not only in Kendrick, but in Catherine Belsey, Francis Barker, Tennenhouse and Armstrong, and many of the contributors to the 1987 *Re-membering Milton*), produces (following an eighteenth-century tendency) an unnecessary bifurcation between Milton the "politician" and Milton the "poet" and "theologian."

But more than that, I should note that I employ this term more generally throughout as a way of demonstrating that Milton remained suspicious of individuation unless it was incorporated within – or *mediated* by – a larger context (whether it be the Christian republic of *Areopagitica* and *The Readie and Easie Way* or, what he calls in *Of Civil Power*, the "common ground" of the scriptures). Thus the parts of this study are focused upon recovering those discourses which *mediate* between what are often now conceived of as contradictory – if not incommensurable – positions. Part I demonstrates how Milton's Christian republicanism mediates between the competing claims of the individual and the *res publica*; Part II, how the radical textualism of *De Doctrina* mediates between the power of individual interpretations and the "inviolable" truth of scriptures; and Part III, how Milton's poetics mediate between the claims of a hermeneutic guided by a commitment to contingency (what I call in chapter 7 satanic immanence) and a hermeneutic guided by a commitment to the Absolute (or what I call angelic transcendence).

Mediation – the means through which Milton joins, *without reconciling*, apparently contradictory positions – serves in the readings which follow to move past the oppositions hypostatized in various competing readings of Milton. This entails neither a polemic against polemic (an attempt at a grand historical reconciliation), nor is it an attempt to employ "devils and angels" as a formalist dichotomy with Milton waiting as the mysterious light at the end of the tunnel. Rather, I want to suggest that the discourses present in Milton's work are unassimilable to certain interpretive paradigms of modernity. To historicize Milton in this fashion is not so much to claim him as occupying a mystical space before modernity (there is no ur-Milton in these pages), or embracing what T. S. Eliot might have called a unified sensibility, but rather to understand Milton as articulating his thought in lexicons which remain at least partly untranslatable into Enlightenment paradigms.

The oppositions that characterize Enlightenment habits of thought may be in accord with – and indeed constitute the reality of the contemporary world – yet they, with the narratives of history upon which they are founded, violate the meanings of Milton's texts. That is, notwithstanding the continuing contemporary debate on the relationship of, for example, reason and authority, and Habermas's trenchant critique of Gadamerian tradition,[13] the unconditional opposition between these two terms, *for Milton*, simply did not exist. This, like the other oppositions which parallel it, were, for Milton, as for Gadamer, in a basically *ambivalent* relation. Because of the fundamental ambivalence implicit in the style and structure of Milton's thought (in both his poetry and prose) Milton at once lends himself to, but strongly and *finally* resists, the antinomies that so preoccupy the "warring angels" of this study.

In the argument that follows, I suggest that devils and angels produce different kinds of "Whig" readings of Milton. If the complexities and paradoxes of Miltonic discourse lead to what Herbert Butterfield has identified as the necessity of "abridgement," then progressive and conservative "abridgements" are equally whiggish: in the reading offered in chapter 1, the authoritarian and angelic *Areopagitica* in which reason and difference are denied is no less whiggish – no less polemical – than the libertarian and satanic one in which they are celebrated.[14] As Butterfield's student, J. G. A. Pocock, has pointed out, the "varieties of Whiggism" include not only "the complacent progressivism" that Butterfield "anatomized," but also the "complacent traditionalism" which he "admired" in his later work.[15] For Pocock, the "varieties of Whiggism," therefore, include a conservative variety which coincides in Milton studies, as I shall argue in chapter 6, with angelic attempts (as in Bentley and Stanley Fish) to correct earlier satanic versions of Milton.

While the methodology of this study may bear some resemblance to that of Thomas N. Corns, whose investigation into "the plurality of Miltonic ideology" has led him (following the historiographical impulse) to affirm that the "multiplicity of Miltons" is "reflective" of "the cultural and political assumptions" of its various interpreters, there are important differences between Corns's assumptions and my own.[16] Though I will not go so far as to agree with Stanley Fish that "there is only one true interpretation of *Paradise Lost*,"[17] the current sets of readings, ultimately intentionalist (and thus more like Fish's than either Corns's or Jameson's), argues for a Milton who produced texts, not "internally contradictory," as in Corns's reading, but *polyvalent*. Where Corns argues for various distinct versions of Milton, each bearing its own aspect of "unity," I am arguing for a unified *reading* of Milton which – to echo the primary metaphor of mediation in the seventeenth century, *discordia concors* – has multiple aspects. In Corns's reading, Milton's critics have extrapolated unified readings from Milton's "convoluted" text; in my reading, it is the critics who have made Milton "convoluted" by insisting upon monolithic readings of his works. This is not, however, to argue an ahistorical or metacritical reading of Milton, but rather to assert that the complex unity of Milton's texts has been occluded by powerful and persistent interpretive paradigms within Milton studies.

The Milton invoked here, like Fish's, may be singular, though made possible by what Gadamer calls, citing Vico, "copia, the abundance of viewpoints."[18] There may be many ways of historicizing *this* study, though the narrative which I would choose to emphasize now is personal: the polyvalent yet singular Milton constructed here, is built on my own *sensus communis* – the various Miltonists with whom I have been privileged to study and work. Despite their critical differences, they have shown me, in their generosity and in their common Miltonic desire to "close truth to truth," that the "war in heaven" may not be the most appropriate paradigm for interpreters of Milton's works.

PART I

Politics

CHAPTER I

"Plainly partiall": the liberal Areopagitica

In considering the "spiritual architecture" of an England overflowing
with "schismaticks and sectaries," Milton in the *Areopagitica* compares the
"great reformation" of a nation to the building of Solomon's temple: "And
when every stone is laid artfully together, it cannot be united into a
continuity, it can but be contiguous in this world ... (II 555).[1] There may
be "many dissections in the quarry," many "schisms" and differences
"among men ... ere the house of God can be built," Milton writes. But
he continues, paradoxically, "the perfection consists in this": "Out of the
many moderat varieties and brotherly dissimilitudes ... arises the goodly
and gracefull symmetry that commends the whole pile and structure"
(II 555). From out of the contiguity and particularity intrinsic to the fallen
world, Milton perceives at least the possibility of "continuity," a
"perfection" organizing and ordering difference.

Milton's temple trope, like the totality about which T. W. Adorno
writes in his *Aesthetic Theory*, preserves particulars even "in their diffuse,
divergent and contradictory condition." For Adorno, the demand for
"unity" does not merely assimilate particularity, but it also, crucially,
preserves "the individual moment." Within the context of Adorno's
negative dialectics, as in Milton's *Areopagitica*, the concrete maintains its
own integrity, though it also reveals "the ever-elusive entirety in itself ...
in line with a pre-established disharmony rather than a pre-established
harmony."[2] As Edward Tayler writes, by both stressing "juxtaposition"
and moving "toward identity," Milton's temple trope balances the
tensions of "differences" maintained "in agreement."[3] Milton's reformed
England, therefore, establishes its "goodly and graceful symmetry"
through "brotherly dissimilitudes," at once mediating *and* preserving the
differences it must acknowledge.

Unmediated particularity – the experience of an untranscendable
"contiguity" – remains for Milton, as for Thomas Hobbes, a synecdoche
for civil war, where the lack of any form of mediation – "no knowledge of
the face of the earth; no account of time; no arts; no letters" – drives

opposing forces "in mutual opposition to nothing." For Hobbes, a disunited multitude is shunned in the way that Hegel was to shun "bad infinity"; difference is only recognized – not to say legitimated – in so far that it is capable of assimilation through public mediation. For Hobbes, the subject's ability to "*personate* ... to *act* ... to represent *himself*" is at once the precondition *and* result of the Leviathan's accession to power. Through the Leviathan's authority, "given him," writes Hobbes, "by every particular man in the commonwealth, he hath the use of so much power and strength conferred on him, that ... he is able to form the wills of them all." The private "Actor," "Author," and "Authority" can only come into being *with* the commonwealth. Individuality, and hence agency, thus only exists for Hobbes when the "commonwealth" – a "plurality of voices" in "one will" – confers subjectivity, a "*persona*," upon its constituents.[4]

"Hobbes," as David Quint writes, "could be the name" for that which all of Milton's "various political strategies ... converge to resist";[5] nevertheless, for both Hobbes and Milton, the individual is understood only in relation to the constraints imposed by varying forms of public mediation. Although Hobbes's statist politics differ drastically from the civic republicanism of *Areopagitica*, Milton's own self-constitution as one who wishes to "promote" his "Countries liberty" (II 487) occurs only within the context of the public realm (which he helped to define) where individual agency is at once independent *and* mediated.[6] For Milton, individual differences, what he describes as "contiguities," are like "the confused seeds" imposed upon Psyche in *Areopagitica*. They threaten, unless the "many cunning resemblances" between them are "discerned" (II 514), to transform into what Hobbes most feared – a disunited and warring multitude.

The notion, in Hiram Haydn's phrase, that the seventeenth century saw "the ultimate desertion of the universal for the particular" through "the decentralizing individuation of the nominalist" continues to persist as part of an historiographical tradition that dates back at least to Dr. Johnson.[7] Johnson's celebrated – though peremptory – discussion of *discordia concors* transforms the world-view of the metaphysicals into a quaint and antiquated trope. The most significant aspect of Johnson's notorious formulation of the poetics of Cowley and his school – "the most heterogeneous ideas are yoked by violence together" – may well be the adverbial phrase. By "violence" their "slender conceits" created only "dissimilar images," thus asserting that heterogeneity – "exility of particulars" – lay beneath the veneer of metaphysical wit. In Johnson's formulation, the oppositions that constitute *discordia concors* were already understood as fundamentally different and opposed – "laboured particularities" – only to be joined "by violence."[8] For Johnson and the eighteenth century, the dualism of the universal and particular had ossified into an irreconcilable opposition. In contrast, for the metaphysical poets, and for Milton, who shared many of their tendencies, individual difference could only come into being as an aspect of similarity: contiguity and continuity emerge at once.

The "paradox" which Raymond Williams points to in his *Keywords*, that "*Individual* originally meant indivisible" is of particular relevance. Individual, as Williams observes "stresses a distinction from others," while indivisible "implies a necessary connection." Milton's texts – which accommodate both senses of the term – may be a part of that "extraordinary social and political history" that "parallels the development of the modern … from the original meaning."[9] But it is Milton's critics, and not Milton himself, who represent the endpoint of that history. That is, the Milton triumphantly proclaiming in "the voice of reason and convincement" his "universal propositions on individual liberty,"[10] as well as the Milton whose "individualism" serves as "the agent of the general disintegration of feudal ties," need to be further interrogated as critical, not Miltonic, creations.

"Our ancient history is the possession of the liberal," E. A. Freeman remarked in his *The Growth of the English Constitution*.[11] And, so we could add, is our literary history. Although the Burckhardtian conception of the Renaissance as the "age of the discovery of man the individual" has undergone considerable critique in the works of contemporary critics,[12] literary historiography still reflects the dualism so often attributed to Burckhardt – that between Renaissance autonomy and feudal obligation. Indeed, Milton is often located as the central figure in this historiographical narrative, as one of, in Michael Walzer's words, the "bold speculators free, more or less, from traditional controls" who overthrew "the old patterns of passivity and acquiescence."[13] While over half-a-century ago, Butterfield's *Whig Interpretation of History* warned against the moralizing triumphalism of Whig history, literary critics persist in abiding by historiographical narratives which alternatively extol or deplore – but assume as given – the emergence of the modern individual in the seventeenth century. Indeed Walzer's is an example of Whig optimism which, as Herbert Butterfield writes, "organizes the whole course of centuries upon what is really a directing principle of progress."[14] By contrast, the historiographical assumptions in Eliot's "dissociation of sensibility," of which Milton is the repressed and canonically effaced agent, is a pessimistic version of the same Whig narrative. Marxists, equipped with a more complex manifestation of the same historiographical paradigm, often retain a similar period scheme: under the guise of categories such as "social collectivity" (against which an emergent market-place individualism is posited), the old periodization, with its attendant antinomies, reappears.[15]

Milton criticism continues to be governed by these antinomies and, moreover, dominated by a paradigm of individualism (one which may be said to have developed simultaneously with liberal discourses of the individual) wholly foreign to Milton's thought. John Toland – whose Milton "thought constraint of any sort to be the utmost misery"[16] – may have inaugurated the paradigm while Sensabaugh's 1952 *That Grand Whig Milton* stands as a testimony to the paradigm's endurance. For Catherine Belsey, the autonomy promised in *Areopagitica* is never completely fulfilled;[17] while for Harold Bloom, reviving the Romantic celebration of Milton the Individual, the autonomy established in Milton's texts is total. "Milton carried within himself," writes Bloom, "the extreme individualism of the Puritan Left Wing" and "finally became a Protestant Church of one, a sect unto himself."[18] Christopher Kendrick similarly emphasizes the "central autonomy of Milton's ... individualism," declaring him to be "an ideologist and poet of emergent capitalism," the agent of the "general disintegration of feudal ties."[19] In all these readings, Blake's Milton – of the devil's party – resisting Divine Providence and asserting the independence of the autonomous individual is celebrated again and again.

No doubt, it may be useful to understand Milton from a perspective that includes critics as diverse as Sensabaugh, Bloom, and Kendrick (remembering, as J. G. A. Pocock does, that Whig and Marxist historiographies dovetail at a certain point).[20] However, before asserting that Milton's works are "produced by a Protestantism pressed into the service of an historically specific form of individualism,"[21] that is, before situating Milton's individualism within the context of the classical liberal and Marxist historiographical schemes, it may be worthwhile to locate that individualism within the discursive contexts from which it emanated. Before, therefore, we attend exclusively to the Milton who calls in *Doctrine and Discipline of Divorce* for the independence of "every mind and spirit ... created each so different each from other," we ought to recall the Milton who enjoins these spirits, "by the skill of wise conducting, all to become uniform in vertue" (II 230). We may then find Milton's texts capable of sustaining, if not producing, ambivalence towards oppositions that the bifurcating tendencies of Milton scholarship have long since hypostatized into irreconcilable extremes. In Milton's civic republican discourses of *Areopagitica*, the competing claims made by the individual – "every mind and spirit" – and the community – "all" those "uniform in vertue" – are both addressed, without assimilating either to the other.

THE LIBERAL *AREOPAGITICA*

Catherine Belsey's recent designation of *Areopagitica* as "one of the founding and canonical texts of modern liberalism"[22] is in consonance with an entire tradition that found in the tract, as Thomson did, an "admirable defense of the best of human rights."[23] Yet even within the Whig tradition that held up Milton – as Sensabaugh would have it, "as an oracle to all young gentlemen in England"[24] – there were those for whom the rhetoric of *Areopagitica* aroused suspicion. Even T. Holt White, the parliamentary reformer and 1819 editor of the tract, expressed some reservations about Milton's commitment to toleration. "From some passages in the early part of this oration," White observes, "incurious Readers might be led to conclude hastily, that there were topics on which Milton conceived Discussion ought not to take an unrestrained course." White, however, is quick to apologize for the Milton who, he claims, was able to "develop principles highly liberal" for his "times." "In a more enlightened era," White argues, appropriating Milton in the interest of constitutional reform, "he would have laid claim to a larger measure of freedom."[25]

In this century, however, some of Milton's critics began to lose their confidence in the tolerationist Milton. Arthur Barker, for example, in his magisterial *Milton and the Puritan Dilemma*, laments Milton's failure to articulate a truly liberal program. If it were not for the "single fundamental condition" that men "believe in scripture," Barker observes, then Milton would have articulated "a complete theory of religious freedom."[26] In similar fashion, Christopher Hill asserts that Milton's theology was "fundamentally individualist" in its emphasis on the powers of "the individual conscience," though, like Barker, he finds Milton wanting: "He was not prepared to trust the spirit in all men"; he was "blind" to, and thus never pursued, "the higher rationality of democracy." This "rationality," what others would call the "logic of capital," provokes Hill to wonder "why Milton could not let go of his hold on God." For Hill, history follows a logical trajectory, which Milton's stubborn prejudices (alternately construed by Hill as "class interest" and "respect for social hierarchy") prevent him from pursuing. From Hill's perspective, Milton's thought – rife with contradictions only to be resolved through history – is rejected as a species of false consciousness. "Milton is not necessarily the worse for his class limitations," Hill writes, "but he lacks the Digger emphasis on human love." He "could never cross the chasm," Hill laments, "which separated him from a man like Winstanley." Thus – for Hill, as for Barker – Milton becomes the avatar of a partial liberalism: the failed or, at best, the proto-liberal.[27]

In John Illo's 1965 article, "The Misreading of Milton," White's ambivalences and Barker's and Hill's reluctant condemnations are articulated from a liberal perspective that locates Milton, especially the *Areopagitica*, entirely outside of the liberal tradition. In Illo's explicit cold-war rhetoric, Milton's London is compared to "Petrograd in 1919 and Havana in 1965" and the *Areopagitica*, not "liberal or libertarian even in its time," is dismissed as a "militant and exclusivist revolutionary pamphlet." It was the Romantics, Illo asserts, who "reinforced the image of a libertarian Milton, venerating in him the same supposed unrestrained tolerance for which Johnson had censured him."[28] Illo's polemical analysis *does* illuminate how post-Restoration (angelic) and Romantic (satanic) judgments of Milton conspire in the same mis-reading, both emphasizing the increased tendency towards "individuation" and particularization in the seventeenth century.[29] Yet Illo's affiliation of *Areopagitica* with "the revolutionary intolerance" of "Che Guevera" is no more true than Dr. Johnson's contention that the *Areopagitica* provided "unbound liberty" for "every skeptick" to "teach his follies."[30] In a critical history where liberty and authority (a corollary of the Johnsonian opposition between the particular and the universal) are viewed as irreconcilable opposites, Milton is classed alternatively as the voice of individual liberty or of an authoritarian intolerance.[31] But the two Miltons – the liberal and the authoritarian – are merely flip-sides of one another.

THE CHRISTIAN REPUBLIC

From Illo's explicitly liberal perspective any synthesis of private and public spheres seems impossible (or authoritarian); when Milton argues for the confluence of these spheres, the liberal Illo perceives only a totalitarian argument. Yet when Milton invokes Euripides on his frontispiece – "This is true Liberty when free born men / Having to advise the public may speak free" (II 485) – he is not operating within a liberal paradigm. Rather, Milton argues implicitly for the superiority of the classical city-states – of "wisest Commonwealths" (II 507) – and attempts to enlarge the discursive horizons of his own Commonwealth. When "complaints" may be "freely heard, deeply consider'd, and speedily reform'd" (II 487), the public sphere – and its available forms of mediation – is expanded.[32] Contemporary scholars, however, continue to read Milton and the seventeenth century through the matrix of negative liberty and, what C. B. Macpherson has called, "possessive individualism"; while the *Areopagitica*, in its very form – the five-part structure of the classical deliberative oration – argues implicitly for the creation of a diffused, inclusive, and corporate authority.[33] Such a corporate authority, reliant as it is upon the language of classical humanism, places the *Areopagitica* within the context of an emergent republicanism. Although, as Quentin Skinner writes, classical republicans may have been "the earliest group of political writers who insist with full self-consciousness on a categorical disjunction between the state and those who have control of it," they make "no comparable distinction between the powers of the state and those of its citizens." On the contrary, writes Skinner, "the whole thrust of classical republican theory is directed towards an ultimate equation of the two."[34]

Yet this alternative strain of political thought remains largely inaccessible to critics who find their views on literary history corroborated in the work of professional historians like Macpherson. For the thesis that the seventeenth century saw the emergence of an individual as "essentially the proprietor of his own person and capacities" owing "nothing to society" renders the presence of civic republican discourses – with their implied equation between public and private spheres – virtually invisible.[35] In his on-going response to Macpherson, however, J. G. A. Pocock has challenged the adequacy of an historiographical model in which bourgeois individualism and "market relations" are determined to be "deeply embedded in the seventeenth-century foundations."[36] We have found, Pocock writes, "that a 'bourgeois ideology,' a paradigm for capitalist man as *zōon politikon*, was immensely hampered in its development by the omnipresence of Aristotelian and civic humanist values."[37] Although Pocock agrees with Macpherson that the liberal individual acquires his role "in the possession, conveyance and administration of things," and not through the "right to govern," he affirms, *contra*

Macpherson, that the conception of negative liberty, which distinguishes between "freedom and authority, individuality and sovereignty, private and public" emerges – and still only haltingly – in the eighteenth century.[38]

Pocock's recognition of the contingency of Whig and Marxist histories, which insist upon the bifurcation of "private and public" in the seventeenth century, allows the civic humanism of the period – including the idiosyncratic republicanism of Milton's *Areopagitica* – to come into focus. Indeed the methodologies of both Pocock and Quentin Skinner combine to inform the works collected in the recent *Milton and Republicanism* which sets Milton squarely in the context of European republican traditions.[39] Though Milton, as Thomas N. Corns suggests in this volume, did not articulate a full-fledged republican political agenda (with all of its constitutional components) until the *Readie and Easie Way*, even Milton's early prose works were informed by what he calls a "republican consciousness."[40]

Milton manifests this "republican consciousness" in *Areopagitica* where the relationship between the private and public is conceived as primary. As Milton insists, it is the relation between the "privat Orator" and the "Commonwealth" that preserves and insures "the utmost bound of civil liberty." Thus Dion Prusaeus, the "stranger" and "privat Orator" who offered "counsel" to the Rhodians becomes – along with Isocrates – the model of "old and elegant humanity" whom Milton seeks to "imitate" (II 489). Milton, fashioning himself as the ideal civic humanist, having withdrawn to Horton to pursue a life "wholly dedicated to studious labours," demands the "honor done ... to men who professed the study of wisdom and eloquence" in the days of the "Parlament of *Athens*." If ever these men "had aught in publick to admonish the State," Milton argues, they were heeded not only "in their own country," but "Cities and Sinories heard them gladly, and with great respect" (II 489-90).

That is, private utterance (as that of Isocrates who "from his private house wrote that discourse" to the Athenian parliament) acquires currency and public authority merely through its articulation. The very fact, however, that the "prudent spirit" of Lords and Commons "acknowledges and obeyes the voice of reason from what quarter soever it be heard speaking" (II 490) testifies to the superiority of the modernization of the classical paradigm. Indeed, Milton finds the Lords and Commons "superior" to those "wisest commonwealths" of old, because, with the advent of the printing press, more voices (more than, for example, that of the lone Isocrates) can be "heard speaking." Publication, as Nigel Smith writes, "was an act whereby the ethos of virtuous speaking was literally extended into a wider forum of public exchange."[41] Thus, in 1644, Milton is not forced to skulk "privily from house to house," but "openly by writing," he can "publish to the world what his opinion is" and "what his reasons" (II 548). Although Jesus justified himself when he "preacht in publick," Milton openly proclaims the superiority of printing: for "writing is more publick than preaching" and "more easie to refutation" (II 548). And therefore, those who write what "they foresee may advance the publick good" (II 486) – barring the interference of some "patriarchal licencer" (II 533) – will not find themselves "wanting such accesse" on account of their "private condition" (II 486).

Indeed, the very publication of the tract of *Areopagitica*, with its translation of the classical epigram printed on its cover (for all to read), affirms Milton's argument. As Milton writes, "the whole Discourse propos'd will be a certaine testimony" for those "who wish and promote their Countries liberty" (II 487). Once "propos'd," the *Areopagitica*, a specific political intervention to "advance the publick good" enacts by entering the realm of "controversie, and new invention" (II 557) the very argument that it proposes. So Milton acknowledges the performative aspect of his own argument: "I now manifest by the very sound of this which I shall utter, that wee are already in good part arriv'd" (II 487).[42]

The printing press enables Milton to envision a civic context – informed by a prophetic spirit – where he can imagine "not only our sev'nty Elders, but all the Lords people are become Prophets" (II 555-56) – a utopian civic republic where all voices are "heard." Though some may be jealous of this prophecy of the multitude as was Joshua, "young in goodnesse," who protested against the spread of prophesy in the Israelite camp, Milton warns against their premonitions: "The adversarie again applauds, and waits the hour, when they have brancht themselves out, saith he, small anough into parties and partitions, then will be our time. Fool! he sees not the firm root, out of which we all grow, though into branches ..." (II 556).[43] While for many in the 1640s, as Smith has observed, "the sheer weight of public outspokenness" seemed to be "unnatural and unhealthy," leading to the multiplication of "private languages" and the disappearance of "consensus," Milton viewed things differently.[44] The proliferation of prophesy does not lead, Milton argues, "as the applauders of our differences" contend, to "parties and partitions" ('corruption" in the lexicon of civic republicanism), but to *"unity of Spirit"* (II 565). And the hoped-for emergence of a nation of prophets does not lead to an autonomous private sphere, what Christopher Kendrick describes, following Macpherson, as the result of the dissolution of the connection between political and religious discourses.[45]

Milton, however, *does* appear to abhor the consequences of the inference that if "we think to regulat Printing, thereby to rectifie manners, we must regulat all recreations and pastimes" (II 523). Indeed, when he delineates the ramifications that follow upon the licensing of printing, he again seems to be remarking on the undesirability of such restraint:

There must be licensing dancers, that no gesture, motion, or deportment be taught our youth ... Our garments also should be referr'd to the licensing of some more sober work-masters, to see them cut into a lesse wanton garb. Who shall regulat all the mixt conversation ... Who shall still appoint what shall be discours'd, what presum'd? (II 523, 526)

Yet here Milton is *not* advocating license, but affirming that "manners" cannot be legislated – that they must and *will* emerge through other means: "These things *will be and must be*; but how they shall be lest hurtfull, how lest enticing, herein consists the grave and governing wisdom of a State" (II 526; emphasis added). "Impunity and remissenes," Milton asserts, "are the bane of a Commonwealth." The "great art" of the commonwealth, therefore, lies in discerning when "the law is to bid restraint and punishment," and when "perswasion only is to work" (II 527). Persuasion – the prerogative of those given the "freedom to choose" (II 527)[46] – permits "debate," "gentle meetings and gentle dismissions" in "liberall and frequent audience" (II 567). The reasoned debate of the prophetic multitude, enabled through the printing press and the expansion of the classically defined public sphere, does not lead to the libertarian cultivation of a thoroughly privatized realm ("lest" Milton be "condemn'd" of "introducing licence" [II 493]), but to the emergence of – and voluntary adherence to – communally defined behavioral norms.

Those who know the "virtue" of "temperance," and who have been trusted with the "gift of reason" can thus live "without particular Law or prescription" (II 513). "God committs" such men to their own "managing," each left to exercise "his owne leading capacity ... to be his own chooser." In this "capacity," they are "sufficient," comparable to the Israelites to whom God dispensed their daily portion of manna: "And therefore when he himself tabl'd the Jews from heaven, that Omer which was every mans daily portion of Manna, is computed to have bin more

than might have well suffic'd the heartiest feeder thrice as many meals"
(II 513). For the Israelites, who Milton holds as a paradigm, there is no
necessity for "Law" or "compulsion" in "things ... govern'd only by
exhortation" (II 514). Yet Milton's representation of Exodus 16 is
misleading in presuming the sufficiency and "temperance" of the
Israelite multitude. Indeed, in this representation, Milton's ambivalence
towards the rationality of classical republican precedents begins to be
evidenced, and the "superiority" of the Christian republic is underscored.
Hughes claims that Milton's account of the biblical narrative "lays stress
on the abundance of the supply" of manna;[47] it does that, but it also
occludes the *intemperance* of the Israelites who, against the directive of
Moses, hoard their daily measure so as to have an abundant supply for
the following day. Thus Exodus 16:20: "Notwithstanding they hearkened
not unto Moses; but some of them left of it until the morning, and it bred
worms, and stank: and Moses was wroth with them." Milton's omission
tends to emphasize the reasoned temperance of the Israelite multitude
while obscuring their need for divine guidance that comes through
Moses' "wroth" (not to mention the direct intervention of God who
brings disease to their hoarded manna).[48] The diffuse and public
mediation of the Jews is sufficient, though the effaced authority of the
prophetic mediator is registered even in its omission.

This omission should perhaps be recalled as a balance to that other
episode of "mis-reading" in *Areopagitica*, where Milton commits what
Bloom calls the "astonishing mistake" of bringing the Palmer to
accompany Guyon into the Spenserian Cave of Mammon (II 516). In the
often-discussed Miltonic rendering of the Spenserian episode, "true
temperance under the person of *Guion*" is realized only through the
accompaniment of the mis-remembered Palmer.[49] Though the appearance
of the Palmer (as a figure of Reason) may seem to emphasize the
sufficiency of independent rational agency, the Palmer's actual *embodiment*
in Milton's text foregrounds the presence of – and need for – a "teacher
guide." Indeed, I would argue, with John Guillory, that the Palmer's
presence as mediator in *Areopagitica*, registers "the danger" implicit in the
"self-reliant posture" argued throughout the *Areopagitica*.[50] By contrast,
in the representation of Exodus 16, Milton not only effaces the "wroth"
of the prophetic mediator, but also the dangers incurred through the
self-reliance of those acting without guidance.

In Milton's representation of the Spenserian text, the figure of
mediation is required and surreptitiously smuggled in, while, by
contrast, in the biblical episode, the figure of mediation – understood as

an obstacle to "virtue" – is surreptitiously smuggled out. In Milton's "mis-readings" of these two episodes, we begin to see the dialectic of *Areopagitica*, how Milton will at once assert that "evill doctrine not with books can propagate, except a teacher guide," and that all "tractates, whether false or true, are ... not to be *understood without a guide*" (II 520, 519). One of the central paradoxes of the tract lies in the ambivalence towards figures of mediation in *Areopagitica*: Milton simultaneously argues for the independence of reasoned temperance (for which the paradigm is the Israelites in the desert) and for the necessity of mediation (for which Spenser's Palmer is the paradigm). The most notable case of such ambivalence occurs as Milton asserts his own pedagogic authority against the power of state authority: "And how can a man teach with autority, which is the life of teaching, how can he be a Doctor in his book as he ought to be ... whenas all he teaches, all he delivers," is "under the correction of his patriarchal licenser" (II 532-33).

The correlate of Milton's ambivalence towards figures of mediation in *Areopagitica* is an ambivalence towards free choice – figured powerfully in Milton's representation of the "perverted Arminius." The experience of the "acute and distinct Arminius," "perverted meerly by the perusing of a namelesse discours writt'n at *Delf*" (II 520), explicitly contradicts Milton's earlier assertion that to "a discreet and judicious Reader" (not "acute and distinct"?) "bad books" serve "to discover, to confute, to forewarn, and to illustrate" (II 512, 513). Maurice Kelley has pointed out that Milton's representation of Arminius is inconsistent with the rest of the argument of the tract; that Milton by this time had "at least tacitly accepted the Arminian position on free will"; and that the argument of *Areopagitica* – stripped of its Arminian implications – "would be an empty one, for trial can purify only those who have freedom of choice." [51] Milton characteristically accepts – and the tract embodies – Arminian doctrine, while he rejects Arminian authority. As Regina Schwartz puts it, writing in another context, for Milton "authority becomes the instrument to de-authorize." [52]

In *Areopagitica*, even as forms of mediation are asserted, they seem to be subverted; thus the "faithful guidance" of the House of Commons is always in some sense limited for Milton by "the strong assistance of God our deliverer" (II 487). For Milton, such conviction manifests itself in epistemological considerations which make the reasoned guidance of even the House of Commons problematic. As Pocock observes, behind "all the acute, rational, and earthly criticism," expressed by the seventeenth-century Reformers, "there lay inseparably an element of apocalyptic and antinomian conviction."[53] The "antinomian element" expressed in *Areopagitica* leads to a revaluation and refinement of the classical paradigm.[54] For religious belief, as Nancy Streuver writes, necessitated changes in the role of the "Christian orator." An epistemological skepticism, Streuver observes, expresses "doubt of the scope and power of the subjective *judicium* of both the addresser and the addressee."[55] Indeed, Milton's skepticism extended to both of these agents, both the "addressee" and "addresser" assumed by *Areopagitica* – that is, parliament and Milton himself.

For Milton, like the "acute and distinct Arminius," the Lords and Commons (as all forms of "state prudence") are susceptible to error: "This I know, that errors in a good government and in a bad are equally almost incident" (II 570). "Governors," he writes, "may be mistak'n" (II 534). Thus, when Milton praises his parliamentary audience, he praises them precisely for their ability to recognize their errors: their "uprightnesse of ... judgement ... not wont to be partiall," "renders" them as "willing to repeal any Act" of their "own setting forth" "as any set forth" by their "Predecessors" (II 490). The revisionary character of truth, and its ultimate inaccessibility, is a recurrent theme in *Areopagitica*. He who "thinks we are to pitch our tents here," writes Milton, "and have attain'd the utmost prospect of reformation, that the mortall glasse wherein we contemplate, can shew us ... that man by this very opinion declares, that he is yet farre short of Truth" (II 549). For Milton, truth lies in admitting error (errors which "known, read, and collated, are of main service & assistance towards the speedy attainment of what is truest" [II 513]); and the ideal Miltonic mediator is left to foreground the recognition of error.

The rhetorical strategy of *Areopagitica* is to effect just this foregrounding. When Milton complains in the midst of his discourse that he has "almost" been "prevented" by his own argument, "by being clear already while thus much hath bin explaining" (II 521), his syntax reveals the tenuous nature of the authority he is assuming. At once "clear already" and set in the past, the argument – as the verb – is *also* progressive, and therefore susceptible to continual revision. For when "Truth ... gets a free ... hand," Milton explains, she "opens herself faster, then the pace of method and discours can overtake her" (II 521). Thus Milton claims that *Areopagitica*, his "whole Discourse propos'd," will be a "certaine testimony, if not a Trophey" to all "who wish and promote their Countries liberty" (II 487). At once a "Trophey," Milton's tract attains authority as a public utterance aiming "to advance the publick good." As "testimony," however, Milton asserts the contingency of *Areopagitica*, how even *its* pedagogy is susceptible of revision, and how the tract, like St. Jerome's "lenten dream," is "plainly partiall" (II 510). *Areopagitica* cannot stand in for the "publick good" (were it to do so, it would become a "Trophey"); but it is part of the continual process of "still closing up truth to truth" (II 551) – a process which, because of the nature of discourse itself (the darkness of the "mortall glasse"), must be perpetual. While others may have seen the emergence of the press in England as creating conditions which, as Smith suggests, "radically destabilized conceptions of truth, trustworthiness, and authority," Milton was able to assimilate such experiences of instability into the very rhetoric of his tract and to that process of closing "truth to truth."[56]

This is not to suggest, however, that *Areopagitica* is entirely "self-consuming," and that its efficacy as a specific political intervention is intended to be negligible. In foregrounding the limitations of its own local claims, *Areopagitica* may insist upon its own particularity (and its mere shadowing of the "immortall feature of lovelines and perfection" [II 549]). This, however, is neither a concession, nor is it a cause, as Stanley Fish would have it, for despair. It is the condition of discourse, always "plainly partial."

Indeed, in Fish's work, there is a tendency to empty Miltonic discourse of its particularity – not to mention its specific political content. In *Surprised by Sin*, for example, Fish constructs an angelic Milton for whom any political engagement is fruitless. In his "larger scheme," Fish writes, "the conviction that man can do nothing is accompanied by the conviction that Christ has taken it upon himself to do it all."[57] For Fish, (and here his "Reason in *The Reason of Church Government*" is also representative),[58] there is the sense that Milton's rational discourse, always acknowledging its own inadequacy, points towards a non-discursive truth only achieved through faith.

In Fish's more recent work on *Areopagitica*, he has moved slightly away from the extremity of his earlier position, and warns that the "impurity of difference must not be denied or lamented but embraced." He goes on to say, however, that the "incompleteness" that characterizes historical discourse "must be at once lamented [*sic*] and protected."[59] For the lamenting Fish, "difference" is only to be "protected" as a pointer to "that bliss" which "awaits us." Nonetheless, the Miltonic model of virtue as John Rumrich has asserted, is *not* Bunyan's Christian "fleeing with his hand over his ears crying Life, Life, Eternal Life."[60] That is, Milton's sense of "bliss" is in a far more complex relation with the historically particular "publick good" than Fish's argument permits. The "incompleteness that characterizes historical discourse" does not lead to its total abandonment – or, in Fish's lexicon, to its total "self-consuming."

Rather, as Marshall Grossman relates, writing of *Paradise Lost*, Miltonic "representation is the mimesis that ultimately negates, yet *preserves* the experience of mundane contingency."[61] "Mundane contingency" – whether it manifests itself in the form of the doctrines of the perverse Arminius or the "Orders" of Parliament – must be preserved, though such preservation is stipulated upon the recognition of the contingency of mundane authority (upon its ultimate negation). Without such negation, Milton writes, there is the "dead congealment" of a "rigid externall formality" (II 564).

Of such "dead congealment," where private utterance claims to offer a definitive embodiment of the "publick good," Milton writes sarcastically: "How goodly, and how to be wisht, were such an obedient unanimity as this, what a fine conformity would it starch us all into? doubtles a staunch and solid peece of frame-work, as any January could freeze together" (II 545). The "publick good" in *Areopagitica* is as evasive as its constituents. "Lords and Commons" make up part of that constituency, and they are praised so long as they evidence their desire "not to be partial" – that is, so long as they refuse a monopoly over the "publick good." The closing of the *Second Defence*, like the implicit argument of *Areopagitica*, enjoins its readers, as David Quint notes, "not to fall from their liberty into a worship of the state and its workings."[62] The Christian commonwealth is "superior" to the classical republic precisely because "accesse" to the "publick good" is not limited to the parliamentary body, and thus neither it, nor its instrument, reason, is likely to become an idol. But such "accesse" to the public sphere is, of course, limited by Milton, in significant and notorious ways: "I mean not tolerated Popery and open superstition," Milton proclaims, "which as it extirpats all religious and civill supremacies, so it self should be extirpat" (II 565). For Milton – from the early *Of Reformation* to the late prose – popery and superstition are synonomous with idolatry. Because idolatry, in its claim to embody truth, defies the very principle – free circulation – upon which Milton's commonwealth is founded, it situates its adherents outside, indeed opposed to, the "publick good."[63]

For Milton, the flow of public discourse and the "unity of spirit" guaranteed by *Areopagitica* are presupposed upon a difference which insures that the social totality – at once always present yet negated in individual utterance – will not materialize into an iconic "solid piece of framework," and the "outward union of cold, and neutrall, and inwardly divided minds" (II 551). The process of assimilating "neighboring differences, or rather indifferences" to such an "outward union," and the failure "to keep truth separated from truth," for Milton is, paradoxically, "the fiercest rent and disunion of all" (II 564). Yet Catherine Belsey, writing from within the long and complicated historiographical tradition outlined above, finds Milton's "acknowledgement of pluralism" insufficient, in fact "coercive," because it "leaves the existing framework of values essentially unchallenged."[64] But as I have argued throughout, the existing "framework of values" in *Areopagitica* is always beyond articulation, or if articulated, always provisional and demanding revision. Belsey's implicit attribution of essentialism to Milton, in her suggestion that "truth" for him in "its singularity" is "the final object of a knowledge based on the exchange of views" (p. 78), seems questionable to me for the same reasons.[65] There is no "final object of knowledge" in *Areopagitica*. We have "not yet found" all the limbs of "the mangl'd body of *Osiris*," Milton writes, "nor ever shall do, till her [Truth's] Masters second comming" (II 549).

Indeed, *Areopagitica* ultimately disappoints Belsey because, though there may be a moment where the text "begins to glimpse a broader, more inclusive humanism," where Milton acknowledges that truth may be "plural," the text eventually clamps down, and the "boundaries of liberal tolerance" are "marked off and policed."[66] For Belsey, the notion that public and private are reciprocally defining – that private utterance exists only in relation to public context – is necessarily limiting (a notion she shares, perhaps surprisingly, with Illo, the champion of the "open society"). Yet Belsey's post-structuralist Marxism, which celebrates the "difference and dissemination" that "mobilize meaning,"[67] may itself have its affinities with liberal politics. The pursuit of difference, so characteristic of a liberal politics resisting any notion of publicly constituted authority, leads naturally to an evaluation of the discourses of *Areopagitica* as "authoritarian."[68]

Belsey's apparent romanticism of a seemingly unmediated subject, like the assumptions of many earlier commentators, renders the republican discourses of Milton's *Areopagitica* inaccessible. For in the seventeenth century, as Pocock has written, it was "impossible to assert even the most radical liberty without asserting some conception of authority at the same time."[69] Indeed, for the Milton of *Areopagitica*, radical liberty and public authority are simultaneously asserted; the conception of agency that emerges in the tract is at once constrained by, and constructed through, the language of civic republicanism. This may be to exaggerate Milton's conception of the individual subject as socially mediated (and to understate the remarkable emphasis he placed on individual autonomy) but it will also, I hope, serve as a useful corrective to earlier constructions of the liberal Milton.

In *Areopagitica*, the individual and the social stand in an intricate and productive tension. The "many dissections made in the quarry and in the timber," though leading to the construction of Solomon's temple, somehow manage to retain their independent particularity. They, like the individual in relation to the "publick good," are accommodated without being wholly assimilated. Indeed, it is just this particularity (the "contiguity" which, for Milton, always adumbrates "continuity") that guarantees the "goodly and graceful symmetry," which "commends the whole pile and structure."

CHAPTER 2

"Not the readiest way": Milton and the abandonment of politics

Although in *Areopagitica* Milton was able to argue that the printing press enabled the virtual identity of public and private spheres and the creation of a diffused, inclusive, and corporate authority, by the time of Milton's *Defence*, that public sphere was already constricting. To justify Pride's Purge, for example, the "minority" who attempted to "preserve their freedom" stand in synecdochically, according to Milton, for all the people of England:

"Did the people," you ask, "do violence to the commoners of the lower house, putting some to flight . . .?" I say it was the people; for why should I not say that the act of the better, the sound part of the Parliament, in which resides the real power of the people was the act of the people? (IV.I 457)

Robert Filmer's acerbic response to Milton's definition of the "people" in his "Mr. Milton Against Salmasius," however, evidences no sympathy for Milton's use of synecdoche.

"Come to our modern politicians," Filmer writes, "and ask them who the people is, though they talk big of the people, yet they take up and are content with a few representors (as they call them) of the whole people . . . neither are these representors stood upon to be the whole people." Of all these "modern politicians," however, "J.M.," writes the author of *Patriarcha*, makes the most outrageous claims: he "will not allow the major part of these representors to be the people, but the sounder and better part of them . . ." If "the sounder, the better, and the uprighter part have the power of the people," Filmer asks, "how shall we know, or who shall judge who they be?"[1] Filmer's question, directed as an attack on both Milton and contemporary republicanism, is reflected – although implicitly – in Milton's prose of the 1650s. For the Milton of this period is forced – in the context of a diminishing public sphere – to re-evaluate the applicability of the languages of civic republicanism, and to wonder himself about the source and authority for virtue.

Although Sharon Achinstein has usefully depicted Milton as having helped to define the "revolutionary public" through "fashioning his audience as a valuable participant in political discussion," by 1660, this project could not be so easily pursued.[2] With General Monk's imminent return to London from Scotland, and the prospect of elections which would return the secluded members (who had been expelled by the Rump in 1649), Milton's tract could no longer adopt the traditional languages of virtue. Indeed, the Rump in late 1659 seems to have been more concerned with rooting out its military opponents (those who had recently supported Lambert and Fleetwood), than any spirited commitment to "the good Old Cause" (VII 462). After February 22, the day the Parliament issued writs for the calling of new elections, it became clear that a restored parliamentary majority would support the Restoration, and that the "revolutionary public" had failed.

Thus, though Milton's proposals in his *The Readie and Easie Way* of 1660 serve as a meditation upon the question of how virtue should be determined, the rhetoric and tone of that tract seem to vitiate the very question. While in *Reason of Church Government*, Milton sought a "covnant" with the "elegant & learned" (I 820, 807), and in the *Animadversions* of 1641, he would argue that "the greatest gaine of a teacher" is "to make a soule vertuous" (III 719), by the 1650s, his confidence in his "elegant" and "learned" audience was dwindling. William Kerrigan has suggested that the Milton of the mid-fifties was already dwelling "obsessively on his own particularity," while Thomas Corns has argued that the "idiom" of Milton's *Letter to a Friend* of 1659 "seems hard to hit, the fit audience hard to identify."[3] By the late 1650s, and certainly by February 1660 (when Milton composed the first version of *The Readie and Easie Way*), the connection, or "covnant," that would guarantee community had been broken. Milton may have attempted, as Achinstein argues, to establish "a revolutionary conception of an active and informed public," but by 1660, this public had betrayed him.[4]

Milton's correspondence with Jean Labadie in 1659, however, still reveals a Milton at least rhetorically committed to the public authority of a civic context: "I still think I have only so much fame as I have a good name among good men" (VII 509). But, as early as the *Pro Se Defensio*, Milton registers a skepticism about the efficacy and virtue of civic authority. Milton concedes that "public testimony is indeed a great ornament to virtue," though the qualification which follows modifies the original claim: "To the extent that any man is virtuous, so stands he less in need of extrinsic testimony; for a good man, content with himself, does nothing to make himself known. If he needs commendation, he has always with him that virtue which is the best commender" (IV.2 791). Because those "who seek public testimony, as well as those who give it, are alike the good and the bad, indeed, evil men, decked out in the false cloak of probity," Milton, "content with himself" and retiring (doing "nothing to make himself known"), must seek an alternate authority for virtue – the origin of which is personal, not public.[5]

Milton intimates the nature of that authority in another of his correspondences of the late fifties. To Emeric Bigot, he writes, "if I can succeed so that I seem in mind and manners as I seem in my best writings, I shall myself both have added weight to the writings and received greater fame, no matter how small, from them in return" (VII 497). The classical model in which private intention and public reputation are reciprocally defining – where private ethos is at once mediated by, and manifested in, the public "fame" – gives way here to a different vocabulary. Milton thus hopes to "seem less to have taken what is honest and laudable from the most distinguished authors than to have brought it forth, pure and unalloyed from the depths" of his own "mind and spirit" (VII 497). Having gestured towards a rhetorical context where "mind and manners" are reflected in "greater fame," Milton qualifies his acceptance of this civic vocabulary with a private, more stoic, discourse (which anticipates and overlaps with the prophetic) where utterance springs forth from a different origin – "pure and unalloyed from the depths" of "mind and spirit." If, as Kerrigan has written, "by the time Milton finished *Paradise Lost*, the solitary watchman" had become "for him the principle of divine truth in human societies," then by *The Readie and Easie Way*, Milton seems well on the way to fashioning himself as that lone figure.[6] Though he had not yet abandoned "the cool element of prose" (II 808), by the time of the publication of the 1660 tract, Milton had already adopted a set of languages which could not so simply be accommodated to virtue.

LIBERTY WITHOUT PROVIDENCE

From Milton's letters of the late fifties and his *Defence*, it becomes evident that his confidence in the applicability of civic discourses to the political realities of the 1650s was already diminishing. Yet the tract which Milton wrote to end the decade, *The Readie and Easie Way*, has been accorded its own role in various Whig histories – by those who place the tract in a tradition of political discourse, while evidencing little regard for its theological resonances. Though *The Readie and Easie Way* has remained unheralded by those who celebrate Milton's individualism (for reasons which will soon become obvious), by relegating the tract to the realm of purely *political* discourses, many of Milton's critics have placed it in the service of a set of classic Whig narratives: the triumph of politics over religion and reason over providence.

The assumption of the emergence of an independent rational discourse, linked with the ostensibly liberal *Areopagitica*, persists, as I have shown, as a primary supposition in the historiography of the seventeenth century in England. The assumption, however, of reason's triumph and immanence in the state – figured as either part of the progressive realization of Whig history as in readings of *Areopagitica*, or what Levinas calls the establishment of "the tyranny of the State" as an anonymous and inhuman universality – remains an anachronism in relation to seventeenth-century texts.[7] This anachronism is enabled, indeed furthered, through the application of contemporary genres and categories of discourse to these texts.

The contemporary tendency to mark separations between genres of discourse is presupposed, Fredric Jameson suggests, upon an "experiential double standard in modern life" which assumes "the eclipse of . . . the religious instance."[8] To speak of the fissure between private and public life, reason and religion, Jameson suggests, is to betray a distinctively modern prejudice. John Toland's 1698 edition of *A Voyce from the Watchtower* – a tract written by Edmund Ludlow in Geneva in 1660 – evidences, in Toland's editorial interpolations and cuts, this eclipse of religious vocabularies. As Blair Worden has shown, there is a considerable discrepancy between the manuscript of Ludlow's *Voyce* and the *Memoirs* published by John Toland. "While the tone of the *Memoirs* is predominantly secular," writes Worden, the "tone of the Bodleian manuscript could hardly be more different." Where "spiritual intensity and apocalyptic prophesy are closely woven" into the manuscript narrative, the *Memoirs* emphasize Ludlow's commitment to "civic principles." Toland has created what Worden calls "Ludlow the country Whig," not least by erasing the lexicon of Christian martyrdom and patience that marks the original. "The publishers did not merely cut and reorder the manuscript," Worden concludes: "They completely rewrote it."[9]

Toland's appropriation of Ludlow – the translation of his language of providence into a language of politics – is part of what Worden calls "the story of the emergence of Whig historiography."[10] By attending to "liberty," and not to the specifically "Christian liberty" of Ludlow's tract

– a liberty *mediated* and achieved through providence – Toland's Ludlow
becomes a spokesman for the efficacy of politics and rational action.
Toland, as Worden points out, assimilated not only Ludlow to his own
political agenda, but Harrington and Milton as well. Indeed, Toland
himself understood how his editions of all three of these authors "greatly
contributed to beget in the minds of men . . . an ardent love of liberty,
and an extreme aversion to arbitrary power."[11]

Although a republican like Henry Neville could boast of being "more
affected by reading Cicero than the Bible,"[12] there were those for whom,
like Ludlow, "providence" remained at "the center of the political
stage."[13] Eventually, an autonomous discourse of rational politics –
emphasizing the agency of human actors – did gain ascendancy, but not
until later. The "translation of Godly politics into Whig ideology," as
Stephen Zwicker has shown, came only after the Restoration.[14] While
sacred history, Zwicker explains, is "the record of men waiting on signs
from God" and the "story of ceaseless intervention," Whig ideologists
found in Rome the "history of a city that raised itself to universal Empire
solely by human endeavor."[15]

This willful suppression of providence in Toland's editorial procedures
– where political and theological discourses are rendered incompatible –
is paradigmatic of later tendencies to hypostatize cultural and generic
categories: as *A Voyce from the Watchtower* becomes a strictly political
document, so *Paradise Lost*, for example, becomes a literary one. As
Bernard Sharratt explains, "the strictly theological dimension of *Paradise
Lost* is no longer recognizable or even intelligible."[16] To be sure, the
tactic served Milton's different apologists equally – though in different
ways. The prose was placed in the service of the image of Milton the
radical politician, while the poetry was placed in the service of the image
of Milton the transcendent poet. With the emergence of the generic
distinction between theological and political discourse in the early
eighteenth century – which paralleled the distinction between private
and public discourses – emerged a set of antithetical vocabularies
through which these very different Miltons were constructed.

In *The Readie and Easie Way*, Milton became, for his opponent Filmer, a
mere "politician." But Filmer's judgment, echoed by many of Milton's
critics, fails to note the extent to which Milton can scarcely be called
political in the modern sense, and the way in which, for Milton, politics
was itself (despite our sense of the fierceness of his political commitments)
a form of idolatry. For where Milton in his *Second Defence* finds "three
species of libertie . . . essential to the happinesse of social life" – the

"religious, domestic, and civil" – the discourses of modernity recognize only two of these levels: "the public and the private, [or] the political and the personal."[17] Which is to affirm that Milton's notions of politics and rational agency were always framed by a commitment to providence. Historiographical constructs – like Toland's – which assume the absence (or displacement) of the Jamesonian "religious instance" insist upon the separation between politics and theology, as the latter category becomes the province of an ever more circumscribed private realm. Yet the place of a specifically religious intensity in the classical republicanism of the 1640s and 1650s cannot be ignored. As Worden cautions, although "historians will always disagree about the explanations, and about the attractiveness of Puritan spiritual intensity, our image of Puritan politics is gravely distorted when we neglect it." "A fuller study of the classical republicans," Worden suggests, "would dwell on the limits as well as the extent of their rationalism."[18] That is, although political argument was dominated by the language of the "state" by the middle of the eighteenth century, that terminology was not fully ascendant in 1660.[19] In the historiographical attempts to marginalize theological discourse in the name of the primacy of rational politics and human agency "lies yet another of the seventeenth-century roads," Worden observes, "which leads us back to Milton."[20]

MILTON AND THE STATE

Just as Toland constructs a Ludlow whose notion of liberty is unmediated by providence, so recent critics of Milton find in his prose tracts adumbrations of the modern state with its "installation and fetishism of reason." "Already in the *Areopagitica*," Rapaport writes in *Milton and the Postmodern*, "we see this turn from the 'state of man' to 'man in the state.'" Lamenting this ominous transition, Rapaport continues:

We see Milton as poet and politician standing before the rise of the modern state not unlike a Faustian character who knows that in the beginning there was the deed and that this deed is morally undecidable . . . It is a perception not lost in our time by those bloody heroes of the state to whom we owe so much: the Stalinists, Maoists, National Socialists, imperialists, and others.[21]

While Rapaport's rhetoric is particularly extreme, the charge that Milton's prose tracts are proleptic of an "instrumentalization of reason" is not unfamiliar: Kendrick, Milner, and Illo all seem to corroborate Rapaport's claims.[22] Not all reaction to Milton's prose tracts is so overtly hostile; but the tendency to render unto Caesar what is Caesar's – that is, to submit the prose tracts to the interpretive vocabularies of the political scientist – is familiar and remains prevalent.

In the eighteenth century, this strategy of divorcing poetry from prose – and of separating theological and literary argument from political discourse – was enabled through casting the Milton of the prose tracts as a republican or a regicide. Thomas Yalden in 1698 helped to inaugurate a tradition that discriminated between poetry – the "sacred lines" which "with wonder we peruse" – and the "seditious prose" which "provokes our rage." Already here we see the attempts made by angelic critics throughout the centuries (in order to preserve the pure image of the transcendent poet) to repress or discredit Milton's political writings.[23]

Richardson, turning to the evidence of Milton's prose, confidently asserted, "'tis Certain he was a Republican," and Newton fifteen years later echoed the judgment, finding Milton to be "a thorough republican."[24] Francis Blackburne, an eighteenth-century editor of *Areopagitica* and *Of Education*, and himself a republican, confirms the view that Milton's politics were categorized, rejected, and then, usually, ignored. If "Milton had adopted for his epic poem a political hero, as it seems he once intended," it may "be justly questioned whether . . . the majesty of his style, would have redeemed it from the fate which befell the *Iconoclastes*" – if, he continues, such a "poem should have fallen into the like orthodox hands." For Blackburne, it is the specific *political* content of Milton's prose writings which accounts for the "absolute ignorance" of these tracts "among his own countrymen."[25]

The edition of *The Readie and Easie Way* published in 1791 demonstrates how Milton's prose became assimilated into the requisites of political argument. The frontispiece of this edition advertised the hope that the tract might "enlarge the stock of *political* information," and that Milton might "offer a rational and satisfactory answer to the splendid sophistry of Edmunde Burke."[26] Similarly, Austin Woolrych, who edited the Yale edition of *The Readie and Easie Way*, identifies non-political discourses in the pamphlets of the late commonwealth, though he contends that the move from "rational politics" to religious discourses represented a form of political expediency: "The Republicans found," he suggests, "that they could best win" support by "enlisting the pens or at least borrowing the language of the saints."[27] While Woolrych recognizes the adaptation of theological argument as an aspect of rhetorical expediency, Zera Fink, in her study of *The Readie and Easie Way*, limits her attention to the "spirit of antique republicanism" that "hovered over Milton." Employing the language of classical political theory, Fink claims that Milton was "an adherent of the theory of mixed government" and concludes that the system he proposed was "truly ... one of checks and balances."[28] Similarly, Barbara Lewalski, in an article on Milton's late prose, emphasizes "Milton the practical politician close to affairs," while Perez Zagorin claims that the "poet's final political counsel" allowed "no scope for democratic rights," and was driven by "mere self-delusion."[29] While many of these judgments may be true, and may indeed help elaborate both the context and meaning of Milton's tract, they tend, in their approaches, to occlude the relationship between seventeenth-century politics and theology. The intricate relationship between these spheres will make both the designation of *Paradise Lost* as a poetic text, or *The Readie and Easie Way* as a political tract, equally problematic.

Though there have been important exceptions to the tendency, much of the criticism of the tract has disproportionately emphasized Milton's commitment to the power and efficacy of reason and human agency.[30] Indeed, critics have tended to ignore the manner in which such commitments are qualified and mediated by a providential discourse which makes any faith in "the instrumentalization of reason" problematic. Even *The Readie and Easie Way*, the tract most explicitly indebted to classical paradigms, evidences an antinomian distrust of rational politics that makes it resistant, if not inaccessible, to appropriation within modern political arguments. Milton's appropriation as a proponent of bourgeois individualism represents one form of Whig history; the erasure of providence from Milton's ostensibly political lexicon represents yet another.

In the current reading of *The Readie and Easie Way*, I do not intend to offer an angelic counter-image of Toland's interpretive indulgences. A tract insisting that "a free Commonwealth" is "held by wisest men in all ages the noblest, the manliest, the equallest, the justest government" (VII 424) and devoting the majority of its argument to concrete political proposals is certainly "political." But politics here, as in *Areopagitica*, sixteen years earlier, provides only "as much assurance as can be of human things" (VII 444). Just as Milton embraced Arminian doctrine while rejecting Arminian authority in *Areopagitica*, he elaborates a political program in his tract of 1660, while manifesting a profound distrust of politics.

Those who, according to Arthur Barker, wonder "how the convictions which inspired the *Areopagitica* ... could be made to support the repressive program" articulated in *The Readie and Easie Way*, presume that for Milton the political sphere was the primary locus for the "trial of virtue and the exercise of truth."[31] Kevin Gilmartin, for example, finds that Milton's proposal for a "perpetual senate" represents a betrayal "of some of his most cherished convictions about the progressive dimensions of human social and political experience."[32] Citing the passage from *The Readie and Easie Way* in which Milton claims that a restored monarchy will "leave the contest endless between prerogative and petition of right, till only doomsday end it," Gilmartin comments: "The millennium figures not as the glorious fulfillment of human progress, but rather as sheer relief from disorder and futile political activity."[33] As if Milton had ever advocated "futile political activity"!

Milton never argued for political faction; indeed, *The Readie and Easie Way* is precisely a response to those who pursue political faction – to those who, through politics, pursue their private interest as an end in itself. In his claim that "*Areopagitica* is as always furthest from Milton's position in 1660," Gilmartin mistakes political faction for *religious* freedom.[34] Milton advocated "schism" and Christian liberty in 1644; in 1659, Milton authored a tract on Christian liberty – *Of Civil Power* – which virtually replicates the position on religious freedom articulated in the earlier tract. "Nothing," Milton writes in *Of Civil Power*, "more protestantly can be permitted then a free and lawful debate at all times by writing, conference or disputation of what opinion soever ..." (VII 249).[35] Milton maintains a continuity of purpose from 1644 to 1660 – though the later period demanded a form of political intervention (towards which Milton himself felt ambivalent) which the former did not. The centrality of religious freedoms – "free debate" and "disputation" – in both the early and later tract nonetheless remains.

Indeed, in *The Readie and Easie Way*, Milton insists on the primacy of *religious* freedoms: "Who can be at rest," he asks, "who can enjoy any thing in this world with contentment, who hath not libertie to serve God and to save his own soul"? (VII 456). In 1660 – as in 1644 – Milton defends the "*sectaries*" (VII 458) and warns that it is the "son of *Charls* returning" who will "*persevere in not the doctrin only, but government of the church of* England; *not to neglect the speedie and effectual suppressing of errors and schisms*" (VII 457). Writing at the end of a decade that began with the Engagement Controversy and closed with the anarchic pursuit to establish a lawful government, Milton attempts with *The Readie and Easie Way* to bring an end to the country's political crisis by asserting that a "free Commonwealth" was most "inclinable" to "libertie of conscience" (VII 458). Yet Milton never saw in parliamentary authority – or any political authority for that matter – the solution to the nation's problems. As Robert T. Fallon writes of the *Second Defence*, the tract "issues no stirring call for a new Parliament, for as [Milton] says, who would think 'his own liberty enlarged one iota by such caretakers of the state.'"[36]

Indeed, Milton's "political" solution in *The Readie and Easie Way* – the establishment of a perpetual "Grand Councel" – seems designed to *minimize* the influence of politics. The life tenure of Milton's Council is an index of its relative indifference, *not* its power. The role of the Grand Council, in fact, is conceived to be so minimal that Milton imagines it sitting "perpetually," unless, he hastens to add parenthetically, "thir leisure give them now and then som intermissions or vacations" (VII 446). Rotation of members of the Council (as argued by Harrington in his *Oceana*, and allowed in the first edition of the tract), Milton argues here, will only "breed commotions, changes, novelties and uncertainties" (VII 434). Indeed every new assembly, finding "no great work to do," "will make it, by altering or repealing former acts, or making and multiplying new; that they may seem to see what thir predecessors saw not, and not to have assembld for nothing: till all law be lost in the multitude of clashing statutes" (VII 434). If, as Zwicker suggests, "the civil wars represented ... a failure to acknowledge the competing interests that party would finally come to legitimate at the close of the century,"[37] then Milton's conception of the Grand Council in *The Readie and Easie Way* can be understood as an attempted – though perhaps ineffective and largely rhetorical – resolution of the factional strife that would, after the Restoration, evolve into party politics.

Milton continues, therefore, to employ in *The Readie and Easie Way*, as he did in *Areopagitica*, a republican discourse which insists that the Grand Council is subordinated "to the general power and union of the whole Republic" (VII 461). The Grand Council, as Quentin Skinner remarks, is conceived by Milton as "nothing more than a means of expressing the powers of the people in an administratively more convenient form."[38] The monarchy, however, according to Milton, makes such representation impossible. For the King sets "a pompous face upon the superficial actings of State," and pageants "himself up and down in progress among the perpetual bowings and cringings of an abject people" (VII 426). In contrast, the people as Milton envisions them are "representers" of their own freedom.

In *The Readie and Easie Way*, Milton requires that the people will have "all public ornaments in thir own election and within thir own bounds" (VII 461). "Offices and ornaments," he further insists, must be "at home in our own ordering and administration" (VII 461). For Milton, monopoly over "public ornament" is the very act that enables political faction to transform itself into an idol of private interest.[39] And what greater idolatry can there be than when those "who might manage nobly thir own affairs themselves, sluggishly and we[a]kly . . . devolve all on a single person" (VII 427) who must be "ador'd like a Demigod" (VII 425)? Here, as in Milton's earlier tracts, epistemological and political questions converge. The author of *Eikonoklastes* knew the power of representation, and anticipated how the King's "masks and revels" would lead to "the multiplying of a servile crew" (VII 425) – to a people "not only in fleece, but in minde also sheepishest" (VII 460). Those mesmerized by the representations of others – "the pompous face set upon the superficial actings of State" – cannot, Milton suggests, represent themselves.[40]

The diffusion of what Milton calls "public ornament" prevents faction from transforming private interest into "the fond conceit of something like the duke of *Venice*" (VII 446). Similarly, Milton's advocacy of a kind of federalism of "subordinate Commonaltie[s]" prevents state centralization and safely limits the business of the Grand Council to "forein affairs" (VII 443), while providing for more general participation of the people in a multiplicity of different local assemblies.[41] Further, Milton's support for "learning and noble education" would be designed to communicate "the natural heat of government and culture more distributively" (VII 460) and thus prevent a "madd or strangely infatuated" nation from falling into the "perpetual bowings and cringings of an abject people" (VII 427, 426). If the nation were to follow these prescriptions, Milton concludes, there could be nothing "that may any way divide or sever the publick interest," and consequently no need to fear the institution of a perpetual senate: "what can a perpetual senat have then wherin to grow corrupt, wherin to encroach upon us or usurp; or if they do, wherin to be formidable (VII 461)?" Milton's "people," rendered "fittest to chuse," are disciplined not to fall into a fetishism of the workings of the state. Moreover, they are disciplined "not to admire wealth or honour," but to "hate turbulence and ambition," and thus "to place every one his privat welfare and happiness in the public peace, libertie and safetie" (VII 443).

Milton, however, prompted by *The Censure of the Rota*, an anonymous Harringtonian spoof on the 1660 tract, carefully distinguishes his republicanism from that of his Harringtonian rival whose emphases were purely rationalist and political. Indeed, Milton's skepticism about the efficacy of political *institutions* – informed by the sense that politics can only provide "as much assurance as can be of human things" – is manifest in his critique of Harringtonian politics. "The way propounded is plane, easie and open before us," Milton proclaims, "without intricacies, without the introducement of new or obsolete forms, or terms, or exotic models" (VII 445). While "Harrington's freedom was defined by elaborate external laws," Milton's "liberty," as Barker suggests, "was to be had ... through a nullification of sin which made external law ... unnecessary."[42] Milton, therefore, found Harrington's political model – with its Agrarian Law, Rotation, and bipartite legislature – unwieldy and intrusive, and concluded that his "ideas ... would effect nothing" (echoing the conviction in *Areopagitica* that the "great art" of the commonwealth "is to bid restraint" when "perswasion only is to work" [VII 445, II 527]). To the contrary, these "new injunctions" would "manacle the native liberty of mankinde; turning all vertue into prescription, servitude, and necessitie, to the great impairing and frustrating of Christian libertie" (VII 445).

What Corns has described as the "absence of a viable theoretical component" in Milton's argument may not only register what Corns calls Milton's "profoundly anti-democratic" position, but also Milton's skepticism towards what Corns calls "theory."[43] To attribute to Milton a properly political "theory" (in the modern sense of the term) would be to attribute to him a belief in the mechanisms of rational politics and legislative constraint that he never fully advocated. Indeed, that many of the contributors to the recent *Milton and Republicanism* volume seem to sense that Milton's works cannot be assimilated to strictly political paradigms testifies not only to the limitations of a certain kind of Skinnerian analysis, but to Milton's indifference to *mere* politics.[44] Milton was not after a political *system* – though he was intent upon establishing a "firm foundation" for the commonwealth (VII 394). Milton's Grand Council would provide a foundation for social harmony, but only, as Nigel Smith argues, so that "there might be activity in the city."[45] This is not, after all, very different from the *discordia concors* of *Areopagitica*; though in 1644 the "firm foundation" (the condition for difference) did not need to be *legislated*.

The commonwealth which Milton sought to legislate was very different from its Harringtonian antecedent. The "truly immortal commonwealth," as Pocock points out, "entailed the anti-Christian concept of *aeternitas mundi*."[46] This Harringtonian ideal – which aspires to a secular immortality through a prudence identical with providence[47] – was surely to be seen by Milton as placing too much emphasis on "human things," and as enforcing civic virtue through an idolatry of reason and the state as ends *in themselves*. That is, where Harrington collapses providence and prudence, for Milton, political and providential agency – though related – can never be entirely identified.

In *The Readie and Easie Way*, Milton evidences a skepticism for all political models, even for the historical precedents to which he referred extensively in his earlier tracts. "The appeal of *Eikonoklastes* to rolls and records and the ancient English constitution," Barker observes, "is scarcely echoed in the last tracts."[48] In his *Defence*, Milton presents the methodology that would inform his investigations of political sovereignty in *The Readie and Easie Way*: "Our dispute is to be conducted by reasoning, not by narrating." "Reason," Milton writes, "will prevail over narration" (IV.1 512).

Although at the time Milton was writing his *Defence* he still flirted with the ancient constitution and the political authority justified through "narration," by the time of *The Readie and Easie Way*, he had completely abandoned arguments for the historical authority of parliament.[49] In fact, he attempts to obfuscate the historical origins of that body when in 1660 he proposes "abolishing that name" of "*Parlament*" as "originally signifying but the *parlie* of our Lords and Commons with thir *Norman* king when he pleasd to call them" (VII 444). While the *Defence* proclaims that "our most venerable documents bear witness that our kings owe their power wholly to the people," Milton, by 1660, had entirely turned away from historical precedent. Indeed, Milton's additions in his "Digression" to his *History of Britain* in 1658 mark his final despair over historical argument.[50]

Instead of claiming, as he did in the *Defence*, that the English people had always been the source of political sovereignty, in *The History of Britain*, Milton asserts that the people "gave to *William* the Conqueror so easie a conquest" (V 403-4), and thereby transferred their sovereignty to the Conqueror. Milton's virtual admission that all of English history had been nothing but the history of conquests leads him to abandon historical inquiry altogether: "What more worth," he despairs in the *History of Britain*, "is it then to chronicle the wars of kites, or crows, flocking and fighting in the air" (V 249). The result for Milton of such an abandonment of history is what Barker calls an appeal to a "legality" which "had a foundation at once more positive and more abstract."[51]

Thus, in *The Readie and Easie Way*, Milton appeals not "to any former covnant" (VII 409), but claims instead that parliament is

not bound by any statute of preceding Parlaments, but by law of nature only, which is the only law of laws truly and properly to all mankinde fundamental;

the beginning and the end of all Government; to which no Parlament or people will throughly reforme, but may and must have recourse ... (VII 412-13)

Asserting his conviction that parliament is "more & more unbound" to previous covenant and historical precedent, Milton attempted to establish a form of political authority somehow unaffiliated with what Skinner calls "the history of politics" which "ever since the time of Nimrod, the first politician, was ... characteristically seen as mainly the history of conquests and subordination."[52] In *The Readie and Easie Way*, Milton struggled to found a notion of political sovereignty that would not simply be an expression of the illegitimate lust for power, and would consequently avoid coalescing into the faction of merely private interest. If Nimrod the tyrant had loomed in the political discourses of the 1650s as a figure of political illegitimacy, then Milton's 1660 tract attempts to establish a form of political sovereignty which would not itself be tainted by associations with the Nimrodic conqueror. All the governments since the Rump had been charged with such usurpation; Milton himself would seek a different ground for political authority.[53]

In his insistence on the abrogation of all previous "covnants" on the authority of the "law of nature only," and on the necessity that the people of England "represent themselves," Milton argued for a political settlement not unlike the one he presumed *already* to exist when he wrote the *Areopagitica*.[54] For, as Mark Kishlansky argues, in the 1640s, "contradictory policies" maintained the "unity" of an "organic political structure" in which party and faction were "a cultural and structural impossibility."[55] That is, notwithstanding Kishlansky's problematic metaphor of "organic" politics, the civic republicanism of *Areopagitica* is presumed upon the prophetic authority of "all the Lords people," while the public sphere in *The Readie and Easie Way*, transformed by faction and "corruption," has contracted so that Milton's own prophetic words are "spoken only to trees and stones" (VII 462). It is Milton's own avowal of the virtual absence of this public sphere that leads him both to adopt the prophetic tones of the Jeremiad and to deny (at least implicitly) the efficacy of the very political programs that his tract proposes. Where the relationship in *Areopagitica* between the sufficiency of reasoned temperance and the "strong assistance of God our deliverer" (II 487) remains intricate, the failure of the public sphere as figured in *The Readie and Easie Way* leads to the virtual fissuring of republican and providential arguments. For providence and human agency can no longer overlap where there are no virtuous men to perform His will.

THE RUMP

Milton's extended defense of the actions of the Rump Parliament in 1649 in *The Readie and Easie Way* provides a primary instance of the failure of civic languages. The Rump, Milton asserts, "knew the people of *England* to be a free people, themselves the representers of that freedom" (VII 411). Yet the proposed identity between public and private authority – sustained in the argument of *Areopagitica* and gestured towards in his letters and *Defence* – collapses here in *The Readie and Easie Way*.

In defending the actions of the Rump Parliament in 1649, Milton's conception of the public sphere again contracts: "many were excluded, & as many fled" (VII 411) though, Milton concludes, there "were left a sufficient number to act ... " (VII 412). The basis for their action, however, is acknowledged even by Milton to be problematic. The influence of those "evil men, decked out in the false cloak of probity," who made their appearance in Milton's letter to Labadie, exert their presence again in *The Readie and Easie Way*. Since Milton affirms that members of parliament "were not to learn [i.e., they already knew] that a greater number might be corrupt within the walls of a Parlament as well as of a citie" (VII 415), he must vindicate the actions of an uncorrupted minority of an already truncated parliamentary body. To the question of the soundness or corruption of parliament, Milton asserts "all men will be judges." Nor shall they "easily permitt," he continues, in an argument too dense to permit paraphrase, "that the odds of voices in thir greatest councel, shall more endanger them by corrupt or credulous votes, then the odds of enemies by open assaults; judging that most voices ought not alwaies to prevail where main matters are in question" (VII 415). In "matters of nearest concernment," as that of determining the corruption of parliament, Milton argues, "all men will be judges." Yet the "greater number" of the already circumscribed group who act on behalf of "all men" has *already* been acknowledged as "corrupt," and it is they, Milton seems to argue, who shall not "easily permitt" themselves to be endangered by "corrupt or credulous votes."

One cannot, in the words of Milton's letter to Labadie, seek "fame from the wicked" (indeed one's "good name among men" is guaranteed by calling down the wicked's "certain hatred and maledictions" [VII 509]); yet here the "public testimony" meant to detect "corruption" is already implicated in a web of previously existing corruption. Milton's assertion, then, "that most voices ought not alwaies to prevail where main matters are in question" is not so much a *non sequitur* (reversing the proclamation of the previous sentence), but an acknowledgment of the difficulty of political engagement where the ubiquity of "corruption" makes classically defined virtue impossible. Virtue – within the republican matrix – needs a public context for its embodiment; yet where the "greater part" is already "corrupt," the link between private virtue and public action is sundered.

As a consequence, the Aristotelian notion, elaborated in Milton's *Of Education*, that actors must "articulate the thought that shaped their choice," is abandoned in *The Readie and Easie Way*.[56] For, in Milton's analysis of the Rump, the omnipresence of corruption makes the intentions of individual actors irrecoverable. And, indeed, the intentions and the virtue of individual actors are, in Milton's account of the Rump, no criteria for evaluating their actions. Members of the Rump Parliament, Milton argues, ". . . examind not whether fear or perswasion carried . . . the vote; neither did they measure votes and counsels by the intentions of them that voted . . ." (VII 414). Thus, "the best affected . . . and best principl'd" of the Rumpers judged events independently of the intentions which formed them: the actions of the Rump (already acknowledged as corrupt) are, however, vindicated by Milton – despite the intentions which underlie them. Although *Of Education* emphasizes "that act of reason which in *Ethics* is call'd *Proairesis*" (II 396), *proairesis*, or deliberative action, is impossible in the context of Milton's account of the corrupt Rump.[57] *Proairesis* – as deliberative action – provides a direct manifestation of ethos and functions as the guarantor of the link between a public sphere of action and private intention. Yet this link also dissolves in *The Readie and Easie Way*, as Milton contends that "intentions either are but guess'd at, or not soon anough known; and although good, can neither make the deed such, nor prevent the consequence from being bad" (VII 414). As Woolrych points out, alluding to the deterioration of republican argument in the tract, these are "dangerous doctrines in a treatise whose central purpose is a perpetual Grand Council" (VII 414).

In so far that Milton's doctrines point to a radical division between intention and action, the question of the responsibility (or agency, for that matter) of political actors – specifically the Rump's members – becomes irrelevant. Milton therefore turns to consequences rather than intentions to evaluate actions: "Suppose bad intentions in things otherwise welldon; what was welldon, was by them who so thought [that is, despite their intentions], not the less obey'd . . ." (VII 414). For Milton, in 1660, it is essential to disregard the moral disposition of agents, for if one were to "foresake . . . a just and noble cause" from the "mixture of bad men who have ill manag'd and abus'd it," then, "what had long ere this become of our gospel and all protestant reformation so much intermixt with the avarice and ambition of som reformers"? (VII 422). Milton's rejection of deliberative action is so complete in these opening pages of *The Readie and Easie Way* that he is led to the somewhat bizarre and novel conclusion that it is better to "follow *Iscariot* or *Simon* the magician . . . preaching, then *Saul*, though in the uprightness of his heart persecuting the gospell" (VII 414-15).

Milton's defense of the Rump in *The Readie and Easie Way* signals his ambivalence about the continued relevance of civic discourses to the contemporary situation in England. His argument against intention is necessitated by his perception of the corruption of the "abject" nation falling into an idolatry of the King and the consequent collapse of the public sphere. No virtue, no "greater fame" can be bestowed by these men. Milton, therefore, turns to an Agent – beyond the realm of the social – who not only bestows virtue, but who orders time.

PROVIDENTIAL HISTORIOGRAPHY

Milton's move from the analysis of deliberative action to the analysis of unintended consequences represents a transition from the methods of classical history to those of providential historiography.[58] In his letter to Henry de Brass of 1657, Milton elaborates the method of the historian, insisting that he inquire into the intentions behind actions: "he who would write worthily of worthy deeds ought to write with no less largeness of spirit and experience of the world than he who did them, so that he can comprehend and judge as an equal even the greatest, and, having comprehended, can narrate . . ." (VII 501). But in so far that the intentions of the actors depicted in *The Readie and Easie Way* are irrecoverable (because of the absence of a public sphere in which virtue can manifest itself), then the "spirit" the historian attempts to approximate must reside elsewhere than in the minds of men. Milton, therefore, is led to seek an explanation for the cause of events beyond the intentions of rational agents. He identifies that cause in another meditation on history where "language" is said to be "unable to match" the "great and wonderful deeds performed . . . by Almighty God himself *rather than by mortal men*" (IV.1 305; emphasis added). Milton, as Kerrigan suggests, did not number himself among such mortals; Milton, like God, would be able to ignore the intentions of actors, and, by means of a providential historiography, see the "future in the present."[59] Though "men were wanting" at the "opportunity for doing the greatest deeds," there was not, Milton writes at the end of the *Second Defence*, "one wanting who could ... make both deeds and doers illustrious with praises that will never die" (IV.1 685) Milton, the prophetic historian, thus ennobles both the "deeds" and "doers" of an otherwise abject history.

In his *Readie and Easie Way*, Milton abandons the intentions of "mortal men" and rational agency for a prophetic voice authorized by God where the words of the prophet reflect the agency – the "largeness of spirit" – of God, not that of rational actors. Milton's approximation of the prophetic voice, therefore, at the conclusion of the tract – added to the second edition of *The Readie and Easie Way* – not only registers his belief in his own authority to "comprehend and judge," and thus to "narrate," but also serves as a barometer of his perceived isolation: "Thus much I should perhaps have said though I were sure I should have spoken only to trees and stones; and had none to cry to, but with the Prophet, *O earth, earth, earth!* to tell the very soil it self, what her perverse inhabitants are deaf to ..." (VII 462-63). Here the stoic language of Milton's letter to Labadie transforms into full-fledged prophetic tones. This prophetic utterance, addressed to a "deaf" nation of "trees and stones," is necessarily incompatible with a republican argument which requires for its articulation the existence of a virtuous and rational audience.

The juxtaposition and incompatibility of providential and republican argument is revealed most strikingly in Milton's discussion of the role of his "perpetual ... Grand or General Councel" (VII 444). Such an institution, Milton explains, would allow for "peace, justice, plentifull trade and all prosperitie," that is, "with as much assurance as can be of human things" (VII 444). This "prosperitie," Milton adds, shall "so continue (if God favour us, and our willful sins provoke him not),"

even to the coming of our true and rightfull and only to be expected King, only worthie as he is our only Saviour, the Messiah, the Christ, the only heir of his eternal father, the only by him anointed and ordaind since the work of our redemption finishd, Universal Lord of all mankinde. (VII 445)

The transition is swift from republican to providential argument, from the authority of the "General Councel" to the "favour" of "our only Saviour," the agent of a "redemption" already "*finish'd.*" The transition back to political argument, however, is equally rapid, and here seems forced: "The way propounded is plane, easie and open before us" (VII 445), Milton matter-of-factly continues. Parataxis of this type may be said to characterize all Miltonic discourse; to be sure, as I have already emphasized, Milton never advocated the identity of reason and providence. For Milton, the assertion of God's immanence in history – whether embodied in the King or Harrington's prudence – could lead only to idolatry, the worship of the state. In *The Readie and Easie Way*, however, the two forms of agency – rational and providential – seem to have fissured entirely.

Milton sets a providential narrative of a cause abandoned, understood only by him in his prophetic role, against a republican argument that presumes the continued existence of a virtuous community and the efficacy of rational politics. Milton's second and revised edition of the tract, published at the end of March, only two weeks after the parliament had voted for its own dissolution (and weeks before the Convention Parliament and the Restoration), would further question the already problematic notion of a community established through virtue.[60] Thus in this revised edition, Milton cuts the optimistic assertion of the earlier edition that there is "part of the nation which consents not" with those who wish to be "slaves." Similarly, and even more tellingly, Milton edits from his second edition the still hopeful assertion that "God hath yet his remnant" (VII 363). Milton, in the revised edition, figures himself as more and more isolated, without even the consolation of the "remnant."

In *Areopagitica* where "all the Lords people are become prophets," providential and republican discourses are maintained in a tenuous balance – reinforcing one another. This nation of prophets at once embodies the dual and sometimes contradictory nature of the Christian commonwealth: like the "distinct Arminius," they are free to choose, but also in need of "guidance." With the corruption of the nation embodied in Milton's representation of the Rump of 1649, the possible confluence of republican and providential arguments, with their distinct forms of agency, becomes impossible. Milton, at the close of *The Readie and Easie Way*, chooses the authority of prophesy "pure and unalloyed" from the depths of his "minde and spirit," as a more public authority is lost in the "epidemic madness ... and defection of a misguided and abus'd multitude" (VII 463).

POLITICS: "NOT THE READIEST WAY"

The fragmenting of republican and providentialist arguments, and the ultimate primacy of prophetic discourse in *The Readie and Easie Way*, casts its shadow even on Milton's explicitly minimalist republican project "to make the people fittest to chuse" (VII 443). For there are insinuations in the tract that Milton's political proposals are themselves, in Milton's mind, affiliated with political usurpation. Milton's ambivalence about the possibly coercive elements in his own political program becomes manifest when he proclaims: "Where is this goodly tower of a Commonwealth, which the English boasted they would build to overshaddow kings, and be another *Rome* in the west? The foundation indeed they laid gallantly; but fell into a wors confusion, not of tongues, but of factions, then those at the tower of *Babel . . .*" (VII 423). Although Milton begins by affiliating the construction of a "tower" with the parable in Luke 16, where Jesus admonishes those who began to build but were not "able to finish," the connotations that accrue to this "tower" are much more invidious. The connection between the factions at Babel and "Nimrod, the mighty hunter of men" is established in Genesis 10 8–10.[61] Milton's *Eikonoklastes*, in consonance with the political lexicon of its time, claims that Nimrod was "the first that hunted after *Faction*" (III 466; emphasis added). Where the construction of the temple in *Areopagitica* assimilated "schisms and sectaries" in the "graceful symmetry" of "brotherly dissimilitudes" (II 555), the very creation of a "goodly tower" – Milton's own apparent objective in *The Readie and Easie Way* – is affiliated, by association, with the emergence of *political* "factions" and Nimrod's political conquests.

But the full force of Milton's ambivalence about political innovation is not registered until Book XII of *Paradise Lost* where the Nimrodic conqueror again figures significantly. In this final book of the epic, Nimrod's desire to "arrogate Dominion undeserv'd / Over his brethren" (XII 27-28) leads him "to build / A City and Tow'r, whose top may reach to Heav'n" (XII 44-45). To his guide and teacher – the archangel Michael – Adam disdainfully dismisses the Nimrodic endeavors at Babel:

> But this Usurper his encroachment proud
> Stays not on man; to God his Tower intends
> Siege and defiance . . .   (XII 72-74)[62]

The notion of Nimrod as one who "hunted after faction" was present to Milton's imagination throughout his career, yet still Milton implicitly affiliates Nimrod with the realization of his own political proposals in *The Readie and Easie Way*. Milton, from *Areopagitica* to *The Readie and Easie Way*, was never interested in (and never recognized) an autonomous realm of politics in which human agency (individual or corporate) existed outside of the realm of providence. His intervention, however, in 1660, registers both his awareness of the contemporary need for specific *political* proposals (which were to be adopted, paradoxically, to escape the dangers of an already emergent modern politics), as well as a profound skepticism about their means and efficacy. This is not to say, however, that Milton was in any way betraying an earlier commitment to the Christian republicanism of *Areopagitica*. Milton sought a return to such an ideal state, where the public realm could mediate – without subsuming – a multiplicity of different perspectives, but he resisted the notion that such a vision was merely a *political* creation (witness his rejection of Harrington). One might be able to protect the community of saints through political innovation; one could not, however, legislate that community into existence.

Although Milton's *Readie and Easie Way* evidences ambivalence about a political proposal which aims to "make the people fittest to chuse," his later description of the Israelites in *Paradise Lost*, who through "the wild Desert," advance "towards *Canaan . . .* not the readiest way" (XII 215-16) figures as a self-correction that acknowledges that the path of rational politics is often forged by Nimrod. Although *The Readie and Easie Way* – in its attempt to avoid associations with other forms of political usurpation – gestures explicitly away from history, precedent, and "covnant," towards "the light of nature or religion," there is the suggestion that to Milton in 1660 even the foundation of the "goodly tower of a Commonwealth" cannot be achieved except under the auspices of Nimrod. Indeed in 1660, with the King's return imminent, it was Milton's proposals, though made in the name of the people, which had the appearance of being factional.[63]

If, as Mary Ann Radzinowicz suggests, the figure of Nimrod shows "the absurd falsity of the heroics of linguistic and political usurpation,"[64] then here Milton's implicit comparison of the English nation to Nimrod and the building of the tower of Babel aligns their political project – however implicitly – with other forms of political usurpation. From this perspective, Milton's *The Readie and Easie Way*, with its implicit questioning of the role of the republic in a "corrupt" and "abject" nation, may belong to a whole class of texts of the later Renaissance, in which, as Victoria Kahn writes, "the authors are finally less concerned with moving the reader to action, or even to a particular attitude, than with forcing the reader to reflect on how *praxis* can be, and in some cases, whether it can be."[65] From this perspective Worden's evaluation of the Milton of the late fifties has particular force. It is doubtful, Worden writes, whether the Milton of this period can "helpfully be called a republican at all."[66] This may be an extreme characterization of the author of *Areopagitica*, though it does register the difficulty in subsuming Milton entirely within a political matrix. Though political argument would soon turn towards the acknowledgment of "passions" and "interests," Milton, in the final meditation on "virtue" before the Restoration, anticipates his own turn towards the prophetic registers of *Paradise Lost*. Even in Milton's "most political tract," rationalist agency finds itself constrained – sometimes overshadowed – by its providential context.

Milton's ambivalences about political engagement, asserted in *The Readie and Easie Way* and amplified in *Paradise Lost*, reach their final articulation in *Paradise Regained*. In this, Milton's final brief epic, Jesus turns his back on the "eloquence" of "all the Oratory of *Greece* and *Rome*" (IV 360) dismissing them as "Statists indeed" (IV 354) – just one more group whose political engagement transforms into political faction and an idolatry of the state.

PART II

Theology

CHAPTER 3

Introduction: Whig metaphysics

It came to me as I lay there, a nightmare that this was the last hour of history. Nothing else explains it. The breakdown. I mean, how *thorough* it is, from top to bottom, like everything from ancient times to now, the civilized values and visions of high culture, have all gone to hell in fine old hamlets filled high with garbage, over-run with Mudmen and Jews, riddled with vital infections and ve-nereal complaints that boggle the mind and cripple whole gener-ations of white children who'll be strangers, if not slaves, in their own country. I saw families killing each other. People were living in alleyways. Sexes and races were blurred. I saw riots in cities and on clippers. Then: the rise of Aztec religion and voodoo as credible spiritual practices for some, but people were still worship-ping stage personalities too. On and on it came to me. Crazy as it seems, I saw a ship with a whole crew of women. Yellow men were buying up half of America. Hegel was spewing from the mouths of Hottentots. Gawd!   Charles Johnson, *Middle Passage*

There are Whig histories of all varieties; "nostalgia," as Raymond Williams has suggested, "is universal and persistent."[1] Not only T. S. Eliot whose "dissociation of sensibility," has been habitually viewed as serving a "cultural elitism,"[2] but Marxists and neo-Marxists, as well, have produced their own Whig histories, drifting into what Pocock calls the "figures of metahistory." Fredric Jameson, though repudiating the affiliation of Marxian paradigms with the gentlemanly and now "extinct" "liberal or bourgeois narratives of progress," nonetheless insists upon a common element to both historiographical strands.[3] The "contradiction," Jameson writes, "which preoccupies much of modern historiography is the whole matter of *transition*" – the "emergence of the modern world," "the miraculous birth of modernity," and "the end of 'traditional' society in all its forms." Although Jameson contends that "the Marxian sequence of modes of production is not a narrative of that kind at all, nor even a narrative at all," he nonetheless contends that

"modernization is the only true Event of history." Jameson denies the
narrativity of Marxism while at the same time invoking "something like
the primal mystery": the "transition from feudalism to capitalism."[4] In
Jameson's reading of the "political unconscious" of contemporary
historiography, "this particular story" of "transition" is what is "being
secretly (or more deeply) told . . . whatever its ostensible content."[5] Thus
Jameson generalizes the content of Burckhardt (and all historiographies
of modernity) to assimilate them into a Marxist narrative. Although
Jameson may attempt to distinguish himself from that liberal antecedent,
his story of "transition" nonetheless has its affiliations with Whig
histories. As Robert Ashton puts it, "the Marxist interpretation may be
open to the same criticism which Sir Herbert Butterfield leveled at the
Whig."[6]

Moreover, as David Aers maintains, it is no longer only Marxists who
remain committed to this vision of history, nor is it only the "feudal" that
stands as the ground-zero for modernity. Rather, Aers argues, there is a
strange and resilient "belief," particularly in literary departments, "that
everything suddenly changed during the period of one's specialization."[7]
Indeed, the problem of historical crisis and transition – even catastrophe
– may not be so easily limited within the bounds of what Jameson
designates as "modernity." While Frank Kermode gamely proposes the
"thirteenth century" as the transition to modernity, and Jean-Luc
Nancy the "Athenian city state," Manis Friedman claims modernity
emerged at the moment when Moses descended from Mount Sinai with
the tablets of the Law.[8] The radical dating of modernity at Sinai suggests
that, for Friedman, the modern functions as does the postmodern in
Lyotard's thought: it is not a periodizing concept, but rather a constant
"state."[9] Whig histories in this reading, with their impulse to constitute a
fallen present in relationship to an unfallen and mythic past, emerge as
recurring responses to what Bloom calls "belatedness."

To be sure, the propensity in contemporary historiography to turn
Hans-Georg Gadamer's binary between mythos and logos on its head,
and privilege the historical pole that the Enlightenment rejected,
requires an expansion of Butterfield's notion of Whig history. If
Sensabaugh, for example, celebrated the emergence of reason and
liberty from the constraints of an unenlightened past, in contemporary
historiography, enlightenment *itself* is often figured as the sign of decline.
Thus, the Whiggism that gained its ascendancy in the nineteenth
century celebrated reason and the autonomy of the independent subject,
while contemporary Whiggism looks towards an historical past (or

future) as a refuge from the modern subject and the reason which it wields. The former tendency manifests a faith in a utopian present that progresses gracefully towards a telos of enlightenment which it already in some sense embodies. By contrast, the latter tendency – Whig pessimism – contains a nostalgia not only for a utopian past, but a utopian future as well.[10] The nostalgia evidenced here is not only political, but perhaps pre-political or metaphysical – the desire for an experience of wholeness and unity. These narratives of decline and fall presuppose Enlightenment distinctions – most specifically that between spirit and matter – which were being articulated by Milton's contemporaries, though not Milton himself.

When, in his *The Immortality of the Soul*, Henry More affirms that "the ancient *Pythagorick*, or Judaic Cabbala did consist of what we call *Platonism* and *Cartesianism*, the "latter as being as it were the *Body*, the other the *Soul* of *Cartesianism*; the unhappy disjunction of which, has been a great evil to both," he is articulating – through a delineation of a dualism – a Renaissance version of what has since become a powerful historiographical trope. Here the golden age is not attributed to the still recent middle ages, but to early antiquity, the "ancient *Pythagorick*" and "Judaic Cabbala." Where varieties of political Whiggism emerge from a tendency to hypostatize freedom and authority, the individual and the sovereign, a kind of metaphysical Whiggism emerges from a specifically philosophical language that insists upon the distinctions between spirit and matter, mind and body.[11] Such distinctions, as in More's language, emerge concurrently with an historiographical myth: the lived experience of a truncated dualism – the perception of the ontologically separate substances of spirit and matter – becomes, paradoxically, the guarantor of an earlier historical unity.

Ralph Cudworth, as J. E. McGuire and P. M. Rattansi suggest, shared some of More's metaphysical, as well as historiographical tendencies. Cudworth, McGuire and Rattansi argue, understood that the "true religious, moral and natural philosophy flows to the Gentiles from the Hebrews," and "came to be fragmented in the course of time."[12] For the Cudworth of the *True Intellectual System*, the first atomist, "Moschus" was "no other than the celebrated Moses of the Jews" whose "authentic atomical philosophy was both older than *Democritus*, and had no such atheistical original either."[13] From More's mythological Platonized Cartesianism, and Cudworth's non-atheistic "atomism" (which he of course contrasted with that of Hobbes and Spinoza) emerges the contemporary experience of fragmentation – what More described as an "unhappy disjunction." Such historiographical narratives as those promulgated by More and Cudworth, suggests Kermode, are "attractive" precisely because they "give design and simplicity to history," and because they explain "in a subtly agreeable way" the "torments and division" of "contemporary life."[14]

The fall into the dualisms of modernity – crystallized for More and Cudworth in the separation of spirit from matter – enacts the inversion of the optimistic versions of Whig history endorsed by the likes of Toland, Sensabaugh, and more recently, Michael Walzer. Where Walzer can celebrate his "bold speculators" who overthrew "the old patterns of passivity," the avatars of "Whig pessimism" see in the emergence of Walzer's "bold speculators" the passing of an historical integrity – what F. R. Leavis called the "organic community."[15] The counterpart of Leavis' "organic community," what Jean-Luc Nancy describes as the "lost, or broken community," can be "exemplified in all kinds of ways, by all kinds of paradigms." But in all of the historical variations of the paradigms, writes Nancy, it is "always a matter of a lost age in which community was woven of tight harmonious and infrangible bonds and in which above all it played back to itself, through its institutions, its rituals, and its symbols, the representation . . . of its own immanent unity."[16] For Nancy, then, the nostalgia for an integrated community, in all of its political, social, and cultural aspects, is ultimately informed by a set of metaphysical assumptions which he calls "immanentism" – "the altogether modern thought of humanity's partaking of divine life." That is, the "exacerbated consciousness of the 'loss' of community" whether located in the "natural family, the Athenian city," or "the first Christian community," is informed, for Nancy, by "the thought of the human being penetrating into pure immanence," which is itself a particular product of *modern* ontological assumptions about the unity of being.[17] Thus, this "nostalgia for communion" is produced by, and related historiographically to, the distinction between mind and body – and the philosophical dualisms which spring metonymically from it: spirit/matter, subject/object – in which what Nancy calls the "intimacy of being-in-common with itself" is no longer felt.[18]

The "unhappy disjunction," then, registered by More and Cudworth, is simultaneously the creation *and* symptom of what for Nancy is a distinctly Western form of historiographical longing. It is an acute form of what Jameson has called the preoccupation of modern historiography – "the whole matter of transition." Indeed, the persistence of what

Nancy calls "immanentism" – the positing of a mythic past in which the dualisms of contemporary life have no place – becomes a primary mode of modern historical explanation. It is this belief in the *reality* of the "immanence" of a "lost communion," accompanied by a no less vehement belief in the *reality* of contemporary dualisms, which informs the historiography of the Cambridge Platonists, and has become one of the primary historiographical tropes through which the seventeenth century is understood. More and Cudworth – in their assimilation of Cartesian dualism to seventeenth-century historiography – helped to articulate a version of history which finds echoes in this century's attempts to historicize early modern thought. These attempts – particularly those of Adorno and Horkheimer and T. S. Eliot – will provide an introduction to the languages and paradigms often employed in the reception of Milton's *De Doctrina Christiana*. Milton's texts, I will argue, though contemporaneous with those of More and Cudworth, resist the historiographical assumptions and oppositions that remain prevalent in literary historians' interpretation of the seventeenth century in England.

Adorno and Horkheimer's reading of Bacon in the *Dialectic of Enlightenment* is perhaps the *locus classicus* in the twentieth century for the interpretation of history which posits what Nancy calls "immanence" at the pre-dawn of modernity. For the two Frankfurt School theorists, Bacon is thought to initiate a modernity where the "leveling domination of abstraction" is "to hold sway over a disenchanted nature" (in the vocabulary of Critical Theory, the disjunction of "abstraction" and "nature" echoes the earlier philosophical distinction between soul and body).[19] This "disenchantment of the world" leads, for Bacon, according to Adorno and Horkheimer, to the "extirpation of animism" and "mystery," and the abandonment of the concepts of "substance and quality . . . being and existence" as "the *idolo theatri* of the old metaphysics." This loss of "quality" and "substance" permits men to "distance themselves from nature in order thus imaginatively to present it to themselves," but only "in order to determine how it is to be dominated." Modernity as embodied in Bacon's thought is presupposed upon the domination of the mind over a "disenchanted nature": "Man's likeness to God consists in sovereignty over existence, in the countenance of the lord and master in command."[20]

The Bacon of the *Dialectic of Enlightenment* is uniquely interested in the "discovery of particulars," in the reduction of "history to fact" and "things to matter," in rendering the "dissimilar comparable by reducing it to abstract quantities." In the Frankfurt Bacon, Henry More's "unhappy disjunction" between Cartesianism and Platonism returns with a vengeance. The Bacon who subordinates a dead nature to an instrumental and quantitative reason initiates the genealogy of modernity which finds its telos, for Adorno and Horkheimer, in the "new German pagans and warmongers."[21]

But Bacon's "particulars," the Frankfurt School notwithstanding, still manifest connections to the universal, and not only that universal by which quality is reduced to abstract and homogeneous quantity.[22] Indeed, in _The Great Instauration_, though Bacon insists "on keeping the eye steadily fixed upon the facts," the Baconian eye discovers more than dead matter, and, in fact, aspires to reveal "an apocalypse or true vision of the footsteps of the Creator imprinted on his creatures."[23] Paradoxically, intrinsic to Bacon's facts, the "disenchanted nature" that Adorno and Horkheimer lament so emphatically, are "imprinted" the "true vision of the footsteps of the Creator." Similarly in the _Advancement of Learning_, Bacon acknowledges the relation of first and second causes, and the inseparability of the universal from the particular:

. . . when the second causes, which are next unto the senses, do offer themselves to the minds of man, if it dwell and stay there, it may induce some oblivion of the highest cause, but when a man passeth on farther, and seeth the dependence of causes and the works of Providence, then, according to the allegory of the poets, he will easily believe that the highest link of nature's chain must needs be tied to the foot of Jupiter's chair.[24]

Bacon's second causes are not leveled, _pace_ Adorno and Horkheimer, into a contiguous mass of unrelated particularity, "disenchanted nature," but they adumbrate the first cause, "tied" as they are "to the foot of Jupiter's chair." That is, there is a simultaneity of different epistemologies in Bacon's work, one tending towards the examination of facts in their empirical difference, and the other extrapolating – by way of correspondence – from particulars to universals. Embracing neither a mythically full "presence," nor a "reality" constituted only by difference, Baconian similarity and difference emerge as a result of epistemological, not ontological categories. Although these appear as irreconcilable and contradictory epistemologies, in Bacon's texts they prove complementary.

Bacon specifies these different epistemologies in Aphorism LV of _The New Organon_:

There is one principle and as it were radical distinction between different minds in respect of philosophy and the sciences, which is this: that some minds are stronger and apter to mark the differences of things, others to mark their resemblances. The steady and acute mind can fix its contemplations and dwell and fasten on the subtlest distinctions; the lofty and discursive mind recognizes and puts together the finest and most general resemblances.[25]

Both, Bacon warns, "easily err in excess." The latter, "prone to abstraction," supposes "more order and regularity in the world than it finds," the former refuses to acknowledge any relation between first and second causes – the "links" between nature and "Jupiter's chair."[26] One tendency, to use terminology from Adorno and Horkheimer, permits the quantification and differentiation of dead matter, while the other responds to the similarities which apparently permeate the world.[27]

Bacon's "metaphysical discourse of *reform*," as Charles Whitney explains, "draws much from the older ideas of the world united by a chain of correspondences and similitudes" while simultaneously informing the emerging view "that dissolves likeness into . . . difference."[28] The latter view anticipates a fundamentally modern ontology where matter is abandoned (and then dominated) by spirit, while the former presupposes a world-view where spirit and matter are *perceived* still, in some limited sense, as co-extensive. For Bacon, as well as Milton, the problem is not ontological, but epistemological: the "facts" and "the footsteps of the Creator" co-exist simultaneously. Ontological arguments with their assumption of a monolithic reality will imply irreconcilable oppositions; epistemological arguments, by contrast, will imply complementary alternatives. As Lord Brooke claimed, asserting the primacy of epistemology over ontology (indeed hinting at the impossibility of a language of being, or what he called "Truth"): "Truth . . . is alwayes and continually one, though it appeareth otherwise to me . . ."[29]

The distinction between mind and body, spirit and matter, in *The Dialectic of Enlightenment*, serves the purposes of the historiographical trope that ends, for Horkheimer and Adorno, with the Nazis and Auschwitz. For T. S. Eliot, these same distinctions (now in the aestheticized modern lexicon, the "intellectual" and the "sensual") became the basis for a literary canon, and for a literary history that seemed to be upheld despite, or perhaps because of, its detractors.[30] The metaphysical poets, Eliot wrote in his 1921 essay, "incorporated their erudition into their sensibility: their mode of feeling was directly and freshly altered by their reading and thought."[31] The integrative sensibility of the metaphysicals, Eliot wrote, "ripens" through experiences "which are at once sensuous and intellectual"; their "keenest sensuous experience" had been "'as if the body thought.'"[32] Out of Eliot's aesthetic preference – for the reflective or inspirited body[33] – emerges an implicit historiography of modernity, for in the seventeenth century, this integrative sensibility was lost, and as the canonical formulation goes, "a dissociation of sensibility set in, from which we have never recovered."[34]

While Donne's sensibility was held to be integrative, "constantly amalgamating disparate experiences," his successors, particularly Milton and Dryden – either too "reflective" or too "crude" – instigated a disjunction of thought and feeling. Elaborating Eliot's theory, Herbert Read wrote that "Milton was conscious all the time of a dualism," while the "true Metaphysical poet is conscious of no such dualism."[35] Eliot's implicit historiography of modernity – corroborated by Read – entails, like its Marxist analogues, a nostalgic longing for integration – for a kind of ontological plenitude – located historically in the middle of the seventeenth century before the fall into "dualism." Where Eliot's Donne, possessing a "unified sensibility," "amalgamated," Adorno and Horkheimer's Bacon, with Eliot's Milton, the harbingers of an impoverished modernity, "differentiated." The dualisms implicit in the historiography of Eliot's "Metaphysical Poets" soon became canonical. Basil Willey, for example, "accepted Eliot's theory as if it were a statement of fact." The "Cartesian spirit" that informed seventeenth-century thought, Willey insisted, hastened the "dissociation of sensibility" and accounts not only for the more "philosophical" dualism between spirit and matter, but "between prose and poetry," "between values and facts," "between what you *felt* as a human being . . . and what you *thought* as a man of sense."[36]

When "Metaphysical Poets" was re-published in 1924, however, Eliot suggested in a new preface that the essay preserved "in cryptogram" certain "notions which, if expressed directly, would be destined to immediate obloquy, followed by perpetual oblivion."[37] Of course, as Willey's enthusiasm attests, Eliot's theory met with no such oblivion; though Eliot himself did have further second thoughts.[38] In 1931, the Donne who years earlier had represented an integrated personality was now a poet who, far from "amalgamating," portrayed "the unrelatedness of things." In Donne, Eliot writes, "there is a manifest fissure between thought and sensibility"; in his work, Eliot affirms, there is only "a puzzled and humorous shuffling of the pieces."[39]

Yet Eliot's essay on Donne does not suggest that the dissociation of sensibility somehow preceded Donne, but rather that the theory – and the historiographical narrative it implies – required severe qualification. Eliot's self-correction suggests that the experience of difference, Donne's "sense of the unrelatedness of things," is as crucial to seventeenth-century thought as its "amalgamating" tendencies; that the seventeenth century does not represent some mythical historical moment of unity. And further it suggests, perhaps, that for Eliot, the "integrated" personality does not emerge from an experience of ontological fullness (or from what Nancy calls "penetration into the divine"), but from a particular kind of epistemological *relationship* to the world.[40]

Eliot's essay on Donne, then, is not only a revision of a particular version of literary history but also of the specific metaphysical assumptions that inform it. Eliot's "integrated personality" – the Donne extrapolated from the 1923 and 1931 essays – experiences both differentiation and similitude. Donne does not, therefore, remain in Eliot's canon as an example of some kind of "unified" sensibility, nor is he represented as a transitional figure *en route* to a disjunctive modernity. Eliot's suspension of the metaphysical question – the question of being – permits the coincidence of apparently contradictory epistemologies where distinctions seem, paradoxically, to be at once static, flexible, and non-existent.

In his aversion to the fixity of philosophical categories, and in his revision of the dualisms of "Metaphysical Poets," Eliot re-capitulates a seventeenth-century mental habit.[41] For whether it is in Donne's trope of "twin compasses," Bacon's divine "footsteps" or Browne's meditation on nature in the *Religio*, identity is affirmed only through the acknowledgment and sustenance of difference. As Browne writes, "even in things alike, there is diversitie, and those that doe seem to accord doe manifestly disagree . . . There was never any thing so like another, as in all points to concurre; there will ever some reserved difference slip in."[42] Contraries, Browne writes, "though they destroy one another, are yet the life of one another."[43] Philosophical argument in quest of an "ultimate reality" can sustain no such paradox, though epistemological argument – harboring no such illusions about the accessibility of reality – can. In Browne's epistemology, oppositions co-exist, revealing themselves as necessary complements to one another.

As the following two chapters on *De Doctrina Christiana* argue, Milton acknowledges the impossibility of penetrating "into the divine"; he had no illusion about the accessibility of "being unconditioned." Milton's work, therefore, resists appropriation in the historiographical narratives in which such access is imagined as a possibility. Moreover, his thought seems to not be entirely assimilable to those categories – especially the dualisms between immanence and transcendence, mind and body, monism and dualism – which have informed the debates about his theological tract. Chapter 4 argues that the scriptural hermeneutics elaborated in Milton's *De Doctrina* explicitly resist the objectivist epistemology (with the possibility of certainty which it held out) which was emerging among his philosophical contemporaries. The subsequent chapter, through examining Milton's account of creation in *De Doctrina*, demonstrates how Milton resists formulation in the philosophical languages of angelic and satanic critics who often adopt the abstract oppositions of Cartesian philosophy. In this analysis, the Cambridge Platonist Ralph Cudworth plays a significant role. For Cudworth's lengthy elaboration of "plastic nature" in *The True Intellectual Systems* manifests a commitment to both ontology and philosophical dualism. The suppositions evidenced in Milton's *De Doctrina* – in which those commitments are absent – come more clearly into focus in relation to the more clearly *philosophical* tendencies of Cudworth's work. The application of philosophical categories to Milton (and especially the attribution of philosophical aims to Milton's work) provides yet another site for the strife between Milton's irreconcilable critical camps.

CHAPTER 4

"Abnormal forms of discourse": Milton's De Doctrina Christiana

I assume that no one thinks you should look for truth among philosophers and schoolmen rather than in the Bible! *Of Christian Doctrine*
(VI 400)

Whig appropriations of Milton – optimistic and pessimistic varieties
alike – have often been presupposed upon philosophical languages
which insist upon the inflexibility of metaphysical distinctions organized
as hostile pairs. The competing claims – raised after the discovery of
Milton's *De Doctrina Christiana* in 1824 – whether Milton was *either* a
philosophical monist *or* dualist, heretical *or* orthodox, mirror in metaphysical terms the controversy over Milton's politics. As we have already seen, for Stanley Fish, claiming to oppose a tradition of liberal
commentators, the polarity is clear: Milton as a poet of "democratic
liberalism," or, as Fish himself advocates, a poet of "revolutionary absolutism." On Fish's horizon, there is either the "democratic" or the
"absolutist" Milton – the Milton of the satanic or angelic camp. The
claims that Milton adhered to and promulgated a philosophical monism
or dualism lead to a variety of similar alternatives: Milton the angelic
apologist for an eighteenth-century Anglican orthodoxy against Milton
the satanic avatar of a radical monist theology, *or*, in a different lexicon,
Milton the orthodox Christian against Milton the antinomian radical.

Recent debates about the provenance of *De Doctrina Christiana*, spur-
red on by William B. Hunter's claim in 1992 that Milton was not the
author of the theological tract, has provided the latest context for the
appropriation and construction of the antithetical visions of the canonical Milton. Indeed, far from being merely an arcane scholarly quibble
about textual provenance, the recent debates played out in *Studies in
English Literature* attest to the extent to which the ambiguities of Milton's
texts continue to produce opposed and conflicting images of the poet.[1]
One could almost say that the latest development – Hunter's "unortho-
dox thesis" that Milton did not author the tract – was, in the history of

Milton's reception, an almost inevitable event. For while earlier readers of *De Doctrina* had their own strategies for dissociating the poet from the theological tract, Hunter's strategy has been more dramatic and direct: to employ the tools of contemporary textual scholarship to demonstrate that Milton was not *De Doctrina*'s author.

Arguably, as Hunter admits, Maurice Kelley's *This Great Argument* "has been the most influential work of Miltonic scholarship published in this century." Hunter, however, aggressively seeks to undo Kelley's legacy, demonstrating that the parallels between *Paradise Lost* and *De Doctrina* are merely felicitous, and often incomplete.[2] Since the tract and the epic share a Reformed Protestant tradition, Hunter argues that there is no reason to be surprised at the many parallels between the Miltonic canon and the treatise (which Hunter finally attributes to John Goodwin). But what needs to be explained and what most "scholars have avoided even mentioning," according to Hunter, are the "contradictions of dogma" between the theological tract and the rest of Milton's works.[3]

It is unnecessary to elaborate fully the nature of these contradictions and Hunter's arguments about them to acknowledge the way in which Hunter stands in a long line of Milton's readers – from Bentley and Toland to Empson and Fish – who are involved in the re-fashioning of the image of Milton. Though Hunter claims a certain scholarly objectivity (distancing himself from the "vested interests" of his opponents), he nonetheless can be seen as part of the pattern of Miltonic interpretation that I have been elaborating – acting the part of the angelic apologist for an orthodox Milton against his radical and satanic-leaning opponents.[4]

Indeed, for Hunter, once the provenance of *De Doctrina* has been properly established, *Paradise Lost* can "be read . . . as orthodox," and Milton can be seen as standing "closer to the great traditions of Christianity" – no longer "associated with a merely eccentric fringe."[5] If there remains any doubt about the rhetorical force of Hunter's claims, then Christopher Hill's response (as part of his extraordinarily learned and extensive reply to Hunter's arguments) should put that doubt to rest. "Those who wish to claim the poet for 'orthodoxy,'" Hill writes, "will no doubt continue trying to explain away the now well-established congruence between the *DDC* and Milton's other writings." But "even if," Hill continues, "*per impossible*," *De Doctrina* were to be "removed from the canon, Milton would not be left any 'closer to the great traditions of Christianity.'"[6] Against Hunter's arguments for an orthodox

Milton, Hill responds with a Milton who – notwithstanding Hunter's canonical revision – remains very much on the "eccentric," not to mention, radical "fringes."

The debate between Hunter and Hill, the latest episode in the history of Milton's reception, is emphatically about the politics of interpretation – all the more so since, as Hunter admits, there is "no 'smoking gun'" to establish absolutely the authorship of the tract.[7] Though some of Hunter's arguments are indeed powerful, and might perhaps lead us to adopt a guarded agnosticism about the actual authorship of the tract, Hunter's claim that the "burden of proof remains on those who think that he [Milton] wrote the treatise" seems to me unfounded.[8] That Hunter in the successive *SEL* articles had to fashion himself more and more as the "one just man" against the persuasive arguments of Lewalski, Shawcross, and especially Hill and Kelley, suggests the burden of proof remains *with him*. That is to say, the inherited weight of *De Doctrina* as part of the Milton canon has created a reality among Milton scholars which has been shaken, though certainly not shattered by Hunter's arguments. Though Hunter claims to be "no longer interested" in *De Doctrina*, it does not mean – and it is indeed unlikely – that other Miltonists will share this lack of interest.[9]

MILTON CONTRASTED WITH MILTON

As Hunter himself relates, he was not the first to try to dissociate Milton from *De Doctrina*. Thomas Burgess, the Bishop of Salisbury, was so incensed at the attribution of *De Doctrina* to Milton, that he not only published his *Milton Not the Author of the Lately-Discovered Arian Work De Doctrina Christiana* in 1829, but he promised a further elaboration of his argument (which never appeared in print) entitled *Milton Contrasted with Milton*.[10] While Burgess's projected work was to elaborate the inconsistencies between the Milton canon and the newly discovered treatise, the title of this promised work provides a gloss on the history of the reception of Milton's theological tract where different versions of Milton oppose one another in polemical debate. In the latest manifestation of this debate, *De Doctrina* appears too radical to appear in Hunter's orthodox version of the Milton canon, where for Hill, *De Doctrina* is simply part of a consistently radical canon. For this study, the inconsistency of these different scholarly accounts attests to a deeply ambivalent – even fissured – Miltonic text subject to vastly different interpretation by various strong readers.

This ambivalence underlies a Miltonic *œuvre* that is only with difficulty appropriated into a single schematic vision. To be sure, our understanding of Milton has been advanced by those like Corns, Smith, and Achinstein, who have worked to recover and articulate the rhetorical contexts for Milton's political and theological utterances. Milton's prose seems at times, however, to overgo the very conventions of polemic, just as the poetry overgoes the conventions of antecedent poetic forms. Though the prose may have been "persistently shaped," as Corns writes, by a "polemical awareness," the polemical energy of Milton's tracts is often compromised by an energy that seems to need to take into account all possible positions.[11] Indeed, as Keith Stavely has suggestively written, if Milton's political tracts "were the only surviving documents of the English Revolution, we would know little about it as a major political event."[12]

Despite the fact that ours is very much a Skinnerian moment in Milton studies, Milton's resistance to his contexts may be as important an aspect of his texts as their functioning within those contexts. Indeed, the Miltonic habit of mind is not at all times best served by a Skinnerian paradigm of "language-games" that insists upon locating and defining utterances within their specific rhetorical contexts.[13] The notion that authors perform, in Skinner's language, "this or that move," and that their "intentions must be conventional intentions in the strong sense that they must . . . uphold some particular position in argument" may not always be salutary for Milton studies.[14]

Skinnerian method, which constructs hypotheses regarding an author's intention within the framework of a particular performative context, often evidences an insensitivity to contradictions and ambivalences – to ways in which a particular utterance transcends, even refuses, the context of its performance. Skinner himself laments the way in which contradictory utterances will in fact thwart the historian's task. Since "the primary aim" of the historian "is to use our ancestors' utterances as a guide to the identification of their beliefs," if "they display no concern for consistency," if "they are willing . . . both to affirm and deny the truth of some particular proposition, then we can never hope to say what they believe about that proposition at all."[15]

Of course, Skinnerian method has provided the framework for Stephen Fallon's brilliant and much-needed recontextualization of Milton's *De Doctrina* and *Paradise Lost*.[16] But though, as Fallon writes, these two texts can be understood as providing a specific response to "an urgent philosophical debate," the texts themselves cannot be fully understood within the emergent philosophical discourses of Milton's contemporaries.[17] Hobbes, Spinoza, and the Cambridge Platonists elaborated their schemes according to the emergent criteria of philosophical truth and objectivity, and in doing so seem to have abided by the rules of the language games which Skinner has so well elaborated. Milton's *De Doctrina*, however, which articulates seemingly contradictory perspectives, is not so easily understood within the contexts of seventeenth-century polemical or philosophical paradigms. Where Fallon claims to recuperate Milton's philosophical "solution," to "characterize," in Skinner's words "what" Milton must "have been doing," I would suggest that it is more productive to consider that Milton may have elaborated a variety of the "abnormal forms of discourse" which "historians" like Skinner occasionally, and, from his perspective, regrettably, encounter.[18]

Indeed, Milton himself seems all too willing to embrace a rhetorical posture which Skinner deplores – "willing both to affirm and deny the truth" of various propositions. Milton may have in *De Doctrina* and *Paradise Lost*, as Fallon argues, offered a "response" to "an urgent philosophical problem," though Milton's own arguments seem sometimes to frustrate the very *philosophical* terms of that context. It is hard to read Miltonic argument as entailing simply a rhetorical choice or "move" in the Skinnerian sense, for Milton's habit of mind refuses conventional polemical constraints just as he refuses or overgoes other conventions – literary and otherwise.

Certainly, as Fallon claims, Milton (with Descartes, Hobbes, and the Cambridge Platonists), was "thinking about the nature of substance and what has come to be called the mind–body problem."[19] But if Milton did offer a solution to this "urgent philosophical" problem, his "response" seems to have been formulated in such a way as to frustrate the very *philosophical* terms of the context which he was addressing. Milton was, as Fallon rightly notes, "interested in the questions of ontology that occupied his contemporaries," but he never fully embraced the language of ontology.[20]

Indeed, Milton explicitly sought to escape what he called in *De Doctrina* "the thick darkness of metaphysics" (VI 580), and his assertion in *The Likeliest Means* that "som where or other, I trust, may be found som wholsom bodie of divinitie ... without school terms and metaphysical notions" (VII 304) is in all likelihood a reference to his own "bodie" of doctrine, a body presumably noteworthy for eluding that "darkness." Certainly, Milton had been excoriating "this monkish disease" since his youth; metaphysics, he claimed was "not an Art at all, but a sinister rock, a Lernian bog of fallacies" (I 301). The "useless technicalities and meaningless distinctions" (VI 580) of the philosophers, the "glosses of metaphysicians," Milton later wrote, were the cause for him of "how many prolix and monstrous controversies" (VI 421). As Milton rejected the language of politics for placing too much emphasis on "human things" and eventually transforming into faction and an idolatry of reason and the state, so he implicitly rejected what he called "the nonsense of quibbling metaphysicians" (VI 262) – the language of "empty philosophy" (VI 212) which was itself the source of dispute.[21]

But Milton's attacks upon philosophy were a commonplace in the seventeenth century, and it is difficult to take them at face-value. For Milton, who in all likelihood learned logic at St. Paul's (and certainly at Christ's College, the Ramist stronghold), seems uncommonly well versed in the intricacies of scholastism, and argues quite forcefully and persistently within the terms of philosophical and even scholastic discourse. But the author of the *Art of Logic* evidenced a predictable Ramist skepticism about the use of scholastic languages. As Ong observes, Milton's Ramist logic was not employed "merely to discern and describe noetic structures, but to get somewhere" – serving as "a context for action rather than a framework for pure speculation." Milton's Ramist logic was, as Ong argues, the perfect corollary of the "Calvinist preference for a world free of statuary," placed in the service of what Frances Yates called an "inner iconoclasm."[22]

Where the politics of the *Areopagitica* and the *Readie and Easie Way* represent a kind of anti-politics, so Milton's philosophical and logical resources were often directed against the traditional scholastic ends of philosophy. Indeed, Milton, in the *Art of Logic*, his translation of Ramus, expressed his own reservations about the applicablity of logical structure to theological argument, arguing against those theologians who

produce rules about God, about divine substances, and about sacraments right out of the middle of logic as though these rules had been provided simply for their own use, although nothing is more foreign to logic, or indeed to reason itself, than the grounds for these rules as formulated by them. (VIII 211)

Of course, despite his protestations, Milton does not hesitate, in the *Art of Logic*, to voice his own "theological persuasions" (as Ong notes; VIII 208n). The inconsistency here points both to Milton's own reservations about the efficacy of logical method to theology, *and* his willingness to employ the traditional languages of scholastic theological inquiry. In *De Doctrina*, there is a similar inconsistency: while Milton seems to play by the rules of both conventional polemic and scholastic argument, his own arguments seem willfully to court contradictions, suggesting an awareness that merely polemical responses to complex theological issues would falsify scriptural complexity in the name of a simple logical or philosophical schema. From this perspective, William Kerrigan's claim about Milton resonates as an implicit critique of those who seek to assimilate Milton within strictly philosophical categories: "By some measures the author of *Paradise Lost* was not a particularly philosophical man."[23] The author of *De Doctrina* was also not particularly philosophical – as evidenced, in the following section, in Milton's unconventional interventions in contemporary debates about the nature of God.

DIVINE NATURE AND FREE WILL

Seventeenth century England inherited the debates about God that had dominated the Continent in the previous century. Where Calvinists and Lutherans celebrated divine power, emphasizing its arbitrary exercise, a humanist such as Erasmus stressed the reasonableness of the divine nature. Hobbes and Bishop Bramhall serve as convenient touchstones for the continuation of this debate in England. Hobbes argued that "the power which is absolutely irresistible, makes him that hath it above all law, so that nothing he doth can be unjust."[24] Bramhall, by contrast, argued God's reasonableness against God's arbitrary power: Hobbes's "greatest error," Bramhall writes, was "to make justice to be the proper result of power." "Power does not measure and regulate justice," Bramhall continues, "but justice measures and regulates power."[25] Where Hobbes articulated a kind of secular Calvinism, Bramhall's rationalist emphasis had an obvious continuity with the Laudian Church and later the Cambridge Platonists.[26]

Milton seems to express an allegiance to this latter rationalist position when he argues that "everyone agrees that an exception must be made to God's omnipotence, namely that he cannot do things which, as it is put, imply a contradiction" (VI 148). God, for example, as Henry More would later argue, could not make a "Football . . . as good an Instrument to make or mend a Pen withal, as a Pen-knife."[27] But notwithstanding Milton's assertion of God's reasonableness, he later argues in *De Doctrina* that "scripture itself bears witness to the fact that his decrees and still more his actions, whatever they may be, are absolutely free" (VI 159). Similarly, in the *Art of Logic*, Milton would argue that "Only God does all things with absolute freedom, that is, He does whatever He wills; and He can act or not act" (VIII 227). Though Milton, in *De Doctrina*, makes a concession to polemical consistency – "in God a certain immutable internal consistency to do good ... can be consistent with absolute freedom of action" (VI 159) – there remains a distance between such conclusive remarks and the processes of thought on display in the tract. Although Milton's more polemical statements can be taken as representative, and placed on a continuum with other Reformed theologies, such an approach fails to register the dialectical energy and tensions of Milton's prose.

The question of the compatibility of free will and predestination – played out on the same set of coordinates as the question of the nature of the Deity – shows a similar Miltonic idiosyncrasy. While Milton certainly answers any polemical or philosophical requisites by providing a notion of "conditional decree" to escape the contradictions between Calvinist predestination and Pelagian free will, Milton's own rhetoric seems again to overgo the constraints and requirements of conventional polemic. Aside from the logical problems – Calvinism seemed to lead to a cosmology where God would be responsible for sin, and Pelagianism (and even Arminianism) to one where God's will was subject to man's freedom – there were scriptural contradictions as well. In the introductory paragraphs to Hobbes's debate with Bramhall, Hobbes classified those texts in the scriptures which might lead to the perception of contradiction: there were "the places of Scripture that make for me" in addition to "those which seem to make against me."[28] Despite Hobbes's own admission of the "contradiction," his capacious intellect was of a decidedly different character from that of Milton. It's not that Milton was any less committed to his conviction that these scriptural texts "may and must be reconciled and made to stand together"; the approaches, however, of Hobbes and Milton were altogether different. T. S. Eliot called Bramhall "single-minded"; Hobbes, of course, could not be considered any less so.[29]

The youthful author of "Whether Day or Night is the More Excellent," however, would never be so "single-minded." Indeed Milton may have employed a classical training that taught the arguing of both sides of an argument (*in utramque partem*), to his rhetorical *disadvantage*. As Leopold Damrosch observes, Milton, unable to "give up either God's omnipotence or man's freedom," is "unusual in repeatedly asserting freedom while giving full play to the logical and theological arguments that tend to cast doubt upon it."[30] Thus Milton attempts to balance the contradictory aspects of his argument: "We imagine nothing unworthy of God," he writes, "if we maintain that . . . those conditions which God himself has chosen to place within man's free power, depend upon man's free will. In fact, God made his decrees conditional in this way for the very purpose of allowing free causes to put into effect that freedom which he himself gave them" (vi 160). Opposed to the argument here which guarantees free will, Milton affirms with equal certainty that such free will can be reconciled with "God's absolutely firm decree" (vi 161). In the notion of "conditional decree," that God, as the Columbia translation puts it, "framed his own decrees with reference to particular circumstances," Milton intends to maintain both God's decree and man's freedom. But this is a position riddled with contradictions (for how can God's will be both "immutable" and "conditional?"), and Milton, continually anticipating the objections of his readers ("But it is said"; "But, you ask"; "But you will object" [vi 159, 161, 186]), never hesitates to entertain the apparent "absurdities" of his own argument (vi 162).[31] Indeed, the concluding remarks of Milton's chapter on "Divine Decree" entails a dizzying shifting of perspectives:

> To conclude, we should feel certain that God has not decreed that everything must happen inevitably. Otherwise we should make him responsible for all the sins ever committed, and should make demons and wicked men blameless. But we should feel certain also that God really does foreknow everything that is going to happen. My opponent, of course, snatches up this last remark and thinks I have conceded enough for him to prove either that God does not foreknow everything, or that all future events must happen by necessity because God has foreknown them. But though future events will certainly happen, because divine foreknowledge cannot be mistaken, they will not happen by necessity . . . (vi 164–65)

The frenetic style of this passage (against all of Hunter's evidence) seems unquestionably Miltonic – if not authentically Milton's own. Here, Milton, as I take it, affirms contrary propositions (man's freedom and God's foreknowledge), anticipates the attack of his "opponent" (who will argue that such freedom ensures that God "does not foreknow everything"), then argues that indeed God does "foreknow everything," though Milton will not allow that this entails any kind of "necessity" or limitation of free will. Milton's answer may provide some rhetorical satisfaction, but a passage such as this evidences a Milton breaking through the constraints of conventional polemic. Which is not to say that Milton's positions here and elsewhere cannot be tidily paraphrased. Dennis Danielson, for example, on the associated issue of the relationship between God's grace and free will, provides this summation: "As

Arminianism teaches, sufficient grace is offered to all human beings, so that their wills are truly decisive, even though they would be incapable of desiring or producing good without that grace." Milton's Arminian position of "sufficiency" enables a "truly decisive" free will, and, as Danielson explains, the "insistence that the power to will comes from God prevents any tendency to Pelagian self reliance."[32] This position, as Milton himself affirms, is thus "absolutely in keeping with justice and does not detract at all from the importance of divine grace" (VI 189).

Milton might have stopped with this formulation, but his sensitivities to the difficulties of the position ("sufficiency" merely displaces the contradictions to a different level), pushes him on. "The power of the will to believe is either the gift of God," Milton continues, "or, insofar as it is inherent in man at all, has no relation to good work or merit" (VI 189). It's not that Milton disproves his argument while attempting to prove it, but the ambivalence that "or" signals suggests – if only for a moment – that free will might be "inherent" (and therefore not "the gift of God"). Though Milton finally rests on the conclusion that such inherency of free will would "have no relation to good work or merit," the continuing shifting of perspectives – which seem to argue alternately from within the perspectives of God's grace and man's free will – suggests that Milton's own rhetorical strategy was pushing the limits of conventional theological polemic. This failure to achieve rhetorical consistency (or perhaps, better, Milton's *resistance* to this consistency) manifests, I would suggest, a reluctance to embrace the singularity of a single, uncomplicated perspective.

Though a rigidly Skinnerian model of interpretation might find itself exasperated with this view, it is not necessary to see Milton's affinity to Skinner's "abnormal forms of discourse" as a failure or even as a liability. The oscillation between perspectives evidenced in Milton's discussion of the divine nature and free will mirrors an *explicit* hermeneutic strategy in *De Doctrina* in which a cultivation of multiple perspectives reproduces the unsystematized complexity of the scriptures. Scriptural multiplicity, militating against both rhetorical coherence and philosophical systems, sanctions the very differences in individual perspective and interpretation already articulated by Milton in *Areopagitica*. In *De Doctrina*, it is Milton's commitment both to language and the multiple images of the scripture which registers, yet once more, the difference between Milton and his contemporaries.

READING SCRIPTURES

Milton's avoidance of the clarity of a single philosophical register is not then a rhetorical failure, but rather a deliberate strategy. What I will call Milton's advocacy of a radical textualism in *De Doctrina* – and a kind of biblical literalism which accommodates a multivalent scriptural text – further registers Milton's skepticism towards philosophical truth, his resistance towards the claims of ontology, and his conviction, to use Emmanuel Levinas's terminology, of the ultimate incommensurability between the "Divine and the human."[33] Indeed, against the demands of both contemporary polemic and emerging philosophical languages, Milton expresses his affinity to both the Bible and its images.

The unknowability of God – in the arguments of *De Doctrina* – underwrites this commitment to language and multiplicity. Thus, Milton writes in "Of God," the second chapter of the first book of *De Doctrina*, that "God, by his very nature, transcends everything, including definition" (VI 137). Milton's radical distrust of language's ability to encompass or make accessible the divine leads him to articulate his idiosyncratic notion of accommodation. God, Milton writes, "has brought himself down to our level expressly to prevent our being carried beyond the reach of human comprehension, and outside the written authority of scripture, into vague subtleties of speculation" (VI 133–34). For Milton, "God must be understood in terms of man's limited power of comprehension." But in acknowledging man's limited cognitive abilities Milton turns to an emphasis on the importance of God's representation of himself in the scriptures. It is "safest for us," writes Milton,

to form an image of God in our minds which corresponds to his representation and description of himself in the sacred writings. Admittedly, God is always described or outlined not as he really is but in such a way as will make him conceivable to us (VI 133)

talem nostro animo comprehendere Deum, qualem in sacris literis ipse se exhibet, se describit. Quamvis enim hoc concedatur, Deum, non qualis in se est, sed qualem nos capere possumus, talem semper vel describi vel adumbrari ... (XIV 30)[34]

That the scriptures – God's accommodation of himself to man – inveigh against "our being carried beyond the reach of comprehension" into "vague subtleties of speculation" is almost a commonplace – even among philosophers.[35] Yet for Milton, the traditional Protestant notion of God's accommodation in scripture as a mere concession to the frailty of human psychology is coupled with a far more radical and idiosyncratic notion of the representation of the divine. Milton's prescribed hermeneutics of the divine do not merely avoid, in Raphael's words in *Paradise Lost*, "what surmounts the reach / Of human sense" (v 571–72), but becomes the privileged locus of truth. For that which is "conceivable" (nos capere possumus), though it does *not*, Milton claims, approximate God "as he really is," provides the *only* access possible to what Milton calls the "divine nature."

Milton's doctrine of accommodation, as H. R. MacCullum explains in his important article, "centres attention unwaveringly on the Bible itself," and "is calculated to encourage the reader to rest in the words and images of the scripture, not to penetrate behind them."[36] For Milton, then, there is no penetrating "behind." In fact, claims to move "behind" or beyond language (the distinguishing characteristic of the ontological enterprise) must have seemed to Milton, like its counterpart in the political tracts – a private monopoly over "public ornament" – a kind of idolatry.

Milton's linguistic emphasis, what Georgia Christopher has referred to as the "distinctively 'literary' cast" of mainstream Lutheran theology, persists throughout *De Doctrina*. Indeed, as Christopher writes, in Reform theology, faith has "an irreducible literary component" for "it is defined by reception of divine words that constitute a 'verbal sacrament.'" While in the tradition that Christopher elaborates, faith is tied to very specific "verbal sacraments" ("the promise of redemption can be inferred simply by the mention of Christ"), Milton incorporates this insistence upon "verbal report" into a hermeneutic that takes in the entire scriptures.[37]

In *De Doctrina*, we find Milton advocating a severe biblical textualism, enjoining biblical readers to "form just such a mental image" (talem prorsus mente nostra concipere [xɪv 30, 32]) of God "as he, in bringing himself within the limits of our understanding, wishes us to form" (vɪ 133). "Let there be no question about it," writes Milton:

they understand best what God is like who adjust their understanding to the word of God, for he has adjusted his word to our understanding, and has shown what kind of an idea of him he wishes us to have. (vɪ 136)

Qualis sit Deus, eos optime capere statuamus qui suum accommodant captum Dei verbo; quandoquidem is verbum suum accommodat captui eorum; qualemque esse valit captum de se nostrum, ostendit. (xɪv 36)

For Milton, the "mental image," "adjusted to our understanding" through the sacred writings, becomes the primary means of access to the "divine nature." "We ought not," therefore, writes Milton, "imagine that God would have said anything or caused anything to be written about himself unless he intended that it should be a part of our conception of him" (VI 134).

From this understanding of divine accommodation emerges the preeminence of the image, for "after all . . . *God is said to have created man in his own image* . . . and not only his mind but also his external appearance" (VI 135). Thus Milton asserts unabashedly: "if God attributes to himself again and again a human shape and form, why should we be afraid of assigning to him something which he assigns to himself" (VI 136). Since "on the question" of "what is suitable for God," there is "no more dependable authority than God himself," Milton reaches the astonishing conclusion that God should be imagined just in the way that he is *represented*: "If *Jehovah repented that he had created man*, Gen. vi. 6, *and repented because of their groanings*, Judges ii. 18, let us believe that he did repent" (VI 134). Similarly, if scripture asserts that God "*grieved in his heart*," that he "*was refreshed*," and that "he *feared his enemy's displeasure*," Milton writes, "let us believe that it is not beneath God to feel what grief he does feel, to be refreshed by what refreshes him, and to fear what he does fear" (VI 135). So insistent, then, is Milton on the primacy of the image, on the represented God, that he insists on the *literal* truth of biblical passages – even when they portray a mutable, re-active, and even passionate God. While Milton adds a concluding, qualifying clause, "provided we believe that what is imperfect and weak in us is, when ascribed to God, utterly perfect and utterly beautiful," the qualification does not wholly temper the force of his claims (VI 136). For as Milton himself writes, "however you may try to tone down these and similar texts about God by an elaborate show of interpretive glosses, it comes to the same thing in the end" (VI 135).

While traditional "theologians" have felt the "need to employ anthropopathy" (VI 134), to move allegorically beyond the literal, Milton argues against the use of this "rhetorical device": If God "wants us to imagine him in this way, why does our imagination go off on some other tack?" (si saltem talis vult concipi, cur noster conceptus alio se vertit [VI 136; XIV 36]). In Milton's hermeneutic, there is the insistence that the imagination stay anchored in the text, and refuse passage into some allegorical beyond. Milton's doctrine of accommodation, as MacCullum writes, requires the acceptance of the descriptions of God "at face value, without any distinction between the 'tenor' and the 'vehicle.'"[38]

To those who feel the need to make this distinction, to move beyond the text, and to transcend the image, Milton bluntly asks, "why does our imagination shy away from a notion of God which he himself does not hesitate to promulgate in unambiguous terms" (cur id [noster conceptus] dubitat de Deo cogitare, quod ipse non dubitat Deus de se clare dicere [vi 136; xiv 36]). For Milton, God must be understood exclusively within the scriptural terms that he himself "promulgates." The original Latin text in which God "does not hesitate to *speak* about himself" (dicere) clearly underlines the fact that Milton's God makes himself accessible to men's minds through *language*. Similarly, when Milton is considering those who "form some other idea of him" (nos contra captum alium de Deo captamus), he wonders "quo id auctore dicimus, quod Deus non dicit" (xiv36). Here a literal rendering – "by what authority do we say what God does not say" – emphasizing as it does, God's spoken revelation, seems preferable to Carey's more abstract translation – "on what authority do we contradict God?" (vi 136).[39] From Milton's perspective, as Sanford Budick argues, "human knowledge, including even knowledge of the divine," lies "in the right perception and comprehension of images."[40] As such, this entails that readers of the scriptures remain steadfast to language, and to the images that God himself supplies.

The radical nature of this approach – and its resistance to consistent philosophical conceptions of truth and certainty – is registered in relation to an emergent Enlightenment philosophy embodied in Spinoza's *Tractatus Theologico-Politicus*. While four years after the publication of Milton's *Paradise Lost*, Spinoza would write conclusively "that revelation has occurred through images alone," and "does not of its own nature carry certainty," Milton was insisting in *De Doctrina* that the language of the scriptures did not contain, but were themselves the very locus of truth.[41] Spinoza, in his rejection of the prophetic imagination, championed a philosophy based "on universally valid axioms" and the study of "Nature alone." The "Books of the Prophets," however, "go far astray," writes Spinoza, in relation to the "demands of our age, of philosophy, and of truth itself." "The aim of philosophy is quite simply, truth, while the aim of faith . . . is nothing other than obedience and piety." While philosophy becomes a source of "certainty," "Scripture and revelation," what Spinoza refers to somewhat pejoratively as "history and language," produce (only) "faith."[42]

Similarly, the Cambridge Platonists, though not expressing the same Spinozan preference for reason over revelation, anticipate the eventual passing of the distinction in English Deism. From their belief that God is a God of reason, and *not* the Hobbesian God of will, revelation and reason begin to converge. "Everything," writes Cudworth in the *Treatise Concerning Immutable and Eternal Morality*, "is what it is immutably by the Necessity of its own Nature" and "not dependent upon an Arbitrary Will of God."[43] For the Cambridge Platonists, the essential rationality of God and his fundamental harmony with his creation places, as Peter Harrison writes, "knowledge and salvation ... under the dominion of that same reason which permeated nature."[44] Whichcote, who found the summary of "all necessary divinity" in a verse from the book of Titus, may have been an extreme case of this phenomenon, though Richard Baxter, Harrison adds, was "substantially correct when he indignantly declared of the Cambridge Platonists that they 'thinke yt Reason must know more of the Divine Being than Scripture.'"[45] When, as in the case of Spinoza and Whichcote, "reason became the criteria and judge of revelation," scripture obviously lost much of its authority.[46]

Milton, however, strongly resisted the tendency to collapse transcendence into the immanence of reason; indeed, he steadfastly insists on the authority of scriptures. Notwithstanding his advocacy of "right reason" (which, as we have noted, is qualified even in his political tracts), Milton, in *De Doctrina*, is skeptical about reason's ability to embody truth. Let "us disregard reason when discussing sacred matters," he writes, "and follow exclusively what the Bible teaches" (vi 213). Milton insists upon the dialectic between authority and reason collapsed in Spinoza's work and argues for the primacy of prophecy: "God either is or is not really like he says he is" (Deus aut in se talis est qualem se dicit esses, aut non est talis [vi 136; xiv 36]).[47] In this remarkable utterance, Milton resists the notion of philosophical certainty – achieved through an unmediated study of nature – for a truth that is divinely sanctioned, though *linguistically* constituted: God is as he *says* he is (est qualis se *dicit* esse). The divine word, without recourse to allegory or anthropomorphism, must for Milton suffice.

The radical textualism expressed in *De Doctrina* is evidenced not only in comparison to an emergent philosophical conception of truth, but to traditional Protestant hermeneutics as well. Where Milton embraces the image, Calvin in his commentary on Genesis insists that the "figure called Anthropopatheia" is simply the way in which God can "expresse that which was necessary to be knowen." For Calvin, the figure, the "means by which humane affections are attributed to God for our capacitie," is employed to accommodate an impoverished human psychology. As "nurses commonly do with infants," Calvin explains in his *Institutes*, so "God is wont in a measure to 'lisp' in speaking to us."[48] From this perspective, anthropomorphism permits the replacement (indeed, the transcendence) of the impoverished 'lisped' text with its spiritual meaning. The various texts – the contradictions and theological problems they pose – are subsumed by a meaning ostensibly prior to or, in MacCullum's phrase, "behind" the text. This Hellenic mode of interpretation, may serve as a precedent for the hermeneutic implicit in Fish's *Self-Consuming Artifacts* (where the material always accedes to the spiritual), but not for that of Milton's *De Doctrina*.[49] For in *De Doctrina*, Milton asserts the primacy, or perhaps the exclusivity of the image: "so far as it concerns us to know," Milton asserts, God "has that form which he attributes to himself in Holy Writ" (vi 136). In the repeated insistence on remaining faithful to the language of the scriptures, Milton not only resists the emerging Enlightenment language of certainty, but also the Calvinist (and Hellenized) hermeneutic where there is a gap between scriptural language and scriptural truth. In his distance from Spinozan certainty, Milton evidences a skepticism towards a truth that can be completely embodied, while in his distance from Calvinist "Anthropopatheia," he evidences a skepticism towards a truth that completely transcends language.

But does Milton's attention to the image in *De Doctrina* mitigate against Paul's injunction, cited in *Reason of Church Government*, of the necessity of "*casting down imaginations, and every high thing that exalteth it selfe against the knowledge of God*" (i 848)? Certainly not. Notwithstanding Milton's insistence that the scriptures "were written for the use of the Church throughout all succeeding ages," and that they are "in themselves . . . absolutely clear," Milton's commitment to the scriptures remains qualified (vi 575, 576). For the "Spirit," the "individual possession of each man," is the "pre-eminent and supreme authority" (vi 587) – an authority which prevents, in the language of *Areopagitica*, the "dead congealment" of a "rigid external formality." That is, the Spirit is the guarantor, against those that claim to "be infallible judges or determiners in matters of religion" (vii 243), that interpretation will remain plural, authoritative for only those who authorize it themselves. Thus Milton remains simultaneously committed to the Pauline emphasis on "casting down imaginations" and the importance of the Scriptures ("the just and adquate measure of truth" [i 700]) – cultivating an iconoclasm placed in the service of what Budick calls "the struggle to attain a truthful image."[50] Indeed, throughout *De Doctrina*, the relationship between Milton's iconoclasm and commitment to the scriptures remains intricate.

"However," Milton writes, "we believe in the scriptures in a general and overall way *first of all*," and "*finally* we believe in the whole scripture because of that Spirit which inwardly persuades every believer" (VI 589–90; emphasis added). Despite the ultimate authority of the Spirit (and the uncertain reliability of some biblical manuscripts),[51] for Milton, the scriptures remain a primary and originary source of authority – "the rule and canon of faith" (VI 585).

Indeed, the iconoclastic Spirit and the scriptural image, as Regina Schwartz argues, are "caught up in a relational configuration." Milton, therefore, writes Schwartz, continually returns "authority to the very scripture" he takes it away from.[52] This on-going process serves its political function in preventing the mediation of the "visible church" from imposing "its own interpretations upon the consciences of men" (VI 584), but it also reflects an interpretive stance which Milton finds implicit in the biblical texts themselves. For in his rejection of anthropomorphic and allegorical explanations of the scriptures, Milton advocates literal readings of *contradictory* biblical passages. Without relying upon Calvinist anthropomorphism through which contradictions can be attributed to God's apparently lisping voice, Milton sanctions two contrary interpretations of the "divine nature." One concrete, embodied, proximate; the other abstract, transcendent, remote.

Thus, according to his reading of Genesis 6, Milton insists that God "did repent," while arguing, according to Numbers 23, that "God has warned us not to think about him in this way: . . . *God is not a man that he should lie, nor the son of man that he should repent*" (VI 135). Milton attempts to temper these remarks, warning his readers "not to imagine that God's repentance arises from lack of foresight" (VI 134). Nonetheless, to imagine a God who at once repents (even with "foresight"), and at the same time "warns us not to think about him in this way" is to push the very limits of philosophy. For "what we are obliged to believe," Milton insists, "are the things written in the sacred books, not the things debated in academic gatherings" (VI 583). For Milton, the ideal reader of the sacred texts, giving no attention to the disputes promulgated in such "academic gatherings," will "form a mental imagine" of a God who does not hesitate "to speak clearly about himself" (se clare dicere) – clearly, but *diversely*. The multiple ways in which God has "shown" himself entail a notion of truth for Milton distant both from Spinoza's "philosophical certainty" and Skinner's search for "consistency." To Milton, the authority of the scriptures and God's representations of himself for the imagination, are at once ultimate and contingent: ultimate as they are experienced, contingent in relationship – to time, to other images, and to "other mens consciences."

REPUBLICAN THEOLOGY

> Interiority is consequently not a secret place somewhere in me. It is that reverting in which the eminently exterior, this impossibility of being contained and consequently entering into a theme, infinite exception to essence, concerns me and orders me by my own voice.[53]
>   Emmanuel Levinas

Although Milton writes with certainty of his own ability to "distinguish correctly in religion between matters of faith and matters of opinion" (VI 121), *De Doctrina* – despite its idiosyncrasies and polemical inconsistencies – is self-consciously situated within a sphere of public debate. Indeed, the same epistemological assumptions that inform the *Areopagitica*, asserting at once the priority, though ultimate partiality and revisability of particular utterances, are foregrounded in Milton's introductory "Epistle to All Churches of Christ."

"I intend," writes Milton, adopting the language of *Areopagitica*, "to make people understand how much it is in the interest of the Christian religion that man should be free not only to sift and winnow any doctrine, but also openly to give their opinions of it and even to write about it" (VI 122). As in *Of Civil Power* where he describes "heresie" as a "Greek apparition" (VIII 247), so here Milton argues that whenever heresy "was used as an accusation" it was "applied only to something which contradicted the teaching of the apostles as it passed from mouth to mouth" ("viva voce traditae" [VI 123, XIV12]). For Milton, it is the "viva voce" – the live voice – of tradition which at once circumscribes and guarantees the open expression of opinion. Milton's *De Doctrina* is then, by his own admission, at once the source of his "greatest comfort . . . a powerful support" for his "faith," *and* ("vel" in Milton's lexicon) a "provision . . . that I should not . . . be unprepared or hesitant when I need *to give an account of my beliefs*" (VI 121; emphasis added). From the dialectical tension between the claims of the self ("fidei") and the "viva voce traditio" which demands from Milton an account of that faith ("fidei ratio") emerges Milton's complex and diffuse notion of authority. Again, as in *Areopagitica*, the individual and authority do not form an abstract antithesis. They remain distinct, though reciprocally defining and in productive tension, like the "brotherly dissimilitudes" of Solomon's temple. In this sense, to adopt the language of Levinas, an unthematizable "exteriority" (which for both Milton and Levinas can be located in both God and community as Other) "orders" Milton, paradoxically, in his "own voice."

Schwartz, though pointing to the "relational" aspect of this authority in *De Doctrina*, nevertheless insists that Miltonic interpretation, like all interpretation, is "essentially an act of violence." Milton, Schwartz continues, is "engaged in just such aggression, even as he is at pains to disguise it" in order finally "to reject the authority of anyone else."[54] In Schwartz's reading, Milton appears in his Bloomian manifestation, "a Protestant Church of one, a sect unto himself." While certainly Milton's faith in his own authority is explicit, he is equally insistent that "any man who wishes to be saved should work out his beliefs for himself" (VI 118). But the Miltonic commitment to the authority of individuals does not degenerate into a chaos of relativized and autonomous authorities. His text, therefore, is ever conscious of its public for whom it exists: "God is my witness that it is with feelings of universal brotherhood and good will that I make this account public. By so doing I am sharing, and that most willingly, my dearest and best possession with as many people as possible" (VI 121).

In the image of Milton sharing his "dearest and best possession," he distributes that "provision" (a distinctly linguistic "provision" as "thesaurus" of the Latin text indicates) to "as many people as possible." And the "thesaurus" that Milton makes public (palam facio) is replete "even to overflowing," not with his own words, but with "quotations drawn from all parts of the Bible" (VI 122, XIV 8). Miltonic authority – in this metaphor – is enabled only through its dispersal, and is, in fact, mediated through the biblical text. So while Schwartz's argument may suggest that Milton's concluding remarks in the Epistle – "Do not accept or reject what I say unless you are absolutely convinced *by the clear evidence of the Bible*" (VI 124; emphasis added) – reveal that Milton was engaged "in an exercise of ventriloquism" whereby "Biblical authority *becomes* Milton authority,"[55] one could suggest the opposite: that Milton subordinates himself to, and becomes subsumed by, what he calls in *Of Civil Power* the "common ground" (VIII 242), of the biblical text and the activity of biblical interpretation.

In this reading, the Miltonic voice of *De Doctrina* becomes a privileged (certainly for Milton himself) though not exclusive mediation of that "common ground." Thus in the opening to the Epistle to *De Doctrina*, Milton can ponder the efforts already "published" on the "subject" of "the chief points of Christian Doctrine." Even though he declares them to be "as exhaustive as possible," he is nonetheless "dissatisfied" with them, and insists that he will not be "discouraged from making the same attempt" himself (VI 118). Milton's resolve to "make a fresh start," through his own "exertions and long hours of study," may testify to the "prejudice" – the "result of habit and partisanship" (consuetudine ac studio partium [VI 120; XIV 6]) – of his predecessors. (It also perhaps testifies to the gap between the "nation of prophets" imagined in *Areopagitica* and the "quibbling" and "prejudiced" "opponents" of *De Doctrina*.)

Milton's dissatisfaction with the work of others, his literal proclamation that "in eo opere non acquieverim" (XIV 2) also testifies emphatically to the fact that "any man who wishes to be saved should work out his beliefs for himself." Anyone who would "rest" in the work of others, and decline the encounter with the biblical text would merely be "unfaithful" (infidus [XIV 6]) to himself. No previous effort "on this subject," no matter how definitive, would have prevented Milton himself from taking up the task. To his adversaries and predecessors, he asks rhetorically: "What is more just, then, than that they should allow someone else to play his part in the business of research and discussion: someone else who is hunting the same truth, following the same track, and using the same methods as they, and who is equally anxious to benefit his fellow men" (VI 204). To "benefit his fellow men," to find "the same truth," Milton sometimes has to take up an adversarial stance in relationship to them – to insist upon difference. "For I take it upon myself to refute," Milton argues, "whenever necessary, not scriptural authority, which is inviolable, but human interpretations. That is my right," Milton continues, "and indeed my duty as a human being" (VI 204).

Nor should *De Doctrina*, Milton suggests, discourage the work and "duty" of others: for "we are ordered to find out the truth about all things" (VI 121). Consequently, he explicitly delineates "those methods that proved profitable" for him "in case desire for similar profit should, perhaps, lead someone else to start out upon the same path in the future" (VI 118–19). To Milton, as to those who would follow him, "work on the subject" may seem as "exhaustive as possible"; though *no matter how* "exhaustive," the task must be repeated. Indeed, to investigate "all things" is, for Milton, by definition an unending process.

In elaborating the qualities necessary for this task, religious and political discourses once more converge as Milton employs a republican language of active virtue to elaborate the qualities necessary for the interpreter of the biblical text. "God does not," Milton warns, offer "his rewards to those who are thoughtless and credulous" (credulitati supinae [VI 120; XIV 6]), for they, like the "people" described in *The Readie and Easie Way*, are "not only in fleece, but in minde also sheepishest" (VIII 460). Political representation, the appropriation of "public ornament" in the language of the 1660 tract, has its correlate in the appropriation of the "common ground" of the Biblical text. Both require action – "men of a mature and manly understanding" (from Columbia [XIV 11]) willing to exert "long hours" with "all possible diligence" (VI 118; excluded from this group, writes Milton, are those who "are ignorant, idle, timid, flattering, doctrinally misleading, avaricious, or ambitious" [VI 805]). But for Milton these active qualities associated with civic virtue are transmuted before "the authority of the Bible."[56] Just as individual political authority is mediated through the never fully articulated public sphere of *Areopagitica*, so the interpretive authority of *De Doctrina* is mediated through a biblical text that can also never be completely embodied or exhausted.

Jean-Luc Nancy's *Inoperative Community*, far as it is from seventeenth-century discourses, has its heuristic applications. "In a certain sense," writes Nancy, "community acknowledges and inscribes . . . the impossibility of community."[57] The implicit notion of community presupposed in Milton's work is built on something like this paradox. Unlike those who extol some version of past or future immanence, Milton's notion of community – though utopian – is not presupposed upon some mythic longing for identity. Indeed, for Milton, political community (in a pejorative sense) transforms into idolatry of the state and corruption; theological community (in the same sense) transforms into popery and "partisanship" ("studio partium," the correlate of corruption). These communities betray themselves – in their very realization. For Milton, however, a community that "inscribes" its own "impossibility" is made (paradoxically) possible by the "common ground" of the scriptures. Like the "public realm" in *Areopagitica*, the scriptures ensure the priority of contingent mediations, while also resisting absolute formulation in any singular utterance or interpretation. *De Doctrina*, then, presupposes a notion of interpretation that at once refuses *and* recognizes the absolute necessity of difference.[58] This difference is inscribed for Milton not only in the manifold images of the biblical text, but the manifold interpretive perspectives upon which his own work is presupposed.

CHAPTER 5

"Milton contrasted with Milton": multiplicity in
De Doctrina Christiana

> ... it was but breath
> Of Life that sinn'd; what dies but what had life
> And sin? The Body properly hath neither.
> All of me then shall die ...   (*Paradise Lost*, x 789–92)

> ... the Spirit of Man
> Which God inspir'd, cannot together perish
> With this corporeal Clod ...   (*Paradise Lost*, x 784–6)

> It is a question which can be debated without detriment to faith or
> devotion, whichever side we may be on.
>   Milton on the death of the soul (vi 400)

Milton's reading of scriptures, especially his account of anthropomorphism
– with its insistence on the compatibility of radically different scriptural
images – could best be called, as MacCullum suggests, *"epistemological."*[1]
This form of argument, as the perspectives about the soul's mortality
articulated by Adam in *Paradise Lost*, resists consistency (and conclusive-
ness),[2] leaving Milton's "system" to appear to more than one commentator
as "contradictory." Milton "was not at all times a philosopher," Arthur
Sewell asserts, "and it is a mistake," he continues, "to impose a logical
system on his thought when in fact there was none complete."[3] Milton,
however, was not so much guilty of contradiction, as Sewell contends;
though the multiplicity of perspectives inscribed in *Paradise Lost* and *De
Doctrina* clearly lend themselves to a tradition in which, in Burgess's phrase,
"Milton" has been "contrasted with Milton."

For critics of Milton since the eighteenth century, monism and dualism
(or in an older lexicon, heresy and orthodoxy) have come to represent
(competing) theories of being. By upholding the abstract antithesis between
monism and dualism, many of these critics have failed to attend to the
ways in which Milton's texts, like their biblical precursor, seem to sustain
apparently contradictory perspectives. Sewell, for example, concludes that
the "inconsistency" of argument in *De Doctrina* implies – against the straight-

forward attestation of the "Epistle" – that Milton could not "have been satisfied with *De Doctrina*." "It seems to me," writes Sewell, "that all his play with the words 'essence,' 'substance,' and the rest reveal a mind unresolved on those questions that touch the nature of Being and the Real."[4]

Sewell's comments suggest a line of argument that may be worth pursing: Milton sometimes employs conventional metaphysical languages in a tropological manner (a practice which underscores his ambivalence – discussed above – towards the efficacy of scholastic languages). Sewell, however, is wrong to suggest that Milton's mind was somehow "unresolved" on these crucial issues. A resolution of these issues, *in the terms that Sewell and other critics have demanded*, would have committed Milton to a philosophical consistency, but, in the process, would have betrayed the complexity of his own position. The apparent inconsistencies of *De Doctrina*, and the tract's articulation of different perspectives on "the nature of Being and the Real," are perhaps not so much part of an explicit methodology, but rather a result of Milton's resistance to the simplicity of the positions which would have rendered him more *philosophically* coherent. Just as Milton's reading of the scriptures does not shy away from apparently contradictory images of God, so Milton's theological treatise expresses itself in a variety of different – apparently contradictory – registers.

For Milton, however, competing and contradictory affirmations about, for example, God and Creation do not entail different theories of *being*, but are rather conditions of different methods of *knowing*. Where the assimilation of Cartesian dualism into historiography and philosophy required a belief (as in Cudworth) in both ontological fullness and its correlate, disjunction or dualism, Milton resists such commitments, and consequently, does not evidence the longing for ontological certainty which so obsessed his more philosophical contemporaries. Rather, for Milton, the orthodox *and* heretical discourses of *De Doctrina* present different – though ultimately complementary – perspectives on what Sewell calls "the Real." These different sets of discourses, expressed together, adumbrate Milton's own ontological commitments (which could not have been expressed with less appearance of contradiction). This is not to diminish the power of Milton's thought, but rather to suggest that Milton's "contradictions" ought not to be, *pace* Sewell, lamented or, *pace* a variety of angelic and satanic readers, summarily resolved and dismissed. As Milton says of God, to whom contradictory intentions are also attributed, so could be said of him: "If we form some other idea of him, we are not acting according to his will, but are frustrating him of his purpose . . ." (VI 136).

For Thomas N. Corns, as we have already observed, "the plurality of Miltonic ideology" reflects precisely an "*œuvre*" that is "convoluted, ambivalent, and internally contradictory."[5] Corns, however, interested primarily in Milton's reception, elaborates on how the "multiplicity of Miltons," extrapolated from an "internally contradictory" text (each bearing its own stamp of "unity"), is "reflective" of "the cultural and political assumptions" of its various interpreters. Bentley's Milton stands as a testimony of eighteenth-century orthodoxy; Wordsworth's to the Romanticism of the nineteenth century. As Gadamer has written, a text's history "determines in advance both what seems to us worth enquiring about and what will appear as an object of investigation."[6] The all-but invisibility of the language of Milton's materialist monism before the publication of *De Doctrina* may be attributed, therefore, to an orthodox prejudice which found his arguments about the unity of soul and body largely unfathomable.[7] (Though, as we shall see in chapter 6, Milton's heretical tendencies were evident to some of his early readers – John Toland and Richard Bentley, for example.) To those for whom the reading of *Paradise Lost* was an integral part of Anglican sabbath worship,[8] the notion of Miltonic heresy (with its inevitable associations with regicide and radical politics) remained a frightening, if not unthinkable, proposition.

This is not to say, however, that the heretical or monist Milton, encountered and then only haltingly with *De Doctrina*'s publication, entirely supplants orthodox interpretation of Milton's works. *De Doctrina* certainly provides evidence for Milton's heretical tendencies, but it also provides reasons for believing that Miltonic argument avoids metaphysical conclusions, and cannot be categorized as either heretical or orthodox, monist or dualist. Indeed, both the proponents and the opponents of the orthodox Milton evidence similar metaphysical assumptions in rejecting the arguments of their antagonists. The ventriloquists for both Milton the angelic dualist *and* Milton the satanic monist present a Milton certain of ontological truths, instead of a Milton voicing a multiplicity of diverse – though – complementary arguments. Indeed, just as in *Areopagitica*, Milton was committed to the Isocratean goal of a knowledge produced through continuous public practice, so Milton's *De Doctrina* reflects a Milton commmited to a multiplicity of interpretive positions, not to the purity of some disembodied and objectivist truth.

Milton's apparent straying from the paths of orthodoxy, and the monistic tendencies of his poetic works are only first registered in print in an anonymous letter to *Gentleman's Magazine* in 1739. Milton, the correspondent observes, is guilty of "corrupting our Notions of spiritual things, and sensualizing our Ideas of heaven." His "heaven," the author continues, "every whit as sensual as the Mahometan's" will inevitably lead to "ill Effects on Religion in General."[9] That Milton seemed to be blurring the distinction between the "spiritual" and the sensual was corroborated by his editor, Thomas Newton, who similarly concluded that Milton "was too much of a materialist in his philosophy."[10] Likewise, in his "Letters Upon Milton and Wycherly," Dennis observes that most of the "Machines" in *Paradise Lost* "have the appearance of something that is inconsistent and contradictory, for in them the Poet seems to confound Body and Mind, Spirit and Matter."[11] Yet despite suspicions about Milton's materialism, Newton, for example, was still able to declare that the poet was "truly orthodox."[12] Todd, Milton's biographer and editor, concurred: Milton was as yet "untainted by any heretical peculiarity of opinion."[13] As Patrick Murray observes, underlining the power of Gadamer's argument, "until 1825," when *De Doctrina Christiana* was published, Milton was regarded as "a poet impeccably sound of faith."[14]

The discovery, however, of the manuscript of Milton's *De Doctrina* in the State Papers Office in London (and the subsequent publication of Charles Sumner's translation) confirmed that Newton's vague suspicions of Milton's materialism were not without premise. The "heresies" that came to be identified in that tract – Milton's Arianism, his mortalism, his apparent belief in the identity of soul and body, and his espousal of *de Deo* creation – all, as Edward Tayler writes, "flow into one another" and constitute a formula for the "integrity" of man. The principle that man is "not double or separable," as Milton puts it, but "intrinsically and properly one and individual" (VI 318), central to all of the heresies, is "finally extended," Tayler writes, "to encompass Christ and Creation."[15] The materialist discourse of *De Doctrina*, therefore, "departs significantly," as John Peter Rumrich observes, from the orthodox dualisms of "Neoplatonic Christianity" – breaking down conventional distinctions between soul and body, matter and spirit.[16]

Yet since Sumner's publication of *De Doctrina*, there has been a continued resistance to recognizing Milton's "heretical" discourses (witnessed most recently in Hunter's claims), particularly as they find expression in the poetic works. A reporter for *The Methodist* in 1826, for example, observed that "those who cherished the memory" of the "author of *Paradise Lost*," and regarded him "as an orthodox believer" were "distressed to be informed that he was the secret advocate of principles subversive to the Christian faith."[17] So distressed, that many discounted, ignored or discredited the "heretical Milton." As Francis Mineka has noted, "even into the nineteenth century," there was "a continued blindness of most critics and readers" in "regard to Milton's heterodoxy."[18] Although a few of the "orthodox expressed the sadness" of those who "grieve the departure of a dearly beloved, yet lost and apostate, leader,"[19] many continued to believe that *Paradise Lost*, as Charles Symons argued, "was orthodox and consistent with the creed of the Church of England."[20] Macaulay's response – his cool dismissal – may have been unusual, though his desire to keep Milton's poetry and prose distinct preserved and continued an old strategy: "It is theological and controversial, and consequently of little interest or value; if printed, it could only add to the lumber of polemical writings of his bewildered times."[21] One of the ways that Milton could continue to appear entirely "orthodox" was to keep his poetry distinct from the prose – what Blunt referred to as Milton's "uncomely parts."[22]

In this century, C. S. Lewis repeated a version of Macaulay's argument: Milton's heresies were merely "private theological whimsies" that "he laid aside" while composing his epic.[23] Sumner's earlier efforts to show the continuity between Milton's prose treatise and his other work (through references to over five hundred parallels between them) were themselves often met with resistance. Frederick Faber's was visceral: "a single thought of that execrable and heretic Milton," who "spent great part of his life in writing down ... my Lord's Divinity," "poisons," Faber writes emphatically, the experience of reading *Comus*.[24]

Faber wanted to preserve Milton's "sacred lines" from the heretical "poison" of the prose, but even in Sumner's translation itself, there is a resistance to Milton's heretical tendencies – or at least an attempt to render them less apparent. John Carey, the Yale translator of *De Doctrina*, points out the ways in which Sumner attempts to fashion a more orthodox Milton: "Where no words corresponding to Milton's Latin proof text can be found in the Authorized Version, Sumner ignores the discrepancy and, instead of translating Milton, prints the Authorized Version reading of the scriptural verse in question." For instance, on the crucial question of Milton's mortalism – which presupposes the identity of body and soul – and therefore assumes that the soul is subject to death, Milton cites Leviticus 21:11, *animas mortuas* – literally translated as "dead souls." Carey observes that Sumner, however, substitutes the Authorized Version "'dead body,'" drawing attention to the "difficulty" by interpolating "'(Heb. "soul").'"[25] Sumner, therefore, provides only in parenthesis the meaning which Milton intended. Milton's citation – an oxymoron to the orthodox believer – undermines the dualisms of orthodox Christianity; Sumner's translation, however, registering a discomfort with the monism of this phrasing, parenthetically notes the difficulty, but then re-inscribes a dualism into Milton's scriptural reference.

The spectacle of the reception of *De Doctrina* evidences orthodox inability to assimilate the heterodox tendencies of Milton's "dearest and best possession" into their conception of Milton the poet. Certainly, the willed blindness to the monist language clearly present in *De Doctrina* registers, as Corns suggests, the "cultural and political assumptions" of the age. It would be misleading, however, to attribute the corollary: that the existence of an orthodox (and dualist) Milton came into being *only* because of prejudice. That is, Sumner's worried interpolation, for example, does reveal the anxieties of the translator, but it also responds to the tensions present in Milton's texts. Thus, we ought to reserve suspicion for those who see *De Doctrina* as providing incontrovertible evidence of the heretical and modern Milton. The "fissured" Milton, in Corns's phrase, engaging the assumptions of a multiplicity of readers, is itself complicit in the production of a multiplicity of readings. The multiplicity implicit in *De Doctrina* registers Milton's own irreducible position; however, neither the monism nor the dualism of the tract fully exhausts Milton's perspective.

MONISM/DUALISM

Though *De Doctrina* would soon, as Macaulay wrote, be "withdrawn to make room for the forthcoming novelties," and "follow the *Defensio Populi* to the dust and silence of the upper shelf,"[26] the twentieth century has witnessed a re-awakening of interest in Milton's treatise on Christianity. Even as the tract regained currency in this century, the issue of Milton's heresies – particularly Milton's ostensible monism – remained central. Some twentieth-century scholars, worried over Milton's monism, were as resistant to Milton's heterodox tendencies as were the orthodox theologians of the previous century; others, like the Unitarians who, at the publication of *De Doctrina*, "joyfully proclaimed Milton one of their own sect," fully embraced the ostensibly materialist Milton.[27]

Not surprisingly, as in the way of all Miltonic criticism, the critics broke up into opposing camps. Saurat, on the one side, appropriating Milton for a secular modernism, suggested that the correspondence of Milton and Overton's "pantheistic schemes" corroborated the claim that Milton revised and republished Overton's *Man's Mortalitie* in 1655.[28] As Empson observes, Saurat wanted "Milton to use the *Zohar* to drive the last remnants of Manichaeism out of Christianity, and therefore argued that God in the epic is already an ineffable Absolute or World-Soul dissolved into the formative matter of the universe."[29] As readers of *Areopagitica*, focusing only on the difference that the tract appears to sanction, transform Milton into an antecedent of liberalism and the modern individual, so Saurat – and readers like him – put Miltonic heresies in the service of a monist and secular universe. Indeed, Saurat and the "New Movement" of the twenties, tended, as James Thorpe has suggested, "to strip Milton of all elements of Puritanism," and represent him "as a rationalistic anti-theologian."[30] And more recently, Christopher Kendrick's claim that an "objective process of differentiation" is "central to Milton's monism" helps to locate Milton within the Macphersonian "possessive individualist narrative."[31] For both Saurat and Kendrick, the discovery of Milton's radical metaphysics only confirms their perception of Milton's radical politics. That is, both critics – attributing a strong monism to Milton – tend to read him either as a Winstanley, a Toland, or even a Spinoza, part of an historical narrative through which the spiritualized creature gains independence from the Creator, canceling, as Kendrick suggests, "predestination in proving it."[32]

By contrast, John Reesing in his "The Materiality of God in Milton's *De Doctrina Christiana*" insisted (presumably against Saurat) that "Milton is not a pantheist," and further that *De Doctrina* "does not contradict orthodox doctrine."[33] More recently, Fish, in his persistent opposition to what he has called the "steady unfolding of the classical liberal vision"[34] in Milton studies has also participated in the rehabilitation of the orthodox Milton. Claiming, as we have seen, to have transformed Milton "from a poet of democratic liberalism to a prophet of revolutionary absolutism," Fish implicitly attacks Saurat's notion of the immanent God which divinizes the creation, and re-constructs a distant God taunting and accusing his wayward creatures. With the re-installment of this absolutist God, there is the simultaneous re-appearance of dualism between, for example, what Fish calls the "dazzling constructs of the carnal mind and the absolute simplicity (unity) of the divine reality."[35]

Here again, in the gulf between Saurat (or Kendrick) and Fish, the binary Milton resurfaces: on the one side, those who proclaim Milton's monism as anticipating or participating in secular modernity, on the other side, those who place Milton's dualisms in the service of conventional orthodoxy. Where one tendency in the criticism on *De Doctrina* acknowledged, indeed celebrated, Milton's monism, the other attempted to demonstrate the dualisms implicit in Milton's text. On both sides, the battle is not 'merely' about metaphysics, but it reflects as well angelic and satanic claims about the nature of Milton and modernity.

But many of these accounts – despite, or actually because, of their sensitivity to detail – seem to be attended by doubt and qualification. In relationship to the parallel issue of the nature of the deity, for example, Walter Clyde Curry worries that God's generation "of among other things, a visible universe" contradicts the Miltonic principle that "God, the ineffable spirit, eternal, infinite, immutable" is "locked securely within an impenetrable numerical unity."[36] In order to resolve the apparent contradiction between a transcendent and an embodied God (which correspond respectively to the different dualist and monist outlooks), Curry insists on Milton's "fundamentally . . . dual concept of deity," and thus invents two new Miltonic categories: "God in the mode of his metaphysical subsistence, and God in the mode of his operational existence."[37] The first would correspond to the transcendent God of orthodoxy, thus echoing an ealier latitudinarian conception of the deity which presupposed the dualist division between spirit and matter; while the second would correspond to the monist God of Milton's heterodoxy which (in its many historical manifestations) presupposes the immanence of spirit in matter.

John Reesing is bothered by a similar problem in *De Doctrina*'s conception of the deity. Contemplating Milton's account of *de Deo creatioii*, Reesing wonders how Milton could "ascribe potentiality to God." Milton, Reesing affirms, "does not intend" this; for "much earlier, he has explicitly and orthodoxly affirmed that God is immutable." "Milton clearly contradicts himself when he ascribes corporeality to God," Reesing concludes, "because if God were corporeal he would be composite," and Milton has "already said . . . that God's essence is in itself most simple."[38] Unable to reconcile the apparent contradiction between the Milton who insists upon the dualist distinction between an immutable God and man and the (apparently monist) Milton who insists that God and man are of the same and therefore "composite" substance,

Reesing feels compelled to dismiss Milton: although Milton "intends to be a logical, honest, devout Christian," Reesing concludes, his arguments are "logically contradictory," and his system "philosophically inadequate."[39]

Reesing's critique of *De Doctrina*, condescending in its attempts to recuperate Milton for orthodoxy, is effective, however, *in its very failure*. For it demonstrates the difficulty of assimilating Milton to either an entirely monist and heretical or dualist and orthodox perspective. Indeed, Milton's "fissured" style permits the orthodox – and the heterodox alike – to re-fashion *De Doctrina* in their own image.

One can, therefore, attend to the Miltonic assertion that "God is PRESENT EVERYWHERE," or to the qualification that follows: "Our ideas about the omnipresence of God, as it is called, should be only such as appear most reconcilable with the reverence we ought to have for him" (VI 144). While the former utterance intends the identity of the Creator and the creation, the latter qualification maintains and insists upon distinction "reconcilable with the reverence we ought to have for" God. As Reesing points out in his attempts to rescue Milton for orthodoxy, when Milton "says that 'the human spirit has no participation in the divine nature, but is purely human,'" he is "plainly thinking of a real, actual, substantial distinction between God and other beings."[40] That is, a creeping dualism – insisting that a gap separates God and man – returns, even as Milton seems to articulate a purely monist "ontology."

Thus Milton, at best, only partially participated in the hylozoism that J. G. A. Pocock attributes to the "mainstream of radical thought" in the seventeenth century. Just as in *Areopagitica*, there is a necessary hiatus between God's providence and human agency (in contrast to Harrington's republicanism in which the two are identical), so in *De Doctrina Christiana*, there is a disjunction posited between God and creation. "The philosophy" of which Christopher Hill writes, which "ended as a kind of materialist pantheism, in which God or abstract reason can be known only in man or nature" is not to be identified with Milton but with Winstanley. For Winstanley, adumbrating tendencies present among the Cambridge Platonists and anticipating the Deists, to "know the secrets of nature is to know the works of God."[41]

Milton's God of *Paradise Lost*, informed by the theology elaborated in *De Doctrina*, remains transcendent, despite Milton's monistic assertion of God's immanence. From an ontological point of view this would entail a contradiction – the simultaneous belief in a world-view in which spirit and matter were separate and a world-view in which they were co-extensive. Milton, however, resolves this apparent contradiction through a perspectivism which incorporates both monist and dualist points of view. In Milton's elaboration of creation in *De Doctrina* (and later in *Paradise Lost*), ontology gives way to a perspectivism which parallels the "epistemological method" of Milton's scriptural hermeneutics.

CREATION

Milton's rejection of orthodox creation relies at the outset upon his reading of Genesis 1:1. Against "the moderns" who "are of the opinion that everything was formed out of nothing," Milton argues that neither the Hebrew *bara* nor its Greek and Latin equivalents "means 'to make out of nothing'" (VI 305). Since it is clear from scriptural sources that God "could not have created this world out of nothing" (VI 307), Milton turns to the question of the origin of matter. Matter, he writes, "must have always existed, independently of God, or else originated from God at some point in time." To the first alternative, Milton responds decisively: "That matter should have always existed independently of God is inconceivable" (VI 307).

The eternity of matter, asserted by Aristotle, is problematic to Milton for two related reasons. For one, "matter is only a passive principle, dependent upon God and subservient to him"; and "in the second place, there is no inherent force or efficacy in time or eternity" (VI 307). To grant the latter – to ascribe agency, "inherent force" to "time" – would challenge the former assertion of God's omnipotence. For if matter is not "dependent upon God and subservient to him," then God would in some sense be subject to matter. The Manichaeism implicit in this notion, acceptable as an explanation for the existence of evil, is, however, no less problematic for its detracting from the omnipotence of the Creator. Those who believe in the eternity of matter and that "all things are created by nature," writes Milton, "are forced to set up as universal rulers two goddesses who are almost always at odds with each other" (VI 131).

Milton therefore seeks an alternative, "guided by scripture, namely that all things came from God." Against the orthodox proposition of *ex nihilo* creation, Milton argues that not even God "could have produced bodies out of nothing . . . unless there had been some bodily force in his own substance" (VI 309). Further, for Milton, "heterogeneous, multiform and inexhaustible virtue . . . exist in God," and he adds, "exist substantially" (VI 308). St. Paul, Milton argues, "himself did not hesitate to attribute something bodily to God" (though the passage Milton cites from Colossians refers to Jesus not God), and Milton concludes for himself "that God produced all things not out of nothing but out of himself" (VI 310).

For Milton, God's "supreme power and goodness" is manifested precisely in that he does "not shut up this heterogeneous and substantial virtue within himself," but does "disperse, propagate and extend it as far as, and in whatever way, he wills" (VI 308). Milton's God of creation, therefore, is at once "heterogeneous" and "multiform" while also, paradoxically, "utterly simple," allowing "nothing to be compounded with it" (VI 140). The presence of "some bodily force" in God's substance does not, however, prevent Milton from asserting that "in his most simple nature," God "is a SPIRIT" (VI 140). Milton's God, "without question, numerically one" ("what could be more plain and straightforward?" [VI 147]), does not, however, hesitate to "disperse, propagate, and extend" his "heterogeneous and substantial virtue." Indeed, Milton argues that the attribution of body to God (which any conventional theology would recognize as ascribing finitude to God) is precisely (not to mention strangely) the source of his infinitude: "I do not see how God can truthfully be called infinite if there is anything which might be added to him. And if something did exist, in the nature of things, which had not first been from God and in God, then that might be added to him" (VI 310). Nothing can "be added" to Milton's God, who is paradoxically "one" and "heterogeneous."

The paradox of a God who is at once embodied and multiform, transcendent and one, is registered again as Milton attempts to explain the problem of the apparent imperfection of matter attributed to his account of *de Deo* creation. Taking aim at the proponents of *ex nihilo* creation, Milton writes: "Those who object to [my] theory, on the grounds that matter was apparently imperfect, should also object to the theory that God originally produced it out of nothing in an imperfect and formless state" (VI 308). That is, those who will argue that the *de Deo* attribution of "imperfect" substance to God is not "reconcilable with the reverence we ought to have for him," will have to examine their own account. "What does it matter," Milton continues, "whether God produced this imperfect matter out of nothing or out of himself?" (VI 308). The problem of the imperfection of matter remains, Milton argues, for the proponents of *ex nihilo* creation. They merely transfer the imperfection from the "material" and "formal" (what Milton calls "internal") causes to "external causes." "To argue" that "there could have been no imperfection in a substance which God produced out of himself, is only to transfer the imperfection to God's efficiency" (vi 308). By Milton's account, it is equally problematic to attribute such imperfection to "God's efficiency" as it is to God's substance. But all this turns out to be merely a rhetorical ploy: Milton brings up the problem of "imperfection" merely to dismiss it. He neither entertains the possibility of an imperfect material nor of an imperfect efficient cause, for "matter . . . came from God in an incorruptible state, and even since the fall it is still incorruptible, so far as its essence is concerned" (vi 309).

Milton, however, is not out of the woods yet: "But the same problem, or an even greater one, still remains. How can anything sinful have come, if I may so speak, from God?" (vi 309). Here, Milton confronts what Dennis Danielson has called the theological problem "in its barest form," the Tertullian question of *unde male*: If "God is both omnipotent and wholly good – how is it that evil can in fact exist in the world?"[42] Although Milton has safeguarded God's omnipotence by dispensing with the proposition that matter "must have always existed, independently of God," he has not dealt sufficiently with this problem of evil. As before, Milton provides his "usual response," turning the question back on the proponents of *ex nihilo* creation: How "can anything sinful," he asks, "have come from that virtue and efficiency which themselves proceed from God?" (vi 309). That is, for Milton, the *ex nihilo* explanation of creation has to contend equally with the problem of sin and evil, originating not from God's substance, but from the "virtue and efficiency" which "proceed" from him.

Here, however, Milton cannot continue to hide behind his attack on *ex nihilo* creation. For while he was able to dismiss the problem of the imperfection in substance, he cannot deny the existence of sin. Nor, he knows, can he attribute this sin to God. So at the crucial moment, the monist cosmology, emphasizing the continuity between a God of "bodily force" and his creation, collapses, and Milton suddenly emphasizes their contiguity and difference:

When matter or form has gone out from God and become the property of another, what is there to prevent its being infected and polluted, since it is now in a mutable state, by the calculations of the devil or of man, calculations which proceed from these creatures themselves. (vi 309)

"Gone out from God" ("egressa" [Patterson, xiv 24]), matter and form are suddenly figured as going beyond the limits of God's provenance – beyond the confines of the Deity. Here, matter and form, by a metaphorical transference, are now "the property of another," possibly "infected and polluted" by "calculations of the devil or man" which significantly "proceed *from these creatures themselves*" ("ratiocinia Diaboli atque hominis ab ipsis produentia" [Patterson, xiv 24]). Indeed, for Milton, as Curry notes, the narrative of creation necessitates that we "speak of God's 'external' efficiency in creation as if he were producing something *outside* of himself." And, further, as Curry continues, it requires that "we speak of the multitude of 'independent essences,' or things composed of matter and form, as if they were independent of God."[43]

Narrative – developing in time – insists on this dualism and on the existence of evil. Because of man's "mutable state" (which is, of course, not to be transcended), evil is understood as independent of God. The narrative components of Milton's version of creation in *De Doctrina*, affirming distinction between God and nature, come to qualify the ostensibly monist ontology implicit in that account.[44] Monism and dualism coincide; both, productions of "man in the mortal state," have the same status as *narratives*.

The different perspectives inscribed in Milton's account of creation may be said to coincide with what Edward Tayler describes as "the time of the creature and that of the creator." "In the knowing Christian," writes Tayler, "there resides the timeless self conferred by God . . . that may radiate throughout a man's being, lifting him momentarily from the temporal to the eternal."[45] It could perhaps be argued that only the (dualist) time of the creature lends itself to narrative articulation, and that the (monist) time of the Creator is a privileged non-narrative form. But in so far that Man in his "mutable state" only intuits the "continuity" of Solomon's temple, knowing "it can be but contiguous in *this* world" (emphasis added), so the time of the Creator is *only* accessible through language, the vehicle of "man in his mutable state." Milton's aspirations, then, do not transcend the bounds of language. Like the contradictory accounts of God in the Bible, so Milton's distinct and contradictory accounts of creation both have their authority and efficacy. Narrative thus comes to accommodate a set of perspectives that cannot be fully rendered in the languages of scholasticism or the emergent objectivist languages of philosophy.

Yet debates on the ontology of *De Doctrina* and *Paradise Lost* continue – and very much along the lines of the debates of mid-century. While there are few critics today who are invested in the way that C. S. Lewis was in preserving a notion of the "orthodox" Milton (though Hunter provides an interesting exception), the most compelling recent expositors of Milton's cosmology, Regina Schwartz and Stephen Fallon, have nonetheless succeeded in producing mirror-images of one another's arguments. The problem of evil – particularly the problem of the status of Chaos in *Paradise Lost* – has been the latest site for this most recent debate on Milton's ontology.

For Schwartz, arguing for the dualism implicit in Milton's cosmology, the Chaos of Milton's *Paradise Lost* represents an independent and sometimes autonomous source of evil. According to Schwartz, Milton verges on a kind of Manichaeism. His "hostile chaos" is "a powerful expression of human fault," existing independently of God's creation. Although "subsuming this hostile other, evil, to divinity is the project" of Milton's theodicy, Chaos is still granted its own autonomy. To Schwartz, Chaos negotiates the "contradiction at the heart of the Christian myth of salvation": that an "omnipotent God has no real enemy," yet requires "the defeat of just such an enemy." When "we have eradicated any hint of an evil principle," Schwartz contends, we are left with "the absurd vision of salvation history as a game or play" in which God, as the Russian theologian Nicholas Berjaev puts it, "'play[s] with himself.'"[46] Without an autonomous and "hostile other," God is, absurdly, according to Schwartz, reduced to unity with his creation. Without the difference of evil, Schwartz implicitly argues, narrative (salvation history), free-will, and evil are impossible and illusory.

Stephen Fallon, arguing for Milton's monism, claims, however, that "Chaos serves in the text" as precisely a "mirage of evil," fulfilling "the requirements of . . . narrative motivation." Like "all mirages," however, "the evil Chaos disappears when we get too close to it."[47] Schwartz, presupposing a dualist Milton, and Fallon, arguing for his monist Milton, in their either/or arguments disagree according to the well-defined precedent of their predecessors: where Schwartz insists on a God distinct from creation, Fallon argues for their ultimate unity. The positions, though logically contradictory, are both equally Miltonic – according to different and finally irreconcilable narrative perspectives of the poem. Evil for Milton is – from different perspectives – both a mirage *and* a reality.

This is the primary tension, as we shall see, in *Paradise Lost* which, as Marshall Grossman points out, "conflates a pre-lapsarian and monistic view of human life with a post-lapsarian and dualistic one."[48] Dualism accounts for, among other things – the existence of evil and free choice – while Milton's monistic discourses anticipate the time when, in the language of *Paradise Lost*, "God shall be all in all" (III 341). When Fallon suggests that the Cambridge Platonists, grappling with the issue of the relationship between mind and body, "subscribed simultaneously to an ontological dualism and monism," he is certainly right. In his reading of Milton, however, he obscures the way in which Milton subscribed to an *epistemological* dualism and monism – which allowed simultaneously for competing perspectives on the nature of God and creation. It is primarily this difference that distinguishes Milton from his contemporaries.

AMONG THE PHILOSOPHERS: MILTON AND CUDWORTH

Without doubt, Milton was, as Fallon suggests, thinking about "what has come to be called the mind–body problem." But Milton's very approach to this problem is at odds with the more philosophical approach of, for example, the Cambridge Platonist, Ralph Cudworth. Milton's stance, represented in his insistence that language always remains inadequate to its object, becomes clearer in relation to Cudworth and his wholly different *ontological* assumptions. That is, Milton does not entertain, as Cudworth does, the emerging Enlightenment notion that reason provides an unmediated access to an objective truth. Further, Milton's epistemological methodology resists both the philosophical and historiographical oppositions present in Cudworth's work. The philosophical languages of the Cambridge Platonist aspire to escape contradiction and to attain certainty, while for Milton, such certainty is not a criterion. For Milton, narratives, elaborating limited and often contradictory perspectives, embody forms of arguments or positions which are not always assimilable to the demands of philosophical language.

In the relationship between spirit and matter, as evidenced in Milton's discussion of creation in *De Doctrina*, is resolved the central issues of any theology: the question of evil, the problem of free will, and *primarily* God's relation to the created world. On this last issue, so much depended. Milton, as we have seen, goes to great lengths in his account of creation to avoid the implication that matter is somehow independent of God. Similarly, Cudworth in his *True Intellectual System* authorizes a metaphysics in which God's presence is manifested in the world through the intermingling of spirit and matter. But where the cosmology of *De Doctrina* does not engage with the more radical ontological assumptions of Descartes and Hobbes – where matter is pure extension and there is no spirit – Cudworth seems compelled to accept certain Cartesian (and Hobbesian) conclusions before denying their ramifications.[49] Milton, unlike Cudworth with his unambiguously modern philosophical language, escapes the constraints and assumptions of this philosophical argument.

Milton's monist and dualist discourses exist concurrently in a tract (and not always harmoniously; witness the attributions of "incoherence") which has been difficult to fully appropriate into either critical camp. For Milton, narrative argument, as opposed to the objectivism presupposed in Cudworth's prose, foregrounds the impossibility of objective certainty attained through language, and thus cultivates a variety of different perspectives. Milton's critics, however, employing versions of Reesing's critical touchstone of philosophical "coherence," have attributed to Milton differing and competing (but usually consistent) ontologies. To apply this criterion of ontological coherence to Milton is to read him through the lens of philosophical categories that do not so much respond to, as violate the assumptions of his thought. In Cudworth, by contrast, we do see the articulation of rival ontologies; he, unlike Milton, is the proper object of a strictly *philosophical* analysis.

The philosophical and theological systems of the Cambridge Platonists, writes Rosalie Colie, were largely "defined to reanimate the machine universe bequeathed by Descartes." Although, as Colie suggests, for the Cambridge Platonists, "the immanent God in all places at all times" was a "basic principle of philosophy," materialist assumptions about the gap between spirit and matter underlie an anxiety at the very foundation of their thought.[50] Certainly Milton's later political tracts (the despairing rhetoric of, for example, *The Readie and Easie Way*) and *Paradise Lost*, in Adam's sorrow at the prospect of his expulsion from Eden, also inscribe an anxious consciousness of God's possible abandonment from the created world. But when Adam laments, learning of his inevitable departure from paradise, that "all places inhospitable appear and desolate, / Not knowing us or known" (xi 305–6), it is a position mediated through Adam's particular consciousness (subject to continual revision through his long discourse with Michael). Indeed, the loss for Adam of the "familiar," God's "blessed countenance ... Presence Divine" (xi 319), is qualified by Michael's re-assurance that "God is as here and will be found alike / Present" (xi 350–51).

Milton represents the consciousness of God's post-lapsarian presence (or absence) through Adam's *experience* in the final two books of *Paradise Lost*. Cudworth, by contrast, in opposition to the Miltonic representation of various forms of experience, speaks in an unqualified and univocal philosophical language: "There is nothing," he writes, "in body or matter, but magnitude, figure, site and motion or rest," and "the whole corporeal World... is nothing else but a Heap of Dust."[51] Methodological difference is inscribed in generic difference: Miltonic epic emphasizes the cognitive and epistemological, while Cudworth's philosophical *Treatise* – meeting the philosophical criteria established in Spinoza's *Tractatus* – tends towards a description of the object itself. In this description of the object, Cudworth did not (*contra* Coplestone) turn his back on the Cartesian interpretation of nature. Rather, as McGuire and Rattansi have argued, Cudworth accepted as his philosophical point of departure a "sharp distinction between spirit and matter."[52]

To mediate between this ontological chasm and to infuse Cartesian mechanism with divine causality, Cudworth described what he called the "plastick power." This plastic power, tying, as More was to write, "Soul and ... Matter together,"[53] negotiated between the poles of the heresies – "Atomical atheism" and "Hylozoist atheism" – that Cudworth himself was to document in his *True Intellectual System*. Where the "Atomick" atheist "supposes the notion or idea of body to be nothing but extended resisting bulk, and consequently to include no matter of life and cogitation in it," the "Hylozoick" atheist "makes all body... to have life essentially belonging to it." The "Atomical" atheism, Cudworth continues, "supposes all *Life* whatsoever to be *Accidental, Generable* and *Corruptible*; But the *hylozoick* admits of a certain *Natural* or *Plastic* life, *Essential* and *Substantial*... though attributing the same only to Matter, as supposing no other Substance in the World besides it."[54] In the "Atomick atheism" associated with Descartes and the "modern atheistical pretender" Hobbes, matter is conceived independent from spirit, having "no matter of life and cogitation in it." By contrast, the "Hylozoick atheism" (linked by M. H. Carré with Gassendi and Bacon, though we might think equally of Spinoza or Toland)[55], attributes "a certain natural or plastic life" to matter, though admitting "*no other substance* in the world besides it." "Unless," therefore, writes Cudworth, "there be such a thing admitted as a Plastick Nature that acts ... *for the sake of something*... one or other of these Two Things must be concluded": the dualist separation of God from the created world as in Descartes and Hobbes *or* the assertion of their absolute identity in what Cudworth called the Hylozoist "nature" or Deity "a very Mysterious piece of Non-sense" (*TIS*, pp. 147, 106).

Cudworth, through his articulation of the "plastic nature," attempts to avoid both "Atomick" mechanical dualism and "Hylozoist" radical monism. For the plastic nature, writes Cudworth, at once "*Domineers* over the Substance of the whole *Corporeal Universe*" and acts "Subordinately to the Deity" (*TIS*, p. 164), linking God to creation though not identifying him with it. This "plastic nature," for Cudworth, represents "*Reason Immersed and Plunged* into Matter," evidencing the "Stamp or Signature of the Divine Wisdom."[56] Reconciling the "*Contrarieties* and *Enmities* of Particular things," this power "passing through the universe," brought them "into one *General Harmony* in the *Whole*" (*TIS*, p. 152). Like the Cartesian "pineal gland," Cudworth's mediating third term, the plastic power – "*acting immediately on . . . Matter as, an Inward Principle*" – permits the resolution of contraries, allowing the manifestation of spirit in the material world (*TIS*, p. 155). But if Cudworth's plastic nature is "*fitly . . . resembled to the Harmony of Disagreeing things*" (*TIS*, p. 152), the *discordia concors* achieved in the *True Intellectual System* is the cosmological equivalent of what Dr. Johnson called Clevelandizing – here spirit and matter "yoked by violence together."

If there is indeed "something perverse"[57] about the "plastic power" and its place amidst Cudworth's massive collocation of heresies, then it lies perhaps in the very power that the heretical atheisms seemed to exert over Cudworth himself. Dryden, sensing Cudworth's affinities towards the very heresies against which he was ostensibly arguing, noted that Cudworth "raised such strong objections against the being of a God and Providence that many think he has not answered them."[58] Shaftesbury, similarly, gave credibility to the judgment of those who "accused" Cudworth "of giving the upper hand to the Atheists for having only stated their reasons and those of their adversaries fairly together."[59] Indeed, just as Cudworth's assertion that the "whole corporeal World . . . is nothing but a Heap of Dust" allies him strangely with the dualism of Descartes and the materialism of Hobbes,[60] so Cudworth's articulation of the "plastical power" allies him with the very "hyolozoist" atheists he so rigorously attacks. In "making orderly activity a quality that matter could possess of its nature," Alan Charles Kors writes, Cudworth, who sought "to identify and analyze ancient atheism, virtually gave lessons in how to think 'atheistically.'"[61]

Of this latter tendency, Cudworth (on some level) was no doubt aware: much of the *True Intellectual System* is devoted to distinguishing Cudworth's own position from "hylozoist atheism" and its "misunderstanding of the Plastic Power" (*TIS*, p. 107; emphasis added). Emphatic in his attempt to avoid attributing intelligence and thus independent agency to matter, Cudworth asserted that the plastic powers "*doth only, but not Know*" (*TIS*, p. 156). This "plastic nature" "is so far from being the

First and *Highest Life*," urged Cudworth, "that it is indeed the Last and Lowest of all *Lives*" (*TIS*, pp. 162–63) – equivalent with what he called the "*Vegetative*" (*TIS*, p. 163). But by personifying the plastic power (it "doth not comprehend the *Reason* of its own Action" [*TIS*, p. 158]), Cudworth cannot help but himself point towards the ways in which his plastic power dovetails with hylozoism. Imputing agency to the plastic power thereby to deny it, Cudworth risks identifying spirit entirely with matter, a consequence he saw embodied in the extreme in "hylozoism" – "the *Breaking* and *Crumbling* of the *Simple Deity*" and "all the several *Atoms* of it" into "*Matter*" (*TIS*, p. 871). If nothing else, Cudworth's tract establishes just how difficult it is to solve these metaphysical problems within a purely philosophical system.

Cudworth, in order to achieve a philosophical reconciliation, both emphatically rejects the mechanism of the "sottish" Hobbes, and obsessively distances himself from the monism of the hylozoists. But in order to do so, he articulates his strange notion of the "plastic power," an "inward principle" acting "*Vitally* and *Magically*" within matter – which, to his critics, identified him with both heresies.[62] On the surface, the phenomenon seems to provide a direct parallel to Milton. Milton, variously condemned and celebrated as a proponent of heresy or a bastion of orthodoxy, seems to have suffered, in his critical reception, the same fate as Cudworth. But no matter what our commitment to a Gadamerian hermeneutic, neither Cudworth nor Milton can be rendered incoherent or contradictory on account of their critical reception. For the parallel between the reception of Milton and Cudworth goes only so far. Cudworth's argument in the *True Intellectual System*, presupposing simultaneously the truncated universe of spirit and matter bequeathed by Descartes and Hobbes, and the resolution of this dualism in the "plastic power," manifests, as Fallon claims, a commitment to both "an ontological dualism and monism." Competing theories of being – contradictory ontologies – are simply that: contradictory.

By contrast, Milton's notion of biblical representation (insisting on both the validity *and* irreconcilability of contradictory scriptural texts) and his notion of interpretation (insisting on both the validity *and* irreconcilability of contradictory scriptural interpretations) explicitly resist the philosophical assumptions of the critics who have come to anatomize him. Employing both a philosophical language and a historiographical paradigm informed by metaphysical distinctions that remained fluid for Milton, generations of critics (sharing many of the philosophical suppositions of Cudworth) have attributed to Milton a variety of differing and competing ontologies. Where these philosophical distinctions may have had reality for Cudworth (as we have noted both in his cosmology and historiography), in *Paradise Lost* Milton avoided the philosophical presuppositions of his contemporary. His texts, inscribing the consciousness of the incommensurability between the "Divine and the human" provide competing perspectives, and never transcend the limitations of language. As Nancy Streuver has suggested, Cudworth's strategy, like Descartes's, involved the "total segregation" of the "Pure Inquirer" engaged "in the search for truth."[63] For Milton, however, the object would have to be mediated through a variety of different linguistic perpectives. Both the pure "inquirer" and the pure "object," for Milton, are unattainable.

The differences in the approaches of Milton and Cudworth are nowhere better manifested than in the strategies they employ for negotiating the crucial relation between spirit and matter.[64] In his articulation of the plastic power, Cudworth struggles to attribute spirit to matter, even as he is at pains to avoid its more heretical implications. Thus, even while insisting that matter's inward principle acts "vitally and magically," he argues:

Now there can be no such Thing as God, if stupid and senseless Matter be the first Original of all Things; and if all Being and Perfection that is found in the World, may spring up and arise of the dark Womb of unthinking Matter; but if Knowledge and Understanding, if Soul, Mind and Wisdom may result and emerge out of it, then doubtless everything that appears in the World may . . .[65]

Compare how Milton voices the same hesitation about the possibility that "all Being and Perfection" arise out "of the dark womb of unthinking Matter" in his description of the third day of the creation in Book VII of *Paradise Lost*:

> forth crept
> The smelling Gourd, up stood the corny Reed
> Embattl'd in her field: and th' humble shrub,
> And Bush with frizzl'd hair implicit . . .
> . . . That Earth, now
> Seem'd like to Heav'n, a seat where Gods might
> dwell . . .   (320–23; 328–29)

The personification of the products of the earth – the "smelling Gourd,"[66] the "corny Reed / Embattl'd in her field," the "humble shrub" – give the impression of the earth's independent agency, suggesting that matter, in Cudworth's words may "be the first original of all Things." Similarly, the "Bush" with its "frizzl'd hair implicit" suggests earthly and material autonomy, acting of its own accord to provide a "seat" where the "Gods might dwell." The egg "Bursting with kindly rupture" (419); the "Libbard, and the Tiger, as the Mole / Rising" (467–68); the "swift Stag" with its "branching head" (469–70), all suggest that the "fertile Womb" (454) of the earth is the Lucretian agent of its own creation. The former image of the "Main Ocean," fermenting "the great Mother," *already* "satiate with genial moisture" to "conceive" (281–82) reinforces the impression of an independent and autonomous creation. This narrative seems even to drift into Manichaeism, as the "torrent rapture," hasting "with glad precipitance" flows with "Serpent error wand'ring" (299, 291, 302). However, against the perspective provided in this narrative, the competing narrative of divine authority is evidenced in the simple assertion that "God had yet not rain'd" (331). The monist account of an inspirited self-generating matter is juxtaposed and balanced by the far more bare account of the "Earth / God made" (335–36). These are articulated not, however, as contradictory ontologies, but as competing narrative perspectives which themselves, what Jean Howard calls "situated" discourses, make no claims about ontological Truth or reality.[67] Though the elegance of this solution has no parallel in *De Doctrina*, the tract's cultivation of apparently contradictory perspectives does, however, anticipate the strategy of the epic.

Although, as Milton explains, "Immediate are the Acts of God, more swift / Than time or motion" (176–77), these "Acts" to "human ears / Cannot without procéss of speech be told" (177–78). There may, as in the more radical moments of Milton's monist discourses in *De Doctrina*, appear to be no hiatus between God and his creation. But God's "immediate" (or unmediated) relationship to his creation can – within the confines of Time – only be rendered mediately, through language. That is, even in *Paradise Lost*, the title of which has been argued to signify every kind of nostalgia, Milton never evidences any longing for a language of pure presence. "Process of speech," in its very contingency, its own acknowledged inadequacy to the object it posits, is for Milton the very locus of ultimacy, of truth. It is to "process of speech," the *narratives* of *Paradise Lost*, and to the reception of Milton's epic to which we now turn.

PART III

Poetics

CHAPTER 6

Those Grand Whigs, Bentley and Fish

In the mid-seventeenth century, the Cambridge philosophers, with an allegiance both to the new science and traditional theology, sought to escape two equally dangerous heresies: both the emergent Cartesian dualism between spirit and matter and the radical monism embodied in ancient and modern "hylozoism." But in Cudworth's *True Intellectual System*, as we saw in the previous chapter, the simultaneous adherence to an ontological monism, guaranteeing God's participation in his creation, and dualism, guaranteeing his separateness from creation, led to explicit contradiction, if not to bizarre conceptual offspring – his "plastic nature" for example. Although the identification of spirit with matter in philosophical argument through the "plastic nature" could be deployed in the assault against Cartesian mechanism, it was itself symptomatic, as the obsessive and compendious discourses of the *True Intellectual System* attest, of the equally unpleasant and "atheistical" alternative of "hylozoism."

Implicit in the ontological monism raised to combat the new science, lay the possibility of – from the point of view of Christian belief – a far more devastating dualism. Matter endowed with its own spirit, divinity interiorized, would leave a disinterested, if not debilitated God, rendered increasingly irrelevant, ultimately to be subsumed entirely by his creation. By attributing "motion to matter and treating the universe as an exclusively material entity," those whom Cudworth called hylozoists broke the link that "connected the individual human being to God." They were thus guilty, as Robert E. Sullivan explains, of advocating atheism.[1] To outflank the mechanists, Cudworth risked the appearance of an alliance with the hylozoists, Deists, and free-thinkers. *The True Intellectual System* reads like one man's confrontation with his alter ego. From a philosophical, as well as personal point of view, the battle was unwinnable.

The history of Milton's reception and appropriation is not unrelated to the heresy that Cudworth identified but could not altogether resist. For hylozoism, as J. G. A. Pocock has shown, persisted – it was the "dark underbelly to Restoration philosophy" – and represented a challenge to an eighteenth-century establishment itself founded upon a marriage of latitudinarian principles and Newtonian philosophy.[2] Both hylozoists and their more orthodox opponents made their claims on Milton's work, portraying him alternatively as an apologist for heretical monism or orthodox dualism. The post-Restoration conflict was conducted in an ontological language foreign to Milton's work, and so ended in antithetical readings – in which Milton was celebrated as the origin of, or, as the antidote to, contemporary reform. Indeed, the philosophical opposition between monism and dualism, like the political opposition between freedom and authority, simply did not have the same authority for Milton as it did for eighteenth-century readers of his work.

Milton's resistance to the demands of philosophy in *De Doctrina*, and the implicit appeal to epistemology and narrative, allowed him to avoid the conflict implicit in Cudworth's *True Intellectual System*. As a consequence, he was able to keep such monsters as the "plastic power" out of his conceptual bestiary. Milton's reliance on narrative did not so much solve the problems posed by seventeenth-century philosophers, but avoid the languages in which these problems were posed. *Paradise Lost*, as *De Doctrina*, does not navigate between monism and dualism; nor does it elaborate some mystical reconciliation of the opposition. Rather, the Milton of *Paradise Lost*, acknowledging that even the inspired poet cannot transcend his perspective for some objectivist view of reality, gives voice simultaneously to competing narrative perspectives – both monist and dualist.

The current chapter explores the Miltonic aesthetic established both on immanence and transcendence – on monism and dualism – and then turns to some representative Whig readings of *Paradise Lost* in the eighteenth century. The eighteenth-century battle among Whigs itself sheds light on contemporary Milton scholarship – demonstrating the resilience of what were already by 1732, the date of Richard Bentley's edition of *Paradise Lost*, entrenched readings of Milton. The linguistic registers of angelic and satanic camps of critics may have, since then, changed slightly, though Bentley's implicit rebuke of various avatars of the radical Milton in 1732 anticipates Stanley Fish's rebuke and usurpation of different contemporary versions of the satanic Milton.

John Rumrich has recently offered an extremely trenchant critique of the "logic of contemporary critical practice" which in his view is dominated by "a corporate, almost institutionalized, view of Milton and his works," initiated by Stanley Fish's *Surprised by Sin*.[3] While this chapter shares Rumrich's sense of the current hegemony of Fish's angelic Milton, I tend to see both Fish *and* Rumrich's account of Milton within a *general* logic of Milton studies in which warring critics vie to replace one Milton with its mirror opposite. In this reading, Rumrich himself is not so much "uninventing Milton," but rather re-instating – with great elegance and argumentative power – a satanic Milton more suitable to the assumptions which inform post-modern critical practices. The warring angels of *this* study can't do without each another: the oppositions instated in the historiography of the Enlightenment West (in which mythos and logos, reason and authority are antithetically opposed) inform a criticism where extremes are *continually* celebrated or condemned, and set polemically against one another. The results of this critical logic are "abridgements," polemical versions of Milton which insure each others' existence – sustained antagonisms that make their own opposition necessary.

The contours of the standard metahistories which I have been describing should by now be somewhat familiar: the metaphysical correlate of the possessive individualism and bourgeois liberty attributed to the *Areopagitica* is the rationalist monism attributed to *De Doctrina* and *Paradise Lost*. Denis Saurat saw the two dovetail in Milton; Milton was for him a "rationalist anti-theologian." Similarly, to refit *Paradise Lost* for the modern world, James Holly Hanford, also part of the "New Movement," "found it necessary to emphasize the power of Milton's 'poetic and philosophic thought' at the expense of the dogmatic aspects of his inherited theology."[4] Re-fashioned as a "rationalist" and "humanist," Hanford and Saurat together tried to "strip Milton of all elements of Puritanism."[5] And Donald F. Bouchard, more radically, has asserted that Milton's monism, paralleling his secular individualism, culminated in "God's eradication before man's freedom."[6]

William Empson, on the other hand, registers Milton's stubborn attachment to transcendence: his "still very disagreeable God of the Old Testament" disqualifies Milton from Empson's embrace.[7] Unhesitant to foreground his own prejudice, Empson wishes that Milton had followed through the trajectory of his monism and forced God to "retire and dissolve into the Absolute."[8] This longing for the disappearance of the transcendent in Milton's metaphysics parallels the longing for the disappearance of authority inscribed in so many Whig readings of

Areopagitica. If only Milton's God had become "totally immanent or invisible," Empson writes, then his epic vision would have been more like the Cambridge Platonists' "graceful picture" of a "better world" (one can only remark here that Empson's Cambridge Platonists are as bizarre as Empson's Milton).[9] As *Some Versions of Pastoral* attests, Empson manifests a preference for Nature as conceived by Wordsworth, where it "appears pantheistically as the muse of all life, a sustaining rather than moral agent" which, moreover, does not conceal "a personal God who will punish sin."[10]

The Wordsworthian world-picture, anticipated for Empson by the Cambridge Platonists, is a "better world" where God has already "abdicated" and become "immanence alone." Thus the Mosaic God who punishes "sin" is dissolved, as Empson claims, "into the landscape" or interiorized, as Bouchard prefers, in Man's reason.[11] This divinization of reason and fading of transcendence, if not achieved then at least adumbrated by Milton, stands as the metaphysical telos of a particular Whig version of history. Indeed, in Empson's thought, the cosmological collapse of the divine into the material parallels the interiorization of God and authority, and the triumph of autonomous reason. Clearly, Empson would have liked to put Milton in the service of this history where the "sustaining" God of reason defeats the transcendent God of power. But Milton's God explicitly resists Empson's Whig principles. As Blair Worden has recently put it: "Ever since William Empson went to school at Winchester and decided that the God that he met in the classroom there was 'very wicked,' the failure of the Old Testament deity to accommodate himself to the moral requirements of twentieth-century liberal agnosticism has been a problem to Milton's readers."[12] Like Empson, Christopher Hill laments this "failure," and regrets Milton's only grudging participation in the teleological progress by which God becomes interiorized in creation. The fact that Milton's God was not Blake's God ("who may be consumed on his own throne") prompted Hill to wonder why Milton "could not let go of his hold on God."[13] The self-consuming God, subsumed into immanence, for Hill, is a God anticipated but not adequately realized in *Paradise Lost.*

By contrast, Bouchard, whom Hill enthusiastically cites, insists that the "real import" of *Paradise Lost* lies precisely in the loss of any "privileged status for the Father" and the subsequent emergence of "a community of Sons responsive to an internalized word."[14] Bouchard's commentary marks *Paradise Lost* as the site of the transition from transcendence towards the independence of an at once divinized and autonomous creation. Following the same currents of interpretation,

Andrew Milner asks rhetorically and *con brio*, "Once God is liquidated into the reasons of particular individuals then what remains of God?"[15] Bouchard and Milner, articulating as a *fait accompli* what Hill and Empson regret as unaccomplished, dispense with Milton's externalized deity altogether, and celebrate the internalized and embodied God. In the reading of Milton as a strong monist ("hylozoist" in Cudworth's lexicon) for whom spirit and matter converge, Saurat, Bouchard, and Milner attempt to appropriate Milton for the cause of twentieth-century secularism – to proclaim in Bouchard's words that "God is dead that man may live."[16] Bouchard's historical narrative – and the central place of Milton in it – realizes the entelechy of hylozoism in close to the way Cudworth predicted.

OLD AND NEW WHIGS

The question of God's dissolution "into the landscape" equally obsessed Richard Bentley, and his reading of Milton can be seen as an appropriation of Milton on behalf of a different, though equally Whig ideology, that of the emergent latitudinarian orthodoxy. Bentley's Milton elaborates the flip-side of immanentism (expounded later by the likes of Saurat and Empson), and it requires the re-instating of orthodox dualisms into Milton's works. It is a phenomenon, we shall see, paralleled in the current century by Stanley Fish's reading of *Areopagitica*. Arguing against what he calls the "liberal vision of Milton" canonized in readings of *Areopagitica*, and replacing it with his vision of Milton the "poet of revolutionary absolutism," Fish pits one version of Milton against the another: the libertarian (or satanic) Milton against his own authoritarian (or angelic) Milton. So Bentley, engaged in his own polemic, argues the dualist against the monist Milton.

Both Bentley and Fish come in the aftermath of the ascendancy of the "Whig Milton," and their readings of Milton come as *responses* to the readings of their predecessors. Just as Fish's "Milton" is an explicit response to the Milton of "democratic liberalism" bequeathed to him, so Bentley's "Milton" emerges in response to the Milton bequeathed by what Sensabaugh called "Whig Theory Triumphant." The strategies of both Bentley and Fish, then, are to reverse the appraisals of the generations that preceded them. In doing so, however, they both answer Whiggism by constructing a polemical counter-image of the Milton they inherited.

To call Bentley a Whig is at once straightforward (he was one), and misleading. For, after the Glorious Revolution and throughout the eighteenth century, the discourses of Whiggism, as Pocock has taken pains to demonstrate, were complex and various. While Bentley, conducting continual battle with the Tory "Christ-Church set," was clearly a "Whig," there were those who believed that Bentley and the Low Churchmen had betrayed the "True Whig" inheritance.[17] There was "a succession of Old Whigs, True Whigs, and Honest Whigs," collectively known as "Commonwealthmen," who, as Pocock says, "kept up a criticism of the principles and practices of the ... 'Whig supremacy.'" Modern Whigs like Bentley identified freedom with "wealth, enlightenment, and progress towards a future," while Old Whigs, among them the publisher and biographer of Milton, John Toland, identified freedom with a particularly republican "virtue" and located it squarely in the past. While Bentley, along with the other Boyle Lecturers, articulated a "rationalist world order," aimed at "repressing, moderating, or replacing the 'enthusiasm'" thought of as an "essential characteristic of Puritanism," Toland, "the leading activist of radical deism" sought to challenge that order ... with a "more radical and illuminist rationalism of hermetic and spiritual origins."[18] Here there was no harmony among Whigs, but a battle for ideological as well as political supremacy. In that struggle between Low Churchmen and free-thinkers, *Paradise Lost* is among the battlegrounds, and our perception of Bentley's infamous emendations becomes sharper when understood as a battle strategy. If Toland, the political radical and "spiritual illuminist," who "provided a system capable of undermining the theological position of the Low Church then in power," had *his* Milton, then Bentley, a spokesman for the Low Church position, would have *his own*.[19]

In his second Boyle Lecture, entitled "Matter and Motion Cannot Think," "preached" in April of 1692, Bentley articulates an attack on hylozoism reminiscent of Cudworth's in the *True Intellectual System*.[20] The "faculties of sensation and perception are not inherent in matter as such," Bentley writes, "for if it were so, what monstrous absurdities would follow! every stock and stone would be a percipient and rational creature."[21] Bentley's weapon against his free-thinking opponents (as against all his opponents) was sarcasm:

If, then, motion, in general, or any degree of its velocity, can beget cogitation, surely a ship under sail must be a very intelligent creature, though while she lies at anchor those faculties must be asleep: some cold water or ice must be phlegmatic and senseless, but when it boils in a kettle it has wonderful heats of thinking and ebullitions of fancy.[22]

To Bentley, "the ideas of matter and thought" were always "absolutely incompatible." He was thus led to lament, in his *Remarks*, the "shame" of the views expressed by the free-thinking Collins "that in these brighter days of knowledge, when *matter* and *motion* have been thoroughly considered, and all the powers of *mechanism* discussed and stated, our author should still contend . . . *that their souls are materials.*"[23] That soul and matter should in any way be identified is patently anathema to the Bentley of the *Remarks*.

Like Cudworth, Bentley rejects emphatically both hylozoism *and* Cartesian mechanism. In contrast to both Cudworth and Descartes, however, Bentley hesitates to describe the "vital conjunction of body and soul" and the "invisible bands and fetters" which unite "them together."[24] To neglect this "conjunction" altogether would be to cede to the worst tendencies of mechanism; to articulate its contours might mean, as in the case of Cudworth, to move in the direction of the hylozoism of his opponents. Hence we find that Bentley was prepared to discuss the resemblances between the spiritual and material worlds but that he was not prepared to provide the kind of excessive theological and philosophical justifications proffered by Cudworth. As R. J. White explains, when Bentley "undertakes to prove that 'there is an immaterial substance in us which we call soul and spirit, essentially distinct from our bodies, and that this spirit doth necessarily evince the existence of a Spiritual Being,'" he "does not prove it," but merely "states it."[25] Regardless, however, of the slipperiness of Bentley's own metaphysics, he undoubtedly sought, as Jacob puts it, "to counteract the influence of the Epicureans, materialists and atheists, whose radical Whiggery threatened the position of the established Church and its religious principles."[26]

Bentley's arguments, as Robert E. Bourdette has suggested, provide "a very specific context" for Bentley's reading of *Paradise Lost*. For the hylozoism to which Bentley again and again addressed himself in the Boyle Lectures had a political analogue: the Old or True Whig politics with which Milton's name was so frequently associated. If Bourdette speculates that Bentley's *Paradise Lost* contributed to the battle with the Deists and free-thinkers to define Christianity, we could add the additional and more limited speculation that Bentley contributed to the battle to define Milton.[27] By 1732, that battle was well under way: in 1688 Milton's literary reputation was already in the process of becoming

established; by 1712 and the publication of Addison's *Spectator* papers, the
"reputation of *Paradise Lost* as a 'classic' was, according to J. W. Mackail,
'already made.' "[28] This reputation, as Mark Pattison further suggests,
"was the work of the Whigs": not only was the "first *edition de luxe* of
Paradise Lost brought out by a subscription got up by the Whig leader
Lord Somers," but "in the height of the Whig ascendancy, the bust of
Milton penetrated Westminster, though in the generation before, the
Dean of that day had refused to admit an inscription on the monument
erected to John Philips, because the name of Milton occurred in it."[29]
Joseph Addison could point to the "one great Moral" of the epic, that
"*Obedience to the Will of God makes Men happy*," and Jonathan Richardson
could read *Paradise Lost* as a paradigm of Addisonian politeness (a poem
"to Calm and Purify the Mind ... to a State of Tranquility and
Happiness"), but there were other (less tranquil) contemporary evaluations
of Milton.[30]

Not least of these (to oppose that "Grand Whig Milton") was the
Milton who emerged from the accounts of that great "spiritual
illuminist," John Toland. In his *Life of Milton*, which appeared as a
preface to the first collected edition of Milton's prose works in 1698,
Toland left discussion of Milton's literary merits largely to others:
Toland's *Life* is essentially a description and celebration of the poet's life
and political career. The Milton of Toland's *Life* was "particulary noted"
not for his poetry, but "for those excellent Volumes he wrote on the
behalf of Civil, Religious, and Domestic Liberty."[31] Thus the "classic"
Milton championed by the Whig supremacy was challenged by Milton
the revolutionary whose "chief design" was, according to Toland, to
"display the different Effects of Liberty and Tyranny."

In his *Amyntor*, written a year after the *Life*, Toland felt compelled to
defend himself against charges that his earlier highly politicized portrayal
of Milton had provoked. "The first Charge against me," Toland wrote,
"should have bin, that I had not fairly represented my Hero." "But far
from that," Toland continued, "the great Crime whereof I am arraign'd,
consists in telling more than some People would have me; or discovering
Truths not fit to be known." It was not that Toland was charged with
*mis*representing Milton, but that Toland had represented aspects of
Milton's political career – through both the publication of the prose and
the *Life* – which did not rest well with the established persona of Milton
the classic poet: "I am expresly told that I ought not to meddle with
Milton's Books, nor to revive his Sentiments, or the Memory of those
Quarrels wherein he was engag'd; which is only, in other Words, that I

ought not to write his Life at all." The *Life*, he concluded, raised "so loud a Clamor" simply because it informed the "World about the Occasion" of Milton's "writing."[32] Toland's efforts clearly worked against those who sought to replace the memory of the radical and politicized Milton (in which the "life" figured prominently) with the Milton who in Richardson's later words would come to "calm and purify the mind."

Once Milton's life was reassociated with his poetry, some – William Winstanley, for example, in 1687 – would come to reject the life, and the poet:

John Milton was one, whose natural parts might deservedly give him a place amongst the principal of our English Poets . . . But his Fame is gone out like a Candle in a Snuff, and his Memory will always stink, which might have ever lived in honourable Repute, had not he been a notorious Traytor, and most impiously and villanously bely'd that blessed Martyr *King Charles* the First.[33]

Thomas Yalden in 1698 concurred with Winstanley's evaluation. He too distinguished, as we noted previously, between poetry – the "sacred lines" which "with wonder we peruse" – and the "seditious prose" which "provokes our rage." Yet, for Yalden, as Winstanley, the impiousness of the regicide must infect the "Repute" of the poet. Though the poet is "worthy to rehearse / Heaven's lasting triumphs in immortal verse," Yalden continues in the vocative with an open condemnation:

> But when thy impious mercenary pen
> Insults the best of princes, best of men,
> Our admiration turns to just disdain,
> And we revoke the fond applause again.[34]

To Yalden, any "applause" that Milton's poems had garnered had to be revoked in light of the activities of Milton's "impious mercenary pen."

Bentley's intervention in this history of reception (of which his emendations are clearly a part) belongs to the tradition of Winstanley and Yalden. But where Yalden and Winstanley find the reputation of their poet permanently marred by the "Stink" of his politics, Bentley turns to the poetry itself in an attempt to dissociate it from any stain of radical politics or metaphysics. While Bentley's emendations to *Paradise Lost* have no *specifically* political content, they not only encode Bentley's hostility to the free-thinkers, but also his desire to extract Milton from their ranks. The emendations seem designed to retain and bolster the reputation of *Paradise Lost* as a poem commensurate with latitudinarian principles – political and theological. That is, Bentley's revisions – most notably in Book VII – not only reveal his disbelief that Milton would embrace a specific metaphysics (i.e., those of the free-thinkers) but also the radical politics that it implied. Indeed, Bentley's emendations reveal just how fluid the distinctions were between metaphysics and politics. While the relationship between politics and metaphysics is perhaps occluded in our current discourse (for politics as the reigning meta-discourse disclaims all metaphysical commitments), in the early modern context the connections were more apparent. As Margaret C. Jacob's work attests, radical politics was perceived everywhere to dovetail with radical metaphysics: there existed an "intimate" relationship "between the world natural" and "the moral and social relations prevailing or desired in the 'world politick.'"[35] Those like Toland who cited Milton in the debates over liberty of conscience and the revolutionary settlement were the very men who were advocating a new and radical metaphysics: Toland's program was not only to celebrate the Milton who "look'd upon true and absolute Freedom" as "the Greatest Happiness of this Life," but also to prove that "Motion" is "essential to matter . . . *and that Matter neither ever was nor ever can be a sluggish, dead, and inactive Lump.*"[36] Indeed, in the eighteenth century, the politics of the Milton whom Toland published and celebrated were often affiliated with the metaphysics of Toland's own philosophical tracts. The motives behind Bentley's emendations of *Paradise Lost* become clearer in relation to the figure of Toland who looms large – as publisher and as author – in the radicalism of the post-Restoration period.

Toland knew, as Jacob shows, that the Newtonian system was being "used as a powerful weapon" by "churchmen like Richard Bentley."[37] Toland's philosophical arguments expressly challenged the cosmology elaborated by Bentley and others in the Boyle Lectures. Indeed Toland in the *Letters to Serena* was so radical in his metaphysics that he rejected not only the Low Churchmen, but even the hylozoists of Cudworth's account as too conservative. These hylozoists, he wrote, "did not take care to free themselves" of the prejudice that "Matter was essentially inactive." Toland, embracing a full-blown monism, insists at the outset on attributing energy to matter. Hence the hylozoists and even Cudworth – ostensibly an opponent of "hylozoism" in all of its forms – were condemned by Toland as dualists. "No less romantic is the plastic Life of other Philosophers," Toland wrote, "which (according to its modern Reviver the universally learned Dr. CUDWORTH) is not material, but an inferior sort of Spirit without Sensation or Thought, yet endu'd with a vital Operation and Energy." Despite their alleged opposition to a monism (which Toland's own philosophy embodied), these "Plastics,"

Toland continues, seem "to differ with the Hylozoics only about words, tho pretending a mighty Disagreement, to keep clear, I suppose, of the absurd or invidious Consequences charg'd on their Opinions."[38] Certainly, Toland's remarks on the similarity between Cudworth and the hylozoists (and the "absurd" charges leveled against them) would have been no consolation to Cudworth. Toland instead helped to confirm the argument that Cudworth failed to distinguish himself sufficiently from the heretical positions that he so wanted to avoid – and that the plastic power was less an argument against hylozoism than a form of it. His interpretation of Cudworth notwithstanding, Toland's remarks indicate the extent of his own radical monism.

Toland's monism is again given expression at the end of his *Two Essays*. According to Robert E. Sullivan, the proclamation at the end of the essays, "Jovis omnia plena," should be taken literally to mean that "everything was full of God, who was in everything." In this, Toland's metaphysics – an unqualified monism – was at least as radical as his politics; in fact it was the corollary of his neo-Harringtonian republicanism, a brand of republicanism which Toland did not hesitate to attribute to Milton.[39]

Thus, as Jacob suggests, "Toland's metaphysics contained a 'social message': the worship of nature entails in effect the worship of the here and now; there is no after-life, no spiritual society beyond our own." Or, as Yirmayahu Yovel more generally puts it, the whole "philosophy of immanentism" was "characteristically a philosophy of emancipation" – a philosophy that, perhaps needless to say, conflicted with the quietest vision of the Newtonian Low Church.[40] Indeed, Toland's "immanentism" directly informed a vision of radical politics and "emancipation" affiliated by him and fellow republicans with mid-century radicalism. Thus, Toland's "religious myth" had a particular "political analogue: seventeenth-century English revolutionaries believed that they had been free-born and self-governed and that the Norman conquest had imposed the yoke of tyranny"; the desire to regain this "ancient freedom" paralleled the desire for the restoration of an "indigenous paganism."[41] While Toland could not successfully attribute to Milton a belief in an "indigenous paganism," he could, for the most part, assimilate him to the requisites of his own political and religious agenda. As Shawcross notes, in the early eighteenth century, "Toland's view of religion . . . was usually transferred uncritically to Milton."[42] To suggest Milton as the source of Toland's own views was in fact Toland's strategy. When, in the *Amyntor*, Toland answers the charges that he had derogated "the sacred

Majesty of Kings, the venerable Order of Bishops, the best constituted Church in the World, our holy Liturgy, and decent Ceremonies, the Authority of Councils, the Testimony of the Fathers, and a hundred other things," he cites Milton as his explicit antecedent. Toland warns his attackers to "betake" themselves "for Reparation," not to himself, but "to JOHN MILTON," and continues, if he is not to be "brought to easie Terms," Toland's own antagonists must learn to "defend" their "Castles and Territories against *him* with all the Vigor" they can. It is thus Milton and not Toland against whom Toland's own detractors had to "defend" their "Castles and Territories." Still, to Toland, there was nothing polemical or invented about *his* Milton: "I assure you," he writes, "I am no further concern'd in the Quarrel than to shew you the Enemy, and to give a true Account of his Forces."[43] It was not Toland, the radical monist, leading the battle against the Whig establishment, but Milton himself, whom Toland portrayed as the "Enemy" of latitudinarian principles.[44]

In the Boyle Lectures and in his later response to Collins's *Discourse of Free-Thinking*, Bentley was to attack the metaphysics of Toland and Blount as well as Collins.[45] Thus, the emendations to *Paradise Lost* represent an attempt to distinguish Milton's metaphysics from those of the free-thinkers, republicans and Deists who claimed him for their cause. If, as Pocock claims, "hylozoist spiritual materialism" represents the "mainstream of radical thought," then Bentley attempts to distinguish Milton from that mainstream.[46] As it was Toland who brought Milton's "seditious prose" into print; who passed off his own radicalism as Miltonic in origin; and who stood behind and influenced other free-thinkers, it seems a likely supposition that Toland was the inexplicit target of Bentley's implicit attack.[47]

"UNDER THE SIMILITUDE OF SENSE"

Bentley's metaphysics comes as much into focus in his role as an editor as in his theological writings. The staunch dualisms argued in the Boyle Lectures and in the *Remarks* on Collins's *Discourse* are evidenced continually in his emendations to *Paradise Lost*. When, for example, in Book VII, Milton anticipates the time when

> ... Earth be chang'd to Heav'n, and Heav'n to
> Earth,
> One Kingdom, Joy and Union without End (VII 160–61)

Bentley responds with vehemence, "I scarce know two viler Misprints in the whole poem; because they lurk undiscover'd under the Similitude of Sense." "Surely," Bentley continues,

... it's little advantage for *Heaven, to be chang'd* to Earth: and Joy and Union come both odly together, and have no cement with the preceding words. The Author gave it;

> And Earth be CHAIN'D *to Heav'n and Heav'n to Earth,*
> One Kingdom JOIN'D IN *Union without End.*   (*MPL*, p. 222)[48]

Of all the "vile" insertions of Milton's supposedly malevolent editor, Bentley finds none worse than the notion of Heaven's eventual union with earth – the attribution of monism to Milton. Thus the *eventual continuity* between spirit and matter, earth and heaven, implicit in Milton's verses is transformed by Bentley into *perpetual "contiguity"*: "CHAIN'D" stands in for "chang'd." Similarly, when Michael assures Adam in Book XI that God's "Omnipresence fills every kind that lives" (XI 337), we find Bentley remarking curtly, it "was not the Author's Intention" (*MPL*, p. 359).

Bentley's commentator Zachary Pearce, in glossing Bentley's vehemence on the question of heavenly and earthly union, explains that "*M*'s meaning" in Book VII "seems to have been this, That Earth would be so happy inhabited by *obedient* Creatures, that it would be chang'd to, i.e., resemble Heaven; and Heaven by receiving those Creatures would thus resemble Earth, that it would be stock'd with Men for its inhabitants."[49] None of Pearce's comments more justify Empson's claim on the similarity of Pearce to Bentley "both in their merits and their limitations." (Pearce "is even more 'rational'" than Bentley, writes Empson, which "may help to make Bentley seem less stupid.")[50] Pearce, as he does often, accepts Bentley's objections. Though here, without accepting Bentley's emendation, he foists Bentley's meaning onto Milton's text. According to Pearce, "Earth" and "Heaven" are never intermingled, not even at the end of days; it is only by *resemblance* through which they are "JOIN'D." For Pearce and Bentley, earth and heaven are joined through resemblance; the fundamental contiguity of heaven and earth always remains.

Bentley's (and Pearce's) reluctance to allow that God makes himself present in "every kind that lives," and Bentley's special vehemence with regard to the possibility that Milton would even have considered the ultimate union of heaven and earth, can be glossed in the language of Toland's *Pantheisticon* and its liturgy for a civic and universal religion:

President: All things in the World are One, And one in All in all things.
Response: What's all in All Things is God, Eternal and Immense.[51]

For Toland, in the *Pantheisticon* and throughout the *Letters to Serena*, the unity of things is possible in *this* world; for Milton, this unity is at best adumbrated. That is, Toland's is a this-worldly, Milton's an other-worldly monism. Bentley may not have recalled Toland specifically (he need not have, for as Sullivan notes, "the impulse to merge man into the universe and deify the result" was "widespread"),[52] but Bentley's emendation clearly evidences that the pantheism of the free-thinkers was on his mind. The emendation, then, not only marks the distance of Bentley from Milton, but also registers the continuing presence on Bentley's psyche of the metaphysical radicalism which he combated throughout his career. Milton, Bentley must have thought, could not have advocated ideas that would have affiliated him with the radical metaphysics of a Toland, Blount, or Collins.

In this response lies a paradigmatic moment in the reception-history of Milton's texts, demonstrating how competing readings ultimately depend upon one another. Bentley's anxiety at the free-thinker's *possible* interpretation of *Paradise Lost* (which was as yet outside of the context of political appropriation and debate) was so great that he seems to have imagined and produced their reading of the poem, only then to reject it (this parallels the bizarre phenomenon of *The True Intellectual System* – namely that it produced the heresies it aimed to attack). Thus one extreme version of Milton is constituted and argued against its polemical opposite. Bentley posits his "Editor" as a free-thinking Toland who corrupts the text of *Paradise Lost*, transforming it into a manifesto of radical metaphysics and politics. To the exaggerated and distorted claims of the Tolandian Editor, Bentley provides the emendations as a response.[53] Bentley's sustained attack on Milton's Editor was thus a continuation of the project that he had begun in the Boyle Lectures – an attack on all forms of radical Whiggism. Via *Paradise Lost*, the Grand Whig Bentley attacked the Radical Whig Toland.

While Pearce and Bentley attribute the "confusion of spirit and matter" – the monism of *Paradise Lost* – to Milton's printer and editor, Dr. Johnson attributes that confusion to Milton himself. Certainly Johnson is right to say that Milton "perplexed his poetry with this philosophy" as his "infernal and celestial powers are sometimes pure spirit, and sometimes animated body."[54] But Johnson's objections to Milton's "philosophy" have, as John Guillory explains, "a markedly post-Cartesian ring," and his entire statement "must be cleared of the charge of anachronism."[55]

Clearly, this charge of "anachronism" is applicable to Bentley as well, as he also objects to any implied identity between spirit and matter in Milton's work. While Johnson cedes Milton to the Whigs (in this and also in the judgment that *Areopagitica* provided "unbound liberty" for "every skeptick" to "teach his follies"), Bentley refuses to do give up the fight. So Bentley: Milton could not have written thus; it was his editor.

Nevertheless, Johnson and Bentley, despite the difference of approach and temperament, were equally hostile to monism of any kind. It is therefore not surprising to find Bentley and Johnson both troubled by Satan's imposturing as a "Toad," squatting, at the end of Book IV, at Eve's ear. Johnson complains that Satan "seems to be mere spirit" while in other parts of the epic, "he has a body,"[56] while for Bentley, the conjunction of the arch-angel Satan with the grossly material toad leads of course to an editorial interpolation. Empson terms it one of Bentley's "worst efforts":[57] "Why may I not add *one* Verse to *Milton* as well as his Editor add so *many* . . .":

> Him thus intent Ithuriel with his spear
> *Knowing no real Toad durst there intrude*
> Touch'd lightly . . .   (*MPL*, p. 136)

Bentley's brazenness is perhaps qualified by his directness, but his antipathy to the materialization of the spiritual is no less apparent in his emendation. For Bentley, just as earth and heaven cannot be joined in Milton's cosmos, so the spirit Satan cannot be joined to the material "Toad." Not surprisingly, Bentley is outraged as well by the habits of Milton's angels. In what Empson calls a "snort worthy of the nostrils of Milton himself," Bentley remarks on Milton's angels, who according to Raphael, "concoct, digest, assimilate, / And corporeal to incorporeal turn" (v 412–13): "If the Devils want *feeding*, our Author made poor Provision for them in his Second Book; where they have nothing to eat but *Hell fire*" (*MPL*, p 162). In Bentley's dualist cosmology, angels simply do not eat.

If *Paradise Lost* conflates monistic and dualistic views of life, then Bentley willfully insists on reading the former in terms of the latter. Notwithstanding Milton's claims that the creation can be "by degrees of merit rais'd," there is (for Pearce reading Bentley reading Milton) still an immeasurable gap between Heaven and Earth, with only resemblance to bridge it. The question of spirit's relationship to matter – the "vital conjunction of body and soul," discerned though never articulated by Bentley – is, for him, a matter of "Similitude" and never of identity. The various discursive and narrative frames of *Paradise Lost*, as we shall see in the following chapter, permit Milton to oscillate between a poetics of transcendence and a poetics of immanence. But Bentley recognizes only the former.

Indeed, Bentley's emendation points worriedly at the identification of spirit and matter and then disqualifies it as a mere interpolation of the editor. Here, as throughout his emendations to *Paradise Lost*, Bentley reveals his horror of embodiment, that matter (or by association, the image) is by any manner spiritual, that it is anything more than a reflection or *signifier* of the spiritual. Offering the mirror-image of the history implied in the "liquefaction" of God in his creation urged on by Empson and heralded by some contemporary critics, Bentley argues for – and creates – a dualist Milton whose aversion to the material matches his own.

The differences between Bentley and Milton can be assayed not only in relation to their respective "metaphysics" but also in relation to the presuppositions about representation that parallel their metaphysics. Remembering Milton's insistence in *De Doctrina* that even the God who repents "is as he says he is," Bentley's own anti-material suppositions in his reading of Genesis 6 come into sharp relief. In his response to Collins, Bentley explains some "frequent expressions of our Bible" to which the *Discourse* has called attention, among them the "wrath of the Lord." Advocating just the kind of "anthropopathy" which Milton rejected in *De Doctrina*, Bentley argues that "the whole herd of Christians" must certainly know "that these are not to be taken literally, but are spoken . . . *in a human manner*, accommodated to our capacities and affections." The "nature of God," Bentley concludes, evading the connotations of the biblical text, is "infinitely above all ruffles of passion."[58] While the Milton of *De Doctrina* does not "shy away from a notion of God which he himself does not hesitate to promulgate in unambiguous terms" (VI 136), Bentley's reading of the "wrath of the Lord" is unapologetically allegorical. Bentley, in contrast to Milton, allegorizes the particular connotations of the biblical passage when it doesn't accord with the requirements of his theology.

Moving from the particular to the abstract, Bentley similarly argues against the problematic connotations of biblical language in his discussion of the "*war in heaven*" represented in Revelation 12:7. "Where has this writer lived," Bentley rails against Collins, "or what *idiot evangelist* was he bred under, not to know that this is all vision and allegory, and not proposed as literal truth?" (It is irresistible to speculate that Bentley was thinking here also of Milton's "war in heaven").[59] Bentley's hermeneutics, in the tradition of conventional Protestant (and Hellenist) hermeneutics, insists on a bifurcation between language and truth whereby the light of the truth consequently stands above any *particular* articulation of that truth.

Bentley's anti-material hermeneutics suffuse his interpretation of Milton, even the Milton he depicts in his "Preface" to the 1732 edition. "*I wonder not so much at the Poem it self, though worthy of all Wonder,*" Bentley writes, "*as that the Author could so abstract his Thoughts from his own Troubles, as to be able to make it*" (*MPL*, p. a3v). The image of the Milton "*confin'd in a narrow and to Him a dark Chamber,*" able to "*abstract*" himself "*through the Compass of the Whole Universe*" (*MPL*, p. a3v) becomes a fit image for Bentley's 1732 edition of the poem, and for the tendencies of Bentley's thought in general.

In Bentley's metaphor of abstraction, Milton overcomes not only the physical limitations of his blindness but also the specific "Cares and Fears" of his old age. Where Milton's "Life" was central to Toland, to Bentley it was something to be overcome. Milton, according to Bentley, thus abstracts from the specificity of his own sufferings, "all outward Uneasiness" (including the revolutionary commitments which Toland so celebrated), to revel in the "Integrity" of "the Human Mind." Likewise, the "dark Chamber" of Milton's personal (and political) history yields to the consideration of "*all Periods of Time from before the Creation to the Consummation of all Things*" (*MPL*, p. a3v). Similarly, Bentley claims, "*the Defoedation of so many Parts*" of *Paradise Lost* "*by a bad Printer*" could "*not hinder*" the Poem's "*native, unextinguishable Beauty*" from "*shining forth*" (*MPL*, p. a3r). Just as Bentley's Milton is able to "abstract" from his personal history and from the "Defoedation" of his printer, so Bentley, an enemy of all forms of immanence and what Collins would call the "miscellaneous," abstracts, allegorizes, or simply deletes passages of *Paradise Lost* that do not conform to his refined image of it.

In this regard, Bentley's attention to the fables in *Paradise Lost* is of particular significance. Indeed, Bentley's emendations (deletions usually) of Milton's fables suggest that he was undoubtedly conscious of, to use Empson's phrase, "the wild gang of comparative anthropologists" who came ready to announce the equivalence between sacred and mythological history.[60] Already in 1656, Cowley implicitly argued for this in his *Preface*, when he asked,

What can we imagine more proper for the ornaments of *Wit* or *Learning* in the story of *Deucalion*, then in that of *Noah*? Why will not the actions of *Sampson* afford us plentiful matter as the *Labors* of *Hercules?* Why is not *Jeptha's Daughter* as *good a woman* as *Iphigenia?*

"All the *Books* of the *Bible*," Cowley continues, "are either already most admirable, and exalted pieces of *Poesie*, or are the best *Materials* in the world for it."[61] In his advocacy of Noah and Sampson as "Materials" for "Poesie," Cowley implicitly equates secular with sacred history, placing Hebrew "mythology" on the same plane with the Greek. The "effect" is, as Empson suggests, an implicit equation of "Christian and pagan views of life as equally solid and possible."[62] Bentley's demand for the "verbal and theological unity"[63] of *Paradise Lost* is thus expressed in his desire to cleanse the pollution of "Fable and Lye" from the "Divine Narrative" (*MPL*, p. 157).

But it is precisely Bentley, not Milton, who sees fable, in Michael McKeon's phrase, as "invested" with "sufficiency of its own."[64] For Bentley, the apparent "sufficiency" detracts from the authority and providential unity of the poem. Milton's famous comparison of "Deucalion and Pyrrha" to "our Adam and Eve," which suggests the equivalence of pagan myth and sacred history, prompts Bentley to ask: "Is *Adam* and *Eve's* History an *old Fable* too, by this Editor's own Insinuation?" (*MPL*, p. 349). Likewise, in Book VII, Bentley renders Milton's "Giant Angels" as "rebel Angels." Pearce, again shadowing Bentley's thoughts, explains the emendation: "Dr. Bentley reads 'the rebel Angels,' thinking that the word *giant* insinuates as if this was as fabulous as that of Jove."[65] The diversity of the poem, and the use of a comparative poetics, can for Bentley only lessen or even subvert the authority of the "Divine Narrative," and must consequently be attributed to the Editor "who had a great talent at Mythology." It is "our Editor," Bentley writes, who "had such an Itching to mix Fable with the most Serious matter," who "blunders on," filling the poem with "his Similitudes" (*MPL*, pp. 353, 156).[66] To Bentley's binary imagination – in which sacred and profane are polar opposites – the comparisons, fables, and myths are literally inconceivable as facets of *Paradise Lost*. As Bentley deletes the following lines from Book II – "*Hesperian Fables* true, / If true, here only" – he asks flatly, "Very quaint: but pray you, Sir, how can *Fables* be true *any where?*" (*MPL*, p. 114). Where Toland praises Bruno, who treated "all miracles as fables," yet maintained at the same time "that the pagan mythology wasn't much more unintelligible or absurd or monstrous than Judaic or Christian theology," Bentley asserts the absolute incompatibility of fable with Christian theology.[67]

In Bentley's aggressive emendations of the fables in *Paradise Lost*, he again evidences his sympathy with the presuppositions of the free-thinkers (Empson's "comparative anthropologists"), even while *rejecting* them. If Toland could point out that Christian mysteries were virtually indistinguishable from other ancient religions in his *Christianity not Mysterious*; if Deists could point to a common natural religion at the root of all the world's religions; and if the radical strand of Protestant thought (Toland included) could equate Christian and pagan myth,[68] then Bentley would respond with a Milton whose Christianity was unique and unalloyed. As if to say, Milton couldn't have authored the comparisons inserted by the editor: if he had, he would have been of Toland's party (and later Blake's) – knowingly or not.

If, in *Areopagitica* and *De Doctrina*, meaning emerges as a function of "contiguity" and "cunning resemblances," striving towards though never achieving "continuity," so in *Paradise Lost* meaning also necessarily emerges through difference. As if to stress this point, Milton introduces his "Giant Angels" with the following lines:

> Great are thy works, *Jehovah*, infinite
> Thy power; what thought can measure thee or tongue
> Relate thee ... (VII 602–4)

To the question, "what thought can measure thee or tongue," Milton responds with the "thought" of the "Giant Angels." For Milton, "Good and evil," as we remember from *Areopagitica*, "grow up together almost inseparably; and the knowledge of good is so involv'd and interwoven with the knowledge of evill ... that those confused seeds which were impos'd on Psyche ... were not more intermixt" (II 514). Bentley's aesthetic, "emending," as Bourdette suggests, "towards a unity," is not interested in Psyche's task: "the identification of so many cunning resemblances hardly to be discerned." Samuel Johnson took note of (and despaired of) the "confused seeds"; Bentley, however, dispensed with them altogether.

In Johnson's formulation, the oppositions that constitute "*discordia concors*" are understood as fundamentally different and opposed, "laboured particularities" – only to be joined "by violence." But in Bentley's far more aggressive and revisionary formulation, the "*discordia concors*" achieved in Milton's juxtaposition of sacred and secular narrative – "*Jehovah*" and the "Great Angels" – is not even allowed. It is the editor who is always "grafting into the Poem his *likenesses*" (*MPL*, p. 160). The poem must have been different; Milton would not, could not, have allowed the multiplying of difference, parading as "likenesses," to detract from the unity of his poem. Bentley, therefore, must refine the poem of its comparison, abstracting from an ostensibly corrupted text to the "Integrity" of the Divine Narrative.[69] Thus we are not surprised at Bentley's emendation of the description of Eden in Book IV: "... *Not Enna says he, not Daphne, nor Fons, Castalus, nor Nysa, nor Mt. Amara, could compare with Paradise.* Why, sir, who would suspect they could...?" (*MPL*, p. 215). Given the tendencies of Bentley's thought, we marvel not at his emendations, but at his restraint, wondering why he didn't find more of the poem unacceptable.

THE UNCONSUMING ARTIFACT

Following the publication of Bentley's emendations, Lewis Theobald observed of him: "It is plain it is the Intention of that great Man rather to correct and pare of the Excrescencies of the *Paradise Lost* ... than to restore corrupted passages." The "chief Turn" of Bentley's criticism, Theobald goes on to argue in his bizarre defense of "that great Man," is "plainly to shew the World, that if *Milton* did not write as He would have him, he ought to have wrote so."[70] More recently Bourdette has elaborated a similar argument claiming that Bentley "helped lay the ground work for the postmodern formulation of the relations between text and critic." Rather than the text "imposing its reason upon the reader," Bourdette continues, the "text submitted to the reason of the critic."[71] Bourdette might have refined this observation even further: in the history of Milton criticism, Richard Bentley anticipates Stanley Fish. Notwithstanding the mockery heaped on Bentley for his brazenness, his emendations do in fact seem restrained in comparison to the far more thorough – though "affective" – emendations of Stanley Fish.

If Bentley's "was perhaps the first evaluation of Milton ... to see him as a universal personality ... awesome in his isolation, greatness of mind and integrity," then Fish repeats and emphasizes this evaluation in the twentieth century.[72] Fish, with infinitely more subtlety and power than Bentley, has constructed a Milton, who also, like Bentley's Milton, seems inimical to difference of all kinds. Fish, like Bentley, has constituted a Milton able to "abstract" himself from his contexts, who is, according to Fish, like his "absolutist" God, "unyielding and dismissive of the texture of reality and plenitudinous human actuality."[73] But to insist, as Fish does, on the chasm between the "carnal mind" and "divine reality"; to eschew the "colour and chaotic liveliness of earthly motions" for the "absolute simplicity (unity) of the divine reality"; to maintain, as a consequence, that *Paradise Lost* be read as a "self-consuming artifact" is to overlook the ramifications of what Milton calls in *De Doctrina* the "heterogeneous, multiform and inexhaustible" virtue of the Deity.[74] One need not argue for the primacy of the theological treatise to see how Milton's cosmology informs, is, in fact, implicit within *Paradise Lost*. For the explicit argument by which God is affiliated with his creation (informing, though never completely defining, Milton's perspective) sanctions, even sanctifies the contingent – whether that be the republican politics of *Areopagitica* and *The Readie and Easie Way*, or the imagery of *Paradise Lost* and the Bible.

Fish's dualist reading of Milton endorses a rejection of everything temporal. This bias is evident as well in his reading of Sir Thomas Browne's *Religio Medici*, a text that by Fish's own admission resists the generic constraints he elaborates in *Self-Consuming Artifacts*. Nonetheless, Fish's chapter on Browne begins by invoking the *Religio* as the "most consistent and overt celebration of the literary vision whose literary effects we have been examining." Much to Fish's pleasure, he can claim that the reader's "reason is exercised (and teased) to the point where its insufficiency becomes self-evident, and ratiocination gives way to faith professing assertion; and in the process, of course, the machinery of reason – linguistic, logical, rhetorical – becomes the vehicle of its own abandonment." As "in the manner of Milton," Fish claims, apparently expanding the hegemony of the "self-consuming" paradigm, "the rationalizing tendencies of the carnal understanding are given reign only so that their dangers can be more fully exposed." Fish applauds Browne when the latter appears to give up on "the promise of distinguishing and particularizing," and he commends the Browne who insists on the "homogeneity of whatever is discreetly perceived."[75] Like his Augustan precursors, Fish prefers this "homogeneity" to the ostensibly false "promise of distinguishing and particularizing." Though Browne's *Religio* obsessively particularizes ("there will ever some reserved difference slip in," Browne remarks),[76] Fish, like Bentley before him, latches on to "homogeneity" and the certainty that in time everything "will be the same."

While the *Religio*, like its author, is "naturally inclined to Rhythme,"[77] modulating between the individuating tendency that emphasizes difference and the expansive tendency that reveals "common harmony," Fish documents only the latter.[78] Thus, he writes that "Browne finally surrenders his identity"; that a passage of the *Religio* "ends in the happy loss of his individuation"; that "individuations" are "transcended on every page of the *Religio Medici.*" All of this, Fish asserts, "involves the denial not only of the differences between persons and nations and sects, but of the more abstract distinctions that mislead us into differentiating qualitatively between aspects of God's perfect whole."[79]

Individuation, the mark of the Renaissance in contemporary historiography, is strangely denied by Fish (as by Bentley, as by Johnson) in favor of a homogeneity that turns difference into a sign of spiritual and, in the case of Bentley and Johnson, political failure.[80] Here again we can identify what I have been calling the "flip-side" of liberal or Whig historiography: where their liberal predecessors emphasize difference, Fish and Bentley emphasize similarity. It is not that Fish is wrong in arguing that "distinctions mislead us into differentiating qualitatively between aspects of God's perfect whole." But, for Browne, such awareness is elaborated only through a difference which is integral to the movement towards unity. For the Brownian investigator, the experience of unity always remains tied to difference: "For even in things alike, there is diversitie, and those that doe seeme to accord, doe manifestly disagree."[81] That is: access to "God's perfect whole" is enabled precisely through individuation in Browne, "as in Milton." Difference is the very site of meaning, the horizon on which "God's perfect whole" becomes visible.

Fish's "self-consuming" aesthetic, by contrast, has little tolerance for such unyielding particularity. For when it turns out that Browne's "sweeping dismissal of human values" is qualified: "'I take it all back, April Fool's, I didn't mean it,'" that Browne seems attached to "particularizing," even to the "machinery of reason," Fish laments that the *Religio* is "not self-consuming, but self-indulgent."[82] For Fish, notably, it is not his paradigm that has failed, but Browne, the "Bad Physician."

STILL SELF-CONSUMING

As recently as 1987, Fish has pointed to the way in which Miltonic texts are, still more than Browne's, "self-consuming." "Again and again," Fish writes, "Milton employs forms (of argument, imagery, justification) that are then discarded or repudiated or denounced." The triptych, "argument, imagery, justification," is triply rejected: "discarded," "repudiated," "denounced" in the name of a non-discursive truth whose "apprehension is negative."[83] "I see Milton," he writes, "continually undermining the forms within which he necessarily moves in order to make his tract a (self-consuming) emblem of its message" (Fish's parenthesis indicates the extent to which his paradigm has itself become one of what he calls the dominant "structures of constraint" for the interpretation of seventeenth-century literature).[84]

The Milton of *Surprised by Sin* encourages us to "distrust our own abilities and perceptions," and to understand that "Life lived or viewed on the human level alone is itself a rhetorical deception." Though we are loath to "be jolted out of a perspective that is after all ours," after being continuously "controlled and mocked" by Milton, we become, Fish argues, "determined not to be caught out again." The reader attached to the sufficiency of reason, the sufficiency of human perception, and the sufficiency of the signified, eventually acquiesces to the admonishing strains of the poet as preacher (though the "learning process," we are assured, "is slow at first"). Here the other half of the Fishian "split-reader," the reader who has internalized Milton's super-ego, begins to perform his revisionary work, recoiling "in the presence of what he knows to be wrong," and imposing "final certainty on the ambiguity of the poetic moment." In that moment of "final certainty," the "experience" of the individual poetic moment" (like, for example, the "ambiguities" of Milton's "'fables'") gives way to the "ever-present pressure of Christian doctrine."[85]

But the achievement of "final certainty" seems an entirely un-Miltonic aspiration, to be affiliated with not only the hubris of Satan, but also that of that other adversary of ambiguity, diversity, and heterogeneity, Richard Bentley. To be sure, Bentley had his own method of guarding against ambiguity, the emendation or wholesale deletion of Milton's text. Although Bentley's method, on the surface, may at first seem far more extreme, I would suggest that the reader of *Surprised by Sin* learns to become an even more relentless editor than his eighteenth-century counterpart. In comparison to Fish, even Bentley's excesses sometimes appear restrained.

For though Bentley insists that the Printer's Faults "*are corrigible by retrieving the Poet's Own Words, not from a Manuscript, (for none exists) but by Sagacity, and happy Conjecture*" (*MPL*, p. a2v), his emendations remain graphically subordinate to the text of the poem. Furthermore, Bentley explicitly leaves it to the reader to evaluate the emendations. All "the conjectures," he writes, "*are cast into the Margin, and explan'd in the Notes. So that every reader has his free Choice, whether he will accept or reject what is here offer'd him*" (*MPL*, p. a2v). In fact, in his preface, Bentley presents himself as acutely aware of the ramifications of his editorial interpolations. Since

"Milton's *own Slips and Inadvertencies cannot be redressed without a Change both of the Words and Sense,*" such changes, he offers are "*suggested, but not obtruded to the Reader: they are generally in this Stile . . . Among several ways of Change this May be one*" *(MPL,* p. a2v). Bentley even forces a moment of humility when he allows for diverse, or at least cooperative, editions of *Paradise Lost:* If "*any Person will substitute better, he will deserve every Reader's Thanks.*" Though "*it's hoped,*" Bentley adds – always reverential for the "Integrity" of the "*Genuine Milton*" – that "*even these will not be found absurd or disagreeing from the* Miltonian *character*" *(MPL,* p. a2v).

Bentley's instructions to the reader, encouraging him to exercise his "free-choice," seem a humbler eighteenth-century version of Fish's "reader-response." Where the formal qualities of Bentley's 1732 edition and his extensive qualification give his text the feeling of a commentary, the corrections of Fish's reader, by contrast, are presented as definitive. Fish can thus insist that, though A. J. Waldock's "reaction to the epic voice is the *correct* one, Milton expects his readers to go beyond it."[86] For Fish, going "beyond" (paralleling Bentley's response to the "wrath of God"), explicitly entails the abandonment of one affective response for another, but entails as well a movement beyond the text. For shifting the "focus of attention from themselves and what is happening in their formal confines to the reader and what is happening in their mind and heart," self-consuming artifacts, as Fish writes, become "the vehicle" of their "own abandonment."[87] "Difficulties" in the poem are transferred from the poem (and from the intentions informing it) to readers whose "ambiguities (crookednesses) are reflected in the interpretations they arrive at." In Fish's reading, whatever ambiguity there may be about *Paradise Lost,* it is not the "poem [that] is finally ambiguous," certainly not as "a moral statement"; it is the readers of the poem to whom the ambiguities belong.[88] In Fish's twentieth-century rendition of Bentley, the "sin" has been transferred from Bentley's Editor and Printer to the reader.

Where Bentley is occasionally surprised by the interpolations and alterations of Milton's ostensible editor, Fish's reader is "continually surprised by sin and in shame." The revisionary attitude of the reader, for Fish no doubt a sign of vigilance, persists in the unending task of fleeing particularity for the certainty of "Christian doctrine." The "rationalizing tendencies of the carnal understanding" (the source of our ostensible "shame") can only be escaped once the ambiguities of the "poetic moment" have been abandoned. The reader of *Paradise Lost* who is able to "resolve a troublesome contradiction" will "reunite with an authority who is a natural ally against the difficulties of the poem." Here the authority and "Integrity" of Fish's ("authoritarian") Milton loom large. This Milton stands above the "difficulties" of his poem, like Bentley's Milton, who shines forth from the "Defoedation" of a bad printer. Thus, Fish's reader, like Bentley's, turns from "plenitudinous human actuality" and "carnal reason" to the "absolute simplicity" and "unity" of "divine reality."

Transcending the "difficulties of the poem" for the "authority" that lurks "beyond" it, Fish's reader begins to supply the "correcting perspectives" that Milton requires.[89] Finally, the reader achieves the position where he can revel in the doctrinal purity and "simplicity" of the poem and join with the authority that proclaims that some readings entail "a distortion that cannot be allowed if *Paradise Lost* is to be read correctly." For, as Fish writes, "there is only one true interpretation of *Paradise Lost*."[90]

Bentley's emendations were polemical; as Empson says, he "hooted as a pedant." There are some bounds, however, that even the "Man who said the Tactless Thing" will not overgo.[91] Though his "Indignation" is raised and Milton's "Editor" berated, Bentley does manage to maintain some semblance of scholarly decorum: his readings are "suggested, but not obtruded to the Reader," and they are acknowledged to be only one, "*Among several ways of Change*." Fish's Milton, by contrast, whom Rumrich calls "an impostor," schooled in a tradition of anti-carnal didacticism, insistently points "beyond" the text to the one "true interpretation." Particularity is rooted out, the "poetic moment" abandoned "continually." Bentley's emendations may be copious, Fish's are unending.

Helen Darbishire remarked of Bentley that he provides "an excellent way-in to what matters in Milton's texts."[92] For a current generation of Milton scholars, it is Fish who has continually pointed to what matters in Milton. But Fish's responses to Milton's text, and the anti-material presuppositions that govern them, at times contradict Milton's own commitment – however qualified – to difference. For difference for Milton, in the politics of *Areopagitica*, the hermeneutics of *De Doctrina*, or the poetics of *Paradise Lost* is the *only* means through which what Fish calls "God's perfect whole" is glimpsed. Fish and Bentley provided what was perhaps a corrective to the liberal (or satanic) avatars of Milton who celebrated difference for its own sake, who in McKeon's words, proclaim the autonomy of the "self-sufficient signifier." That is, where Empson and Hill (heirs to the cosmology advocated by Toland) long for the *subsumption* of God in his creation, Fish advocates the *consumption* of the creation before God (the self-consuming of the "artifact" of humanity before God's transcendence).

Following Fish's own account of his critical genealogy – specifically, his rejection of the "steady unfolding of a classical liberal vision" in Milton criticism – one can simply turn to his "liberal" predecessors to understand whose Milton is being toppled.[93] The Milton fashioned by the "New Movement," and still in vogue at mid-century, was one whose "*moderate* religious views" could "coexist harmoniously with the claims of humanism." It is the "humanist" and "rationalist" Milton, aligned not only with the Milton of "the classical liberal vision" but with the Milton engaged in "human actuality" who comes continually under Fish's critical attack.[94]

Milton clearly is not Saurat's monist "rationalist anti-theologian," though neither is he the Milton who is everywhere proving the "insufficiency" of reason and the "poetic moment." Fish, in responding to his predecessors, like Bentley before him, initiated a "change" – a change "from the celebration" of Milton the poet "of infinite variety" to a "celebration" of Milton the poet "of a single monolithic vision." This "change" in Fish's work parallels another one: the change of the poet of "liberalism" into the poet of "revolutionary absolutism." But the "change," as I have stressed, is only of emphasis: the dichotomy remains. That is, in constructing and celebrating this "monolithic" Milton with only a grudging connection to the particular, to what Milton calls "heterogeneous" and "multiform" reality, Fish and Bentley have also participated in the struggle between devils and angels, producing their own readings of Milton, also, in the language of *Areopagitica*, "plainly partiall."

CHAPTER 7

A *"noble stroke"*: *representation in* Paradise Lost

"Eternity in a grain of sand" – or perhaps on two kernels of wheat. Walter Benjamin, Hannah Arendt recalls, was particularly enamored of an exhibit in the Musée Cluny of two such kernels upon which the entire *Shema Yisrael* was inscribed.[1] Here in what Dr. Johnson would disapprovingly call *"discordia concors,"* the timeless meets the temporal – the concrete particular resonates with the eternal. Johnson himself would have had no truck with Benjamin's fragmentary aesthetic; he had enough of that, as we have already noted, in Cowley, Cleveland, and Donne. Of these metaphysicals (for Johnson of course, it was a *perjorative* designation), Johnson averred:

Their attempts were always analytick: they broke every image into fragments, and could not more represent by their slender conceits and laboured particularities the prospects of nature or the scenes of life, than he who dissects a sun-beam with a prism can exhibit the wide effulgence of a summer moon ...

The metaphysical sensibility was hopelessly local and disjointed. This may have been bad in itself, but it was made worse by the propensity to place this fragmentary sensiblity in the service of "illustrations, comparisons, and allusions." One can only wonder what Johnson might have thought about Benjamin's kernels of wheat.

By the time of the *Lives of the Poets*, the analogical universe had lost much of its power, and a new *episteme* with a less paradoxical but ultimately more rigorous sense of totality had emerged. Indeed, already in the 1650s, Hobbes was revising his notion of wit from a concept which relied upon fancy and judgment – the power of discerning resemblance and difference respectively – to one which relied exclusively upon the latter. Resemblances could be forced – as in Johnson's image of the "most heterogeneous ideas ... yoked by violence together" – but the sign of true wit (not to mention political judgment) was the capacity to make distinctions. Not the fragmentary "analytick" distinctions that turned up in the metaphysical habit of "Clevelandizing," but *rational* distinctions. To be sure, Johnson's was not a celebration of difference, but rather of *rational* multiplicity where such multiplicity could be safely subordinated to the regulative and unifying power of rational aesthetic *and* political norms.[2] In the Enlightenment version of the relationship between the particular and the universal, the particular was *subsumed* under the universal – thus losing the fragmentary individuality that Benjamin's irridiscent empiricism so longed to preserve.

According to John Rumrich, in angelic readings of Milton now so dominant, it is precisely Benjamin's sense of concrete individuality which has been sacrificed. Fish and his angelic legacy, anticipating the New Historicist paradigm of subversion and containment, only accommodate rebellion or individuation as mere fantasies that can never be successfully realized, and are in actuality "the pretext for the assertion and confirmation of power." There is, Rumrich writes, only an "appearance of dualism within a totalitarian system"; in reality, Rumrich suggests, the totalitarian logic of the angelic model merely recuperates – or better coopts – difference for an orthodox Christianity.[3]

Rumrich's association of such interpretive paradigms with totalitarianism is instructive, and indeed the application to Fish's model, in which – as we saw in chapter 6 – difference is constantly eschewed, does not seem altogether inappropriate. Rumrich's invocation against totality succeeds in placing the angelic Milton beyond the fascist pale, justifying the project of salvaging Milton (from his recent regrettable past) for "indeterminacy." But the incorporation of difference within an imagined Christian unity does not follow the model of totality (at least as it is often currently glossed), and does not justify what amounts to throwing out the baby with the bath water. *Discordia concors*, before Johnson memorialized it and Fish coopted it, allowed for an individuation placed in the service of unity. To associate *discordia concors* with the much-despised and minatory totality of the second half of this century is to project our own anxieties about systems and closure upon a rhetorical trope which – in its ideal form – imagined a cultural dynamic that at once tolerated difference, but ultimately articulated a unity.

Miltonic representation in *Paradise Lost*, the current chapter argues, at once inscribes difference, but finally moves towards (though never reaching) such a unity. The chapter thus begins by stressing what Fish continually seeks to deny: the Miltonic emphasis on difference and the ineradicability of the contingent in Miltonic representation in *Paradise Lost*. But while the chapter begins with a reading of *Paradise Lost* that argues against those over-zealous angels – like Fish – who attempt to transcend materiality and difference, it concludes by showing the way in which the text argues against the satanic hermeneutic for which materiality and difference is an end in itself. This is not to argue for a totality which either eschews or coopts difference, but for a *discordia concors* (akin to that embodied in Benjamin kernels of wheat) – not yet Johnson's dead letter, nor Fish's impoverished version of the trope.

Though poetics, with politics and theology, constitute the heuristic and generic perspectives of this study, it, with the others of course, remains an insufficient and ultimately artificial category – falsely demarcating Milton's works into separate generic realms. Thus, the question of divine embodiment, and the correlative question of divine representation in *De Doctrina*, is crucial to an understanding of representation in *Paradise Lost*. Similarly, the principle of political representation in *Areopagitica*, in which individual political interventions represent, but do not *embody* the "public good," stands as an analogy to poetic representation in *Paradise Lost*. In all three realms, that of political representation, biblical interpretation (which might be glossed as the *representation* of the biblical text to the self and others), and poetic representation, the same principle maintains: representation – in all its acknowledged deficiencies – is the locus of truth, contingent upon a totality (i.e., the Bible or the "commonwealth") that it can attempt to mediate though never fully embody.

To elaborate the question of representation in *Paradise Lost*, I want to return to *De Doctrina* – first to the radical and apparently contradictory statements that God is somehow simultaneously "utterly simple" and "multiform," "heterogeneous" and "one." Understood separately, as I have argued, the perspectives collapsed in Miltonic paradox imply either God's involvement or separation from the created world. Indeed, this is the central metaphysical issue that separates critics like William Empson and Christopher Hill from critics like Richard Bentley and Stanley Fish. God's heterogeneity, and the monist metaphysics that it underwrites, sanctions God's presence in the created world, while his simplicity and unity argue for his distinctiveness and transcendence. But, as the previous chapters on *De Doctrina* suggest, the proponents of Milton the monist and Milton the dualist are both dealing with powerful partial truths. For Milton asserted competing cosmologies that must be understood to be complementary.

Arthur Lovejoy testifies to the ostensibly dual conception of God present in Milton's work – the co-presence of what he identifies as the God of Descartes and the God of the Cambridge Platonists. According to Lovejoy, the Cartesian God of Will, whose Power is "irresistible" and "above the law" is juxtaposed, in *De Doctrina*, with the God of the Cambridge Platonists whose primary attribute is "Wisdom." This conflict, which Lovejoy locates throughout Milton's prose, recapitulates the conflict about Miltonic and seventeenth-century ontology. The Cambridge Platonists, by arguing the intrinsic rationality of God, guaranteed the "vital conjunction" between the Creator and creation. The Cartesian (and Hobbesian) emphasis on God's attribute of Will, by contrast, produced a "Divine voluntarism" in which the created world becomes dependent on the arbitrary "will, or even whim" of a thoroughly transcendent Creator. The God of "Wisdom" is present and accessible to his creation, while God conceived as pure power, by contrast, leaves a creation absolutely opaque to its inhabitants.[4]

In his reading of *De Doctrina*, Arthur Sewell, like Lovejoy, manifests a similar attachment to such irreconcilable binaries. Sewell also finds "two hostile conceptions of God in Milton's mind," one "the vision of God as Power and awful Omnipotence" (suggesting Descartes) and the other "the vision of God as Goodness" (affiliated explicitly in Sewell's account with Cudworth). Sewell's solution to the apparent contradiction provides a prime example of what I have been calling metaphysical Whiggism:

This view of God as Incomprehensible Absolute was in keeping with Milton's earlier Calvinist belief. Another view sprang from something deeper in his nature. Where the treatise is second-hand and unoriginal, the Calvinist view governs the thought; and God appears as Absolute Will. Where the treatise is alive and adventurous, this other view vitalizes the new outlook.

"So soon as Milton abandoned the Calvinist notion of God's 'pure will' and denied that God's decrees were absolute," Sewell continues, "he approached very nearly to agreement with Cudworth's view." "God's will," Sewell hastens to add, "is not indifferent," but "determined by his wisdom and his goodness." Where Milton represents a God who, like the God of Cudworth's account, infuses his creation, his views are "alive and adventurous."[5]

What Sewell calls the Calvinist notion of a God of "pure will" is, to borrow from a different lexicon, simply residual, and obstructs the realization of an otherwise "new outlook," emerging from something "deeper" in Milton's "nature." Sewell's language – notwithstanding its biases – does underline the contradictory commitments evidenced in Milton's work. These contradictory commitments, however, are both present in Milton's theology, and should not be de-coded in the context of some telos of metaphysical, political, or poetic embodiment. Just as Milton argues for the sufficiency *and* insufficiency of reason in *Areopagitica*; just as he simultaneously articulates providentialist *and* republican discourses in *The Readie and Easie Way*; so Milton in *De Doctrina*, as we saw in chapter 4, simultaneously advocates the God of Will *and* Reason. This strategy permits the positing of a God who is at once present and absent to his creation, at once constrained and beyond constraint. But where many critics register their objections to this kind of Miltonic paradox, evidencing a version of what Christopher Norris has called Empson's "rationalist antipathy to . . . mystery-mongering," Milton, himself, can be said to embrace paradox as a form of argument.[6] That is, where Empson finds paradox a form of obfuscation, for Milton it becomes a *mode of explanation* – permitting, among other things, the possibility of the co-existence of God's providence and man's free will, the transcendent God of Will and the immanent God of Reason.

In this crucial paradox, embodied for Milton in the notion of God's simultaneous transcendence and constraint, it becomes evident how metaphysics underwrites poetics, and how ostensibly ontological issues inform the problem of representation. Where a monist metaphysics underwrites a poetics in which the signifier is self-sufficient, sanctioning the interchangeability of the material and the spiritual (and leading in Sewell's idiom to a "new outlook"), a dualist metaphysics underwrites a poetics in which the signifier is wholly insufficient, separated from the signified by an unbridgeable chasm.[7] Like his metaphysics, however, Milton's notion of representation does not fit neatly into either of these categories. The coincident monism and dualism of Miltonic cosmology will therefore have specific consequences for theodicy: just as God is simultaneously present and absent to his creation, so "God's ways" are simultaneously implicit within, though always in part inaccessible to, the language of poetry – even the inspired poetry of *Paradise Lost*.

What I have been calling Milton's epistemological monism and dualism informs, as Herman Rapaport argues, conflicting "linguistic ideologies" in *Paradise Lost* – one in which "matter and spirit are one," the other in which "they are radically split apart."[8] This conflict underlies the tension implicit in Miltonic representation, manifested in the simultaneous affirmation of the sufficiency and insufficiency of language as the medium for theodicy.

The fifth book of *Paradise Lost*, with its various songs, orisons, prayers, and dreams, represents Milton's most focused statement on representation and theodicy. Indeed, here Raphael provides an account of the eventual telos of history (and matter), an explanation that underwrites the monist vision of the poem and the "linguistic ideology" that "matter and spirit are one." Raphael's discourse on metaphysics, however, is itself complicated by an implicit dualism, which will become crucial for the discussion of Miltonic representation. For Raphael's claims about the ultimate destiny of matter (despite the obvious monist implications) reveal that though matter *tends* towards spirit, it remains a gesture or direction, *not*, however, an arrival or achievement. Indeed, against the telos implied by Raphael's initial assertion that "All things proceed, and up to him return," follows the qualification: "If not deprav'd from good" (v 470–71). Thus the upward direction of matter, first figured as ineluctable and inevitable, turns out to be subject to the inertial forces of evil. Continuing, Raphael reveals that the eventual return to "perfection" and "one first matter all" is a *process*. Those "various forms" and "various degrees / Of substance," Raphael declares, become

> ... more refin'd, more spirituous, and pure,
> As nearer to him plac't or nearer tending ...
> Till body up to spirit work, in bounds,
> Proportion'd to each kind.   (v 475–79)

The comparatives – "*more* refin'd" and "*more* spirituous," and "*nearer* to him ... or *nearer* tending" – and the temporal adverb – "Till" – reveal that for Milton monism is always figured – even in Paradise – as a direction, not an end. Indeed, though those "various forms" of "substance" are moving towards a monist unity with spirit, they are for the moment "Each in thir several active Spheres assign'd" – thus both upward tending, yet static, "plac't."

Though Adam and Eve learn the cosmological principle by which "substance" is "refin'd," that matter is by "gradual scale sublim'd" (v 483) and that their bodies,

> ... may at last turn all to spirit,
> Improv'd by tract of time, and wing'd ascend
> Ethereal ...   (v 497–99)

the very language which Raphael employs emphasizes that this transformation is as yet incomplete, and that at the very origin of Milton's monism lies what will always appear in *this* world as an ineradicable dualism.

To be sure, while the "monism" of Raphael's discourse has, as we shall see below, interpretive, as well as cosmological ramifications, what

John Guillory calls Milton's "ideological monism" is even further qualified by the conclusion of Raphael's excursus. For Raphael insists that Adam and Eve be cognizant of the limitations of their current state:

> ... Meanwhile enjoy
> Your fill what happiness this state
> Can comprehend, incapable of more.   (v 504–6)

In "this state," Adam and Eve are limited by what they can "comprehend." It is precisely at this level of comprehension that representation and dualism are fully reinstated. Notwithstanding the monism articulated here by Raphael, there remains, as Guillory writes, "a dualistic problem at the level of representation." As Edward Tayler more succinctly puts it, "dualism necessarily precedes monism."[9] Paraphrased again: difference precedes, is the necessary condition for, unity.

DIFFERENCE AGAIN

If we expect Books XI and XII to register Adam's consciousness of God's abandonment from the created world, then we might also expect the middle books of *Paradise Lost* (which Marshall Grossman has rightly affiliated with Milton's monism) to provide an unambiguous testimony of God's continuing presence. Even here, however, in these middle "monist" books – even in the "morning hymn" – God remains "invisible" "or," at best, "dimly seen / In these thy lowest works" (v 157–58). Despite Raphael's later rhetorical assurances, "For where is not hee / Present" (VII 517–18), the apocalyptic promise of the return to "one first matter all" seems not to have any consequences *even* for the pre-fallen Edenic pair searching for His presence. Miltonic language, even in striving towards representing unity, in the attempts to assert "continuity" between the Creator and the created world, inscribes difference, "contiguity."

That is, language may gesture towards an expression of the eternal in the temporal, but the temporal can never be said to *contain* the eternal. As Milton was not, as were the Fifth Monarchy Men, an advocate of the transparency of contemporary history (with their emphasis on what R. S. Capp calls the "imminence of the millennium"), he likewise did not advocate the transparency of poetic language.[10] The absence of such linguistic transparency in even the so-called monist books of *Paradise Lost* attests to both Milton's critique of immanence and his critique of the transparency of the signifier. Notwithstanding the monist discourses in

De Doctrina and *Paradise Lost* (not to mention Fallon's aggressive claims about "Miltonic monism"), Miltonic representation is presupposed upon difference, upon the ultimate inadequacy of the signifier to the signified.

If Richard Crashaw, for example, can be said to have advocated an incarnationalist poetic in which the presence of the metaphysical is evidenced in the physical, where the "Divine / Idea" will "take a shrine / Of Chrystall flesh, through which to shine," Milton emphatically denies such a possibility of linguistic transparency.[11] Even Milton's monist vision (that "God shall be all in all") is only available through representation, which, in the language of *Areopagitica*, is emphatically the realm of "contiguity."

The fifth book of *Paradise Lost*, opening as it does with the "Matin Song / Of Birds on every bough" (v 7–8) serves as a meditation on the efficacy of "Song," and on the problem of how God is made accessible – rendered present – through song. If, as Mary Ann Radzinowicz claims, Milton "conceives of the whole poem, which he calls 'my Song,' as an act of praise,"[12] then the morning hymn, modelled, as Newton first noted, on Psalm 148, stands as a synecdoche for the "praise" of *Paradise Lost*. Even in this most intense form of lyrical praise, Milton calls attention to its *mediate* form. That is, the medium of poetic expression described in Milton's *Of Education* as "more simple, sensuous, and passionate," is not transcended (or self-consumed) even as Adam and Eve direct their praise heavenward (II 403).

In Adam and Eve's morning hymn, Milton alternates between presenting creation as opaque (neither divine, nor acknowledging the divine), and a creation disclosing God's "goodness beyond thought." In this, the Psalms, as Radzinowicz has demonstrated, provided Milton with a clear precedent. Although the Psalmist confidently intones: "The heavens declare the glory of God; and the firmament sheweth his handywork. Day to day uttereth speech, and night to night sheweth knowledge," the confident opening is followed by a sudden reversal: "There is no speech nor languages . . . their voice is not heard" (19:1:2). The testimony of nature, to the Psalmist, is at once expressive, and yet paradoxically mute: "their voice is not heard." In *Paradise Lost*, Adam and Eve's hymn locates the same ambiguity in the created world. Although they proclaim that God remains "invisible," their perspective shifts as, reassured, they find that God's "works" do in fact "declare / Thy goodness beyond thought, and Power Divine" (v 158–59).

Milton pursues the paradox of Psalm 19 as Adam and Eve invoke the testimony of Nature:

> Vary to our great Maker still new praise.
> Ye Mists and Exhalations that now rise
> From Hill or steaming Lake, dusky or grey ...
> In honor to the World's great Author rise,
> Whether to deck with Clouds th' uncolor'd sky,
> Or wet the thirsty Earth with falling showers,
> Rising or falling still advance his praise.
> His praise ye Winds ...
> Melodious murmurs, warbling tune his praise ...
>   ... ye Birds ...
> Bear on your wings and in your notes his praise ...
>   (v 184–86, 188–92, 196–97, 199)

Notwithstanding Fallon's claims that the hymn "confers" upon Nature "the ability to act," the "animism" of the passage and Nature's autonomous praise of God is not altogether straightforward.[13] Although Nature's testimony seems unqualified and might be construed itself as praise, the repetitions of the pair's invocations ("Vary ... still new praise"; "advance his praise"; "tune his praise") suggest that Adam and Eve are engaging in what becomes a performative utterance – that the praise is *their own*, not the created world's. Indeed, it is only Adam and Eve who convert the waving of "Pines" and "every plant" into a "sign of worship" (193–94). That Adam and Eve transform the contingent acts of Nature into praise of God is a possibility suggested in the last lines of the hymn:

> Witness if I be silent, Morn or Even,
> To Hill, or Valley, Fountain, or fresh shade
> Made vocal by my Song, and taught his praise.
>   (v 202–4)

Adam and Eve seek to fend off silence, but the witnesses they invoke are paradoxically "made vocal" by their own song. The created world is "taught his praise" – but only by Adam and Eve's song which precedes them, and upon which their "praise" ultimately depends. Just as in Book XII, where there is a disjunction between the voice of the guide Michael, and the visions that Adam no longer has access to ("I see him," Michael says of the vision of Abraham, "but thou canst not" [XII 128]), here there is a similar disjunction, and a similar privileging of the aural over the visual.[14]

Even in Paradise, the presence of God is mediated by language: as if

Hobbes had made his way into Milton's Paradise to insist that faith only comes by hearing – that even here pure presence would be unavailable. But this is not to register a Miltonic longing for lost immanence or a nostalgia for transparency, but rather to re-affirm a notion implied throughout *Areopagitica*: that the incompleteness of representation does not so much signal a lack, but rather a perfection. This incompleteness is, in fact, Paradise; and its corollary, completion (which Satan attempts to achieve) is idolatry or Hell.

Not only does the Miltonic emphasis on the aural register a sharp (Old Testament) resistance to idolatry (and its embodiment of the divine), but in a more contemporary lexicon, it resists the seduction of unmediated presence.[15] The specular, providing an illusion of presence, gives way to the oracular – to the insistence on the mediation of language (paralleling the movement from the visions of Book XI to Michael's narration of Book XII). What T. S. Eliot described as "the limitation of visual power" in Milton's poetry, and the consequent difficulty "to *see* very clearly any scene that Milton depicts" corresponds with the need, Eliot writes, that the reader's "*hearing* . . . become more acute."[16] For Milton, hearing – the realm of language – displaces the visual realm where embodiment would be possible.

Nowhere is Milton's distance from the nostalgia for immanence (a nostalgia understood by Jean-Luc Nancy as the distinguishing characteristic of Western philosophy) more in evidence than in this disjunction inscribed into the "morning hymn" in the very bliss of Paradise. It is a disjunction – already present in Eden – that fully anticipates (or perhaps registers) the Fall and Adam's "evil Conscience" which then "represented / All things with double terror" (x 849–50). Thus in Adam's later invocation:

> O Woods, O Fountains, Hillocks, Dales and Bow'rs,
> With other echo late I taught your Shades
> To answer, and resound far other song . . .   (x 860–62)

the rupture between the creation and Adam's "song" appears complete, as Nature merely echoes the shattered song of Adam's "evil Conscience."[17]

But strangely, not only for the Adam of Book x, but even for the pre-lapsarian couple, the search for the embodied God is frustrated. Nature not only does not transparently manifest divinity but it contains forces antithetical to it. So Adam and Eve end their hymn with a supplication:

> Hail universal Lord, be bounteous still
> To give us only good; and if the night
> Have gather'd aught of evil or conceal'd,
> Disperse it . . .   (v 205–8)

Even in Paradise, Nature is not only potentially opaque, but also a possible refuge for evil "conceal'd." Just as Milton's monist account of creation in *De Doctrina* fragments, allowing for the "calculations of the devil or of man, calculations which proceed from these creatures themselves" (vi 309), so Adam and Eve, in the midst of Paradise, feel the threat of evil. This experience of evil inscribes dualism, perhaps, as Regina Schwartz might suggest, even an *apparent* Manicheanism in the midst of Eden. Evil, what Raphael in Book v refers to as "depravity," is the very site of difference – registering the appearance of an ostensible "reality" unassimilable to God's goodness. Even here, as worship gives way to the pressures of theodicy, narrative – its stubborn contingency before God's non-narratable providence – registers the experience of difference. But the appearance of evil and difference, for the Milton of *Paradise Lost* as well as for the Milton of the 1640s, is not only the guarantor of free will, but also the guarantor of that unity figured at history's end.

a "noble stroke"

Raphael's description of Abdiel's confrontation with Satan during the War in Heaven in Book vi emphasizes the limitations of language, and consequently of epic narrative and theodicy as well. Language, straining towards the eternal, returns, ineluctably for Milton, to the temporal and contingent – to the limitations of what man in this "state / Can comprehend." During their face-to-face struggle, after Abdiel's "stern" reply to "the grand Foe,"

> . . . a noble stroke he lifted high,
> Which hung not, but so swift with tempest fell
> On the proud Crest of *Satan*, that no sight,
> Nor motion of swift thought, less could his Shield
> Such ruin intercept . . .   (vi 189–93)

Raphael's description insists upon the necessity of narrative temporality – "a noble stroke he lifted high" – but in the qualification – "Which hung not" – he seems to erase its possibility. As Fish writes of another passage, the effort to accommodate the two different perspectives, "strains the mind to its capacities."[18] For the interpolation, "Which hung not," simultaneously places the reader within two different perspectives. While the phrase can be read to be consistent with narrative continuity (Abdiel doesn't leave his sword in the air but strikes swiftly), it can also be read to affirm the unreality of action (Abdiel's sword doesn't hang *at all*). This latter perspective emphasizes that belief in agency, drama, or narrative is nothing more than a temptation in a world which, as Fish explains, "Christ has taken it upon himself to do it all," and where man "can do nothing." But the Miltonic allusion to a timeless realm where Abdiel's "noble stroke" is acknowledged, as Fish writes, to be truly "pointless" is itself qualified by the return to action and to the concrete.[19]

Though the epic narrator writes from a perspective in which the action of the poem is already complete (both anticipating and already aware of the time when "one greater Man / Restore us" [I 4–5]), Abdiel's actions nonetheless retain their significance. From the perspective of the telos of the narrative (the realization of "one first matter all"), Abdiel's actions, like all those who "each on himself reli'd, / As only in his arm the moment lay / Of victory" (VI 238–40), do seem "pointless." Abdiel, however, acts *in time*, the medium of narrative. Thus the timeless yields to the temporal: Abdiel's "noble stroke . . . so swift with tempest fell."

Raphael's affirmation that "no sight, / Nor motion of swift thought, less could his Shield / Such ruin intercept" furthers the paradox of the previous lines: the twin subjects of the line ("motion of swift thought" and Satan's "shield") pull in two different connotative directions, suggesting simultaneously the narrativity and non-narrativity of providence. In its most obvious sense, the lines assert the incompatibility of "swift thought" to its object, affirming that providential history resists the temporalizing effects of narrative. That is, the drama, or rather lack of drama of providential history cannot be intercepted – rendered – in language. No matter how "swift" the thought, such a thought temporalizes and thereby represents (and in representing, mis-represents) a non-narrative event.[20] The interpolation of a second subject in the clause "less could his Shield," however, throws the reader back into a history (what Fish calls the "security of sequence") where both agency and drama have significance.[21] Raphael's insistence on the very non-narrativity of providential history is ultimately rendered *in narrative*: Satan's "ruin" *is* finally represented. Even his "proud Crest" cannot withstand the "noble stroke" – that very "stroke," paradoxically, which Raphael had declared to be beyond "motion of swift thought."

This must be seen as the primary tension that underlies theodicy: utter inaction, as in the case of Abdiel in *Paradise Lost*, or inaction accompanied by silence, as in the case of Jesus in *Paradise Regained*, may represent ideal responses of faith, but they do little to "justify the ways of God to men" (1 26). In this, the "noble stroke" becomes an emblem for Miltonic theodicy, at once foregrounding its own inadequacy, but acknowledging its ultimate sufficiency. Thus, if the vehicles of Miltonic theodicy can be said to be "self-consuming," they are never completely so. The trace of language, of the materiality of poetic representation, is always evident. The "noble stroke," therefore, inscribes another in the litany of reader-temptations (one which Fish himself seems unable to identify and to which he often succumbs): the *angelic* temptation to transcend language for God-like certainty, for a perception not constrained by the "motion of swift thought." "Process of speech," however, constitutes the very horizon of human knowledge. God's immediacy, like his presence, is never completely accessible to the temporalizing characteristics of narrative. That is, representation in its very essence violates the promised unity – the monistic identity – of God with his creation.

The Miltonic reliance on representation and "process of speech" do not merely represent concessions, part of a Miltonic accommodation to a limited human capacity. In arguing, as we saw in *De Doctrina*, against a Hellenic notion of a truth beyond discourse, Milton, unlike Calvin, does not embrace a defensive notion of accommodation in which language serves as an inadequate medium for a truth outside of it. Although Milton shares the Calvinist skepticism about the transparency of discourse, Milton's epistemology is more aggressive than defensive: language is itself the limit of truth. The turn towards language for Milton is not regrettable, but necessary, a point driven home as the "noble stroke" crashes down on Satan's "proud Crest." The idea that poetic language, as Fish claims, is simply "self-consuming" before a non-linguistic truth, enacts the temptation of omniscience – the temptation of moving beyond representation to the clarity of a divine perspective. This perspective may, as Isabel MacCaffrey suggested, be "transposed into the poem's mythic structure."[22] Notwithstanding this claim, however, Milton is not open to the attack of those who like Donna Haraway argue that "the god trick" underlies an objectivist, "non-situated" epistemology. Although what Jean Howard describes as a "disembodied, all-seeing, hidden eye" is inscribed in Milton's text, the "god trick" in *Paradise Lost* throws Milton (and the reader) back to the "situatedness" of language.[23]

In *Paradise Lost*, Milton insistently points the reader back to that realm of language. When Ithuriel, with his "spear" in hand, comes at the end of Book IV to rescue Eve from Satan, who "Squat like a Toad" sat close at her ear, he comes confident that "no falsehood can endure / Touch of Celestial temper, but returns / Of force to its own likeness" (IV 811–13). "Ithuriel's spear" which Guillory elevates "to something like a poetic principle," though representing an "ideal relation between the object and the process of representation," is not completely efficacious.[24]

Before Satan can return to his "own likeness," before, in Guillory's words, "Ithuriel's spear translates, as it were, 'like a toad,'" Satan undergoes a further transmutation:

> ... up he starts
> Discover'd and surpris'd. As when a spark
> Lights on a heap of nitrous Powder, laid
> Fit for the Tun some Magazin to store
> Against a rumor'd War, the Smutty grain
> With sudden blaze diffus'd, inflames the Air:
> So started up in his own shape the Fiend.   (IV 813–19)

The desire to "translate" poetic language and to undo the "falsehood" of Satan's appearance only leads to *further* poetic elaboration. Satan's unmasking is in fact elaborated four times: once in the abstract articulation of lines 811–13; again in the description of 813–14; again in the simile of the "spark"; and finally in the simile's conclusion of line 819. The repetition and multiplication of perspectives serves to emphasize the impossibility of complete "translation." The astronomical triangulation of Galileo who spied the moon from "the top of *Fesole*, / Or in *Valderno*" (I 289–90) becomes itself, in *Paradise Lost*, an epistemological principle. The Galilean multiplication of perspectives (again, in Book v, in "*Delos*" or "*Samos*"; [265]) emphasizes the limitation of knowledge, but it also defers (perpetually) the move out of language to some transcendent perspective.

The extended simile enacts that deferral as the ostensible vehicle of translation, the comparison to the "spark" on "a heap of nitrous Powder," yields to the digressive history of the "Powder" itself. "Fit for the Tun some Magazin to store," the story of the "Powder" wanders listlessly into the past, receding into the unreality of some "rumor'd War." Although the simile's eventual translation of the "Smutty grain" into a "sudden blaze diffus'd" enacts the "turn" from "corporeal to incorporeal," we are left with the realization that this Miltonic translation has not left the bounds of simile. "Like a toad" is translated into the extended simile of the "nitrous Powder." That is, even though Satan re-assumes his "own shape," the return to his "own likeness" is not to be confused with a return to, or the establishment, of identity. The transformation enabled in poetic language is relational and, therefore, never complete. Notwithstanding Bentley's impatience with the whole passage, the materiality of language continually re-asserts itself. As Guillory affirms, "we can never manage to see the 'thing itself.'"[25]

MEDIATION

If the desire for unmediated truth or "the thing itself," associated with Milton's angelic readers, is rendered problematic, the drift into materiality and the fetishism of narrative, associated with Milton's satanic readers, poses its own problems. Just as the "Smutty grain" is almost forgotten in its "Magazin," so in Satanic discourse the material is its own final refuge, an end in itself, becoming at best like Satan himself, a presumed "Idol of Majesty Divine" (VI 101). Satanic discourse in *Paradise Lost* enacts the materialization of language divorced from spirit – language left, figuratively, in some "Magazin," long after the "rumor'd War" had been forgotten. Where Milton insists on the inter-relation of divine and profane discourse, Satan insists on their utter separation. This relationship between heavenly and profane is rendered most forcefully in Books V and VI – especially in the "war in heaven" in which, as Leslie Moore claims, paraphrasing John Dennis, Milton is able "to generate an aesthetic equaling the power of Satan's."[26]

But these central books of the epic are also the locus of Satan's refusal of heavenly narrative:

> ... wee style
> The strife of Glory: which we mean to win,
> Or turn this Heav'n itself into the Hell
> Thou fabl'st ...   (VI 289–92)

The satanic insistence that it is God who fables levels the vertical scale by which matter is by "gradual scale sublim'd" into a horizontal scale of equivalent and equally material narratives. From this perspective, Satan's outraged railing at the Son's anointing seems understandable:

> Thrones, Dominations, Princedoms, Virtues, Powers,
> If these magnific Titles yet remain
> Not merely titular, since by Decree
> Another now hath to himself ingross't
> All Power, and us eclipst under the name
> Of King anointed ...
> With what may be devis'd of honors new
> Receive him to coming to receive from us
> Knee-tribute yet unpaid, prostration vile,

Too much to one, but double how endur'd
To one and to his image now proclaim'd?

(v 772–77; 780–784)

Armed with the rhetoric that Milton himself employed in the *Readie and Easie Way*, Satan resists the primacy – what becomes *for him* the idolatry – of the Son, and the worship of "his image now proclaim'd." There is a difference, however, between the application of Milton's anti-monarchical language in the 1660 tract, and Satan's application of that language to Jesus in *Paradise Lost*. Jesus, who continually recognizes his subordination to the Father, is not to be confused with Charles who "ingross't" titles for *himself*.

For Satan, the Son's "magnific Titles" and "Power" "ingross't" do argue for the throwing off of "this Yoke" (v 786). But the Satanic challenge to the primacy of the Son – in the words of *De Doctrina* that there is only "*one mediator between God and men: the man, Jesus Christ*" (vi 217) – evidences the projection of Satan's own aesthetic on to that of God and Jesus. If Satan himself articulates a critique of a mode of representation in which the worship of the Son's "image" is "now proclaim'd," it is only because he wants to embrace that notion of representation for himself: to become, as Satan *wrongly thinks of the Son*, an "Idol of Majesty Divine" (vi 101). Thus in competition with the Son, Satan,

> Affecting all equality with God,
> In imitation of that Mount whereon
> *Messiah* was declar'd in sight of Heav'n . . .
> . . . thither he assembl'd all his Train
>
> (v 763–65, 767)

Where God anoints the Son, Satan, in a perverse "imitation" seeks to anoint himself. For Satan, as Sin says of him, is "enamor'd" by his own "perfect image" (ii 765, 764). Thus Satan assumes that by reclaiming his titles, he can compete with the Son's "Power":

> *Thrones, Dominations, Princedoms, Virtues, Powers,*
> For in possession such, not only of right,
> I call ye and declare ye now, return'd
>
> (x 460–63; emphasis added)

Without first asserting that the Son is a mere idol "to be cast off," Satan cannot raise himself up to a level of equivalence to compete with the Son and the heavenly narrative, what by Book x is described with greater and greater frequency as God's "Sentence" (x 805). Indeed, it is the priority of this divine "Sentence" (and here the juridical and linguistic connotations of the word both have relevance) that render Satanic "counterfeits" more and more secondary.

As Dennis suggests, it is precisely Jesus' mediatorial agency that provides a challenge to the Satanic aesthetic of equivalent and competing iconic narratives. At the virtual center of the poem, Jesus' intervention in the "war in heaven" radiates outwards sanctioning the inter-relation of sacred and profane narratives. In Jesus' ascension into the divine "Chariot" in Book VI, Milton comes as close as he ever does to *representing* immanence – as his entrance into the heavenly fray enacts divine history. Thus, upon hearing of his anointing, Jesus proclaims:

> ... this I my Glory account,
> My exaltation, and my whole delight.
> That thou in me well pleas'd, declar'st thy will
> Fulfill'd, which to fulfil is all my bliss.   (VI 726–29)

"When the great Ensign of *Messiah* blaz'd," Jesus, "Sign in Heav'n" (VI 775–76), manifests the "will" of God "Fulfill'd." In his response to the divine command, however, the Son, himself apparently in a Satanic mode, emphasizes his own agency in the fulfillment of divine narrative: "this I my Glory *account*" (emphasis added). "My exaltation, and my whole delight," as appositives to "my Glory," continue to assert the Son's independent role in the accounting of God's "Sentence" (while also seemingly bearing out Satan's claims against him). However, the appositives, understood as subjects of the relative clause – "That thou in me well pleas'd" – emphasize Jesus' subordination to God's "will." While Satan, in apparent "imitation" of the Son, asserts his own self-sufficiency ("We know no time when we were not as now / Know none before us, self-begot, self-raised" [V 859–60]), Jesus asserts his own *insufficiency* and dependence on the Father. Though he wields "Sceptre and Power," he acknowledges them of "thy giving," and though he proclaims *himself* the "Image of thee in all things," and anticipates *himself* sending the "undying Worm" to the "chains of darkness" (VI 739), he also includes himself in the numbers of the "Saints unmixt" who will "Unfeigned *Halleluiahs*" to the Father "sing" (VI 742, 745). In this reading, even the privileged accounting of Jesus acknowledges its own insufficiency, as the agent of this narrative anticipates the time when he, too, "gladlier shall resign" – that is, resign himself to the democracy of "Saints unmixt" who will join in praising the Father (VI 742).

The asserted subordination of the Son to the Father not only answers to the narrative demands of epic, it also reflects the theology elaborated in *De Doctrina*. In the Son's relation to the Father, the consistency between the heresies of *De Doctrina* and the poetics of *Paradise Lost* again comes into focus. For in his theological tract, Milton wrote that "the attributes of divinity belong to the Father alone, and ... even he [the Son] is excluded from them" (vi 227). So Jesus, unlike Satan, recognizes his subordinate role and gives "back to the Father everything," and is consequently, according to *De Doctrina*, "unwilling to accept the flattering titles" which were habitually bestowed upon others (vi 229). Jesus deflects just the idea of immanence – "Titles" and "honors" "ingross't" – which Satan attributes first to Christ and then to himself.

On the level of representation, the fundamental "difference in essence" (vi 216) between the Father and Son asserts the ultimate incommensurability between sign and signified, even the privileged "Sign" represented by Jesus in the war in heaven. In Milton's very specific and repeated formulations in *De Doctrina*, Jesus is a "mediator," a function which clearly distinguishes him from God. It is "quite inconceivable," Milton writes,

that anyone could be a mediator to himself or on his own behalf. According to Gal. iii. 20: *a mediator however is not needed for one person acting alone, but God is one.* How, then, could God be God's mediator? How is it that the mediator constantly testified when speaking of himself that he did nothing by himself... and that he did not come from himself... It must follow that he does not act as mediator to himself, or return as mediator to himself. (vi 218)

If God and his mediator are essentially the same, and "he is his own mediator between himself and us," then we are left with what Milton calls "a quite inexplicable state of affairs" (vi 218) where the three poles of the interpretive triad – interpreter, mediator (Christ), and God – are collapsed into two, as the latter term, God, is cancelled.

For Milton it is a manifest absurdity that "God be God's mediator," and thus in delineating what is for him the primary relation between the divine and the created worlds, he insists on their difference – the ultimate incommensurability between God and Jesus.[27] For "Christ," as Milton continues in *De Doctrina*, "did not come to make himself, but his Father, manifest" (vi 244). Milton's explanation of Christ's role as a *mediator* of God is consistent with the ways in which mediation (in the way I have used the term) functions throughout Milton's works. Just as in *Areopagitica*, individual mediations (political interventions) are never to be considered identical with the public sphere; just as in *De Doctrina*, such mediations (interpretations) are never to be considered identical with the scriptures;

so narratives (even those accounted by Jesus) and theodicies (even those rendered by inspired poets) are not to be considered *completely* identical with "the ways of God."[28] Even Jesus, for Milton the ultimate mediator, is not considered identical with the Father.

"God," as Milton writes in *De Doctrina*, *"was made manifest in flesh,* that is, in the Son, his image." As Milton continues, however, he immediately qualifies the assertion of immanence: "in any other way he is invisible" (VI 244). Thus when God calls the Son "Effulgence of my Glory, Son belov'd, / Son in whose face invisible is beheld / Visibly, what Deity I am" (VI 680–82), Milton emphasizes the paradoxical nature of representation. At once, the Son is the straightforward "Effulgence" of God's glory, by which invisibility is "beheld Visibly." By contrast, the ambiguous syntax of the line suggests an opposite meaning: that "invisible" is not the subject of the sentence that follows, but the adjective that qualifies the previous noun. In this reading, it is the Son's "face" which is invisible, suggesting not only God's inaccessibility through representation, but also anticipating the time, after the Fall, when God's creation will seem to conceal even "his utmost skirts / Of glory" (XI 332–33).

FANTASIES OF IDENTITY

Where divine representation continually re-inscribes difference – even in the privileged relation between the Father and Son – satanic representation continually re-asserts identity. Satan thus nurtures his own fantasy of identity, collapsing one pole of Milton's interpretive triad, interpreter–mediator–God (or perhaps, reader–sign–signified), becoming, in the words of *De Doctrina*, his "own mediator between himself and us." This "quite inexplicable state of affairs" becomes the very condition for idolatry, the identification of the mediator with the object of mediation. This satanic emphasis on unity is, ironically, the ultimate sign and guarantor of a critical tradition which would celebrate Milton's ostensibly satanic emphasis on difference. Satan's celebration of his own materiality, and his refusal to acknowledge that mediation requires the acknowledgment of a third term (God), invests Satan with an autonomy and independence from God which later critics would hold up as a model for Miltonic politics and theology. A mediator to himself, Satan has no need for God.

The war in heaven not only enables "the expulsion" of God's "Foes" (VI 785), but it also permits a kind of anatomy of narrative, distinguishing Satan's "calumnious Art / Of counterfeited truth" from Jesus' "account" and God's "sentence" (v 770–71). From the time of the composition of *L'Allegro* and *Il Penseroso*, Milton had been committed to the depiction and discrimination of various poetic modes; in *Paradise Lost* this reaches epic proportions. Thus the war in heaven represents, among other things, a war of conflicting narratives and modes of representation; Satan, more than any one else, sees it so. For him, the military battle against the angelic hosts is figured as a kind of linguistic competition: the satanic "invention," gunpowder, is deployed through "hollow'd bodies made of Oak or Fir" (VI 574) – cannons with a strange resemblance to pastoral pipes. The military and pastoral metaphors again overlap as one of these cannons is described as flanked by a Seraph "in his hand a Reed" [VI 579]). The "Reed" here doubles as the "incentive" (what Hughes glosses as the "kindling" for the "gunner's match" [VI 519]) and the symbol for pastoral, what Milton calls in Book XI, the "Pastoral Reed" (XI, 132; we also can recall, from *Comus*, the "pastoral *reed* with oaten stops" [345; emphasis added]).

Indeed, if Milton's *Masque* represents a kind of Virgilian competition between the poetic of "the good Shepherd" Comus and the "rural minstrelsy" of the Attendant Spirit, then *Paradise Lost* provides a variation on that same theme. Throughout the war in heaven, Satan looks for linguistic equivalents to his military actions, as he propounds "terms / of composition" (VI 612–13), advances an "overture" (VI 562), offers "proposals" (VI 618), discharges his "part" (VI 565), and entreats a response ("and loud that all may hear") to what "we propound" (VI 567). Belial, "in gamesome mood," again in the mode of *analogia antithetica*, stresses the relation between military and linguistic "invention":

> Leader, the terms we sent were terms of weight,
> Of hard contents, and full of force urg'd home
>
> (VI 620–22)

Belial's interjection, more than simply an occasion for some bad punning, quite literally literalizes the war in heaven, emphasizing the satanic failure in not only military but linguistic terms as well.[29] Satanic language and satanic warfare, linked in their materiality and ostensible self-sufficiency, continually fail in relation to God's all-powerful "Sentence." While the very materiality and doubleness of the puns themselves indicate satanic fallenness, the triumph of Christ also emphasizes the superiority of providential narrative over classical generic forms – a step on the way to Christ's final rejection of the "Harmonious Airs" and "charming pipes" of *Paradise Regained* (II 362–63).

As Belial's description suggests, satanic "invention" is emphatically and exclusively material: Belial believes the war in heaven can be won in "terms of weight" and "hard contents." Where Miltonic theodicy, on the model of angelic invention, is presupposed on the "lik'ning of spiritual to corporal forms" (v 575), satanic invention begins and ends in the corporeal. Thus, Satan ignores the *potentia* of meaning (or spirit) in the material world. To one with an "erected wit" or what Donne in the *Anniversaries* would call a "potent receiver," the distinction between matter and spirit (the sign and the signified) begins to collapse. This monist *aspect* of representation is the means by which theodicy – the relating of the "secrets of another World" – becomes possible.

In angelic invention, like angelic digestion, the "sensuous" is gradually "refin'd." Milton compared this process (upon which his own theodicy is modelled) to the occult arts of the "Empiric Alchemist":

> Of sooty coal the Empiric Alchemist
> Can turn, or holds it possible to turn
> Metals of drossiest Ore to perfet Gold
> As from the Mine.   (v 440–43)

Angelic invention begins in "drossiest Ore" and ends in "perfet Gold." By contrast, in the satanic correlate to this process in Book VI, matter is not, as in the case of the angelic process, "by gradual scale sublim'd."

Preparing for battle, with "dev'lish machination," the satanic host turns to their own mode of "invention," looking themselves to "devise / Like instrument to plague the Sons of men":

> . . . in a moment up they turn'd
> Wide the Celestial soil, and saw beneath
> Th' originals of Nature in thir crude
> Conception; Sulphurous and Nitrous Foam
> They found, they mingl'd, and with subtle Art
> Concocted and adjusted they reduc'd
> To blackest grain, and into store convey'd
>   (VI 504–5, 509–15)

Where the angels (in eating as in inventing) are able to "concoct, digest, assimilate" (v 412), and eventually with "concoctive heat . . . transubstantiate" (v 437–38), the "dev'lish" arts "concocted and adjusted" an already "crude" Nature until it is still further "reduc'd / To blackest grain." Echoing the simile from Book IV, the creation of the satanic arts, "blackest grain," is like the "Smutty grain." Here the material, in its ostensible sufficiency, is truly forgotten, and "into store convey'd."

In *Paradise Lost*, these processes of satanic and angelic concoction are figures not only for representation, but for interpretation as well. That is, the epistemological relationship to the image underlies both its production and reception (and in this sense invention and interpretation, both creative acts, are flip-sides of a similar process). Both the inventor (Satan, Jesus, the epic poet) and the interpreter always run the risk of supposing that the mediator, in the words of *De Doctrina*, "acts as mediator to himself." The risk of identification – the collapse of the third term – leads to the dominion of what Milton describes in *The Readie and Easie Way* as the "two most prevailing usurpers over mankinde, superstition and tyranny" (VII 417). To be sure, in the Miltonic imagination, the two are mutually enforcing – "superstition," as in *The Readie and Easie Way* prepares the mind for "tyranny." Indeed, in the 1660 tract Milton demonstrated how eagerly the "mob" would mistake the mediator for the object of mediation – the King for the commonwealth. In *Paradise Lost*, as in the political tract, Milton continually demonstrates the mind's propensity to lose itself in the material, and thus prepare the way for tyranny. In this most obvious sense, then, *Paradise Lost* is a "political" poem in that the same cognitive vigilance that obviates idolatry also obviates tyranny. That the transformation of "drossiest Ore to perfet Gold," however, is, as we have seen, held only "possible," evidences the Miltonic conviction in the power of the "usurpers" – and also in the mind's desire to rest in, and fetishize, the material.

Given this conviction, interpretation as figured in *Paradise Lost* requires a special kind of cognitive vigilance. It is a vigilance that seems to be embodied in the "Cohort bright" who descend with the Archangel Michael in the beginning of Book XI. As Raphael describes them, Michael's angelic retinue of "watchful Cherubim"

> . . . four faces each
> Had, like a double *Janus*, all thir shape
> Spangl'd with eyes more numerous than those
> Of *Argus*, and more wakeful than to drowse (XI 128–31)

But even this angelic vigilance is put in doubt. While the syntax of the allusion affirms the wakefulness of the angelic "cohort," the wandering final clause has the opposite effect, suggesting that their "wakeful" vision might be compromised as was Argus', who was "Charm'd with *Arcadian* Pipe, the Pastoral Reed / Of *Hermes*, or his opiate rod" (XI 132–33). It does not take a Comus with his "Charming Rod" and "dazzling Spells" to "cheat the eye with blear illusion" (154–55): even the mediatorial efforts of Michael are associated with the potentially misleading power of discourse.[30] This, then, represents not so much an attack on angelic, divine, or even Miltonic authority, but a recognition of the problems inherent in mediation and interpretation as such.[31] All discourse, irreducibly material, elicits the *temptation* of idolatry.

It is not, then, that the fables in *Paradise Lost* represent, as Bentley's emendations everywhere indicate, a threat to the unity and "Integrity" of the poem. But given the Satanic and human propensity to wander in the mazes of self-sufficient and autonomous narrative, they represent possible anchors for the idolatrous gaze. Nowhere is this interpretive literalism more evidenced than in Satan's own interpretation of God's "Judgment" in Book x. Strangely, in this judgment, God seems constrained to punish the "Serpent" as he seems

> ... unable to transfer
> The Guilt on him who made him instrument
> Of mischief ...
>
> (x 165–67)

God's failure to punish the agent of evil, Satan – but only the "instrument" (or "mediator"), the Serpent – accords with the sense in the final books (which Schwartz brings out so well) of the ineradicability of evil. As God continues, however, we learn that Satan does eventually suffer punishment, and that the Serpent's fate is not unconnected with Satan's "doom":

> ... yet God at last
> To Satan first in sin his doom appli'd
> Though in mysterious terms, judg'd as then best
> And on the Serpent thus his curse let fall.   (x 171–74)

In these lines, "at last" represents more than a simple linear chronology of events (that is: first the Serpent, then Satan), but refers as well to the last days, the end of time, when God's judgment will be manifest in other than "mysterious terms." Within history, however (even Edenic history), God's "Sentence" is literalized only in these "mysterious terms." The clarity of divine judgment, Milton implicitly argues, is only evidenced "at last"; in history the material sign of the "Serpent though brute" (x 165), "judg'd as then best," needs to be deciphered.

Of course, to the satanic perspective, these "mysterious terms" remain totally indecipherable; for Satan the mediator remains always sufficient to itself. Satan's interpretation, as we soon discover, begins and ends in the "brute" sign of the Serpent. Thus, Satan triumphantly asserts that God has "judg'd . . . the brute Serpent," though "Mee not" (x 494–95). For him, the *protevangelium*, God's promise to Adam and Eve, is understood in only the most literal of terms:

> ... I am to bruise his heel;
> His Seed, when is not set, shall bruise my head:
> A World who would not purchase with a bruise,
> Or much more grievous pain?   (x 498–501)

Just as Satan does not see himself implicated in the judgment of the "brute Serpent," so he sees his conquest of a "World" resulting in a mere "bruise." Although Satan acknowledges the possibility of a "much more grievous pain," his understanding remains firmly anchored to the physical.[32]

In what Waldock calls the "cartoon" scene which follows, however, Satan undergoes something like the literalizing of divine sentence.[33] Although anticipating the "universal shout and high applause" (505) for the "account" of his "performance" (501–2), Satan instead suddenly finds himself transforming:

> ... supplanted down he fell
> A monstrous Serpent on his Belly prone,
> Reluctant, but in vain: a greater power
> Now rul'd him, punish't in the shape he sinn'd,
> According to his doom ...   (x 513–17)

Despite this "humbling" (576) in which God's "mysterious terms" are unpacked as Satan takes on the material form of the "Serpent," the devils persist in their deceit: "some tradition they dispers'd ... how the Serpent ... had first the rule / Of high *Olympus*" (x 578, 80, 82–83). Immediately following the experience of having been "rul'd," of having been literalized in the divine sentence in the most abject and material terms (terms they can certainly understand), the satanic host again argues for their own priority, asserting that they had "first the rule." The materiality of satanic narrative, always asserting its own autonomy, thus becomes a means for competing with God's "Sentence." This illusion of satanic autonomy is presupposed upon Satan's willful ignorance of all of the connotations of the divine "Sentence."

Thus, the "annual" divine "humbling" of Satan becomes an especially fit punishment for Satan: for the repetition of the narrative in which even Satan experiences that "a greater power / Now ruled him" offsets the compulsive and fetishistic return to narratives of satanic autonomy. It provides an object lesson in the divine aesthetic, where the signifier inevitably points away from itself – suggesting a register in which angelic and human agency are qualified. The literalism which underlies Satan's fetishistic compulsions, what Schwartz calls the satanic "refusal to confront a genuine Other," are related symptoms of an impoverished epistemology.[34]

Unable to acknowledge anything exterior to itself, Satanic discourse remains trapped in its understanding of its own sufficiency and its confidence in the absoluteness of its own "mediations." The cognitive vigilance, dependent, as Budick suggests, "upon the recognition of an image component that is excluded from our imaginative control, which stands as a sign of our incomplete cognitive power,"[35] remains completely inaccessible to the satanic interpreter. Satan, incapable of understanding a God whose justice is not always transparently rendered, mistakes the sign for the signified, the mediator for that which is mediated, the Serpent for Satan himself.

By contrast, mediations in Miltonic epistemology always inscribe their difference from their object. Milton's Arianism – in which Christ stands as *mediator* between the Father and mankind – embodies the more general principles of Miltonic representation, where the mediator never "acts as a mediator to himself." The consequences of such self-mediation – enacted in myths of satanic, Nimrodic, or Stuart self-sufficiency – are first superstition, then tyranny.

To escape the idolatry of the contingent and the fetishism of reason is not, however, to trancend the limits of what Gadamer calls "the hermeneutic situation," and thus to attain the "absolute simplicity" of "objective-reality."[36] Mediations for Milton – whether political interventions, biblical interpretations, or epic justifications – constitute, in their multiplicity *and* their inter-relationship, the very limits of knowledge. Although, from one perspective, Abdiel's efforts are merely "pointless," from another, equally valid in the discursive universe of *Paradise Lost*, his "noble stroke," falling on Satan's "proud Crest," has significant, though *local* consequences. History – the medium of the action in *Paradise Lost* – though qualified by a divine perspective, still, as Jameson might say, "hurts." It remains the locus for action – actions, moreover, for which its agents remain responsible. To remain fixed to matter (to see only the agency of the mediator), or to attempt to fly unimpeded to spirit (to efface the agency of the mediator) reflect – as I shall argue in the conclusion – the twin and mutually reinforcing positions of Milton's satanic and angelic interpreters.

Conclusion: devils, angels, and Milton

To attend to the role of irreconcilable oppositions in Milton criticism – institutionalized in "angelic" and "satanic" camps of critics – is to acknowledge that Milton appears as one of the figures in literary history who, as Marcus and Taylor suggest, "invite and even attract dichotomous, polarized readings." One answer to their question, "How and under what conditions do figures of cultural significance acquire dichotomous images?", lies, as this study suggests, in the realm of historiography. Indeed, the competing and opposed claims made for Milton in the history of his reception – delineated in political, theological, and poetic arguments – have their origin in specifically Enlightenment oppositions. These oppositions are constituted, on the one side, by the "satanic" fetishism of difference, individuality and matter, and, on the other, by the "angelic" fetishism of unity, authority, and spirit. Milton's resistance to those oppositions – which are themselves hypostatized in the still on-going debates between satanic and angelic camps of critics – comes through most clearly in *Paradise Lost* where representation, as in the "brotherly dissimilitudes" of *Areopagitica*, is presupposed upon the acknowledgment of both difference *and* unity, on the assumption that representations will be both like and unlike their posited object.

If "Fancy," as described by Adam in Book v of *Paradise Lost*, "forms Imaginations, Aery shapes," then "Reason" "frames / All what we affirm or what deny" by "joining or disjoining" (v 105–6).[1] Fancy asserts resemblances; reason, by both "joining" and "disjoining," preserves difference.[2] Milton's critics often posit "difference" or "unity" as ends in themselves, where for Milton the two exist in productive tension.

Unassisted, fancy (as we saw in Locke's account) leads the mind to be "misled by similitudes." So Eve's dream in Book iv prompts Adam to elaborate fancy's propensity for "ill matching words" and strange "resemblances" (v 113–14). When fancy "wakes" after reason "retires," "misjoining shapes," it "Wild work produces oft." For Milton, as for

Hobbes, both similarity and difference are necessary to the imaginative process: "Fancy without Judgment," as Hobbes writes, "is not commended a Vertue."[3]

In Book v, Raphael's anatomy of the "intellectual" soul largely corroborates Adam's account of the imagination:

> Fancy and understanding, whence the Soul
> Reason receives, and reason is her being,
> Discursive or Intuitive; discourse
> Is oftest yours, the latter most is ours,
> Differing but in degree, of kind the same.
>
> (v 486–91)

The parataxis here of "fancy and understanding" forms the first part of a double chiasmus with "discursive" and "intuitive" reason. Jonathan Richardson's gloss on the latter pair aptly distinguishes the human intellect from its angelic counterpart. Discursive reason, Richardson explains, engages itself in "Tracing Truth from Argument to Argument, Discerning, Examining, Distinguishing, Comparing, Inferring, Concluding." Discursive reasoning, literally meaning the "running to and fro of the human mind in reasoning," is contrasted with the "*Intuitive*" intellect, which Richardson explains, "Instantly perceives Truth."[4] Thus, Milton's discursive and intuitive reason parallels the tendency and function of fancy and understanding.

Understanding, like discursive reason, is presupposed upon eliciting difference – "Discerning, Examining, Distinguishing, Comparing." The chiastic relationship, however, between fancy and intuitive reason is not quite so straightforward. For where fancy is associated with satanic repetition and assertion of similitude, "intuitive" reason is associated with the angelic instantaneous apprehension of truth. Both, however, as the chiastic structure makes plain, represent *equal* temptations in *Paradise Lost* – temptations enacted in different ways in the history of the interpretation of Milton's texts.

Although in the double chiasmus, discursive reason is squarely affiliated with human understanding, and intuitive reason with that of the angels, in neither are the kinds of understanding mutually exclusive: ". . . discourse / Is *oftest* yours, the latter *most* is ours" (emphasis added). Even the angels have to rely on discourse, and thus have no direct access to truth. In this, Milton departed from the common seventeenth-century notion that angels were endowed with an "intuitive knowledge that transcends man's bondage to 'discursive reason.'"[5] In *De Doctrina*, Milton was to observe that even the "good angels do not see into all

God's thoughts," and further, that there "are many things of which they are ignorant" (VI 347, 348). Direct access without recourse to, in Richardson's terms, "Argument," the materiality of "discourse," is likewise a temptation, no less so for being associated with the unfallen angels. Jacques Maritain has referred to this very temptation – that of moving beyond the situatedness of language for the supposed absolute intuition of "Truth" – as the "angelic heresy."[6] The satanic heresy, diagnosed from every angle in Fish's work, is no more dangerous than its angelic counterpart.

Though both fancy and intuitive reason, satanic and angelic heresies, to continue in a different lexicon – that of the Frankfurt School – may act as though they had "the object assuredly in hand," reason must act out the consciousness of "discrepancy foregrounding . . . unfinishedness."[7] Milton, throughout his poetry and prose, is not unlike the "un-naive thinker" of Adorno's thought whose consciousness of "how far he remains from the object of his thinking" is combined with the conviction that he "must always talk as if he had it entirely."[8] Having "it entirely" expresses itself in two ways in *Paradise Lost*, both in the satanic temptation to identify the mediator and the mediated, and the perhaps more angelic, though no less problematic practice, of rejecting the mediator and claiming the instantaneous perception of "Truth." Satanic repetition, on the one hand, clings to matter; pretenders to angelic apprehension, by contrast, cling to a truth which they claim to be beyond discourse.

Both angelic and satanic intepreters typically represent themselves as though they have "it" (the object, Truth, God) "entirely," producing readings of Milton's texts which emphasize autonomy or authority, immanence or transcendence, the contingent or the Absolute. Thus, in every generation Milton seems to be taken captive in either the "angelic" or "satanic" camp. Those in the satanic camp of Milton criticism typically celebrate the contingent – reason, politics, immanence – while angelic readers, from their otherworldly perch, berate their wayward antagonists with the rod of the Absolute – authority, theology, transcendence.

In Butterfield's spirit, it may be possible to understand these competing readings of Milton as emerging as a necessity of "abridgement" – a process that governs the interpretation of any set of texts or events. From this perspective, the complexity of Miltonic argument, what Corns calls the "plurality of Miltonic ideology," would lead inevitably to paraphrase – abridgement. But in the history of Milton's reception, these paraphrases have been defended, often with tendentious fervor, as

Milton is appropriated for the cause of bourgeois individualism or authoritarian intolerance, the Devil's Party or God's, free-thinking heresy or high-Church orthodoxy, contingent or Absolute truth. Milton's resistance to assimilation to any of these positions is not only to affirm Corns's argument, but to assert Milton's resistance to Enlightenment paradigms of knowledge in which oppositions are determined to be irreconcilable and contradictory.

In politics, Milton avoided the emergent distinction between liberty and authority; in theology, he avoided the distinction between monism and dualism becoming ossified in philosophical debate; in poetics, he embraced a notion of representation based at once upon the immanence and non-immanence of poetic meaning.

These positions – or perhaps non-positions – are all mutually informing, producing a bizarre consistency of Miltonic inconsistencies. They center, perhaps, on the question of representation which for Milton, as I have argued throughout, is always the limit and untranscendable ground of truth. This ground is established in *De Doctrina* as Milton defends his method of disputation:

> ... I take it upon myself to refute, whenever necessary, not scriptural authority, which is inviolable, but human interpretations. That is my right, and indeed my duty as a human being. Of course, if my opponents could show that the doctrine they defend was revealed to them by a voice from heaven, he would be an impious wretch who dared to raise so much as a murmur against it, let alone a sustained protest. But in fact they can lay claim to nothing more than human powers and that spiritual illumination which is common to all men. (VI 204)

To follow the rhythms of Milton's thought here is not only to understand the politics of Milton's prose, but the politics of his appropriation, and the power – though partial – of the competing interpretations of his work. At first, Milton seems to be defending, as he has been often accused of defending (and most lately by Catherine Belsey), an unmediated truth, that of "scriptural authority which is inviolable." As he continues, however, he appears to reverse course, eliding that "scriptural authority" with his own personal authority. So long as his defendants are not inspired "from heaven," it is his "duty," he says, to refute them. In the face of "scriptural authority," he appears to argue, what can be the authority of mere "human powers"?

Within the space of just two sentences Milton seems to be embracing both the angelic and satanic heresies that I have outlined above: first asserting the inviolability of a non-mediated truth, then eliding the mediator and the object mediated (the scriptures) to assert the sufficiency of the mediator, here himself. The pejorative characterization of his opponents, however, possessed of "nothing more than human powers," eventually gives way. For Milton, at once limiting the authority of his antagonists, also articulates the foundation for his own authority: "that spiritual illumination which is *common to all men.*" Though Milton will acquiesce in the face of a doctrine "revealed ... by a voice from heaven," *there is no such voice.* Not even his own. The fierce polemicist in Milton, however, nurtured by a visceral and continually renewed acceptance of "duty," cannot help but assert the primacy of *his own interpretation* – the immanence of meaning in the individuated utterance of John Milton.

But Miltonic fierceness has another aspect, one which emphasizes that individuation is itself presupposed upon commonality (the "spiritual illumination common to all men"), and consequently that "inviolable" truth defies complete embodiment and individuation. The intricate nature of Miltonic discourse, its constant self-qualification and refinement, seems to embody Joyce's challenge from *Finnegans Wake* to entertain "two thinks at a time." But the "thinks," more often than not, are more easily understood separately, producing the tendencies among "devils" and "angels" to which this study has called attention. The historical and critical "abridgments" – based on the assimilations and appropriations addressed in these pages – have led to the bifurcation of Milton. Set one against the other, the two Miltonic personae, fierce as are both, have clashed on the stage of literary history.

For the Milton of *this* study, however, there is not so much a balance as an unresolved conflict – *within* his works – between the individual and the *res publica*, interpretation and the "inviolable" truth of scriptures, contingent and Absolute truth. In the center of *Paradise Lost*, the *discordia concors* of Milton's thought (not Dr. Johnson's version of the trope) expresses itself in the figure of Christ's intervention in history. Thus Raphael describes the "four Cherubic shapes" (VI 753) which flank Christ's Chariot as

> Distinct with eyes, and from the living Wheels,
> Distinct alike with multitude of eyes;
> One Spirit in them rul'd ...   (VI 846–48)

Simultaneously "Distinct with eyes," and "Distinct alike," the manifestation of the "Chariot of Paternal Deity" (VI 750) stands as a figural analogue for the "brotherly dissimilitudes" of *Areopagitica*, asserting similarity though registering difference. In this image, politics, theology, and poetics converge as the representation of the heavenly host becomes a potential paradigm of heavenly and republican politics, where a "multitude of eyes" are ruled, still "Distinct," by "One Spirit."

Notes

INTRODUCTION

1 Christopher Hill, *Milton and the English Revolution* (New York: Penguin, 1978), p. 261.

2 John T. Shawcross, *Milton: The Critical Heritage: 1732–1801* (New Jersey: Barnes and Noble, 1972), p. 66.

3 Hans-Georg Gadamer, *Truth and Method* (New York: Crossroad, 1991), p. 296.

4 James Thorpe, *Milton Criticism: Selections from Four Centuries* (London: Routledge, 1951); Nancy Armstrong and Leonard Tennenhouse, *The Imaginary Puritan* (Berkeley: University of California Press, 1992).

5 A. S. P. Woodhouse, "Notes on Milton's Views on the Creation: The Initial Phases," *Philological Quarterly* 28 (1949): 211.

6 Steven Marcus and Charles Taylor, "Calls for Papers," *Common Knowledge* 1 (1992): 6.

7 Gadamer, *Truth and Method*, p. 273.

8 Herbert Butterfield, *The Whig Interpretation of History* (New York: Norton, 1930), p. 101.

9 *Ibid.*, p. 4.

10 For an analysis of the "hegemony" of Fish's Milton in contemporary criticism, see John Rumrich's *Milton Unbound* (Cambridge University Press, 1996).

11 Fredric Jameson, "Religion and Ideology," *1642: Literature and Power in the Seventeenth Century*, ed. Francis Barker et al. (University of Essex, 1981), p. 333.

12 On the complex issue of the "provenance" of *De Doctrina* (raised recently by William B. Hunter), and the historiographical issues that have emerged around Hunter's radical claims, see chapter 4 below.

13 See, for example, Habermas, "A Review of Gadamer's *Truth and Method*," *Understanding and Social Inquiry*, ed. Fred R. Dallmayr and Thomas A. McCarthy, (University of Notre Dame Press, 1977), p. 361.

14 Butterfield, *Whig Interpretation*, p. 98.

15 J. G. A. Pocock, *The Ancient Constitution and the Feudal Law* (Cambridge University Press, 1987), pp. viii-ix.

16 Thomas N. Corns, "'Some rousing motions': the Plurality of Miltonic Ideology," in *Literature and the English Civil War*, ed. Thomas Healy and

Jonathan Sawday (Cambridge University Press, 1990), p. 140. Corns's attitude towards contradiction may have changed somewhat – at least in the context of his more recent treatment of Milton's polemical prose. In his *Uncloistered Virtue* (Oxford: Clarendon Press, 1992), Corns judges Milton's use of contradiction as strategic, placed in the service of targeting the "prejudices and assumptions" of a diverse readership (p. 58). For more on Milton's strategic use of contradiction, see chapter 4 below.

17 Stanley Fish, *Surprised by Sin* (New York: Macmillan, 1967), p. 272.
18 Gadamer, *Truth and Method*, p. 56.

I "PLAINLY PARTIALL": THE LIBERAL *AREOPAGITICA*

1 All citations of Milton's prose – unless otherwise noted – are from *Complete Prose Works of John Milton*, ed. Don E. Wolfe (New Haven: Yale University Press, 1959), cited parenthetically in text with volume and page numbers.

2 T. W. Adorno, *Aesthetic Theory*, trans. C. Lenhardt, ed. Gretel Adorno and Rolf Tiedemann (New York: Routledge, 1984), p. 207; and *Negative Dialectics*, trans. E. B. Ashton (New York: Continuum, 1983), pp. 13–14, 24.

3 Edward Tayler, *Milton's Poetry: Its Development in Time* (Pittsburgh: Duquesne University Press, 1979), pp. 203–4.

4 Thomas Hobbes, *Leviathan*, ed. Michael Oakeshott (New York: Collier, 1982), pp. 100, 125, 132.

5 David Quint, "David's Census: Milton's Politics and *Paradise Regained*," *Re-membering Milton*, ed. Mary Nyquist and Margaret Ferguson (New York: Methuen, 1987), p. 144.

6 On the construction of the public sphere in seventeenth-century revolutionary writing, see Sharon Achinstein's *Milton and the Revolutionary Reader* (Princeton University Press, 1994).

7 Hiram Haydn, *The Counter Renaissance* (New York: Scribners, 1950), pp. 142–43.

8 Samuel Johnson, "Cowley," *Johnson: Prose and Poetry*, ed. Mona Wilson (Cambridge, Mass.: Harvard University Press, 1963), p. 799. For more on the "restricted sense of wit," emerging, with Hobbes, in the 1650s, see the introductory essay to Edward Tayler's *Literary Criticism of Seventeenth-Century England* (New York: Alfred A. Knopf, 1967): "When wit is used precisely," Tayler writes, "it usually refers to the power of seeing resemblances in things apparently unlike (or really) unlike and is therefore subordinated to the more admirable power of discerning differences" (p. 30). The faculty of judgment, as Locke writes in the *Essay*, "lies . . . in separating carefully one from another, *Ideas*, wherein can be found the least difference." Fancy is thus distinguishable and superior to wit. For Locke, wit becomes affiliated with a fancy which may lead one to be "misled by Similitude" and "by affinity to take one thing for another" (as quoted by Tayler, p. 31). For more on Johnson's understanding of *discordia concors*, see chapter 7 below.

9 Raymond Williams, *Keywords: A Vocabulary of Culture and Society* (Oxford University Press, 1976), p. 133. For observations on Milton's place in this

history, see Mary Ann Radzinowicz's "Politics of Paradise Lost," in *Politics of Discourse*, ed. Kevin Sharpe and Stephen N. Zwicker (Berkeley: University of California Press, 1987): "A good deal of emphasis has been given to Milton's individualism, and rightly given by students of his political thought, but Milton himself uses the word 'individual' to signify aggregation not segregation, to mean non-dividual as in the phrase 'united as one individual Soule'" (p. 225).

10 George Sensabaugh, *That Grand Whig Milton* (Stanford University Press, 1952), pp. 204–5.

11 As quoted by J. W. Burrow, *A Liberal Descent: Victorian Historians and the English Past* (Cambridge University Press, 1981), p. 3.

12 For an account of this critique, see Jean Howard's "The New Historicism in Renaissance Studies," *English Literary Renaissance* 16 (1986): 13–43.

13 Michael Walzer, *Revolution of the Saints* (Harvard University Press), p. 310. Ben Jonson has also been located as a transitional figure between feudalism and bourgeois individualism. Don E. Wayne thus describes Jonson as "an apologist for an older feudal ideology which stressed the importance of the social collectivity over the individual" (As quoted by Howard, "New Historicism," p. 16) Here, in the perpetuation of the category of "the feudal" or the even less precise, "social collectivity" (bearing a strange resemblance to Tillyard's regularly maligned "Elizabethan World Picture"), both the possibilities for autonomous selfhood and unreflective obligation to authority re-emerge: the feudal is still seen as the locus of obligation (bearing the marks of subjection or "wholeness" depending upon the historiographical take), while the post-feudal (the modern or the bourgeois) permits the possibility – however circumscribed – of individual autonomy.

14 Butterfield, *Whig Interpretation*, p. 101.

15 David Aers's recent "Reflections on Current Histories of the Subject," *Literature and History* 2 (1991): 20–3, begins to take issue with the "particularly dematerializing and idealist versions of medieval culture and society" implicit in contemporary radical histories of the subject. Taking the historiography of Francis Barker as his starting point (which asserts that "pre-bourgeois subjection does not properly involve subjectivity at all, but a condition of dependent membership ... in the body politic which is the king's body in its social form"), Aers finds Marxist histories resembling their conservative antecedents: "the basic picture is still of a static homogeneous collective in which there simply could not be any self-conscious concern with individual identity or subjectivity" (pp. 26, 24).

16 Cited by Dustin Griffin, *Regaining Paradise: Milton and the Eighteenth Century* (Cambridge University Press, 1986), p. 16. Toland himself understood that his editions of Milton, Harrington, and Ludlow "greatly contributed to beget in the minds of men ... an ardent love of liberty, and an extreme aversion to arbitrary power" (as quoted by Blair Worden in his introduction to Edmund Ludlow's *A Voyce from the Watch Tower* [Royal Historical Society, 1978], p. 54). Worden confirms that these editions "were to be among the

most central and widely read texts of eighteenth-century Whig doctrine in England" (p. 54). For more on Toland's Milton, see chapter 6 below.

17 Belsey's nuanced historiographical argument – which suggests the influence of Habermas's work on the emergence of the bourgeois public sphere – suggests a coercive "authoritarianism" present even in liberalism. To Belsey, *The Subject of Tragedy* (London: Methuen, 1985), the illusion of self-authorship held out by liberalism is presupposed upon the emergence of the "unified, knowing, and autonomous" human being, seeking a "political system which guarantees freedom of choice." There would be, without doubt, a certain irony in calling Belsey a Whig (her disdain for the liberal subject is unapologetic); though an interpretation of history which finds evidence of the predominance of liberal discourses "in the seventeenth century with the emergence of the individual . . . and the consecutive English Revolutions of the 1640s and 1688" is undeniably whiggish (p. 8).

18 Harold Bloom, *Modern Critical Views: John Milton* (New York: Chelsea House, 1986), p. 2.

19 Kendrick, *Milton: A Study in Ideology and Form* (London: Methuen, 1986), pp. 4–5. For Kendrick, the "central event" in *Areopagitica* is the "creation of a literary subject that registers . . . the full weight of a specific personal and historical juncture" (p. 51). Kendrick follows Christopher Hill who argues, *Milton and the English Revolution* (London: Faber, 1977), that "Milton's is a bourgeois conception of liberty: the right to be left alone, to work, to make money, to trade freely" (p. 263). Andrew Milner makes a similar case, *John Milton and the English Revolution* (New Jersey: Barnes and Noble, 1981), p. 100: Milton's "rationalistic individualism," Milner contests, "reveals a remarkable formal similarity with later explicitly atheistic or agnostic rationalisms." Similarly, Herman Rapaport, *Milton and the Postmodern* (Lincoln: University of Nebraska Press, 1983), argues that "in the political texts of Milton, the bourgeoisie takes over the culture entirely" (p. 202), and that "indeed, Milton was a capitalist" (p. 170). The "aim of Milton's poetic *œuvre*," Rapaport concludes, is "to dismantle the legacy of feudalism and forge with that inheritance a new bourgeois tradition" (p. 204).

20 Pocock, in his "The Myth of John Locke and the Obsession with Liberalism," *Papers read at a Clark Library Seminar* (Los Angeles: University of California Press, 1980), suggests that "classical and socialist critics converge – and nearly unite – in perpetuating a distortion of history which consists in vastly exaggerating the role of liberalism (or of possessive individualism or of bourgeois ideology)" (p. 17). He puts the point polemically elsewhere, "Cambridge Paradigms and Scottish Philosophers," *Wealth and Virtue*, ed. Istvan Hont and Michael Ignatieff (Cambridge University Press, 1985): Marxists are "so obsessed with their hostility to a Lockean modern or bourgeois liberalism that they can see nothing on the stage of history but the arrival and triumph of their antagonist" (p. 240).

21 Mary Nyquist, "The Genesis of Gendered Subjectivity" in *Re-membering Milton*, pp. 114–15.

22 Catherine Belsey, *John Milton: Language, Gender, Power* (New York: Basil Blackwell, 1988), p. 78.

23 In his "prefatory remarks" to the 1819 (London: R. Hunter) edition of *Areopagitica*, (which includes Thomson's 1738 introduction to the tract), T. Holt White observes that "succeeding advocates for the Freedom of Printing have copied not unfrequently as well as largely from this Oration" (p. lvii). As Sensabaugh notes, Milton contributed even to "the first phases of the attempted Whig revolution through Charles Blount's *A Just Vindication of Learning* in 1679 and William Denton's *An Apology for the Liberty of the Press* in 1681, two unlike but unmistakable adaptations of *Areopagitica*" (p. 55). For these and other Whig appropriations, see Sensabaugh, *That Grand Whig*, pp. 55–64 and pp. 157–62. White's edition includes a collection of "Commendatory Testimonies" of which Warton's – "The *Areopagitica* . . . is the most close, conclusive, comprehensive, and decisive vindication of the Liberty of the Press that has yet appeared" – is typical (p. cxxvii).

24 Sensabaugh, *That Grand Whig*, p. 4.

25 White, *Areopagitica*, pp. 201, 197. Similarly, in this century, George W. Whiting, "The Politics of Milton's Apostate Angels," *The London Chronicle* 163 (1932), contended that "the considered judgment of unprejudiced students of Milton" would have to conclude with the eighteenth-century critic John Upton in favor of the toleration permitted by constitutional monarchism: had Milton "known the sobriety, the toleration, and decency of our laws, our liberties, and our constitution ascertained . . . he would never have been an enemy to such a church and such a king" (p. 385). More recently, the University of Colorado invited Leo Miller to "deliver a full hour plenary address" on "John Milton and the American Constitution." Proclaiming Milton "as a poet of struggle for freedom," Miller cited "specific provisions in the American Constitution which embody Miltonic principles," and "read recent newspaper items which report current departures from these principles on university, state, and federal levels" ("Colorado World Affairs Conference Dedicated to Milton," *Milton Quarterly* 12 (1987): 123).

26 Arthur Barker, *Milton and the Puritan Dilemma* (University of Toronto Press, 1942), p. 244.

27 Hill, *Milton and the English Revolution*, pp. 244, 258, 242, 266, 250.

28 John Illo, "The Misreading of Milton," *Columbia University Forum* 8 (1965): 40–41.

29 In his *Truth and Method* (New York: Crossroad, 1991), Hans-Georg Gadamer offers a similar analysis of a Romantic historiography reliant upon the Enlightenment categories that precede it: Romanticism, Gadamer writes, "shares the presupposition of the Enlightenment and only reverses its values" (p. 273). Both Enlightenment and Romantic historiographies insist upon the binary between freedom and obligation, both require viewing reason and authority as an "unconditional antithesis" (p. 281).

30 Illo, "Misreading of Milton," p. 41; Johnson, "Milton," *Prose and Poetry*, p. 823. Illo's more recent "*Areopagitica's* Mythic and Real," *Prose Studies* 11 (1988), catalogues recent "tolerationist" and "libertarian" readings of

Milton. He still insists that the "real" *Areopagitica* is "illibertarian," a "political document of repression" (p. 21).

31 In 1986, Stanley Fish, "'Transmuting the Lump': *Paradise Lost*, 1942–1982," *Literature and History*, ed. Gary Saul Morson (Stanford University Press, 1986), was still advertising the "coming attractions" for a Milton criticism based upon "the transformation of Milton from a poet of democratic liberalism to a prophet of revolutionary absolutism" (p. 55). Fish continues to fashion himself as a critic in opposition to the liberal vision of Milton in his more recent "Driving from the Letter: Truth and Indeterminacy in Milton's *Areopagitica*," in *Re-membering Milton*. It "is precisely my method to find tension and discontinuities," Fish writes, "where others before me had found only the steady unfolding of a classical liberal vision" (p. 248). Fish's absolutist Milton maintains the Whig, what Gadamer calls the Enlightenment, antithesis between freedom and authority. Though the emphasis is different, the dichotomy prevails. For the relationship between Fish and Dr. Bentley, who attempted to distance himself (and Milton) from his own "liberal" precedessors, see chapter 6 below.

32 This is not to invoke Habermas's "bourgeois public sphere," which presupposes a separation of private from public realms. Milton's notion of public and private, as I argue below, is reciprocally defining (really identical) where in the "bourgeois public sphere," "public authority" is "consolidated into a palpable object confronting" those who are "merely subject to it." See Habermas, *The Structural Transformation of the Public Sphere*, ed. Thomas Berger (Cambridge: MIT Press, 1989), p. 18.

33 See Ernest Sirluck's Introduction to volume II of the Yale *Complete Prose*, p. 170.

34 Quentin Skinner, "The State" in *Political Innovation and Conceptual Change*, ed. Terence Ball et al. (Cambridge University Press, 1989), p. 112.

35 C. B. Macpherson, *Possessive Individualism* (Oxford University Press, 1979), p. 263. In a Macphersonian mode, Lawrence Stone has argued that the sectarian or violent social behavior of Puritans reflected the divisions and animosities of an atomized society. Patrick Collinson, "The Cohabitation of the Faithful with the Unfaithful," *From Persecution to Toleration: The Glorious Revolution and Religion in England*, ed. Ole Peter Grell et al. (Oxford University Press, 1991), counters that "occasional and regrettable disturbers of the social peace" were redressed "by law ... with the concealed motive of restoring social harmony" (p. 71). The debate about historiographical paradigms thus continues.

36 Macpherson, *Possessive Individualism*, p. 270.

37 From Pocock's most extensive treatments of the emergence of classical republicanism in the seventeenth century, *The Machiavellian Moment: Florentine Political Thought and the Atlantic Republican Tradition* (Princeton University Press, 1975), pp. 460–61. See also Zera S. Fink's earlier *The Classical Republicans* (Evanston, Ill.: Northwestern University Press, 1962), Ruth Nevo's *The Dial of Virtue* (Princeton University Press, 1963), and Blair Worden's "Classical Republicanism and the Puritan Revolution," *History*

and Imagination, ed. Hugh-Lloyd Jones (London: Duckworth, 1981), pp. 188–200.

38 Pocock, *Virtue, Commerce, and History* (Cambridge University Press, 1986), pp. 40, 44.

39 See especially, Martin Dzelzainis, "Milton's Classical Republicanism" (pp. 3–24), Thomas N. Corns, "Milton and the Characteristics of a Free Commonwealth" (pp. 25–42), and Cedric C. Brown, "Great Senates and Godly Education" (pp. 43–60) in *Milton and Republicanism*, ed. David Armitage et al. (Cambridge University Press, 1996). For an analysis of *Areopagitica* in its republican context, see Nigel Smith's "*Areopagitica*: Voicing Contexts, 1643–5," in *Politics, Poetics, and Hermeneutics in Milton's prose*, ed. David Loewenstein and James Grantham Turner (Cambridge University Press, 1990), pp. 103–22. Smith's *Literature and Revolution 1640–1660* (New Haven: Yale University Press, 1994), provides an important contextualization of Milton's republicanism; see especially, pp. 178–200. For Milton's involvement with the "English Republic," see Corns's *Uncloistered Virtue* (Oxford: Clarendon Press, 1992), especially pp. 194–220.

40 Thomas N. Corns, "Milton and the Characteristics of a Free Commonwealth," *Milton and Republicanism*, p. 42.

41 "In the political and religious works of the 1640s and 1650s," Smith writes, "it was assumed that oratory could be transferred to the printed pamphlet, and that such printed oratory would play an active role in what was understood to be a war of words" (*Literature and Revolution*, pp. 36, 38). Sharon Achinstein, *The Revolutionary Reader*, further demonstrates how the printing press enabled the extension of the classical public sphere: "Publication," she observes, was a means by which writers were able to address "readers as responsible actors in the public forum created by the press" (p. 32).

42 Although Milton is obviously arguing for the superiority of the printing press, he often shifts the rhetoric of his tract as if to assert that his discourse would be "heard" in public debate. Such a strategy may be linked to the Aristotelian distinction (*Rhetoric* 3.12) between types of discourse and their respective styles. The public style of deliberative oratory that deals with matters of importance to the entire community (and which, not surprisingly, is the discourse that Isocrates held in highest esteem) requires "voice," sometimes a "loud one." In contrast, forensic or epideictic oratory, appropriate to the more circumscribed realm of the legal courts or private readings, requires a written form. Milton's deliberative ends place *Areopagitica* in a public context. To explicitly adapt its style to prospective listeners, and not readers, is to save the tract from associations with the more private – and less universal ends – of the other two modes of oratory. For the distinction between oratorical styles, see Wesley Trimpi's *Muses of One Mind* (Princeton University Press, 1982), pp. 133–35.

43 In *The Readie and Easie Way*, Milton shifts from admonishing his "adversaries" to enjoining the remnant of "chosen patriots." By "relapsing," he argues, the nation will "verifie all the bitter predictions of our triumphing enemies,

who will now think they wisely discern'd and justly censur'd both us and all
our actions as rash, rebellious, hypocritical, and impious" (VII 422). That the
prophetic powers of the King's party may have been more acute than his
own became, for Milton in 1660, a horrible reality.

44 Milton, Smith adds, did not share the common contemporary belief that
"the rhetorical practices of the ancient Greeks . . . could lead to social chaos"
(*Literature and Revolution*, p. 36).

45 The influence of Macpherson's historiographical perspective, evidenced in
Kendrick, *Ideology and Form* (pp. 8, 14), is also present in Francis Barker's
The Tremulous Private Body (New York: Methuen, 1984). Barker argues that
Milton's tract founds itself on the separation "between the public arena of
the state apparatus and another domain of civil life," and thus creates "a
more direct ideological control through subjectivity" (p. 46). Mary Nyquist's
"The Genesis of Gendered Subjectivity," *Re-membering Milton*, focusing on
Paradise Lost and the divorce tracts, explores "the kind of female subjectivity
required by a new economy's progressive sentimentalization of the private
sphere" (p. 120). The story of the "encoding" of a new realm of
subjectivity, and the emergence of a "new liberty," which acts as "an
effective support of the emergent pattern of domination" (Barker, p. 47) is
also told with reference to eighteenth-century aesthetics in Eagleton's *The
Ideology of the Aesthetic* (Oxford: Basil Blackwell, 1990), especially pp. 13–28.
One can, however, find accounts of the emergence of "negative liberty"
(Barker, p. 47) outside of the Marxist tradition. For the transition from a
language of civic "virtue" to a language of civil "rights" (located after the
Glorious Revolution of 1689), see Pocock, *Virtue*, especially pp. 37–50, and
also the essays by Pocock, John Robertson, and Nicholas Phillipson in
Wealth and Virtue.

46 The contracting of this category, as we shall see in the following chapter,
parallels the trajectory of Milton's republicanism in the fifties. In *The Readie
and Easie Way*, the "better part" shrinks into a "remnant," leading Milton to
assert "that most voices ought not alwaies to prevail where main matters are
in question" (VII 509). For more on the doctrine of the "better part," see
Barbara K. Lewalski, "Milton: Political Beliefs and Polemical Methods,
1659–1660," *Publications of the Modern Language Association* 74 (1959): 96; for a
recent study of Milton's republicanism in the fifties, see Blair Worden's
"Milton's republicanism and the tyranny of heaven," in *Machiavelli and
Republicanism*, ed. Gisela Bock et al (Cambridge University Press, 1990),
pp. 225–45.

47 *John Milton: Complete Poems and Major Prose*, ed. Merrit Y. Hughes (New York:
Macmillan, 1985), p. 727.

48 In *Eikonoclastes*, Milton refers explicitly to the hoarded manna of the biblical
episode. Writing of the uniformity imposed by the liturgy of the
"Commonpraier Book," Milton argues that even if such prayers were
"*Manna* it self, yet if they shall be hoarded up and enjoynd us, while God
every morning raines down new expressions into our hearts, in stead of

being fit to use, they will be found like reserv'd *Manna*, rather *to breed wormes and stink*" (III 505).

49 For accounts of the "mis-reading" of Spenser, see Ernest Sirluck, "Milton Revises the Faerie Queene," *Modern Philology* 48 (1950): 90–96; Bloom, *A Map of Misreading* (Oxford University Press, 1975) p. 127; Tayler, *Milton's Poetry*, p. 194; and John Guillory, *Poetic Authority: Spenser, Milton, and Literary History* (Columbia University Press, 1983), pp. 130–45.

50 John Guillory, *Poetic Authority*, p. 135.

51 Kelley, Yale *Complete Prose*, vol. VI, p. 82.

52 Regina Schwartz, "Citation, Authority, and *De Doctrina Christiana*," *Politics, Poetics, and Hermeneutics in Milton's Prose*, p. 238.

53 *The Political Works of James Harrington*, ed. J. G. A. Pocock (Cambridge University Press, 1977), p. 26.

54 In the conflict between rational critique and the epistemological uncertainty engendered by antinomian conviction, we can see, with Victoria Kahn, *Rhetoric, Prudence, and Skepticism in the Renaissance* (Ithaca, N.Y.: Cornell University Press, 1985), "a questioning of the early humanist belief in the compatibility of skepticism and prudence, cognitive doubt and practical certainty" (p. 53). The questioning of both the humanist paradigm and the efficacy of prudential judgment, as we shall see, is articulated by Milton with the greatest urgency in *The Readie and Easie Way*.

55 Nancy S. Streuver, *Theory as Practice: Ethical Inquiry in the Renaissance* (University of Chicago Press, 1992), p. 206.

56 Smith, *Literature and Revolution*, p. 358.

57 Fish, *Surprised by Sin*, p. 45.

58 Stanley Fish, *Self-Consuming Artifacts* (Berkeley: University of California Press, 1982), pp. 265–302.

59 Fish, "Driving from the Letter," p. 247.

60 John Peter Rumrich, "Uninventing Milton," *Modern Philology* 87 (1990): 262.

61 Marshall Grossman, *"Authors to Themselves": Milton and the Revelation of History* (Cambridge University Press, 1987), p. 190; emphasis added.

62 Quint, "David's Census," p. 141.

63 If Milton's "intolerance" fails to register among contemporary expositors, then so equally, and perhaps more surpisingly, does the "intolerance" of Locke. Locke's pleas for tolerance "cannot be interpreted," writes John Dunn, "as an anachronistic cipher for a broader and more general entitlement to think as one happens to think." Though tolerating Jews, Muslims, and Socinians, Locke too draws the line at those beliefs which he finds to be "an inherent menace to every other human being." The "belief which he especially singles out," Dunn continues, "is the belief that there *is* no God to worship: atheism." See "The Claims of Freedom of Conscience," in *From Persecution to Toleration*, pp. 179–81.

64 Belsey, *Milton*, p. 78.

65 *Ibid.*

66 *Ibid.*
67 *Ibid.*, p. 104.
68 Providing an implicit critique of Belsey, Jonathan Dollimore warns in his
   Radical Tragedy (University of Chicago Press, 1984) that a Foucauldian
   "pursuit of difference," may "render the subject so completely dispersed as
   to be incapable of acting as any agent, least of all as an agent of change" (p.
   271). Perry Anderson, writing in a different context, *Arguments within English
   Marxism* (London: Verso, 1980), fears that only an "arbitrary relativism" will
   follow from unmediated subjectivity: "Why should the intersection of rival
   collective wills not produce the random chaos of a log-jam" (p. 51)?
   Anderson continues a debate begun in this century by Lukács controversial
   espousal of totality. The eventual dismantling of this totality, and the
   emergence of "*post*-Marxism" has been enabled by what Ernesto Laclau
   and Chantal Mouffe have called the "deconstructive logic of hegemony."
   Belsey's post-structuralist Marxism and her notion of subjectivity may be
   informed by the "*post*-Marxism" articulated and defended by Mouffe and
   Laclau (see their *Hegemony and Socialist Strategy* [London: Verso, 1985]).
   Laclau, however, in his "Universalism, Particularism, and the Question of
   Identity," *October* 61 (1992), argues that "an appeal to pure particularism is
   no solution to the problems we are facing in contemporary societies." The
   "assertion of particularism" he continues, "independent of any appeal to a
   universality, is a self-defeating enterprise" (p. 87).
69 Pocock, *Virtue*, p. 54.

2 "NOT THE READIEST WAY": MILTON AND THE
         ABANDONMENT OF POLITICS

1 Sir Rober Filmer, *Patriarcha and Other Political Writings*, ed. Peter Laslett
   (Oxford: Blackwell, 1949), p. 252.
2 Sharon Achinstein, *Revolutionary Reader* (Princeton University Press, 1994), p. 16.
3 William Kerrigan, *The Prophetic Milton* (Charlottesville: University of
   Virginia Press, 1974), p. 175; and Thomas N. Corns, *Uncloistered Virtue*
   (Oxford: Clarendon, 1992), p. 278.
4 Achinstein, *Revolutionary Reader*, p. 32.
5 A similar tension between what Blair Worden calls "enthusiasm for civic
   action" and "stoic detachment" ("Classical Republicanism," *History and
   Imagination: Essays in Honor of H. R. Trevor-Roper*, ed. Hugh-Lloyd Jones
   [London: Duckworth, 1981], p. 183) is evident in the poetry of Ben Jonson.
   The opening lines of his "To William, Earl of Pembroke," for example,
   suggest that individual virtue is contingent upon, and mediated through,
   public context, that Pembroke's name is "an epigram on all mankind" – a
   name addressed at once "against the bad, but of, and to the good" (*Ben
   Jonson: The Complete Poems*, ed. George Parfitt [New Haven: Yale University
   Press, 1975], p. 71, lines 2–3). That is, Pembroke's virtue, and, by extension,
   the vice of others is inscribed within an already existing hermeneutic circle:

the authority of Pembroke's name is contingent upon a community in which the distinction between virtue and vice is already presupposed – always already recognized. Jonson, however, like the Milton who considers doing "nothing to make himself known," eventually suggests that the authority for Pembroke's virtue is circumscribed in his "one stature still" (13). Indeed, Jonson anticipates Milton in that the commonwealth, that most public place – the potential locus of a civic virtue enabled through the active life – becomes "still and safe," internalized in Pembroke in whom, paradoxically, public virtue is privately constituted. Although Milton's relationship to Shakespeare and Spenser has been well documented, much work remains to be done on Milton and Jonson's shared ambivalence towards a "virtue" which cannot be manifested publicly. See my " 'Man to Man': Self-Fashioning in Jonson's 'To William Pembroke,' " *Texas Studies in Literature and Language*, forthcoming.

6 Kerrigan, *Prophetic Milton*, p. 177.
7 Emmanuel Levinas, *Totality and Infinity: An Essay on Exteriority* (The Hague: Martinus Nijhoff, 1979), p. 46.
8 Fredric Jameson, "Religion and Ideology," *1642: Literature and Power in the Seventeenth Century*, ed. Francis Barker et al.(University of Essex, 1981), p. 333.
9 Edmund Ludlow, *A Voyce from the Watchtower*, ed. A. B. Worden (Royal Historical Society, 1978), pp. 5, 51, 4.
10 *Ibid.*, p. 72.
11 *Ibid.*, p. 54.
12 As quoted by Worden, "Classical Republicanism," p. 195.
13 Ludlow, *Voyce*, p. 10.
14 Stephen N. Zwicker, "Lines of Authority: Politics and Literary Culture in the Restoration," in *Politics of Discourse* ed. Kevin Sharpe and Stephen N. Zwicker (Berkeley: University of California Press, 1987), p. 233.
15 Stephen N. Zwicker, "England, Israel, and the Triumph of Roman Virtue" in *Millenarianism and Messianism in English Literature and Thought: 1650–1800*, ed. Richard Popkin (New York: E. J. Brill, 1988), p. 45; emphasis added.
16 Bernard Sharratt, "The Appropriation of Milton," *Essays & Studies*, ed. Suheil Bushrui, 35 (1982): 42. The change in "ideological atmosphere" which "made theological explanations and vindications of political events seem increasingly redundant" (p. 41), Sharratt argues, gave rise "not merely [to] a reading of the poem as literature, but almost [to] the very emergence of that notion of 'literature' " (p. 42). "By the time of Macaulay's *Edinburgh Review* article on Milton in August 1825," Sharratt adds, "the idea that Milton's own theology might be at all relevant to *Paradise Lost* can be casually acknowledged and perfunctorily disposed of in a sentence" (p. 42). On the specification of literature as an autonomous category, see also Michael McKeon, "Politics of Discourse and the Rise of the Aesthetic in Seventeenth-Century England" in *Politics of Discourse*, p. 36.
17 Jameson, "Religion and Ideology" p. 322.
18 Ludlow, *Voyce*, p. 10; Worden, "Classical Republicanism," p. 195.

19 See Quentin Skinner, "The State," in *Political Innovation and Conceptual Change*, ed. Terence Ball et al. (Cambridge University Press, 1989), p. 123.
20 Ludlow, *Voyce*, p. 72.
21 Herman Rapaport, *Milton and the Postmodern* (Lincoln: University of Nebraska Press, 1983), p. 188.
22 *Ibid.*, p. 70. Andrew Milner, *John Milton and the English Revolution* (New Jersey: Barnes and Noble, 1981), for example, commenting on a passage from *Tenure of Kings and Magistrates*, asserts that, for Milton, "divine plans are achieved only through the exercise of the rational free wills of men." Citing this "future triumph of reason," Milner can dispense with God and sacred politics: "For once God is liquidated into the reasons of particular individuals then what remains of God?" (pp. 58–59).
23 Sharratt, "Appropriation of Milton," p. 32. Toland, however, as we shall see more fully in chapter 6, celebrated Milton's political commitments, and published Milton's collected prose in 1698 – the year of his publication of Ludlow's *Voyce*. Certainly, Milton himself did not think, as his biographer Mark Pattison did, that "the second act" of his life was wasted writing "that most ephemeral and valueless kind of prose." As Sharratt remarks, ". . . it has been plausibly suggested that Milton, by 1654, saw himself as having fulfilled his task of writing a national epic, precisely his authorship of his *Defensio*" (p. 39).
24 As quoted by Dustin Griffin, *Regaining Paradise: Milton and the Eighteenth Century* (Cambridge University Press, 1986), pp. 13–14.
25 John T. Shawcross, *Critical Heritage: 1732–1801* (New Jersey: Barnes and Noble, 1972), p. 313.
26 John Milton, *A Ready and Easy Way* (London: Printed for J. Ridgway, 1791), pp. iii–iv; emphasis added.
27 Austin Woolrych, "The Good Old Cause and the Fall of the Protectorate," *Cambridge Historical Journal*, 13 (1957): 159–60.
28 Zera S. Fink, *The Classical Republicans* (Northwestern University Press, 1962) pp. 99, 117, 90.
29 Barbara K. Lewalski, "Political Beliefs and Polemical Methods," p. 195, and Perez Zagorin, *A History of Political Thought in the English Revolution* (Great Britain: The Humanities Press, 1966), p. 119.
30 Exceptions include Turner and Loewenstein's collection of essays, *Milton and the Drama of History* (Cambridge University Press, 1990), which has done much to move Milton out of a purely rationalist matrix by showing the "conjunction of literary and political discourse" in the prose. L. L. Knoppers, "Milton's *The Readie and Easie Way* and the English Jeremiad," pp. 213–26, is especially significant for this context.
31 Arthur Barker, *Milton and the Puritan Dilemma* (University of Toronto Press, 1942), p. 272.
32 Kevin Gilmartin, "History and Reform in Milton's *Readie and Easie Way*," *Milton Studies*, 24 (1988), 37.
33 *Ibid.*, p. 31.

34 *Ibid.*, p. 29.
35 "Heresie," according to the Milton of 1659, is "another Greek apparition" and "signifies no word of evil note" (VII 247). One who "holds in religion that beleef . . . which to his conscience and utmost understanding appeer with most evidence or probabilitie in the scripture, though to others he seem erroneous, can no more be justly censur'd for a heretic then his censurers" (VII 248). There is, however, the characteristic addition that distinguishes – as in *Areopagitica* – Christian liberty from liberty: "and therefore a true heresie, or rather an impietie; wherein a right conscience can have naught to do . . . that a magistrate can hardly err in prohibiting" (VII 254–55). For the corresponding restrictions in *Areopagitica* on "Popery and open superstition," see II 565. Gilmartin finds the Milton of 1660 to have abandoned "his most cherished convictions about the progressive dimensions of human social and political experience" because he likely overestimates Milton's commitment to these ideals in 1644.
36 Robert Thomas Fallon, "Milton and the Anarchy, 1659–1660: A Question of Consistency," *Studies in English Literature*, 21 (1981): 128. We might also recall here that Milton's minimalist conception of politics and parliamentary intervention extends back to *Areopagitica* where he praises parliament for its ability to recognize its own errors. Dennis Saurat, *Milton: Man and Thinker* (London: J. M. Dent, 1946), summarizes Milton's position: "government is only a necessary evil; therefore there must be as little as possible. The best government is that which governs least" (p. 158).
37 Zwicker, "Lines of Authority," *Politics of Discourse*, p. 233. Terence Ball, "Party," *Political Innovation*, acknowledges that until "the late seventeenth century there was neither the vocabulary nor the necessary stock of images in which anything like the recognizably modern notion of party could be conceived, much less publicly articulated and discussed" (p. 158). In so far as party legitimates private interest – "corruption" in the lexicon of civic republicanism – then it would be equally anathema to the Milton of 1660 *and* 1644.
38 Skinner, "The State," *Political Innovation*, p. 113.
39 Elisa New, "'Feminist Invisibility': The Examples of Anne Bradstreet and Anne Hutchinson," *Common Knowledge* 2 (1993), suggests that in an early American feminist lexicon "all outward organization" is understood "as antithetical to the workings of spirit" (p. 101). Bradstreet, argues New, "investigates how a female pursuit of presentability, of a vindicating image, can exacerbate intracommunal tension," and enacts what she calls "the fall into politics" (p. 107). For Milton, as for Bradstreet, private struggles for representativeness, the appropriation of "offices and ornaments," whether on the level of politics or poetry, is an indication not of "political maturity," but, as New writes, "spiritual crisis" (p. 117).
40 Thus David Norbrook, "Marvell's 'Horatian Ode' and the Politics of Genre," in *Literature and the English Civil War*, ed. Thomas Healy and Jonathan Sawday (Cambridge University Press, 1990), demonstrates how

the "republican sublime," for both Marvell and Milton, represented a rejection of the "courtly beautiful" and the "Caroline aestheticisation of politics" (p. 156).

41 Robert Fallon, "Milton and the Anarchy," suggests that Milton also conceived of the army as "a force for the preservation of freedom, one that would inhibit the natural propensity of the executive ... to accumulate power" (p. 141). Milton warns in *The Readie and Easie Way* that under the King, the army would "be soon disbanded, and likeliest without arrear or pay" (VII 454).

42 Barker, *Puritan Dilemma*, p. 268.

43 Corns, *Uncloistered Virtue*, pp. 282, 290. Corns affirms this judgment in his more recent "Milton and the characteristics of a free commonwealth" in *Milton and Republicanism* (Cambridge University Press, 1996) where he admits that Milton, as a political thinker (who never articulated a systematic republican theory) "falls far short of Machiavelli or of Harrington" (p. 41). In the same volume, Martin Dzelzainis, "Milton's Classical Republicanism," echoes this conclusion, "noting Milton's lack of interest in precise constitutional forms" (p. 20). Blair Worden, also in this volume, "Milton and Marchamont Nedham," affirms that Milton's "interest in constitutional architecture proves to be distinctly limited," and that he "quickly loses patience with disputes about the 'intricacies' of constitutional forms" (p. 170).

44 Although the editors of *Milton and Republicanism* may have come to affirm that Milton was a "transmitter of republican values," many of the volume's contributors seem to share the sense that a single focus on Milton's political discourses – even in the "polemical tracts" – will not do full justice to Milton's work. Cedric C. Brown, in his "Great Senates and Godly Education," for example, concedes that he does not "wish to deny that there is political theory in [Milton's] works, or to refuse to see them as political interventions in themselves." Brown (whose defensive tone attests to the power of Skinnerian argument in contemporary Milton studies), nonetheless affirms that Milton's "political language was never free from the categories of religious and moral definition" (p. 60). For more on the limits of Skinnerian methodology, see chapter 4 below.

45 Smith, *Literature and Revolution 1640–1660* (New Haven: Yale University Press, 1994), p. 195.

46 Pocock, *Political Works of Harrington* (Cambridge University Press, 1977), p. 17.

47 Writing on Israelite theocracy in his *Art of Lawgiving*, Harrington asserts the identity of rational action and Divine Will: "That God elected the King in Israel is certain; and that the people, no less for that, did also elect the King is as certain." Not "God, nor Christ, nor the apostles," Harrington continues, "ever instituted any government ecclesiastical or civil upon other principles than those only of human prudence" (*Political Works of Harrington*, pp. 627 and 652).

48 Barker, *Puritan Dilemma*, p. 261.

49 In the *Defence*, Milton cites, for example, "a most ancient volume on the law

entitled *Mirror of Justices*, which reports that, after the conquest of Britain, the first Saxons when appointing their kings were accustomed to demand an oath of them that, like any other citizen, they would obey the laws and the courts" (IV.1 490). In this account, the joint sovereignty of king and parliament – by compact – insures the parliament's claims for its own historical authority.

50 On the date of Milton's "Digression" – which is contested – I am following Woolrych. For Woolrych's arguments and a record of the controversy, see his "The Date of the Digression in Milton's History of Britain," *For Veronica Wedgwood, These*, ed. Richard Ollard and Pamela Tudor-Craig (London: William Collins Sons, 1986), pp. 217–46. Hugh Trevor-Roper, "The Elitist Politics of John Milton," *Times Literary Supplement*, June 1, 1973, argues that Milton had once looked back to his own history as "a heroic age in which liberty, true religion and high civilization coincided." In the *History of Britain*, Trevor-Roper observes, Milton "lit on the fifth century, when Britain found itself free from the Rule of Rome and when the court of King Arthur, the pattern of Christian virtue, kept the pagan Saxon at bay." Though, "on closer inspection," he found in his historical investigations "only a sour and dismal chronicle of general decline, in which Arthur himself, if he existed (for that was now doubtful), marked no real revival" (pp. 602–3).

51 Barker, *Puritan Dilemma*, p. 261.

52 Quentin Skinner, "History and Ideology in the English Revolution," *Historical Journal*, 8 (1965): 163. The figure of Nimrod was common in the political discourse of the fifties. The "type of the conqueror," J. G. A. Pocock writes in his *The Machiavellian Moment* (Princeton University Press, 1975), "was not William the Conqueror so much as Nimrod of the Bible, the primeval despot whose power was not unwilled by God" (p. 37). John M. Wallace in his *Destiny his Choice: The Loyalism of Andrew Marvell* (Cambridge University Press, 1968) similarly suggests that in "political controversy Nimrod was not always the villain he is reported to be, because his empire, although founded and maintained by the sword, was recognized to have prospered by God's ordinance" (p. 83). For Marvell's comparison of Cromwell to Nimrod, see Wallace, pp. 98–105; Nevo, *Dial of Virtue* (Princeton University Press, 1963), pp. 93–118; and Joseph Anthony Mazzeo, "Cromwell as Machiavellian Prince in Marvell's 'An Horatian Ode,'" *Journal of the History of Ideas*, 21 (1960): 1–17.

53 In this respect, Milton's arguments of 1660 parallel those of the Levellers for whom all forms of government were seen, as Christopher Hill writes, as "the badge of the Norman bondage." For the historiography of the Norman Conquest in England, see Christopher Hill, "The Norman Yoke" in *Puritanism and Revolution* (New York: Schocken, 1958), pp. 50–102, especially p. 82, and J. G. A. Pocock's *The Ancient Constitution and the Feudal Law* (Cambridge University Press, 1986).

54 Indeed the late thirties and forties serve, in the rhetoric of *The Readie and Easie Way*, as a time of greater national unity. As Corns has noted, Milton, who

wanted in *The Readie and Easie Way* "to incorporate the Presbyterians into the Good Old Cause," had to drastically revise "his account of events leading to the formation of the republic." Milton, Corns writes, pushed this account "back towards the 1630s and early 1640s, which permits him to describe issues on which all elements of the parliamentary opposition to Charles I were substantially united" (*Uncloistered Virtue*, p. 288).

55 Mark A. Kishlansky, *The Rise of the New Model Army* (Cambridge University Press, 1979), suggests that the argument for *discordia concors* implicit in *Areopagitica* was reflected in the political discourses of the forties. Kishlansky further presumes that it was only later that "party came to describe a new method of political action, one that implied a corruption of the old political system – more explicitly the pursuit of self-interest against the common good" (p. 15).

56 See Janel Mueller's interpretation of Milton's argument in her "The Mastery of Decorum: Politics as Poetry in Milton's Sonnets," *Critical Inquiry*, 13 (1987): 475–508, where she argues that classical sources (specifically Aristotle's *Poetics*) provide the "immediate context" for Milton's poetry of the forties.

57 As Mueller argues, "Mastery of Decorum," Aristotle, in the *Ethics* and *Politics*, conceives of *proairesis* as "a course of voluntary action based in reason," which informs "the kind of choice that defines moral virtue" (p. 482). For a further explication of deliberative action (*proairesis*) in Aristotle, see Kathy Eden, *Poetic and Legal Fiction in the Aristotelian Tradition* (Princeton University Press, 1986), pp. 39–42.

58 This movement is mirrored in Whig and Marxist historiography. As Christopher Hill remarks in "A Bourgeois Revolution," in *Three British Revolutions*, "the outcome of the Revolution was something which none of the activists had willed" (p. 111). Hill does not hesitate to point out the confluence of Christian and Marxist historiography, as he quotes approvingly George Wither's *Dark Lantern*: "He that would, and he that would not too / Shall help effect what God intends to do . . . " (p. 135). Like it or not, Wither suggests, God is the agent behind all human action; the substitution of "History" for "God," presumably, reveals Hill's historiographical suppositions. Peter Laslett, *World We Have Lost* (London: Methuen, 1983), offers a critique of Hill's argument for "unintended consequences," and sees "A Bourgeois Revolution" as a "retreat" from Hill's earlier more classically Marxist assumptions about England from 1640 to 1660 (p. 187).

59 Kerrigan, *Prophetic Milton*, p. 177.

60 The date of the publication remains speculative; though see Corns, *Uncloistered Virtue*, p. 288.

61 On the genesis of this connection in the Church fathers, see *The Poems of John Milton*, ed. John Carey and Alastair Fowler (New York: Longman, 1971), pp. 1028–29, note to XII, lines 24–63.

62 Nimrod's political and architectural enterprises, ending in "a jangling noise of words unknown" (XII 55), are affiliated in *Paradise Lost* with Satan himself.

In Book 1, Satan stands "above the rest / In shape and gesture proudly eminent . . . like a Tow'r" (1 589–91) who "with fear of change / Perplexes Monarchs" (1 598–99).

63 The people, of course, as Pepys explains, were as "abject" as Milton could have imagined, as they greeted news of the King's return with bonfires and roastings of "the Rump": "But the common joy that was every where to be seen! The number of bonfires . . . and all along burning, and roasting and drinking for rumps. There being rumps tied upon sticks and carried up and down. The butchers at the May Pole in the Strand rang a Peal with their knives when they were going to sacrifice their rump. On Ludgate Hill there was one turning on the spit that a rump tied upon it, and another basting of it. Indeed it was past imagination . . ." (*The Diary of Samuel Pepys* 11 vols. [London: G. Bell, 1924], vol. 1, p. 55).

64 "The Politics of *Paradise Lost*," *Politics of Discourse*, p. 228.

65 Victoria Kahn, *Rhetoric, Prudence and Skepticism* (Ithaca, N.Y.: Cornell University Press, 1985), p. 54.

66 Blair Worden, "Milton's Republicanism and the tyranny of heaven," *Machiavelli and Republicanism*, ed. Gisela Bock et al. (Cambridge University Press, 1990), p. 227.

3 INTRODUCTION: WHIG METAPHYSICS

1 As quoted by Jonathan Hayes, *The Birth of Popular Culture* (Pittsburgh: Duquesne University Press, 1992), p. 7.

2 See for example, Hayes, *Popular Culture*, p. 138.

3 Fredric Jameson, *Signatures of the Visible* (New York: Routledge, 1990), p. 226.

4 For an analagous moment in contemporary Marxist economic theory, see Stephen A. Resnick and Richard D. Wolff, "Marxist Epistemology: the Critique of Determinism," *Social Text* 6 (1982), 31–72. While they critique the "essentialism" of contemporary Marxists, including the still "faint determinism" of Althusser, Wolff and Resnick nonetheless maintain "class-relations" as a privileged "entry-point" for Marxist analysis (p. 71). Although claiming to escape the "essentialism" of their predecessors, Wolff and Resnick seem to merely repeat it in a different form.

5 Jameson, *Signatures*, p. 227.

6 Robert Ashton, "Tradition and Innovation in the Great Rebellion," in *Three British Revolutions*, ed. J. G. A. Pocock (Princeton University Press, 1980), p. 208.

7 David Aers, "Reflections on current histories of the subject" *Literature and History* 2 (1991): 31.

8 Frank Kermode, *The Romantic Image* (New York: Random House, 1967), p. 141; Jean-Luc Nancy, *The Inoperative Community*, ed. Peter Connor (Minneapolis: University of Minnesota Press, 1992). Friedman offered his comments in a lecture, "Orthodox Jewish Responses to Modernism," *Judaism and Modernism*, Jewish Theological Seminary, December 1990.

9 Jean François Lyotard, "What is Postmodernism?" in *The Postmodern*

Condition, trans. Geoff Bennington and Brian Massumi (Minneapolis: University of Minnesota Press, 1984), p. 79.

10 For an account of this "nostalgia for the future" among contemporary cultural materialists, see Howard Felperin's "'Cultural poetics' versus 'cultural materialism,'" *Uses of History: Marxism, Postmodernism, and the Renaissance* (Manchester University Press, 1991), pp. 76–100. Employing the "peculiar" phrase, "nostalgia for the future," Felperin wishes to distinguish the practice of contemporary British Marxists from "a straightforward, prospective utopianism also endemic to Marxism." This "utopianism expresses itself not in projection, forward or backward, but in nostalgia, literally understood as a communitarian longing for home, for an England that in certain respects once was and might be again" (p. 92).

11 As I will suggest in chapter 5 below, both More and his contemporary Ralph Cudworth were engaged – sometimes obsessively – in attempts to defy this dualism and, as Rosalie Colie, *Light and Enlightenment: A Study of the Cambridge Platonists and the Dutch Arminians* (Cambridge University Press, 1957), explains, to "reanimate the machine universe bequeathed by Descartes" (p. 57). Their starting-point, however, was an acceptance of the philosophical languages and distinctions inherited from Descartes. As J. E. McGuire and P. M. Rattansi explain, "Newton and the Pipes of Pan," *Notes and Reports of the Royal Society* 21 (1966), reacting against "hylozoistic magical philosophies" as well as "against Deists . . . and Socinians, the Cambridge Platonists adopted a sharp distinction between spirit and matter" (p. 131).

12 McGuire and Rattansi, "Pipes of Pan," p. 133.

13 Ralph Cudworth, *True Intellectual System of the Universe* (Stuttgart, 1964; reprint of the 1678 edition), p. 12. Hobbes, according to J. G. A. Pocock, similarly depicts "Hellenic superstition in opposition to, and as encroaching upon, the prophetic religion of Moses and Christ." "The Gentiles," writes Hobbes, "being ignorant of the physical processes of vision, took things which they imagined they saw for gods and disembodied spirits; and later, being equally ignorant of the mental processes of the formation of ideas, took the words which they coined in excessive profusion for the names of real entities. In this way was built up the kingdom of darkness, an empire of insignificant speech . . ." "All this," Pocock argues, "was the result of the importation of Greek thought and mental habits into the revelation made by God to the Jews and Christians." See Pocock, *Politics, Language and Time: Essays on Political Thought and History* (University of Chicago Press, 1989), pp. 199–200.

14 Kermode, *Romantic Image*, p. 140. Where Kermode suggests that Eliot's "dissociation of sensibility" registered a "particular and far-reaching catastrophe," not "in the seventeenth century, but the twentieth" (p. 143), I would suggest that the language of "dissociation" – the sense of what Kermode calls "a pregnant historical crisis" – was produced by the twentieth, but *also*, as in More and Cudworth, the seventeenth-century mind.

15 Felperin suggests a "strange" connection between Leavis' nostalgia and the nostalgia implicit in the works of the contemporary British cultural critics,

Francis Barker and Catherine Belsey. "What links so apparently ill-sorted a trio as Leavis, Barker and Belsey," Felperin writes, "is not only their common desire for a restored univocality of the sign, poetic and social, but their nostalgia for a time when it is supposed to have actually existed" ("Cultural Poetics," p. 97).

16 Nancy, *Inoperative Community*, p. 9.

17 *Ibid.* "It would be quite as reasonable," writes Kermode in his critique of Eliot, "to locate the great dissociation in the sixteenth or the thirteenth century as in the seventeenth." And "if we were to pursue the dissociation back into the past," Kermode argues, "we should find ourselves in Athens" (*Romantic Image*, pp. 141, 142).

18 Nancy, *Inoperative Community*, p. 17.

19 Theodore Adorno and Max Horkheimer, *Dialectic of Enlightenment*, trans. John Cumming (New York: Continuum, 1987), pp. 13, 4.

20 Adorno, *Dialectic of Englightenment*, pp. 5, 39, 9. The dominion of the subject over the "disenchanted object" in Adorno and Horkheimer's historiography has significant correlates in other Marxist histories. The Marx of the *Economic and Philosophical Manuscripts*, for example, presupposes a primitive unity between subject and object (lost by virtue of "alienated labor"). Such a unity is even romanticized in Marx's notion of the "*genuine* community" of feudalism where labor continues to have a "*social* meaning" (Karl Marx, *Early Writings*, trans. Rodney Livingstone et al. [Harmondsworth: Penguin, 1984], p. 337). So also Walter Benjamin, in *The Origins of the German Tragic Drama*, trans. John Osborne (London: Verso, 1977), associates the disjunction between subject and object with the genres of an emergent modernity. In the allegorical – as opposed to the historiographically prior symbolic – there "is not the faintest glimmer of any spiritualization of the physical" (p. 187). Where the symbol reconciles the immanent and the transcendent (matter and spirit), modern allegory ostentatiously demonstrates their separation.

On man's disjunction from nature – again figured in relation to modernity – see also Martin Heidegger's "The Age of the World Picture," *What is Called Thinking* (New York: Harper and Row, 1968): "The World Picture does not change from an earlier medieval one into a modern one, but rather the fact that the world becomes picture at all is what distinguishes the essence of the modern age" (p. 130). The "fundamental event of the modern age," continues Heidegger, "is the *conquest* of the world as picture" (p. 133; emphasis added). Although Lukács in *Theory of the Novel* (Cambridge: MIT Press, 1985), laments the lost unity of the Homeric world in which the "object" itself was "meta-subjective, transcendent," it is finally the genre of modernity, the novel, which "understands the limited nature of mutually alien worlds of subject and object, and by thus seeing through them allows the duality of the world to subsist." The novel, the distinctly modern genre, writes Lukács, "reveals a rift between inside and outside, a sign of the difference between the self and the world" (p. 29).

21 Adorno, *Dialectic of Enlightenment*, pp. 5, 7, 31. Analogously, Herman Rapaport, *Milton and the Postmodern* (Lincoln: University of Nebraska Press, 1983) finds Milton actively complicit in Nazism which, claims Rapaport, has its genealogy in the seventeenth century when "God left the world" and man was "deprived of a physical universe." "Not only Descartes and Corneille," writes Rapaport, "but Milton as well were only too willing to underwrite such a cultural breakup: in fact, Milton is not the only of such figures militantly to propagandize for the 'tragic' rupture Goldmann outlines in terms of the justification of armed violence" – a violence which "in our day appears as the legitimation of storm troopers, death squads, and other political apparatuses of terror" (p. 171).

22 It is this totalizing gesture, for Adorno and Horkheimer, that beginning in "nominalism" ends in fascism. Adorno's post-Enlightenment philosophy, however, seeks "to adhere as closely to the heterogeneous" as possible, aiming towards "total self-relinquishment" in the "diversity ... of the objects it seeks." "To yield to the object means to do justice to the object's qualitative moments" (*Dialectic of Enlightenment*, pp. 13, 43).

23 Francis Bacon, *A Selection of His Works*, ed. Sidney Warhaft (Indianapolis: Bobbs Merril, 1982), pp. 323–24.

24 *Ibid.*, p. 205.

25 *Ibid.*, p. 341.

26 Bacon, *Selection*, pp. 341, 337.

27 Henry Reynolds, in his *Mythomystes* of 1629, elaborates the apparent contradictions implicit in these competing epistemologies, attacking Bacon's different approaches to the "wisdom of the ancients": "... suppose that a man ... shall have taken pains in four or five fables of the Auncients to unfold and deliver us much doctrine and high meanings in them, which he calls their wisdome; and yet the same man in an other Treatise of his, shall say of those auncient Fables – I think they were first made, and their expositions devised afterward ... What shall we make of such willing contradictions, when a man to vent a few fancies of his owne, shall tell us first, they are the Wisdome of the Auncients; and next that those Auncient fables were but mere fables, and withoute wisdome or meaning" (from Tayler, *Literary Criticism of Seventeenth Century England* [New York: Alfred A. Knopf, 1967], p. 257).

To Reynolds, in the first case, Bacon insists on the inherent quality of the objects, their intrinsic "wisdome," while in the second case, the fables are, inexplicably, mere objects, "without wisdome or meaning," their "expositions devised afterward." For Bacon, the strategy represents two complementary, though legitimate, ways of knowing. To the irritated Reynolds, it is merely a "contradiction."

28 Charles Whitney, *Francis Bacon and Modernity* (New Haven: Yale University Press, 1986), p. 23.

29 Robert Lord Brooke, *The Nature of Truth: Its Union and Unity with the Soule* (London: R. Bishop, 1641), p. 103.

30 For a documentation of this strange phenomenon, see Jeffrey Perl's

Skepticism and Modern Enmity (Baltimore: Johns Hopkins University Press, 1989), pp. 25–40.

31 T. S. Eliot, "Metaphysical Poets," *Selected Essays* (New York: Harcourt Brace Jovanovich, 1964), p. 286.

32 T. S. Eliot, "A Skeptical Patrician," *Athenaeum* 4747 (May 13, 1929): 362.

33 This preference was canonized for the New Criticism with Wimsatt's notion, *The Verbal Icon* (Lexington: University of Kentucky Press, 1982) of the "concrete universal" (p. 69). For the "objective correlative" of this critical *desideratum* in Eliot's early poetry, see, for example, "Whispers of Immortality" (roughly contemporaneous with "Metaphysical Poets": "Donne, I suppose, was such another / Who found no substitute for sense, / To seize and clutch and penetrate; / Expert beyond experience / He knew the anguish of the marrow . . ."

34 Eliot, "Metaphysical Poets," p. 288.

35 As quoted by Patrick Murray, *Milton: The Modern Phase* (London: Longman, 1967), p. 34. "It was not long after the emergence of 'dissociation of sensibility' as part of the vocabulary of literary criticism," writes Murray, "that various critics began to use it to establish the superiority of various Metaphysical poets to Milton." Leavis, for example, borrowing the terminology of "Metaphysical Poets" lamented "the laboured, pedantic artifice of the diction" of *Paradise Lost* that seemed to be "focussing rather upon words than upon perceptions, sensations, or things" (p. 36).

36 As quoted by Murray, *Modern Phase*, p. 38.

37 T. S. Eliot, "Donne in Our Time," *A Garland for John Donne*, ed. Theodore Spencer (Cambridge, Mass.: Harvard University Press, 1931), p. 9.

38 Thus, in his 1947 essay "Milton," *Selected Prose*, ed. John Hayward (London: Penguin, 1954), Eliot wrote, that "if such a dissociation did take place, I suspect that the causes are too complex and too profound to justify our accounting for the change in terms of literary criticism." "All we can say," Eliot continues, is that "something like this did happen; that it had something to do with the Civil War; that it would be unwise to say it was caused by the Civil War, but that it is a consequence of the same causes which brought about the Civil War; that we must seek the cause in Europe, not in England alone; and for what these causes were, we may dig and dig until we get to a depth at which words and concepts fail us" (p. 132). In 1947, in so far that the notion continued to have any historiographical efficacy for Eliot, it was stipulated upon a web of determinants outside of the Civil War, England, and even "words and concepts" themselves.

39 Eliot, "Garland for Donne," p. 8.

40 Indeed, Eliot's own critique of metaphysics and ontology from the perspective of epistemology should make us pause before attributing to Eliot a foundationalist historiography. A 1913 seminar report on Kant, for example, "describes as 'pathetic' the philosopher's attachment to 'ultimate reality which haunts us like the prayers of childhood.'" And in another paper Eliot laments that metaphysical inquiry, in Western philosophy,

became a futile "quest to reveal being unconditioned" (Perl, *Skepticism*, pp. 69, 71).

41 Aspects of the historiography implicit in Eliot's "dissociation" were of course to die hard. Eliot's own relationship to Milton, evidenced in his consecutive "Milton" essays, was based on an "antipathy" towards Milton – an antipathy which continued to figure significantly in Eliot's canon. Eliot, in his particularly virulent strains of Whig pessimism in *After Strange Gods: A Primer in Modern Heresy* (London: Faber, 1934), finds the "key to the understanding of most contemporary literature" in the "decay of protestantism" (p. 38), and he thus describes the "Inner Light" as "the most untrustworthy and deceitful guide that ever offered itself to wandering humanity" (p. 59). The sentiments expressed here are also perhaps uncomfortably autobiographical (providing the motivation – with the unfortunate expression of his disdain for "free-thinking Jews" – for Eliot's suppression of the work). Ironically, the modernist exclusion of Milton may have resulted from Eliot's own troubled relationship (and identification) with his Puritan predecessor. As Kermode writes, "A Babylonish Dialect," *T. S. Eliot: The Man and his Works*, ed. Alan Tate (New York: Delacorte Press, 1966), "the more we see of the hidden side of Eliot, the more he seems to resemble Milton, though he thought of Milton as a polar opposite" (p. 234). Thus it is not altogether surprising that we find in Eliot's praise of F. H. Bradley an unmistakable echo of *Areopagitica*. Bradley, Eliot avers, was able to acknowledge the "continuity and contiguity of the various provinces of thought" ("Francis Herbert Bradley," *Selected Essays*, p. 454).

42 Sir Thomas Browne, *The Prose of Sir Thomas Browne*, ed. Norman Endicott (New York: Stuart Editions, 1968), p. 70.

43 *Ibid.*, p. 73.

4 "ABNORMAL FORMS OF DISCOURSE": MILTON'S
DE DOCTRINA CHRISTIANA

1 Hunter's "The Provenance of the *Christian Doctrine*," *Studies in English Literature* 32 (1992): 129–42 is followed by a "Forum" which includes responses by John T. Shawcross, pp. 155–62; Barbara Lewalski, pp. 143–54, and a further reply by Hunter himself, pp. 163–66. In the following year, Hunter sought to bolster his argument with his "The Provenance of the *Christian Doctrine*: Addenda from the Bishop of Salisbury," *Studies in English Literature* 33 (1993): 191–208. Hunter's position came under attack in 1994 in Christopher Hill's "Professor William B. Hunter, Bishop Burgess, and John Milton," *Studies in English Literature* 34 (1994): 165–93, and Maurice Kelley's "The Provenance of John Milton's *Christian Doctrine*: A Reply to William B. Hunter," 153–63. In the same issue, Hunter contributed what seems to be a final reply to his critics in "Animadversions upon the Remonstrants: Defenses against Burgess and Hunter," 195–203.

2 Hunter, "Provenance," p. 129.

3 Hunter, "Animadversions," pp. 202, 198.
4 "I think it is true, and I observed this at the symposium, that scholars with a vested interest in believing that Milton authored the *Christian Doctrine* tend to argue in favor and those with a vested interest in believing that he did not argue against it. My own vested interests, as I have previously published them, are all with the former group. On the other hand, from this new perspective I find a less contradictory, more interesting, and richer understanding of the man and his works." Hunter, "Forum," p. 166.
5 *Ibid.*
6 Hill, "Professor William B. Hunter," pp. 168, 184.
7 Hunter, "Animadversions," p. 195.
8 Hunter, "Forum," p. 166.
9 *Ibid.*, p. 165.
10 For Hunter's account of Burgess's arguments, see his "Addenda," pp. 191–201; for Hill's response to these arguments, see "Professor William B. Hunter," pp. 165–68.
11 Corns's explanation of Miltonic contradiction is most persuasive in his account of the contexts for *Areopagitica* which, following Sirluck, argues that the split registers of *Areopagitica* comprise "various appeals to Independence, Erastians, and Presbyterians." For the Corns of *Uncloistered Virtue* (Oxford University Press, 1992), Milton compromises "philosophical coherence" for a series of complex arguments that engage with the variey of "prejudices and assumptions of his target readership" (pp. 56, 58).
12 Keith Stavely, *The Politics of Milton's Prose Style* (New Haven: Yale University Press, 1975), p. 112.
13 This is not by any means to deny the fact that Skinner has done much to re-historicize political philosophy and move it away from the consideration of "universal truths" and "perennial problems." For Skinner's methodology, see his "Meaning and Understanding in the History of Ideas" (pp. 29–67), and "Motives, Intentions, and Interpretations" (pp. 68–78), collected in *Meaning and Context: Quentin Skinner and his Critics*, ed. James Tully (Princeton University Press, 1988).
14 Tully, *Meaning and Context*, p. 77.
15 *Ibid.*, p. 258. Pocock's *Virtue, Commerce, and History* (Cambridge University Press, 1986), with its introduction to the "State of the Art," re-formulates Skinnerian method to incorporate this kind of critique. "Political language," Pocock argues, "is by its nature ambivalent; it consists in the utterance of what have been called 'essentially contested concepts' and propositions." It follows, therefore, that "any text . . . in a sophisticated political discourse is by its nature polyvalent." Sensitivity to what Pocock calls the "patterns of polyvalence" will be especially significant in contexts where the registers of political, theological, and poetic discourse are not clearly delineated. As the "author may move among these patterns of polyvalence," Pocock continues, "employing them and recombining them according to the measure of his capacity," what to one "investigator looks like the generation of linguistic

muddles and misunderstandings may look to another like the generation of rhetoric, literature, and the history of discourse" (pp. 8–9).

16 Stephen M. Fallon, *Milton among the Philosophers: Poetry and Materialism in Seventeenth Century England* (Ithaca, N.Y.: Cornell University Press, 1991), explains that he aims to provide a "description of what Milton and other intellectuals in the middle third of the seventeenth century were thinking about" and he situates his project in relation to the "hypothetical thousand volume *Intellectual History of Europe*" imagined by "Richard Rorty, J. B. Schneewind, and Quentin Skinner" (pp. 17, 16).

17 Fallon, *Among the Philosophers*, p. 18.

18 Tully, *Meaning and Context*, pp. 76, 258.

19 Fallon, *Among the Philosophers*, p. 17.

20 *Ibid.*, p. 193.

21 As well as decrying the methods of the schoolmen, Milton was also opposed to what we might call the professionalization of the study of divinity. Although Milton advocated the public interpretation of scriptures by "whoever God has appointed as apostle or evangelist or pastor or teacher," he explicitly excluded "those who are appointed to professional chairs by mere men or by universities: of these it can often be said, as in Luke xi. 52: *woe to you, interpreters of the law, for you have taken away the key of knowledge . . .*" (VI 584).

22 Yale *Complete Prose*, vol. VIII, pp. 161, 203.

23 William Kerrigan, "Milton's Place in Intellectual History," *The Cambridge Companion to Milton*, ed. Dennis Danielson (Cambridge University Press, 1989), pp. 266–67.

24 Thomas Hobbes, *The Questions Concerning Liberty, Necessity, and Chance* in *The English Works of Thomas Hobbes*, ed. Sir William Molesworth [London: John Bohn, 1840], vol. V, p. 146.

25 *English Works of Hobbes*, vol. V, p. 136.

26 Milton, as A. O. Lovejoy suggests, *The Great Chain of Being* (New York: Harper, 1963), hesitated between these poles, admiring at once the God of Descartes and the God of the Cambridge Platonists (a suggestion that interestingly anticipates and partially explains Empson's impatience for Milton's God to "turn into the God of the Cambridge Platonists" [see *Miltons God* (London: Chatto and Windus, 1965), p. 132]). Milton, writes Lovejoy, "rejects at times the extreme nominalist doctrine of Descartes; the essences of things, and the truths concerning the intrinsic relation of essences are logically prior to any will, so that not even God could alter them." Against this notion of a God limited by a "certain immutable and internal necessity of acting right" (*De Doctrina*; Lovejoy's translation), Milton also posits a "motiveless" God whose intentions, according to Lovejoy, can only be described as "ineluctable" (p. 160).

27 As quoted by Aharon Lichtenstein, *Henry More: The Rational Theology of a Cambridge Platonist* (Cambridge, Mass.: Harvard University Press, 1962).

28 *English Works of Hobbes*, vol. V, pp. 6, 10.

29 *Ibid.*, vol. v, p. 10; T.S. Eliot, *Selected Essays* (New York: Harcourt Brace Jovanovich, 1964), p. 315.
30 Leopold Damrosch, *God's Plot and Man's Stories* (University of Chicago Press, 1982), pp. 83, 85.
31 Milton spells out these "absurdities," and explains how belief in free will may lead to the conviction "that something temporal may cause or limit something eternal" (vi 163) – i.e., that man's will could limit that of the Deity. Hobbes also elaborates on the "absurd conclusions" which arise from such a position. Those who believe that "*if man will, then God concurs,*" Hobbes writes, "subject not the will of man to God, but the will of God to man" (*Hobbes*, vol. v, p. 18) The difference, of course, is that Hobbes makes his point *against* Bramhall.
32 Dennis Danielson, *Milton's Good God* (Cambridge University Press, 1982), pp. 86, 76.
33 Emmanuel Levinas and Richard Kearney, "Dialogue with Emmanuel Levinas" in *Face to Face with Levinas*, ed. Richard A. Cohen (Albany: SUNY Press, 1987), p. 19.
34 I cite Milton's Latin text (from *Works*, ed. Frank E. Patterson [Columbia University Press, 1931]) selectively, primarily to illustrate that Milton's language of the imagination in *De Doctrina* tends to be much more graphic – less abstract – than Carey's English translation. When the English and Latin texts are quoted consecutively, I cite Carey and then Patterson.
35 See for example, Henry More who writes: "All Pretenders to Philosophy will indeed be ready to magnifie Reason to the skies, to make it the light of Heaven and the very Oracle of God: but they doe not consider that the Oracle of God is not to be heard but in his Holy Temple, that is to say, in a good and holy man" (as quoted by Lichtenstein, *Rational Theology*, p. 64). Baxter's *Arrogancy of Reason* (London, 1655) offers similar versions of the commonplace: "When God hath put his Seal to it, and proved it to be his own; if after this you will be questioning it, because of the seeming contradictions or improbabilities, you do but question the wisdom and power of the Lord: As if he had no more wisdom then you can reach and fathom" (p. 46).
36 H. R. MacCullum, "Milton and Figurative Interpretation," *Union Theological Quarterly* 31 (1961–62): 403.
37 Georgia Christopher, "Milton and the Reforming Spirit," *Cambridge Companion*, pp. 198, 199, 201.
38 MacCullum, "Figurative Interpretation," p. 403.
39 Similarly, where Milton claims that "sufficient care has been taken" that the scriptures do not "quid vel ipsa indecorum aut indignum Deo scriberet" (xvi 32), Carey again opts for a less graphic, and less precise, rendering: "the holy scriptures *contain* nothing unfitting to God or unworthy of him" (vi 134; emphasis added). Not only does Carey's metaphor suggest that words *contain* meaning (a notion, I am arguing, which contradicts Milton's understanding of scriptural language where text and meaning are inseparable), but it lacks the concreteness and allusiveness of Milton's "scriberet."

40 Sanford Budick, *The Dividing Muse: Images of Sacred Disjunction in Milton's Poetry* (New Haven, Yale University Press, 1985), p. 71.

41 Baruch Spinoza, *Tractatus Theologico-Politicus*, trans. Samuel Shirley (Leiden: E.J. Brill, 1989), pp. 63, 71.

42 *Ibid.* pp. 226, 73.

43 Ralph Cudworth, *Treatise Concerning Immutable and Eternal Morality* (London: Knapton, 1731), p. 34. Where for Hobbes, as J. G. A. Pocock writes, "faith in God's word is little more than acknowledgement of his power" (Pocock, *Politics, Language and Time* [University of Chicago Press, 1989] p. 185), for Cudworth, "infinite will and power" cannot be made "to devour and swallow up" "infinite understanding and wisdom" (as quoted by Frederick Copleston, *A History of Philosophy* (London: Burnes, Oates and Washbourne, 1959), vol. v, p. 62. More's 1647 "Psychathanasia," *Philosophical Poems*, ed. A. B. Grosart (London, 1878), parallels Cudworth: "If God do all things simply at his pleasure / Because he will, and not because it's good. / So that his action will have no set measure / Is't possible it should be understood / What he intends? . . . Can any be assur'd, if liberty / We give to such thoughts, that thus pervert / The laws of God, and rashly do assert / That will rules God, but Good rules not God's will" (p. 85). For More, as for Cudworth, the emergence of the Hobbesian or Cartesian God of will marks God's abandonment from nature, and the loss of his immanence in the created world.

44 Peter Harrison, *'Religion' and the Religions in the English Enlightenment* (Cambridge University Press, 1990), p. 30.

45 *Ibid.*, pp. 30–31.

46 *Ibid.*, p. 32.

47 God "is," in the Columbia edition, "or is not, such as he represents himself to be" (xiv 37).

48 As quoted by Kelley, Yale *Complete Prose*, vi 137. Milton's response to anthropomorphism, asserts Kelley, has its precedent in Lactantius, though he suggests that Milton avoided the extremes of Lactantius' position (vi 137).

49 As Daniel Boyarin suggests, *A Radical Jew: Paul and the Politics of Identity* (Berkeley: University of California Press, 1994), in the Hellenizing hermeneutics of Philo and Paul, the text yields to its source and origin, "the invisible, ideal, and spiritual reality that lies behind . . . the body of language" (p. 15). In this Hellenic mode, Fish argues that the "dialectical presentation" of the seventeenth-century text becomes the "vehicle of its own abandonment." "A self-consuming artifact," writes Fish, "signifies most successfully when it fails, when it points *away* from itself to something its form cannot capture" (*Self-Consuming Artifacts* [Berkeley: University of California, 1982], p. 3). In Fish's reading of the seventeenth century, the image or the text (and by association any kind of political intervention) necessarily "self-consume" and accede to a transcendent truth beyond them.

50 Budick, *Dividing Muse*, p. 71.

51 Milton most doubted the authenticity of the New Testament, as the "law of Moses" was "unquestionably . . . handed down" in "an uncorrupted state."

To underline both the authority of the written scriptures, and to ground the authority of the sometimes corrupt New Testament in the more certain written traditions of the Old Testament, Milton assures his readers that "almost everything in the New Testament is proved by reference to the Old" (VI 588, 576).

52 Regina Schwartz, "Citation, authority, and *De Doctrina Christiana*," in *Politics, Poetics, and Hermeneutics in Milton's prose*, ed. David Loewenstein and James Grantham Turner (Cambridge University Press, 1990), p. 233.

53 Emmanuel Levinas, *Otherwise than Being* (Martinus Nijhoff: The Hague, 1981), p. 147.

54 Schwartz, "Citation," pp. 230, 239.

55 *Ibid.*, p. 230.

56 See J. W. Burrow, *A Liberal Descent: Victorian Historians and the English Past* (Cambridge University Press, 1981) on these qualities: "*Virtú* gives mastery over the flux of circumstances and one's own weaknesses, by self-control, daring, self-assertion . . . *virtú* becomes public spirit, patriotism, the sacrifice of private interest to civic duty, which includes political participation, but also still, significantly, courage, martial virtue and energy" (p. 86).

57 Jean-Luc Nancy, *Inoperative Community*, ed. Peter Connor (Minneapolis: University of Minnesota Press, 1992), p. 15.

58 Richard Rorty, invoking Isaiah Berlin invoking Joseph Schumpeter, argues that to "realise the relative validity of one's convictions and yet stand for them unflinchingly, is what distinguishes a civilized man from a barbarian" (*Contingency, Irony, and Solidarity* [Cambridge University Press, 1989], p. 46). This liberal lineage, however, is not to be confused with the perspective represented in *De Doctrina*. Though Milton may accurately be said to have "combined commitment with a sense of the contingency" of his own "commitment" (*Contingency*, p. 61), this contingency is mediated through a *common* public realm – in *De Doctrina*, the Bible – which insures the ultimate commensurability of different "contingencies." Against Rorty's "liberal ironist," Milton stands as a "Christian ironist." Though as well as being an anachronism, the phrase is also probably redundant.

5 MILTON CONTRASTED WITH MILTON: MULTIPLICITY IN *DE DOCTRINA CHRISTIANA*

1 H. R. MacCallum, "Milton and Figurative Interpretation," *Union Theological Quarterly* 31 (1961–62): 403.

2 Milton's acknowledgment of difference on this question does not, of course, prevent him from arguing one side of the issue (see the argument in *De Doctrina*, VI 400–14). Milton acknowledges the ambivalence of scripture, but the ultimate superiority of his own argument, when he closes: "What more is there to say? There is virtually no scriptural text left which cannot be countered by one or other of the arguments which I have already produced" (VI 414).

3 Arthur Sewell, *A Study in Milton's Christian Doctrine* (Norwood Editions, 1975), p. 180.
4 *Ibid.*, p. 203.
5 Thomas N. Corns, "Some Rousing Motions: the Plurality of Miltonic Ideology," *Literature and the English Civil War*, ed. Thomas Healy and Jonathan Sawday (Cambridge University Press, 1990), p. 110.
6 Hans-Georg Gadamer, *Truth and Method* (New York: Crossroad, 1991), p. 300.
7 "For the orthodox in religion," as John W. Yolton, *Thinking Matter: Materialism in Eighteenth-Century Britain* (Minneapolis: University of Minnesota Press, 1983), writes, "it was important that there be two substances, one material, the other immaterial... Any suggestion that the two substances be reduced to one (i.e., to material substance) eliminated the soul" (p. 4).
8 "By devoting his *Saturday* essays to Milton, Addison indicated and encouraged the suitability of *Paradise Lost* for Sunday reading, and throughout the eighteenth and nineteenth centuries, Milton's poem shared the privileged and widely influential status of 'Sunday Book'" with *Pilgrim's Progress* and *Robinson Crusoe* (Bernard Sharratt, "The Appropriation of Milton," ed. Suheil Bushrui, *Essays and Studies* 35 [1982]: 35).
9 John T. Shawcross, *Milton: The Critical Heritage* (London: Barnes and Noble, 1972), p. 101.
10 As quoted by Leslie E. Moore, *Beautiful Sublime: The Making of Paradise Lost* (Stanford University Press, 1990), p. 18. Another anonymous pronouncement from 1738 declared, "whatever *Milton* may have as a poet, I'm afraid he will have but little to plead in his religious character" (Shawcross, *1732–1801*, p. 95).
11 As quoted by Moore, *Beautiful Sublime*, p. 23.
12 Richardson's discussion in the *Explanatory Notes* that for Milton "Matter... is Varied and Mov'd Perpetually still aspiring," is, according to Leslie Moore, *Beautiful Sublime*, "as close as the eighteenth century came to discerning Milton's theory of creation *ex deo*" (p. 22).
13 Francis Mineka, "The Critical Reception of Milton's *De Doctrina*," *Studies in English* (Austin: University of Texas Press, 1943), p. 116. Todd, however, later came to his senses, and attempted to explain his earlier evaluation: "The dormant suspicion of schism was unawakened, while I dwelt upon the magic of his invention; and like others, I was all ear only to his sweet and solemn-breathing strain" (as quoted by Mineka, "Critical Reception," p. 116).
14 Patrick Murray, *Milton: The Modern Phase* (London: Longman, 1967), p. 85.
15 Tayler, *Milton's Poetry: Its Development in Time* (Pittsburgh: Duquesne University Press, 1979), pp. 209–10.
16 John Peter Rumrich, "Uninventing Milton," *Modern Philology* 87 (1990): 256. These divisions were emphatically reasserted, according to J. G. A. Pocock, at the Restoration. Though a "hylozoistic spiritual materialism," Pocock argues, *Virtue, Commerce, and History* (Cambridge University Press, 1986), formed the "mainstream of radical thought," the "scientific Revolution of the Restoration period" functioned "in ideological terms" as a conservative

reaction aiming at the separation of spirit and matter in the name of authority and rationalism" (p. 52).

17 As quoted by Mineka, "Critical Reception," p. 125.

18 Mineka, "Critical Reception," p. 117.

19 Maurice Kelley, *This Great Argument* (Gloucester, Mass.: Peter Smith, 1962), p. 4. "Ivimey," Kelley writes, "could weep over the defection," and Theodore Hunt felt that "it was to 'be deeply regretted that Milton ever penned such a treatise and defended such views.'" Others, as Kelley points out, "merely denied the authenticity of the document" (p. 4). There were those, however, who recognized the importance of *De Doctrina* to the interpretation of *Paradise Lost.* Masson found it "an indispensable commentary to some obscure parts of *Paradise Lost*," while *The Monthly Review* of 1825 hailed it as "indispensable to all critical readers of our illustrious epic" (Kelley, p. 5).

20 As quoted by Mineka, "Critical Reception," p. 116. Gadamerian "prejudice" runs deep. Balachandra Rajan's *Paradise Lost and the Seventeenth-century Reader* (Ann Arbor Paperbacks, 1967), offers a similar apology for the orthodox Milton in 1947: "Milton is willing to subdue his unorthodoxies, to subscribe them to a general system of assent, to organize his inner poetic feeling so that it issues in a universal pattern of belief . . . Milton *wanted* his poetry to look orthodox" (p. 142).

21 Thomas Babington Macaulay, *Essay on Milton*, ed. Edward Leeds Gluck (New York: American Book Company, 1903), p. 58.

22 Although, as James G. Nelson, *The Sublime Puritan: Milton and the Victorians* (University of Wisconsin Press, 1963) suggests, there was a renewed interest in the prose in the nineteenth century, especially among "Chartist and other radical groups" who "found Milton's defense of freedom and republican government . . . congenial" (p. 83). Blunt's views, expressed in his review of *De Doctrina*, tended to be more typical. "The Politics of Milton," he wrote, "had been consigned to oblivion by common consent, until recent circumstances accidentally revived them; and now to oblivion they had better return." Of his poetry, however, Blunt wrote, "it would require a tongue like his own to speak the praise" (as quoted by Nelson, p. 90).

23 As quoted by Rumrich, "Uninventing Milton," 251.

24 As quoted by Kelley, Yale *Complete Prose*, vol. VI, p. 10.

25 John Carey, "Translator's Preface," Yale *Complete Prose*, vol. VI, p. xv.

26 Macaulay, *Milton*, p. 58.

27 Kelley, *Great Argument*, p. 4. Against the Baptists who celebrated the disclosure of Milton's heterodoxy, one orthodox periodical, *The Evangelist*, countered, "If Baptists *will* boast, they must not forget that he was an Arian, a Polygamist, a Materialist, a Humanitarian, and, in fact, an abettor of almost every error which has infested the Church of God" (as quoted by Mineka, "Critical Reception," p. 119).

28 Dennis Saurat, *Milton: Man and Thinker* (London: J. M. Dent, 1946), p. 277.

29 Empson, *Milton's God* (London: Chatto & Windus, 1965), p. 143.

30 James Thorpe, *Milton Criticism: Selections from Four Centuries* (London: Routledge, 1951), p. 16. "To refit *Paradise Lost* for the modern world," Patrick Murray writes, James Holly Hanford, also part of the 'New Movement,' "found it necessary to emphasize the power of Milton's 'poetic and philosophic thought' at the expense of the dogmatic aspects of his inherited theology" (*The Modern Phase*, p. 80).

31 Kendrick, *Milton: A Study in Ideology and Form* (London: Methuen, 1986), p. 68.

32 *Ibid.*, p. 12.

33 John Reesing, "The Materiality of God in Milton's *De Doctrina Christiana*," *Harvard Theological Review* 50 (1957): 162, 171.

34 Fish, "Driving from the Letter: Truth and Indeterminacy in Milton's *Areopagitica*," *Re-membering Milton* ed. Mary Nyquist and Margaret Ferguson (New York: Methuen, 1987), p. 248.

35 Fish, *Surprised by Sin* (New York: Macmillan, 1967), p. 91.

36 Walter Clyde Curry, "Milton's Dual Concept of God as Related to Creation," *Studies in Philology* 47 (1950): 193.

37 *Ibid.*, p. 210.

38 Reesing, "Materiality of God," pp. 171, 170.

39 *Ibid.*, p. 171. Reesing's sympathies, however, are with the Milton who tends towards "orthodoxy." "No man is a pantheist," Reesing argues, who tries "to prove with every scrap of evidence he can lay his hands on that those two creatures, the Son and the Holy Spirit, are emphatically not of one substance with the Father" (p. 162).

40 *Ibid.*, p. 162.

41 Christopher Hill, *The World Turned Upside Down* (New York: Penguin, 1980), p. 142.

42 Dennis Danielson, *Milton's Good God* (Cambridge University Press, 1982), p. 2.

43 Curry, "Milton's Dual Concept," p. 200.

44 Though just as soon as Milton dispenses with the problem of evil, he returns to his monist account of creation. Replying to the possible charge that "body cannot emanate from spirit," Milton argues that "spirit, being the more excellent substance, virtually, as they say, and eminently contains within itself what is clearly the inferior substance" (VI 309). Thus Milton again affirms the equivalence of the Creator and the creation.

45 Tayler, *Milton's Poetry*, p. 17.

46 Regina Schwartz, *Remembering and Repeating: Biblical Creation in Paradise Lost* (Cambridge University Press, 1988), p. 35. Schwartz in her reading follows the 1963 study of A. B. Chambers, "Chaos in *Paradise Lost*," *Journal of the History of Ideas* 24 (1963), in which Chaos and Night are described as "the enemies of God" (p. 65).

47 Stephen M. Fallon, *Milton Among the Philosophers* (Ithaca, N.Y.: Cornell University Press, 1991), p. 91.

48 Marshall Grossman, *Authors to Themselves* (Cambridge University Press, 1987), p. 180.

49 Margaret C. Jacob, *The Newtonians and the English Revolution: 1689–1720* (New York: Gordon and Breach, 1990), describes this reaction as a general phenomenon among the Cambridge Platonists who first saw "Descartes as an ally." Their subsequent rejection of his "natural philosophy rested not simply on the inconsistencies and inaccuracies" of Descartes's "scientific explanation; it also had much to do with their fear that his mechanical philosophy led straight to materialism" (p. 28). But More's relation to Descartes and the "new science" was complex. As Marjorie Hope Nicolson, "Milton and the *Conjectura Cabbalistica,*" *Philological Quarterly* 6 (1927), observed: "More was too keenly interested in the new science to be content with a theology which was contradicted by experiment; yet he was too devout a Christian to consider for a moment a completely mechanical explanation of the universe" (p. 4).

50 Rosalie Colie, *Light and Enlightenment: A Study of the Cambridge Platonists and the Dutch Arminians* (CambridgeUniversity Press, 1957), p. 57.

51 As quoted by Frederick Copleston, *A History of Philosophy* (London: Burnes, Oates and Washbourne, 1959) v, pp. 59–60; Ralph Cudworth, *A Treatise Concerning Eternal and Immutable Morality* (London: James and John Knapton, 1731) p. 295.

52 Copleston, v, p. 60; J. E. McGuire and P. M. Rattansi, "Newton and the Pipes of Pan," *Notes and Reports of the Royal Society* 21 (1966): 131.

53 Similarly, More developed his own notion of the plastic power: there is a "substance incorporeal, but without sense and Animadversion, pervading the Whole Matter of the universe, and exercising a plastic power therein . . ." On More and the plastic power, see Aharon Lichtenstein, *Henry More: The Rational Theology of a Cambridge Platonist* (Cambridge, Mass.: Harvard University Press,1962), pp. 9–10, and p. 171. For a review of the plastic power in the seventeenth century, see Hunter, "The Seventeenth-Century Doctrine of Plastic Nature," *Harvard Theological Review* 43 (1950): 197–213.

54 Ralph Cudworth, *The True Intellectual System*, p. 105. All citations from Cudworth, unless otherwise noted, are from the Stuttgart (1964) facsimile of the 1678 edition, and abbreviated within as *TIS*.

55 See M. H. Carré, "Ralph Cudworth," *Philosophical Quarterly* 3 (1953): 345 and Rosalie Colie, "Spinoza and the English Deists," *Journal of the History of Ideas* 20 (1959): 27.

56 As quoted by C. A. Patrides, *The Cambridge Platonists* (Cambridge University Press, 1980), p. 303.

57 Fallon, *Among the Philosophers*, p. 59.

58 As quoted by Thomas Birch in his introduction to *The True Intellectual System*, (London, 1738), p. xv.

59 *Ibid.*

60 Birch cites Bayle's critique of Cudworth: "Monsieur Bayle . . . endeavor'd to shew, that if these Writers had consider'd the plastic Natures only as instruments in the hand of God, this System would have been exposed to all

the difficulties to which the Cartesian hypothesis is liable and which they intend to avoid." For "if God could communicate such a plastic power," Bayle explains, "then it is not inconsistent with the nature of things that there be such agents ... whence it would also follow, that the regularity, which we observe in the universe, may be the effect of a blind cause, which was not conscious of what it did" (*True Intellectual System*, (1738), p. xv).

61 Alan Charles Kors, *Atheism in France: 1650–1729* (Princeton University Press, 1990), p. 237.
62 As quoted by Patrides, *Cambridge Platonists*, p. 301.
63 Nancy Streuver, *Theory as Practice: Ethical Inquiry in the Renaissance* (University of Chicago Press, 1992), p. 224.
64 Arthur Sewell, *A Study in Milton's Christian Doctrine* (Norwood Editions, 1975), argues for the similarities between Milton and Cudworth, especially on the issue of creation: "There is a clear correspondence between the view of Cudworth and the implication of Milton's remarks on the origin and nature of created things" (p. 193).
65 Cudworth, *Treatise*, p. 299.
66 The text is more probably, and aptly, "swelling," as in Bentley's emendation. See *Milton's Paradise Lost*, ed. Richard Bentley, D.D. (London: Jacob Tonson, 1732), p. 228.
67 Jean Howard, "Towards a Postmodern, Politically Committed, Historical Practice," in *Uses of History: Marxism, Postmodernism, and the Renaissance*, ed. Francis Barker et al. (Manchester University Press, 1991), p. 115. For Milton, the two competing narrative perspectives are contained in his rendering of divine fiat: "Boundless the Deep, because I am who fill / Infinitude, nor vacuous the space / Though I uncircumscrib'd myself retire" (VII 168–70). Milton's God is at once present in his creation, filling infinitude, though paradoxically, "uncircumscrib'd" *and* retired – simultaneously transcending and constrained by his creation. On the divine character of space in More and the Cambridge Platonists, and their understanding of "the totality of extension as a realization of the divine presence," see Lichtenstein, *Rational Theology*, pp. 170–71.

6 THOSE GRAND WHIGS BENTLEY AND FISH

1 Robert E. Sullivan, *John Toland and the Deist Controversy* (Cambridge, Mass.: Harvard University Press, 1982), pp. 177, 75, 179. "The principle of immanence," as Yirmiyahu Yovel writes, *Spinoza and Other Heretics: The Adventures of Immanence* (Princeton University Press, 1989), implies that "this-worldly existence" is "the unique source of ethical value and political authority." "All being," Yovel continues, "is this-worldly and there is nothing beyond, neither a personal creator-God who imposes His divine will on man, nor supernatural powers or values of any kind" (p. ix).
2 Pocock, *Virtue, Commerce and History* (Cambridge University Press, 1986), p. 63.
3 The power of Fish's "invented Milton," and its relative hegemony in

contemporary Milton studies is the subject of John Rumrich's *Milton Unbound* (Cambridge University Press, 1996). The "invented Milton," Rumrich claims, is "a rhetorical artifact or paradigm foundational to contemporary Milton scholarship" (pp. 2, 4). Rumrich here brings to fruition arguments he initiated in his "Uninventing Milton," *Modern Philology* 87 (1990): 249–65.

4 Patrick Murray, *Milton: The Modern Phase* (London: Longman, 1967) p. 98.

5 James Thorpe, *Milton Criticism: Selections from Four Centuries* (London: Routledge, 1951), p. 16.

6 Donald F. Bouchard, *Milton, A Structuralist Reading* (Montreal: McGill–Queen's University Press, 1974), p. 64.

7 William Empson, *Milton's God* (London: Chatto and Windus, 1965), pp. 132–33.

8 *Ibid.*, p. 273.

9 *Ibid.*, pp. 139, 268.

10 William Empson, *Some Versions of Pastoral* (London: Chatto and Windus, 1935), p. 188.

11 Empson, *Milton's God*, p. 133. Tillyard, like Empson, wonders about (and despairs over) the perpetuation of hebraic legalism in Milton's texts. Milton, he writes, "insists with an emphasis he could have avoided had he wished, on the legalism" inherent in his account of the redemption. Milton, Tillyard continues, was "powerless either to free himself or to impassion" this legalism. E. M. W. Tillyard, *Studies in Milton* (London: Chatto and Windus, 1951), p. 164. For a different view of Milton's "deuteronomic" legalism, see Jason P. Rosenblatt, *Torah and Law in Paradise Lost* (Princeton University Press, 1994).

12 Blair Worden, "Milton's Republicanism and the Tyranny of Heaven," *Machiavelli and Republicanism*, ed. Gisela Bock et al. (Cambridge University Press, 1990), p. 240.

13 Christopher Hill, *Milton and the English Revolution* (London: Faber, 1977), p. 242.

14 Bouchard, *A Structuralist Reading*, pp. 64, 99.

15 Andrew Milner, *John Milton and the English Revolution* (New Jersey: Barnes and Noble, 1981), p. 59.

16 Bouchard, *A Structuralist Reading*, p. 64.

17 For the context of Bentley's conflicts with the "Christ-Church set," see Joseph Levine's *The Battle of the Books: History and Literature in the Augustan Age* (Ithaca, N.Y.: Cornell University Press, 1992), pp. 54–58.

18 Pocock, *Virtue*, pp. 215, 231, 219, 220, 233. See also Margaret Jacob, "John Toland and Newtonian Ideology," *Journal of the Warburg and Courtault Institute* 32 (1969): 307–21. "Low Churchmen," Jacob writes, "endeavored to maintain the Church as a bulwark of social stability by indoctrinating their public with a particular metaphysical and religious world-view that would give support to their mission. Part of that mission was the purging from society of the dissident and extreme republican element which, far more than their High Church counterpart, threatened the delicate relationship formed between church and state after the revolution of 1689" (p. 302). For

the persistence of ideas affiliated with civil war republicanism after the Glorious Revolution, see Mark Goldie, "The Roots of True Whiggism 1688–1694," *History of Political Thought* 1 (1980): 195–236.

19 Jacob, "Toland," p. 313.

20 It is possible that Bentley was setting his sights on the Locke of the *Essay Concerning Human Understanding.* "We have the ideas of *matter* and *thinking*," Locke writes, "but possibly shall never be able to know whether any mere material being thinks or no: it being impossible for us, by the contemplation of our own *ideas*, without revelation, to discover whether Omnipotency has not given to some system of matter, fitly disposed, a power to perceive and think, or else joined and fixed to matter, so disposed, a thinking immaterial substance." Thus for Locke, as John Yolton writes, *Thinking Matter: Materialism in Eighteenth-Century Britain* (Minneapolis: University of Minnesota Press, 1983), it was "possible for God – that omnipotent, eternal, cogitative being – to add to a system of matter the power of thought" (pp. 14, 17).

21 *The Works of Richard Bentley*, ed. Alexander Dyce (New York: AMS Press, 1966), vol. III, p. 35.

22 As quoted by R. J. White, *Dr. Bentley: A Study in Academic Scarlet* (London: Eyre and Spottiswoode, 1965), p. 79. See also Bentley's attack on the other sort of atheism identified by Cudworth, atomism: "For is it not every whit as likely, or more, that cocks and bulls might discourse, and hinds and panthers hold conferences about religion, as that atoms can do so? that atoms can invent arts and sciences, can institute society and government, can make leagues and confederacies, can devise methods of peace and strategems of war" (Dyce, vol. III, pp. 49–50).

23 Dyce, vol. III, p. 309.

24 Ibid., p. 47.

25 White, *Academic Scarlet*, p. 70.

26 Jacob, "Toland," p. 314.

27 In his "A Sense of the Sacred: Richard Bentley's Reading of *Paradise Lost*," *Milton Studies* 24 (1988): 73–106, Bourdette is concerned primarily with Bentley's reading of *Paradise Lost* in relation to the attack on sacred texts leveled by Collins, Toland, et al. Bourdette thus explores the role of *Paradise Lost* in what Mark Pattison called "the endeavor to 'prove the truth' of Christianity" (p. 85).

28 J. W. Mackail, "Bentley's Milton," *The British Academy: Warton Lectures on English Poetry* (London, 1924) vol. XI, p. 11.

29 Mark Pattison, *Milton* (London: Macmillan, 1909), p. 217.

30 Joseph Addison, *The Spectator*, ed. Donald F. Bond (Oxford: Clarendon Press), vol. III, p. 391 (no. 369); and Jonathan Richardson, *Explanatory Notes and Remarks on Milton's Paradise Lost* (London: James Knapton, 1734), p. clxiii. A Whig like Addison, as Nicholas von Maltzahn argues, "The Whig Milton, 1667–1700" in *Milton and Republicanism* (Cambridge University Press, 1996), came to "recommend Milton's politeness at the expense of his politics and prophesy" (p. 230). "In the flowering of Whig literary culture in the 1690s,"

von Maltzahn continues, Milton came to have a wider appeal not because of his politics but because his politics might be more readily overlooked" (p. 242). Milton thus became, von Maltzahn observes, a "literary figure of a milder sobriety, increasingly freed from the languages of faction and revelation" (p. 253).

31 John Toland, *A Complete Collection of the Historical, Political, and Miscellaneous Works of John Milton* (Amsterdam, 1698), p. 5.

32 John Toland, *Amyntor: or, A Defence of Milton's Life* (London, 1699), pp. 3, 5, 6, 8. At least part of the "Clamor" to which Toland refers can be attributed to his claim in the *Life* that King Charles I had not authored *Icon Basilike*, and to his further insinuation that his contemporaries might also be mistaken about the authenticity of many early Christian writings. Offspring Blackall took this opportunity, as the *DNB* notes, to hint to the House of Commons "that their pious designs would not be of much effect if the foundation of all revealed religion were thus openly struck at." A year following the controversy (1700), Blackall was chosen Boyle lecturer. See *Dictionary of National Biography*, ed. Leslie Stephen et al. (Oxford University Press, 1917), vol. II, pp. 579–80.

33 As quoted by Thorpe, *Milton Criticism*, p. 5.

34 Thomas Yalden, "On the Reprinting of Milton's Prose Works," *The Works of the British Poets*, ed. Robert Anderson (London, 1795), vol. VII, p. 762.

35 Margaret C. Jacob, *Newtonians and the English Revolution 1689–1720* (New York: Gordon and Breach, 1990), p. 24.

36 George F. Sensabaugh, *That Grand Whig, Milton* (Stanford University Press, 1952), p. 192; John Toland, *Letters to Serena* (London: Bernard Lintot, 1704), p. c3.

37 Jacob, "Toland," p. 313.

38 Toland, *Letters*, pp. 209, 211.

39 Sullivan, *Deist Controversy*, pp. 177, 75.

40 Margaret C. Jacob, *The Radical Enlightenment: Pantheists, Freemasons, and Republicans* (London: Allen and Unwin, 1981), p. 217; Yovel, *Spinoza*, p. 184.

41 Jacob, *Radical Enlightenment*, p. 154.

42 John T. Shawcross, *Milton: The Critical Heritage 1732–1801* (New Jersey: Barnes and Noble, 1972), p. 89.

43 Toland, *Amyntor*, pp. 7–8.

44 The association of Milton and radical monism was an undertaking not only of Toland but Collins, Blount, and others. The same Charles Blount who adopted *Areopagitica* in his *Reasons Humbly offered for the Liberty of Unlicens'd Printing* also elaborated his own version of radical theology (Sensabaugh, *That Grand Whig*, pp. 155–62). In his *Animus Mundi*, for example, Blount sought "to trace the concept of the human soul to the cosmology of the 'ancient philosophies' – which had presumed the immanence of the Deity" (Sullivan, *Deist Controversy*, p. 274). Likewise, at the end of *A Discourse of Free-Thinking*, Milton becomes an advocate of Collins's politics and theology. Indeed, Collins's *Discourse* (London, 1713) lists Milton as among those who are "already know[n] for their Penetration, Virtue and Free-Thinking" (p. 139).

45 Roger L. Emerson, "Latitudinarianism and the English Deists," *Deism, Masonry and the Enlightenment: Essays Honoring Alfred Owen Aldridge*, ed. J. A. Leo Lamay (Newark: University of Delaware Press, 1987), links Bentley's Boyle Lectures directly to Blount. Bentley, Emerson argued, alluded to Blount when he "wrote that deists 'understand [God to be] no more than some inanimate Matter, some universal Nature, and Soul of the World, Void of all Sense and Cogitation, so far from being endowed with infinite Wisdom and Goodness'" (p. 27). On the close relationship between Toland, Blount, and Collins, see Sullivan, *Deist Controversy*, pp. 232–33.

46 Pocock, *Virtue*, p. 52.

47 Toland's work could hardly be disentangled from that of other radicals. Collins, James O'Higgins, *Anthony Collins: The Man and His Works* (The Hague: Martinus Nijhoff, 1970), explains, was an acquaintance of Toland, and he dedicated his *Adeisidaemon* of 1708 to "Carissime Antoni" (p. 14). Collins's *Discourse* was, as A. De la Chapelle notes, first falsely attributed to Toland: "Les prémiers souçons tombérent sur le fameux *Jean Toland*, parce qui l'on y voyoit tous ses Sentiments, & que l'on crut y reconnoitre aussi son Stile & sa Méthode. Le bruit en courut même fort loin, & dura long temps dans les Pays étrangers . . ." For De La Chapelle, See Giancarlo Carabelli, *Tolandiana: Materiali Bibliografici per Lo Studio Dell'Opera e Della Fortuna di John Toland* (Firenze: La Nuovo Italia Editrice, 1975), p. 286.

48 Citations of Bentley's emendations and comments are from *Milton's Paradise Lost*, ed. Richard Bentley, D.D. (London: Jacob Tonson, 1732), abbreviated within as *MPL*.

49 Zachary Pearce, *A Review of the Text of the Twelve Books of Milton's Paradise Lost* (London: John Shuckburgh, 1733), p. 240.

50 Empson, *Versions of Pastoral*, p. 149.

51 As quoted by Jacob, *The Radical Enlightenment*, p. 154.

52 Sullivan, *Deist Controversy*, p. 193.

53 Levine, *Battle of the Books*, also suggests that Bentley created his editor as a kind of rhetorical straw man: "When all is said and done, then, it seems unlikely that Bentley truly believed in his nefarious editor, though as he warmed to his task and piled on alterations and emendations through all the twelve books, he may well have convinced himself of his fiction . . . If so, instead of laughing *at* Bentley for his evident fiction, we should perhaps be laughing *with* him" (p. 262).

54 Shawcross, *Milton: 1732–1801*, pp. 306, 305.

55 John Guillory, *Poetic Authority: Spenser, Milton, and Literary History* (New York: Columbia University Press, 1983), p. 148.

56 Shawcross, *Milton: 1732–1801*, p. 305.

57 Empson, *Versions of Pastoral*, p. 156.

58 Dyce, vol. III, p. 403.

59 *Ibid.*, pp. 403, 404.

60 Empson, *Versions of Pastoral*, p. 179.

61 Abraham Cowley, *The Essays and Other Prose Writings*, ed. Alfred B. Gough (Oxford University Press, 1915), p. 16.

62 Empson, *Versions of Pastoral*, p. 180.

63 Bourdette, "Bentley's Reading," p. 90.

64 Michael McKeon "Politics of Discourses and the Rise of the Aesthetic in Seventeenth-Century England," *Politics of Discourse*, ed. Kevin Sharpe and Stephen N. Zwicker (Berkeley: University of California Press, 1987), p. 41.

65 Pearce, *A Review of the Text*, p. 265.

66 Bentley thus also cuts the lines from Book IV in which "*Pan, Sylvanus*, and *Faunus*, salvage and beastly Dieties, and acknowledg'd *feign'd*" are "brought ... in comparison" to Eden (*MPL*, p. 132).

67 Jacob, "Toland," p. 314. Similarly, in his translation of Aesop, Toland, as Stephen H. Daniel argues, joined Collins in "the endorsement of fables as non-religious inspiration to virtue, praising Aesop as an author whose every syllable tends 'to the discrediting of Vice'" and "'the encouraging of Vertue.'" See Daniel's *John Toland: His Method, Manners, and Mind* (Montreal: McGill–Queen's University Press, 1984), p. 33.

68 This tendency had its pedigree in the Cambridge Platonists, specifically Cudworth, who, according to Peter Harrison, '*Religion' and the Religions in the English Enlightenment* (Cambridge University Press, 1990), aimed to "show the continuity of true religion" (p. 45). The "Egyptians, like the Persians, Syrians, and Indians, as well as having a 'vulgar and fabulous theology,'" had an "arcane and recondite theology." "The conclusion drawn by Cudworth," Harrison explains, "was that there existed 'a theology of divine tradition or revelation, or a divine cabala' amongst the Hebrews which was 'from them afterwards communicated to the Egyptians and other nations'" (pp. 135–36).

69 Here, Pearce defends Milton from Bentley's charges. After "he has shew'd the common resemblances" in "his Similitudes," Pearce writes, Milton "often takes the liberty of wandring into some unresembling Circumstances; which have no other relation to the Comparison than they gave him the Hint, and (as it were) set fire to the Train of his Imagination" (II 636). John Gillies, like Pearce, could discern that "unresembling Circumstances" did not always stand as evidence of editorial meddling or poetic ineptness. Milton, Gillies writes, "resembled Bezaleel, who was to make the furniture of the tabernacle. Like him, he was endowed with extraordinary talents: and, like him, he employed Egyptian gold to embellish his work" (as quoted by Henry John Todd, *The Poetical Works of John Milton* [London: Bye and Law, 1801], vol. III, p. 337).

70 John T. Shawcross, *Milton: 1732–1801*, p. 66. Dr. Johnson took a similar, if not so respectful tack. Bentley, he wrote, who was "perhaps better skilled in grammar than poetry, imputed "frequent ... verbal inaccuracies" to the obtrusions of a reviser whom the author's blindness obliged him to employ." This, Johnson continues, is a "supposition rash and groundless, if he thought it true; and vile and pernicious, if, as is said, he in private allowed it to be false" (Shawcross, p. 304).

71 Bourdette, "Bentley's Reading," p. 102.
72 Peter M. Briggs, as quoted by Bourdette, "Bentley's Reading," p. 86.
73 Fish, "'Transmuting the Lump': *Paradise Lost*, 1942–1982," *Literature and History* ed. Gary Saul Morson (Stanford University Press, 1986), in this reading, follows Kingsely Widmer, whose resurrection of the "absolutist" Milton "allows for the rehabilitation of Books xi and xii" of *Paradise Lost* (p. 52). For Widmer, see "The Iconography of Renunciation: the Miltonic Simile," *English Literary History* 25 (1958): 258–69.
74 Fish, *Surprised by Sin* (New York: Macmillan, 1967), pp. 91, 88. Despite the dualistic language that jumps out from every page of *Surprised by Sin*, in a brief discussion of creation, Fish does acknowledge Milton's "monist" cosmology. "There is no dualism," Fish writes, "except that provided by the Manichean reader" (p. 150).
75 Stanley Fish, "The Bad Physician: the Case of Sir Thomas Browne," in *Self-Consuming Artifacts* (Berkeley: University of California Press, 1982), pp. 353, 370, 364.
76 Sir Thomas Browne, *The Prose of Sir Thomas Browne*, ed. Norman Endicott (New York: Stuart Editions, 1968), p. 70.
77 *Prose of Browne*, p. 87.
78 In his musings on charity and friendship, for example, Browne cannot but begin by thinking of the distance and difference that separates men. Of the unity for which friends yearn, "of being, truly each other," Browne explains, "it is impossible," and he continues ruefully adding that "their desires are infinite, and must proceed without a possibility of satisfaction" (*Prose of Browne*, p. 75). Indeed, at the moment he professes his desire to apprehend the sorrows of another "within" his "owne reason," he also affirms his isolation: the distance between the circle of his "own reason" and the "circle of another" which exists "without" seems insurmountable as Browne delineates an atomistic, almost Hobbesian view of human relations. But even in Browne's isolated and contiguous circles, one can see the art of what he calls, the "skilfulle Geometrician," the work of the divine "Compasse" (p. 22) in which distinct and divided circles can be rendered continuous. "For," as Browne writes, "though indeed they be really divided, yet are they so united, as they make rather a duality then two distinct souls" (p. 75). Where distinction and integration are the twin tendencies of the *Religio*, Fish wants to collapse all difference into similarity.
79 Fish, *Self-Consuming Artifacts*, pp. 359–60.
80 There may be a further parallel between Fish, Johnson, and Bentley, who all seem deaf, if not overtly hostile, to the specifically political arguments of Milton's tracts. Politics have no place in Milton's "larger scheme," Fish writes, because "the conviction that man can do nothing is accompanied by the conviction that Christ has taken it upon himself to do it all" (*Surprised by Sin*, p. 45). The confluence of this ostensibly Miltonic position with the attitude towards politics in Fish's theoretical work certainly requires further investigation.

81 *Prose of Browne*, p. 70.
82 Fish, *Self-Consuming Artifacts*, p. 372.
83 Fish, "Driving from the Letter," pp. 248, 249.
84 Fish, "Unger and Milton," *Doing What Comes Naturally* (Durham, N.C.: Duke University Press, 1989), p. 426.
85 Fish, *Surprised by Sin*, pp. 19–20, 15, 14, 42.
86 *Ibid.*, p. 17; emphasis added.
87 Fish, *Self-Consuming Artifacts*, pp. 371, 3.
88 Fish, *Surprised by Sin*, p. 272.
89 *Ibid.*, p. 43.
90 *Ibid.*, pp. 37, 272.
91 Empson, *Versions of Pastoral*, pp. 152, 149.
92 As quoted by R. J. White, *Academic Scarlet*, p. 221. Earlier, Richardson had also found this to be the case. "Bentley has cut me out a good deal of work," Richardson remarks, "not to answer Blunders, Conundrums, and Impertinences, but to read Milton with more care and attention." Thus, as Levine notes, "Bentley's critical perceptions" had "the paradoxical but undoubted effect of stimulating the serious study of *Paradise Lost*" (*Battle of the Books*, p. 262).
93 Fish, "Driving from the Letter," p. 248.
94 Where Fish's "theological" reading of the poem displaces the "humanist" Milton of the "New Movement," the New Movement's "humanist" Milton tended to displace the "Puritan" Milton of Victorian criticism. Although, according to Thorpe, the Victorians disapproved of Milton's thought, he was thought of only as "a strict theologian who set down in poetry severe Puritan dogmas" (p. 13). Now – almost predictably – John Rumrich, who objects to contemporary scholars' "penchant for the angelic perspective," has come to displace Fish's "invented" orthodox Milton ("a mistake, a big one") with a Milton more open to "uncertainty, doubt and division" (*Milton Unbound*, pp. 7, 22). And so it goes.

7 A "NOBLE STROKE": REPRESENTATION IN *PARADISE LOST*

1 Walter Benjamin, *Illuminations*, ed. Hannah Arendt (New York: Schocken, 1968), p. 11.
2 For an account of this phenomenon in Enlightenment Europe, see Terry Eagleton, *The Ideology of the Aesthetic* (Oxford: Blackwell, 1990), especially pp. 13–30.
3 John Rumrich, *Milton Unbound* (Cambridge University Press, 1996), p. 8.
4 A. O. Lovejoy, *The Great Chain of Being* (New York: Harper, 1963), pp. 160–62. This helps to explain why even Bentley, the enemy of immanence, queries *Paradise Lost*, v 159: "Thy goodness beyond thought and Power Divine." "Here's only God's *Goodness* and *Power* mention'd; his chief Attribute in the Creation quite drop'd. Would it not have been better thus? *Thy Goodness*, WISDOM, POWER, ALIKE *DIVINE*" (p. 159). Where Bentley's emendations most frequently redress Milton's spiritualization of the

material, untangling God from his creation, here his comments move in the opposite direction, assuring the "vital conjunction" between God and the world. Bentley, while arguing consistently against the immanent God, may have had, like Cudworth, another conceptual antagonist in mind: the Hobbesian God who manifested himself primarily through his *"irresistible power,"* and not his Reason (Hobbes, *Leviathan*, ed. Michael Oakeshott [New York: Collier, 1962] p. 262).

5 Arthur Sewell, *A Study in Milton's Christian Doctrine* (Norwood Editions, 1975), p. 175.

6 Christopher Norris, *Spinoza and the Origins of Modern Critical Theory* (Oxford: Blackwell, 1991), p. 211. Christopher Kendrick, *Milton: A Study in Ideology and Form* (New York: Methuen, 1986), foregrounds the paradoxical notion of God's constraint. Milton's God, he writes, "submits his own activity, which must on any orthodox view justify *itself*, to an external imperative to that fate or telos inscribed in and presiding over all 'free' or 'true' action, and guaranteeing its unity." There "are few moments," Kendrick continues, "I think in which the poem is so embarrassing at its official level, not just to Protestantism, but to all Christian theology" (p. 115).

7 Or, as in the case of Hobbes, for whom the relationship between sign and signified is merely conventional: "A *name* or *appellation* therefore is the voice of a man *arbitrary*, imposed for a *mark* to bring into his mind some conception concerning the thing on which it is imposed" (*De Homine* in *The English Works of Thomas Hobbes*, ed. Sir William Molesworth [London: John Bohn, 1840], vol. IV, p. 20.

8 Herman Rapaport, *Milton and the Postmodern* (Lincoln: University of Nebraska Press, 1983), p. 17.

9 John Guillory, *Poetic Authority: Spenser, Milton, and Literary History* (Columbia University Press, 1983), p. 149; Edward Tayler, *Milton's Poetry: Its Development in Time* (Pittsburgh: Duquesne University Press, 1979), p. 194.

10 R. S. Capp, *The Fifth Monarchy Men: A Study in Seventeenth-century English Millenarianism* (London: Faber and Faber, 1972), p. 181. Certainly Kendrick is right in asserting that in the last books of *Paradise Lost* the "harshness of Milton's depiction of the historical quotidian is transparently motivated by his political disappointment" (*Ideology and Form*, p. 217). The Milton of Books XI and XII of *Paradise Lost*, like the late Marx, may be said to have lamented history's "gray on gray." But to suggest as David Loewenstein does, *Milton and the Drama of History: Historical Vision, Iconoclasm, and the Literary Imagination* (Cambridge University Press, 1990), that Milton confronts the problem of reconciling "the coherence of a typological interpretation of historical events ... with a tragic vision ... that so unrelentingly dramatizes the conflicts and terror of human history" (p. 94) is to implicitly attribute to Milton a notion of the historical process that he never embraced, not even in *Areopagitica*. Loewenstein's assertion that we "are left with competing interpretations not completely resolved in the poet's historical consciousness" (p. 124) implies that Milton himself sought such resolution. Even in the

idealistic days of the 1640s, Milton explicitly resisted such a resolution, asserting that all the limbs of "the mangled body of Osiris" will not be "found" until "her [Truth's] Master's Second Coming." Clearly, Milton's late works betray a desire that "degenerate" and "redemptive" history be more intricately related, though he would have *always* held their identity "in this world" to be impossible. Of course, this identity was eventually asserted, though by Bentley, *not* Milton. In his emendation to the last lines of *Paradise Lost* (XII 648–49), he erases any hint of Adam's "Anguish" or the Reader's "Melancholy': "THEN *hand in hand with* SOCIAL *steps their way* / *Through* EDEN *took*, WITH HEAVEN'LY COMFORT CHEER'D."

11 I am grateful to Victoria Silver for the formulation of this notion. This deferral of embodiment has a parallel in Milton's early works, particularly his "On the Morning of Christ's Nativity." Though there is the promise that "Heav'n" will "open the Gates of her high Palace Hall," for the moment, "wisest Fate says no, / This must not *yet* be so" as the "Babe lies yet in smiling Infancy" (147, 148, 149–50; emphasis added). Thus the poem seems to end prematurely, deferring the revelation of Jesus' divinity: "But see! the Virgin blest, / Hath laid her Babe to rest. / Time is our tedious Song should here have ending" (237–39).

12 Mary Ann Radzinowicz, *Milton's Epic and the Book of Psalms* (Princeton University Press, 1989), p. 137.

13 Stephen M. Fallon, *Milton Among the Philosophers* (Ithaca, N.Y.: Cornell University Press, 1991), p. 200.

14 This has a pedigree, in among others, the Calvin of the *Institutes*. Describing Mosaic prophecy, Calvin writes: "Although a vision was exhibited to his eyes the main point was in the voice; because true acquaintance with God is made more by the ear than by the eye. A promise indeed is given that he shall behold God; but the latter blessing is more excellent, that God will proclaim his name so that Moses may know Him more by this voice than by His face." As quoted by Thomas Luxon in "Calvin and Bunyan on Word and Image: is there a Text in Interpreter's House?," *English Literary Renaissance* 18 (1988): 440.

15 Thus, Milton's account of the sons of Lamech in Book XI not only echoes the narrative from Genesis but also the more general injunction that the Israelites not "turn after . . . their eyes." The "Men, though grave," who "let thir eyes / Rove without rein," will be tempted by the "fair female Troop" whom Milton decries as "fair Atheists" (XI 585–86; 614, 625).

16 T. S. Eliot, *Selected Prose*, ed. John Hayward (London: Penguin, 1954), pp. 144–45. Eliot's notion that Milton's poems require the "readjustment of the reader's mode of apprehension" (p. 145) towards the "auditory imagination," parallels what Thomas Docherty has identified as a dominant tendency in postmodernism. Culling from the works of contemporary theorists, Docherty, *After Theory* (London: Routledge, 1991), asserts that the postmodernist project represents not only a "turn away from the eye," but also from the "prioritization of specularity" implicit in the Enlightenment project from Descartes to Habermas. Citing Jacques Attali's assertion that "the world is

not for beholding," but "for hearing," Docherty claims that postmodern practitioners are developing a "different (non-visionary) imagination: an imagination without the tyranny of the iconic image." Such an iconoclasm, Docherty concludes, "is itself a dominant part of postmodernism." It is perhaps not too much of an anachronism to suggest that the emphasis on aurality in postmodern and Miltonic "iconoclasm" are placed in similar service: the critique of immanence and embodiment (p. 148).

17 Marvell's lyrics thematize this disjunction. In the "Mower against Gardens" for example, "Luxurious Man, to bring his Vice in use, / Did after him the world seduce," and as a consequence, the "Pink grew then, as double as his mind" (*Poems and Letters of Andrew Marvell*, ed. H. M. Margoliouth [Oxford: Clarendon Press], 1927, vol. I, p. 27).

18 Fish, *Surprised by Sin* (New York: Macmillan, 1967), p. 33.

19 *Ibid.*, pp. 45, 188.

20 Sir Thomas Browne would attempt such narration in his *Religio Medici*: "*Before Abraham was, I am*, is the saying of Christ, yet is it true in some sense if I say it of my selfe, for I was not onely before my selfe, but *Adam*, that is, in the Idea of God, and the decree of that Synod from all Eternity. And in this sense, I say, the world was before the Creation, and at an end before it had a beginning; and thus was I dead before I was alive; though my grave be *England*, my dying place was Paradise, and *Eve* miscarried of mee before she conceiv'd of *Cain*" (*The Prose of Sir Thomas Browne*, ed. Norman Endicott [New York: Stuart Editions, 1968], p. 65).

21 Fish, *Surprised by Sin*, p. 32.

22 Isabel MacCaffrey, *Paradise Lost as "Myth"* (Harvard University Press, 1967), p. 53.

23 Jean E. Howard, "Towards a Postmodern, Politically Committed, Historical Practice," in *Uses of History: Marxism, Postmodernism, and the Renaissance*, ed. Francis Barker et al. (Manchester University Press, 1991), p. 115. The "god trick," and its "silently naturalizing a partial perspective as a universal or total perspective" (p. 115), as Howard's comments indicate, was deployed as a method of domination primarily in "Enlightenment philosophy and historiography" (p. 106), and needs to be distinguished from its Renaissance, specifically, Christian embodiments.

24 Guillory, *Poetic Authority*, p. 149.

25 *Ibid.*

26 Leslie Moore, *Beautiful Sublime: The Making of Paradise Lost* (Stanford University Press, 1990), p. 123.

27 Milton's belief in the difference between the Father and Son did not transform into a full-flung Arianism where the Son's individual "personality," as Maurice Kelley notes, "is maintained at the expense of his divinity" (VI 49). While the conventional Arian position maintained that Jesus was created *ex nihilo*, in Milton's account Jesus is, like the rest of creation, created out of God's substance. Thus Milton affirms the *essential* similarity of Jesus and God, even as he insists upon their difference.

28 In *De Doctrina*, Milton responds anxiously to scriptural verses which have been construed as asserting the identity between the Father and Son – for example, "1 Tim. iii. 16: *God made manifest in flesh*" and "Tit. ii 13: *the appearance of the glory of the great God and our Saviour Jesus Christ*" (VI 244, 45). Milton challenged both the authority and clarity of these verses. Of Timothy 3:16 Milton argues, "neither Ambrose nor the *Vetus Interpres* reads the word *God* here, and many of the old copies corroborate this" (VI 244). Of the latter verses from Titus, Milton asserts, we should not "believe in something which has to be lured out from among articles and particles by some sort of verbal bird-catcher, or which has to be dug out from a mass of ambiguities and obscurities like the answers of an oracle" (VI 246).

29 On satanic punning as symptomatic of the fall from "*integritas* or oneness into duality," see Tayler, *Milton*, pp. 96–97.

30 And so, too, Milton implicates the "potent rod" of Moses in this metonymic chain (I 338; XII 211).

31 Bentley, not surprisingly, rejects the comparison to Argus altogether: "great Character indeed of the Cherubim," Bentley comments, "that they were more wakeful than a Country Cow-herd *Argus*" (*MPL*, p. 353). Bentley's usual snideness notwithstanding, what comes through clearly is his rejection of the equivalence of sacred and profane narrative. Here, as in Bentley's other rejection of pagan fables, his dualist consciousness manifests itself. Thus, Bentley cannot allow for the possibility that sacred narrative could be compromised by its affiliation to pagan myth. To Bentley, the integrity of Michael's doctrines undoubtedly paralleled the "Integrity" of "Milton's mind" and could not be tainted with the "illusion" of pastoral.

32 Though Satan represents an extreme case of literalism and misinterpretation, Adam and Eve are susceptible to similar misinterpretations. Thus, despite Georgia B. Christopher's claim, "The Verbal Gate to Paradise: Adam's Literary Experience in Book x," *PMLA* 90 (1975), that Adam's "grasp of the *protevangelium* or promise is a dramatization of . . . [him] as the first Christian who is rehabilitated by a heartfelt grasp of the promise," Adam, blundering in Book x, similarly misinterprets the promise (p. 72). Hoping, in the most satanic of terms for "revenge," Adam worries that "death brought on ourselves, or childless days" will lead the Serpent to "'scape his punishment" (x 1037, 1039). Adam's extremely local notion of Satan's bruising, represented in his limited understanding of the divine "Sentence," suggests that the ostensibly "heartfelt grasp of the promise" is somewhat incomplete. Clearly, as Loewenstein suggests, it takes Michael to turn Adam "into a kind of semiologist, training him in the art of reading and interpreting God's signs in fallen history" (*Drama of History*, p. 108). Though arguably even Michael is not completely successful at his task. Thus Book xi opens with a comparison of Adam and Eve with Ovid's Deucalion and Pyrrha (xi 10), who evidence their own resistance to instruction and a consequent inability to read what Loewenstein calls "the signs of fallen history." In the *Metamorphoses*, ed. F. J. Miller (Cambridge, Mass.: Harvard University Press, 1977), upon hearing

the oracle of Themis, the two "stand in dumb amaze . . . and refuse to obey the bidding of the goddess" (p. 29). Adam and Eve, like their pagan antecedents, often "stand in dumb amaze" in front of a history that remains opaque to them.

33 A. J. Waldock, *Paradise Lost and its Critics* (Cambridge University Press, 1966), p. 91.

34 Regina Schwartz, *Remembering and Repeating: Biblical Creation in Paradise Lost* (Cambridge University Press, 1988), p. 100.

35 Sanford Budick, *The Dividing Muse: Images of Sacred Disjunction in Milton's Poetry* (New Haven: Yale University Press, 1985), p. 90.

36 Fish, *Surprised by Sin*, pp. 91, 87.

CONCLUSION

1 Milton is echoing contemporary definitions of "wit" which in Hobbes's, and later Locke's analysis, was said to be composed of fancy and judgment. In the *Leviathan*, however, "wit" is only identified with the former faculty. "Those that observe their similitudes," writes Hobbes in *Leviathan*, "are said to have a *good wit*; by which, in this occasion, is meant a *good fancy*. But they that observe their differences, and dissimilitudes; which is called *distinguishing*, and *discerning*, and *judging* between thing and thing . . . are said to have a *good judgment*" (*Leviathan*, ed. Michael Oakeshott [New York: Collier Books, 1962], pp. 59–60).

2 Eve's culinary preparations seem to follow the aesthetic principles as described by Adam: "What order, so contriv'd as not to mix / Tastes, not well join'd, inelegant, but bring / Taste after taste upheld with kindliest change" (v 334–36). Eve provides an example of something like reasonable cooking.

3 Indeed, "without Steddiness, and Direction to some End, a great Fancy is one kind of Madnesse." As quoted by Clarence DeWitt Thorpe, *The Aesthetic Theory of Thomas Hobbes* (Ann Arbor: University of Michigan Press, 1940), p. 106.

4 Merrit Y. Hughes p. 313, note to line 488; Richardson, *Explanatory Notes and Remarks on Milton's Paradise Lost* (London, 1734), p. 229. On *"intueor"* or "immediate enlightenment" in Milton and Donne, see Edward W. Tayler, *Donne's Idea of a Woman* (Columbia University Press, 1991), p. 32.

5 Isabel MacCaffrey, *Paradise Lost as "Myth"* (Cambridge, Mass.: Harvard University Press, 1967), p. 53.

6 As quoted by MacCaffrey, *Paradise Lost as "Myth"*, p. 53.

7 Terry Eagleton, *Ideology of the Aesthetic*, (Oxford: Blackwell, 1990), p. 360.

8 T. W. Adorno, *Aesthetic Theory*, trans. C. Lenhardt, ed. Gretel Adorno and Rolf Tiedemann (New York: Routledge, 1984), p. 19. For Adorno, this double consciousness brings the "un-naive thinker" to the "point of clowning." Here Adorno raises Lukács specifically historical notion of "irony" to the level of a philosophical principle. Authors of the modern novel, Lukács writes, "must show polemically the impossibility of achieving

their necessary object and the inner nullity of their means" (*Theory of the Novel*, [Cambridge: The MIT Press, 1985], p. 38). Undoubtedly, Adorno's notion of "clowning" also has a pedigree in Benjamin's "baroque."

In the seventeenth century, such "clowning" reaches its limits in the poetry of Andrew Marvell – particularly in "Upon Appleton House." The intransigence of the object before reifying thought (thematized in the "Mower Poems") is demonstrated most acutely in "Appleton House" – especially at the moment when the narrative voice refers to the mowers as "*Israelites*." He "call'd us *Israelites*," Thestylis objects (*Poems and Letters of Andrew Marvell*, ed. H. M. Margoliouth [Oxford: Clarendon Press, 1927], lines 389, 406). In Thestylis' complaint, Marvell enacts a refusal of allegory, and consequently emphasizes the disjunction between subject and object. (For more on this moment, see Leah Marcus, *Politics of Mirth* [University of Chicago Press, 1986], p. 249). The hesitancy of Marvellian poetry before its object, implied in the almost manic shifting of perspectives of "Appleton House," may in fact inform Marvell's later poetry, where a more thoroughly relativized aesthetic – implying the ultimate break between sign and signified – lends itself more easily to politics.

Index

A Jewish Boyhood in Poland

The Isak Saleschütz family, Kolbuszowa, 1934.

A Jewish Boyhood in Poland

Remembering Kolbuszowa

Norman Salsitz ❧ *As told to Richard Skolnik*

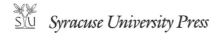 *Syracuse University Press*

Library of Congress Cataloging-in-Publication Data
Salsitz, Norman, 1920–
    A Jewish boyhood in Poland : remembering
Kolbuszowa / Norman Salsitz ; as told to Richard Skolnik.
— 1st ed.
        p.   cm.
    ISBN 0-8156-0262-6 (alk. paper)
        1. Salsitz, Norman, 1920– —Children and youth.
    2. Jews—Poland—Kolbuszowa—Biography.
    3. Kolbuszowa (Poland)—Biography.
    I. Skolnik, Richard.   II. Title.
    DS135.P63S24   1992
    943.8'6—dc20   91-17841

Contents

Norman Salsitz was born in Kolbuszowa, Poland, in 1920 and spent the first twenty-two years of his life there. After being forced to take part in the brick-by-brick destruction of his town by the Germans, he escaped the Holocaust, unlike so many of his family and friends, becoming a ranking officer in the Polish military and surviving the terrible years of World War II. In 1947, he and his wife, Amalie, came to America to make a new life for themselves. He is coauthor, with his wife, of *Against All Odds: A Tale of Two Survivors,* which recounts his struggle for survival after the destruction of Kolbuszowa, and a contributor to the *Kolbuszowa Memorial Book* (1965). They now live in New Jersey. They have a daughter, Esther, a lawyer, and three grandsons.

Richard Skolnik was born in New York City, earned a Ph.D. in history at Yale University, and ever since has taught history to students from all over the world (Poland included) at the City College of New York. His wife, Louise, is a Professsor of Social Work at Adelphi University. They have four children.

Illustrations

Acknowledgments

It was certainly my good fortune when several years ago a friend, Roger Gaeckler, introduced me to Norman Salsitz. In short order I realized what a treasure he was, able to step back in time some fifty to sixty years and recreate in exquisite detail a world that no longer exists. His capacity to recall names, places, and incidents was simply astounding. As a historian I understood how rare such people are and what a loss it would be were his story not told.

What followed were countless taped sessions, each hours long, in which Norman responded to every manner of question I posed. Occasional memory lapses generally proved temporary, so adept was he at summoning forth pertinent information. Remembering and explaining was to him a labor of love, a way of reaffirming his attachment to Kolbuszowa, his birthplace and home for the first twenty-two years of his life (where he was known to all as Naftali Saleschütz). I listened carefully, raised issues that prompted him to elaborate, and posed questions suggested by the general literature, including information found in the Kolbuszowa Memorial Book (1965) published in the United States and containing, in typical fashion, collections of photographs, family memorial pages, historical sketches, and individual recollections.

Some corroboration was available from Norman's brother David, but by and large what follows are Norman's own recollections. His story is important for many reasons, not the least being that it offers insights into a way of life not described in detail elsewhere. We have had numerous accounts of life in the large Polish cities and small villages before World War II, but few if any from places like Kolbuszowa, a provincial town of local importance in which lifestyles and perceptions reflected realities not present elsewhere.

As Norman reconstructed life there I began to see what he saw, even grew comfortable in places where I had never been, with people I had never met. He reviewed every word of the book most meticulously, patiently correcting me where I missed a certain nuance or overlooked a point he wished to make. What follows is my writing, but I have tried to capture his unique style and buoyant spirit and to illuminate as he would the rich textures of Kolbuszowa, a place that fate would in the end treat most cruelly. There is, of course, no way to restore the community of Jews that was destroyed, but thanks to Norman Salsitz and his special gift of memory we now have a vivid record of their lives.

Norman survived the terrible years of World War II. Indeed, incredibly enough, by the end of the war he had become a ranking officer in the Polish military. Still he saw no future for himself and his new wife in postwar Poland, and in 1947 they came to America to begin life anew. As with countless immigrants before them there followed years of hard work and hardship; but in time they prospered, raised a daughter, and entered fully into the American mainstream. Many, many years now separate Norman Salsitz from Kolbuszowa, but the passage of time has not diminished his devotion to this special place, to this other world now gone.

Special thanks must go to Amalie Salsitz, who from time to time helped clarify aspects of the prewar situation in Poland and to amplify her husband's statements. Not only did she welcome me into her home on innumerable occasions, but she prepared countless welcome and tasty lunches in the intervals of our lengthy interviews.

That a manuscript finally emerged is owing to the encouragement and exceptional tenacity of my typist and word processor, Dorothy Hanley. Undaunted by impossibly messy pages, undeterred by my incomprehensible scribbling, she stuck to the task with remarkable fortitude. Working together with her made an otherwise onerous task a joy.

Finally, I would also like to offer gratitude and appreciation to my wife, Louise, who waited patiently for me to return from many a trip to Norman in New Jersey during the course of a year in which we were celebrating the first twenty-five years of an uncommonly happy marriage.

Rockville Centre, New York   RICHARD SKOLNIK
October 1991

Introduction

In the chapters that follow there are only occasional indications that we are witnessing the final chapter of an extended historical era, one many centuries old. The Jewish presence in Poland was nearly coextensive with the emergence of a Polish sense of peoplehood, the Jews having been invited to settle there by leaders of the Polish nobility as early as the twelfth and thirteenth centuries. The Jews, it was hoped, would contribute to vitalizing a region notably backward and overwhelmingly agricultural.

To render services in exchange for sanctuary and encouragement had considerable appeal to Jews seeking refuge or laboring under severe restrictions in other regions. Still the relationship between the Polish elite and those who settled on their lands was a difficult one. Regarded as "foreigners" by the local populations, resented for occupying a pivotal position in the economy, and scorned by officials of the Catholic Church, Jews had no guarantee of security and freedom. Indeed, over the centuries Polish Jews saw restrictions imposed on their places of residence and limits placed on their economic activities, besides suffering periodic attacks on their persons and property.

Nonetheless they stayed on, increased in numbers, and succeeded in creating a varied and vital culture in both the religious and secular spheres. In the 1920s and 1930s, according to one writer, "Jewish culture was more alive and functioning on a larger scale [in Poland] than anywhere else in the world." This was so even as pressures on the Jewish population intensified, the leaders of a now independent Poland declaring that no longer was there a place for most Jews in the new nation. Well before the invading Germans introduced their plans for extermination Poland was anxious to see its Jewish population reduced substantially.

Jews had resided in and around the town of Kolbuszowa for centuries. Many had been farmers, tilling their small plots of land in much the same way as their Polish peasant neighbors. A majority lived in the town itself, their labor as artisans, craftsmen, peddlers, merchants, and businessmen contributing significantly to the local economy. In the two decades prior to the outbreak of World War II the many burdens imposed on Jews throughout Poland were not felt as heavily by those living in Kolbuszowa. Not that life was easy there. At least half of the town's Jewish residents were impoverished, nearly all were discriminated against by authorities, and many were subjected to attacks and beatings by elements of the Polish population.

Still, several moderating factors were evident. Whereas Jews represented about 10 percent (or 3.1 million in 1931) of the overall Polish population, the 4,000 residents of Kolbuszowa were equally divided between Jews and Poles. Additionally the Jews conducted practically all the business of the town, with little or no Polish competition. On the other hand, the instruments of government and official authority belonged exclusively to the Poles. (For example, despite the equally divided population, the town's mayor was always a Pole.) In this sense a relatively stable balance was achieved that throughout the period went mostly unchallenged. Furthermore, the Jewish community of Kolbuszowa was a most traditional one, with orthodox Jews long in ascendance. It was disposed to leave most secular concerns to others and to occupy itself with the daily pursuit of religious obligations. Kolbuszowa harbored few Socialists and Bundists (though Zionism did flourish); those who took issue with existing circumstances and conditions, those disposed to challenge the status quo, generally chose at some point to leave Kolbuszowa. Accordingly persistent dissent, let alone militancy, never took root.

It was possible for particular Jews in Kolbuszowa to lead rich, fulfilling, and relatively secure lives in this period. Certainly our story of Naftali Saleschütz and his family demonstrates as much. These were good years for all of them. Isak Saleschütz, his father, was a well-to-do businessman highly regarded in the town, generous in charitable undertakings, and active in religious affairs. His wife bore him nine children, five girls and four boys, all of whom survived infancy. They lived in a well-constructed two-story house in the marketplace. They lacked none of life's basic necessities and could enjoy many of its comforts. Three daughters were married and well married, all to scholarly men who then chose to live in Kolbuszowa. Within the family harmony generally prevailed. What more then could one ask from life?

Still, there was cause for concern. All of Isak's brothers had long ago left Poland, as had two of his sons. Hopes that his sons would follow his example and observe the Jewish faith in strict fashion came to naught. He was a leader in the Jewish community, but that meant little to the Poles. His business was a successful one, but the hard times of the 1930s, growing peasant discontent, and government policies that undermined the economic standing of the Jews produced a growing sense of insecurity.

Problems like these were always a part of life, and workable accommodations could generally be reached. But then came catastrophic events over which there could be no control. In a brief time all was destroyed, almost everyone swallowed up by the relentless killing machine introduced by the German invaders. The Jewish community of Kolbuszowa perished; the lines of continuity stretching over the centuries were brought to an abrupt end, and the tangible signs of the community's presence were reduced mostly to rubble.

But there were a few survivors, most notable among them Naftali Saleschütz. Most notable because Naftali remembers. He recalls to a remarkable degree all that he saw and much of what he was told in the years before 1939. And through him we can return and reconstruct Kolbuszowa as it was, glimpse part of a vanished world and a way of life that was full of both promise and pain.

A Jewish Boyhood in Poland

Dedicated to the Jews from Kolbuszowa
who were murdered in the Holocaust

Poland, 1921–1938

Time Is Not the Enemy

I t's been over fifty years, but time is not the enemy; it does no violence to my memories. I have little sense of having left or of the distance I traveled. I remain and always have been an inhabitant of Kolbuszowa. I walk its crooked streets, trail along with those in black coats, broad hats, and long beards as daily they make their way to the synagogue, watch as peasants stream into the square on market day and wait impatiently before the town well for cool water that will bring relief on a hot summer day. No one in Kolbuszowa was a stranger to me. I knew almost everyone's name, more often nickname,* and most people's sto-

---

*Certainly everyone had his or her family and given name, but often these names were put aside in favor of nicknames. Indeed, only a small number in our community were known by their legal names. It was common when a person was born outside of Kolbuszowa to refer to him or her by the place of birth. Thus my father, Isak Saleschütz, was known to practically everyone as Itche Dubaser, having been born in the village of Dubas. Also names told of generational ties, linked the past to the present. I, for example, was known as Naftali Itche Dubasers. A contemporary, Mendel by name, was the son of Itches, so his daughter predictably was to us Chaya Mendel Itches, and when she in time had a son, David, he patiently accepted the name David Chaya Mendel Itches. It was most common for nicknames to incorporate occupations, ways of making a living. Thus another Mendel, because he worked as caretaker of the public baths, was known to us as Mendel Bader; Fischel Salz, who served the Jewish community as scribe, was referred to as Fischel Sopher (Scribe); and a family of musicians in town were always called the Klezmers (Musicians). Finally there was a tendency to create nicknames around personal features and peculiarities. The

ries—the respectable and the wretched, the devout and those beginning to doubt, Jews and Poles alike. The days of my youth I spent among them all, ever curious, insisting always on being at the center of things. From them I learned about the world even as we were, all of us in Kolbuszowa, set apart from it.

I was the favored child, the youngest of nine. It fell to me to stay, to carry on the name and the family business. But it was with misgivings that I considered such a future for myself. A thriving business would, I knew, produce a comfortable living and eventually an established position for me within our community. The security of familiar patterns, the supports of family, the bonds of tradition—these were assured. But would they be enough? Would they in fact be too much, too confining to a person as attracted as I was to the new, as tempted by the possibilities just then beginning to appear? Kolbuszowa's Jewish community, you see, took enormous pride in its faithful adherence to tradition. Resistance to change, a refusal to compromise—such was its response to the modern world.

But the prescriptions of the orthodox did not always prevail. Here and there questions were raised and challenges mounted. How I welcomed them! Here were the seeds of my own liberation, my chance to become what I otherwise could not be. But such thoughts I dared not express openly. My challenge became that of fitting in yet planning for the day that I might leave Kolbuszowa, growing attached but still preparing to sever my ties. In the end I suffered a violent, wrenching, painful separation, but by then Kolbuszowa was no longer my town, the one I am so anxious to describe. So let me introduce you and allow you to see the place I knew so well, the place I have always considered home wherever I have lived.

Neither a glance at a map nor a quick tour of our town would lead you to conclude that Kolbuszowa deserves any special attention. With 4,000 inhabitants it was hardly a bustling metropolis.

Blinder Avram could not see well; the Toybeh Melamed was a teacher with a hearing defect; Mechuginer Meyer was a mentally defective man who roamed around the town. We never saw this practice as cruel. Rather it brought them closer to us, established for them a fixed, rightful place in our universe.

With no railroad passing through or located nearby, it was isolated from and without easy access to Poland's centers of population. In its physical outlines it was far from impressive, lacking even the redeeming quality of quaintness. As for architectural wonders, Kolbuszowa was not the place to look. Many of the town's buildings were in disrepair, and even the intact ones were often depressingly drab.

But out in the Polish countryside appearances were not always what they seemed; metropolitan standards did not apply. Inhabitants of the region had reasons enough to hold Kolbuszowa in special regard, to depend on it and to consider their own well-being tied to its fortunes. Indeed, Kolbuszowa was very much at the center of things, at the hub of the political, economic, and religious life of the area. It was, above all, the county seat for sixty-five villages and four small towns, a designation that brought county offices and officials to the town along with those seeking their services or otherwise summoned to appear. To the town also came tens of thousands of peasants who lived on the surrounding lands. Kolbuszowa, you see, was a market town, a place where farm products and town goods were exchanged, a commercial center where by countless individual acts of buying and selling basic needs were met and livelihoods provided. Kolbuszowa was also home to the Catholic Church, presided over by Monsignor Dunajecki, a parish center whose priests ministered to the spiritual needs of the faithful and whose extensive cemetery and burial grounds offered a final resting place for the departed.

Kolbuszowa might well have developed quite differently during my years there if a projected railroad line had been built. At one time walls for a railway station were put in place, and a path was cleared for tracks from Rzeszow to Sandomierz. But then everything stopped when the Great War began in 1914. Nothing more was ever done. It would still take hours of travel by wagon to the railroad at Sedziszow, where the tracks headed off to Cracow and elsewhere.

Roads we had. Several of them in fact passed through Kolbuszowa and on to the larger towns of Rzeszow, Mielec, and Tarnow, repeatedly branching off into narrow paths before ending among the numerous peasant villages scattered about the countryside. Travel almost always meant wagon trips along narrow gravel roads, passable in dry, warm weather but otherwise a challenge to both man and beast, especially after rains or through the snowdrifts of winter, when wagon wheels gave way to sled runners.

Though the train never came, a bus did, connecting our town with Rzeszow and Sandomierz, important regional centers. The bus completed two round trips each day. Its midday return from Rzeszow was always a high point for us, for on board were the daily newspapers, Polish and Yiddish, from Warsaw, Lvov, and Cracow. Also by that time Kolbuszowa's two postmen were usually well along in their rounds. Additional news might arrive by radio, the word being spread by the three or four people in town with receivers. Unfortunately all were crystal sets and could never be relied on, especially, it seemed, when important events were unfolding. Precisely at such times they faded out or failed altogether.*

Let me not forget to tell you that Kolbuszowa was situated alongside a waterway, the River Nile no less, though it was scarcely deserving of so grand a name. Back at the end of the seventeenth century a count who owned much of the land in our area journeyed to the Middle East, visiting Egypt, the Sahara, and the Nile River Valley. His trip, one must conclude, left a powerful impression. Entering the town our river passed through a rather

---

*Yes, we had telephones in town, six if I remember correctly—three in private hands, one at the post office, and two associated with government offices. Most people never had occasion to use them. (Calls were costly. For the same price ten letters could be sent.) We made a call now and then for the business, usually in order to find out when a shipment of goods had been sent so that we could send wagons to the railroad station to pick them up and save on storage costs. Arranging calls across Poland was an elaborate, time-consuming procedure, often involving hours of waiting for a connection to be established and the other party to be summoned. Over the phone the quality of the sound was poor and scratchiness was common. Most users were convinced that unless they shouted into the headset their words would be lost. During the German occupation the phone assumed greater importance; I was able, being friendly with the operator, to learn of developments in Rzeszow, the administrative center of our area, and therefore could at times anticipate events in our town.

barren stretch of sandy yellow soil that reminded him of the Egyptian landscape. Accordingly on his return he directed that the stream be called the Nile, and the sandy area the Sahara.

As rivers go this one surely was of modest proportions, being no more than twenty yards across at its widest point near the town. Its water, however, could reach up to the ears, but only, it was solemnly declared, if you stood on your head! Still there was no ignoring the river. Peasants fished in it and brought their catch of small fish to the marketplace, where each fetched a few groschen. In warm weather elderly Jews often preferred its waters to those of the ritual bathhouse. Heading out of town on a Friday afternoon they reached a tree-lined section of the river. Here they undressed and waded in, the water enveloping their unclothed bodies except for their covered heads and long beards. They enjoyed no leisurely bath, however. If the authorities arrived and caught them, they would be fined for public nakedness. What use then having saved the few groschen, the charge at the bathhouse? On oppressively hot summer Sunday afternoons young girls from the town took to the river for relief. Modest they most certainly were, but the high aprons they wore into the water were noticeably deficient in the rear. Women's bathing suits (which evoked stern, disapproving looks from orthodox Jews) would not make their way to Kolbuszowa until the 1930s.

Those living near the Nile at times found it a convenient place to wash their clothes. But like its namesake the river had its less benign moods, times when it refused to stay within its banks. Every so often it flooded, damaging the nearby fields and sending water spreading across portions of the town.

Kolbuszowa rose out of the countryside but to no great height, the typical structure being a one-story stucco building. Any building of more than one story commanded attention, there being just a handful of them about the town. Most prominent was the Catholic Church, a tall building made more impressive by its steeple and surrounding stucco wall; others that deserve mention were City Hall, the synagogue, the courthouse, the county office building, and the Sokol [Falcon], the local headquarters of a national honorary society. The two public school buildings, one for boys, the other for girls, and the private Gymnasium were all well-constructed, as were the homes of some of the more prominent citizens of the town, notably Jakob Ekstein, Abraham Wagshal, and Dr. Leon Anderman.

In contrast stood large numbers of dilapidated houses, actually little more than fragile huts, occupied by Kolbuszowa's abundant poor. Not the least pretty or picturesque, Kolbuszowa was at best plain. Most buildings, to be sure, were relatively new, a good portion of the town having been rebuilt after fire destroyed large sections early in the century. Nonetheless their stucco walls were peeling, roofs were crumbling and in disrepair, and broken fences and windows were everywhere.

All across Poland it was the same, a situation one Prime Minister, General Slawoj Skladkovski, found most distressing. After visiting many towns in 1937, including a brief stopover in Kolbuszowa, he announced an ambitious national renewal project. Orders went forth that across the land fences and exterior walls were to be repaired, then painted. Beautification became the watchword of the day. But were painted walls and mended fences the answer to our problems in the late 1930s? Not according to "Crazy" Meyer of Kolbuszowa. While Skladkovski gave orders to paint fences, "Hitler," he said, "gave orders to build airplanes." But then Meyer, considered the town fool, was much given to bizarre and delusional utterances.

Conveniences were few and late in coming to Kolbuszowa. Of indoor plumbing little need be said; until 1938 no one in town knew of such things. In that year, however, Dr. Leon Anderman became the first to install this exceptional contrivance in his new home, perhaps the finest in Kolbuszowa. The rest of us made do with outhouses as we always had. And for this the peasants were grateful. Once a year homeowners in town invited them to clean out their cisterns. Oblige us they did, arriving in the evening, working through the night, then carting off what had been collected (mixed together with straw) in their wagons. Back home the waste was spread over the fields. Our need to dispose matched their need to fertilize, so everyone benefited.

Drinking water we obtained from the large community well located in the marketplace. Those who could afford it had their water delivered by the town's three water carriers. They knew their customers, understood the weekly needs of each family, and saw to it that the water in the barrels set inside their dwellings did not run out. A barrel's water level could be high but even so a water carrier might empty and refill the barrel if he discovered that live fish had recently been stored there. Just a sniff and he had his answer.

Safe passage through the night's darkness required skill. There was little in the way of public outdoor lighting in Kolbuszowa. In fact there were only three outdoor lamps in the entire town. One was located in the middle of the marketplace near the well; the second stood at a nearby square, where young people frequently gathered for conversation as long as the light stayed on; and the third illuminated an area adjacent to the City Hall. Later on a fourth light was added near the post office.

Each night at dusk Szymek the policeman moved from lamp to lamp, lighting them always in the same sequence, a crowd of children following his every move. All enjoyed watching this bringer of light. He first turned a crank to lower the fixture, then removed the glass and poured in the kerosene. As he lit each light we all cheered. The light, not very bright to begin with, ordinarily lasted till midnight or 1:00 A.M. After that, darkness descended. This being so, everyone learned how to get around in the dark. Ordinarily, though, a person out at night carried a light, usually a lighted candle in a glass container. Later storm lamps fueled with kerosene became available. Toward the end of the 1930s flashlights and batteries arrived. Such rapid changes in just a matter of years!

Small as it was, Kolbuszowa still contained several distinct areas, some little more than a block long, others stretching over several blocks. On the outskirts of town stood sprawling flour and lumber mills. An area of crooked streets around the synagogue, noticeably shabby in appearance, served as a magnet for those Jews who put great value on living as close as possible to their house of prayer and study. Butchers and bakers occupied separate streets on which fellow tradesmen lived and worked. Then there was New Town, an area exclusively Polish; the name was in no way misleading, the houses there having been built after World War I. There working-class Poles, especially shoemakers, lived. There were several lovely tree-lined streets with fine houses and well-kept gardens on the fringes of town, the residences of well-to-do Poles and some Jews.

Finally there was the marketplace, the most vital section of Kolbuszowa. A very large area was enclosed on all four sides by one- and two-story houses. Located here were a good many of the wholesale and retail establishments of the town, and also Kolbuszowa's only hotel and several of its taverns. Here as elsewhere people mostly lived and worked together in the same spaces, living quarters being adjacent to or coextensive with the workshop or retail shop. One was always at home and always in the store or workshop.

Every Tuesday the marketplace became the commercial center of the region as thousands poured into it from the surrounding countryside to buy and to sell, to look and to talk. All day long the pace of activity was feverish. Only as evening drew close did the area begin to clear; peasants headed back to the villages and vendors packed their wares, preparing for the journey that same night to yet another town and still another market. A week would pass before the marketplace once again became its exuberant self, resuming its role as the economic lifeline of Kolbuszowa and the surrounding region.

Except for the hustle, bustle, and clamor of commerce on market day Kolbuszowa was normally a quiet town. No factory whistles, locomotive blasts, or automobile horns upset the general tranquillity. What was there to hear other than the occasional shouts of wagon drivers urging their horses on or the sounds of children playing in the schoolyard during recess? Church bells rang every day at 12 noon,* and in the event of severe illness priests

---

*Throughout the month of May, each day at 6 P.M. a bugler mounted the church steeple to play a special series of notes recalling a dramatic episode in Polish history centuries before. The original event occurred in Cracow, at St. Mary's Cathedral. A bugler appeared at the top of the church to alert the people to a Tartar invasion; but before he could complete the warning signal, he was struck by an arrow. For that reason the bugler in Kolbuszowa stopped abruptly,

on their way to administer last rites to the afflicted shook a bell as they passed through the town in a wagon. In our town no one ever complained about noise.

One sound there was, however, that never failed to strike fear into all of us—the two trumpet blasts that signaled fire. Nothing was more chilling. Not a townsman was ignorant of the great blazes that had devastated Kolbuszowa in the past. That the town was hundreds of years old but its buildings were mostly of recent construction was no mystery. Fires had repeatedly swept buildings away over the years. One blaze, early in the twentieth century, had wiped out nearly the entire town. Accounts of that period never failed to date events before or after the Great Fire. We did have a volunteer fire department, even some pumping equipment, but we lacked horses. Only by commandeering a passing wagon could men and equipment arrive at the scene of a fire. That worked well enough during the day, when there were wagons and horses about town, but the nights were a problem. A trumpet sounding after dark brought almost everyone outside to try to spot the location of the fire.* Especially at night all felt threatened.

Except for Tuesday's market, weekdays in Kolbuszowa revealed much the same pattern of activity. At daybreak local vendors climbed onto peasant wagons bound for markets in nearby towns. Soon afterward Jewish men hurried off to the synagogue in time for one of the morning prayer services. As 8 o'clock approached the pace quickened, with children heading off to school and people traveling to Rzeszow hastening to the corner of the marketplace nearest the City Hall to catch the bus. Somewhat later, maybe ten to fifteen people gathered in front of the post office, where they

---

leaving the series of notes uncompleted. He did, however, remain there, and after a pause proceeded to play several religious melodies celebrating the month of May.

*Some of those who appeared on the street could expect to be pressed into service pushing the fire wagon or forced to operate the pumps. Since mostly Jews lived in the area where the fire pumps were stored, several of them, dressed only in nightshirts, might be seen on occasions where horses were unavailable, huffing and puffing, pushing and pulling the fire equipment through the dark streets. Often we simply looked on, watching a distant glow from a neighboring village, hoping the fire there could be contained.

expected or hoped to receive a special letter or package. Eager, impatient, they would not wait for the postman to make his rounds, but would intercept him as he emerged and request their mail. Among those gathered were always one or two especially sad souls who arrived almost every day to await a letter from a family member—maybe a son, daughter, or husband who had left Kolbuszowa. Only rarely were they rewarded. Still they came early each morning, waiting, hoping for word.

The early morning "rush" over, the town turned quiet once more; empty streets were the rule. Peasants either on foot or aboard wagons might be seen now and then heading through town to attend the courts, visit a doctor, or take care of some business or shopping, but otherwise few people passed by. Most people remained at home, a place that during the day became a workshop or a store. The most notable exceptions were the butchers, who all headed off to work at adjoining shops located between the Public Baths and the City Hall. Butchers, tailors, bakers, and shoemakers generally had work to do in their shops. Storekeepers, on the other hand, mostly sat and waited. With customers generally scarce and often with little to sell in the store, they faced long, depressing periods of inactivity. It saddened me greatly to see them sitting there waiting in their stores. How they managed day after day I never really understood. Many merely went through the motions and didn't manage at all.

Of all the people who on occasion passed through Kolbuszowa—marketplace vendors, itinerant beggars, visiting rabbis, theatrical performers—none made so great an impression as the gypsies. Several times each year, most often in the summer months, bands of gypsies would appear. Word of their arrival spread quickly ("Gypsies in town!"), a fact soon confirmed by townspeople who witnessed their covered wagons (ordinarily between twenty and twenty-five) rolling into a wooded area on the outskirts of town. Usually the children were the first to venture out to watch as the gypsies set up camp. They were a sight—the oversized mustaches of the men, the big, baggy pants, the red kerchiefs, the boots, the earrings, the long, flowing skirts worn by remarkably large-bosomed women. There was no mistaking the "king" of the gypsies, the unquestioned leader of the band. Neither could one overlook the exceptional quality of the gypsies' well-cared-for horses.

The gypsies came to Kolbuszowa mostly on business; altogether they might stay two to three weeks. In addition to crafting jewelry they also manufactured copper utensils, producing pots and pans of fine quality that they sold on market day. They also bought and traded horses; but given their reputation for shrewdness, plus the fact that they soon would be leaving town, many people were reluctant to deal with them. Some gypsies offered entertainment, hoping onlookers would show their appreciation with a few coins. Trained bears and monkeys performed tricks of all sorts in the marketplace, and musicians played stirring gypsy music that was always well-received. Meanwhile gypsy fortune-tellers were busy spinning out wondrous tales of the future (although when we listened in they seemed always to tell the same story, of how this girl would meet a tall military man with a saber . . .), and others performing card tricks were attracting curious but wary audiences. At night the gypsies would be back in town in the marketplace area, strolling from house to house, playing their fiddles, basses, and tambourines, making music that rarely failed to bring people out of their houses (and reaching into their pockets for a few groschen).

The gypsies brought excitement, color, and entertainment to Kolbuszowa, but given their reputation for thievery they also made people uneasy. Was it just coincidence that often after they left, items seemed to be missing? Was it not foul play the day some very pretty gypsy women visited several stores in the marketplace? They were hoping, they said, to exchange paper currency for two-zloty silver coins, which they intended to use to create jewelry pieces. The women all wore low-cut blouses, partly exposing their ample bosoms. All managed to bend forward sufficiently so that the shopkeepers, however strict their religious upbringing, were tempted to let their eyes drift in that direction. With money drawers open somehow these women were able to reach in and help themselves to a portion of the contents. Little surprise that several businessmen reported money missing after these visits.

It was also accepted that gypsies would on occasion steal horses. More than once after the gypsies departed, complaints about them came streaming in to the authorities. In one instance that I recall, the police chased after a gypsy caravan, led all the wagons back into the marketplace, and proceeded to search for missing goods. I don't remember anything being found; but I do recollect the gypsies rebuking the police for accepting the word of Jews, who were, after all, the killers of Christ. So it was that the gypsies, both when they came and when they departed, managed often to become the center of attention.

The gypsies notwithstanding, daily patterns typically varied little. But we did not lack for special occasions. There was of course the Sabbath, which lifted us out of the ordinary, allowing us to set aside the burdens of the week. It was a day of rest, of renewal, a day of prayer and of looking one's best. The elaborate preparations, the festive Friday night and midday Saturday meals, the gathering of family and friends—these made for a day that was eagerly awaited, altogether different from the rest. For me it was the long walks with my friends that stand out and set the Sabbath apart. Such joy it was to stroll the length of town (the walk taking perhaps twenty minutes) and see almost every other young person in Kolbuszowa. As I grew older my eyes fell often on groups of young girls shuffling past who glanced shyly at us before passing on. To stop and talk would have been unacceptable to our elders, and so we didn't. But how I envied those whose beliefs and courage led them to disregard such restrictions! Boys and girls walking together, some even holding hands—truly a revelation.

Although the following day, Sunday, was the Christian Sabbath, Jews regarded it as the first workday of the week—a complication eased by certain adjustments. Local law required that businesses be closed, and they were—at least for those passing by the front door. In reality it was business as usual, except that customers arrived at open back doors, a practice condoned by the authorities. Religious holidays, however, could produce strains between Polish Catholics and Jews. We Jews were never comfortable at Christmas or Easter time or during other major Christian celebrations and parish festivals; these were times when our separateness was most pronounced, times when we imagined the engines of anti-Semitism were being fueled. On the other hand, our many religious holidays over the year—Rosh Hashanah, Yom Kippur, Passover, Shavuoth, Succoth—produced confusion and inconvenience for our Christian neighbors. Uncertain about the Jewish calendar, they were on occasion taken by surprise during holiday periods when stores they expected to be open were not. And since Jews operated most of the businesses in Kolbuszowa, the disruption of commercial activity was no small matter. It was easy enough to blame a peasant for forgetting about the holiday and traveling to town for market day, but what of the resentment such disappointments surely produced?

Poles and Jews were together, however, in celebrating our great national holidays in Kolbuszowa. On May 3 [the anniversary of the Polish Constitution], November 11 [Independence Day], and March 19 [the name day of Józef Piłsudski], almost everyone felt a common pride, shared a sense of national unity. Festivities on those days reflected this spirit. Assemblies and special events took place in the church and the synagogue, in the public schools, and on the athletic fields. All turned out to watch the parades through town and to listen to and applaud the speeches and speechmakers. Through the streets marched the two Polish bands followed by the Jewish band, all playing the same patriotic songs. Sports on occasion could produce a similar sense of unity. In Kolbuszowa sports mostly meant soccer, and it was not taken lightly. Three teams contended for superiority in town, and rivalries, as we shall see, were keen. But when Kolbuszowa took the field against an opponent from another town it assembled a squad recruited from all of its teams. These athletes represented all classes, all citizens, and were the pride of Kolbuszowa.*

---

*By the early 1930s there were three soccer teams in town: one representing Kolbuszowa itself, clearly the best of the three; another consisting of students from the Gymnasium, whose two best players were Jews; and the Jewish team, the Maccabees. Our attention usually focused on the two very excellent Jewish players (from Rzeszow) on the Gymnasium team. We lamented the fact that when the Maccabees contended against the Gymnasium, these two became "traitors" and played with the latter. We felt much better, however, when in matches

Joys and sorrows, expected or not, also turned us from everyday matters. A priest borne by a carriage moves rapidly through town, in his hand a bell that he rings repeatedly, prompting people to kneel in the street as he passes by. All know that a fellow human being, a member of the community, at that moment stands close to death's door. A funeral procession leaves the synagogue, the plain pine box carried aloft by mourners, one of whom, cup in hand, shakes coins within and summons all onlookers to charity and compassion. Weddings, by contrast, lift the spirits. Should the groom's family be arriving from outside Kolbuszowa, word of their presence passes quickly through town as if to remind all to be on their best behavior. An outdoor ceremony under the *chupah* [wedding canopy], followed by an indoor feast, concludes as a community affair as all are invited in to attend the evening's comic and dramatic entertainments.

Joys and sorrows might mingle in uneasy balance amid uncertainty and expectation. Individuals or families leaving for America or Palestine diminished the community, often symbolized its defeated hopes. But their departure also produced a sense of renewal and the realization that a larger community was in the process of being formed and strengthened. With family, friends and the curious often numbering in the hundreds, we gathered first at the marketplace near the well, then marched to the post office, where Freifeld's wagon was waiting for the trip to the railroad. If the people were leaving for Palestine (not America), Hazamir, the Jewish band, would accompany us playing Hebrew melodies. We then said our goodbyes, wondering all the time whether one day we would ourselves set sights on a place far beyond the borders of Kolbuszowa.

---

between Kolbuszowa and the Maccabees they joined in with the other Jewish players, which meant an occasional victory for the Maccabees. The two were also members of the Kolbuszowa all-star team, which, despite its best efforts, was never able to beat the superior athletes representing Rzeszow. Sundays, the day when most soccer games were played, often were sheer torture for me. I wanted so much to be at the games, but this was also the day when in religious school we received the main lesson for the week. To miss this lesson put a student at a distinct disadvantage for days on end. There were times, however, when that just didn't seem to matter. Almost always the game was worth it.

Even as they left us many signaled their intention to maintain relations, to serve in a new capacity. What precious moments when their letters arrived and were read aloud, once, twice, repeatedly, each sentence an opportunity for extended comment, for questions often left unanswered. What joy when, in addition to letters, there came packages, almost always containing clothes. These clothes would, we knew, distinguish us in the community, send a message that new bonds had been forged, that guardians of our welfare, however distant, could be summoned.

Time passed until one day word would come to expect a visitor, a former townsman returning for a stay. Such anxious anticipation and lengthy preparations! When finally the day arrives it is filled with tearful reunions, endless exchanges and mutual assessments. So much news to pass on, so many questions begging for answers. The visitor is, it's plain to see, not the same person who left years ago. The gifts he brings offer clear proof that the fates have been kind. Word of his presence circulates rapidly about town. Many come round to press him for news of overseas friends and relatives. He remains for days the center of attention, the unchallenged source of worldly wisdom. When he leaves, life resumes its regular course, except that he has left some people with an enlarged view of life's possibilities, suggested a different path that they might in time themselves consider.

Those who returned for visits had improved themselves by leaving Kolbuszowa. That's certainly the message we received as we accepted the gifts and money they offered us. What reasons had we to doubt their success? Life was anything but easy in Kolbuszowa. It almost certainly had to be better elsewhere. Making a living—very few wanted much more out of life than that—was for most of us a constant struggle. Certainly the peasants understood that only too well, since their small plots of land were barely able to sustain them. At certain times of the year, before the harvest was in, survival for them came to be measured a day at a time. Potatoes, cabbage, sour milk, beans, a piece of bread—only these basic foods kept them from starvation. Pigs, chickens, eggs, butter, and milk they also produced, but could not themselves afford to eat. Such products had to be sold in town so that there might be money for taxes, money for kerosene, seeds, shoes, cloth, and kerchiefs, money also for whiskey and beer. And when the land at times became stubborn, the margin of existence grew even narrower, especially when plots were divided among one's children. Beyond the land there was little or no work to be had, few jobs to soften the crush of bad times. And most times were bad times. What of the celebrated patience of the peasants? A mounting restiveness, a willingness to act together and bring about changes— such signs were unmistakable. How would it turn out? Who would be caught up, perhaps swept away, in this coming wave of change? When Kolbuszowa became the scene of mass peasant rallies in the late 1930s, new trials and troubles surely lay ahead.

In town also, life was hard. Nothing came without effort. Everything had to be attended to, usually each day: basic matters, endlessly repeated. Otherwise life could not go on. There had to be wood; without it there'd be no cooking, no heat. Dry wood was relatively easy to light; wood that was green and moist was a challenge—it smoked and gave off little heat. But the poor had no other choice. Interiors could be illuminated, but only at the cost of repeated effort. One had first to have the money to buy the kerosene. Then the lamp needed to be filled, lit, later refilled, the wick replaced every so often.

Water we had, as I've already mentioned, in the town well located in the center of the marketplace; but it had to be first pumped up, and buckets had to be filled and carried home. Water carriers could be hired for a price; but many could not afford the price and fetched their own water, a tolerable task in good weather but a severe trial otherwise. In the winter, for example, water in the well often froze, producing an irregular supply. Then, too, the water carriers did not arrive daily to refill one's barrel, so day after day one's water stood. At times live fish were put in the water barrel to swim about until the next fish meal for the Sabbath. This same water was then used for cooking, washing, and cleaning, notwithstanding the fish odors unmistakably present.

Outhouses, as the name implies, were outside our houses, conditions there varying with the weather. (One always prepared toilet paper in advance by tearing newspapers into strips.) In the winter one dared not linger. The nights were another problem. Only rarely were outhouses used at night. Instead we performed in pots, placed these under our beds, then tended to them when we arose. Many a morning did we awaken amid distinctly foul odors.

Cleanliness we valued, but achieving it was a real struggle. There was no shortage of rats; only the presence of cats in practically every Jewish home kept the rat population under control. The struggle against bedbugs and roaches was never-ending, victories few and rarely complete. Housecleaning was a less demanding task if for no other reason than that there were few rooms to clean, most families occupying just one or two. Nevertheless floors were a challenge because the streets of town often were muddy or dusty.

In a large majority of households food was always scarce. People worried all the time about having money to buy food, even in small amounts, and about having enough food, particularly for the Sabbath. The food that was on hand had to be doled out carefully, made to last, extended in all manner of ways, but it also had to be quickly consumed because there were few ways to keep food from spoiling. In the poorest of houses "false soup" was often the order of the day, with garlic or onion added to boiling water to give it a little taste. Many meals consisted of little more than a plate of potatoes or cereal, a piece of bread rubbed with onion or garlic and a cup of tea, chickory, or sometimes coffee. (With so little to eat, how long could meals take? Leisurely meals were possible only on the Sabbath.) The concern over food mirrored the general scarcity that was everywhere to be seen. Life was hard because so much around us was crude and old-fashioned. Life was harsh because there was rarely enough to go around.

Hard times and desperate circumstances were only too common in our town. I would estimate that half the Jewish population was impoverished, living under the most trying conditions, surviving only by the slimmest of margins. This included many who were businessmen. They had stores, set out goods for sale, but, alas, saw few if any customers in the course of a day or even a week. Others were struggling middlemen trudging from village to village buying small amounts of eggs, butter, or grain from peasants, collecting these goods, then selling them to a wholesaler in town. Profit margins were small, so small in fact that by the end of the week funds were exhausted. Only by borrowing money, usually from more substantial townsmen such as my father (at no interest), were such traders able to keep going. Each week brought the same round of hand-to-mouth existence. Some people stayed at home laboring at a sewing machine all day and long into the night, assembling shirts or pants or stitching the tops of shoes. Piecework rates were never generous, nor was there even the assurance of steady work.

How all these people got along I never really understood, especially when most had to support large families. But they made do with very, very little—the barest of living quarters, one set of patched clothes, the most basic of foods, supplemented by frequent acts of kindness and charity from fellow Jews. Distributions of potatoes and firewood, food supplies for the holidays, money and clothes sent by relatives overseas—such gifts could make the difference, avert catastrophe. Yet however unfortunate the poor might be, most were not tragic figures. Many were warm, friendly, dare I say contented, people who expected little from life but were content to be alive, to have their families, and to find comfort in their God and in their religious obligations. Not blaming the world or cursing their fate—there was dignity in their endurance.* Not that a change for the better would be unwelcome, but

---

*This dignity extended even to several mentally defective people who could be seen almost every day about the town. (Those inclined to be violent we usually sent out of Kolbuszowa to hospitals or asylums.) It is true that children often taunted them, even on occasion threw stones at them; but always doors opened when they knocked, and people saw to it that they had enough to eat. Several belonged to one family. There was Rachel, ever smiling, endlessly embarrassing boys by embracing them in public, professing her love for them and predicting they would one day be married. There was also her cousin, "Crazy" Meyer, a young man of talent who composed original humorous topical songs of exceptional merit. Meyer, however, always complained of hearing noises in his head, which he tried to silence by smearing his head with grease. Unlike Rachel and Meyer, another brother, Yossel, though not normal, had a job, as one of the three water carriers in town. Also there was Stoj, a gifted young man who had attended the Gymnasium in town. A crisis in his life—a girlfriend ended their

it was an unlikely prospect, most sensed, so long as they remained in Kolbuszowa. (Unless a "good" marriage produced more comfortable circumstances.) And so a goodly number headed off to other parts of Poland, or left the country for America or Palestine. But most stayed, some simply unable to leave, others fearing the risks, the sacrifice of community, the persistent struggle to maintain a tradition and a faith.

On the other hand, half the Jews of Kolbuszowa did manage, some (perhaps 10 percent) quite well. These were the businessmen, shopkeepers, retailers, and wholesalers who did not lack for customers; the bakers, butchers, tailors, and shoemakers whose services were in demand; and some professional people—doctors, dentists, and lawyers—whose special knowledge and skills did not go unrewarded. Such people were able ordinarily to make a living, which, along with giving to charity, supporting the rabbi, and finding suitable marriage partners for their children, represented for them all that was of real substance in this world. Some set aside inherited orthodoxies and found in Zionism a new secular faith, but most saw no reason to question what had always been. Indeed, a good many saw no special merit in their success in business compared to the rewards and joys of religious study and prayer. Their great hope was that a daughter of theirs might marry a scholar, a man who each day devoted himself to the greater understanding of religious texts. It would be an honor to support such a man in this endeavor for all the years of his life.

For those able to make a living, life in Kolbuszowa had its plea-

---

relationship—caused him to fall apart and never recover. All he did each day was walk and walk endlessly around the marketplace. Children ran after him and shouted for him to stop ("Stoj! Stoj!"), and he would stop until they "permitted" him to continue.

Everyone in town knew of "Bulbes" [the local word for potatoes], who was forever begging potatoes from everyone he encountered. For some reason children in town mistreated him terribly. They beat him, stoned him, left him with scars about his body. Never did he complain or fight back. I remember the day he died and how sorry I felt for him. After his death, townspeople reflected on the way he had been abused yet never complained concluded that he was likely to have been one of the "thirty-six righteous people" placed on earth to prevent God from destroying it out of anger and despair at people's wickedness. That such a man had lived among us—it was an awesome realization.

sures, comforts, and rewards. Always there was enough to eat on the table, and on the Sabbath and holidays there was food in abundance and tasty food indeed. Dry wood, enough for well into the following year, stood stacked up outside, and inside kerosene lamps with large wicks provided effective, cheerful illumination. Clothes for the Sabbath and other special occasions there were for each family member, garments usually tailor-made, distinctive outfits that could scarcely go unnoticed. Outside the home there existed a true community in which joys could be shared, griefs lightened, and mutual support exchanged. An easy familiarity prevailed—first names, nicknames. Family matters were freely discussed; it was hard to keep a secret in Kolbuszowa. Those who made a living had standing in the community, positions of honor and responsibility in the synagogue. They gathered together with their Polish counterparts in Kolbuszowa, confident, as successful men of affairs usually are, in the leadership they were expected and able to provide.

I have been speaking so far mostly of my fellow Jews, but their story is only a part of the doings in Kolbuszowa, actually only half the story. Of the approximately 4,000 residents of the town, half were Polish Jews and half Polish Catholics. This balance held out at least the promise of mutual tolerance, even acceptance. Such apparently was the wish of an earlier generation of townspeople, an intention symbolized in the official seal they created for Kolbuszowa, which in my day was still prominently displayed on the front of our City Hall. There was no mistaking the message here: two men clasping hands, one a Pole, the other a Jew, a Jewish star on the bottom, a Polish eagle and a crusader's cross on the top. True, it acknowledged a division within Kolbuszowa, and certainly it portrayed Jews as separate from other Poles; but given the usual hostility Jews encountered, this was a marvel of moderation, a remarkable gesture of recognition.

And I suppose for a time a certain mutual respect prevailed, but I must tell you that what we experienced in my day was something rather different. Actually it was not a simple situation, not without its contradictions. The Poles both disliked us and depended upon us. We lived among them but not with them. Each day brought countless dealings between Jews and Poles, but then we went off in our separate ways. Though we were equal in numbers, no one doubted who held power. We did not challenge, we did not question; we tried only to live in peace, to fashion a measure of permanence and predictability amid circumstances that were often precarious.

Relations could proceed without overt incident much of the time. Economic ties and daily necessities usually operated to keep tensions and hostilities below the surface. Every peasant had his "Jew," a shopkeeper he relied on for the goods he needed. The relationship had developed over time and had produced a satisfactory degree of mutual understanding and trust. In the marketplace Jewish vendors supplied many basic items and purchased much of the produce and farm products brought there for sale. Out in the villages Jews lived much the way Poles did, resulting in unusually close relations between the two. Together Jews and Poles celebrated Poland's national holidays in a spirit of unity and fellowship. Men of standing in Kolbuszowa, whether Jews or Poles, clearly commanded the respect of all inhabitants.

But we knew our place. If there was any doubt what that was, it was dispelled, at least for my generation, on May 6, 1919, when the rumors proved true and thousands of peasants descended upon Kolbuszowa; the town experienced its very own pogrom (9 Jews killed, 200 wounded). Death and destruction cut a swath through our community;* my father, among others, lost all that he worked so hard to build. The authorities investigated; two persons who had been involved in the murders and general mayhem were executed, and one, Sus by name, a most vicious anti-Semite he was, received two years in jail. Yet on his release he returned to his residence in Kolbuszowa and resumed his dealings in the

---

*Yet one Jewish woman about to give birth was carried right on her bed by peasants out of harm's way. The baby, Nussin Schrek, born that very day in the midst of this terrible violence, was for the rest of his life known to us as Nussin Pogromchik. I was born one year later, May 6, 1920, and nearly died the next month when barely six weeks old during a smallpox epidemic. Indeed I was given up for dead, my body placed in a makeshift coffin (a wooden yeast box). Just when the box was to be taken for burial sounds were heard from within. I was, they discovered, still alive. Surely this was a miracle.

town, many of them with Jews. He was accepted once more as a member of the community in good standing. When his son Kazik later became an anti-Semitic bully, it surprised no one.*

We kept mostly apart. We had our synagogue, they had their church; we celebrated our religious holidays, and they gathered separately for theirs. Intermarriage? Conversion? It almost never happened. We had our political and social organizations, and they had theirs; the only exception was the Town Council, where, however, Jewish representatives were expected to follow the lead of the Poles. Poles marched in their band, Jews in theirs. Kolbuszowa supported a soccer team on which there were no Jews; Jews organized their own squad. In the marketplace area nearly all the residents were Jewish; in the district known as New Town all residents were Poles. The town's volunteer fire department had not a single Jew, nor did the police.

There was, we knew, no point in aspiring to a position with the government at any level; nor was there much hope of gaining access to the professions, especially when laws passed preventing Jews from changing their names. No Jews, for example, taught in the town's two public schools or in the private Gymnasium. (All schools remained in session six days a week including Saturday, the Jewish Sabbath, though no Jew could attend on that day.) Though relatively few Jews aspired to become army officers, the officer corps pointedly rejected Jews. Jews were represented on the Town Council in Kolbuszowa, but never would a Jew be mayor of our town. Discrimination was a matter of public policy; Jews had come to expect it as a matter of course. In Poland a Jew was always considered a Jew first and foremost, never a Pole.

But discrimination too often encouraged more destructive activity. Attacks against Jews were not uncommon and almost always went unpunished. Jewish youngsters expected periodically to be beaten up by Poles. I was attacked and, as you will see, on

---

*Neither was it very surprising that Poles in Kolbuszowa later composed a song commemorating this bloody encounter. Using a familiar church tune for the month of May, they sang a song that included these ominous words: "Beat the Jew, kill the Jew, for the Pole it's a pleasant day. . . . Third of May, Sixth of May, break all Jewish windows."

one occasion even stoned. At wedding celebrations young Poles delighted in pulling the hair of Jewish girls arriving for the festivities. In the marketplace Jews young and old were assaulted by groups of Poles who insisted that Jews relinquish the sidewalks to them. When the Kolbuszowa soccer team played the Jewish team, our players were subjected to consistently rough treatment on the field and Jewish spectators were attacked in the stands. During draft month, when peasant boys streamed into Kolbuszowa for physical exams, they delighted in overturning wagons and beating up Jews they met along the way. In Kolbuszowa a Jew could never be safe.

In the face of this hostility what did we Jews do? Not much, I grant you. We knew, of course, that complaints brought no changes. We thanked God that things were not worse, that it was still possible to lead lives that to most of us seemed almost normal, at least for Jews. We kept to ourselves as much as we could and took comfort in the support we provided one another. But I should tell you that my brothers and I never could get used to it, could not find it in ourselves simply to turn the other cheek. So we took action on more than one occasion and turned on our tormentors in a way they certainly did not expect. Later I shall speak of the effect this had on the morale of the Jews here.

As the 1930s wore on, Jewish morale needed to be bolstered. All around Kolbuszowa peasants by the tens of thousands were organizing against the government, attempting to establish producer cooperatives while boycotting the marketplace in town. Their actions were aimed against the government and not expressly at Jews, but we knew it was just a matter of time before we would feel the force of their anger. I well remember watching from the attic of my house as 40,000 to 50,000 peasants rallied in the marketplace. Not a Jew was to be seen. Certainly it was prudent to keep out of sight, with the situation potentially so explosive (though rally leaders actually met in our house to devise strategy!).

These intensifying pressures forced those Jews still living in the smaller surrounding villages to leave their homes and take up residence in Kolbuszowa. Off in Warsaw leading government officials and members of the Catholic hierarchy continued to mutter darkly about the Jewish problem. The need was urgent, they said, for Poland to regain control of its economy and reduce sharply the number of Jews permitted to remain in the country. Nor were any of us unaware of developments in Germany. We all spoke German, had access to German newspapers, and knew Jews who had fled from or been forced out of Germany. What we knew, what we suspected, was chilling; we feared greatly for the future.

Still Poland, we were told, could repel any German forces sent against our country. We were confident that England, France, and certainly the United States would if necessary come to our aid. But such hopes, frail at best, shattered in the summer of 1939 as our radios began cackling out the news that Polish armed forces, battling alone, were being pushed back, unable to halt the on-rushing German assault. Polish soldiers and Jewish refugees early in September began streaming into Kolbuszowa, the soldiers looting our shops as they retreated. One week after the war began a German tank rattled into town. The next day Kolbuszowa fell to the invaders. My world, the world all of us in Kolbuszowa had created and sustained for so long, was about to collapse. My people were about to face the severest of trials.

Family Matters

I had the "perfect" family. That was not necessarily my view but rather how most people in Kolbuszowa regarded the Saleschützes. We were considered exemplary, a model Jewish family. In fact we had much to be thankful for. To my mother were born nine children, of whom all survived (although as mentioned I was given up for dead shortly after birth and recovered only at the last moment). We were well off, the owners of an established general wholesale store that provided for our needs and comforts. My father was a respected member of the community and exceedingly active in town affairs. A pillar of the synagogue, he was a faithful follower of Jewish orthodoxy, ever mindful of its requirements. My mother did what was expected, keeping house, feeding and clothing all of us, and helping in the business. She was devoted to her children, loving them without exception, keeping their needs uppermost in her mind. When it came time for my older sisters to be married, proper suitors were selected and most desirable matches arranged. Even then we remained close; all three sisters remained in Kolbuszowa and continued to work in our business. There was, you see, good reason to consider our family specially blessed.

But our family also was caught up in the tides of change that were gradually altering our small town. The traditionalists and the orthodox rejected all new developments outright, condemned those who adjusted to the "new world," considered them "spoiled."

But many others, even if they didn't welcome change or even understand it fully, absorbed bits and pieces here and there, and in so doing furthered a process destined to transform Kolbuszowa in ways never before imagined. Traditional Jewish practices were abandoned by secular critics and by others tired of the network of restrictions, prohibitions, and obligations associated with orthodoxy. A change in clothing style or haircut, a cigarette dangling from the lips—in these ways one could trace the muted rebellion under way. Then, too, romance was in the air. Matchmakers grumbled, parents resisted, but many young boys and girls were intent on going their own way, preferred dating to dictation when it came time to select partners for life. So in these and in many other ways the modern era entered Kolbuszowa long after it had settled in elsewhere. In my family much remained as it had been for generations, but there was no mistaking the meaning of those distinctly novel attitudes, unconventional behaviors, and unexpected directions many of us began to pursue. Would we have remained the "perfect family" had the process been allowed to proceed? That we'll never know.

My father's father was born and spent his life on an estate not far from Kolbuszowa. The estate belonged to Jacob Eckstein, certainly the most estimable Jew in our town. Naftali Saleschütz, my grandfather, served as manager, which brought him into close relations with many peasants who worked in the fields belonging to Eckstein and gave him a sense of connection with the soil. (The Jews had lived in the area since the sixteenth century; they were originally farmers but had in time moved off to the towns and villages and lost direct contact with the land.) Estate revenues came from farming and from toll collections. When a public road crossed private lands the owner retained the right to erect barriers and collect fees from wagons and drivers passing through, a most happy arrangement for the Eckstein estate.

My grandmother, Gela, had her own business to attend to on the estate. Strictly religious people would never drink milk unless they knew how it was produced and handled. It was a short walk beyond the outskirts of town to where the peasants kept their cows, and my mother and I took this walk daily. We brought along a clean bucket, one used only for milk, and saw to it that the milk flowed directly in and was not contaminated by contact with anything else. I went along to help, also for a taste of the fresh milk. Such a treat, the warm, sweet liquid with the foam I so much enjoyed, all of which my mother assured me was very healthy.*

Understanding the concern orthodox Jews had about pure milk makes it easy to appreciate the service provided by my grandmother. She could be trusted to milk the cows and properly fill the buckets and jars, relieving people of the need for on-site inspection. Accordingly she attracted numerous customers in Kolbuszowa, many of them friends dating back to the time she had lived there before marrying my grandfather. Every morning she dispatched a wagon from the estate into town, with the jars of each family marked and filled with milk. On Sundays she came to Kolbuszowa herself to deliver milk, along with butter and cheese that had been produced from the extra milk, and to collect money she was owed. Always, however, collections lagged, customers being often unable to pay. What did she do? She did nothing except continue her deliveries. Hers was a business notably deficient in business principles. Few people were more kindhearted.

There were seven children in all in my father's family: two girls and five boys, of whom my father was the youngest. My grandfather arranged that his children be taught on the estate along with the children of certain local peasants, and for that purpose hired both a Polish tutor and a teacher for Jewish subjects. As a result my father learned Polish, unlike most Jews, who, in the absence of public schools, tended to speak Polish haltingly or not at all. That fact, along with his early and close attachment to the land, probably explains why all his life my father was a Polish patriot,

---

*Even "healthier" was goat's milk. Often when I was not well my mother prescribed this remedy. This involved no excursion to a peasant's farm; instead peasants selling goat's milk came to town almost nightly and knocked on doors looking for customers. Orders were filled on the spot. The peasant brought along a stool on which she sat and milked the goat right in front of your doorstep, directly into your glass. On a given evening you might see several children lined up waiting for their glasses to be filled. Goat's milk, as I recall, was not as sweet as cow's milk, but it was certainly easier to swallow than any medicine we might otherwise have been obliged to take.

perhaps the most patriotic Polish Jew in all of Kolbuszowa. All his brothers and sisters left for America in the latter part of the nineteenth century. He alone remained in Poland.

All my father did was to leave the estate for Kolbuszowa, where he was sent to study in the house of the distinguished scholar and teacher Leibush Avrumalis. Study he did, for he was a serious, intelligent young boy; Leibush Berl accepted only such boys into his classes. But my father did more than study; he also took notice of Leibush's daughter Esther.* In 1900, when he was eighteen and she twenty, they were married. He established a small retail shop in town and managed each year to improve his fortunes. He was helped by his previous ties to the estate and the peasants there, for they now patronized his store, preferring to deal with someone they knew. He also benefited from his growing involvement in community and town affairs. An inveterate joiner, he devoted much energy to the organizational life of the town. So his customers increased because Isak Saleschütz became a name known and respected around Kolbuszowa.

That my father would have a large family was no surprise. Just about everyone who could did, peasants primarily because children were valued for working the land, most Jews because their religion encouraged fertility and viewed large families as a blessing from God. Both groups also realized that in old age who but the children would be there to provide support and comfort? Smaller families there were in Kolbuszowa, primarily among the Polish civil servants, but most Jews then would have been disappointed with a household of fewer than five children. My father and mother raised nine, born between 1901 and 1920. To provide for a household of this size was a formidable though not exceptional task. Unless business was good the burden of supporting such a family could be severe indeed.

The hard work, the progress that had been made, all of it was swept away during the Great War. Not at first, though. In the early stages my father and two other merchants in town prospered,

---

*Later on those eager to find fault with my father pointed to these years and hinted at indiscretions. While he was supposedly occupied with his studies, they charged, in truth he was paying undue attention to Esther.

thanks to being officially authorized by the Austro-Hungarian government to distribute sugar, which was rationed at the time. The "Sugar King"—that's what they called him as he doled out this precious commodity to those with valued ration cards. Because not all people in the region claimed their sugar allotment, the remaining sugar was eagerly sought by persons who hoped to profit from reselling it on the black market in places like Cracow and Vienna. Not everyone was lucky enough to acquire this "extra" sugar, and many were disgruntled. Inevitably my father was accused of favoritism, hoarding, and selfishness. For many years stories about the "Sugar King" would circulate in Kolbuszowa.

The Russians occupied Kolbuszowa twice. The Jews' experience was so bad the first time that when the Russians returned, perhaps half the Jews in town fled to the west, some to Vienna, others to places along the way.* My father, my mother, and their seven children left also, with no specific destination in mind, with only a horse and wagon and hopes to make it through the war. After wandering about they arrived in a place called Kaliwaria, some two hundred miles away near the Czech-Austrian border. Fortunately my father met a rich Jew there who agreed to let them occupy one room of his house, and in that room the nine of them stayed until the Russians evacuated Kolbuszowa. Always my mother referred to this period as "the difficult times." How could it be otherwise—seven children, far away from home, no assured livelihood, and a war going on? Nevertheless they managed. With a horse and wagon my father made a living by carrying foodstuffs to Vienna.

A year and a half passed before it was considered safe to return home. They returned to Kolbuszowa, sharing the roads with Austro-Hungarian soldiers moving eastward, to find their house still standing but otherwise stripped completely bare, the windows all broken. Zach, a Polish neighbor, assured them that he had kept

---

*The Russian troops were undisciplined and usually helped themselves to whatever they wished, especially civilian property. My father, I remember him telling me, took to wearing one boot and one shoe on his feet. That way the Russian soldiers, who prized boots, would be less inclined to demand his footwear. This was a lesson I later applied during the German occupation.

a watchful eye out on the house, but just what had that accomplished, my father wondered. The family was back home, but how was it now to survive? There was nothing beyond the little they had brought back. Soon enough much of that was gone, and my father was obliged to sell the horse and the wagon for money to feed the family.

But then, just when prospects seemed darkest, good fortune arrived in a most unexpected manner. Rummaging around the debris in the basement of the house, they discovered a 25-liter container of vinegar concentrate. Perhaps because of its size and weight it had not been taken. Nearby lay two bags of baking soda. Now those two items might not at first seem like the key to economic recovery, but indeed they were. Together with cool, delicious water from the well in the marketplace, they were the ingredients for seltzer water. In short order my parents were in the beverage business, dispensing this delicious drink from a bench in the marketplace. Customers abounded, for passing through Kolbuszowa at the time were soldiers of the Austro-Hungarian army retaking territory surrendered by the retreating Russians. These soldiers were thirsty and willing to pay for a cool, refreshing drink while heading through the marketplace. Unlike Russian troops, these were disciplined soldiers; they would even wait in line as my mother filled up cup after cup from morning till night.

In this strange way was my family rescued from further misfortune. The proceeds from this beverage business enabled my father to reestablish his general store. You can well imagine how often I heard the story of these remarkable remnants and of our dramatic recovery. Few overlooked the resemblance to the story of Chanukah. Back in that ancient time a small quantity of oil discovered untouched in the ruined temple lasted not one day, as expected, but fully eight days. That had been judged a miracle. Was there any other way to view the vinegar concentrate and baking soda?

Thus far we've barely glimpsed my mother's side of the family, noting how my father arrived to study in the house of Leibush

Avrumalis. Leibush, as you will see, had not intended to be a teacher, and but for a series of misfortunes would have spent his days in some other calling. That he was a serious and gifted Talmudic student there was no doubt. In fact it was his reputation as a scholar that led to his marriage with my grandmother, Matil, the youngest daughter of Yozeph and Rana Komito. Now Yozeph was a plain, uneducated man, but one who had managed through his own efforts to amass a handsome fortune indeed. Fattening and selling oxen was what led to his extraordinary success. There was a large brewery in Kolbuszowa that in the course of production disposed of substantial quantities of mash. This residue was beloved by oxen. Komito had only to drive oxen into the field alongside the brewery and in no time they were gaining weight, pound after pound. Once fattened they were driven or shipped off to be sold in Vienna, Bohemia, and Hungary.

When it was time for Yozeph's daughter Matil to be married, there was no shortage of suitors, for he was a rich man who would provide a large dowry and a substantial commission for the matchmaker. But at this point his wife intervened, suggesting that her husband select for their daughter a scholar, a man of learning, a religious man of the highest credentials. The idea pleased him greatly, for nothing brought more favor to a family than to have such a man as a member of the household. In fact the custom known as *kest* had long been common. According to this custom, a poor but learned man would marry the daughter of the house and then move in with his in laws, whose support would enable him to devote all his time to study. Such an arrangement, far from being a burden, was considered a blessing to the house, a way of obtaining God's favor.

And so Leibush came to live in the Komito household. In fact Komito also provided him with a convenient side business, involving cattle skins. The skins were stored in the attic, dried there, and then sold. For a time all went smoothly, but then disaster struck. A fire destroyed the house and ruined the skin business. Shortly thereafter Komito died and his business dissolved. Leibush and his wife were left on their own. What could he do? He was not a worldly man with skills to make a living. He did what many others like him did. He became a *melamed* [teacher], but only of advanced students who came to his home for instruction.

To be a student of Leibush Avrumalis was no small accomplishment. But still Leibush (with four children, one boy and three girls) could barely make a living from teaching, and so the family struggled. Many times my mother contrasted the abundance of our household with the near-starvation that she had endured under the roof of her parents. She recalled how at the seder on Passover the customary egg was usually divided into quarters so that each child could have a piece. Nicknamed "Potato Soup," Leibush on most days ate little more than that. Who could doubt that the prospect of marrying my father kindled hope in Esther, the youngest daughter of Leibush and Matil? For sure he would be a better provider.

Remarkably, Leibush Avrumalis was the author of a book that has always haunted and intrigued me and always will. On occasion I saw my father open it and begin reading; but whenever he heard me approaching he quickly put it away, in fact hid it. I could see that it was beautifully written in Hebrew by hand on pages yellowed by age. And in time I learned about some of the ideas it contained, but to my great regret I never managed to read the book. Once the Germans swept in, the book perished along with everything else.

What then is so remarkable about this book by Leibush Avrumalis? Its very name provides much of the answer: *Yehoshua Hanotzri,* "Jesus of Nazareth." Here was a nineteenth-century man of ultra-orthodox background writing on a subject that nearly every Jew would take pains to avoid. Jesus Christ was at the very center of a rival religion whose followers too often had lashed out viciously against the Jews. To write about Jesus Christ was an act of singular courage by an independent thinker. The emphasis, I learned, was on Jesus as a most exceptional man, one whose greatness derived, Leibush explained, from his standing outside of established society and abstaining from its common indulgences. Jesus, Leibush suggested, never intended to be anything more than a man. As for the originality of these and other ideas of his about Jesus, I could not judge at that time. But how proud I was that my grandfather had dared to do what most others considered unthinkable, that he had broken through the sometimes arid scholasticism of traditional studies to investigate a subject so central to Jewish history.*

I was born in 1920, the last of nine children. The previous year had seen a pogrom in Kolbuszowa in which Jews had been killed and much property destroyed. Recovery followed swiftly, but the incident was enough to convince my oldest brother, Avrum, that it was time to settle elsewhere. He left, going first to Germany, then Canada, and settling finally in the United States. Everyone else remained, and the family flourished throughout my early years. We had moved into a two-story building in the marketplace (there were only about twelve in the entire town), and thus lived in relative comfort for that time. Our general store did well, providing money enough for most of our needs and enabling the Saleschützes to be counted among the leading families of Kolbuszowa.

Piety and prosperity—that was the much sought after but rarely attained ideal in Kolbuszowa. Actually there was a popular phrase used to describe our situation: "Torah and merchandise in one place." Ours was a strictly orthodox family, so the Torah portion of that saying fully applied. As for merchandise, there were few items our general store did not carry. "In one place" was literally true for us, as for almost every other family in town. People lived and worked in the same house. The largest portion of the ground floor was our place of business; and the business was open as long as we were in the house, which was nearly all the time.

It was without question a family business. At one time or another every member of the family was involved in some part of its operation. My sister Malcia, for example, worked hard in the store,

*Tragedy surrounded Leibush's last days on earth. When a painful appendix condition was diagnosed, he agreed to journey to Cracow for an operation. Somehow he was placed in St. Lazar's Hospital. It was not long before he noticed a crucifix in his room. As a pious Jew, he refused to remain there a minute longer and demanded to be taken home to Kolbuszowa. During the long and painful return trip (by train and sled) his appendix burst, and he died on the way. Often my mother referred to this tragic incident to register her disapproval of the rigidities of the past.

and another sister, Matil, was responsible for writing the bills. When I was old enough I was given the task of bringing up additional goods nightly from the basement storeroom to replenish our stock. Later on, at age fourteen or fifteen, I handled some purchasing for the store, traveling to nearby towns to obtain goods. Every Tuesday, which was market day, brought the family to a peak of activity, for on that day transactions in the store continued from early morning till dark almost without letup. Even after my sisters married and set up separate households, they all continued to come to the store and assist when needed, especially on market days.

It was a family business in yet another way. It spawned other related enterprises in town. My brother Leibush (after the departure of Avrum, my oldest brother) established a wholesale general store much like the one we operated. There was the appearance of competition with us, but his store was in truth an extension of ours. We often bought merchandise together, and when specific shortages developed we exchanged goods. When my sister Malcia married, her husband, a very religious man, had no trade or obvious means of support. Accordingly my father turned over most of our wholesale flour business to him, and he prospered. Where do you think we bought our flour? A similar story can be told of my sister Lieba. For her new husband my father set up a wholesale textile business in town, where his principal customers were manufacturers of underwear.

Aside from Avrum, who left before I was born, the family remained together throughout my early years. It was customary that when girls married husbands from outside the town they would leave home to live with (or near) their husbands' parents. In no instance did that happen with us. My three married sisters all remained in Kolbuszowa; their husbands came to live with us. All three were pious, learned men who would have had to struggle to earn a livelihood elsewhere. As I have already mentioned, my father arranged for all three to make a living in Kolbuszowa, turning over a portion of his business to them or helping them set up enterprises of their own. But he did even more. For Malcia and Lieba and their husbands he bought houses not far from us; and

Gela, his eldest daughter, and her husband came to live in our house. This was supposed to be a temporary arrangement, but in fact they never left. My father could afford to do all this; what's more, he wanted to do it. His three daughters had married well, all to respected, learned, scholarly men. A Jewish father could wish for nothing better.

We were a family living close together, but we were also close. Rivalries, jealousies, petty feuds—somehow we were not afflicted. With some families in town, especially a family of bakers who lived nearby, you could stand outside their door at almost any time of the day and hear shouting, screaming, always conflict. But not with us. Peace prevailed, you might say, because there was enough to go around; but as I observed life in Kolbuszowa, property did not always guarantee harmony. More often the closest-knit were the poorest families, whose members did all they could for each other because they know their survival might depend on it. Just what made us close I cannot say for sure, though it was probably my mother, who loved all her children dearly.

My sisters came to our house and took what they needed from the store. Sometimes they paid, sometimes they promised to pay, occasionally they didn't. They often came to eat with us and left their children at our house. It seemed so natural, altogether without friction. Every Friday night the entire family gathered. First we had our meal and then, toward the end, my sisters and their families began to arrive. There we would be, some fifteen to twenty people together in one room.* Tea, cake, and dried fruit would be served, and then all would sing, men and women together, the traditional songs of the Sabbath.† Friday nights, how-

---

*People often remarked on how crowded we seemed to be, with so many people often in a single room. But I'll tell you: we usually felt nothing of the sort. I suppose we were used to it. Most people lived together in close quarters, slept together with others in the same bed, and squeezed together in one part of a room while the rest of it was devoted to business activities. Maybe people got along more easily with each other because they just had to, on a minute-by-minute, day-by-day basis. To have a room for yourself then—that was sheer fantasy.

†The family would also gather on weekday nights, especially in the winter. We would sit and chat and watch as the women talked and plucked goose feath-

ever ordinary they were, were memorable, a family at prayer and song, a family at leisure, a family gathered together.

My father was a busy man, the head of a large family, in charge of a sizable business, a pious Jew active in Jewish community life and involved in the general affairs of Kolbuszowa. He managed somehow to be all these things. Of course, in the business he received plenty of help from all of us. And with the family he wasn't that much involved. He loved us all, that much was clear, but it would not be correct to say that he was very close to any of us. That kind of thing, after all, was what he expected his wife to do, and what my mother in fact did so well. He was anxious that all his children follow him closely along the path of orthodox Judaism, so much so that progress in our Jewish studies mattered more to him than our grades in public school. No doubt it disappointed him that none of his sons became deeply committed to the daily practice of Judaism. But then he did have his sons-in-law, all of whom he selected, to fit the proper pattern—scholars, men of learning, good singers even, a notable asset in the synagogue.

My father had a quick temper, a trait supposedly characteristic of Cohanim.* Usually he was able to control it, but not always. He might discipline the children, but that happened only infrequently and never involved the girls. In general we were all good children, did what we were told, and caused little trouble. There were the usual misdeeds, especially involving my brothers—getting our pants wet in the snow, getting our shoes dirty, cutting off our earlocks—but serious misconduct was rare. My father could hit us and occasionally did, but I can remember only one time when he actually struck me. It came about because of something I either said or did in *cheder* [Hebrew School]. For this in-

---

ers. Goose feathers filled our quilts, but not before a section containing a sharp point had been removed. It was tedious work, involving one feather at a time. It was best to do this together with others so that the time would pass agreeably and the task seem less onerous.

*Descendants of Aaron, the brother of Moses, and the High Priest of Israel, Cohanim had special religious functions to perform, among them blessing the congregation on particular important holidays and officiating at the "redemption" ceremonies for firstborn sons.

discretion I was whipped. Had the same thing occurred in public school I probably would have gone unpunished.

Much of my father's displeasure with his children was provoked by complaints from his religious associates, some of whom were always on the lookout for unacceptable behavior on the part of children, a sure sign of an unfortunate relaxation of standards. When such complaints reached him, he became angry—not so much, I think, at the behavior itself as at having been made to lose standing in the sight of others.

When left to himself, he could react quite differently. By the late 1930s flashlights had begun to replace kerosene lamps for many families in Kolbuszowa. As a result batteries became an important part of our business in the store. I was fascinated with the potential of batteries and on this one particular holiday, Succoth, I devised a way to put them to use. Succoth is a time when Jews construct temporary wooden structures alongside their homes and take their meals there. We of course had one set up in the back yard. What a wonderful idea it would be, I decided, to light it up with scores of bulbs illuminating the area. Such a sight, so entirely unique, would be certain to attract people from all over the town. And so I set about creating the desired effect by hooking up scores and scores of batteries (without, however, removing the seals) to bulbs. The batteries I simply "borrowed" from our store.

Sure enough, the display was successful, and became the talk of the town. In the course of producing this extravaganza, however, I exhausted a large number of batteries. I then arranged to have them sent back to the company, claiming that they were defective. But I had gone too far. A company representative came to town, unconvinced that in one shipment so many batteries could have malfunctioned. In the end my father had to pay for them, but I went unpunished despite my misguided attempt at deception. After all, I had acted in "good faith" for the greater enjoyment of the festive holiday of Succoth.

To me one of my father's most endearing and remarkable abilities was his storytelling. Among us this was not uncommon. People related stories or told tales to illustrate a point, to drive home a lesson, or simply to entertain. Jewish scriptures and traditions often supplied the subject matter, as did folktales and the everyday lives of the people. People tended to be patient listeners, to enjoy hearing a drawn-out tale. Some possessed the gift of storytelling, and my father was one of them. Put a question to him, and he would answer "Let me tell you a story. . . ." Almost everyone enjoyed his digressions, for despite their roundabout way they usually made the intended point. My mother, I should add, was an exception. His tales she had heard all too often; the time spent telling them, she insisted, could be put to better use. Never did this deter my father, however.

I could spend days relating some of his stories, but there is one that long remained a special favorite of his. It concerned a business relationship he had with a supplier whom he paid regularly each month. On one occasion, however, he ordered additional goods before he had paid for certain previous shipments. When pressed for the money, my father instead related a story about a peasant who came to town to purchase a cow from a supplier who enjoyed a reputation for honesty and fair dealing.

"I want a good cow," said the peasant.

"You've come to the right place," responded the other. "I have just the one for you."

A price was agreed upon and the transaction concluded. But soon afterward the peasant returned, dragging the cow with him, clearly displeased.

"This cow doesn't give any milk," he said. "You said this was a fine animal, but I find there's no milk to be had from her."

"There is no misrepresentation," replied the seller. "You came to me asking for a good cow, and surely you have one. She has a marvelous disposition, don't you agree? I assure you that if she had any milk she would not hesitate to give it to you. Indeed, I am sure she would offer you her last drop of milk if she had it, so good a cow is she."

And with that he assured listeners that at the conclusion of his story he had been granted an extension by his supplier.*

*Then there was the time the internal revenue agent in Kolbuszowa raised

His sense of humor and occasional absentmindedness may be clearer once I tell you of his unusual drinking habit. Always in his tea he put seven lumps of sugar, counting them so as to be certain of the total. Once the sugar had accumulated along the bottom of his glass, however, he refrained from stirring it. "Why don't you stir your tea?" he was often asked by those observing this ritual. "Because I don't like sweet drinks" was his unvarying response. If his sugar count chanced to be interrupted before he had reached seven, he always started all over again from the beginning. Such was his distaste for sweet liquids.

My father's life was a busy one, but was it any different from my mother's? Working in the business, maintaining the house, preparing and cooking the food, raising the children—the idea of leisure time would have made little sense to her. Woman's place was to be in the home and with the family constantly.* To both my mother was devoted. Although my father could on occasion be a distant figure, unaware of or even concerned with domestic matters, my mother always was in the midst of things, seeing to it that everything was as it should be. She loved all her children, considered us all exceptional prizes. So perfect, for example, was

---

his estimate of my father's gross income, on which an income tax was based. Naturally my father went to the official, and by way of protest he related a story about a peasant harvesting a large wheat crop. It started to rain, and the peasant despaired of getting the wheat into the barn before it was ruined. He and his wife hurriedly piled all the wheat into one huge wagonload, but this did not solve the problem. How would they get the wagon through the barn door, which was clearly too small to accommodate it? The peasant hit upon a solution. Rushing into his house for a magnifying glass, he held it up to the barn door and instructed his wife to drive the wagon through the artificially "enlarged" entrance. That, my father concluded, was precisely what had occurred in this tax situation: the revenue agent had applied a magnifying glass to his gross income, thereby enabling the income tax to fit what the agent wished to collect from my father. The point was made, and the original assessment was adjusted.

*It's hard not to conclude that the burdens placed on women exceeded those borne by the men of our community. For women there was no relief from the multitude of tasks they were expected to perform. Whereas the men could head to the synagogue, attend study groups, join organizations, or go off to see their rabbis, the women were largely confined to their crowded homes. Certainly the women complained more about their situation and, compared to the men, seemed more unhappy and depressed.

my brother David in her eyes that never, she insisted, would there be a girl good enough for him.

Our accomplishments filled her with pride. How she looked forward to visiting my teachers at the public school! She would put on her best dress and go forth fully confident that she would hear only the highest praise of my performance. Since I was in fact a good student, she was always greatly pleased. She generally indulged us, rarely disciplined us, and always defended us. A threat to any of us and she became a lioness committed to thwarting any attacker. My mother stayed mostly at home, but I remember one time when my brother Leibush was threatened with eviction and the loss of his store. She stormed out of the house and headed directly over to speak to those who had dared treat her son so cruelly. Actually she didn't speak; she screamed and protested bitterly. Anyone who dared make life difficult for one of her children could not easily escape her wrath.

To many in Kolbuszowa we were, as I stated, a perfect family. And from what I've said so far one might so conclude. But perfection, of course, is not an earthly measure, and in reality all was not quite as rosy as it might seem to an outsider. There were the usual disputes and differences of opinion between my mother and my father. Much of it related to my father's ongoing involvement in community life and organizational activities. Because my mother paid almost exclusive attention to home and family, she resented my father's "dabbling" in what for her were foreign affairs. Always he was mixing in. There were meetings in the town that he was obliged to attend; there were get-togethers at our house; there were disputes, controversies, rivals, enemies. Who needed all this, she asked. Then, too, she thought my father was entirely too free and easy with his money. Called on to invest in this project or that about town, he usually agreed. He was unfailingly generous in lending money to people who lacked sufficient capital to conduct a business. Week after week, year after year, people came to him and he gave. When it was time to collect for charities, he organized the collection and saw to it that the money was properly distributed. My mother's priority was almost exclusively the family; my father, though he certainly did not neglect us, cast a wider net.*

My father counted himself among the loyal followers of the Dzikiver Rebbe.† He was very active in the Jewish community in Kolbuszowa, a prominent figure in our synagogue, but if you asked about his religious views he'd tell you of his devotion to the teachings of this rebbe, who resided elsewhere. Naturally the Dzikiver Rebbe relied on his followers for support and solicited funds on a regular basis. My father, it turned out, gave repeatedly, responding also to special appeals launched from time to time. Most of us suspected that he was giving the rebbe money, but it was not until my mother discovered a series of receipts that we learned the extent of his contributions. Rarely had I seen my mother as angry as when she confronted my father with the evidence of what she deemed his excessive generosity. He listened to her and said nothing. He had, it was clear, no intention of changing his ways.

One other related issue often led to arguments. Once a year at Shavuoth it was traditional for my father to travel to another town to be with his rebbe and his followers. How eagerly he awaited this occasion! My mother understood and offered no resistance to his leaving for the few days. It was different when my father left to be with rebbe again later the same year, usually around Succoth. She considered this excessive and resented the additional burdens it placed on her.

Whenever a dispute arose between my parents, my mother possessed the ultimate weapon, which rarely failed to send my father into a hasty retreat, defenseless at least for the moment. All she had to say was "Rifka"—that did it. Argument over. Rifka represented the shame of my father's family. The daughter of my fa-

---

*For all my father's civic interests and involvement he was often wronged and disappointed by his friends and acquaintances. Political "allies" occasionally deserted him; borrowers failed to repay him and then resented his requests for repayment. Invariably my mother's response was "I told you so," but my father never ceased being generous, open, and loyal even to those who had not appreciated his kindnesses. When for example he was told that a certain person had spoken ill of him, he responded "I don't know why, I never did him any favors."

†A *rebbe* is a spiritual leader of a Hassidic sect.—RS

ther's sister Raizel, Rifka, had gone to America by herself, no less, and once there committed the unpardonable sin of marrying out of the faith. She married an Italian—a fine man, it seemed, but that was of no consequence since he was not Jewish. Rifka's "sins" were visited on the entire family, to the point that my father simply withered when my mother invoked her name.

My father, as I've told you, was not much pleased with the religious practices of his sons. Nothing would have given him more pleasure than to see them follow his orthodox ways; but neither Avrum nor Leibush nor David did, and as for me, despite a promising beginning, I gave notice that this was not to be the direction my life would take. Of all of us Avrum was the least sympathetic to orthodoxy, often openly. Certainly that was the message when he began to smoke. More shameful, he violated the sanctity of the Sabbath by secretly smoking on that holy day; and worse still, he was caught doing it. Then there was the time he and a friend entered a Polish butcher shop and bought kielbasa. Imagine belonging to a strictly kosher home and doing something like that! Avrum also angered my parents by frequenting a candy store in town owned by two sisters with somewhat sullied reputations. He went there, he said, for tea and cookies, which invariably prompted my mother to inquire whether there were not sufficient quantities of tea and cookies at home. The sense I had from listening to my parents is that Avrum's decision to leave Kolbuszowa did not break my father's heart.

All four of us, no doubt, did not compare favorably with the men who married my three sisters. My brothers-in-law, all strictly religious and very scholarly, were welcomed into the family, and all went well with them except for one unfortunate incident. We learned about it when one day Malcia came to us in tears. She had had a quarrel with her husband, Szaja David. What was it about? They were childless, and he said it was her fault. The argument intensified, and at some point he hit her. She then fled the house and in front of us began crying. Shocked and angry, my father immediately wrote to Szaja David's parents requesting that they come to Kolbuszowa. They arrived in short order, refusing at first to believe what their eldest son had done. Eventually matters were settled, less I think because of reasoned attempts to resolve the problem than because of the not too subtle threats directed at Szaja David. Were such an incident to recur, my father swore he'd throw him out and Malcia would leave him. If that was not enough, Leibush, a man of exceptional strength and uncommon bluntness, threatened to break his neck. In time two children were born to my sister.

These disputes and frictions were what you might anticipate even in a "perfect" family. Far more unexpected were the changes that filtered into our world and affected our lives. I must tell you, for example, that my father was in love—but not only with my mother! Love, you say—what place did such unstable emotions have among the traditional practical arrangements that determined the pairings of men and women? Well, before the twentieth century generally not much, but that, of course, began to change. That love had in some way affected my father was for me an astounding fact. Naturally there was much about the affair that I didn't know, but I knew enough. I knew about this pretty woman, Sarah Feiga, a cousin of his, who lived in Kolbuszowa. He was very fond of her and she of him. Still she married another man, someone it was said she did not especially like, had children, and left Kolbuszowa for America in 1920.

But in 1934 she returned to visit her father, and during her stay my father managed to see her almost every day. It was clear, too, that my mother was jealous. An intended two-week stay turned into a six-month visit after her father suffered a stroke and she decided to stay on to nurse him. She ate at our house every Saturday, a situation not entirely comfortable under the circumstances. Ultimately her father died and she made plans to return to America. I remember that my father took her to the train in Cracow. What they must have said to each other is for romantics to imagine. I do know my mother's reaction afterward, however. She spoke out. She admitted she knew of his affection for Sarah Feiga, which had been obvious even before their marriage. Though she spoke of this on several other occasions, never once did he respond. Life continued as before for them both. And I never sensed much of a change in their relationship, but in all honesty it was not something I wanted to look for or to see.

Now that we've opened up the subject of love and romance, I can offer some additional evidence as it affected our family. My older sisters, Gela, Malcia and Lieba, and my brother Leibush all had their marriages arranged, as had generations of young people before them. Matchmakers provided them with whatever choices they were allowed. Ordinarily the two parties had never met, but were complete strangers destined to be matched up and expected to spend their lives together. It was for the most part a workable system, but not one likely to appeal to a younger generation eager to make its own choices and bridling under a multitude of traditional restraints. So it was that David went off to Palestine, and naturally, once there, married a woman of his own choosing. My sister Rachel dated several boys and would have considered the idea of a matchmaker laughable. I fell in love at age twelve, no less, then waited years before I could declare my feelings for her. My father objected to "my" Rozia not so much because I had taken the initiative, but because he considered the religious practices of her family to be somewhat deficient. Nevertheless three members of our family had declared our independence. In this "new world" love and romance had a part to play.

With the exception of Rachel, all my other sisters seemed content to live out their lives in Kolbuszowa. It was different for me and two of my brothers. Avrum, as I've told you, left home before I was even born. I saw him for the first time in 1934, when I was fourteen and he returned from the United States for a visit. David, as you will see, was caught up in the wave of Zionist enthusiasm that arrived in our town toward the end of the 1920s. He joined a Zionist organization, went off for a year to Cracow to a Zionist-sponsored workshop to prepare for a new life, and in 1933 left for the Promised Land. No one really wanted to see him go, but there was nothing we could do. My mother cried at the "loss"; my father wondered how he could get along in the business without David, who at age twenty was in a position to shoulder additional responsibilities. My youngest sister, Rachel, also joined the Zionists and had plans at some point to go off to Palestine. By the late 1930s, however, she had met a boy, they had become engaged, and together they were preparing to leave for America. Fate, however, would play a terrible trick on Rachel.

By the time I was fourteen or fifteen I let it be known that in time I too would leave Kolbuszowa. There were too many things I wanted to do that could never be done there. I would go to America if a way to do so could be found, but I was most eager to emigrate to Palestine. In fact, plans to smuggle me in were already well under way when war exploded over Europe.

By the middle 1930s the Saleschützes of Kolbuszowa were still likely to be seen as the "perfect family." But by then standards had probably changed. We were not, I think you might conclude, nearly as "perfect" as we once were.

My Youth

What was it like growing up in Kolbuszowa? I recall wonderfully warm, full, rich years in a place where I was known and where I knew everyone. In a town the size of mine this was not unusual. Family relationships extended far and wide; aunts, uncles, cousins were all about. When I walked down the street everyone knew me, Naftali Itches—that counted for something, for my father, a successful businessman and active in civic affairs, was accounted among the leaders of the community. It had its drawbacks, too, I should add, for always I knew I was being watched, my appearance evaluated, my behavior scrutinized. And were someone to find fault, word would most certainly get back to my father. On the other hand, everywhere you went people greeted you, and many, though I was but a youngster, found time to stop and talk, to explain, to tell stories, even to teach. Naturally there were some who wouldn't let you go, who bent your ear, who needed someone to talk to, but mostly I welcomed the attention.

With large families the rule, there was no shortage of children. Though our time was usually occupied, there were still sufficient occasions to meet with friends, to play games, to talk, to dream together, and naturally to do mischief. It was a small town, but there was much to do and to see. There was a river, nearby lakes, and woods all about us; there was a hill on the edge of town where military maneuvers were staged, also the castle of a count just up the road at Werynia. There were two flour mills, three lumber mills, and a brewery, the Catholic cemetery in town, and the partial structures of a railroad station destined never to be completed. And there was, of course, the marketplace area, which each Tuesday, on market day, became a carnival of commerce, an emporium of entertainment, with sights and sounds I as a child could never forget.

There were the national holidays, featuring lively parades with bands playing and flags flying everywhere; the theatrical groups passing through and performing for us; the gypsy troupes camping out in the woods, then coming to town to perform and enthrall. There were lively weddings to which most of the town would be invited. There were warm, festive reunions of friends and relatives visiting from overseas, admired people who would spin tales of their adventures, accounts of the exotic certain to excite young minds. Many of the Jewish holidays were joyous affairs offering dramatic, mysterious rituals and uncommon treats. Passover, for example, when some of us got new clothes "from top to bottom," was the only time of the year that this happened. That was special, you can be sure.

My youth was spent safe and secure in the midst of a large, comfortable, harmonious family. My father looked out for my spiritual welfare, my mother attended to all my more immediate needs, and my sisters, especially Rachel, who was closest to me in age, saw to it that I was included in everything. As the youngest child I suffered from no want of attention. No one doubted that to some degree I was being pampered, that I was a bit spoiled. I welcomed the attention and motherly concerns of Malcia; admired my brother Leibush, unquestionably the strongest man in Kolbuszowa; and basked in the spotlight because I had a brother (Avrum) in America and later on another brother in Palestine (David). And as the son of Isak Saleschütz I already counted for someone. I enjoyed helping out in the store, going on market day to shop with my mother, also heading off with her to a peasant's farm each day for fresh milk. Who could forget my sisters sneaking me into the movie house on Saturday nights or pulling me out of *cheder* to watch an acrobatic troupe that had come to perform in the marketplace? These were good times, secure times; no child growing up could wish for more.

So now when I tell you I couldn't wait to leave Kolbuszowa, you may be tempted to question the soundness of my mind and wonder at how much of a misfit I was. Had I been born at an earlier time, maybe in my father's generation, such dissatisfaction as I was to express would have defied explanation. But I grew up in Kolbuszowa in the years after the close of the Great War, at a time when many of the age-old traditions of our people were being questioned, when the world outside started to intrude on our changeless patterns, when novel ideas and modern ways challenged a way of life that people had always taken for granted. In such an atmosphere I could no longer be considered strange. Add to that the fact that I was restless and ambitious and had a touch of the rebel in me. A growing disenchantment with Kolbuszowa could not then be altogether surprising.

Kolbuszowa, even in the 1920s, was not a place that welcomed or encouraged such energetic spirits. It took pride in its steadfast resistance to the modern and dismissed those who advocated flexibility. I understood that and realized the conflicts that awaited me if I tested the narrow boundaries that defined the lives of the Jewish inhabitants of town. It may be I understood this from the earliest days when I was sent all day to *cheder* to learn about Judaism, to speak another language, all the time dressed in a way that set me apart from the non-Jewish Polish population.

Certainly it was clear that my father expected me to follow his ways, the path of orthodox Judaism, bound to an all-encompassing universe of prayer and prescription. But although I learned to do as he did and appeared headed in that direction, it was mostly pretense. I did not believe in his religious observances and obligations or find the satisfactions he felt in his daily rounds. Naturally I was never asked to provide an account of my religious convictions; and as long as I adhered to the outward signs and displays of the faith, difficulties were averted. Besides, it took time for me to sense this uneasiness, to recognize what it represented, and to marshal the courage to place obstacles in the path of my father's plans for me.

With my eldest brother off in America, Leibush in his own store, and David in Palestine, it was expected that in time I would run the family business in Kolbuszowa. It was some business—long established, well-run by the family, clearly something to be proud of. There were problems, of course—there always are in business—notably the threat of competition from peasant cooperatives, but in the short run the business would continue to provide handsomely for all of us. And I very much enjoyed business; I liked the hustle and bustle and welcomed the additional responsibilities given me, especially the journeys to purchase supplies in near and far-off towns.

But my ambitions led in other directions; my talents seemed to flow along different channels. Not that I was entirely sure what I wished to do. I knew how much it would mean to me to continue my secular education, to go on to the Gymnasium and then beyond. I wanted to be a physician. This was more than a childhood fantasy, as I shall make clear. I had a keen interest in the field, real ability to help those in distress, and much practical experience in doing so. But I also longed to be an actor, to be on stage entertaining an audience. I was a mimic, a storyteller, a singer, not in the least uneasy when the center of attention, something I tried very often to be. When I read of boys running off to join the circus, I imagined myself doing the same. When there were plays put on in school or by different organizations in town, more often than not the leading role went to me. I was good; I was natural. To be an actor was, I thought, a worthy ambition. But in Kolbuszowa? Not a chance. Nor could I expect to become a physician there either. My secular education came to an end at age fifteen, and there were no plans for me to continue. To fulfill my ambitions would take me well beyond the borders of Kolbuszowa.

Probably beyond the borders of Poland as well. I loved Poland and considered myself, just as my father did, a loyal citizen—more, a patriot. Both of us spoke Polish fluently; both of us felt considerable pride displaying the flag on national holidays and watching the parades and celebrations that followed. But, alas, our love and devotion went unappreciated. Relations between Poles and Jews, comparatively good in Kolbuszowa, were nevertheless strained, occasionally tense. There had been the pogrom the year before I was born; and there were certainly enough incidents in my early years, both in and out of school, to convince me that Polish hostility and Polish domination had not in any way relaxed. In fact by the middle of the 1930s attitudes all across Poland had hardened. Voices were becoming more shrill, our future security more in doubt.

I was a fighter; unlike most Jews, I was unwilling to turn the other cheek, overlook an intended slight, keep out of the way, accept circumstances as they were. But could I really expect to win such a struggle? Why insist on staying in a place where I was not wanted, where I was resented and, more critically, kept from advancing into fields and into positions of my choice, according to my capacities? Why stay on when America beckoned and offered so much? Why remain in the minority when in Palestine there was the chance once more to fulfill God's promise to the children of Israel?

I left home at age three to attend *cheder*, along with about twenty other boys my age. Of course the *cheder* was but a short walk from our house, but the fact is that I arrived there at about 9:00 in the morning and usually did not return until 5:00 or 6:00 in the evening. This was no play group. My father paid the *melamed* to instruct me in the Hebrew alphabet, to teach me the prayers and other Jewish rituals. On the first day I was wrapped in a prayer shawl and carried by my father and mother to *cheder*, where raisins and almonds were dropped on the pages of the alphabet and honey spread on my fingers in the hope that my learning experience would be sweet. Just about everyone cried that first day, and for many days after. We were just three years old! We were away from our families with a strange man in an unfamiliar place, and he was talking to us of things in which we had little interest. What's more, we had to listen—or else.

Some *melameds* were good and some were bad, but either way the *melamed* was not usually held in high esteem, was often considered a worldly failure, a teacher because he had no other way to support himself and his family. Not that he was paid very much or could expect to make a living from instructing us. Nearly all the teachers I had were poor, some desperately so. And the surroundings reflected their circumstances. Here we were, young boys, sometimes twenty or even thirty of us in one room. It was not much of a room, cramped, poorly lit, inadequately ventilated. Indeed conditions in places were so dismal that the Polish government began a campaign to close down these unlicensed schools for reasons of health and safety. Many a time word passed that a government inspector was on the way to investigate *cheders* in our town. That sent everyone scurrying off. We were ordered home, and an attempt was made to conceal the use to which the room had been put. Even when shut down by government order, these schools quickly reopened and life continued as before.

When I say we were gathered in one room, don't for a moment think we had the room to ourselves. Our classroom also was the bedroom, kitchen, and workroom of the *melamed* and his family. While we sat in a corner of the room on benches reciting our lessons, the rest of his family was right there with us—doing their work, eating, having disputes, living their lives as best they could in our presence. Meanwhile for hour after hour we sat and listened, sat and recited—no formal breaks or recess, no naps or play periods. To this day I have no idea how we as three-year-olds managed to endure.

I understand somewhat better, however, how at least some *melameds** were able to control so many children for so long a period of time. They yelled at us in a most frightening manner, and few hesitated to hit us. And even if they didn't hit, they could still intimidate us. One I remember had those he wished to punish stand, wearing a woman's hat, on his oven in the canopy-like area where the smoke normally accumulated. Several *melameds* simply scared us by their appearance or erratic behavior. There was "the deaf one," who would hear little or nothing unless everyone shouted at him; and then, when I was five, there was Chaim "Da-

---

*I studied with a number of *melameds* because each year or so I would "graduate" from one to another who took boys of a certain age. Some, to be sure, managed to conduct classes for children of different ages and levels of preparation.

dik." Chaim, to his great misfortune, was plagued by psoriasis. Always he was scratching, and always there were pieces of skin in his beard, pieces of skin falling on the table, everywhere. That he cursed incessantly and hit on occasion I found far less distressing than the fact that he scratched and scratched.

Did we learn anything? I think we did. Certainly we spent enough time at it. When called upon we would just get up from our workbench and go over and sit next to the *melamed*. Together we would recite the letters, sound out the punctuation, and recite the prayers. Then we would return to our seats and do some writing in our notebooks. The procedure varied little, day after day, practically all day except Saturdays and holidays. Little wonder, then, that I loved it when my sisters came, usually unexpectedly, during the day to pluck me out of *cheder* and take me off to some activity they thought I would enjoy. Such diversions were not appreciated by my father; he worried that I might be missing something during my brief absences. So to make sure that I kept up, he would inquire nearly every week what I had learned, and even test me.

Cheder students had one obligation in which we all delighed. When a Jewish male child was born, we were expected to gather briefly each night for a week in the same room with the mother and the newborn. There we would say a prayer in unison with the *melamed* that was intended to ward off evil spirits and protect the child. Who's to say whether our prayers were helpful enough to offset the likely harm we caused bringing in germs? But that was the custom. The reason we liked it so much, beyond being able to leave our classroom, was that each of us, as we departed, received a special cookie with a candy in the middle. You can't imagine how excited we were looking forward to that cookie. To a child such things are important.

But there were never enough such cookie treats, and there was not much else about *cheder* that I enjoyed. So you can well understand why it was that I looked forward to entering public school when I turned six. Not that *cheder* ended for me. I still had to go each day, all afternoon and into the evening, but at least public school would be something different, a place that was neat and clean, that was not cramped and so terribly cold in winter. I entered the boys' school in Kolbuszowa along with others my age from town and from the small villages and the surrounding countryside. The school day was from 8:00 A.M. until noon six days a week excepting Sunday. But Jewish boys could not attend on Saturday either, it being the Sabbath. That wasn't a problem. In our absence the teachers used the time for review and introduced no new material.

Each class divided into three distinct groups. Half usually were Jews. Many of the orthodox families in town were not at all comfortable with the public schools; they resented the schools' secular emphasis and the complete absence of Jewish teachers. But attendance was compulsory, and those who tried keeping their children home were fined and forced to obey the law. Still, it was obvious that the orthodox children cared little for school; their commitments were elsewhere. Orthodox or otherwise, all the Jewish boys tended to sit together in the classroom. Different from the other boys they certainly looked; all wore the same black garments. As we shall see, the teachers were not at all pleased to have them in the class. Nor were they particularly happy with the second group, the boys from outlying villages, who almost always made it clear that school held no interest for them. Indifferent to almost all the other subjects, they excelled only in woodcraft. As a result they often were left behind and made to repeat a grade, sometimes more than once. Imagine their interest the second or third time around!

Who the best students were was obvious; they tended to sit up near the front. The children of the Polish civil servants and professional people who lived in town, they looked well, dressed properly, were respectful, and clearly were favored by the teachers. Members of these three different groups generally kept to themselves, sitting together in the classroom except when inspectors came to visit the school. When the inspectors came, a funny thing happened. The teachers split up the groups, putting the better students in and around the dull ones. When the inspectors entered the classroom and began asking questions of the students, the hope was that the smarter ones would assist the others. As one of the "smarter" ones I never liked doing this, but it was expected.

My school, like all the public schools, was administered by the

Polish government. The nationalistic component was unmistakable, the emphasis always on Poland, its glorious army, its marvelous government.* There was no overlooking the presence of the Catholic Church either. Placed inside each room was a crucifix with a figure of Jesus. Teachers were with few exceptions highly respected, and the atmosphere in the class was consistently formal. Teachers, for example, sat on a raised area in front of the class. When a teacher first entered the room, however noisy the class, all the students immediately returned to their seats and there stood silent and erect. The Catholic boys then recited the Lord's Prayer (Jewish boys were excused), whereupon the teacher instructed us all to sit down. Students called to perform an exercise at the blackboard were without exception expected first, in a show of respect, to click their heels and bow toward the front. Omitting this gesture brought a quick reminder from the teacher. In performing this ritual most Jewish students were deficient. Slow and clumsy, their gestures seemed ever out of joint. It was altogether different with the Polish students. Could they click their heels! And their bows—quick and crisp. How I envied their ability! Try as I might to improve on my click and polish up my bow, I was unable to duplicate the precision of my Polish classmates.

Teachers commanded automatic respect, an attitude reinforced no doubt by their power to punish students, which usually meant hitting them. "Give me your hand!" These were not words one took lightly. With a special stick or ruler the teachers would deliver five, six, ten, smart blows across the hand. Both pain and shame were attached to these encounters. One teacher of mine took special delight in raining blows on the ignorant. At times when I did not know the answer, I usually managed a knowing look that convinced him the correct response was on my lips. And sometimes when I raised my two fingers in the air (the standard gesture for responding to a question) he would pass me by deliberately. "You'll be the last one," he said, explaining that he first wished to beat up the others.

*In each classroom hung the Polish eagle, along with portraits of President Ignacy Moscicki and Marshal Józef Piłsudski.

Students encountering their teachers outside in the streets of
Kolbuszowa were expected to come forward and remove their
hats. My teacher for the first three years was Zofia Gottwaldowa
(otherwise known as "De Lange," for she was over six feet tall),
an old maid who lived in town. Every time we saw her coming,
my friends and I ran away, preferring to avoid the formal ritual of
the hats. Besides, there were times when she was clearly displeased
with us. Her house, you see, was located along the path down to
the river, and each year she planted a large area of rye on her land.
At a certain point the rye seeds made for a delightful treat, and as
we passed by her property we would often strip the plants clean.
At harvest time you could always see a section of her rye field
entirely picked, as if locusts had descended upon it, a lost crop.
Of course she warned us about this; but since she did not know
which boys were directly responsible, there was not much she
could do about this plague of human pests.

As much as I disliked *cheder* I found myself enjoying public
school. Here I performed with distinction. After a single explanation I usually understood whatever was presented. Whenever I
didn't there was always my sister Rachel, just three years older and
very smart, to explain it to me. Fortunately, too, I had an exceptionally good memory. I especially loved geography; I think to
this day I can still name all the rivers and streams that flow into
the Vistula as it makes its way from the Czech border in the south
north to the Baltic: the Sola, the Skawa, the Raba, the Dunajec,
the Wisłoka, the San, the Wieprz, the Bystrzyca, the Bug, the
Narev . . . Unlike most of the other Jewish boys in the class, who
spoke Polish haltingly, I spoke it with ease. Also I was clean and
neat and thus did not provoke the wrath of the teachers, who were
visibly disturbed at the rumpled appearance of some of my Jewish
classmates. I did not sit at the rear with most of them, but rather
was seated at the front alongside the brighter Polish boys.

I liked school in part, I'm sure, because I did well there. Several
times a year, on Sundays, parent-teacher conferences were scheduled. Always my mother went, after dressing up in her finest
clothes. The reports consistently were glowing, and her pride
showed on her face as she related the news to her friends, then

listened sympathetically because their children had not fared nearly so well. Report card time brought its special tension to the class, for in truth a competitive environment prevailed, but rarely did I have any cause for alarm. My report cards were good—somewhat surprisingly, I should add, because the Polish teachers were usually eager to find fault with the Jewish boys. In case you find it hard to believe I was so good, here's proof of what I'm saying.*

Each time I requested and paid for a second copy of my report card. This was because my father wanted his brother Shulim in America to see how smart I was and to be kept abreast of the progress I was making. (Usually a good report card led Shulim to reward me with a gift of two dollars.) So year after year my report cards from public school in Kolbuszowa made their way across the Atlantic to America. My good report cards were also a source of puzzlement to my father. Why, he often asked, did I do so well in public school yet appear so deficient in the Talmud Torah [advanced Hebrew School]? I wasn't so bold as to explain why. I knew well how much happier it would have made him if I had excelled in my religious studies. But that was not to be.

Probably nowhere else in Kolbuszowa did Jews and Poles come together in such close contact for so long a period of time as in the boys' and the girls' public schools. Relations in the school reflected for the most part relations everywhere else in town. In general they were not good. All teachers were Polish (with the exception of a religious teacher who came in once a week for an hour to teach us Judaism while at the same time a priest instructed the Catholic boys), and, as I have already said, they were not well-disposed toward the Jewish boys.

Some of their feeling, I'm sure, had to do with the indifferent attitude many Jewish boys had toward their schoolwork. Remember, most of the peasant boys were equally uninterested, and indeed the teachers displayed the same animosity toward them. But there was more to it. The Jews looked different, spoke strangely, kept to themselves, did not say the Lord's Prayer, and refused to drink the milk provided by the school during recess because it was

*See the report card in the section of illustrations following p. 240.—RS

not kosher. Moreover, they ran away when the other boys opened sandwiches containing kielbasa for fear of inhaling even the odors.

On our annual field day, which featured gymnastic displays at the stadium, the Jews were certainly at a disadvantage. Whereas the Polish boys looked smart in their short pants and well-fitting athletic shirts, what a bedraggled group the Jews were! Short pants were never a part of the Jewish wardrobe. And you can well imagine the look of rolled-up pants along with yarmulkas [skull-caps] and *tzitzis** hanging out. Not surprisingly the performances of the Jewish boys matched the impression left by their clothes. Ordinarily few Jewish parents were on hand for these festivities.

From the teachers the Jewish students could expect caustic comments, verbal abuse, and, on occasion, severe reprisals. No one in the school expressed this hostility more openly and more forcefully than Mr. Wisniewski, a fourth-grade teacher. The way Jews looked was not to his liking, so he took it upon himself to "correct" the situation. One day in school he announced that he was going to snip off one of the *payes* [earlocks] of all the Jewish boys in the first four grades. Jewish law forbade cutting off the *payes*. No doubt Wisniewski understood what an affront his action was. Determined to proceed, but unwilling even to touch "those slimy Jews," he put a glove on one of his hands and in the other began aggressively to wield his clippers. By posting a woman teacher ("De Lange") at the door he kept us from escaping.

Moving from seat to seat, he cut off one of the *payes* of each child. There were cries and screams—we were terrified. This was especially true of Moishele, who sat behind me. His father was the *dayan,* one of the judges who sat on the rabbinical court in town. Moishele had by far the longest *payes* of all of us and was immensely proud of that fact. As Wisniewski drew closer, there was no controlling Moishele. His screams could be heard above all the others. It was about this time that I decided I would try to escape, sound the alarm, and attempt to save Moishele and some of the others. Jumping over the desks I headed straight for the

---

*The *talit katan* (small prayer shawl), with four *tzitzis* (fringes), hanging on the corners, was worn by orthodox Jews under the vest and by the not so orthodox under the shirt.

door and collided with "De Lange," knocking her down. It was but a short run to my house. All the time I kept yelling *"Tateh, m'shnat payes! Tateh, m'shnat payes!"* [Daddy, they are cutting off earlocks!].

My father, hearing the commotion, came running out of his store and, joined by Mr. Greenstein, the director of the Jewish bank, hurried to the school. There he found some fifty wailing children, each missing one of his *payes*. My father immediately summoned the principal and the police, and later a photographer. He would not let the matter rest. Word of the incident spread quickly, and over the next few days pictures of the crying children with their missing *payes* appeared on the front pages of newspapers across Poland. Wisniewski was suspended and the matter taken to court. My father's friends, however, urged him to withdraw the charges, which they insisted would unnecessarily provoke our Polish neighbors. In the end the whole matter was dropped.

And Wisniewski returned to school, resentful and clearly unrepentant. But the affair of the *payes* changed me. I would not in the future back away from his insults. There were times even when I challenged him. Why, he asked on one occasion when there had been a succession of rainy Saturdays, had God caused such weekly downpours on the Jewish Sabbath—"So there should be mud on Sundays" was my hostile, impertinent response. Another time he proclaimed that the Poles could do anything the Jews could, but not vice versa. I raised my hand. "That is not true," I said, and proceeded to place my *payes* in my mouth. "Let a Catholic boy do that!" Wisniewski sought opportunities to show up the relative frailty of the Jews. In charge of athletics, he always insisted that the Jews compete against the Poles. Never could we beat them. In winter he suggested snowball fights, again the Jews versus the non-Jews. As usual we got the worst of it.*

No doubt the presence of Wisniewski encouraged a sharp division of the school into Polish and Jewish groups, although even

---

*By and large Polish children the same age seemed more robust and healthier than their Jewish counterparts. This was especially true of the children from the village.

without him the outcome would likely have been much the same. Take note, though, that a somewhat different situation prevailed at the girls' public school. Here anti-Semitic feelings were far more subdued, overt hostility almost nonexistent. Jewish girls, you see, did not stand out in their dress and demeanor the way Jewish boys did. Perhaps, too, the level of competition there was less keen. (The Jewish girls were usually judged to be better students than the Polish girls.) Whatever the reasons, the Jewish boys mainly bore the brunt of Polish aggressiveness.

Contacts between Jewish and Polish boys in school were severely limited. The only exceptions to this rule were some Jewish boys whose families were educated professionals and not very religious. These boys tended to mix more readily with the Poles, and indeed to keep a distance from their fellow Jews. In all my years there I had only two close contacts with Polish boys. One was with Wladek Drewnicki, whose father, a well-to-do man, owned a grocery store in town as well as Kolbuszowa's only gasoline pump. He encouraged our friendship, expecting me to help his son with schoolwork. Frankly I enjoyed the visits to Wladek's house. He had some very nice toys and games. Besides, his mother treated me to some exotic fruits that we didn't have in my house. But beyond my tutoring efforts no true friendship developed. This was also the case with Jedrek Przybyło, the son of the principal. We were friendly in school, but once classes ended we went our separate ways.

The separation of Jews and Poles would have been tolerable except that there was more to it. It happened quite often that the Polish boys beat up Jewish boys during recess or just after school was dismissed. By and large the Poles were physically more imposing to begin with, but in addition many of those in our classes had been left back, sometimes once, occasionally twice. Naturally they were older and bigger than the rest of us, and they took great delight in assaulting us. They tended, however, to leave me alone. I had a reputation; I fought back. It stemmed mostly from an incident with Vika, a village boy in my class who one day decided, for no reason I could discover, to attack me. Not long after, I waited for him after school and beat him bloody with a stick. That brought his father storming into town demanding to meet with my father. In the end my father agreed to pay the medical bills. It was a cheap price to pay, for although other Jewish boys continued to be beaten up, for the most part I was left alone.

In spite of all I have just described, my years in the public school were for me exceptionally happy ones. I did well, I enjoyed almost all the subjects, I was regarded as a star pupil, and even won some grudging acceptance from my Polish classmates. When it was all over, when we were about to graduate, which for most of us meant an end to further secular schooling, I alone mourned my fate. While other students shouted slogans like, "Thank God, the end of our tortures," I was sad, even cried. My father needed me in the business, and besides put little stock in the value of a secular education. I would not, like certain of the Polish boys in my class, be going on to the Gymnasium.

My father had no quarrel with the secular world; indeed, for a man of his intense religious convictions, he moved comfortably within it. But there was never any question about his priorities or what he expected from me. So while the years at the public school passed, I was at the same time attending Talmud Torah. Actually I spent more hours there each day than I did at the public school. And after supper each night I would gather with others at the synagogue to continue my Jewish studies. Not until I returned home at about 9:00 P.M. was I able to begin my homework and preparations for the next day in public school. Leisure time was not something I knew much about.

Some of my Talmud Torah teachers were good, challenging; and given my reputation, they were sometimes surprised when I bestirred myself to raise sharp, knowledgeable questions, which they could not always answer. I'll admit also that their discussions of Jewish tradition, history, and interpretation of texts were often immensely fascinating. Who knows, if I had applied myself I might have become a creditable Jewish scholar. But my heart was never in it. I was there because it was expected of me. And though each year I drew away further and resisted with greater success, my father, powerful and persuasive as he was, still kept the upper hand.

I tried to provoke teachers, developed the reputation for being a troublemaker in Talmud Torah, and succeeded on several occasions in getting myself kicked out. I had no quarrel with God; it's just that the yoke of orthodoxy left me with few opportunities for self-expression. Playing the bad boy was more comfortable for me. When strict dress codes were observed by all, I deliberately chose to alter my appearance. When it was expected that facial hair would not be removed, I proceeded to trim mine. Because so frivolous an activity as riding a bicycle was unacceptable, I learned how to ride one. When the idea of sex education was not something anyone would dare discuss openly, I found a sex manual and introduced it to my friends, one of whom became so upset by its revelations that he turned me in.* When it was absolutely forbidden to be in the presence of a female, I had the temerity to ask a girl out for a walk.

All these affronts were undertaken when I was only a youngster, but all, I think, reflected my basic rebelliousness. What's more, each one succeeded in getting me suspended from Talmud Torah. (A sign placed inside the school announced my various suspensions.) But always I would be invited back, not simply because my father was a member of the school's board of directors, but often because I was needed to take a leading part in an upcoming school play. Again and again I was forgiven, my singing abilities being sufficient to overcome whatever doubts they had about my religious credentials.

Although I resisted the rigidities of Jewish orthodoxy and was a less than enthusiastic follower of all orthodox rituals (I delighted, for example, in eating milk chocolates shortly after having eaten meat, a succession of events forbidden by Jewish dietary laws), there was much of Jewish practice in which I found delight. Weddings were for me a real treat. When not invited I managed nevertheless most of the time to get myself in by arranging with the band to help carry their instruments into the wedding hall. Once inside I danced and drank cold seltzer water and felt very much at ease. I usually was present at the wedding ceremony itself,

*See pp. 194–95.—RS

right up front, almost under the *chupah,* where I could watch and listen to all that went on. This I accomplished by agreeing to serve as a prompter for the *shamus* [caretaker of the synagogue], Chaim Scher, whose job it was to sing a certain prayer while the bride, followed by her mother and future mother-in-law, marched around the groom under the *chupah* seven times. Unfortunately he couldn't remember how to begin the melody, so my offer to start with him was promptly accepted. The trembling bride, the frightened, pale groom, the crying relatives—always the same scene. I never tired of it.

Many of the Jewish holidays held out special delights for children, and I joined in enthusiastically. In addition to the strictly religious rituals, other traditions, often irreverent ones, somehow became attached to certain holidays. Well-known, of course, was Chanukah, when children were permitted to play with dreidels [four-sided tops]. We were also allowed to play cards on Chanukah, even for money. On another holiday, Simchat Torah, Jews looked forward to dancing with the Torah, a time when emotions usually ran high. Even the children were permitted on this occasion to have a drink, something that of course we were eager to do. Everyone became a bit tipsy, some more than others, and naturally most of us pretended to get drunk, to lose control. Drinking also was associated with Purim, a joyous holiday celebrating the heroism of Queen Esther and her uncle Mordechai and the destruction of Haman, a bitter enemy of the Jews. A drink on such an occasion was not out of place.

Some of the things we did I certainly can't account for, but the fact remains that they were tolerated, sometimes even encouraged. A week before the High Holy Days of Rosh Hashanah and Yom Kippur came Selichot, an entire night given over to prayer before the arrival of these days of awe. What we children did on this night, however, was something quite different: we stole fruit off the trees and out of the orchards of the townspeople and peasants. Why we did it no one seemed to know. The Poles, of course, knew of this practice and tried their best to protect their property. Dogs were set upon us, and if Poles caught up with us we could expect a beating. But year after year it was the same all over again. Instead of actually taking fruit, too often we just managed to break off the tree limbs and ruin what was on them. I went out with the others a few times, but rarely with much enthusiasm.

The practices surrounding Tisha Ba'av were much more to my liking. First understand that this holiday was a mournful one indeed, commemorating as it did the destruction of the first and second temples in Jerusalem, perhaps the most tragic event in all our history. Jews generally observed Tisha Ba'av by denying themselves anything that gave pleasure, by debasing themselves, sitting, for example, not on chairs but on special low boxes, placing ashes in their hair, and not eating or drinking for twenty-four hours. Throughout the entire day my father wore torn clothes specially set aside for this time. Understand this and try to explain why it was that children were allowed to do what they did.

At this time of the year [summer] a certain kind of prickly thistle grew abundantly in our region, which we proceeded to collect. In short order these thistles were being used as missiles within the synagogue, children taking aim at the long beards of the congregants and then throwing them. When accurately thrown they became entangled in the beards and very hard to remove. Here were men absorbed in mournful prayer forced to be on the alert for annoying thistles aimed at them! Women were considered off limits, but not young girls. Here the object was to direct the thistles at their heads. It was also "permitted" to sneak up on a girl and rub a thistle into her hair. Once in, it was not easily removed; at times girls were forced to cut off parts of their hair. They were not without some protection against us. Most of them wore tightly fitting kerchiefs throughout this period, a strategy that complicated our task. But the truth is that many of them enjoyed this whole business as much as we did and resisted rather weakly when we launched our thistles.

You would think such disruption would tax the limits of everyone's patience, but there was more. On Tisha Ba'av in the synagogue, children threw bricks! In the midst of solemn prayers, bricks were sent skidding along the floor! Naturally when things got out of hand people complained bitterly, but never did anyone insist that such doings ought not to be tolerated. It was accepted; it was tradition.

Yet another "tradition," this one associated with the Saturday before Passover, began when a group of children located a wagon and dragged it throughout Kolbuszowa, stopping at houses in which one occupant had a scalp disease that appeared as a loss of hair and a flaking of the skin. In front of each such house the children shouted *"Parches ka Mizrayim!"* [All scalp sores to Egypt!] The afflicted person, if he came to the door, was always visibly embarrassed. Then we were off to the next house and the next. What it all meant—who knew? We did it, we enjoyed it, no one stopped us.

Of all the Jewish holidays none brought forth higher levels of expectation than Passover. The special, elaborate preparations for the seder, the baking of the matzoh, this I will discuss another time. Actually much of the excitement surrounding the holiday had to do with clothes. Kolbuszowa was not a wealthy town; a great number of its people were dreadfully poor. Getting new clothes was not something that happened very often if at all. Even for those who were relatively comfortable, new clothes were special. And that special time almost always came in the spring just before Passover.

"I have new from top to bottom" was the proud boast you would hear from those who had just been newly outfitted. How unusual that was is clear when you realize that we wore the same clothes year after year, repairing them often, replacing them infrequently. So when Passover came, on went the new clothes and off you went to be seen by as many people as possible. What was most comical were the boys wearing new shoes. Why were so many of them standing on one foot? There they stood, rubbing one shoe, then the other, against their pant legs to maintain the original shine. A cap, a kerchief, a pair of shoes, pants, a new dress—any one of these could make for a memorable Passover.

Religion might be clothes; religion could also be singing. If there was anything that kept me observant, it was the singing associated with the religious service. If songs were all there was to the practice of my faith, I would have been a religious zealot my entire life. I just loved singing, harmonizing with others, learning new melodies. (Hearing a melody just once or twice was usually sufficient for me. I was able to repeat it almost exactly.) It was part of my love of performing, being in the spotlight. That I had a good voice everyone agreed, at least up until age thirteen. At that point my boy soprano departed pretty much on schedule, although my singing voice after that remained a pleasant one.

For me the highlight of the year came on the High Holidays when I stood in the synagogue to sing along with my brother-in-law. Then there was the annual coming of the famous cantor Israel Bakon to perform in our synagogue. He organized a choir, for which I was usually selected. Several times I was chosen to sing a solo. You can imagine just how proud I was, the youngest choir member, to be singing before the congregation in the presence of this well-known cantor. My mother always assured me that amidst the blending of voices she could hear only mine.

Despite an outward religious conformity, I was, you now understand, inclined more to challenge than to concede, to be skeptical rather than accept matters on faith, to behave in ways no orthodox boy would dare. When I was about sixteen and on a bus trip to Rzeszow for my father, I recall deciding to stay overnight in order to attend a movie. A Hassidic boy in a movie theater certainly was no ordinary sight, and the truth is I was terribly uncomfortable as I waited on line outside the theater for a ticket. No one else was dressed as I was: in a long black coat with a traditional Hassidic cap, wearing *payes*. Everyone, I was sure, was gazing at me. Not knowing where to look myself, I was certain my discomfort was obvious to everyone. I couldn't wait for the lights to go out. As I waited I suddenly felt a tap on my shoulder. Were they going to ask me to leave? Why? No, they were just requesting tickets. But where was mine? Somehow I had lost it after taking a seat. The attendant stands over me as I frantically search my pockets. Meanwhile everyone turns to see what is happening. I couldn't imagine a worse situation. Mercifully someone sitting nearby recognized my plight and placed an extra ticket in my hand, which I then presented to the usher. Had all this embarrassment been visited upon me as punishment for my decision to attend a movie?

On another occasion, this time in Tarnow, I encountered two yeshiva students, boys my age. Like me they were free spirits, ready for adventure. What daring exploit do you think we decided on? To attend religious services at a reform synagogue! Why was that such a brazen act of defiance? None of us had ever seen a reform synagogue, let alone entered one. To the orthodox, reform Jews hardly qualified as fellow religionists. Even to acknowledge their existence by attending reform services was an unspeakable sin. So off we went, located the synagogue, and went in, dressed as we were in the orthodox manner. Unlike attending the movie, this was something I couldn't have done by myself. All eyes turned toward us as we sat down, and a noticeable buzzing could be heard. To them we were the freaks. What in God's name were we doing there? For our part we couldn't believe what we were seeing. These were Jews and this was the Sabbath, yet people were arriving not on foot but in carriages! These were Jews, but none wore any covering on their heads! Men and women were sitting together!! It would be some time before I could get over that bewildering scene.

The service ended early, and emboldened by our first adventure we were determined to press on, to throw off all restraints. There could be nothing more shocking, we concluded, than for all three of us next to see a movie. Three Hassidic boys attending a movie on a Saturday night! On further reflection we realized that this would be going too far. The decision, mind you, was still to go—but not as Hassidim. We would attend in disguise. The first thing we did was to buy three berets to cover our heads; we then tied up the *payes* on top of our heads. Our long coats were still a problem, which was resolved when we realized that they could be folded under and then tied in place. So there we were, three ordinary boys out for a night at the movies. So it might have appeared to others, but surely none of us had ever had a more exciting night than we did that time in Tarnow.

In the ordinary course of things young boys my age found many things in Kolbuszowa to occupy them. We attended school together, went off to the Talmud Torah each day and gathered to study at night, and met one another again at synagogue services, where we found opportunities to talk, stroll about, and poke fun at whatever we found amusing. Naturally we also met in more informal settings. None of us had much in the way of toys or commercial games, but that certainly didn't stop us from playing. Play, to be sure, was not much encouraged by many of the older folks, since it took time away from more serious and important matters. My father regularly pointed out to me that while I was off playing, Schlomo Greenstein and Noah Hutner among others were no doubt hard at work studying and learning, activities that were of infinitely greater value.

A bunch of rags tied tightly together became our soccer ball, which we kicked around in the streets after dividing up into teams selected by two "captains." Up and down we'd run with a stick and a round metal ring from a large barrel. We'd continue hitting it to speed it up, keeping it upright until it fell or we did from exhaustion. Less demanding physically was the game *kitzka,* in which a stick was placed at an angle into a hole in the ground, then struck by another in a way to make it pop up out of the hole. The object was to hit it as far as possible.

Another game we often played began by bouncing a coin off a wall, after which we took turns throwing our own coins against the wall. The one landing closest to the original was declared the winner, and its owner was entitled to gather up the other coins. A variation involved propping a board up against a wall, then rolling coins down in an attempt to have them come to rest near a target coin.

There was also a game played with penknives, one our mothers discouraged but to little effect. The knife had to be thrown toward the ground from a variety of positions and land in prescribed ways, which were designated by a series of German names. While the boys were so engaged the girls were off jumping rope, playing tag or blind man's bluff, or hopping on one foot while kicking a piece of wood into different boxes marked off with chalk.

When we were not playing games there were places to go around Kolbuszowa that we enjoyed. A series of bald, sandy hills on the edge of town was a special attraction. It was used by a pre-army cadet group for firing practice, and by the army itself for maneuvers. It afforded us an opportunity for a treasure hunt, the treasure being shell casings from the bullets. The flour and lumber mills also had their attractions. Climbing up on top of the piles of wood was not easily accomplished, and the element of danger added to our excitement. There was nothing especially exciting about watching firemen care for the fire engine and clean the big brass water container, but for some reason we gathered round and looked on with interest as they did this work. The count's castle at Werynia, about a mile or two out of town, was a place we walked to from time to time. We couldn't go in but were content just to look at it. I wouldn't say it was breathtaking, but it was after all a castle, and for Kolbuszowa it was impressive.

In the wintertime there were many opportunities for ice skating and sledding. Jews did not have ice skates, but no matter. We had iron plates attached to the heels of our shoes, not for skating but so they would last longer. Now if you began running on the ice, built up speed, then put your weight on these plates, you might slide for some distance. You might, but in fact most of us somehow never managed to get very far. With sledding it was another story. We had sleds; I in particular had a very good one with metal runners, built for me by my brother David. Off we went to the hill in town, and from morning till evening went up and down. (Public school and *cheder* both were likely to be closed after a particularly heavy snowfall.) There were snowball fights mixed in as well. It was great fun. The problem was that most of the children's shoes were in such bad condition that their socks and feet quickly got wet and stayed that way. Naturally they caught colds, which usually lasted the entire winter. Actually it wasn't any different for those with good shoes. All winter long my nose dripped, a patch of raw skin appearing under my nose from constant wiping. Invariably my mother noted how the cold I caught on the High Holidays lasted without fail till Passover!

Boys were boys and some manner of mischief was to be expected. Most of it was relatively harmless. An opportunity developed each time a wagon driver sped through town. There was one peasant in particular, the proud owner of a pair of uncastrated horses (in an effort to improve the stock many horses were castrated by agents of the Polish government), who was our favorite target. On those occasions when he sped by us we'd go running after him, loudly shouting "Mister! Mister!" Finally catching his attention, we caused him to rein in his horses, assuming that we had something important to tell him. After great effort he finally came to a stop and turned to us for our vital information. "We wanted to let you know," we said, "that your wheels are turning." We laughed heartily, thinking how great a joke it was. Rarely was the peasant amused.

It was highly unusual to see automobiles. But from time to time they did appear, most of them belonging to estate owners who, after hunting, arrived for lunch at Zach's restaurant in the marketplace. Even as their chauffeurs watched us we drew near to observe these exotic machines. And when the chauffeurs turned away we rushed forward to write our names in the dust that covered the cars. Usually we were caught in the act and dispersed, but after a time we would return to complete our inscriptions.

I was especially fond of a prank that involved placing a dead mouse in a finely wrapped box. Usually we left the package on the main street of town, sometimes near the movie theater. Then we stood at a distance, watched, and waited. In time someone (usually a woman) picked it up, but not until she had looked all about to make certain she had not been noticed. Generally she placed it in her purse, then continued walking. We never saw the box opened, but it was not hard to imagine the scene when the "lucky" lady discovered her prize!

A certain well-to-do man in Kolbuszowa was known for being absentminded. There were times, for example, when we'd watch him holding up an open umbrella even when it wasn't raining. Often when we spotted him out for a walk we would go into action, ducking into an alley and calling out to him as he passed by, "Mister—excuse me, Mister!" He would then look up, to see who it was addressing him in this way. But by that time we had run off, heading through rear passageways so as to get into position in another alley to repeat the scene when he walked by. Having done this two or three times in succession without tipping off what was going on, we usually stopped, very much pleased with ourselves.

To several of the mentally disturbed people about town some

of my friends were less than considerate. "Crazy" Meyer, whom everyone enjoyed because he made up "love" poems about certain of the boys and girls, fared well, but "Bulbes" usually suffered at our hands. "Bulbes," wherever he was, always asked for potatoes. Instead he often got kicks and was beaten. In the winter he became the target for snowballs. Please believe me when I tell you I didn't join in here; I could never see the fun of doing something I regarded as sadistic. On the other hand I couldn't get my friends to stop, and at times I didn't even try.

Before you form too flattering a picture of me, let me tell you of the time I played devil's advocate, scoffing at the presumed holiness and omniscience of a famous rabbi who was about to visit Kolbuszowa. My friends insisted that he was wise beyond all belief, knew all there was to know, could penetrate into the minds of mere mortals. I scoffed at such pretensions, wondering why everyone was planning a special visit to the *mikvah* [ritual bath] so as to be properly pure when they met with him face to face, shook hands, and offered the greeting *"Sholem Aleichem"* [Peace unto you]. "I'll prove he doesn't know everything," I told them. Instead of purifying myself I will desecrate myself, I informed them, adding that I was sure this rabbi would not know the difference. Well, what did I do? I blush when I mention it now, but I had my friends urinate on my hands. Certainly such impurity he would detect. When he arrived in town I managed to meet him and to shake his hand. He said nothing. I had, I assumed, made my point.

The national holidays were something special in Kolbuszowa, especially for the children. It meant time off from school and included festivities that set the day apart. The town certainly looked different, with flags flying from every house. Was it that everyone was so patriotic? Many were, of course, but it was also the law. Every family, under penalty of a fine, was obligated to display the flag on national holidays.

For some reason I took it upon myself to see that this was done, at least along the streets adjacent to where I lived. That meant getting up at 6:00 A.M. because not much later Shimek, the policeman, would be on patrol checking to see who had failed to put out the flag and issuing a five-zloty fine for each offense. So there I was walking along the streets in the early morning chill, looking for a flag at each house, and where one was missing, knocking on the door, warning the owners that Shimek was on the way.

Sometimes there was a flag on display, but a second look revealed that it was not the right one. "How could that be?" you will ask. The fact is that flags could not be bought. They had to be made, usually from two pieces of cloth, one red and one white. Here's where the problem began. Many people sewed the red segment on top of the white; but that unfortunately was the Czech flag, and flying such a flag brought a fine. In the Polish flag the white area was above the red. Whenever I noticed this mistake I knocked on the door to warn whoever answered. What then took place I can well imagine—a frantic scurrying about, a cutting up of the flag, and a hasty job of sewing together the two pieces and putting it out the window once again. No wonder so many of the flags looked as bad as they did! But I had done my job as a Polish patriot and as a defender of the Jews.

The highlight of the day's events surely was the parade through town, which was followed by speeches given by local dignitaries. Naturally it was the parade that held our attention, as the town's firemen, the army unit from Rzeszow, members of the various Polish organizations, and the students from the Gymnasium came marching by. In between the groups came the town's three bands. Everyone took considerable pride in the firemen's band, which was always first in the line of march. The band from the Gymnasium came next and was always well-received. That was not always the case with the third band, Hazamir, the Jewish band, which was closely associated with certain Zionist organizations in town and the most recently organized of the three. I'll admit that this band's performance level was not always up to that of the other two, but the real issue no doubt was that it was a Jewish band. Very often non-Jewish townspeople would express their displeasure at the approach of Hazamir by walking away from the parade route. They did not wish to be seen listening to Jewish musicians playing on a Polish national holiday.

My group of friends, Noah Hutner, Yankel Schifman, David Friedenreich, and Kalman Kerenweiss, was much like any other bunch of youngsters. We came together whenever we could for talk, for play, for mischief, and for mutual support. I was the talker, the mimic, the storyteller, the entertainer; these were all parts I always enjoyed playing.*

I was also the one, as you will see, who guided them through the mysteries of the male and female anatomies, thanks to a most revealing book given to me by my sister Rachel. Awakening in all of us at about age thirteen or fourteen was a notable interest in girls, but as orthodox boys there was absolutely nothing we could do about it except talk among ourselves, which we certainly did. At this stage that's all we could do, all that was permitted. What drew my friends and me even closer together was the fact that several of us had "girlfriends." Certainly none of us had ever been alone with a girlfriend, and we had rarely even talked with them, but still we had no doubt we were in love. My girlfriend at this time was Rozia Süsskind (about twelve years old), "my" Rozia, to whom I was greatly attracted although I knew it would be years before anything could develop between us.

There was also a serious side to some of the get-togethers with

---

*I was also the group's photographer. My brother Al (once Avrum), in response to my request, brought a camera with him from America when he came to visit us in 1934. Unfortunately it was a rather crude model, dating back to 1890. Still it worked, and I delighted in taking pictures of everything and everyone in town, pictures that were developed for me by Joel Shapiro, a professional photographer. Picture-taking was a risky business because most orthodox Jews frowned on such an activity. I managed, for example, to take but one informal picture of my father when he wasn't looking. Because man was made in the image of God, the orthodox wished to have little to do with photography.

When the Germans occupied Kolbuszowa, they ordered that all radios and cameras be turned over to them. I could not hand over my camera, so greatly had I become attached to it. I continued to take pictures surreptitiously, though in doing so I incurred great risk. Finally, when we were confined to the ghetto, my parents insisted that I give up the camera. Smashing it to pieces was one of the most painful acts I was ever obliged to perform. But the pictures I had taken over the years were not lost. Many of them in fact appear in this book. During the war I managed to hide many packages of photographs in the straw roofs of peasant huts (without informing the peasants). In 1945 I returned to these various locations and without exception the packages were still there, safe and untouched.

my friends. When we were about thirteen or fourteen we began meeting to read out loud to one another, to engage in discussion. During the summer we might go off to the woods for perhaps two hours for this purpose. One of my friends had a relative in Werynia, so for a time we walked over there almost every Saturday afternoon after our get-together to enjoy fresh bread, butter, and sour milk. We talked about many things. I enjoyed Polish writings immensely and delighted in reading some of the classics out loud to my friends. Nor did we overlook Jewish literature. Of course, newspapers were usually a standard feature of these readings; from them we learned of developments across Poland, in Germany, and in the rest of the world.

Later on, when some of us had been aroused by the promise of Palestine, we read Zionist materials to each other and dreamed of the time we might ourselves get the chance to leave for the land of Israel. These get-togethers continued until we were old enough to include girls in our sessions, but then the flavor changed. It was apparent that the girls were not as serious as we were; indeed, they were surprised that we persisted in our readings and discussions when they preferred that we consider other possibilities. Actually it's when the girls joined us that we took more to singing together, Zionist songs from Palestine as well as the popular songs of the day.

I certainly had fun with my friends, but there was much in Kolbuszowa to enjoy all by myself. Every Tuesday on market day the town was transformed from a quiet, uncrowded place into a bustling, exciting center for commerce and entertainment. I found myself in the midst of it all, enjoying every minute. I wandered over to the area in town where animals were traded and sold, gazing at the cows and especially the horses as the big and little ones dashed about, first this way, then that. In the marketplace itself I walked around for a time with my mother as she did her shopping, especially for vegetables, which I then carried. Much more fun was watching the photographer position the mostly young couples who were having their pictures taken against exotic and romantic painted backgrounds.

I could stand for hours on end and watch the organ grinder

and his parrot, Laura, who with its beak would open a drawer to reveal a special prize; "Let me see what this man just bought for this girl," the organ grinder would exclaim as he pulled out a cheap ring or glittering necklace to the delight of everyone around. There might be acrobats putting on a show, then passing the hat, or chickens breaking free and dashing about madly with two or three people in hot pursuit.

Usually, too, there were fights involving boys from the villages who had come into town with little to do other than to get into trouble. There was one peasant boy, probably the biggest of all the bullies, who for a time was my idol. He certainly looked impressive to me carrying a thick walking stick, his hat perched at a jaunty angle on his head, wearing a scarf, a red tie, and a stiff collar with a fancy pin. Judging from the number of girls who gathered round him, they too found him irresistible. He didn't walk, he swaggered—there was no mistaking him in the crowd. Pretty soon I took to walking the way he did, and not long after that I began hearing about it, especially from my mother, whose friends had complained that I no longer walked properly but rather appeared to sway from side to side.

Without doubt the greatest treat for me on market day was heading over to where the pickle barrels stood, inhaling the aroma, then selecting the largest pickle I could find. I next bought a loaf of dark bread, inserted the pickle, sat down, and ate the whole thing. It was a meal of prodigious proportions, largely eliminating any appetite I might have for the next two days. My mother saw no point to it all. Why did I need to fill my mouth with pickles when at home there was so much good food to eat? I took note of her advice but continued each week to buy a delicious oversize pickle.

On other occasions walking about town brought me face to face with merchants, tradespeople, and workers who at times welcomed the opportunity to talk, even though as a young boy there was not much I could tell them. Some were lonely and simply enjoyed the company, others had stories to tell and welcomed anyone who would listen, and some felt a kind of obligation to instruct the young, to make sure they had a proper view of things.

Rozia's uncle loved to discuss the Bible and philosophy with me; he even lent me his copy of the New Testament, which he said merited serious attention. Shmuel Berl, the photographer, had lived in Vienna and told endless stories about it, as did Yossel Weitzen. Weitzen also loved to sing operas, and finding an attentive listener proceeded through his lengthy repertoire. Melech Kirschenbaum was a conversationalist par excellence; when I or my friends approached, he would come out of his house to talk, tell stories, and teach songs. He was a most friendly man. Leibche Kaiser had been to America, smoked a long pipe, and had a gift for explaining things that could only be envied. To listen to him was to be enchanted as he mixed in stories from America, the Talmud, and the Bible.

At times I entered the shops of artisans, watched them at work, and listened to their tales. Moishe Feld was a maker of pants and an ardent Zionist. On many an occasion I dropped in and soon was hearing all about Zionism, Palestine, and his plans for leaving for the Holy Land. The shoemaker David Scher was a different story; his conversation was full of coarse jokes and trivial matters, but I had no complaints. It was different again with Haskel Derschowitz, the manager of the Jewish bank. Often I encountered him outside the synagogue, and what seemed always to interest him was how much I knew, usually about geography, history, and Polish literature. He fired question after question at me; it was a regular examination, but I must say I enjoyed the challenge and usually knew the answers. The point is that even though I was young I was taken seriously. People had patience and the interest to share their experiences, impart their knowledge.

I also gave in return. In the steamroom of the public bathhouse I volunteered to bring buckets of cold water to the elderly as they sat and sweated in the steam. As you will see later, I became the town expert in applying *bankes* [pressure cups], which many used to draw off the "poison" from their bodies and thereby cure themselves. I was most adept at placing them on at just the right time and in the proper way so that they exerted their maximum effect. At about twelve or thirteen I also became one of the visitors of the sick. There was an organized Jewish activity in Kolbuszowa, a society for that purpose [Bikur Cholim], that had long been in existence. It assumed responsibility for sending people to stay overnight with sick people when there was no one else to care for them or when a persisting illness exhausted those who were in attendance. Naturally women took care of women and men sat with men. Both my father and my mother were members of the society; my father, unfortunately, contracted smallpox after one such visitation.

Visiting and caring for the sick was a noble idea, but in practice it did not work out so well. The problem was that those who arrived near the end of the day were themselves exhausted from work, and almost as soon as they sat down they fell asleep. And so it happened that one time when my father was scheduled to stay with Ephraim Harr he sent me instead. Harr, it seems, had severe pains in his legs that could be relieved only by rubbing. I started rubbing his legs when I arrived and continued doing it at intervals throughout the night to his great satisfaction. Word spread of what I had accomplished for Harr. Soon requests started coming in for my services and off I would go, taking things very seriously. Maybe once every two weeks or so I stayed the night, doing what had to be done—applying compresses, giving medication, talking as long as the sick person wished to talk. I never went to sleep. It's no wonder my services were in demand.

Good times there were with my friends in and about the town, but most free time was spent at home. I've already spoken of the kind of family we were, how I was the youngest of nine, pampered, probably spoiled. I felt especially close to my sisters Matel and Rachel, and I admired my big brothers Leibush and David. My mother, Esther, loved me without reservation. Itche, my father, had some difficulty with my religious attitudes and would not display much emotion whatever the circumstances, but clearly he regarded me with favor. In turn I tried to be cooperative and not a problem. I saw one of my tasks to be entertaining and amusing my family, mimicking people they knew, telling lengthy stories of my experiences. Generally they were patient with me; sometimes they even laughed at my stories. My sisters knew I enjoyed going to the movies on Saturday night; and though this was not a proper thing for a Hassidic boy to do and I might as a result be suspended from Talmud Torah, they usually conspired to sneak me in unobserved.

Knowing how much I enjoyed appearing in plays, singing, and performing, my sisters arranged for me to attend when various theatrical groups came to Kolbuszowa to perform. I remember so well when the Vilna Troupe arrived with famous actors Jonas Turkov and Deana Blumenfeld. I saw two of the shows, "The Sacrifice of Isaac" and the Abraham Goldfaden operetta "Shulamith." I hoped also to attend their third presentation, "Baranovich," but it was canceled because of insufficient attendance.

What I did see, however, convinced me anew that my future should be on the stage. I wanted to be an actor: I already was a performer. I loved to sing, to act in plays, to tell stories, to be the center of attention, to be a ham. When I went to the movies I immediately was transported, saw myself as the characters on the screen. When I heard that the famous actor Maurice Schwartz had arrived in Poland, I considered the possibility of running off to Warsaw to meet him and beg him to take me with him. I would shine his shoes, be his servant, do anything to be around him and learn about the stage. From time to time I read of boys running off to join the circus. That would be me, I thought. Why shouldn't I do what I wanted, follow my dreams?

Thanks to my sisters I shared in the pleasures of the popular culture. My sister Malcia and her friends had taken dance lessons and soon invited me to join them as they practiced. In short time I was doing the shimmy and the one-step. At weddings I was not shy. Out onto the dance floor I went to show off my newly acquired skills. I learned all the popular songs of the day. My sister Rachel was instrumental in opening up this world to me. They were beautiful songs, I thought. To this day I can still sing them.

Some parts of them were kept from me, my sister apparently believing them to be indelicate and unsuited to my ears. I remember in particular the song about a pimp and a prostitute in Lvov. It was so beautiful. It told of how the pimp beat her and sent her out to make money, but still he loved her. Every night she went out to the corner of the street to sell. But what was it she sold? I couldn't imagine. They would not let me find out. Each time the song came to that particular point my sisters would interpose "tra-la-la-la." Was it matches? Cigarettes? Each time I asked them they only laughed. Who dreamed she stood there for the purpose of selling her body? Had I been told that, it would have left me only more puzzled.

Life with my family mostly involved working together in our store. It started when at about seven years old I was instructed to stand on a ladder and watch the customers, some of whom might otherwise at times be tempted to fill their pockets with our goods. Later on I graduated to stockboy and was given the laborious duty of going down to the cellar each day to unpack goods and bring them upstairs to replace goods that had been sold. Real responsibility came when my brother David, who had been expected to be my father's right hand, caught the Zionist fever and departed for Palestine in 1933. That left me to shoulder major responsibilities at age thirteen. Clearly whatever plans I might have for additional schooling, for going to a Gymnasium, would not come to pass.

Not that working in the store was a hardship for me. I took to it easily, enjoyed much of the activity. This was especially true when I became the purchaser of goods for the store. I had often accompanied my father on his trips to buy supplies in Rzeszow, Tarnow, even Cracow. For a young boy such journeys were adventures, exciting, filled with unexpected sights. Imagine, then, what it might have been like when at about age sixteen my father called on me to make these trips by myself. Without hesitation I agreed.

Almost every Wednesday, the day after market day, I took the bumpy trip by wagon to Rzeszow (on occasion I took the autobus). Once there I scurried about all day buying the goods on the list, often in a way that upset some of our normal suppliers. My father, when he had gone, had been accustomed to buying from certain people and never much compared prices or shopped around for the best available deals. With me it was different. I was young, energetic, eager to save a zloty here and there. And so I raced around from store to store until I was satisfied I had bought right. Sometimes that meant passing up our regular suppliers or bargaining them down in price after telling them what a competitor was charging. I saw it as a challenge, though I knew they regarded it as a headache and told my father so on occasion. He was not at all displeased; nor was my brother Leibush, for whose store I also bought goods. My father especially appreciated the fact that I was always on the lookout for new goods that we could add to our stock. It was hard work, the round trip, the running around, the packing and loading the wagon, but what an experience for a young boy! I had established contact with the "outside world," made new acquaintances, and developed a degree of self-confidence that would not have been possible if I had not been given this responsibility.

That I matured rapidly as a businessman is due in no small measure to the fact that already for years I had been in business for myself. A succession of business enterprises had not made me a rich man, but they had bolstered my self-esteem (not something that needed too much of a boost) and enhanced my reputation, at least within some circles in Kolbuszowa.

My business career began rather modestly at the age of six when my father bought me a viewer into which one looked to see certain pictures. Nothing occurred to me until I befriended the man who ran the projector in the movie house. Not only did he let me sneak up to the projection room and watch movies from there, but he cut off extra pieces of film and let me have them. Often they were scenes from the movie. It was then that the thought struck me. I would put together ten of these pieces of film, cut them to the size of my viewer, and charge my friends one groschen to see all ten of them. It must have been an attractive offer because I had many takers.

Next I entered the chocolate business. That was simple enough because we sold chocolates in the store, and thus I could get the wholesale price. The problem was distribution. Easily solved. I brought boxes of chocolates to school in order to sell them during the recess. Also, when our religious teacher came to teach us one hour a week, practically no one paid attention to him, so instead he let me sell my candies then. But I realized the need for representation in order to expand my market. Accordingly I hired an agent in the girls' school and another in the Talmud Torah. I also discovered the house in which some of the orthodox men played cards during the winter months, and appeared there with chocolates for sale. Business never boomed, but I made a living.

After that I entered the collection business. Many charitable organizations in town periodically went from house to house for donations. Usually they hired young boys to do the legwork, giving the boys 10 percent of what they collected. I began doing this but was not satisfied. The urge to expand could not be suppressed. What I did was buy up the routes that others had, paying them a lump sum and then hiring people to collect for me. They were quickly found, and in short order I was the collection king of Kolbuszowa.

From collection I turned to manufacturing. This was made possible by my brother David, who designed a most beautiful wooden mold for me for producing dreidels, which were so popular during Chanukah. I intended to produce lead dreidels, melting the lead in the kitchen oven and then pouring it into the mold. Getting sufficient lead proved easy enough, although some of the sources were surprising. In the lining of women's suits, lead weights were placed at the bottom of the jacket to make it hang straight. I encouraged my friends to seek out such jackets, cut the linings, and remove the lead weights. I would pay them five groschen for each, which would leave a sufficient profit when I sold the dreidel for fifteen groschen. Off many of them went, and it wasn't long before my mother began receiving complaints from her friends that their sons were cutting up their jackets at my request.

Clearly a new source was needed. Toothpaste tubes, which contained lead, seemed to have potential until I realized that not many people in Kolbuszowa used toothpaste. More promising were the siphons on seltzer bottles. Melting down one siphon could yield enough lead for ten dreidels. Once the word got out, boys started breaking the siphons off the tops of the bottles. Soon the manufacturer discovered the cause of his losses and complained to my father. That ended my use of siphons, but by that point I had stockpiled a sufficient supply of lead.

My dreidels sold well directly to Hebrew teachers and to agents in the surrounding smaller towns because I undersold the market. My price was fifteen groschen, whereas the going rate was twenty-five. Before the driedel season ended I might sell about 200 of them. But I was forced to move on. The mold for the dreidel finally broke, and my brother David, who had made it for me, was now away in Palestine. Furthermore, my mother put her foot down. Melting down the lead in the oven created a foul odor in the room, and she would tolerate it no longer.

My next undertaking was to manufacture petroleum jelly for use in keeping boots soft and waterproofed. I bought paraffin, mixed in oil, and in no time had my finished product; I sold the jelly to my father and my brother, who displayed it in their stores. The item sold, but the profit margin for me was not great because the paraffin was costly. I then hit on the idea of melting down the candle fragments that were always left over in the synagogue after Yom Kippur. I paid my friends to gather these up, and this solved my supply problem. There was a steady business here, though not one to arouse the envy of competitors.

Talk about quick money and I have to tell you of the time my aunt came for a visit from Berlin and brought us a pineapple. No one in our house had ever eaten a pineapple, or probably even seen one. When we opened it the aroma was like nothing we had ever experienced. Because I was so entranced by it I assumed my friends would be also. So the business I decided on, obviously one of short duration, was to charge people to enjoy the smell of the pineapple. Each day I would rub the pineapple skin on my hand, and for a fee would let my friends inhale near my hand ten times. A sufficient number were curious enough to pay the price and to keep me in business for several days.

In a similar manner I enjoyed a brief career in the cigarette business. It all came about when my brother Al and two other former residents of Kolbuszowa arrived from America for a visit. All of them smoked cigarettes one after the other, and all, in the United States, had gotten into the habit of taking only a few puffs, then tossing the cigarette away. This was my opportunity. I gathered up the scarcely consumed cigarettes and before long had accumulated a goodly number. I removed the tobacco, mixed it with tobacco available to us in Poland, enclosed the mixture in cigarette paper, and sold the resulting product as American cigarettes. They sold at a high premium. Thanks to these visitors I enjoyed a short-lived but lucrative business.

Probably the enterprise that gave me the most satisfaction and in which I did the most good was the skin plaster business. It began with a conversation with a salesman visiting my father. He had plasters that would eat away bunions when you applied them directly to the skin. Now I knew bunions plagued many of the Jews in town. One had only to go into the public bath to see just how many had these unsightly protrusions and lumps on their feet. How wonderful if these plasters actually worked, and possibly profitable too. My place of business became the baths, where I began to apply the plasters, cutting them to fit, each one to a different size. The following week when my customers returned, I put on a fresh one. After two or three times the condition invariably cleared up; the plaster had eaten away the bunion. The number of customers began to increase. (With most people wearing tight-fitting shoes, it was no wonder so many were plagued by bunions.) At one point I was treating about twenty men each Friday, fitting the plasters to the size of their bunions. My reputation in this field couldn't have been better. These men would never have gone to a druggist; they would simply have endured the discomfort year after year. I was pleased to be of service and to be making money besides.

There were other businesses that I won't mention because I think by now it's sufficiently clear that I had become a restless, energetic, enterprising young man. Even so, that's not how I wished to spend my life; no more than I was prepared to accept the dictates of religious orthodoxy. I complied when it was politic to do so, but my thoughts always were elsewhere. As each year passed, the idea of staying on in Kolbuszowa became more and more distasteful to me. There I could never become what I wanted to be, maybe an actor, even a doctor. The secular education I so much wanted to continue I could not pursue there. I would be obligated to remain in the family store—a fine living, no doubt, but not the life I wanted. The unbending rigidity of so many of the townspeople would always be a barrier to my aspirations, to the expression of my true self. There was also no question that as the 1930s wore on and I passed into young manhood, Poland was becoming an increasingly hostile place for Jews. The future could only be worse.

I made it clear to my family that before long I would be leaving Kolbuszowa, just as my brothers Al and David had. There was no hand-wringing, no cries of anguish on their part. They lamented my decision, but they understood. Besides, they knew me; they recognized that they were helpless once I had made up my mind. I would attempt to get to America or, better still, to Palestine. I tried very hard for both places. But in the end the decision was taken abruptly out of my hands.

Making a Living

Kolbuszowa was no garden spot. It never had been, nor would it ever be. Centuries before, the town and the surrounding lands had been cut out of a thickly forested region (the wilderness of Sandomierz), whose soil was not of the highest quality. Still an agriculture sufficient to support a sizable peasant population developed. Farming, along with small-scale manufacturing and handicraft activities, created a local economy that embraced both town and countryside. The fields began at the edge of Kolbuszowa and stretched in all directions. Had the soil been richer, peasants would have grown mostly wheat; as it was, they settled for rye, along with barley, oats, and beans.

The great staple (more than half of all that was grown), at times the only difference between starvation and survival, was the potato. Day after day, meal after meal often consisted of little more than potatoes, excluding the skins, which were removed, mixed with chopped straw, then fed to the cows. In the morning it might be mashed potatoes and milk; at noon, boiled potatoes, cabbage, and buttermilk; in the evening, baked potatoes, beans, and sour milk. Chickens and geese there usually were, but not to be eaten. Off to town they went to be sold for desperately needed money. It was much the same story with cows; peasants consumed little of the milk, butter, and cheese they produced.

Beyond the tilled lands lay the forests. Their trees supplied the town's lumber mills and also the wood that peasants in desperate straits took for themselves or sold to others. On the edge of the forests, berries and mushrooms of many varieties were gathered for sale in the marketplace. Not far from the forests lay the fields of lubin, a small bean much like the lentil that grew in great abundance. In summer the lubin blossomed in spectacular fashion, waves of deep yellow flowers producing an intoxicating aroma. The arrival of millions of bees offered us a unique opportunity to collect honey. In my day Poles showed a strong preference for vodka, but the national drink once was something altogether different. Just read the heroic legends, recall the traditional tales of the country, and you will discover repeated reference to mead, once the most popular of drinks. Much of this honey wine came from our region; and though vodka's popularity grew steadily, mead continued to be produced and to provide jobs and income for our area.

But there is more to the lubin story. When our local forests were cut back they sometimes gave way to marshy ground that was well-suited to the creation of artificial lakes. Once these filled, they became perfect for raising fish, especially carp, a fatty fish, a favorite among Jews. There were many such lakes in our area, most of them on lands belonging to Count Tyszkiewicz. Here the carp grew rapidly, and the waters were thick with fish that could reach twenty-five pounds or more.* On hot summer days you might find me along with friends heading for these lakes, not for the carp but for a dip in the cool water. The swimming could end abruptly, however, if we were spotted and chased away by caretakers.

Peasants rarely were well off. The overwhelming majority barely scraped by. Either they worked the fields for others and received a portion of the harvest, or they cultivated their own plots (a large majority owned their land), few of which were large enough for

---

*What made them grow so large was the lubin. Once gathered, these beans would be brought to the lakes and fed to the fish, which consumed them in great quantities. In the winter holes would be cut in the ice, and in time fish would darken the waters below in anticipation of the beans. The carp, always in demand, were easily sold in town. From time to time peasants risked fines and imprisonment to poach in these lakes. More than once my father struck a deal with someone who had happened to come upon an "extra" carp.

subsistence, let alone surplus. Most led a hand-to-mouth existence, and worse than that in the early summer months, when
reserve provisions were nearly exhausted and the desperately
needed new crop was still not ripe. Most made it through, season
after season, year after year, even as additional mouths arrived and
scant provisions were stretched even further. They survived in part
because they made do with so little and because of Kolbuszowa,
where they might find an occasional job. Also in town were customers prepared to buy from them and to supply the seeds and
equipment they needed, together with clothes and other basic
provisions. Was the condition of the peasants likely to improve?
As matters stood, no, especially when all across Poland the peasant
was held in almost universal contempt. What reason was there to
expect any change for the better?

For many a citizen of Kolbuszowa existence could be just as
harsh and unrelenting, and for those without either land or livestock, even more precarious. Food came from outside the town;
to eat one had first to earn. But what was there to do? How was
one to make a living? Business—that was the answer heard most
often. Open a store, sell something, become a businessman. After
all, what did it take? Exceptional skills? Rarely. Lengthy preparations? No. Take in some goods, open the door, stand around
and wait, and in time customers will come. God will take care;
He will provide. A good many of the Jews of Kolbuszowa did just
that. Not so the Polish residents, who operated very few of the
businesses in town.

There were businesses in our town with extensive, wide-rang-
ing operations and others that barely operated at all. Certainly our
family business was among the more highly developed and successful. It is best understood as a general store selling primarily
wholesale, mostly to other businessmen. We stocked anything and
everything. There was hardly an item that we didn't carry, or so
it seemed. For this I was partially responsible. I was always urging
my father to stock this or that product, and in time it would arrive
and be added to our inventory. Supplies could come from just
about anywhere in Poland; shipments were arriving at our store
all the time. Where to put everything—that was the great chal-

lenge. Barrels, burlap sacks, boxes and crates, all competed for scarce space. Every available area was taken up with this or that, items hanging from the ceiling, displayed along the walls, set out in large sacks on the floor, or held in reserve in the back rooms and the basement. Few products were packaged ready to be sold. Most were displayed in bulk, needing first to be measured out and after purchase wrapped up in newspaper or plain brown paper.

What better way to see how we lived than to survey a portion of our inventory? For sheer bulk there was probably nothing to compare with our stocks of grease, salt, and kerosene. Without a greasing of the wheels, transportation in and around Kolbuszowa might well come to a standstill, or at best to a crawl. Nearly everything moved by wagons, whose moving parts periodically became cranky and stubborn until appeased with a coat of grease. Machines had to be treated in much the same way. Salt we bought by the carload. A gray variety sold for 20 groschen a kilo, the white for 35 groschen. There were also 25- and 50-pound blocks of rock salt, which peasants bought for their animals.

Because we sold kerosene all year round it seemed as if I was forever carrying cans of kerosene up from the basement to replace empty containers upstairs. In town almost all lighting came from kerosene lamps. We sold kerosene lamps numbered 3, 5, 7, and 11, the numbers referring to the sizes of the wicks. The peasants usually could only afford those with the smallest wicks, which gave off little light but consumed the least amount of kerosene. We also kept some gasoline on hand, which was generally bought for use in cigarette lighters and for cleaning purposes.* Later, in the 1930s, flashlights arrived in Kolbuszowa and we did a lively business in batteries.

Most of our items—*kasha* [cereal], sugar, oil, margarine, rice, flour, chicory, coffee, tea, sewing supplies, paint ingredients, chocolate, candies, soap, socks, china, lamps, glassware, brooms,

---

*It was illegal to sell cigarette lighters without a special permit that was not readily available. Match production, you see, was a government monopoly (though matches were actually produced by a Swedish company), which explains the effort to make cigarette lighters unavailable. Because matches were so precious, peasants usually divided a single one into four parts.

and brushes—were standard everyday products. More unusual were the huge quantities of flypaper (never could we keep enough in stock) and the barrels of castor oil, for which there was never a shortage of customers. Our sales of Christmas ornaments were always very strong; and for Lent we did an especially active business in herring (of which I smelled for weeks on end), which we brought in by the barrel from Danzig. Clearly ours was a most active business, among the largest in town.

I would estimate our yearly volume to be in the vicinity of a million zlotys.* Still, margins were very small, and profits as such were something we never really calculated.† We saw little need to. We took what we required from the store and used the money that came in for other family purchases and to replenish inventory. If there was money left over, well and good. Such money was no doubt profit, though we never referred to it as such.

Ours was a family business, but then so was almost every other one in our town. My mother and father and all my brothers and sisters worked in the store. Home and store were just a doorway apart, so getting to work each day was never a problem. But such convenience had its drawbacks. Living next to the store meant extended working hours. My father rose at 6:00 A.M., headed off first to the synagogue for morning prayers, and was back to open the store at 7:30. He took a half hour for dinner at midday, then returned to the store until 9:00 P.M. If there were no customers, he'd sit in the kitchen, which was adjacent to the store—especially in the winter, when the living quarters were heated and the store area was not. Actually, "closing time" was never quite fixed. It could be as late as 10:00 P.M.; and even after that, if the bell over the entrance door rang, he'd always admit a customer.

The work week created certain problems for Jewish storekeepers in town. The law required almost all businesses to close on Sundays (the exception in Kolbuszowa being the ice cream and

---

*Equivalent to approximately U.S. $200,000 in 1930.—RS

†Costs, which we used to determine prices, were marked on most items in a special lettered code that all family members could interpret. Bookkeeping was performed in a most elementary fashion when it was done at all.

candy stores), but this requirement worked an undue hardship on Jews, who were obligated to keep their shops closed on Saturday in observance of the Jewish Sabbath. The solution, as noted earlier: subterfuge. Officially all stores remained closed on Sunday, with their front doors shut. Back doors, however, remained open, and customers entered through the rear. Thus legal niceties were preserved and business went on. When policemen stopped by on New Year's Day to pay their "respects" to Jewish shopkeepers, they clearly expected to be remembered for their Sunday favors.

Because Jews owned nearly all the retail establishments in town (the only exceptions being the pharmacy, Drewnicki's store and gasoline station, Zach's private restaurant, Szpara's pork store, and Karakiewicz's tavern), non-Jews tended to accept Saturday closings. They were less understanding, however, when businesses closed on other Jewish holidays throughout the year. These often arrived "unexpectedly," producing inconvenience and creating resentment.

Our business was unusual for the wide variety of items we carried. More typical were businesses that specialized, whether they catered to local residents and area peasants or to far-off markets. Several wholesalers found it profitable to buy up local agricultural products and ship them to distant markets, especially England and Italy. Lumber, grain, butter, and livestock were handled in this fashion. So were eggs. Ordinarily these middlemen made their purchases from peasants in the marketplace. A second source of supply was itinerant traders who visited the villages and bought up farm produce in small quantities for eventual resale to the wholesalers. Wholesalers generally made a secure living. For the peasants and itinerant traders the outcome was less certain.

The business of the Hoffert family was typical of those extending beyond Kolbuszowa. Thick forests in the region made the production of wooden products a most natural enterprise. Peasant carvers made all manner of wooden churns, looms, utensils, toys, basins, and plungers that the Hofferts bought and in turn sold in Kolbuszowa, in the marketplaces of other towns, and across Poland itself. The Hofferts themselves made sieves for sifting and separating. Every Sunday, when it was not too cold, you could watch the family working together outside making sieves, and every Tuesday there they were in the marketplace selling their wooden products.

Shoemaking, involving both Poles and some Jews, was not an inconsiderable element in the economy of Kolbuszowa. Everyone needed shoes, though people were not likely to wear them all the time, as I have already mentioned. A person owned one pair, at most two (aside from winter boots), and did everything possible to preserve them. Considerable variation existed both in the way shoes were produced and in the way they were distributed. At the top of this business stood two Jewish shoemakers who produced fine custom-made shoes. A customer brought leather to them, watched them take careful measurements, then returned some two to three weeks later for the finished shoes, which were always black. A few Polish shoemakers also did custom work and less expensively, but Jews generally patronized Jewish shoemakers.

There were about five or six leather stores in town. Much of their business involved farming out the leather to individual shoe-makers from whom they ordered specific quantities and sizes of ready-made shoes. Polish shoemakers, working at home and as-sisted by their wives and children, filled these orders and brought the completed shoes to the leather shops, which then shipped them off to retail stores across Poland. Specialization advanced further when six Jewish families were hired to produce only shoe uppers, leaving it to other shoemakers, responsible for the bot-toms, to assemble the finished product. I'm talking now only about men's shoes. The women of Kolbuszowa had their choice of two stores featuring ready-made shoes, which were supple-mented from time to time by much fancier shoes sent over from America by relatives.

No one threw out shoes. God forbid! There were five shoe-makers in town, all Poles, whose business was strictly repair work, with "Pucak" Skowronski clearly the best of them. Because people customarily had but one pair of shoes, when repairs were neces-sary you waited at the shop until the shoes were ready to go back on your feet. I knew the business quite well because we supplied many of the shoemakers in town. To us they came for their glue, hooks, nails, needles, and thread. Actually one way or another we were involved with many of the town's businesses.

We had in town a sizable clothing industry with all manner of producers and all levels of skill. The Singer sewing machine, powered by the foot pedal, reigned supreme in Kolbuszowa. Sewing machines were to be found in most homes; women were expected to know how to sew and to use the machine for minor repairs and for producing simple items such as quilts, sheets, and pillowcases. We also had an abundance of tailors, maybe thirty or forty, many of them with young apprentices who were learning the trade, though for the first year or two they did little more than assist with household chores. Tailoring was not accounted among the prestige trades in town. Many who entered intended to remain only until better prospects appeared elsewhere.

Most tailors made ready-to-wear garments, usually pants, by sitting hour after hour at their machines in a room that was at once a kitchen, a bedroom, and a workplace. (The idea of "working hours" didn't mean much to us. One kept working as long as there was something to do.) Plain garments these were, garments like the ready-made shirts, pulled over the head and with only two buttons in front, that tailors produced by the hundreds. Another such garment was the underwear intended for peasants. Made from unbleached yellow muslin, it was cheap but strong. All day long, starting at 6:00 A.M., the tailor Mendel Schul's wife sat at her sewing machine producing this underwear. She would cook and sew, or nurse and sew (she had ten children), so that there'd be enough to sell to the peasants in the marketplace. Unlike Mendel's wife, most people worked for contractors who supplied the material to people working at home, then collected the finished pants and jackets. Paid on a piecework basis, even those who worked day and night earned paltry sums.

The shining glory of the garment business such as it was in Kolbuszowa was one very tall and distinguished man, the aforesaid Mendel Schul, a master tailor trained in Vienna, no less. You wouldn't go to him for everyday garments; only for something special, a suit, a wedding coat, above all for something that would fit well. But getting Mendel to produce was no simple matter. Only customers with exceptional patience and perseverance would in the end be rewarded.

The process began unceremoniously enough when he accepted from you the cloth intended for the garment, including material for the lining and horsehair for filling. (The buttons Mendel provided.) Nothing seemed amiss when he then proceeded to take measurements. When asked about a completion date, he was most reassuring although somewhat evasive. Little would you suspect the strange odyssey that was about to begin for your material.

Almost always Mendel first found uses for it other than what was intended. It might serve as a blanket or sheet for his children, then for a time be used as a tablecloth, perhaps also for a floor covering. When sufficient time had elapsed, customers naturally began to wonder how matters stood. Off to Mendel they would go to inquire. Standing there always with a tape measure about his neck, sucking candy, needles protruding every which way from his clothes and a cigarette dangling day and night from his lips, Mendel, ever sympathetic and polite, would indicate that the cloth had already been cut. A search for it ensued, one doomed to failure, given the impossibly disordered condition of his one room. Customers departed, still confident that the material would turn up.

They usually returned shortly thereafter. Indeed the material had been discovered, Mendel assured them; it had in fact been cut. Most encouraging! "Try on the jacket," Mendel would suggest. Almost always it proved too large. A frown appeared immediately on Mendel's face, and he proceeded to scold whichever apprentice happened to be close by. There was no reason to worry, though; he would take it in and make things right. Although the customer did not know it, what he had tried on was not his jacket but another's. Since almost all suits were either black or navy blue, substitution was easy. In all likelihood the customer's cloth had not been cut; indeed it probably had not even been cleaned yet by Mendel after the multitudinous uses to which it had been put.

The next time around the customer was likely to find his garment too tight and thus in need of additional alterations. The stalling continued even as the special occasion approached. But Mendel never failed; your garment would always be ready—just in time. (It should be said that Mendel had Polish customers as well, with whom he tended to act in a more responsible fashion. But the material they brought to him was usually quite distinctive in color and pattern, so that one customer's material could not easily be confused with another's.) Always it was worth the wait, the final product a work of genius, a once-in-a-lifetime purchase, good enough to be passed down to the next generation. There were two other custom tailors in town, both with far more orderly work habits than Mendel, but neither possessing his talents or enjoying his prestige.

Tailors were also needed to alter garments. In large families alterations were frequent as clothes passed back and forth among members; and of course ready-made clothes nearly always required tailoring to fit properly. Then there were the items that arrived from America. These had to be altered for all the usual reasons plus a few unexpected ones. When such clothes were too extreme or too immodest, few dared risk public exposure and censure by wearing them. So it became necessary to alter them, tone them down, keep them from violating community standards. Although it was a source of pride and status to wear clothes from America, in the end the expectations of the people of Kolbuszowa dictated appearances.

Everyone sewed in Kolbuszowa; still tailors had plenty of business. Nor were bakers superfluous simply because most wives baked. My mother baked every week for the Sabbath, arising at 2:00 A.M. Friday morning to prepare *challah* [braided loaf of white bread], rye bread, and cookies. Still we all enjoyed freshly baked goods the rest of the week as well, and for these my mother and others relied on the bakers. There were seven bakers in all, one Pole, the rest Jews. They baked where they lived, the ovens located in their basements, and they all lived on the same street, which was called, quite properly, Baker Street. Two of them operated retail stores. The others baked all night and then sold their goods in the various town markets during the course of the week. One baker had his son go from house to house each morning selling fresh-from-the-oven products. Ah, the baked goods—they were incomparable! The rolls, and especially the bagels and pretzels. Nothing I've tasted since can compare to them. Their taste had something to do, I was told, with the wood used for baking. Without exception the bakers earned a respectable living. Later, when the war came, bakers were in a favored position; they managed more easily than others to have something around to eat and to sell on the black market.

For Jewish families the bakers performed a most valuable service: keeping the *chulent* pot hot for the Sabbath. I'll explain. *Chulent* was a delicacy, a rich, heavy, fatty stew frequently eaten during the main meal on the Sabbath. The problem was that cooking was prohibited on Saturday. Heating up food likewise was forbidden. Enter the bakers. Though their ovens were shut off Friday evening, the heat trapped inside remained. So women brought covered pots of *chulent* to the bakers late Friday afternoon, and into the ovens they went to stand simmering in the heat. (Those who were extremely orthodox sealed their pots with dough so that fumes from the pots of those less observant would not drift into their *chulent*.) Between noon and one o'clock the next day the bakers opened their doors so that the pots could be retrieved and the hot and heavy Sabbath meal get under way.

The people of Kolbuszowa were equally dependent on the butchers, a great number of whom were clustered along one street, like the bakers, in a row of buildings belonging to the municipality. Space was rented from the town, which in turn required that the shops and meat sold there be subject to inspection. On Tuesdays, market days, an area of Kolubuszowa was set aside for buying and selling animals brought in from the surrounding countryside.* A ready supply of meat was therefore usually on hand. Twelve butcher shops could be found on this block, one

---

*Actually most of the transactions were concluded in one of the five taverns in town, four of which were owned by Jews. The taverns enjoyed a steady trade almost every day of the week, but on market day they did especially well. Buyers and sellers of cattle and horses found that the bargaining progressed more easily in the cozy corners of taverns. Besides, a peasant "under the influence" was less likely to hold out for a higher price.

non-kosher, the rest serving the Jewish community. When a kosher butcher purchased an animal, he brought it to the *shochet* [ritual slaughterer] in the municipal slaughterhouse, who then slaughtered it in accordance with Jewish law. Once the town's veterinarian certified the meat, it went on sale at the butcher shop.

Overall the kosher butchers of Kolbuszowa fared quite well, and some became exceptionally well off. In another part of town were six or seven butchers (all non-Jews) dealing exclusively in pork and pork products. They served customers in their stores and also set up stands every Tuesday in the marketplace, where peasants in town for the day delighted in their kielbasa and sausages. Ironically the largest pig dealer in Kolbuszowa was Abraham Rappaport, a Jew, though obviously a nonobserver, whose wholesale enterprise involved the shipment of pigs to markets outside the region. How a Jew could prosper in such a business no one ever explained.

We did not lack for agile hands and clever minds among the workers in Kolbuszowa, Jew and Pole alike. Shuniek Arzt must be counted among the most talented, though his rewards were meager. Arzt owned a jewelry store, and what business he did came from the watches he repaired. Truly a genius, he would reconstruct a watch from parts he himself had produced. Well-known was the story about a French clock that occupied an entire wall of a room in Count Tyszkiewicz's castle. When it suddenly stopped and could not be made to start again, the count sent directly to France for a repairman. The man arrived and spent two or three weeks at the castle working on the clock, but without success. He gave up and returned to France. It was at this point that Arzt was called in. He soon discovered the problem, proceeded to make the necessary parts himself, and returned the clock to working order.

Haskel Green, on the other hand, did nothing to advance the art of watch repairing in our town. When one left a watch for him to repair, there were few grounds for optimism if the problem was the slightest bit complicated. Haskel had no difficulty taking a watch apart; his trouble was in putting it back together. Weeks would go by, during which time he would insist progress was being made. In the end he often conceded the task to be beyond his ability. Green was sometimes compared to one of the town's ritual slaughterers, a man whose skills were also deemed deficient. When Green the watchmaker, it was declared, fixes a watch, the watch stops; and when the slaughterer kills a chicken, the chicken keeps on walking!

Mendel Springer, the candlestick maker, was a craftsman par excellence. Out of brass and copper he created graceful candlesticks, menorahs [ritual candleholders], and chandeliers. He produced exceptionally beautiful pieces, but few could afford his products and as a result he had to rely upon repair work to make a living. By contrast, the two blacksmiths in town (both Poles, although Jewish blacksmiths were commonplace elsewhere) had no difficulty finding customers. They made their own horseshoes and fitted them to horses brought to their shop. They also produced a variety of iron products including plows, sickles, door hinges, iron bars, and window grates. Two tinsmiths, both Jews, were kept busy providing roofing around town, especially after municipal ordinances banned straw or wooden roofs. They produced many of the utensils and measuring cups we used, and in addition repaired and patched pots and pans.

Once in the distant past Kolbuszowa had enjoyed a reputation for producing fine furniture. Craftsmen of the highest order created pieces destined for the castles and estates of the aristocracy across Poland and in France. Finely designed and elaborately carved, these were treasures passed down over the generations. The tradition had ended long ago, as had Kolbuszowa's involvement in the production of fine violins; but there were still furniture makers in town—four in fact, two Jews and two Poles.

I remember each time one of my sisters was about to marry we would go to a furniture maker and order two single beds, some wardrobes, a couple of night tables, and a large table with chairs. Everything was produced by hand, custom-made from the finest wood and veneers. Next we headed over to Moishele Letzter, the only upholsterer in town (in Kolbuszowa, upholstered furniture was rare), to have him make a mattress for us. Mattresses were anything but common in my day. Instead most people slept on burlap bags stuffed with straw that would be changed twice a year, usually before winter and prior to Passover. But we had mattresses made for us by Moishele. Unfortunately these mattresses, for reasons I never could understand, came in sections, three to a bed. This made them uncomfortable, and we had to place cushions between the sections to reduce the discomfort. Eventually there came a notable improvement—a mattress in two sections. Not until I came to America did I discover the marvelous one-piece mattress.

Could there be a commercial town, a place where business was transacted, without the presence of lawyers? There were five in Kolbuszowa, four Jews and one Pole, the last an arrogant fellow who handled mostly government and county cases. Most Poles in Kolbuszowa were not at all reluctant to employ Jewish lawyers, whom they believed to be highly skilled and able to get results. (Besides, these lawyers were "modern" men who adhered but casually to Jewish religious practices.) I remember my father used Benedict Pomerantz, who served also as attorney for Count Tyszkiewicz and the municipality. Except for Pomerantz, lawyers conducted their business in their homes. Without exception they were well off.

Two judges held court in Kolbuszowa, both Poles and both openly biased against Jews. On more than one occasion my father suffered at their hands. Once when he appeared in court the sitting judge made fun of him, mouthing a singsong mannerism, supposedly mimicking the way Jews talked. In fact my father spoke Polish perfectly, without the slightest trace of an accent. He took considerable pride in this. Few times in my life had I seen my father cry, but when he returned from court that day he was in tears. The next time my father came before the court he was once again his feisty self. He had been sued by a Pole over a personal insult.* "You are low," my father had said to his accuser. The judge, after hearing the charge, fined my father ten zlotys. "Then I give you twenty," my father responded, and turning to the plaintiff, he shouted, "And I repeat—you are low!"

*The Poles had a strict sense of personal honor. When it was called into question, they were quick to rush to its defense.

The doctors of Kolbuszowa commanded the respect of all. My father, influential as he was, always took off his hat when the doctor arrived at our home to care for a sick member of the family. For years there were just two doctors in town, Dr. Leon Anderman and the official county doctor, a Pole, who among other functions administered inoculations in the school but who also had his own private practice. In 1935 or '36 a third doctor, Marek Marienstraus, a Jew, settled in town, struggling at first but in time advancing to a comfortable living such as the two others enjoyed. Few were disposed to call for a doctor unless the ailment became severe. The charge: three zlotys.

The county veterinarian lived in Kolbuszowa. One of his principal responsibilities was certifying the condition of horses for the army. Once a year horses in the area were examined and their suitability for army service determined. An owner whose horse was selected had no choice but to deliver it up to the army, though he could expect fair compensation. Reaction to this draft varied. At times owners announced proudly that their animals had been selected, but on other occasions there was grumbling and resentment at being deprived of the services of a valuable asset. The veterinarian also assisted the Horse Commission when it arrived in town to examine horses as part of its effort to improve breeding stock. If commission members determined a horse to be in some way deficient, it had to be castrated. When a horse passed inspection, its proud owner was not only pleased but also assured of added income from stud fees.

Kolbuszowa also had two dentists (one a Russian woman who left Leningrad for our town shortly after the Russian Revolution) and four barbers. The barbers were assuredly the most versatile. Cutting hair was only one of their skills. They could also pull teeth and draw blood, a therapy valued by many as a cure for whatever ailed them. For drawing blood they employed leeches, which could be seen in jars displayed in their store windows. The leeches could be purchased, or the barber could be summoned to your home to apply them. The peasants in particular placed great faith in the therapeutic power of leeches.*

*I never did, for after all I was a modern person; also, as noted earlier, I had

Judaism was our religion; it governed the way we lived. But for some it also provided a living, however meager. The Jewish Council in town, the organization officially representative of the Jewish community of Kolbuszowa, raised money and employed several people. Most of its revenues came from the ritual slaughtering franchise it sold.* No animals could be eaten unless they had first been killed in the prescribed manner, and for this a fee was paid to the kosher slaughterers selected by the Jewish Council. Slaughtering fees ranged from twenty-five groschen for a chicken to a half zloty for a goose, one zloty for a calf, and five zlotys for a cow. The slaughterers, in addition to their salaries, made additional money on the side when Jews from the villages arrived and negotiated special fees that were kept "off the books."

The Jewish Council, which employed a paid secretary, Hersh Gewirz, also provided funds for our rabbi, Yechiel Teitelbaum, and his assistant, the *dayan,* Mendel Rubin, though the amount was most meager. Fortunately the rabbi was able to supplement his income, as for example when he sat as a judge settling disputes on the rabbinical court. Both parties in the controversy before the court were expected to contribute an identical amount of money to the rabbi in return for his decision. Of course, our rabbi was called on almost daily to answer questions regarding Jewish law and ritual—"With pimples on its liver or nails in its stomach, tell me, Rabbi, is the chicken still kosher?" The rabbi resolved these

---

a vested interest in the healing powers of *bankes,* small glass cups that were applied to the skin (usually the back) to drain out the sickness and fever from the body. To apply these cups to best effect required no little skill and dexterity, and that's why I was called upon often for this service, usually assisted by my sister Malcia. First a lit candle was used to ignite the alcohol applied to the inside of the cup. Even before the flame was extinguished you quickly placed the cup, mouth down, on the skin. The vacuum produced by the flame led the cup to adhere to the skin. The more complete the vacuum, the tighter the cup pressed on the skin, indeed drew the skin into the cup. Nimbleness and speed of transfer were required here, and that's where I excelled. I would apply up to twenty to thirty cups at one time. The success of this therapy was thought to correlate with the size and darkness of the welts left after the cups were removed, welts that could be seen up to two months later! If the *bankes* therapy proved disappointing, there was always the doctor.

*For years that franchise belonged to Hersh Ulan.

questions and countless others like them at no charge. But when he was invited by congregation members to attend their parties and celebrations, he could count on receiving something for his presence.

In Kolbuszowa we had a *sopher* [scribe], Fischel Saltz, a man with an angelic face, a most contented man. He enjoyed a reputation for piety that extended far beyond our town. Because of this he was much in demand to produce handwritten prayers, which were then placed within *tefillin* and *mezuzahs*.* It was painstaking work, for which he received only modest payment. For him it was a labor of love, which explains why so many sought him out. To produce a completed Torah, for example, might take a year, probably two. In part this was because every element he prepared himself, including the parchment from the skin of an unborn calf, thread from its veins, and the ink and the quills with which he produced the letters, then the words. That a scribe should be worthy to write the holy words was an obligation he assumed with awesome seriousness. Such purity, such exceptional holiness! Little wonder that all treasured what came forth from his hands.

On many occasions I witnessed just how singularly sincere he was. Fischel didn't live far from us. There would be times when I saw him five or six times in one day. There he was walking at a rapid pace from his house in the direction of the *mikvah,* the ritual baths. What he was about was no mystery; it was in fact what accounted for his reputation as a scribe. That the name of God would appear quite often in the text he was preparing was well understood. But before writing the Holy Word he had first to ensure his own purity, and that meant a trip to the *mikvah.* There he would undress and submerge himself completely in the purifying waters. Back home he would go, and then, appropriately prepared, he could set down on paper the awesome word. That the name of God might appear once again after an interval of a few words did not disturb Fischel. Putting his quill aside, he once

---

*Tefillin, small leather boxes containing Bible passages, are worn during morning prayers. *Mezuzahs* are small cases or lockets affixed to front door jambs of Jewish homes that contain parchment with biblical verses.—RS

again headed off to the *mikvah,* ever concerned that the name of God should not be inscribed by a man not altogether cleansed, not entirely pure.

At the *mikvah,* Fischel would be attended by Mendel Gertner, keeper of the ritual and public bath. His job was to see that everything was in readiness when people arrived. Women usually went on Thursday nights to purify themselves before Friday, the night usually reserved for sexual relations with their husbands; men ordinarily went the following day, for the steam baths. Mendel, who lived right across from the baths, was a pleasant man and a learned one. From the baths, however, he could not make a sufficient living, so he like many others had a side job—selling religious books and religious articles. Were you in need of a *chumash* [Bible], a *sidur* [prayer book], or religious articles such as *tefillin, tzitzits* or a *tallit* [prayer shawl], there was Mendel to sell them to you.

Certain seasonal religious jobs also existed, notably around Passover time. On that occasion we ate a matzoh, a special unleavened bread that had to be prepared under closely supervised conditions. Only Passover flour could be used, flour that had been produced by mills specially cleansed for the occasion. Once such flour had been obtained, it was brought to the houses of two bakers authorized each year to bake the Passover matzohs. Even so no chances were taken; a religious Jew stood by in each baker's house to guard against violations as the Passover matzohs were prepared. Once completed the matzohs were collected and the bakers paid for their labors.

Melameds, religious teachers of the young, were a fixture of every Jewish community, and we had the usual assortment of types who eked out a living in this manner. There were different teachers for each age group, starting with the boys at age three. Each year one passed on to another teacher, each one trying to impart something to the young "scholar" and hoping also to attract a class large enough so that he might make a living. A living it sometimes was, but never a comfortable one.

A teacher worked hard with the young day after day, pounding into their heads the basic elements of Hebrew and the fundamental precepts of our faith. With a scholar it was altogether different.

It was enough that he was dedicating his life to studying the holy scriptures and the principal religious texts. This was a higher calling, one requiring no explanation, no justification. I have already spoken about such men, how eagerly they were sought out by fathers who were anxious to have them marry their daughters, willing to provide for them in all ways, and ready to allow them to follow their scholarly pursuits for years on end. Mostly their wives felt the same way; honored to be married to a scholar, they accepted his detachment and his almost total immersion in books and study. Willingly would a scholar's wife bear his children, run the household, and go out and work, leaving him free to follow his "higher" pursuits. What choice did she have? He could do little to help her, so unsuited was he for almost anything other than endlessly poring over texts and engaging in scholarly interpretations and exchanges.

When on occasion a scholar was called upon to help out, as for example when his pregnant wife was about to deliver, he was likely to demonstrate just how unsuited he was for the real world. A story about one scholar in Kolbuszowa and how he got his name is most instructive. We knew him as Moishe Gdziezona, and I'll tell you why. His wife, who operated a bridal shop, asked Moishe one day to take charge of things while she prepared to give birth (they would have twelve children). He did not object to this diversion and agreed to watch the store. Unfortunately he spoke no Polish. A Pole soon walked into the store and asked, "Gdzie zona?," "Where is your wife?" Assuming that the customer referred to an item sold in the store, Moishe began opening every box and drawer in search of a gdzie zona. The customer repeated the question, but that only sent Moishe looking even more frantically through the shop. By that time the customer had departed. When his wife asked if all had gone well, he suggested that to her existing stock-in-trade she consider adding a gdzie zona!

The story was always told in good-humored fashion, for you see in scholars the absence of a certain worldliness was in no way considered a liability. Their singlemindedness was accepted without question. Their indifference to business, to making a living, and to bringing up children was entirely forgivable given their dedication to the word, to perpetuating the wisdom of the sages. In Kolbuszowa, however, such independent scholars, once quite numerous, were in my day becoming fewer in number.*

Jewish tradition required that a woman about to be married cut off the hair on her head the day after her wedding night. This was primarily to make her unattractive to other men, but also to ensure that no part of her—not even a single hair—remained out of the water when she entered the ritual baths. In public, of course, married women would always appear with their heads covered, usually with a kerchief. On the Sabbath and other special occasions the kerchief was replaced by a wig, often a finely made and costly one. Wigmakers therefore could count on a steady demand for their creations. As time went on, the younger and more progressive girls of Kolbuszowa began paying more attention to their appearance, stopped cutting their own hair, and began patronizing a beauty parlor in town that was operated by a sister of the wigmaker.

As noted earlier, Jews ran the majority of the businesses in Kolbuszowa and Poles monopolized the positions in the municipal and county governments, including the schools. Just about every official—policeman, teacher, clerk, caretaker, street cleaner, dog catcher—was Polish. There were just two exceptions: one Jew worked as collector for the internal revenue bureau, and another, Weinglass, served as a clerk in the County Office. Both qualified for the same reason—their association with Piłsudski's Legion, the famed fighting force that halted the Bolshevik advance in 1919–20 and preserved the independence of Poland. Heroes all, Legionnaires received preferential treatment throughout the country. The revenue official had himself served with the Legion;

---

*I must not forget to mention Leon Tauh, the only Jewish teacher in our public schools. A Jewish teacher was acceptable only because religion was a required subject in the curriculum. Once a week the Jewish children received an hour of religious instruction from Tauh while the Catholic youngsters were taught by a priest. Religious instruction was the one thing we didn't need, having been constantly subjected to it ever since we were three years old. That's probably why Tauh's appearance in the classroom became the signal for all of us to misbehave. Never was he able to control our class.

Weinglass, the clerk, occupied the post on the basis of his father's war service. These two, in positions of no particular distinction or importance, were the only Jews holding salaried jobs with the government.*

A comparative economic survey of Kolbuszowa would show that although the wealthier people tended to be Jews, Poles generally occupied the middle levels. You could probably identify no more than five to ten very well-to-do Poles, but a great many earned good, steady, secure middle-level incomes (150 to 250 zlotys a month). More Jews than Poles were very well off, but a considerable number were poorer. I would estimate that 10 percent of the Jews were very comfortable, lived well, could afford lavish weddings and large dowries, and contributed generously to charity. About 40 percent got by, enjoying few comforts but escaping the fears associated with living from day to day. That leaves about half of the Jewish population in the lowest category, poor people for whom life was a daily struggle and existence precarious. Still, such people worked hard to get by, looked for help, begged, borrowed, and held on, all the while maintaining their dignity, not cursing their fate, sometimes even counting their meager blessings.

To say that a large portion of the Jews of Kolbuszowa were in business is true, and a variety of businesses at that. Although some

---

*A further example of discriminatory separation could be seen in the Fire Department. It was a volunteer organization, but not a Jew served in it. If I had been of age, I would certainly have attempted to join. All members, however, were Poles, mostly shoemakers from the section of Kolbuszowa known as New Town. Why this should be I never understood. Had word gotten out that it was two Jews who set what turned out to be the Great Fire of 1908? Probably not, so well kept a secret it was that two Jewish brothers in the grain business had decided to salvage their family enterprise by burning it down and collecting the insurance. Unfortunately their plan to start a fire, allow it to take hold in their warehouse, and then sound the alarm went awry. As the story goes, they set the fire but delayed giving the warning to ensure the total destruction of their place of business. So by the time they began shouting "Fire!" it was too late; the flames had spread and could not be contained. Utter devastation followed; few buildings in town were untouched. It became for us an unforgettable event, the great dividing line in the modern history of Kolbuszowa. We would suffer another major blaze in 1927, this one burning down perhaps 15–20 percent of the town, the section untouched in the 1908 fire.

were substantial undertakings, many, as I've said, were businesses in name only. Often the place of business was little more than a hole in the wall (doubling as a residence as well), containing little if any merchandise and producing meager sales. Small, dirty windows made it difficult for "shoppers" to determine just what was inside. In time picture windows were installed in some of the newer stores.

Whatever the prospects for business, the proprietor and his family waited each day in the shop from morning till nighttime hoping for at least a few customers. When sales were disappointing, everything would depend on market day, when peasants arrived in town. Some peasants shopped around, especially when seeking out white flour at the lowest prices; but most had their favorite "Jew," a storekeeper whom they liked and trusted. Here they believed they would be treated properly and dealt with fairly.* A few such steady customers often meant the difference between staying in business and closing down.

A precarious existence, that was the predicament faced by half of Kolbuszowa's Jewish population. As I've said, it was easy to enter a business, to section off a portion of your room and declare it a store, to purchase a few items and call them your stock, but then what? Would people come? Would you have anything they wished to buy? That was the awful reality. I remember a drawing I saw many a time with a message no one could mistake. It was a picture of a businessman in his store with all the shelves empty— a businessman without merchandise and presumably without money. Without stock there could be no sales and therefore little possibility of acquiring items to sell.

*One way authorities ensured fairness was by strict regulations governing weights and measures. Once a year a special commission arrived in town from Rzeszow to check every scale and ruler in town, a charge taken quite seriously. Members went from store to store examining scales, checking weights, and then, if all was well, affixing an official brass stamp to the scale. Some shopkeepers evaded the law, hiding scales before the inspectors arrived. It was not so much that they were bent on cheating the public as that they wished to avoid paying the fee for each scale checked. If during the year the municipal police discovered scales that lacked official inspection stamps, owners were subject to substantial fines.

There were times when a retailer in town, with a customer waiting in his shop, raced over to our store to buy an item he didn't have (promising to pay us later) and then promptly sold it at a slight markup. That kind of marginal operation was all too common with us, and not just among retailers. Many tried to find ways to scratch out a living, desperate to find something to do, some angle, some function, however minor, anything to stave off destitution. There was, for example, Baruch Kanner, whose business it was to buy used burlap sacks, then resell them to small flour mills and animal feed outlets. Every so often he spent the day outside our store sorting out rice, cereal, flour, and sugar sacks, which always left his face, beard, and clothing almost entirely white. He had any damaged sacks sewn up before setting out to resell them.

Then there was Zalman Wasserman, the umbrella fixer, who went from house to house in town and then out to the surrounding peasant villages knocking on doors and offering to repair damaged umbrellas. There was no mistaking him with his long beard and the knapsack on his back containing wires and clippers. Usually he received no money but accepted grain, eggs, or cheese for his services. The two glaziers in town (brothers whose father had been a glazier—it was generally expected that sons would follow the father's vocation) went about their business in much the same way. They walked from village to village carrying their pieces of glass, offering to fix broken windows. They were quite poor. Most people, if they bothered at all to replace cracked glass, did it themselves.

And of course everyone knew Berish Bilfeld, the scavenger of Kolbuszowa. Whatever you had no use for he would likely take, often paying you for it. Old rags, scrap iron, lead, animal bones, fat, bottles, discarded machines—he took it all, then tried to resell it. Poor he was, but there wasn't a kindlier or more compassionate soul. He stored all his junk in a shed on the edge of town, a place he made available to any poor person visiting in town or just passing through. All visitors were welcome to sleep on a pile of rags amid the junk.

Many townspeople stayed alive by functioning as low-level middlemen between peasants and wholesalers. Their work week was spent walking along the paths that connected village to village, going from peasant hut to peasant hut buying small quantities of eggs, chickens, animal skins, grain, or butter. Most specialized in one item. At the end of the week they sold their goods to a wholesaler in town, hopefully earning an amount sufficient to keep them and their family going. What made this kind of operation possible were no-interest loans, many of them from the Free Loan Society (financed by Jews from Kolbuszowa living in America), others from well-to-do Jews. Middlemen used the money from such loans to pay the peasants, then paid off the loan at the end of the week with money received from the wholesalers.

I remember one man who came every Sunday evening to our house to borrow 200 zlotys from my father. He was a butter man, getting his butter from the peasants in the early part of the week, then heading off to Cracow by truck every Wednesday night. On Thursday he sold the butter there, and on Friday he returned the money my father had loaned to him. But he was always back two days later to borrow once again. This went on for years. He was never able to accumulate enough money; always he had to borrow to keep going.

My father lent money to a number of other people on the same basis. They borrowed it and then returned it shortly thereafter. Week after week, year after year, it was the same pattern. Why did my father do it? It was a *mitzvah,* a good deed, a charitable act, a good turn, a favor. He had always done it. What reason was there not to do it? Others felt the same way, even some who themselves had no money to lend out. Here was Kivche Leistner, a kindly, open-hearted man, an early Zionist, the owner of a notions store that barely provided him with a living. What he did was to borrow money from my father and several others and then lend it out, interest-free, to people in need of the funds. For years he did this. Most of the borrowers never knew it wasn't his money they were borrowing. He went to all this trouble, making nothing himself, because performing such good deeds was, he felt, an obligation.

Where there beggars in Kolbuszowa? Actually there were four families in town who everyone knew survived by begging.* Every

*A few who begged did so to supplement earnings that were clearly insuffi-

Friday the wives went from house to house. No one questioned why they were there. Everyone knew and would give them two, five, maybe ten groschen. On the following day, the Sabbath, they would be back. A knock on the door and there they were, holding out an open cushion cover, expecting that some pieces of *challah* would be placed inside.* They didn't go to every household, only to those they knew were in a position to offer them something. Nothing had to be said; their visits had gone on too long to require any explanation. If there had once been any shame attached to their begging, it had long since passed. It was their life; everyone accepted it.

Some people, it's true, couldn't get themselves to ask for money. This was the case with one of my *cheder* teachers, an old man with a gray beard. He couldn't ask directly, but still he managed. About once a week, when he would see me, he'd start circling around before finally coming over. "What's doing?" he would ask, the unmistakable signal that he was in need. At that point I usually took out twenty-five groschen and handed it to him. Then there was the very learned, scholarly man who loved to smoke but was in no position to buy cigarettes. When he stepped into the store my father knew why he was there and usually gave him five or six cigarettes.

Every Saturday afternoon Golde Mirel, an elderly woman who lived alone, came over to our house knowing my mother would give her something. Usually it was *challah,* soup with a piece of meat in it, a glass of tea, and a piece of cake. "Good Sabbath," said she, and in she came to sit down on a bench in the kitchen and eat her portion. In perhaps five or ten minutes she would finish and leave. A week later she would be back again.

When certain holidays were on the way, the level of charitable activity quickened, especially before Passover. Money from America would usually arrive in time for the poor to purchase and pre-

---

cient. For example, the gravedigger's wife came to us for some money every Friday and returned the next day for *challah.*

*This was not just confined to Jews. For example, the janitor of the synagogue, who was Polish, came to us every Friday for money and then again on Saturday afternoon for *challah.*

pare the special foods that marked the celebration. Always ways had to be devised to get money to those who had once been self-sufficient but had fallen on hard times.* Embarrassment often kept them from accepting assistance openly.†

Jewish administrators of large land estates in the area usually saw to it that food supplies were distributed to the needy before the holidays. Wagonloads of potatoes might be sent to town, unloaded in an empty store, and given out from there. These same administrators usually were the first to arrange shipments of firewood to the poor once the weather turned cold. For well-off people wood was never a problem. It was always bought in advance,

---

*The distribution of funds to such people was arranged by Leibtche Beck. Beck had lived in America for a time and then returned to Kolbuszowa, where he built a most successful wholesale business. He was known to donors in the United States and so was the natural "transfer agent" for money from that country. The "established" poor in town rarely were satisfied with the amounts of money they received; they always resented that funds were given to the "hidden" poor.

†I should emphasize how sensitive our community was to this issue. The poor should be assisted, we believed, and spared embarrassment whenever possible. Especially during the summer months, itinerant Jewish beggars passed through Kolbuszowa, going door to door asking for charity. Eventually an organization was established to raise money for these unfortunate people and spare them the humiliations that begging occasioned. When these same beggars came to the synagogue on Friday night, they would always wait near the door after services, hoping to be invited home for a Sabbath meal by a member of the congregation. Always they were, but the process of waiting to be asked was demeaning and we put an end to it. Another organization was formed to recruit people willing to take beggars into their homes for the Sabbath on a regular basis. Assignments were made beforehand, so that every beggar knew to whose home he'd be going after services concluded. For months on end, a guest ate at our table every Friday night and Saturday noon.

With us charity was not an afterthought or a matter of minor importance. It stood at the very center of our religious beliefs, an obligation of the highest order. Men of standing in the community simply had to give and give in many ways, not only directly to the needy who came knocking on their doors regularly (I would estimate that in a given week we had ten such requests), but also to the many charitable organizations in town. Giving anonymously was considered a most elevated deed (the stories were many of famous rabbis who gave in this fashion), but naturally many preferred their generosity be public knowledge. Charity began at home, but it did not end there. When at times it did, the town exacted its revenge on the uncharitable person after his death. How? The Burial Society simply refused to prepare the body and stage the funeral until a large sum of money was "donated" to the society by the family of the deceased.

usually over the summer, and stacked in piles outside the house. We always, it seemed, had enough on hand to last us several winters, and were therefore in a position to use only the driest wood, wood that would produce smokeless, hot fires. The poor, by contrast, had to buy wood almost every day in the winter. I'd watch the same women coming to the marketplace day after day, able to afford only a few pieces of wood at a time. Usually it was fresh, wet wood, soft pine, which smoked to excess and gave off relatively little heat. For people in these circumstances a supply of firewood meant a great deal.

Charity was not exclusively an individual affair, whether it came from residents in Kolbuszowa or from former townsmen now in America.* The municipality accepted some obligation to help those in need. In the winter, for example, it distributed wood and kerosene to the poor. When my father was on the City Council, one of his responsibilities was to certify those in need of such assistance. (Just as he also authorized these same people to receive a free medical exam and medication. My father always approved such requests.) The Jewish community also maintained a poorhouse, or at least a few rooms in the same building where the ritual slaughter of chickens was conducted for travelers who were poor or Kolbuszowa residents who had suffered a serious misfortune. The town would provide rent money for a period of time.

Being poor never is easy, and certainly the poor of Kolbuszowa suffered. Still it was not in anger or with constant complaints that most lived their lives. You could be poor, but what did you need? A roof over your head, some clothes, bread, potatoes, soup. Most managed that, much of the time. Besides, Kolbuszowa was a poor town. To be poor in a poor town was no great shame. No one singled you out or thought it necessary to account for your condition. It needed no explanation. Anyway, God owed no one a living. On the other hand, together with God you could live as a person should. The humblest person who walked with God

---

*Certain people in town were able to get by thanks primarily to money sent them by relatives living in America [see pp. 206–7].

walked with dignity, was respected. He did not ask much of God, nor did he expect material benefits. For his devotion, for living in the prescribed manner, he hoped only for a long and healthy life. Riches were not to be expected, at least in this world.

Still there was the chance for improvement. It had happened, even without the Messiah appearing. A son or a daughter marrying into a family of means—why not? Moving off to a larger town, to Rzeszow, Tarnow, even Cracow—might not life be better then? Certainly it would be better in Palestine or America. But what about Kolbuszowa? Was one's place in life fixed unalterably? To be sure, we had our success stories. Many who were well off in my time certainly hadn't begun that way. We Jews had never been an aristocratic or privileged group in this region. Still there was Bezalel Orgel, who early in life had been nothing more than a messenger in a bank but whose fortunes rose dramatically after World War I when he bought lumber and flour mills and forested land. Then consider Abraham Insel, a very, very poor, uneducated person who started by transporting the goods of others with his horse and wagon, then during World War I began buying and selling his own items, and finally opened a general merchandise wholesale business and enjoyed considerable success.

My father's experience deserves mention. Originally a villager, he had for many years owned only a small retail store in town. Business improved as he took an active role in town affairs, joining one organization after another. But he lost heavily during World War I, and then again lost everything in the pogrom of 1919. Still, he kept at it and rebuilt his general merchandise business, which soon became the largest in town.

These men and others like them were very well off and made excellent livings. There was little flaunting of wealth—a fur coat here, there a few diamonds. You could see it, though, in the weddings some gave, in the amount of charity they provided, and in their contributions to the synagogue and to the rabbi. There was little need to show off because everyone in town knew. There were few secrets in Kolbuszowa, certainly not when it came to money. Nothing was sadder than those, once comfortable, who attempted desperately to conceal a sharp decline in fortunes. When, for example, a woman began wearing her Sabbath dress each day of the week, you knew the family had suffered reversals.

One danger there was in acquiring wealth, however, that threatened our community more than any resentments that might have arisen against the well-to-do. It was a tendency, often remarked upon, that wealth promoted strong secularist tendencies, a drifting away from the religious community. Certainly that had not been true of my father, and I could point to other affluent men who deviated not an inch from the traditions and the faith. But with lawyers, doctors, engineers, and others it was frequently a different story. With their education and entry into professional life they had, it seemed, entered a different world and drawn apart from the rest of us. Few reached the extreme of Rappaport the pig dealer, but all who had drifted away, to whatever degree, became a cause for concern, a challenge to what the Jewish community of Kolbuszowa had always stood for. I for one welcomed this challenge, with its message of choices that might at some point be openly available, but my sentiments were not those of most others.

Even if the Germans had never come it would not have gone well for us in Poland. It had not in fact been going well for some time. By the late 1930s the signs were everywhere, were unmistakable. We Jews faced a dismal future. Our economic position, always insecure, was beginning to erode as the result of a deliberate effort by Poles to bring us low. We faced growing political attacks as well as a direct campaign against a variety of Jewish economic targets. From on high, authorities made it clear most Jews were no longer welcome in Poland. Cardinal Chlond, the head of the Catholic Church in Poland, was not in the least subtle. "We have in Poland three and a half million Jews," he declared; "in my estimation, three million too many." This assertion was repeated by Foreign Minister Joseph Beck, who thought that three million Polish Jews definitely would have to go.

Atheists, Bolsheviks, white slavers, thieves—our accusers exercised little restraint in describing our supposed misdeeds. Stirring up economic resentment and producing convenient scapegoats became the general order of the day. "The houses are Jewish and the streets are ours" went an all too familiar slogan.* "Poland is ours" became the automatic response to any attempt to defend Jewish economic activities and contributions. The efforts to oust Jews from their positions in the Polish economy needed to go forward, according to Prime Minister General Slawoj Skladkowski. "I will not allow people," he said, "to beat or kill Jews. But to destroy them economically? *Owszem*—by all means."

In Kolbuszowa the attacks we experienced were of two kinds. One originated from below, its target being Jewish small businesses in rural villages. The organization of peasant cooperatives and the insistence that members buy supplies from the cooperative, helped along by the slogan "Everybody to his own, for his own," undermined the position of Jewish businessmen.† In village after village their small enterprises simply disappeared, and the former owners were forced to relocate in the towns. The other kind of attack was from above. The Polish government moved to subsidize Polish manufacturers so that they could in time displace Jewish producers.‡

Was our family's wholesale business under siege? Yes and no. We withstood the first assault, actually benefiting at first when some of our competitors in the villages were forced out of business. The new peasant cooperatives began organizing wholesale operations; but inexperienced as they were, there was much mismanagement and failures were frequent. As a result our Polish peasant customers remained with us. Yet this reprieve, we knew, was only temporary. The effort to oust us and other Jews in our

*Just as familiar was "Jews to Palestine."

†In our area, at least, the government attempted to suppress the growing peasant movement, often in a brutal manner.

‡There were also various kinds of harassment. Efforts to eliminate ritual slaughter did not succeed, nor did pressure to switch market day in Kolbuszowa to Saturday bring any results. The Polish government did, however, force Jews who had changed their first names to Polish-sounding ones to revert back to their original names. You could see that Jews, especially professionals, complied with this new law. On plaques identifying a resident and his profession, quite often the first name was chipped out and a new name painted in.

position would continue, and that they would in time succeed I had no doubt. Hostile attitudes toward the Jews in Poland were of long standing and becoming more and more intense. Merging with the anti-Semitic propaganda pouring out of Germany, they produced a lethal mixture. Progressively squeezed and shoved into a corner as we were, our situation was becoming all too clear. Set upon as we were from all sides, what kind of a future could there be for Jews in Poland?

In the Marketplace

Times like these I would never know again. The exhaustive preparations, the nervous energy, the bustle, the smells, the crowds, the sights—all this, all day, every week, year after year—all right outside my door! We lived, you see, in the marketplace. No one who had ever lived in Kolbuszowa or been present on market day could ever forget the throbbing excitement of the occasion. Even after the passage of years I find myself still awaiting Tuesdays, imagining myself bracing for the challenge. What happened or, God forbid, didn't happen on Tuesdays was a matter of considerable gravity. For many, too many in fact, to do at least some business that day was altogether essential. A bad day put everything in jeopardy. This was serious business.

The reason Tuesday was market day in Kolbuszowa was that market day was on Monday in Maydan, Wednesday in Sokolow, Thursday in Ranizow, and Friday in Rzeszow and in Sedziszow. When had all this started? Who had ordained these days? I'm not sure anyone knew the answer. But as far back as people's memories stretched, that was the way it had been. And so it remained during all my years in Kolbuszowa.

On market day town and country met for the purpose of exchange. Each depended on the other, knew what to expect, understood the terms of trade. From early morning on, thousands of peasants poured into the marketplace; hour after hour vendors stood beside their wares hoping for customers. At the end of the day peasants trekked back to the villages; the vendors, some from Kolbuszowa, the rest outsiders, packed up, and many prepared to move on to the next town, where as dawn broke yet another marketplace would begin to stir.

Our marketplace was large (easily the size of a football field) and enclosed on all four sides. On a busy day there might be some five thousand peasants milling about at any one time, looking at and often bargaining over the offerings of hundreds and hundreds of vendors. Tuesday was market day whatever the weather. On clear days with pleasant temperatures a festive, relaxed air prevailed, with business and pleasures mixing easily. During the rainy days of early fall and the icy, snowy, dark days of winter, it was altogether different. The market then became a trial, a severe test of endurance, with buyers and sellers alike exposed to the elements. My sympathy always went out to the vendors, who were obliged to stand about all day bracing against the soaking rain, the ice forming on their clothes, the cold cutting through unsparingly. Exposed, unprotected, hot coals in a pot placed nearby were their only source, however deficient, of warmth. But they stood their ground. Every sale was vital; what choice had they but to endure?

Peasants headed into the marketplace, many having first to sell before they could buy. What they needed largely determined what they brought along with them. A coat, shoes, tools, kerosene, a kerchief, flypaper, seeds, whatever it was, they knew what they would have to pay. Would a cow have to be sold? A horse? Might a few chickens or some geese be enough, or just some eggs and butter? Selling ordinarily was no problem. Customers there were, plenty of them, wholesale merchants accumulating large quantities of eggs or chickens or pigs and townspeople awaiting the fresh supplies of the countryside. Some peasants completed their business quickly, selling to customers who met them along the streets even before they arrived in the market. Others had arranged beforehand to supply certain store owners in town and headed off directly to complete the transaction. That was how we often obtained our supplies. My mother simply informed peasants she knew of our needs—a chicken, eggs, potatoes—then waited while they were delivered directly to us.

One notable exception was buying geese. Jews liked to eat goose. Actually, it would be more accurate to say we hungered for it, especially in winter. A goose, particularly a fat one, was a prize valued so highly that extraordinary efforts were made to acquire one. Once my mother let it be known that she'd be wanting a fat goose* I knew well what was expected of me. I had to head out of town, a distance of maybe half a mile, early in the morning and wait along the road for peasant wagons carrying geese to come along. However early I left, others were already there waiting,† both men and women, prepared as I was to spring into action.

The mad dash began as soon as a wagon came into view, everyone running toward it, hoping to get on and lay claim to the fattest geese. This was no simple task, since it involved leaping aboard a moving wagon, then simultaneously holding on and thrusting one's hand into the cages to size up the birds. Now everyone knew just where to feel for the fat, either under the wings for the telltale lump or near the goose's behind. Goose after goose might have thus to be examined before a sufficiently plump one was found. Once a choice of one or two had been made, the challenge became that of hanging on to them whatever ensued, which was also no easy matter, as I shall explain.

But first, let us set the scene. Quite a few people had by now climbed onto the wagon and were standing on the poles that ran along the sides; others were still attempting to. People's poking around the cages naturally agitates the geese, which begin to screech hysterically. Meanwhile the peasant driver has become quite furious and begins urging his horses on, both to escape those still in pursuit and to shake the grip of the people clinging

*A fat goose because we prized the *schmaltz* [fat], which we separated and kept, then later smeared onto bread—a treat almost everyone relished—and also used during Passover for cooking and on matzohs.

†On occasion poor women came out to wait for the geese, which they planned to sell in town at a slight profit. The peasants usually charged the same price for a goose, fat or thin, so a fat goose could often be resold at a somewhat higher price.

both to the wagon and the geese. A torrent of curses accomplishes little, so he turns his whip on the unwanted riders, who stubbornly hold their ground. A rising chorus of pounding hooves, abusive shouts, and cackling geese greets onlookers as the wagon careens into town with its original cargo and its recently acquired and remarkably persistent passengers, sometimes as many as five or six. Once in the marketplace the wagon comes to a stop, and the situation gradually returns to normal. Claims to particular geese are advanced and honored, and the peasant collects the money due him. Weary and bruised, the customers depart triumphantly, their heroic efforts rewarded. Can you understand now why fetching a fat goose was for me always a challenge? I never tired of the chase.

Market day itself was an adventure, especially for those peasants who rarely moved off their land. A day in town instead of at hard labor certainly was an exceptional treat and eagerly awaited. Indeed, once business had been concluded there was time for amusement and for talk, time for eating and drinking or just wandering about with family or friends. Market day was a boon for the taverns, which filled up quickly and stayed busy the entire day. Sellers of kielbasa and sausages in the marketplace also enjoyed brisk sales; the peasants eagerly lined up for these treats and then gobbled them down.

Peasant boys often brought girlfriends along to sample the entertainments and delights of Kolbuszowa. But the presence of these young people sometimes led to trouble. Their high spirits and aggressiveness could not always be contained. Few market days passed without fights breaking out among the younger peasants. Nor were these always minor flareups; at times vicious, bloody encounters took place. Young men frequently arrived in town carrying thick walking sticks, stout weapons indeed, in the event of a fight. On occasion knives were produced with grisly results. Upwards of five to seven policemen patrolled the area on market day, but their presence could not always contain the violent outbreaks.

Preparations for market day began for some on Monday evening. Some vendors from outside Kolbuszowa preferred to arrive on Monday night so as to be ready for business early the following morning. Always this was the pattern of the "Biala Gentiles," year after year a fixture in the marketplace. Late each Monday I would watch as they rolled into the market area before nightfall, all together perhaps twenty-five to thirty wagons. These robust, sturdy peasants, men and women from the village of Biala, south of Rzeszow, had been in the business of raising and selling vegetables as far back as anyone could remember. Weary after the four-hour trip to Kolbuszowa, they unharnessed the horses, then prepared supper for themselves, cooking sausages and a variety of vegetable dishes after buying vinegar from us. Then it was time to settle in for the night, and the entire group of twenty-five or thirty bedded down on blankets under their wagons. Summer or winter, mild or frigid, rain or snow, it didn't matter—the peasants of Biala went to sleep under their wagons, arising early the next morning, usually before everyone else, to make ready for the day.

Tuesday was no time for wasted motion. Jews first headed off to the synagogue for morning prayers that were on this day uttered somewhat in haste. Then came a quick walk back home and an abbreviated breakfast, followed by last-minute preparations before the start of business. Meanwhile the marketplace began steadily to fill up. Hundreds of wagons rolled into the spacious open area, and countless individual vendors filed in and prepared to set up wares in their accustomed places. What may have seemed like a disorderly scramble was in reality largely an orderly process. A first come, first served situation it was not. People knew where they belonged; everyone had a place, usually the same one he had occupied week after week, year after year. For this place vendors paid the municipality a modest fee, which was collected by two policemen who circulated through the crowd during the day.

In the bitter winter months the number of vendors fell, leaving room enough for all who wished to conduct business. The return of more moderate weather brought forth additional sellers, producing real congestion. Still everyone squeezed in; somehow places were found for all. Not that complete harmony reigned. Disputes there were, usually over charges of encroachment. Had a vendor, deliberately or otherwise, expanded into another's space? On this and other issues arguments could become heated, especially among the fruit vendors, and often had to be settled by the police (usually in favor of vendors from Kolbuszowa). Hardly a market day passed without spirited exchanges between fruit vendors.

By 8 A.M. the market was already buzzing, the entire area filling up rapidly, its distinctive sounds and smells much in evidence. Parked wagons occupied a good portion of the market. Of necessity they were there for the day, even if their owners wished to depart early. All were jammed together, the wagons along with the horses, by the hundreds. Except for those positioned along the perimeter none could leave until the general exodus began.

Follow along now as we survey the vendors and their wares, a tour that can be readily accomplished because of the organization of the market: regular lines of sellers on each side of the square. Let's begin along the end, where the Biala vegetable vendors traditionally set up shop. These peasants were better off than most because the vegetable business was ordinarily a reliable source of income. Usually you could tell by the way people looked whether their lives were harsh or they enjoyed some measure of comfort and security. The Biala peasants were fat, their horses were fat, their wagons large and heavy—all unmistakable signs of a general well-being. In the spring they came to market with seeds of all kinds along with fresh vegetables harvested from their own fields. The onions, cucumbers, turnips, and the like were laid out not on tables but simply in sacks on the ground.

I remember accompanying my mother when she shopped for vegetables here, basket in hand (always you had to bring along your own bags or containers), moving from one large sack to another scrutinizing the vegetables. These peasants knew their customers and on the Jewish holidays would bring appropriate special items like beets, onions, dill, garlic, and horseradish, making certain that supplies of these items were plentiful. Similarly, they stocked large numbers of wreaths around Christmastime. Week after week, season after season, year in and year out, the same peasants from Biala came among us with their produce. We knew them, they knew us; we depended on their supplies, they relied on our consistent patronage. Up to the end, we never failed each other.

Past the vegetables one came to the fruit vendors, Jews from the towns of Ropczyce and Glogow, all related to one another. From midsummer until the beginning of winter they supplied fruits of almost every variety. When winter came they turned to selling dried fruits. They sold both to wholesalers and to individuals, the former arriving early in the morning for the best selections. There was no ignoring the fruit vendors. Always they could be heard across the marketplace, especially one called Binem, proclaiming their presence and announcing their fine merchandise and exceptional prices. Without signs, how else advertise your products and attract attention?

But that's not all they shouted. As I have said, they were easily among the more cantankerous and argumentative vendors in the market. Each week, almost without exception, they unleased withering verbal attacks against one another. It mattered little that they were related. Spreading out over too large an area, encroaching on one another's territory, stealing customers, offering inferior goods at high prices—these were among the milder accusations flung back and forth. The curses flew even as the day wore on. To ignore their presence in the market was almost impossible. Notorious they were—the fighting vendors.

Past the fruit stands—for no logical reason I know of—were stationed three dealers offering equipment for horses. Bridles, harnesses, whips, ropes, and straps aplenty, all indispensable items because just about everyone and everything that didn't walk moved by horse-drawn wagons and carriages. There were always plenty of peasants gathered in this area, probably because right alongside were three or four women selling sour pickles out of barrels. Whatever the reason, steaming hot or freezing, these same women stood out there all day long peddling their pickles, which were made from cucumbers bought from the Biala peasants. There was no shortage of customers, since the peasants regarded pickles as exceptional treats.

Wood products were next in line, inexpensive items brought to market all the way from Sokolow each Tuesday in three or four wagons. Josel Hoffert was for a long time the presiding patriarch here. Cheap painted bunk beds, folding chairs, and tables, all made of soft pine or spruce and intended for the peasants, stood on the ground in front of the wagons. And servicing wagons was the specialty of the next business in line. The principal product here was wheels, which were made by hand out of hardwood (oak, beech, maple) and fitted to iron rims that protected them. Axles and other wagon accessories were also available here, along with a variety of equipment for horses.

Along the next side, though still on the outer rim of the marketplace, were shoe dealers, three or four of them, also from Sokolow. Several long boards, perhaps ten yards in length, were set up off the ground, and slung across them were the shoes in pairs, starting with those for children on one end and gradually moving up to adult sizes and boots. Peasants usually arrived barefoot. If anything they wrapped rags around their heavily calloused feet, which allowed them to traverse the roughest, most uneven surfaces. A small chair alongside allowed customers to sit down and try the shoes on. After that the bargaining might begin. Next to the shoe sellers from Sokolow were vendors from Kolbuszowa, shoemakers who sold a better-quality product. It was a relatively simple operation for them: they had only to load their goods on pushcarts at their shop, then wheel them over to the marketplace. Unlike many other vendors they would not move on to the Sokolow market the following day.

The next corner was among the busiest in the market. Peasants gathered here to sell what they had brought with them from the countryside. Business proceeded briskly, with sellers eager to dispose of their products so they could themselves join the ranks of the buyers. Chickens were easily the most common item. Hundreds upon hundreds were available, packed three or four to a basket and placed on the ground awaiting purchase. But not waiting quietly. Every so often one or two would break loose and begin scurrying about, desperate to elude their pursuers. When passersby joined in the chase, the level of confusion rose measurably.

Not just any chicken would do; again the fattest were deemed to be the finest, and shoppers moved from basket to basket sticking their hands inside, intent on selecting plump birds. In this, individual buyers competed with wholesalers, who bought up large numbers of chickens and shipped them to Cracow. The chickens sold off quickly; relatively few were left by afternoon. Chickens generally were priced at one and a half zlotys each, but that didn't rule out bargaining. Early in the morning sellers held their ground, but as the hours wore on they came round to accepting a lower price so that they could conclude their affairs. Practices here typified those prevailing across the market. Buyers generally went to sellers they knew, people with whom they had done business on other occasions. They shopped around to some extent; but mostly they ended up doing business with people familiar to them, those they had come to trust (and who might agree to barter—your goods for my butter and eggs, delivered next week).

Along with live chickens came eggs, brought to the market in wicker baskets. Here again, individual customers competed with wholesalers. Bakers, particularly bagel makers, went directly to special containers set aside for broken eggs, which they then bought at a discount. About five or six merchant wholesalers were on hand to buy eggs. They came with long crates (eight feet long, two feet wide) filled with straw. They filled and packed their crates right on the spot in preparation for shipment out of Kolbuszowa.

The place to buy your turkeys, ducks, and geese was right alongside the egg section. Here, too, wholesalers were active, some buying as many as fifty to seventy-five geese at a time and moving them to a prearranged area of the market where they remained throughout the day while additional purchases were made.

Moving past the eggs and the fowl brought you to the grain merchants. They stood, sacks on the ground, waiting to buy what peasants brought them. In time peasants came by, sacks on their backs, prepared to bargain a little, insisting always that what they had was of the finest quality—clear, dry, and fresh. Little by little the merchants' sacks filled up with rye, wheat, barley, beans, and corn.

That brings us to the inside row, to those locations closest to the center of the marketplace. Here one shopped for heavy ear-thenware goods and sampled the wares of four or five families who sold wooden products of all kinds—spoons, spools, sieves, churns, buckets, plungers, and vessels of every variety. In the sum-mer peasants also stood at this location selling wild strawberries, blackberries, and raspberries that they brought along in heavy, thick baskets. People stopped by with cups of all sizes and filled them with their favorite berries. Sometimes these same peasants would also have wild mushrooms for sale.

Actually the peasants sold many more berries on Friday, when they returned to the marketplace and gathered near the well. The berries they sold mostly to the Jewish women, who bought them for the baked goods they would prepare for the Sabbath. Some berries never were sold but instead were filched by youthful raid-ers, myself included. My friends and I missed few chances to sneak up to the baskets and run off with a handful of berries. Why did we do it? The berries we enjoyed, of course, but there can be no denying the thrill that stealing the berries brought us, especially when the peasants gave chase for a short distance in a vain effort to retrieve what rightfully was theirs.*

At the main market on Tuesday, thefts were not common. Ven-dors generally stayed close to their wares; potential thieves would have a hard time going undetected. Besides, the police patrolled the area throughout the day. Walking about with rifles and fixed bayonets, they were an imposing sight, especially with their hat-bands tucked under the chin. That's when you knew they were on duty.

The market assumed a different look once you reached the inner area, which was occupied by hundreds of small covered stands. Scores and scores of vendors displayed the same mixed merchan-dise: soap, powder, needles, thread, shoelaces, pencils, odds and ends of all sorts. Many of the items were purchased at our store.

---

*In my defense (though we were all about seven or eight years old), I argued against this sport with my friends. Snatching a few berries didn't bother me as much as the large number we crushed when we made our grab. There were times when I warned peasants of planned raids on their berry baskets and felt relieved when their watchfulness discouraged my associates in crime.

Working on the narrowest of margins, they made very little on each sale. Bakers were also out in force, occupying perhaps twenty stands; mostly from Kolbuszowa, they sold white and dark bread and a variety of rolls. Throughout the day fresh goods arrived from their bakeries in town. Pork vendors stood nearby, maybe ten or twelve of them, fat women and men outfitted in white aprons, doing a lively business from their stands, with sausages heaped all about them. Ordinarily peasants brought no food along when they came to town. Instead they gathered around the pork stands buying up and relishing the sausages, kielbasa, and salt pork.

Kerchief stands occupied a prominent place in this area. Most women wore kerchiefs and so were always potential customers. Each stand was covered by a small canvas roof to protect the merchandise, which was displayed from ropes attached to the sides of the stall. Wool kerchiefs, silk kerchiefs, plaid kerchiefs, flowered kerchiefs, they made a most colorful display. Women, peasant women particularly, might well spend the entire day trying to make up their minds about a particular kerchief. Around to all the vendors they would go, checking prices, returning to the original location for some bargaining, then repeating the process once, maybe twice. Peasants struggled for every groschen, so bargaining for them was a most serious business. A final decision might not be made until just before the goods were being packed away at the end of the day.

Textile stands there were in abundance, with vendors from several different towns displaying their bolts of cloth and competing intensely with one another. Here bargaining was standard practice. Looking for underwear? There it was, lots of the crude unbleached muslin variety hanging from stands, with Mendel Schul's wife among the sellers. Poor-quality underwear it was for sure, but undeniably cheap. Watch as customers come by, then try on the underwear—always on top of their clothes!

Next to the underwear came pants, maybe twenty vendors selling work pants, Sunday pants, small and large trousers. Shirts followed, along with ready-made suits hanging from racks. Nearby stood two vendors selling fur jackets for men. Were you to count the number of all these small stands (no one ever did), it would not surprise me if the total approached five hundred. For many these stands were their only source of income; smaller business-men there could not be.

What I haven't mentioned yet is that we actually had two mar-ketplaces in Kolbuszowa, the one I've been describing plus an-other a few blocks away. The second market, even larger than the first, was far more specialized. It was here that animals were sold and traded: cows, calves, pigs, and horses. Nowhere was the bar-gaining more intense and the inspection of animals so rigorous. It might easily go on the better part of the day, helped along at times by a strategic retreat into a nearby saloon (and on occasion an agreement by buyers not to compete and bid up prices). A stylized hitting of hands by the two parties signified that an agree-ment had been reached.

Ever present here were butchers looking to supply their shops. Meat dealers also purchased large numbers of pigs, which were then driven immediately to the slaughterhouse and prepared for shipment to some of the larger cities. The animal market lacked the color and variety of the main show and attracted far fewer people. Still much business took place here each Tuesday, includ-ing the auctioning off of goods seized by officials for failure to pay taxes.

The marketplace wasn't all business; amusements and enter-tainment had their place as well. An organ grinder was almost always on hand. Quite a center of attention he was, never failing to attract a large and appreciative crowd of children as well as adults. Interest focused on the prizes he gave to those willing to part with ten or twenty groschen. The prize was selected by Laura the parrot, who at his command opened a drawer with her beak to disclose a small envelope containing the gift. Always it was a cheap but uncommonly bright and colorful ring, necklace, or bracelet. Few ever complained about Laura's selections.

A second organ grinder over at the far side of the market op-erated in the same way. Instead of a parrot, however, he was ably assisted by a white mouse. All watched as the mouse, held by its tail, motioned toward a particular envelope that contained a prize.

No one, it seemed, ever tired of seeing the mouse perform; people were always eager to see what gift had been chosen. Peasant girls waited impatiently as peasant boys purchased a chance and looked on appreciatively as the parrot or mouse selected a colorful item. Such simple pleasures! I for one never tired of them.

Another special feature of the marketplace was the photographer. Cameras were not everyday items in Kolbuszowa. In fact, in the entire town there were only two of them, making a photograph very much a prized possession. Along with his equipment the photographer brought along a variety of painted backgrounds against which people might pose. For the boys and girls from the village, having their picture taken represented an exceptional treat. The process was very much a public affair, with everyone looking on as the pictures were taken and then returning later to gaze and comment on the developed photos. In the meantime one might choose to patronize a gypsy fortune-teller, who for a fee revealed fortunes and other mysterious matters. During the summer months it was also quite common for a group of acrobats to appear for a show in the market. Jugglers, fire-eaters, dancing bears—there was much to see. People gathered round and at the end left money for the performers.

Once the light in the sky began to fade it was time, everyone knew, to start packing up. All across the market vendors began folding up their stands, gathering up their wares, and heading over to their wagons. Clearing the area would be no easy matter, especially with hundreds of wagons having to maneuver past each other. In the market and along adjacent streets peasants could be seen staggering about or lying drunk on the sidewalks. Alongside stood their wives, sometimes their children, alternately pleading and screaming at them to get up and be gone. Ahead of them might be a lengthy wagon ride; or worse, a walk of many miles back to the village. Still nothing could be done until the effects of the liquor began to wear off. Either that or wait for the following day. But where?

The day was over, but much had still to be done. Jews headed to the synagogue for their evening prayers and afterward lingered for a while to discuss the day's doings at the market. Money changers went about exchanging currencies at rates above official levels; American money, when it appeared, was particularly prized. Those owing money began counting out what needed to be repaid. Others calculated the day's proceeds and thanked God there was enough to carry on. Some viewed their meager returns and despaired of the future. For many there was no rest, no chance to recover. Tomorrow, Wednesday, was again market day, this time in Sokolow. Goods had to be readied and a wagon prepared for the trip very early the next morning. Before then, hopefully some sleep.

With the people and wagons gone, the marketplace stood empty again. An incessant din had given way to silence once more. But there was no mistaking what had taken place earlier. Odors told much of the story. Hundreds of horses had stood around all day. What they left behind was substantial: the smell enveloped the area, especially in the summer months. In the summer sweepers entered the marketplace that very night to begin the lengthy cleanup. It would take them through the better part of the next day to finish. In the winter their work would not begin until Wednesday; and if it snowed on Tuesday night, there would be no cleanup at all. The debris would then simply be covered up, packed under the newly fallen snow. Not until a major thaw or the arrival of spring would there be any effort to remove it.

From Wednesday through Monday Kolbuszowa was a quiet town, with affairs proceeding at a leisurely pace. On Tuesday it became something quite different—a bustling, energetic little city, its population suddenly swollen, a vital center of exchange between town and countryside, between Pole and Jew, between buyers and sellers. This weekly awakening produced whatever vitality existed in Kolbuszowa. It helped sustain many, however precarious their existence, and to nourish whatever dreams some of us had for a better life.

The Railroad Never Came

hat if the railroad had come to Kolbuszowa? Would we have remained as backward, as traditional, found life so difficult? Who is to say? Such things were not for us to decide anyway. The Austro-Hungarian government had determined that we should have a railroad, that a line should be built from Rzeszow through Kolbuszowa to Sandomierz on the Vistula; and we were perfectly prepared, when it was proposed in 1910, finally to join the twentieth century. In town the walls of a railway station were put into place, and embankments heading off in the direction of Sandomierz and Rzeszow were constructed. Clearly it was only a matter of time now. But the railroad was never completed; World War I came and everything stopped. Afterward the new independent government of Poland found itself with more pressing matters to attend to. Kolbuszowa would survive, but without a railroad.

Still, the walls of the station remained, and when I was a boy they made for a fine place to play, such opportunities for the imagination! But when the Germans arrived in town in 1939, they saw things quite differently. To these same walls people of our town were dragged, lined up, and shot. If only the railroad had come, might not some of these same people have left town and been out of harm's way when the Germans marched in?

No, we weren't isolated or cut off from the rest of Poland. It's simply that we had to accept the limits set by our feet and the endurance of our horses. We got around mostly as people had for centuries. Everyone knew how fast and how far he could go with a sack on his back, without shoes, along a road made slippery and soft by the rain. It was common knowledge that the wagon trip from Kolbuszowa to Rzeszow, a distance of nineteen miles, would take anywhere from three to three and a half hours. People moved about, of course, but never easily. Joyrides we didn't have.

The well-being of Kolbuszowa, such as it was, depended on a whole series of interconnections with the surrounding country-side, with nearby towns, and with some faraway cities. Roads from our town headed off in several directions, branching here, then there, into paths leading to the villages all around us. Of paved roads we knew nothing. Our better roads were of gravel, which when pressed down served our needs—though it was a tight fit when wagons going in opposite directions passed each other. Trouble came when wagon wheels cut into the surface, producing no end of bumps, depressions, holes, ruts, and ripples. Winter therefore brought certain benefits. The snow came and stayed, one layer after another covering the roads and resurfacing the pathways. By December and up through late March wheels were replaced by runners, our wagons converted into sleds. The roads remained useful though not entirely necessary; we were now free to go off in directions not possible at other times of the year.

Our destinations had long been established, as had the purpose of our travels. Because the railroad never reached us we were obliged to meet it, at Sedziszow, about twelve miles away. Among other things, Sedziszow was where we got our mail, that precious link to all of Poland and to the rest of the world. Each day at 7:00 A.M. Mordechai Freifeld set out from the post office for Sedziszow carrying the town mail in his wagon. Freifeld, with his long, uncommonly wide gray beard, was unmistakably a Jew, and that is a fact worth mentioning, for you see he served in an official position, for which he was eligible by virtue of having served in the cavalry over four years during World War I.

Husky and strong, Mordechai inspired confidence that the mail would arrive on time. Just to make sure, he carried a big revolver.

Each morning he would take it from the post office and strap it around his waist over his heavy fur-lined coat, and there it stayed the entire time. When he was finished for the day, he would return the gun to the post office. For this alone I admired him, and many others I imagine did also. He was, you see, the only Jew in town with a gun, the only one displaying this outward symbol of power. With very few exceptions Jewish assertiveness had to be muted to reflect the realities of Kolbuszowa and the way things were in Poland.

Waiting at that early morning hour for the mail wagon to leave were townspeople (numbering as many as ten, for that was the capacity of the wagon) who were heading for Sedziszow. Some went to pick up packages and goods they were expecting by rail, others to greet visitors and guests arriving by train, and still others to catch trains to faraway places. By five or six o'clock in the evening the wagon was back in town. The mail wagon, however, did not have a monopoly on this route. Two Jews, Aaron Spielman and Shmuel Weiss, owned horses and a wagon and made the round trip nearly every day. Mostly they were employed to carry merchandise. Often they transported supplies my father had ordered for our store, picking them up at the railroad station and bringing them directly to us. They attracted passengers because they charged less. To go with Mordechai would cost you 1.25 zlotys; their charge was 80 groschen. To be sure, their wagons took longer and were often loaded up uncomfortably with goods, but saving money was always a major consideration.

There was still another option when you wanted to make an impression, to do something special, as might be the case when visitors were expected from another part of Poland, of Europe, or especially from America. Arriving in a slow-moving, crowded, uncovered wagon would produce something less than a grand entry into Kolbuszowa. Better to hire and travel with the Pole who had a covered carriage or fiacre going back and forth to Sedziszow or Rzeszow. This was more expensive, naturally, but also faster and fancier. Why not show visitors that we of Kolbuszowa were not so far behind the times?

Between Rzeszow, the largest town in the area, and Kolbuszowa there was much coming and going. Many shopkeepers in town went there to buy goods; most traveled by wagon. I myself made the trip (beginning when I was about thirteen years old) far too many times to count. After market day on Tuesday we almost always needed fresh supplies of goods for our store. So my father produced a list, made certain I understood it, and counted out the money, and early Wednesday morning I was off to Rzeszow. Usually I went to sleep, but not before hiding the money away on the wagon. A smooth ride it wasn't, but I was young and didn't mind the pounding. The older passengers, I know, felt otherwise. It was a nonstop trip, but we stopped whenever someone on board needed to relieve himself.

Most trips were without incident, though one heard of an occasional highway robbery, or wagons stopped by peasants and Jews taken off and beaten up. It happened, not too often, but still it happened—and you came to accept that possibility. Also it could rain, a matter of great concern in an open wagon. Getting wet didn't bother us, but the goods were another matter—especially the flour. The three-hour trip to Rzeszow, the buying, the loading of goods onto the wagon, and the trip back—altogether exhausting.

Fortunately there was another way to get there: a regularly scheduled autobus made the round trip twice a day. It took only one hour each way unless we suffered a flat tire, which could take hours to fix; but it cost two zlotys, compared to the wagon charge of 1.20. Naturally I preferred the bus and traveled by bus when we needed only a few items in Rzeszow. Jews usually went by wagon, Poles by bus. Many of the Poles who used the bus were municipal or country workers and so were entitled to a reduced bus rate, but certainly not to exclusive use. Still I remember once when the military commission was in town to supervise the drafting of men into the Polish army, some of its members, including a colonel, prepared to board the bus to Rzeszow and would not let any Jews on. As one woman attempted to step up, the colonel took hold of her hair and pulled her head back, tearing off her wig. She stood there furious, humiliated; still what could she do?

Now it so happened that my brother Leibush was also waiting

for the bus when this took place. Leibush, you should know, was a powerful man, probably the strongest person in Kolbuszowa. Seeing what had happened, he approached the three Poles, all officers in their uniforms who were standing one behind the other. Thrusting out his arm he pushed the colonel so forcefully that all three of them fell down like dominoes. He then opened the bus door and waved the Jews in.

As you might imagine, the incident did not end here. The police were called, and my brother was arrested for assault. The colonel then sued Leibush. I remember our pleading with the woman to testify, but she was afraid and would not. The case came before a superior court in Rzeszow, so we had to hire a prominent criminal lawyer there for Leibush. The case dragged on for years—a most costly and inconvenient affair. In the end we paid and it was settled. Still Leibush had stood up to the Poles, an act of defiance few Jews in Kolbuszowa would have dared risk.

The bus to Rzeszow left our town each morning at 8:00, returned at noon, then left again at 1:00 P.M. and was back at 6:00. Each time it arrived in Kolbuszowa it drew a crowd, mostly of children who ran alongside until it came to a stop. A fair number of the simply curious waited as well, looking to see who was arriving in town and hoping to be the first to pass on the news. The noon bus brought passengers but also the daily papers from Cracow, Lvov, and Warsaw. They circulated widely in town and were our major connection to the outside world, helping ease the isolation we often felt living in Kolbuszowa.

Now, having heard me speak of buses, you won't be surprised then about talk of automobiles. It was not until 1927 or '28 that cars first were seen in Kolbuszowa. Certainly no one in town owned one, but every so often a few would appear. As noted earlier, the very first cars we saw belonged to several rich landowners. After their hunting parties, their chauffeurs would drive them to town and into the marketplace, where they dined at Zach's private restaurant, which was open only on occasions like these.

Automobiles appeared more regularly when a number of large Polish businesses began sending out traveling salesmen. These were not quite your ordinary cars, however, designed as they were to advertise the company's product. Take Erdal, a company that produced a very popular shoe cream and had a frog as its symbol. Perched on top of their salesman's car was an immense lifelike frog. When the Erdal salesman came to town everyone knew it. And they also noticed that he usually came to my father's store first because we were substantial customers. While he was inside doing business with my father, there's no need to guess where I was. Exactly so—in the front seat, delighted as can be. But there's more. After leaving my father he usually visited my brother's store. It wasn't far, and that's probably why he let me sit next to him as he drove over. Each time he came so did that special treat. How my friends envied me! The Solali salesman also came by car, on top of which was a huge tube: his product was the tubes of cigarette paper into which people put tobacco to make their cigarettes. From him, however, I received no rides.

In Kolbuszowa no one dreamed of owning a car, but then one day it happened. It was in 1935, and the proud owner was the head of our volunteer fire department, a skillful fellow who could fix practically anything. No matter that the car was a used one and not very impressive; it belonged to him and made him a big shot in town. In his new position he assumed new responsibilities. Now when people got very sick, it was he who drove them to a hospital in Rzeszow.

Wagons and horses were in no immediate danger of being displaced by engines and mechanized transport in Kolbuszowa, but at least we had tasted of the modern world. The horses, among others, were not pleased. It happened regularly that when a car came within earshot, a horse reacted violently; probably terrified, it would rear up and try to bolt. Whenever peasants spotted a car approaching, they moved quickly to their horses and tried to keep them calm. Sometimes it worked; but sometimes the animals bolted, creating a scene of unending amusement for the children about town, who anticipated such fun whenever they saw a moving car.

Automobiles generally were not as appealing to young people, especially in the villages, as bicycles. If anything could be said to have become the rage in and around Kolbuszowa in the mid-1930s, it was bicycles. When a boy became sixteen or seventeen he dreamed about getting a bicycle; and thanks to Hirsh Kleinman, a storekeeper in town who sold on payments, many could become proud owners. Almost any two-wheeled bicycle would do, but if a boy had his choice it would be one with thick wheels—the thicker the better.

Riding about was a thrill, but what a village boy really looked forward to was pedaling into Kolbuszowa, going up and down the streets and across and around the marketplace. With a bicycle he was king, able to impress any girl who saw him. There was no shortage of bicycles around our house. We had none ourselves, but because many peasants did business with my father their sons knew us and asked permission to leave their bicycles in our back yard when they came to town. We refused no one, and at one time or another some ten to twenty bicycles might be parked outside.

Mostly Polish boys rode bicycles, not Jews. That doesn't mean that I was not interested. I was, and actually learned to ride one. Unfortunately someone saw me and promptly reported the incident to my religious school teacher. For that I earned yet another suspension from Talmud Torah. When the war came, prohibitions eased and many things changed. I rode about on my own bicycle—unpunished!

Without a doubt the most dramatic moment in the history of transportation in Kolbuszowa was the time a plane flew in and landed in our town. We had watched planes fly over our town on occasion, but never had anyone seen one close up. It was in 1937 that we got our first chance. A Polish boy from town named Przywara had gone off to Warsaw and joined the Air Force. One day, it was on a Friday, he decided to pay his family a visit and off he flew to Kolbuszowa in his Air Force plane. Did he receive permission, or had he just decided to do it on his own? No one ever found out. Anyway, he landed practically in his back yard on a large field alongside the Catholic cemetery in town. Word of this unprecedented event spread quickly, and everyone rushed to see this marvelous device that had descended from the sky. The plane had double wings and was about the size of a car. Impressive it wasn't, but all day Saturday and Sunday people came to look and many returned again and again. No one touched it; all stood nearby simply observing. It stayed there in the field motionless the entire time.

Word circulated that the pilot planned to leave Monday morning, and probably half the town gathered to see the incredible machine soar into the sky. Quite a few doubters there were who said the pilot would surely be unable to get the plane off the ground. But the engines started up, and the plane began to move. It moved very slowly at first, bumping up and down as it gained more speed across the field. And then it was off the ground, heading higher and higher. Only when the tiny speck in the sky disappeared did anyone stir. It was gone, but for years afterward people would reckon time from the day the airplane landed in Kolbuszowa.

However narrow our lives, we were, as you can see, not strictly confined to Kolbuszowa. Still there were many people in town who never once went beyond the limits of Kolbuszowa. Here they were born, lived their lives, married, had their children, and died. Yet even they knew there was a world outside our town that was altogether different, filled with possibilities. People living in Kolbuszowa who had come from a large city, had lived elsewhere for a time, or had simply traveled about were regarded as most fortunate and in some ways even superior. To have been born or once have lived in Vienna, Berlin, or Warsaw, let alone America, made you automatically an exceptional person, a man or woman of substance. Just about everyone understood there was no future for us here. In order to improve our lives, to increase our prospects, we had to leave. But leaving Kolbuszowa was not that easily accomplished. As the years passed, fewer and fewer managed to leave. The leash grew shorter, then tightened. After that it was too late.

The Faith of our Fathers

A very long time ago God went in succession to the sixty-nine different peoples then inhabiting the earth, and to each he offered his Torah, his law. From each he received the same answer: "We wish first to look at the contents; then we will make our decision." But not when God approached the Jews. "We will take it," they said; "later you will explain what it is." From that time on, our legend tells us, we became God's "chosen people," devoting ourselves century after century to following the letter of His law, steadfastly maintaining faith in Him, the Almighty One.

There were probably few places where this was done with greater conviction than in Kolbuszowa. Certainly we liked to believe that this was so. For an authoritative view of the matter you could not find better proof than in the words of the Apte Rebbe, that most distinguished spiritual leader of the nineteenth century who early in his career served as rabbi in Kolbuszowa. One of the first places the Messiah will visit when he returns to the world, he declared, will be Kolbuszowa. Given such a testimonial, little wonder the piety of our people seemed never to waver.

But remember well who is doing the talking here—it is Naftali Saleschütz. Brought up in the strict faith of our people and discovering much in it of beauty and meaning, I nevertheless found early on that I could not believe as deeply as others had, could not focus my vision as was required, could not restrict my life and deny the world to the degree expected. I did not, like others, reject it all, but I did relax; certainly I did stray from the prescribed path. The change took place early on in my thinking, but I lacked the resolve to have my actions reflect it. And so outwardly it seemed to all as if the youngest son of Isak Saleschütz would become as devout, as good a Jew, as his father.

In time, however, appearances and my behavior suggested otherwise. By then I was not alone. Changes were under way in the Jewish community of Kolbuszowa; challenges were mounted to the old traditions, at least by the younger generation. But my intention is not to chronicle this erosion of orthodoxy; rather it is to describe the Judaism that existed in my town, to present the abiding faith of my people and the special forms that it took, even as some began to lose their way. Though some may disagree, I think the task is a proper one for me, raised as I was in a family where religion was taken very seriously but also where mutual respect and love permitted me, in the end, to make my own choices.

There were about 2,000 Jews in Kolbuszowa, about 95 percent of whom were observant, pious people. Mostly when I describe our practices and beliefs I will be thinking of people like my father, whose orthodox credentials could withstand close scrutiny. But there were those in town who considered even him excessively lax, guilty of too many compromises. These ultrareligious people may even have been in the majority, although they kept mostly to themselves. Nothing that their faith prescribed was for them too minor to observe; nothing that was part of our worship service could ever be omitted. Nothing associated with Jewish tradition could be altered in the name of novelty, or for the sake of convenience or change. These people were altogether serious, ever vigilant, quick to uncover threats to their ways. They were also ever ready to criticize; for people who allowed themselves little latitude it was easy to see laxity in others.

Before a Jew went to sleep at night he had to put a glass of water near his bed. This was because the first thing he was obliged to do on awakening in the morning was to cleanse himself, wash his fingertips, then say a prayer of thanks to God for having restored him to life after sleep. From this simple practice there is much to be learned. Never was God far from the thoughts of any Jew, or from our lips. Few sentences passed without a "thank God." On the top of pieces of correspondence we inscribed the letters Beth and Hay, the opening letters in the phrase "Baruch Hashem," "Blessed is God." From the morning on and throughout the waking day the Jew was mindful of his religious obligations, woven as they were into the fabric of everyday life. Never could we become so immersed in the world as to forget who was the arbiter of it all, whose children we were, who it was to whom we owed thanks. Rather we would pause, say our blessing or prayer, and only then resume whatever activity we were about.

Eating food always brought forth prayers. One said a prayer before drinking water, but the responsibility did not end there. Later on, drinking another glass of water brought you to a repetition of the prayer. Prayers before putting on new clothes, prayers before going to sleep—such occasions for prayer are not surprising. But in the course of a given day prayers might also be given in response to lightning or thunder, or even on sighting a rainbow. The prayers were a common vocabulary taught to us as children; they were as natural to us as anything else we did.

We wet our fingertips in the morning just as we washed ourselves at other times, to declare that we were pure and wished in no way knowingly to defile our Lord. We washed our hands before each meal and immersed our bodies in our ritual baths,* some more than others. Our rabbi often could be found in the *mikvah,* as could our scribe, as noted earlier. The body must not in any way diminish the purity of the prayer. For that reason most men

---

*The bathhouse in town contained two such baths, one that most people used and the other a nineteenth-century facility (once used by the revered Apte Rebbe) that had been restored years before by a group of very religious townspeople. To reach the latter was no easy task; it was thirty-five steps down before you came to the water. And your problems were then only beginning. The water always was icy, so plunging in required great strength of character. How well I remember going there with my father on the day of my Bar Mitzvah. Slowly we descended the steep steps. How I survived the frigid waters I'll never know. But it was worth the effort, since the superior efficacy of the deep *mikvah* was generally acknowledged.

wore a *gartle* about their waists, a band that served as a dividing line separating the upper and lower portions of the body. Above it were the heart and the brain, capable of performing our highest functions; below were housed the body's lower functions. Before prayer the body needed to be purified, and this was interpreted to include the bowels. They needed to be emptied, the foul matter evacuated. The many outhouses alongside our synagogue testified to just how seriously we took this obligation. If you were to ask why most Jews had hernias or why we were so likely to have hemorrhoids, I think the explanation is clear. We paid a price for our purity.

Prayer began each day, as I've told you, at home, but in short order it moved to the synagogue. Religious services began as early as 4:00 A.M. to accommodate people heading off that day for business in another town. Even at that hour it was possible to assemble the required *minyan* [ten men] in order to pray. On weekdays from Sunday through Friday groups of worshipers gathered throughout the morning up to about 11:30 for a service usually about thirty minutes in length. It was not unusual to see the same people attending more than one service in order, as they put it, "to catch another *kedusha*."* Later in the day the evening services brought us back to the synagogue. Clearly this house of worship was the center of our religious activities, the principal focus of our spiritual energies. Every day of the year found us there, and on Saturdays and holidays we remained for many hours at a time. No surprise, then, that many Jews wished to live in the immediate vicinity of the synagogue and that in Kolbuszowa the surrounding area was densely populated.

But I would be leaving a false impression if I spoke only of the synagogue. In truth it was less of a religious focus than you might think, less than at other times and in other places. Polish Jews, especially in the larger cities, belonged not so much to synagogues as to *shtibels,* clusters of like-minded Jews, members of a particular group or sect or followers of a specific spiritual leader, who en-

*The *kedusha* was a particular prayer that was regarded with special reverence.—RS

joyed gathering together for prayer. It might be in a hall or a group of rooms, in someone's apartment or house, or in a special section of the synagogue.

A city like Warsaw or Cracow might be home to hundreds of different *shtibels,* each service varying in certain respects from all the others under way at the same time. In Kolbuszowa it was possible to identify four *shtibels,* each of which attracted a particular following. In the rabbi's house men gathered who were followers of that rabbinical dynasty to which the rabbi belonged. The *dayan,* an assistant rabbi, attracted worshipers loyal to the Dzikiver Rebbe, a contemporary spiritual leader. A third group worshiped in the main synagogue, and a fourth, mostly artisans and craftsmen, gathered in one of the rooms of that synagogue.

The rabbi of Kolbuszowa, as you already know, prayed separately with his followers in his own house; it was only on special occasions that he appeared at some of the other gatherings of Jews. He came to the synagogue, for example, for special prayers ushering in each new month. He was also present for Simchat Torah, that joyous occasion marked by singing and dancing with the Torah.

How was it, you're likely to ask, that we could do without a rabbi most of the time? The answer is that in a real sense everyone was a rabbi if by rabbi we mean someone well-acquainted with the service, the appropriate rituals, and all the prayers. We needed no one to lead us in worship, to call out the pages, or to read the Torah. Nearly everyone in the room had that ability. As we shall see, the rabbi performed important functions for our community, but very few were related to worship.

We gathered to pray at least twice every day, so for us it was second nature. The prayers everyone knew by heart; rushing through them in whirlwind fashion, mumbling at breakneck speed—that was standard practice. But let me assure you, most of us knew just what we were saying. True, not many spoke Hebrew, but back in *cheder* we had translated each prayer into Yiddish, and so the words had meaning for us. On the Sabbath, however, no one rushed; there was time then for praying and singing, for a lengthy service perhaps four hours long.

We Jews lived for the Sabbath, a day of rest and prayer, a day for enjoying the most leisurely meals of the week. Every Saturday my father had an important job to perform in his position as *gabai* [synagogue manager]. Arrangements for the morning proceedings were up to him and another congregant, which meant designating who would lead the prayers during various portions of the service. The selection process was no minor matter. It was an honor to receive a part (an *aliyah*), especially being asked to read a portion of the Torah, so the element of competition always was present, even though many of the readers had received the same assignments many times before. The general rule was that a *jahrzeit** during the upcoming week entitled you to an *aliyah* the Sabbath before. My father, drawing on a mental filing system of impressive proportions, was able to recall just whose turn it was to be honored each week. The other rule governing such matters was that if a particular person was awarded an *aliyah* at a specific time for three consecutive years, he was entitled to it for however long he wished.

Inevitably there were disputes about such matters and questions of priority. At such times the rabbi was called upon to engage in delicate negotiations to resolve the matter. One other element entered into this equation: the quality of your voice. Congregants might well tolerate a monotone for a regular Saturday service, but on those special Sabbaths through the year more was expected. Then people looked forward to hearing the prayers led by those with pleasant voices, those capable of singing sweetly, and best of all, those able to introduce new melodies. On such occasions you couldn't help but notice how much more attentive everyone was, how much less people talked or wandered outside.

Not everyone had a specific part in the service, but all had their own seats. Seating was no casual matter. Each seat was spoken for, paid for, a personal possession likely to remain in the same family for generations. Naturally the better seats commanded fancier prices. (Usually one in the men's section was coupled with

---

*A time when one remembered the anniversary of the death of a departed family member.—RS

one in the area reserved for women.) By "better seat," I mean those located near the holy ark, which was close to where the service was conducted, and particularly those along the synagogue's eastern wall, east being the direction of Jerusalem. As a family grew, additional seats were needed. When your daughter married, for example, your new son-in-law would require a place. Whose seat might then be available? A death, a move, a need to raise money—any of these could produce a seat for sale. Where you sat generally determined your circle of friends. Sitting in the same place year after year meant that next to you were people you would see regularly. They were your true "neighbors," and more often than not you developed the closest of ties with them.

The synagogue was largely a man's world, as was our Judaism. The more orthodox the Jew, the more insignificant the religious role assigned to women. No one really noticed or complained about this; it was just the way things were. Unmarried women were not expected even to attend worship services except on the High Holidays. Married women, aside from the holidays, came to synagogue only for Saturday morning services. They sat not with the men, but upstairs with the other women. What's more, thanks to a partition, they could not be seen by the men below and could not themselves see what was going on beneath them, except for a few seated beside small gaps cut into the partition.*

Women, you must understand, were regarded as a distraction; it was thought that the sight of them would divert the men. Likewise women's voices, if heard, might be too disruptive, might cause men to become less attentive to their prayers. Only one time in the entire year were women permitted to come down and be with the men. That was on Simchat Torah, a holiday when many customary restraints were relaxed as we celebrated the final weekly reading from the Torah and prepared to begin yet another cycle. The women, mostly young, gathered together off on one side and watched as the men took turns dancing joyfully with the Torah.

*Many, unable to read or understand Hebrew, could not follow the service either. But usually there was one who could, and she would gather around her a circle of other women who, by listening to her and repeating what she said, were able at times to join in.

For dramatic effect there was nothing quite like what happened from time to time when, with services under way, a woman would burst into our midst, rush up to the holy ark, thrust it open, and begin a lengthy, emotional appeal—not to us, mind you, but to God. However irregular this seems, and only those present could appreciate the extraordinary impact it had, it was accepted practice. The woman was there on a desperate mission, to intercede with God on behalf of a critically ill relative. There she was, alone in front of all those men, pleading (in Yiddish) with all the emotion she could summon, praying for a miracle.

Her dramatic entry and presence was enough to stop whatever else might be happening. No one would ever dare deny her. No matter that she brought our service to an abrupt halt. Some women simply could not muster the courage to act in such a bold and uncharacteristic manner. Actually it is surprising that so many could. Those who could not do it found others prepared to act in their place. And certain women were more than willing to take up the cause of others.*

No matter who appeared, it was an extraordinary scene: a silent hall, attention riveted on the lone distraught woman (sometimes several women entered together) alternately crying, shrieking, and begging for God's intervention. Why was God bringing down such pain and distress? Did He not recognize how righteous and worthy the person was? What would become of the family? When the case was made, the pleas directed to God, the emotions completely discharged, it was over. As quickly as the woman had appeared, she closed the ark and left, and in a moment the service resumed. Even though this happened with some regularity, it never failed to stir all who witnessed it, to send a shiver through everyone present.†

*The usual choice was Rivkah Dershowitz, who had herself lost an only son, age 22, to typhus.

†Often the woman would head out to the cemetery after she left the synagogue to pray at the gravesites of relatives, hoping they would intercede before God in behalf of the stricken person. To further "assure" recovery a name change might ensue. To his existing name a male would have *alter* [old one] or *chaim* [life] added, a female *alte* [old one] or *chaya* [life]. Might the addition of such a name make long life more likely for the one now so gravely afflicted? All prayed it would be so.

"Thank God I was not born a woman"—this was a prayer a man offered, but I think we should explain.* A man was happy, considered himself fortunate, because of the many opportunities he had, when compared to women, to display his love of God. With so many obligations to fulfill, who could doubt his commitment to the Almighty? In truth our Judaism rested far more lightly on women than on men.† Not only did many women never go to religious school, but women (married women, that is) were obliged to attend worship services only on Saturday. Unmarried girls remained at home—quite a contrast to the busy religious schedule of unmarried boys. Perhaps women's highest religious obligation involved keeping a kosher home, which all did with exceptional care all their lives.

Then there were those wives who worked to support husbands who devoted their days almost exclusively to prayer and study. They accepted this heavy burden in the belief that their husbands, by pursuing this higher calling, brought blessings to the entire family. For this reason and many others I cannot help but think that the women of Kolbuszowa had far more difficult lives than the men. The difference was most obvious in their appearance. By age forty to forty-five or so many looked old, fragile, much of their vitality gone. Each Friday night at home, after coming from the synagogue, we sang "*Ayshes Chayl,*" ["Woman of Valor"]. We praised women's goodness, devotion, beauty, and valor. I think we understood the significance of our words, the need to pay tribute to those who sacrificed probably more than men could ever know.

Jews were known as people of the book, and for good reason. Our lives in many ways were based on a set of rules and regulations, reflected the spirit of principles written down in a book thousands of years before our time, a most remarkable circum-

*Women, on the other hand, blessed "God, who has made me according to Thy will."

†Probably for this reason women were less likely than men to challenge religious orthodoxy or throw off its restrictions. My older sisters, for example, remained strictly attached to Judaism while all three of my older brothers drifted away.

stance. When I was only a few years old, I was taught from that very book, the Bible, and had my mind and imagination filled with its stories. How I thrilled to those tales—of creation, Adam and Eve, the tower of Babel, Noah and the flood, the crossing of the Red Sea, Moses on Mount Sinai, David and Goliath, Samson, and countless others. So often did we hear these stories, so much a part of our lives were they, that at times we seemed to exist suspended somewhere between the past and the present.

A religious book for us was a precious possession. Even the poorest Jew labored to own the Bible, a prayer book, and whatever other books he could. Jews who were better off bought many religious books, especially the Talmud, had them bound in the best leather and embossed with gold letters on the cover, and gave them a place of honor in the home. If you dropped a book of this sort, it was expected that you would kiss it, as a sign of reverence, after picking it up. Our Beth Hamidrash [house of study] maintained an impressive library of books, which was kept up to date with the help of a special book fund to which most contributed.*

Books were not for collecting or for display; they were for studying and learning. Judaism drew its substance from the Old Testament, naturally, but beyond this, the written word, there had developed an oral tradition that over a period of time had been set down in writing. What it all meant, however, was not always clear. And so down through the ages rabbis, sages, and scholars chose to comment and interpret, and in time what they wrote was itself subjected to the same kind of scrutiny. All this meant that there were books upon books to be studied and understood before one could claim a close familiarity with our religious traditions. And so was born Jewish scholarship, the commitment to study, the endless, lifelong search for deeper and deeper understanding of texts and teachings.

*Religious books were never thrown out or destroyed, but rather were kept in the attic of the synagogue year after year. There was also a subscription library in town located in a room belonging to Hashachar, a Zionist organization. For a small monthly fee one could borrow books from it. Among its members were several Polish residents, making it probably the only institution run by Jews (aside from businesses) that was patronized by these townspeople.

A scholar—that's what my father wished I would become, but I didn't see the point of it. Too much of it I viewed as splitting hairs, dwelling on minor points, mindlessly reciting the words of others. Most people, however, thought otherwise. There was no shortage of study groups, whose members gathered together in earnest examination and careful consideration of the written word. Those who excelled at this, who were able to lead discussions and guide others, were much admired.

How did we rate such people? The more authorities they could summon forth in support of their point of view, the more direct quotations they could invoke, the greater their ability to cite chapter, section, and page, the higher the esteem in which they were held. They might know little of the world around them, but they possessed the capacity to retain and expound upon an immense amount of information. My father never ceased to remind me about my friend Shlomo Greenstein, who, because he possessed such abilities, won a scholarship to the world-famous yeshiva in Lublin. If I had been able to follow in Shlomo's footsteps, nothing would have made my father prouder.

It was a remarkable phenomenon. Here we were mostly a poor people, living in a small, remote town amid a Polish population that had little or no interest in such matters, and still our faith in books remained unshakable. They were our strength, our solace, our salvation, the tangible products of the tradition that bound us together with endless past generations who valued the same ideas we did.

Books also offered the path to prestige and community esteem. A real scholar—that was the highest praise we could bestow on a person, instantly transforming him in the eyes of others, replacing economic standing, the usual means of judgment, with a more elevated standard of worth. It was remarkable that an impoverished man, a man barely able to survive, the kind of person who might otherwise attract sympathy but never respect, could be given a place of honor in our community because of his piety and learning. Men poor beyond description were admired and consulted because of what they knew and because of their intense commitment to their faith. Where else were humble and otherwise obscure persons accorded such respect and looked to for guidance?

Many Jews looked beyond Kolbuszowa for instruction and religious inspiration. Throughout Poland, indeed all over eastern Europe, rabbinical dynasties claimed loyal followers in hundreds of separate communities. A certain rabbi who enjoyed a reputation for profound learning or for exceptional wisdom, or one seen as a worker of miracles, could expect to attract a large following. Continuity was assured because sons usually accepted the affiliations of their fathers. I knew, for example, that in time I would attach myself to the Dzikiver Rebbe as my father had.

As I have noted, my father's attachment was a source of friction between him and my mother, not only because he faithfully complied with the rebbe's requests for money, but also because my father insisted on seeing his rebbe more often than my mother thought necessary. One visit a year, usually for a weekend at Tarnow, she accepted, but others displeased her greatly because of the burden they placed on the rest of the family.

Still, my father would travel a few times each year, not only to Tarnow but to other towns in the region that the rebbe often visited to meet with his followers. Every few years, the Dzikiver Rebbe came to Kolbuszowa for a weekend, causing considerable excitement among his adherents in town. Just as my father stayed with members of the rebbe's sect when he traveled to other towns, so they found lodging in private homes when they came to Kolbuszowa. Spending time with the rebbe was a joyous occasion for those who gathered around him. To be in his presence, usually after a long absence, was sheer ecstasy. Such feelings were evident when they joined together in song, often with melodies unique to their group.*

At a certain point the rebbe would address his followers, often

---

*One reason my father took me along on occasion when he visited with his rebbe was my ability to remember new melodies. Many of those heard in the synagogue were of course traditional ones and not subject to change. But much credit went to those who were able to introduce new melodies into the service where this was allowed. Introducing new melodies was probably one of the few changes permitted in the otherwise very traditional proceedings.

to elaborate on ideas found in a book that either he or a predecessor in his rabbinical dynasty had written. Naturally they all dined together, the wives usually preparing special foods for the occasion, often *kugel* [noodle or potato pudding]. Ordinarily the rebbe broke off a piece for a follower whom he named, then had it passed along from hand to hand to that person. It was such a thrill to be "fed" by one's rebbe that no one thought to question the hygienic consequences of this hands-to-mouth procedure.

Without a doubt the most eagerly awaited moment was a private interview with the rebbe. Such sessions were managed most methodically, an assistant seeing to it that people kept moving in and out of the rebbe's presence. When finally it was your turn, you presented him with a slip of paper (*kvit'l*) on which was written a request for advice, perhaps on a matter of business, or on a possible marriage partner, or on an intended move out of the country. An answer came immediately, and was generally in accord with what the rebbe supposed your wishes to be. Such weekends left everyone invigorated, their loyalties confirmed.

Other religious figures came to town from time to time, their visits helping to dispel our isolation and allowing us to feel part of a larger religious community. Cantors arrived now and then to perform in the synagogue. Some sang alone; others brought along a choir or assembled one once they arrived. I have warm memories of the times a cantor from Berlin came to Kolbuszowa. I became a member of his choir, and my boy soprano voice was valued highly. If Judaism had been only about singing, no doubt I would have remained a devoted follower throughout my life.

You may be surprised to learn that no sermons were delivered at our services. In part this was because there was no formal leader, usually no rabbi in attendance. In part it was because a sermon would have been repetitious given the many study groups we attended. We suffered from no shortage of explanations and interpretations of the law and traditions of Judaism. We did hear sermons sometimes, but only from the *magids* [itinerant preachers] who came to Kolbuszowa periodically and offered us their thoughts, usually in gatherings on Saturday afternoons. Some were little-known and attracted relatively few listeners, but others were major figures, highly regarded men who could command large audiences. Usually they commented on the Torah portion from the Sabbath service, and for upwards of two hours people sat and listened attentively to their words. On Sunday the lesser *magids* would themselves go door to door in town taking up a collection. Those who were better-known left the collecting for others to do. In this way did they support themselves as they traveled from place to place wherever a Jewish community was to be found.

We did have a rabbi in town, Yechiel Teitelbaum, the son of the previous rabbi of Kolbuszowa. That's usually how it went; the eldest son of the rabbi would succeed to the position not by virtue of any special learning or certification, but simply by descent. Second and third sons were obliged to look elsewhere for such a position, not infrequently in the United States.

Clearly our rabbi hasn't figured prominently in my discussion thus far because although he was respected, even loved, he could not be classified among the great rabbis of our day. He had his close followers and supporters, but he was not a man of overriding intellect; and in everyday worldly matters he was regarded as unsophisticated, even naive. It was his misfortune to have been born in Kolbuszowa and to have performed not so brilliantly in *cheder* among youngsters later to be his congregants. It was not uncommon to hear jokes circulating in town that portrayed the rabbi as a comic figure. In contrast, his wife and daughters were seen as uncommonly intelligent and probably the source of many of the decisions he made as rabbi.

There's no better indication of his limitations than the fact that though he represented the Jewish community, he never learned to speak a word of Polish. With us that mattered little, but there were occasions when he was obliged to address a wider audience. These occurred during the national holidays, when Poles and Jews together gathered at the synagogue for a brief ceremony. The rabbi was naturally called upon to make a few remarks, and everyone who knew him realized he'd be speaking in Yiddish. Knowing he would need to mention the name of the President of Poland, Dr. Ignacy Moscicki, he did his utmost to learn the proper pronunciation of the name; yet when it came time he could never get it right.

The rabbi prayed together with his own followers in his small house; only rarely did he appear at services conducted by the various other groups of Jews in town. But there were some important functions that he performed for all of us. When it came time to circumcise a newborn male child, he presided. So also was he called on to officiate at weddings, but not at funerals except on special occasions. Funerals were the special responsibility of the Burial Society, which prepared the body and the coffin, then brought both to the Jewish cemetery outside of town. It was considered a major *mitzvah*—a deed of the truth, we called it—to attend a funeral even if the deceased was not a dear one or a close acquaintance. Many good acts, it was said, were performed for others in the expectation of one day in turn becoming the beneficiary, but attending a funeral was a pure deed free of ulterior motives.

The rabbi and the town's ritual slaughterer enjoyed a close relationship. The rabbi supervised the activities of the ritual slaughterer, making certain he observed all proper procedures. It was important, therefore, for the slaughterer to be on good terms with the rabbi, to which end he often supplied the rabbi with meat, usually those parts that he kept for himself after slaughtering the animals.

The rabbi, moreover, was the final authority in all things kosher.* In this connection he visited business establishments about town looking for violations. In these rounds he was always accompanied by the *shamus*. The rabbi could never be on the streets

---

*A major scandal erupted after suspicions were aroused about one chicken wholesaler in town. This man, a very religious resident of Kolbuszowa, purchased chickens on a large scale on market day for shipment to markets across Poland. Suspicions were aroused when the slaughterer complained about not receiving any revenues from this business. Spies were sent out to observe the wholesaler's operation and on one occasion found him personally slaughtering scores of chickens. No need for further explanations! Here was an attempt to make additional money by a shameful act, deceiving customers who never imagined that a religious man with a long beard from a town noted for its orthodoxy could commit a deed so foul.

alone lest certain "problems" arise. He could not, for example, pass between two women, or speak to or shake hands with a woman. The *shamus* went with him to prevent such awkward situations.

Each year it was important that the rabbi give his approval to the large quantities of flour arriving in town for the baking of matzoh for Passover. We brought in considerable amounts of such flour for our store, always careful to have it transported from the railroad on wagons on a clear day without threat of rain. Should any moisture penetrate the flour, the rabbi, who inspected each sack carefully, could declare it unfit for Passover because water had caused the process of fermentation to begin.

But there was a further complication. We had in Kolbuszowa a *dayan,* Mendel Rubin by name, who might also be described as the assistant rabbi. His judgment on matters kosher also had official standing. The *dayan* happened to be a follower of the same Dzikiver Rebbe with whom my father was associated, and for this reason my father sometimes called upon the *dayan* to certify that our flour was kosher. Unfortunately this aroused the ire of the rabbi, who was upset that he had been deprived of the small sum of money usually given for this service. One time in response to this slight, the rabbi came to the synagogue and, speaking more clearly and forcefully than usual, declared an embargo on our flour! No matter what the *dayan* had said, no one in town would risk using our flour. A crisis was thus at hand. Quickly my father acted to smooth ruffled feathers, after which he asked the rabbi to reexamine our flour. This he did, declaring it now to be acceptable. At the next Sabbath service came the announcement: the ban was lifted.

Such instances provided additional fuel to those in town who were openly critical of rabbis in general and who scoffed at rabbinical authority. There was, for example, Shuniek Arzt, an exceptionally talented craftsman, who almost always could be heard uttering the phrase "rabbi's cow." This referred to a long-winded story about a cow which fell into a town well on the Sabbath, prompting the residents to rush to their rabbi to get his advice. The cow, he said, could not be rescued, since work could not be performed on the Sabbath. "But Rabbi, it is your cow," they declared, causing him to reexamine the matter and decide that a rescue was indeed appropriate. For Arzt the "rabbi's cow" story punctured the bubble of pretentiousness that often surrounded discussions of rabbinical learning and wisdom.

For decisions on matters kosher most people dealt directly with the rabbi. Not most people, but most women, since it was women who rushed off to him with problems, then awaited his decisions. Maintaining a kosher home, as I have said, was women's primary religious responsibility, and in their daily efforts to do so they encountered unexpected perplexities. They were, for example, obligated to keep dairy and meat products separate and apart, but mistakes happened. What was to be done, for example, if a meat knife happened to be placed in the butter? What if milk overflowed while being boiled and part of it splashed onto a pot used for cooking meat? Was a duck still kosher if a nail was discovered in its stomach? What was one to do when pimples were seen on the liver of a chicken?

Immediate answers were required; otherwise an entire meal could be ruined. Precious, costly meat might have to be thrown out. Worse still, a problem could arise just before Passover, perhaps a grain of wheat or rye found in the meat. Here was a potential disaster, given the elaborate preparations required for this holiday. It was to the rabbi that everyone went for answers— straight to his home, no appointments necessary. The laws of *Kashruth* [dietary rules] were specific and well-established; tractates of the Talmud were devoted to such matters. These the rabbi studied, then rendered his decision after checking the meat or inspecting the broken wing or leg of a chicken.

Many of the problems did not pose novel questions. For example, it was no complicated matter for the rabbi to decide how pots, pans, and utensils that had been tainted could once more be made kosher. Elaborate purification procedures were often involved, among them the temporary burial of items, the placing of red-hot stones in pots, and the continuous filling and emptying of containers. When matters were more complex, not everyone trusted the judgment of the rabbi alone; in such cases people were likely also to consult with a respected scholar in town. Sometimes the scholar refused to intervene, fearful of the divisions that his intervention might encourage. When he did offer an opinion, it almost always coincided with the rabbi's. In all fairness, when cases were complex or ambiguous the rabbi himself did not hesitate to consult other authorities.

Jews preferred to steer clear of the local court system, uncomfortable as they were with courts and judges they considered biased against them. When both parties to a dispute were Jewish, especially when they were small businessmen, most likely they would bring their case to the rabbi for settlement. Not only the rabbi sat in judgment, but with him on the rabbinical court were two other judges. Upon hearing the evidence, they consulted the appropriate sections of the Talmud, then rendered a verdict. Though some decisions might take up to a week, most came speedily. Whatever the verdict, both parties paid equally for the judicial finding. When the court wasn't examining a business issue, it might be involved in a divorce proceeding or deciding who was entitled to a specific *aliyah* in the synagogue. The rabbi, it's now clear, served less as a spiritual leader than as a guardian and judge of the community's religious practices.

I've yet to mention the rivalry that existed between the rabbi and the *dayan*. This was no petty matter that could be readily healed, but a long-standing, mean-spirited dispute that split our community for years. Anyone who thought that harmony reigned among the Jews of Kolbuszowa was either blind or hopelessly naive. The fight stemmed not from matters of doctrine or religious practice, but from personal rivalry and jealousy. Although the two were cousins, our rabbi could not accept having the *dayan* serve as assistant rabbi, being convinced that the *dayan* wished to become the rabbi himself. Followers rallied behind each of the men, and the bitterness intensified with the passing years.

Finally there was an ugly incident that years later still embroiled the town. It happened on Simchat Torah, the joyous holiday on which congregants paraded around bearing the sacred Torahs. With the rabbi dancing about, carrying one of the Torahs, a follower of the *dayan* ran up and attempted to snatch it from him. A battle then ensued between the two sides. The fight ended quickly; but the matter was taken to court, where the *dayan*'s supporter was convicted for "disturbing religious services" and received a five-year prison term. Other heated legal issues between the two sides dragged on year after year.

Whatever our divisions, there was nothing like the holidays to bring us together. Over the course of each year we as Jews joined in to celebrate and commemorate significant episodes from our past and to rededicate and reconsecrate our lives. Whether joyous or sorrowful, the holidays succeeded in lifting us out of our ordinary lives, lending new impetus to our prayers and added meaning to our rituals. Each holiday had its own special flavor and appeal and required a unique round of preparations. Of course, this was a pattern we well understood, given the weekly arrival of the Sabbath and our efforts, whatever the circumstances, always to make this a special time for ourselves and our families. Naturally some of the holidays were considered more significant than others and brought forth greater efforts as well as higher expectations on our part.

When I speak of the various holidays, it is mostly through the eyes of a youngster that I remember them. Elsewhere I have mentioned some of the ways we young people observed these holidays, sometimes with practices notably at odds with the prevailing mood. But let me describe how our community in general approached those special occasions.

Shortly after the New Year was celebrated, in late summer or early fall, came the awe-inspiring Day of Atonement or Yom Kippur. It was a time when sin and forgiveness were the principal themes, a solemn holiday because it was then that God decided one's fate for the coming year. The holiday began at sundown with *Kol Nidre,* perhaps the most compelling and unforgettable prayer in the entire liturgy.* But events occurring before sundown are perhaps more interesting to relate. That afternoon Jews gathered in the synagogue to humble themselves, to accept punishment for sins committed during the year. There was no misun-

---

*The eve of Yom Kippur was the only time in the entire year that unmarried as well as married women attended the synagogue.

derstanding the ritual. Hay was laid upon the ground in a portion of the synagogue, and a whip was prepared by the sexton for the occasion. One by one men knelt on the hay and were subjected to five or six strokes from the whip. Rich, poor, young and old, each man in turn, kneeling upon the floor, was beaten by the sexton; each accepted his humiliation and punishment.

After this these same people scurried about, looking to discover the whereabouts of enemies and competitors who during the year they had slighted or offended. On encountering them they would ask for forgiveness. Imagine all this peacemaking going on at one time. My father was especially busy then. Because he was often embroiled in disputes arising from competing with others in business, many were those whom he asked for forgiveness. How well did this ritual of reconciliation work, you ask. It ushered in a momentary lull in whatever conflict was then under way, but there were very few instances of long-term pacification that I can recall.

Entering the synagogue the day before Yom Kippur one came upon a long table on which were collection plates, some twenty-five in all, from the many charitable and service organizations in Kolbuszowa. Behind each plate sat a representative from the organization. Here at a glance one appreciated how rich an organizational network there was, how much life in Kolbuszowa depended upon the work of charitable people and institutions. (For many years no Zionist organizations were permitted to put a plate out on this occasion.) Here was a plate to assist those buying new books for the synagogue; here was one to supplement the funds loaned out by the Free Loan Society. There was a plate for the rabbi and another (naturally) for the assistant rabbi, plates for widows and for women who had little or no money for a dowry, a plate for the orphans of Kolbuszowa. The Burial Society sought funds, as did the Hebrew schools for boys and for girls. It was customary for one entering this area of the synagogue to place a few coins in each plate as one proceeded down the line.

Let me return to the day for the moment. The minute the last whipping was completed, the young boys looking on made quick dashes for the hay, then with their arms full returned to where their fathers would be seated for the evening services and spread the hay on the ground. Naturally this requires some explanation.

On Yom Kippur, this holiest of holidays, the men did not wear shoes in synagogue, rejecting leather because it was from the skin of an animal slain deliberately. Instead they came in their socks and remained in them throughout the entire holiday. My father and the others arrived at the synagogue well in advance of *Kol Nidre,* then proceeded to stand for this prayer. He never again sat down while praying until the following evening, at the conclusion of the holiday. He stayed on his feet so long that it was no wonder he and the others appreciated the hay we spread along the floor.*

On Yom Kippur each member brought to the synagogue a three-foot-long candle, which was expected to burn for twenty-four consecutive hours. (One similar to it was used at home.) These candles were placed on tables in front of the long benches beside which the men stood. Given the smoke and distinctive aroma they produced, imagine if you will the atmosphere in some of the smaller rooms. Even in the larger halls the sight was impressive and solemn, each worshiper standing in prayer in his stocking feet, dressed in his black coat covered by a *kittel* [a long white outer garment], wrapped in his *tallit,* the entire room bathed in the warm but flickering light of scores of candles.

For me Yom Kippur was extra special, for it was then that I sang with my brother-in-law, Reuben Weinstein, before the congregation. But I had an even more valuable service to perform on this holiday. Yom Kippur, as you know, is a day on which everyone fasts. Add to this the strong emotions felt on this occasion and the aroma of scores of burning candles, and the result was that many congregants became faint. Every year it happened, and always I was prepared. I made certain to bring along *shmeckehts* [bottle of ammonia] with which to answer the call of swooning worshipers. This made me an important figure as I ran here and there responding to requests for the *shmeckehts*. If needed I raced up to the women's section, where the bottle was then passed along to the person in distress. One woman in particular was known to faint away each year just as a certain prayer sounded, so I made certain to be in the vicinity when that time arrived. It just may be

---

*My father and many others would also speak no Yiddish during this entire period because it was too common for this holy occasion. They limited their conversation to Hebrew.

that the emergency relief work I did on Yom Kippur and the kind words it brought were what first awakened the desire to be a doctor that I've already mentioned. No doubt many more worshipers remained conscious that day than might have if I had not been there to help clear their heads.

Other holidays had their special arrangements and memorable moments. There was Succoth, when we all took our meals for seven days in the outdoor *succa* [booth], along with several neighbors whom we invited to join us. Simchat Torah, which marked the annual conclusion of the reading of the Torah and the return to the beginning once more, was probably the only holiday on which everyone was allowed to drink wine, perhaps a little too much of it, and become tipsy. It was the only time of the year that women were permitted to come down to the men's section and look on as men carried and kissed the Torah in a jubilant procession. It was also the occasion when all boys three years and older were given *aliyahs,* usually performed collectively, something to which we as children eagerly looked forward.

Both Chanukah and Purim were happy occasions. On Chanukah some of the normal restrictions were relaxed. Card-playing, for example, was allowed, and of course spinning dreidels was always a prominent feature. On Purim it was customary for my father to read the Megillah [Book of Esther] in our house, which was usually jam-packed for the occasion by anywhere from twenty-five to fifty women from the neighborhood who had been invited in to listen. The children all had noisemakers and managed to create a deafening din each time they heard Haman's hated name. It disturbed my father that we interrupted his readings for so long with our noise, but wait he did until we quieted down. After the reading my mother served *Haman tashen,* sponge cake, honey cake, and other refreshments to our many guests.

To most of us the most tragic event in all of the Jews' less than joyful history as a people was the destruction of the temple in Jerusalem by the Romans. Each summer when we commemorated this event the town assumed the attitude of collective mourning. No weddings could be held in this period or any other happy occasions scheduled. Only dairy products could be eaten: no meat meals whatsoever. The three weeks before Tisha B'av, the day when the Romans encircled the walls of Jerusalem, were marked by special prayer and the removal of meat from our table. The nine days before the destruction, when the Romans broke through the walls, were also declared a time to lament and to remember. Even those Jews who ordinarily shaved refrained now from doing so. Once Tisha B'av itself arrived, the signs of mourning intensified; people fasted, wore old, torn clothes, and sat on boxes instead of chairs and sofas. In this way did we mark and identify with the tragic conclusion of what had been a glorious era in Jewish history.

Almost all of us regarded Passover as the central holiday of the year. There were many reasons for this. It came at a time when winter was behind us and the warming breezes of spring were on the way. It lasted fully eight days, which meant that extensive preparations were necessary, especially in view of the dietary laws and special dishes and utensils associated with this celebration. And as I have mentioned, it was the time when those who could afford it usually acquired new clothes for themselves and family members, a prospect that was positively exhilarating.

The length of Passover allowed for family reunions; members residing in other towns or even outside Poland would return for visits. Some returned because those living on their own knew how difficult it was, away from home, to prepare properly for the holiday, to meet all its many requirements. Passover might also be the occasion when a prospective son-in-law from out of town came to visit, giving the community its first opportunity to size him up, see how well he performed in the synagogue, take the measure of his voice.

Passover was no easy time for many of us. Often it produced much anxiety and considerable uncertainty. The poor wondered and worried how they could afford to make the necessary arrangements, to buy the foods that would be needed. Even those who were better off shuddered when they thought of all the work ahead, of the need for an early start to avoid the panic of last-minute preparations. They even worried about the new clothes. Many others had also placed orders; was it not possible that the garments, almost all made by hand, would not be ready on time? True, the economy of Kolbuszowa displayed more life in this period than at any other time of the year, but the pressures on people now intensified. Businessmen, for example, worried greatly in those years when Passover came before Easter. When this happened, matters were dreadfully complicated, given the necessity of preparing for Passover while at the same time catering to the many needs of their Polish customers at this time of the year.

Passover meant spring cleaning. All homes had to be purged of food items not allowed during the holiday, notably bread and bread products, so why not use the opportunity for a top-to-bottom cleaning? That's exactly what just about everyone did, and dramatic evidence of the results could be seen up and down the town about a week before Passover. Piled up on street after street were practically all the possessions of every household. Sadly one saw just how little many families had. Alongside the various pieces of furniture were religious books spread out on blankets, their pages allowed to turn in the wind, so that moths hidden among the pages would be blown away. Women could be seen pushing feathers dipped in acid into furniture cracks in an attempt to dislodge the *vancen* (bedbugs). This was the only time of the year the battle against these pests would be taken up in earnest and sometimes won. Also when the house was almost empty was an excellent time to paint the rooms, and so walls that had grown dark once again became white.

Along with this serious housecleaning came a ritual act of purification undertaken in every household the night before Passover to ensure that the *chumetz* [foods forbidden during Passover] had been removed. Each year it proceeded in the same fashion, at least in our household. My mother would hide ten small pieces of bread at various locations around the house, and once my father returned from synagogue the search would begin. Finding the *chumetz* was my father's task to perform by himself. The children knew where it had been hidden but were forbidden to assist him. What we did, of course, is follow him about and giggle quite a bit, especially when he was wide of the mark. Meanwhile my father proceeded through the house in a more or less systematic manner, carrying a turkey or goose feather and a wooden spoon. On locating a piece of bread he pushed it onto the spoon with the feather, then continued his quest.

So many years had he done this that many of my mother's favorite hiding places were known to him. But sometimes he forgot, or my mother became especially inventive; on such occasions time passed and still he had not found all ten pieces. There was nothing he could say, however, obliged as he was to remain silent until the search had been completed. The frustration sometimes showed on his face, especially when our laughing signaled that he was off target. His search could take hours, but finally it was done. The feather, the spoon, and the breadcrumbs he wrapped in a rag, and the following morning it all was burned in the oven located in the public bath.

A choice had to be made about the dishes and utensils used throughout the year. They could be used during Passover if first they underwent an elaborate process of ritual purification. Or, as was the case with us, an entirely new set of dishes and utensils saved especially for this holiday could be substituted. This, too, involved much work, taking down dishes packed away carefully upstairs in the attic and removing the everyday set. It's not that I enjoyed the work, but I did look forward to seeing some of the very beautiful items we put aside for Passover. The year-round pieces remained in our house, but they no longer belonged to us. As was the custom, they were temporarily "sold," together with the *chumetz* food, to a non-Jew, a handshake usually confirming the transaction. With the *chumetz* dishes, utensils, and food no longer ours, the laws of Passover were thus upheld.

We had holiday dishes, and normally new clothes, but many in town did not. For them preparations depended on outside assistance, which was forthcoming at Passover in greater amounts perhaps than at any other time during the year. Months before the holiday, money usually arrived from America earmarked for the purchase of wheat by the poor for their matzohs. In charge of distributing the money to the poor was Leibtche Beck, who compiled the list of those in need and proceeded to distribute the funds. That wasn't always easy. On the one hand, there were those truly needy persons who were too proud to come for the money. How to get it to them as discreetly as possible was the first challenge Beck faced. On the other hand there were the regular beneficiaries, who were typically dissatisfied with what they received and demanded more. Beck was obliged to make his case to them, pleading generous intentions that were unfortunately limited by funds actually available. Money from America was supplemented by contributions raised in Kolbuszowa itself and distributed separately. In addition to the money, Jewish estate managers in the vicinity sent in wagonloads of potatoes intended for those in need. Passover remained a major problem for the poor, but they were not forgotten during this period.

Without doubt the primary symbol of Passover was matzoh, the unleavened bread eaten by our forefathers after their hasty departure from Egypt. Weeks before the holiday, bakers, who did nothing else in this period but prepare Passover matzohs, opened for business with ovens used only at this time of the year. People brought flour to them, then watched as it was converted into matzohs. My mother and sisters looked on intently as their flour was made into dough. This could take no longer than seven minutes; beyond that the dough would begin to ferment and could not be used. Then into the ovens it went, and after a minute or two the round, perforated matzohs were ready. Before leaving, my mother distributed chocolates to the employees who had prepared our matzohs. Walking over to each she placed the chocolates directly into their mouths, keeping them from having to touch food that was not kosher for Passover. She and my sisters then carried the matzohs home in big baskets covered with clean sheets. Back at the house they were brought upstairs and placed in new pillowcases in an unused room.

So much did matzohs symbolize Passover that we used them as gifts for Polish friends, who considered them treats—ironically enough, given the ancient Christian charge that Jews baked their matzohs with blood from Christian children. I was the one selected by my father to deliver these gift matzohs, usually two or three packed together. It was also customary for Jewish children to bring matzohs for their favorite teachers in public school. Unfortunately matzohs wrapped in newspapers and not handled carefully usually arrived at school broken into many pieces. My mother urged us to be careful and see to it that our matzohs remained intact. She placed them in clean pillowcases and had us deliver them this way; the pillowcases were later returned to us. Mostly our matzohs arrived in one piece.

The matzohs brought home by my mother were good enough for everyone in our family except my father. To him more rigid requirements were in order, more stringent procedures whose every step would be closely supervised. It all started on a small patch of land owned by a cousin, Szymon Storch, in a nearby village, Przedborz. There each year in the fall my father observed as the seeds were planted that would in time yield the wheat for his matzohs. The following spring he visited his "field" regularly to watch over his crop and see that no outside plants intruded. When the wheat was ready to be cut, he was there again making certain that it dried out properly and that no drops of rain fell on it. Once it was in the barn he saw to it that it stood in a secure, clean area not used for any other purpose and that it was properly threshed.

When the time came, he placed the wheat in a pillowcase and brought it home; paper bags were not kosher because they were constructed with glue made with flour. Back in our house he spread the wheat out on a table upstairs; then he and his friends carefully examined every kernel to make certain that it contained no impurities and that no other seeds and flowers were mixed in. This examination was laborious work performed over the course of several weeks. Once it was completed, the wheat was ready to be ground into a dark whole wheat flour by Szymon Storch. It was this flour that my father brought to the establishment that baked the other family matzohs. The outcome of this lengthy process was what we called *shmira* matzoh. *Shomer* meant "watchman," and as you can see from my description, these very special matzohs seemed aptly named.*

---

*It even went further than this. There were, if you can believe it, super *shmira* matzohs! My father saved some of his prepared flour for the eve of Passover, at

The careful production of matzohs was just one of the many vital tasks required for the holiday. For months before, my father had been preparing various wines in our basement, usually emerging from his work down there a bit red-faced and slightly light-headed, and my mother was busy storing *schmaltz* that would be put to good use at Passover. As the holiday approached, chickens, turkeys, and geese were bought. Cookies and tarts made with potato flour were prepared in advance. We took some of our matzohs to Berish Bilfeld; he crushed them to make matzoh meal flour, which my mother then used to make cakes. Four weeks earlier my mother had placed beets and a few raw eggs in a barrel of water, which she had then let stand and ferment in our warm kitchen. This would later become the borscht we so much enjoyed at Passover.*

No one was ever quite ready for Passover, but it arrived anyway. For many it could not be soon enough, given the excitement and treats it brought. The first treat actually came in the afternoon before the holiday began but when *chumetz* could no longer be eaten. On special earthenware plates we ate potatoes, *schmaltz,* and borscht. Was it our eagerness to begin? Was the borscht so exceptional? Whatever the explanation, we all agreed that the meal was uncommonly delicious.

Passover, of course, brought the seder, a lengthy ceremony conducted at home at night in which the story of Passover was told and a festive meal enjoyed. Always at our table were some friends or family members who for some reason could not make their own seder. My father put on his *kittel* for the occasion† and, as was the

---

which time he and other orthodox men baked matzohs in an oven that had been very carefully inspected, using water taken from the town well in special bottles two weeks earlier, at the time of the new moon. All the time the baking was under way the men prayed and sang psalms by the oven. This combination of prayers, special flour, special water, and a scrupulously clean oven put everyone's mind at ease; truly this matzoh was kosher for Passover. These super *shmira* matzohs were used only for the first two days of Passover.

*Some of the eggs were left in the water till they turned a beautiful purple and were later used as ornaments.

†A man wore his *kittel* on his wedding day and then each Yom Kippur and Passover. When he died he was buried in it.

custom in the ancient Middle East, sat on his bed propped up by cushions like a king. The reading of the Hagadah, which contains the story of the exodus from Egypt and the ceremonials of Passover, could take upwards of four hours. The youngest asked the four questions in Hebrew or in Yiddish about the meaning of Passover, and my father took over the conduct of the service to explain. Over the course of the evening we sang the many holiday songs together.

As children we had studied the Hagadah in *cheder* and so were familiar with its contents. Mostly the children paid close attention throughout the entire evening. Always we watched carefully when the door was opened for Elijah the Prophet, and all eyes focused on Elijah's cup filled with wine. We were certain we saw its level fall, clear proof he had come among us. At some point it was time to steal the *afikomen*, a piece of matzoh set aside earlier and required in order to conclude the seder. We children would return it, of course, but only after gifts had been promised as an inducement. After the service ended, my married sisters and their husbands and children would come over for tea, dessert, and plenty of singing. It was very late by the time everyone left and all was put away. We were all very, very tired from the work and all the excitement. No one ever complained, however. Once we were slaves in Egypt, and now we were free.

Preparations for and celebrations of every holiday on the Jewish calendar each year were only one indication of the enduring strength of traditional Judaism in Kolbuszowa. But at a time when most of the Jewish population maintained their orthodox ways, this is not surprising. Judaism was the most important fact, the principal focus, of our lives; each and every day the obligations of religion took priority over everything else.* The strictly orthodox, for example, would never read newspapers, which were con-

---

*Sometimes it required some fancy footwork to remain true to religious prescription. Because walking too far on the Sabbath would constitute work and thus not be permitted, orthodox Jews planning a Sabbath walk would on Friday set out some water and bread, usually under a tree, at a point midway in their planned journey. That spot became "home," and the walk from there to their destination was now not deemed excessively lengthy.

sidered too worldly. No one complained that these obligations were inconvenient; very few cut corners or avoided performing the countless rituals when they thought they were not observed. Too much was at stake; too much tradition pressed down on us. We prayed to God because we knew He was listening. We studied our sacred texts and religious commentaries because we craved deeper understanding. We gave to charity because we understood that giving was a primary obligation of our faith. And though not all of us had the same degree of assurance as Pinchas Mesheach,* most of us would not have been that surprised to witness the coming of the Messiah.

For all our deeply held religious faith and commitment to learning, we were still in certain ways a plain, isolated, unsophisticated people. Among other things, we were receptive to folk beliefs and superstitions, though to a lesser degree than the surrounding Polish population. We would not cross the path of a black cat, walk under a ladder, be indifferent to a broken mirror, or avoid "cures" that were more superstition than science. Talismans were seen as potent objects; numbers were scrutinized for their significance. The evil eye was a living presence among us. To praise a child, for example, might be tempting fate, so we were quick to spit three times in order to avert any evil consequences. When it thundered we went quickly to place a cup of water on the windowsill as a form of protection.

We were sure that Ashmadai, the king of the evil spirits, and his wife, Lillis, were out in the world opposing all that we held dear. No one doubted that Ashmadi would attempt to strangle a newborn Jewish male the night before his circumcision (to prevent a further addition to the Jewish people), and so on what we called "watch night" the mother and baby were closely guarded to prevent this from happening. At a wedding ceremony the bride

---

*Pinchas Mesheach [Messiah] spent his entire life convinced that the Messiah was about to return and that one needed to be prepared for that moment. Pinchas always slept in his pants and socks so as not to lose a moment's time when the blessed event occurred. A conversation with Pinchas left no doubt as to the depth of his conviction. Each day one could hear him say, "This night the Messiah will come." Pinchas, I assure you, always believed it would be so.

walked around the groom under the *chupah* seven times as a precaution to thwart the designs of Ashmadai, who, it was believed, wished to prevent the marriages of Jewish couples. We worshiped Almighty God, but we were also wary of evil spirits who inhabited our world and attempted to disrupt our lives.

But our beliefs were changing. My generation did not accept as readily the traditions so revered by our fathers. It was becoming modern, restless, questioning, less willing to go along with all that it had inherited. Books, newspapers, new products, visitors, and philosophies from the outside world were offering new possibilities, holding out new prospects. Certainly there was no rush to leave Judaism, but strict adherence could no longer be expected automatically. Outward appearances told much of the story—cutting the *payes* short, shaving the face, wearing more modern clothes and neckties, smoking cigarettes. Among the girls short-sleeved blouses, short dresses, brassieres, the use of lipstick and makeup, dating, and the rejection of matchmakers all reflected the same tendencies.*

These changes did not go unopposed. Unofficial town censors lurked everywhere, usually orthodox adults who did not hide their disdain for what was taking place. Disturbed by some change in appearance that they deemed inappropriate, they might inform the culprit directly—and not always in a kindly manner—or they might express their disapproval to older family members and call for correction. We were being spoiled—of that they were certain.

Judaism as it once had been would no longer be. But that, as you know, would come less from our doing than at the hands of those who had come to hate us so.

*By the 1930s numerous married women refused to cut off all their hair, insisting that portions of it remain in front and along the sides so as to produce a more modern and attractive "look." How well I remember a serious confrontation between my father and my sister-in-law Chancia on just this issue.

Of Matchmakers and Marriages

Love, romance, individual preference—all these counted for very little, were plain foolishness, certainly not to be relied upon. Marriage, almost everyone agreed, required more solid foundations. What sense did it make to leave so important a matter to inexperienced young people, especially young men whose strictly orthodox upbringing kept them from even looking directly at a girl? So it wasn't. And as far back as people could remember, it never had been in Kolbuszowa. But as I was growing up, as I have said many times, things were beginning to change. As you can imagine, this suited me just fine. Young people, some of them at least, began to take once forbidden paths, started behaving in ways few had ever dared to do. That we were entering a new world there could be no doubt. Unfortunately time ran out on us before it was clear just where we had arrived.

Tradition prescribed all things and in that respect simplified life. Uncertainties largely disappeared, resolved by appeals to the past. How it had always been done: that was the proper path to follow. Of course, marriage was among the oldest and most hallowed of traditions. Holy matrimony it certainly was, endowed with scriptural authority, biblical blessings. So it was expected that at the appropriate age boys and girls would be paired off, pledged to one another by parents who were anxious to maintain family security and status but were just as eager for continuity and for grandchildren. Marriage followed, then children, usually in large

numbers; in Kolbuszowa anywhere from five to ten was acceptable. It had always been so. Anything else didn't make sense,
would have been rejected. By and large it worked, as each generation awaited its turn, indeed eagerly anticipated the rites of
passage, release, and renewal.

Tradition prescribed, but nothing happened by itself. The
wheels had to be set in motion, the different parts played out.
When a boy turned nineteen or twenty, a girl seventeen or eighteen, it was time. People expected things—this despite the fact
that there had been, shall we say, few if any preliminaries. By this
I mean that boys and girls had been kept apart, rigidly segregated
even as they moved into young adulthood. What could they know
of one another? Inherited beliefs, observations made from afar,
inferences from one's family life—that was the sum total. Instead
of intimacy there was innocence; no familiarity, simply faith. But
the young people themselves knew it was time, felt nature calling,
had desires that had to be, if not ignored, certainly suppressed
while they remained single.

Likewise a mother was not blind to the situation; in fact she
was expected to take the lead. This could be seen most dramatically with her son. That a person so nearly perfect in her eyes could
find a suitable wife with qualities quite as remarkable as his was
for her a dubious proposition; still, as God was her witness, she
would try. That the campaign was under way there could be no
doubt, not once you laid eyes on the boy. He had been transformed, clothed now in a resplendent new dress coat and a black
velvet hat. No one missed the significance of this change. He
looked different, acted differently, but still by himself there was
not much else he could do.

Although girls also began to dress differently, their prospects
hinged not so much on appearances as on their dowries. The
larger the dowry, the less likely the girl would meet with disappointment. Homely girls with respectable dowries had little need
to worry; pretty ones with deficient dowries might have to wait.
That those with poor dowries envied, even hated, those more fortunately positioned was common knowledge in Kolbuszowa.

Enter the matchmaker, the pivot around which marriageable

youths revolved.* One might, I suppose, be tempted to see matchmakers as colorful characters, even legendary figures blessed with
a special insight into character and compatibility that was denied
mere mortals. But in truth, busybodies in business—representing
more cupidity than Cupid—that is a more accurate picture. For
most, matchmaking was a sideline, a way of supplementing meager earnings from regular occupations. As always, you got what
you paid for. The more highly regarded practitioners were well
connected and could produce on request all manner of likely prospects, as long as a client's status justified such close attention to
details and dowries.† Working along with other matchmakers,
they created a network that embraced numerous towns and villages in a given region. It was their job to know the territory, and
some of the better ones went at it with a zeal unmatched even by
local tax collectors. Because it was their business, they stuck their
noses in everyone else's, eager to detect and uncover the first indications of eligibility, of marital intentions.

One's fate to a large extent was in their hands, rested on their
ability and willingness to propose a match in which compatibility
was of as much concern as their compensation. The trouble was
that the compatibility of the young folks involved was rarely con-

*Could it be that matchmakers served simply as God's messengers on earth?
According to Talmudic tradition, while they labored mightily to bring young
people together they were actually just following paths already prescribed. Surely
this was the meaning of the Talmudic statement that forty days before a child
leaves the womb there is a voice in heaven declaring that this boy will be married
to the daughter of this person. Then were not marriages made in heaven?

†Shulim Korn from Tarnobrzeg was a decidedly upscale matchmaker. First
and foremost he was a land agent, engaged in buying and selling large parcels
of land in the region. Such easy entree to the well-to-do encouraged him to
branch off into matrimony. So with Shulim land deals and marriage contracts—
both of the highest quality, mind you—went hand in hand. Then there was
Mordechai from Majdan, who belonged quite obviously in another category.
This lively, playful man of scholarly inclination could not compete with Shulim
among the upper strata, but he certainly had a following of people who adored
his genial manner and lack of sophistication.

Competition among matchmakers often was fierce. They initiated matches,
offering their services to all in need but not with the expectation of exclusivity.
Often it would happen that several would be in pursuit of a suitable mate for a
given family. That they had to scramble and use their wits and their wiles hardly
comes as a surprise.

sidered; what was important was satisfying the desires of the respective parents. They needed to be appeased, to be assured that they were getting full value. Was the family sufficiently religious? Was its reputation beyond reproach? The girl's dowry—was it worthy of the boy? Could not this princely sum attract a more accomplished young man? You want a girl for your son who is beautiful, intelligent, educated, skillful, healthy, strong, patient, and sensible? Do you seek just one girl or ten? Does not the young man's Jewish education warrant a more substantial dowry? Could he be expected to support a family?* At what level of comfort? You don't say!

Matchmakers collected their fee (usually a few percentage points of the dowry) only when a match was concluded.† Eager to move things along, they were inclined toward enthusiastic endorsements far more than sober assessments.‡ That certainly is the point of this story of the two matchmakers:

"Is she intelligent?" – "Ah! such wisdom."
"Some looks." – "Yes, she's a beauty."
"Is she rich?" – "Oh, such wealth."
"Just a small hunchback." – "And what a hunchback!"

Or a similar anecdote that extols to ruinous excess:

"This young woman," gushed the matchmaker, "is truly excep-

---

*Because scholars were revered among our people, a scholar had more leverage than most others. Only when a scholar was involved was there much likelihood that a match would be arranged between persons from markedly different social strata.

†Before a match was set there could be much give-and-take between the two parties. Because they would not meet face to face until agreement was reached, it fell to the matchmaker to travel back and forth conveying terms, acting as a middleman, surely an early example of "shuttle diplomacy." Rarely were matchmakers overpaid for their efforts, which at times were most strenuous.

‡Of course, few people relied solely on information supplied by matchmakers. Quite often my father wrote to friends and acquaintances who might have knowledge of the other party, seeking information and asking for confirmation of "facts" furnished by the matchmaker. Often a rabbi entered the picture, especially when both parties were known to him. This often represented a delicate issue for the rabbi, who was expected to furnish reliable information but who also had to avoid offending either side. Rabbis generally emphasized positive features wherever possible and endorsed most matches.

tional. She is very well off, beautiful, dutiful, and intelligent, she has a clever hand, and oh, she bears so easy children"!!

A girl's prospects, I've said, improved in direct proportion to the size of her dowry. A substantial dowry brought matchmakers on the run and had them quickly on the lookout for suitable partners. If it was a professional man that the father wanted for his daughter, certainly he'd have to pay more than for a clerk. Did not the young man need money to support his education, then later an office?

What of the poor? Matchmakers offered their services to all, accepting from the poor a small or even token payment. A poor boy, for his part, understood that he would be offered a limited choice of girls. Why not then make his own selection? Many did. Even so the matchmaker would arrive to make official what had already taken place. This way no one complained: everything seemed as it should be, as it always was.*

Marrying off five daughters, as my father had to do, was no casual undertaking; it required long-term planning. Remember that to my father, as a man of standing in our town, suitable matches were a necessity. Since he was also a man of substance, they were also quite likely.†

Still, preparations had to be made years in advance. I remember him putting aside funds for that purpose whenever he could. When money arrived from relations in America, that's where it

---

*Every young person in town was expected to get married. The number of unmarried adults in Kolbuszowa was never more than a handful, most of whom suffered from severe physical disabilities or were known to be mentally disturbed. (Those with physical or mental defects considered only mildly disabling would marry but could not expect to command full value in the marriage marketplace.) There was even an organized group of town elders whose function it was to assist in any way necessary when obstacles blocked the marriage of some of Kolbuszowa's less fortunate. If some additional dowry money was needed, it was provided; so was a wedding hall if necessary. If it proved necessary to look in neighboring towns for a suitable partner, that too was done. Matchmaking and marriage, you see, were everyone's business.

†My father never deviated from insisting on certain qualities he expected in prospective sons-in-law. They should be scholarly, come from Hassidic and preferably rabbinical backgrounds, and have good voices so as to be able to sing well in the synagogue.

went. So did any other American paper money obtained when customers or debtors paid my father in this much prized currency. He would go down to the basement and dig up a box he had hidden away, and into it would go the dowry money.* He had promised each daughter a dowry of $2,000, a princely amount. And he made good on his word; each received what he had promised, plus a house and a business. In each case he took a portion of his own general merchandise operation and turned it over to the couple. That way all the families could remain in Kolbuszowa, each with a means of supporting itself. It was, I grant you, an exceptional arrangement. That's the kind of man my father was.

What most impressed matchmakers about him and made their job easier was one outstanding fact: he had four brothers, two sisters, and a son in America. Why, you might ask, should that be? How could family in America produce suitable matches in Kolbuszowa, Poland? Because America was a special place for us, a magical land whose very mention conjured up dreams, hopes, fantasies—the kind never possible here. So having family members there assumed great significance. Seven members, no less—such connections!

But there was more. Think of it as an insurance policy, as money in the bank or an ace in the hole. With family members there you could be sure of wedding gifts from America, something special that was automatically valuable—made in America! There would be more such presents: annual dividends, you might say. Certain holidays would bring parcels, some containing cash, which was better than gold in Kolbuszowa. There would also be "old" clothes, worn by American standards but ever so precious to us. An alteration here and there made them as good as new. Such pride we took in wearing them! This is what America meant. Fam-

---

*In only one instance that I remember did he have trouble accumulating sufficient funds. Rather than the $2,000 promised to my sister Malcia he had only $1,800 on deposit in the basement box. In a letter to my brother Avrum in America he mentioned this deficiency but said nothing else about it. You can imagine his joy when the next letter from Avrum contained $200 in cash. He had not been asked for the money but understood just how important such things were to our father. Later, when I arrived in America and asked him about this, he remarked that he had gone out and borrowed the $200.

ily there became the equivalent of a guarantee, a source of ongoing support and direct assistance if needed. And maybe even the assurance of a place to go to, a refuge, should one ever wish or need to leave Poland. With family "there" you were a "somebody" here.

My father's ability to provide so handsomely for his daughters aroused the envy of other men in town with daughters as yet unmarried. What else accounts for the following incident? Not long after a match had been planned for my second oldest sister, an envelope arrived sent by the prospective father-in-law. Inside was a six-page letter he had received. It was anonymous, the writer identifying himself only as an "honest man." There was no doubt of the man's purpose, which was to sow doubts and to disrupt ongoing wedding plans. Keep in mind that such letters, supposedly revealing matters unknown to at least one of the wedding partners, were not all that unusual. We even had a name for them: *paszkwils.**

Over and over again my father read the extraordinarily detailed letter, wondering who had written it and defending himself against certain of the accusations. Why it was sent was no mystery. We stood accused, my father most particularly, of numerous unacceptable departures from religious orthodoxy, clear proof of our unworthiness. Had not my father fallen in love with my mother at a time when he was supposedly studying scripture with her father? Falling in love, pursuing a girl on his own—unthinkable, scandalous, and under the guise of religious instruction, no less!

There was more, much more. My father was held to account for going to a dentist. Now that does take some explaining. It should be understood, of course, that few people in town patronized dentists; instead they allowed their teeth to rot away. If a tooth did not fall out by itself, they went to the local barber and town quack (in whose windows jars of leeches were always on

---

*This word, a Polish term, had its origins in the eighteenth century at a time when Poland was partitioned among Germany, Russia, and Austria. Among those who opposed this destruction of Polish sovereignty were a number of writers who in sharply satirical essays castigated certain Polish nobles who had cooperated with the partition process. Such critical comments came to be known as *paszkwils,* and the term was later adopted for letters offering objections to proposed matches.

display), who took a pair of pliers and yanked out whatever remained of the tooth. As a consequence, many adults in town and
certainly most older folks walked around with few if any teeth in
their mouth. My father, a progressive man for all his traditional
beliefs, saw no harm in having cavities filled rather than suffering
the loss of all his teeth.

All this might have been all right if the town's dentist had not
been a woman. That in itself was sufficient to keep all the orthodox
Jews away from her door. What really irked the writer of the letter
was that by going to this dentist my father could not avoid "intimate" contact with the woman. Would she not in treating him
have to get up close, even touch him? With such close contact
inevitable, my father obviously was looking for trouble. Better his
teeth should rot! (My mother had no such aversion to a toothless
state. She avoided the dentist. When my father's youngest brother,
Max, a dentist in Brooklyn, offered to send her a set of false teeth
fashioned from an impression of her mouth, she refused.)

The discussion of my father's teeth apparently led the writer to
consider certain related matters. My father, the letter continued,
ate tomatoes, a charge no doubt assumed to carry considerable
weight. It was true both that my father ate tomatoes and that others would hold this against him. Some orthodox Jews, at least in
Kolbuszowa, did not eat tomatoes. Why, you ask. I'll tell you, although I'm not sure you will believe me. In town were two non-
kosher restaurants whose front windows displayed Swiss cheese
covered by an outer layer of red wax. The color of that wax, not
unlike the color of tomatoes, was the reason for placing tomatoes
on the forbidden list! The restaurant was not kosher, the Swiss
cheese was *traif* [non-kosher], the red wax reminded one of tomatoes, and thus, in this strained and clearly coincidental muddle
of circumstaces, tomatoes were associated with foods that were
impure.

My father, the letter continued, had also acted improperly when
he distributed scarce sugar in our county during World War I.
Accumulating extra sugar, trying to sell it on the black market—
such practices were common then. My father was besieged with
requests for additional sugar beyond what the ration cards might

allow. He did what he could to satisfy the demand; still people left disgruntled, having received less than they wanted. In their anger, he became the "Sugar King." Now years later the charge was arising again as part of an effort to sabotage the wedding of his daughter.

A lengthy letter, it didn't end there. Next the bill of particulars cited my sisters. The charge: singing the special Friday night songs at the table, a breach of behavior that my father apparently condoned. It was true. We were a singing household: men, women, girls, boys, we all sang together, even harmonized, at the dinner table. But orthodox Jews, you see, did not permit women to sing, especially not together with men. So why did we do it? Because we enjoyed it. Religious we were, but not ultra-orthodox. Still, how someone came to know of this particular dereliction was another matter. Was it a person living close by who might have overheard us? We had our suspicions.

Finally a parting salvo, this time involving my father's sisters. (Our accuser left few stones unturned!) Their sin: leaving for America. A curious charge, you say. Allow me to explain. As I've already said, it was perfectly acceptable, even admirable, for young men to head off to America to make their way. But this was not so for women; at least that was the judgment of those with a conservative turn of mind, namely most of the Jews in Kolbuszowa. For women to go produced a stain on their character, was construed as an immoral act. Women were not expected to leave home, certainly not on their own. Leaving home, especially for America, where standards in general were lax, clearly was courting trouble and thus made such women unsuitable. Such were the charges; we did not take them lightly.

Endlessly my father read and reread the letter, studying even the envelope itself. Then it was off to his rabbi for an opinion on who might have sent it and how to respond. An encouraging response here. "If it is destined by God," the rabbi declared, "then this letter will mean nothing." Less enigmatic was his comment that since the other family had forwarded the letter to us, one could assume they hadn't taken its contents all that seriously.

Still not satisfied, my father went further. In our region lived a man we all recognized as possessed; he had psychic powers and was able to see beyond the limits of ordinary people. Surely such a person could study the handwriting for clues or otherwise identify the sender. Into his hands we put the evidence and we watched as he analyzed it. In time he began describing the person who wrote it, adding that the man had two daughters! All uncertainty vanished. We had long suspected this neighbor, supposedly a friend of my father's. Little wonder: both his daughters were unmarried!

This story, it should please you, had a happy ending. We lived with our suspicions but said nothing to our neighbor. The marriage plans went forward, the charges notwithstanding. After all, my sister was beautiful and intelligent and her dowry was substantial. What reason to be deterred by a troublemaker, a sore loser? As for our Mr. Anonymous, his two daughters eventually married.

Were *paszkwils* generally frivolous, the rantings of disappointed competitors or habitual spoilers? Not always. Some people, it seemed, took it upon themselves, conceived it perhaps as their civic duty, to reveal information, supposedly unknown and assuredly damaging, to one of the two parties contemplating a match. I personally knew of instances in which letters arrived with information about business distress, previous bankruptcies, even an undisclosed illness. I recall one family in which a number of the children had died at early ages of heart trouble. When word circulated that a match had been arranged involving another member of this family, a letter arrived revealing this medical past. The result: a canceled wedding.

Is it any surprise that the elders of Kolbuszowa attempted to cover up the frailties of their children or their own failures? Was it ever any different anywhere? Many were the fanciful stories poking fun at such efforts to marry off less than perfect progeny. All knew of the anxious father who despaired of marrying off his three daughters, each with a speech impediment. When a suitor would come to look over the daughters, they were warned to say nothing in his presence. The young man arrives; tea and cookies are served. Meanwhile the three say nothing; the boy is doing all the talking.

Then suddenly one of the young ladies notices a spider crawling up his collar. She can no longer remain silent. "A sp . . . sp . . . spider i . . . i . . . is crawlin' on ya," she cries, at which point the second sister blurts out "Maame sssaid nnnot t' taalk," whereupon the last sister stammers "Sssee, I' . . . mm being kkkwiet."

Or take the young man whose speech was commonly sprinkled with vulgarisms. He is warned not to speak when the matchmaker is present. Everything proceeds according to plan until cups of tea are served and the matchmaker asks why the young man, who unbeknownst to him received no spoon, has made no effort to drink his. "What am I supposed to do, stir it with my *putz* [penis]?" he blurts out!*

There were other real obstacles, to be sure; then, too, many ignored realities and placed unrealistic demands on matchmakers. The dowry often proved a source of difficulty. It was one thing to set a figure, another to deliver when the time arrived. Such misrepresentations or perhaps sudden changes of circumstances found their way into song. In the words of one song, "He promised 100 dollars when he really meant, 90, but he had in mind 80 so he started to talk 70 when he hoped it might be 60 . . ." The song continues all the way down to 10, and even then not actually in cash.†

A dowry had to be cash, not any substitute, because this was serious business. So serious, in fact, that more than one matchmaker might actually arrive at the engagement party claiming a share of the dowry as his or her rightful fee. This became something of a racket; certainly it was an embarrassment. Here they were, two matchmakers intruding at the last minute, claiming either that they somehow had been involved in arranging the match or that at that very moment were, however inconveniently, in touch with another interested party. Insistent they certainly were, and not beyond screaming and causing a general commo-

---

*In another type of test, girls would be asked to unravel a tangled ball of wool, so that their dexterity and level of patience might be evaluated.

†When no dowry funds were available, there developed a "futures" tradition involving the pledge of a grandmother's inheritance. Payments, as you can see, could get distressingly vague.

tion; nor would they agree to go away. What point was there in challenging them at this time or denying their involvement? To accept their interpretation and offer them something for their "efforts"—that clearly was the best solution. Usually this brought the matter to a close. Unfortunately, paying them off guaranteed that they would strike again at yet another inopportune moment.*

A dowry agreed on, a match arranged—remember, the young man and woman had probably met each other but once or twice—all energies now turned toward the engagement party, which was held at the home of the groom or at a neutral site. An important event it surely was, in some cases second only in significance to the wedding itself. It was on this occasion that the boy and girl might see each other for the first time. Of greater importance was the fact that the terms of the marriage, including the date,† were here spelled out and the marriage agreement signed. And also, of course, there was the all-important counting out of the dowry money. A shortfall here could jeopardize the entire affair. Slowly the money, which was almost always in small denominations, was counted out, and when the agreed-on sum was reached, smiles were the order of the day. A fine gentleman, the bride's father—truly a man of his word!

Then followed the presentation of gifts, which was certainly the highlight of the gathering for the two young people. If the boy was fortunate, he would receive from the girl's father a gold watch and chain. Not any gold watch, mind you; it was absolutely vital that it be a Swiss Schafhausen watch. That was the boy's dream, to receive such a watch and display it from the front of his vest. It was said, only with slight exaggeration, that boys entered marriage primarily to obtain such a wondrous thing. The girl, for her part, looked forward to receiving a diamond ring. Ordinarily that

*Matters were not always resolved that easily. Trying to determine the relative contributions of each and assigning each a proper percentage of the dowry based on his or her efforts often occasioned heated disputes. Only adjudication could settle matters, and so it was off to the rabbinical courts for a solution.

†Choosing the date was a matter that was not taken lightly. A girl could not be married in the seven days before and after her period of menstruation. Anywhere from six months to a year in advance, therefore, it was necessary to calculate a date that on the basis of past performance, at least, would be acceptable.

meant a ring with a stone of perhaps a quarter or even a half carat. Small though the stone was, the ring was displayed with supreme pride, especially once it was pronounced dazzling by those in the know.* The engagement party came to a resounding conclusion with the plate ceremony. The signal given, every woman present tossed a plate she had been holding to the ground. Amid this shattering of dishes and exuberant shouts of *"Mazel tov!"* [good luck] the ceremonies concluded in joyous confusion.

All thoughts now turned to the wedding day, which was usually a year after the formal engagement. Not only the family but often the entire town eagerly awaited the event.† With us serious preparations began a week before the wedding day. Rachel the caterer and Rishel, her helper, moved into our house and for an entire week cooked and baked and otherwise made ready for the big day. Never before had I seen vessels so large, containers so spacious, pots and pans of so many different sizes and shapes, all absolutely clean and sparkling, shined to perfection. Aromas filled the house for days as the cooked food was stored in the always chilly basement, where it would remain fresh.‡

Weddings were always held in the bride's town, and Sunday weddings were the most common. To make an impression, one

*Diamond critics abounded among the town's older women, who had viewed many a cut stone in their day. Usually there was one woman whose opinion was prized above all others. She need but declare that the diamond "burned out your eyes" for all to be greatly impressed.

†Especially the town's poor. It was customary to distribute bread, sugar, and other foodstuffs to needy families just before the wedding. I remember accompanying my mother from house to house offering freshly baked goods to people who rejoiced in our good fortune and recognized that such charity often helped them to get by.

‡One must not forget certain ceremonies for both the bride and the groom that took place in the days before the wedding. About a week before, on a Saturday, the boy was called forward in the synagogue to read from the Torah. After the service he was greeted with a shower of nuts and candy tossed his way by women in the congregation. The girl underwent a far more elaborate ritual. The night before the wedding, escorted by her mother and usually another female relative (frequently an aunt), she entered the *mikvah* to prepare for the ceremonial bath. She submitted first to a thorough cleaning (nails cut, calluses removed) and then to a ritual immersion, both intended to ensure purity. This process of sanctification would continue into the wedding day, since it was required that both parties fast until the marriage ceremony was concluded.

family often arranged to meet the other at some point outside of town, from which the arriving party was escorted to the wedding site. Usually that meant heading out of town in a fancy carriage drawn by special horses, gathering for formal toasts, then riding together back into town, where a good many people lined the streets to watch the procession.* Occasionally more spectacular ceremonials were arranged. For years residents of Kolbuszowa spoke of the time a corps of local Poles dressed as Cossack horsemen in full uniforms were hired to ride out to where the families were scheduled to meet and escort the group back. Some show that was! Years later, "Remember the Cossacks" was all people had to say to prompt admiring recollections of that spectacular occasion.

Even as a youngster I loved weddings. I enjoyed the excitement, the festivities, the way the town lifted itself out of the ordinary. When there was a wedding, I would always manage to be there. No matter who was getting married, I went. So what if I wasn't invited? I was young, about ten years old; what difference did my presence make?

Actually it made quite a bit of difference to Hanka the Russka, the hired Russian woman who zealously guarded the entranceway to all weddings in Kolbuszowa. You might say it was her job, even her profession, to do this. She knew—I don't know how, but she knew—just who was invited to each party, and she saw to it that only those people were admitted. If you had seen Hanka or could imagine her bulky, formidable presence (she was over six feet tall), you would understand why she had no difficulty performing her task.

Never could I outwit or deceive her, but I did find ways to get in nevertheless. You see, there was the Durak family in town, all of whom were musicians, and this family was often hired to play

---

*Most of them had probably been invited to the wedding. There were no written invitations. Instead, about two weeks before the event an employee of the synagogue, following a lengthy list given him by my father, went from house to house inviting people by word of mouth. This effort always prompted him to request that in the future my father simplify the process by providing not a list of invitees, but the much smaller list of those not to be asked.

at such affairs. The leader of the orchestra happened to play the drums and fortunately for me often needed assistance taking them from place to place. The deal I made with him was simple enough. I agreed to carry his drums (my sister Rachel volunteered as well) any time he had a wedding engagement in town. With the drums in hand we automatically gained admission to the wedding. Even Hanka the Russka could find no reason to stop us.

At weddings I particularly enjoyed being with the girls, watching them dance, even dancing along with them. They danced by themselves, of course. The men, you see, were in a different room celebrating. They danced as well, also by themselves, moving about to the rhythms of their singing. The women, on the other hand, had the benefit of a band hired for the occasion. So there I was dancing,* always with my sister Rachel, three years older, especially enjoying it when their whirling bodies brushed ever so slightly by my face. There was, I must admit, another reason why I got up to dance. Only those who danced were entitled to refreshment—that was how it worked. And the refreshment was for me an exceptional treat (actually everyone loved it)—cool, sparkling seltzer water. To be able to sip this drink after dancing—such pleasure!

These preliminary ceremonies over, it was time for the wedding ceremony itself, which was held outdoors under the *chupah*. Because I could not bear to be away from the action I often had to squirm through the dense crowd so as to get up front, alongside the *chupah* itself. That was before I made a certain arrangement that at every wedding guaranteed me an unobstructed up-front position alongside the *chupah*. The arrangement came about because Chaim Scher, the *shamus,* suffered from a glaring weakness: he had trouble recalling melodies. He was expected to sing a particular tune as the groom approached the *chupah*; but try as he might, he could never get it straight—which was a source of considerable embarrassment to him and everyone else present. Since I knew the melody, a deal seemed in order. If he saw to it that I

---

*"Modern" dances like the shimmy, the one-step, and the Charleston, along with the waltz and the polka, all of them taught to me by my sisters Lieba and Malcia, who had received lessons and knew them all.

gained a position in the front of the *chupah,* I told him, I would always be present and begin humming the tune until he could pick it up. Agreed. In fact he arranged to have me help him carry the folded-up *chupah* to the site of the ceremony and remain with it throughout the proceedings.

Arriving first, accompanied by the two fathers, was the groom, always solemn, with the expression of one destined for the gallows. Formally dressed, he wore a *kittel* over his black silk outfit, as tradition prescribed. On his head was a *shtraml* [ceremonial hat], which as a groom he was now permitted to wear for the first time. With a velvet crown and the tails of fourteen sables serving as a brim, it was the ultimate status symbol.* How proudly he wore it!

Onto the scene came the bride, accompanied by the two mothers, the entire scene illuminated by candles lit now by all the women in attendance.† Together they stood, the groom and the bride, largely strangers to each other. Could that be the reason why brides, along with their mothers, always wept at such times? Actually I never did understand why so many tears were shed on this supposedly joyous occasion. By tradition such outbursts were accepted, but what was behind them? Was the bride, who may have just laid eyes on her husband for the first time, lamenting her

---

*The fur hat seems to have derived from the Middle Ages, at which time Jews in certain districts in Germany were ordered to wear hats made up in part from the skins of rats. To remind themselves of this one-time indignity yet demonstrate how far they had come, Jews later turned to another kind of hat, this one of sable, the most expensive of furs.

†Before coming to a halt under the *chupah* the bride and the two mothers circled around the groom seven times. It was absolutely vital to do this, you see, for also at the wedding, although quite invisible, were the head of the devils and his wife (Ashmadai and Lillis). No mystery as to their presence: it was a day of joy, and their role was to attempt to sabotage the proceedings. They would likely succeed if the bride failed to circle the groom seven times. Seven, you see, represented God in Jewish mystical thought. Introducing Him onto the scene neutralized the presence of the devils and thwarted their evil designs. Still, they were powerful and needed to be appeased. Customarily one appeased them by deliberately making a mistake and omitting a ritual somewhere in the course of the proceedings. In effect this was throwing a bone to Ashmadai and Lillis, allowing them some measure of satisfaction even while blocking their more sinister efforts to destroy the marriage and prevent the birth of future generations of Jews.

fate? Might she be mourning the forthcoming loss of her hair, which would be cut off the next day? Was she, sexually so very innocent, terrified at the prospect of the physical encounter to come? (Both bride and groom had not long before each been specifically, separately briefed on sexual matters, the bride by the two mothers, the groom by the two fathers.*) Whatever the reason, the ceremony and the sobbing went hand in hand.

The service concluded, it was now time for feasting. The fruits of all that cooking, all that preparing, were now to be savored. The room was cleared of furniture, tables were set up, and separate eating places for the men and women were prepared. Jams made especially for the women were passed around, a spoon in each jar. Each dipped the spoon into the jam, placed it in her mouth, then lovingly licked the spoon until no trace of the treat remained. That same spoon then was passed on to the next woman, who did exactly the same thing. No one, it seemed, paid the last attention to hygienic considerations.

With the main course there were few surprises. The basic ingredients of wedding meals were well-established and eagerly awaited: *challah* and gefilte fish, followed by almost pure (192 proof) vodka, a special wedding soup featuring round small dumplings called the "golden soup," goose, beef, chicken, *kugel,* kishka, *tsimes*† washed down with beer (Vishniac or Rosola for the women), and slivovitz (plum brandy), which the men enjoyed. Enjoyed but not to excess; you would not find drunkenness here. It just didn't happen; it wasn't expected and certainly wasn't accepted. People drank to elevate their spirits, to offer up a toast, not to get drunk. Besides, all looked forward to the conclusion of the meal, to the special treats: chocolate, walnut, and honey tarts for the women; sponge, honey, and egg cakes for the men.

Dessert meant that it was just about time to move on to the

---

*As a prospective groom he had the benefit at least of being able to study the tractate of the Talmud entitled "Nidah," which provided specific instructions regarding standards of female purification and the conditions for permissible sexual activity. Generally he read it alone. He called on no one else for interpretation or illumination.

†A dish made of carrots or prunes, honey, raisins, and sugar.—RS

long-awaited occasion: the presentation of gifts. What made this so special? Curiosity, of course, but also the way the gifts were presented. Quite an entertainment it was. Many a wedding, you see, featured a *badchan* [performer, master of ceremonies], whose job it was throughout the long evening and night to keep things moving and to amuse, even at times to instruct. Some performers, such as Tuviah from Tarnow and Weintraub from Chrzanow, were known far and wide, and their services were eagerly sought. Their presence at an affair usually guaranteed its success. Almost always they took charge of announcing the gifts, introducing the dignitaries, poking fun, telling stories, transforming the occasion into a wondrous show that few would soon forget. In fact the start of the gift-giving usually was the signal for outsiders, townspeople not invited to the wedding, to appear. All who wished to enter were now ushered in, welcomed to watch the entertainment. And come they did, many having waited patiently outside until this moment. It was the closest many of them would ever come to witnessing a theatrical performance, for that is what awaited them.

The gifts, though eagerly anticipated, were nearly always predictable: candlesticks, menorahs, glassware, ladles, teakettles, silver teaspoons, dishes. Still, the tales the *badchan* told about the gifts, his outlandish descriptions of the uses to which they would be put (there were usually so many duplicate gifts that only his humor and bizarre descriptions could overcome the potential tedium of continuous repetition)—all this skillfully and playfully woven together in rhyme (in which most *badchans,* spontaneously it seemed, were gifted with the ability to speak) brought a steady stream of laughter from the crowd packed solidly into the room.

More amusement followed, this time in the form of a special show performed on a makeshift stage erected in the center of the room. The *badchan* now appeared, usually in costume, with a prepared offering: a skit, a story, a dramatization, songs—humor mostly, but here and there a serious theme. I remember one father-and-son team presenting a most touching piece involving conflict between the generations. It began with the father, clearly a man of deep religious convictions, admonishing his son for his waywardness, for neglecting his religious obligations. The son admitted he had been lax but inquired why his father had chosen to give a desperately poor peasant far less money for his cow than it was worth. Whose sin was worse, the son asked his father. Pretty serious stuff, but it was enjoyed and welcomed by the guests as much as the uproarious clowning that came before.

It was by now perhaps 10:30 or 11:00; still there was more to come. First the seven blessings and songs, then the *mitzvah* dances with the bride herself. This was not the kind of dancing you might expect; touching the woman was forbidden, but the man and the bride moved in step together, linked by a handkerchief whose end each held. Every important person at the wedding came forward, announced first usually in a highly original and humorous fashion by the *badchan*; each got his chance, however brief, to dance before the other women present pulled the bride away, a signal for the remaining men to join in and finish the dance. What dancing! Such joy! As if in a trance, the men whirled about in each other's grasp. The same melody repeated, feverish, hypnotic, repeated again, perspiration accumulating on every dancer. Then it all began again, this time another man (never the husband) dancing with the bride, each tightly grasping the handkerchief that separated them. Once more she is pulled away and the menfolk regain the dance floor. A ritual carefully prescribed, joyously pursued.

The long wedding day now was at an end. The newly married couple, perhaps for the last time in many a year, would get one last special gift, the opportunity to be alone for the night.* A room in the bride's house had been set aside for them, its occupants cleared out for the occasion. Husband and wife would now be alone together for the first time. What would they say? What would they do? Each had received advice and formal instruction—they were provided, as it were, with a crash course in coupling—but was that enough? Neither had any experience, innocents both. But somehow they managed; almost everyone did.† The follow-

---

*For the next year or two they would most likely live in the house of the bride's parents (a practice known as *kest*), since financially they were in no position to establish their own household. One of my married sisters planned to stay with us for six months and remained for eighteen years.

†Ordinarily when a couple married they placed their beds on opposite sides

ing morning curious eyes would take note of the blood on the sheet; heads would then nod approvingly.

Still there was more: a post-wedding celebration lasting an additional seven days. Special family guests were invited to stay on, and all gathered daily for festive midday dining, the hired cooks still on the scene to prepare each of the meals. Whatever life would in time bring for the newly married couple, trials more often than triumphs, they would not forget how it all began amid uncommon gaiety, generosity, and hope. Our town would also remember such things as the entourage of "Cossacks," a particularly memorable *badchan,* or the time several grandchildren of someone in town arrived from Hungary to play the violin so beautifully at a wedding. Such matters recurred in conversations for years, fixing the celebration in the collective memory, where it nourished our traditions.

Not that all individual decisions always followed tradition, nor did conformity consistently dictate practice. Violations did occur, followed always by strong community disapproval. How could it be otherwise? Few doubted the sad fate that would befall those who rejected the wisdom of their fathers and the generations before them. Our stories and folktales never failed to make this clear. Often they were tales of young people running off and marrying outside the faith, converting, abandoning Judaism, cutting themselves off from the lifeblood of an ancient tradition. When in real life such a thing happened, the shame felt affected all. Was there a Jewish resident of Kolbuszowa who did not know the story of Miriam, even the fateful details of this terrible tale?

When Miriam was sixteen or seventeen her parents contracted with a tutor, a young man of twenty-two from a prominent non-Jewish family, to help with her studies. Miriam's family was wealthy, Miriam herself was a very pretty girl, and before long

---

of the room. When sex was in the offing, the husband indicated his intentions by placing his yarmulka on his wife's bed. As times changed and restrictions were relaxed, the beds began to come closer to each other; at first they were separated by a night table, but later they were placed side by side with no separation. You can well imagine my surprise, however, when I visited one family in town and discovered that instead of two separate beds, there was only one for both husband and wife!

love blossomed between the two of them. They wished to be married. Her parents, of course, would have none of it. Were they to marry, Miriam would be expected to convert to Catholicism. So one day she ran off, and word arrived that the two had been married in a church service. Miriam's family was devastated. But the worst was yet to come. It arrived with dramatic suddenness when Miriam's mother, burdened by shame, overwhelmed by grief, threw herself into one of the town wells and fell to her death. Soon afterward the family disappeared from Kolbuszowa. They could no longer remain in town and be reminded each day of the double tragedy.

Miriam and her husband, whose family lived in Kolbuszowa, returned every so often. When visiting, she usually attended church service in town and kept herself apart from former friends and acquaintances. The well into which her mother had thrown herself, located in front of the synagogue, was not used for many a year afterward. It was returned to use only when German troops arrived and established the Jewish ghetto in that very area. In these new circumstances the well, despite past associations, was needed to sustain life.

Miriam's transgression led—predictably, many would have said—to tragedy; other sinners experienced retributions less severe. Consider the story of the father of one of my friends, a religious man with a long beard whose wife had already borne him ten children. A family of such size needed help, so he took a poor Jewish girl into his household as a maid. Now it came to pass that both his wife and the maid became pregnant. Tongues began wagging almost immediately. There was no way to avoid the suggestion of scandal, which was made even worse by the fact that the babies were born not far apart and looked very much alike. Later on they would attend the same school. Memories of that incident lingered for years. The town's youngsters never tired of taunting the man's other children with the name of the illegitimate child.

It was no sin to marry above or below your station in life, but barriers were many and objections certain to be raised. People, after all, were expected to marry at their own social level, well-to-do families maintaining their exclusiveness, poorer folk resigned to the fact that marrying their own kind was part of the natural order of things. Occasionally expectations were upset. Ordinarily the match involved a poor girl, usually pretty, and a well-to-do boy; rarely a poor boy and a rich girl. Some parents resigned themselves to these matches, but others intervened and ended the relationship. So it was with my cousin from nearby Sokolow. He fell in love with a young lady named Pesha Gold, who was very pretty, in fact the town beauty, but undeniably poor. His parents would not hear of the match, he gave in, and soon afterward he married someone more suitable. Heartbroken, his former sweetheart left Poland for Belgium, where she perished in the Holocaust.

In the face of unbending tradition it's no surprise that some people chose to mount direct challenges against its rigidities. Their challenges might even at times succeed, but never at the expense of the tradition itself. Indeed, such frontal assaults often had the opposite effect—reaffirming in people's eyes the value of the received wisdom, the established practices. Far more dangerous to the old ways were less dramatic deviations, shall we say adjustments, that evolved gradually. In time these would gather momentum to the point where they did not so much topple the established ways as replace customs that came to be regarded as needlessly old-fashioned.

Take the practice by which the parents of the boy and girl, along with the matchmaker, entered into a marriage contract based on considerations of property, necessity, and acceptability as they saw it. The young watched and waited as their drama unfolded, the script already prepared for them. They were told and probably believed that marriages were best handled in this manner. Would not parents safeguard their interests and be alert to considerations likely overlooked by less experienced eyes? What were individual preferences when family interests were all-important? Besides, why question a system that had tied generation to generation? Had not strong families with close ties been the result? Had not young people brought together into marriage by others come to accept one another—even more, to forge deep bonds of mutual affection? To allow the young their own choices, based on indi-

vidual fancy or considerations of the moment, clearly was a reck-
less departure, a risky business with unpredictable consequences.

Such explanations, which once had served so well and had defied challenge, began to lose their force. They no longer satisfied
everyone. Young people, exposed to new ideas, sensing new opportunities, inevitably discovered new ways. They had only to
watch some of the American films shown at the Kolbuszowa
movie house (open for just three showings a week on Saturday
and Sunday nights) to see how different were the ways of modern
society. They had simply to observe activities of the secular Jewish
organizations in town, where young boys and girls mixed socially,
to realize that such things might happen and still the world would
not come to an end.

The matchmakers were certainly among the first to sense the
shift, and for obvious reasons. What was happening, after all,
threatened their livelihood. How could they be complacent when
a growing number of Zionist organizations brought young people, boys and girls, together in a variety of informal social situations? It required no exceptional insight to predict where all this
would lead. So matchmakers, too, began to change their ways, to
make adjustments. If young people wanted more choice, so be it.
If they wanted greater involvement in the final decision, why not?

So new procedures began to appear alongside the old. Take the
practice known as *beshau* [looking over], which was introduced
so that a bride and groom would not be total strangers. Preliminary meetings between the boy and the girl, arranged by the
matchmaker, offered an opportunity to get together, to look one
another over, to talk, to determine whether one wished to enter
a relationship expected to last one's entire life. Such a "date" took
place under a veil of secrecy in a neutral town, a site generally
accessible to both parties. Someone in that town, a friend or a
family member, would be asked for permission to use a room in
his home for the purpose of this meeting.

Why a neutral town? To keep tongues from wagging. That way
if nothing came of the meeting no explanations need be offered
and busybodies would be thwarted. I recall our home being used
on occasion for a *beshau,* the boy and girl meeting in one of the

rooms we had prepared. They spoke, drank tea, maybe even went for a walk together. I remember my sister Matil preparing for one herself, dressing up and along with my father or mother journeying to a neighboring town to meet a boy for the first time. She returned a second time, then a third. After that, nothing. We never heard from the other side. But that was exactly the point: young folks were gaining the right to decide on particular partners. With freedom came new disappointments.

More refinements followed. Even when preliminary meetings went well and the prospects seemed good, some boys and girls insisted on additional get-togethers prior to any formal engagement. Again the neutral town, the larger the better so that there was little chance of being recognized. Again the two were alone with each other, without chaperones or relatives—quite different from the way it once was. When a formal engagement was announced, the two continued to see each other up until the wedding. It became acceptable for the man and woman to exchange visits, to stay with each other's families. Typically this is what happened during holiday periods. Such arrangements offered a chance to get to know each other better and for community members to observe the young couple, to pass judgment (as inevitably everyone did).

My own family is a perfect place to look for the changes I am describing. My father, although certainly a religious man, nevertheless displayed fewer of the orthodox rigidities than the majority of Kolbuszowa's Jews. He might not welcome many of the changes, but neither was he prepared to dig his heels in. Remember, too, that there were nine of us, five girls and four boys, ranging widely in age. Think how much time elapsed before all of us grew up and were married. As it happened, my three oldest sisters entered marriage in the traditional way, with matchmakers handling all the arrangements. Not so my next sister, who asked for and obtained meetings with prospective husbands (still by way of a matchmaker) before a final decision was reached.

It was for my youngest sister, Rachel, to reject all that had come before. She had boyfriends and went out with them on dates, to the movies, to the woods, unchaperoned, unconcerned with what "others" might think or say. All this my father knew; he was not pleased, but he took no steps to retrain her. Rachel's first serious relationship ended in a most disappointing manner: her boyfriend left for Palestine to study. Then she met and began dating Avram, became engaged, and set marriage plans in motion. But the fates again turned unkind, then most cruel. The two planned to go to America and applied for the proper documents. Hers came; his didn't, and she would not leave without him. When they reapplied, the situation reversed itself; his papers arrived, not hers. He decided to leave first for the United States. Once matters were in order she would follow. Within ten days of his departure (just prior to his leaving they had become formally engaged) came the outbreak of World War II. Their marriage was not meant to be. He left in time; she perished, an innocent victim of the madness that swept across Europe.

Then there was me, not a wayward, rebellious son but also not one disposed to unquestioning paths. I received a traditional Jewish education and certainly by dress and long earlocks looked much like everyone else; but early on I started working for my father, buying and selling for him in neighboring towns and villages. What better way to gain self-confidence and the sophistication that came from exposure to ways that were not those of Kolbuszowa? Then, too, I was born in 1920, so that by my teens I found myself in an era of quickening change, a time when traditions were losing some part of their grip. I never saw myself as socially precocious, and surely not as sexually adventurous; looking back though, I can see that my experiences did set me apart.

That I became an overnight expert on sex I will not dispute. But mostly that was because of my sister Rachel. Seeing to my secular education was a task she took upon herself. Leaving books for me to read became her standard approach. Well, one day, I must have been twelve at the time, I discovered a book that she had left beside my bed: *The Secrets of the Beginning of Life*. Now my friends and I imagined we had such matters pretty well figured out at this point, although admitting to a certain vagueness regarding some details. The book put all doubts to rest. It was a serious, almost technical work, yet to me it was a real eye-opener.

Never had I, or any of us, received such specific information. And there were pictures as well, illustrations of penises and vaginas (who dared imagine such details?) and talk of condoms and warnings about venereal disease. I remember one especially ominous statement about venereal disease. "If you're not afraid of God," it advised readers, "be afraid of this sickness."

Well, all this newly revealed information was far too exciting a discovery to keep to myself. I could scarcely wait to tell my friends about it and watch their reactions. I decided on a formal presentation, the formation of a sex study group, you might say. It took the form of a Saturday get-together at my house with five or six of my closest friends. We locked ourselves into a narrow passageway behind the staircase of our house, then turned to the book. Step by step I conducted them through its wondrous details. No doubt they were impressed with what they learned, especially with what they saw for the first time. All the deficiencies in their education were suddenly remedied. Many a hallowed misconception collapsed that day. There was no going back to the Dark Ages.

The story didn't end here. One of the boys in the group, Wolf Ehrlich, I never understood why, decided we had somehow transgressed and informed on us. In short order I was summoned before the directors of the religious school. They were scandalized and were not at all reassured by my insistence that it was a science book containing purely factual material, not dirty stories. They didn't ask to see the book (the pictures, I'm sure, would not have helped my cause), but still I was expelled, even though my father was president of the governing body that controlled the school. I was not allowed to return for some time.

The suggestion of pornography in this incident may cause you to wonder about the extent to which such materials circulated in Kolbuszowa. I doubt very much if there was any pornography around. What we did have were a variety of off-color stories that made the rounds among the menfolk; the cruder ones were not likely to be repeated by the more religious of us, the milder ones quite likely to be passed on. The following is representative of the milder variety:

On the death of her husband, the wife, angry at him for having fooled around with other women, insists that he be buried entirely naked, without a shroud.

Sometime later, on visiting his grave, she discovers a note on his gravestone that reads: "I was too cold. Don't pray for me here. I'm with Mrs. Berkowitz."

Then there is the story involving a large crowd of women who had gathered outside of the *mikvah* on Thursday night. Why had such a crowd come there? Because it was considered especially praiseworthy to have sexual relations with your husband on Friday night—on the Sabbath, when every man was a king.

Approaching the line is the rabbi's wife, who has no intention of waiting along with the others: "Do you know who I am? It's Thursday night and the rabbi will be waiting for me tomorrow night."

Also on line is Cipka, a well-known prostitute in town. It is she who answers the rabbi's wife: "Oh, so your rabbi is waiting for you! Still, I want to go first. You see, for me the entire congregation waits."

I was probably about thirteen before I attempted my first "serious" talk with a girl. It happened at my cousin's wedding, an occasion when I was feeling pretty good about myself. My mother had let me wear my best Sabbath coat, and I had been invited to sit at the groom's table. I must have looked somewhat grown up because I was offered and accepted a home-made cigarette. It was all I could do to suppress the coughing spasm that followed.

Once the ceremonies began, I noticed a girl I knew from town. Suzia lived not far from us and occasionally came in to purchase goods at my father's store. I had taken a liking to her, and we had at times spoken briefly. I decided I would talk to her at the conclusion of the ceremony. What made me act so brazenly I'm not sure. I had never approached a girl before. I planned to ask her to go for a walk with me. Had she declined I would have been greatly embarrassed, but instead she agreed without hesitation. Since going off by ourselves was risky—it was simply not done— we conspired together. I would leave the gathering first; then some five minutes later she would leave. We planned to meet at the outskirts of town near a wall that ran alongside the Catholic cemetery.

I left the party and headed directly toward the spot, excited, also nervous. Would she actually come? Assuming she did, what would I talk to her about? What if we were seen alone together? Maybe it would be better if she changed her mind. I didn't have to wait long. We started to walk slowly, not saying a word, both of us not daring to talk. There's no telling how long this silence might have continued, but then in the distance I noticed a group of four or five boys coming in our direction. As they drew closer I recognized them, Polish classmates who lived in a village nearby. All were older, having repeated the same grade more than once. It would be embarrassing, I felt, to meet them; I hoped they would turn off, but no such luck.

When they spotted the two of us, they began taunting me ("Naftalina! Naftalina!"), and without any preliminaries or any warning they started throwing stones at us. Young Poles beating up on Jews was hardly a novelty. Provocation? That never was necessary; they just did it seemingly as a sport. For them to do so at this point, just when I was with a girl—you can imagine the shame I felt. We ran, but they ran after us, continuing all the time to throw stones in our direction. I wanted desperately to protect Suzia, since it was on my account that she was there in the first place. I held part of my long black coat behind her, as a shield. I could think of nothing else.

Fortunately only I was hit, not she. We didn't stop running, and finally our pursuers abandoned the chase. All the time we said nothing to each other. Back to the wedding we went, entering separately and staying apart for the rest of the evening. Such was the story of my first "date." We saw each other again from time to time, but neither of us ever chose to recall that night. The stone throwers, however, bragged about their exploits, and word got out about my being alone with a girl—sufficient cause to earn me yet another suspension from religious school.*

*There is a final chapter to this story that must be told. For this I jump ahead to 1945. World War II was winding down, and I, under the alias Tadeusz Zaleski,

If I tell you things were changing in Kolbuszowa, it's largely because of what I myself experienced while growing up there. What I am about to tell you just wouldn't have taken place before my time. But it happened to me, and I was not consumed by fire and brimstone because of it. I fell in love. Her name was Rozia Süsskind. I couldn't have been more than thirteen or fourteen when I first recognized what I felt. Of course, I could say nothing and do nothing. Still, that special feeling stayed with me, could not be denied. Five years would pass before I even dared approach her. Meanwhile I did what I could to learn everything about her, to watch her from a distance, to be with people who knew her. The fact that she knew nothing of my feelings troubled me, but times had not changed that dramatically. There was just nothing to be done at this stage. In Kolbuszowa someone in my position, from my background, was bound to the tradition that kept males and females apart, that rejected the idea of romantic attachments, that warned of love's dangers.

I fantasized about her, imagined ways to impress her and to have her notice me. A recurrent dream involved a fire at the flour mill that her family owned. Naturally I arrive in time to rescue her from the flames. What pleasure when she acknowledges my he-

---

was an officer occupying a lofty military post with the Polish Army stationed in Breslau. On the street one day I was passed by a tall soldier: an artillery man, to judge from his insignia. The instant he passed it hit me in a flash: Wladyslaw Plaza, a name I had never forgotten because he was one of the stone throwers who had so mortified me. Years had passed, but the idea of revenge still seemed altogether fitting, not so much for myself but for Suzia, who had been so frightened that day—Suzia, who was killed early in the war by the Germans.

I ordered him to stop, then reprimanded him for an improper salute. He had no idea who I was. When I learned that his commanding officer was a friend of mine, a plan took shape in my mind. I instructed that officer to proceed to make life miserable for Plaza, which he did. Week after week Plaza came under mounting pressure—endless drills, laborious work assignments, leaves canceled—altogether a nightmare. When I thought enough punishment had been meted out, I sent for Plaza. Still he did not recognize me, but he was astonished to hear how many of the details of his early life I knew. When I revealed my identity, he just stood there in utter disbelief. He had assumed, he said, that I had long ago been killed by the Germans. I then told him why I had become his tormentor. The particular incident he remembered, but he denied having thrown any of the stones; he claimed that he had merely accompanied the actual culprits. I doubted his story, but the incident was closed. Now we were even.

roics! Each day I headed off to a place where I could watch her going to school. I befriended people who knew her and ever so carefully steered the conversation so as to mention her. This way I maintained "contact." I even spent time with an uncle of hers from whom everyone else fled, putting up with his endless stories and windy philosophizing and supplying him with cold water every Friday while he sat sweating in a steam bath. Why? Because I felt closer to her there. But certainly not close enough. I envied those who joined the local Zionist youth organizations, where boys and girls were able to gather and enjoy each other's company. As for me, I had no such opportunities. My social life consisted of little more than strolling with a few friends back and forth down the town's main street, watching while groups of girls did likewise. Looking each other over, not stopping to talk—that was it.

I loved from afar. Rozia knew nothing of my feelings. My sisters did and mostly laughed at my predicament. But as I've said, there was nothing I could do. No allowances had ever been made for such feelings. Still, because times were changing, I wasn't without hope. Never did I imagine that my fate would rest in the hands of matchmakers. In time I summoned the courage to talk to Rozia. I was eighteen, she sixteen, when that happened. Better yet, we joined the same Zionist youth organization and so could begin to spend time together in a manner considered not entirely reprehensible, although there were those who still viewed it in just that way. We grew close and worried less and less about revealing our emotions, though outwardly our behavior remained formal, quite restrained. Kissing? You couldn't do anything like that. But we did hold hands—not in town, mind you, where we would be seen, but elsewhere when we were alone.

When the war began, we quickly agreed on our plans for the future. In a strange and unexpected way the war by undermining existing standards and restrictions, actually liberated many of us, making possible what would have required many years of gradual change. In a word, we intended, when the time was right, to run off to Palestine and marry there. Who knew that the Germans would have other plans for us? When all fell before them, having each other and sharing our love allowed us to cling to the hope of surviving the ever-mounting toll of death and destruction. We relied on each other, sacrificed for each other as never before. In the end, this was not enough. Rozia perished at their hands. I escaped, left only with the precious memories of how far we had come and what might have been.

Only in America

I t was a magical place, the perfect object of our desire. Citizens of Kolbuszowa, still we were in love with America. Nothing could change that; nothing ever did. To us America could do no wrong. Fall in love with a woman and you overlook all her blemishes, ignore all her shortcomings. Such unqualified affection we had for America. Did we know much about this land? Yes and no, as I shall soon explain. But whatever the realities, it was the idea of America that captivated us. Freedom, individual worth, abundance, possibility—such a combination we found intoxicating.

Nor did we merely worship from afar. Beginning in the late nineteenth century, more and more people from our town made their way across Europe to America. It would be fair to say that in time, if you added up the number of Jewish families in Kolbuszowa, half that total could be found in America. That created a very real bond, a solid connection, aside from the ties of sentiment that would always be there. To tell the story of twentieth-century Kolbuszowa without introducing America would for me be as negligent as recalling the American Revolution and omitting Pulaski and Kosciuszko.

In all fairness, not everyone shared this enthusiasm. Kolbuszowa's poor had little to lose by leaving, and by and large they were the ones most eager to go. But the well-to-do, those firmly established in the economic and religious life of our town, found the prospect less attractive.* Too much would have to be sacrificed in exchange for the uncertainties that awaited them in America. Of course, one could live better there; but life was comfortable enough here, secure enough at home. Why look for trouble, especially if you were along in years? America was better for young people.

Remember, too, that if America was the land of the free, it was also all too free. What could happen to people there was common knowledge. The religion of their fathers, the faith of our ancestors, once in America it no longer was the same. Incident after incident reaffirmed this lamentable fact; so did many popular stories. Just look at those who had returned from America to visit us. Beards trimmed or shaved off, *payes* removed, long coats gone. What kind of Jews were these?

It was so. I remember when my brother came for a visit. Saturday arrived, the sacred Sabbath, but he continued to smoke his cigarettes. True, he didn't do it in front of my father; he never would have dared to. Still, he went to the outhouse or hid elsewhere and just kept on smoking. Then he had someone go over to the local Polish store and buy pork sausages. What happened to kosher in America? Excuses—all you heard were excuses. It was too hard. It no longer made sense.

One story, heard often in Kolbuszowa, tells this tale all too well:

A young man arriving from America to visit his mother is asked how well he is maintaining his religious obligations. "Are you, my son, saying your morning prayers?"

"One must work very hard in America," he replies. "There is no time for such things."

"Are you still attending the synagogue on Saturday?"

"Mother, in America there is so much to do. Keeping the Sabbath is very inconvenient."

*My father, for example, although a pogrom in our town in 1919 did cause him to give the idea serious consideration. Then in 1920 he received tickets from his brother Shulim in America, enough for the whole family to go to the United States. For months he hesitated, concerned about the religious well-being of his children in the overly tolerant atmosphere there. The tickets were never used. He did plan to travel to America for the 1939 World's Fair, but on account of illness he had to forgo this long-awaited visit.

"Well, I certainly expect that you are keeping kosher?"

"I try, but it's just not possible in America."

"Well," the mother replies in obvious exasperation, "tell me, my son, are you still circumcised?"

Then there is the mother who suspects that her son will be tempted, once in America, to stray from the faith, and decides to test him. Before he leaves she places a coin in the case used to contain his *tefillin*. Surely it will fall out in the course of using them each day. Years pass and the boy returns for a visit. "Are you praying each morning and wearing your *tefillin?*" she asks him. "Of course I am, mother." Whereupon she opens the case and out falls the coin. Clearly the *tefillin* had gone unused in America.

But for all those who hesitated to go, who were fearful of what might happen, scores couldn't wait to leave, the magnetic attraction of America being almost impossible to resist. Some had special reasons for wanting to go. On occasion you'd hear about people who had faced jail sentences, but more often the reason was the draft. Particularly for Jews military service could mean long stretches of harsh treatment and unrelenting prejudice. Better to leave than endure.

But the fundamental fact was simply that most left to better themselves, leaving behind a place that offered few rewards, fewer prospects, little hope of improvement. Kolbuszowa was too old, too crowded, too poor, too set in its ways, in short claustrophobic. The future was likely to be much like the past, probably worse. Hope lay outside its borders, stagnation within. America was so big, so rich—how could one not succeed there? This was not speculation; this was fact. Story after story was told of people, really poor people, who had left Kolbuszowa for America and soon afterward were sending back money. These stories could only mean one thing, that there was work for all in America and money in abundance:

"You remember what's-his-name who left Kolbuszowa for America? Well, he's become a millionaire."

"You mean he has more than $20,000?"

"Well, he doesn't have that much, but he's a millionaire."

We never knew that most of those who settled in America not only didn't strike it rich, but led wretched, impoverished lives. True, they saved money and sent some of it back, but to do so they endured years of quiet deprivation.

The obligation to help those back home and the need to provide tangible evidence of success combined to produce a steady flow of funds from the New World to the old town. I remember marveling at how this one young man, Leibush, who had had few prospects in town, had been able, once in America, to provide for his mother and crippled sister in Kolbuszowa. I was convinced that he had made a success of himself, that he was probably on his way to becoming a rich man. I made it my business after I arrived in America to look him up. Surely he would be well-established and able to lend a hand to someone like myself groping for a foothold. I located him, all right, but what a surprise it was to discover that he was hardly a rich man. An upholsterer, that's all he was and had been all along. Somehow he had managed to put enough money aside to help support his mother and sister.

What those of us in Kolbuszowa saw as enviable success turned out to be mostly incessant sacrifice. It was not until the second generation that we began to sense the true meaning of American opportunity. More and more we heard of the children of immigrants becoming doctors, lawyers, professionals of all kinds. Such accomplishments provided satisfactions even greater than those associated with economic success.

For those of us in Kolbuszowa an American connection was among the most valuable of possessions. Elsewhere I have spoken about how such ties improved marriage prospects many times over. Indeed, matchmakers were quick to point this out, for the advantages were obvious. But there was more. Picture America as the rich uncle to be relied on for gifts and timely aid. Oh, those treats and the joy they brought to us! The very thought of a "package from America" made one tingle with excitement and boundless anticipation. We knew beforehand, you see, that packages would be arriving. Letters sent to us from America alerted us and advised us to be on the lookout. Since a package would take two months or more to get here, there was time, plenty of it, to work up excitement. Then would come the day. The postman would go out of his way to deliver the package to us before heading off to his rounds, a kindness for which he knew he would receive a special gift from my father.

I had no trouble telling a package was from my Uncle Shulim, since he made it a practice of packing everything in a white flour bag. For me the most impressive feature of these packages was the red wax seals on the outside. Though not unknown to us, seals were used sparingly in Kolbuszowa, only for important official documents prepared by the town's notary. To see them on all these packages from America added immeasurably in our eyes to their value.

Not that what was inside proved much of a surprise. It would be clothes, of course, but just what kind and who they were for— that was the exciting part. No sooner did I bring the package into the house (with everyone standing by, having dropped whatever they were doing) than I ripped it open. All rushed to snatch an item or two to put on display. Joyous moments these, full of surprises, some confusion: "How are you supposed to wear this?" "Are you sure?" "You mean someone actually goes out in public with a tie like this?" Much laughter: "Now who do you suppose would ever put on a hat like that, with feathers no less?"

These were, to be sure, "old clothes" for the most part, but no less precious in our eyes. They were, after all, from America and styled in ways we had never before seen. Not that we would wear them that way. God forbid! Most were unsuitable for Kolbuszowa, where the type of permissible clothing was severely limited and for the most part rigidly prescribed— though I was once the center of attention in school after I wore a rain cap and cape sent from America. No, what we would do was have them altered. To the dressmaker we would go: she would know what to do to transform the stylish into the sedate, what was modern into what was plainly modest.

Except for the shoes. These were not altered. Can you imagine how we felt wearing shoes that were not uniformly black, as nearly all of ours were? Black and white, brown and white, designs— they were truly a revelation, though clearly not for everyday use.

More than any other item it was the shoes that spoke to us of what America was like—rich, flashy, individualistic, decidedly modern.

Cash, when it arrived, came not in the packages but in envelopes, and most commonly in five- and ten-dollar bills. The envelopes, usually manila, were also sealed impressively with red wax. American currency—there was no higher standard of value. Money, always scarce in Kolbuszowa, appeared easy to come by in America. Even the money itself testified to America's special standing. Whereas our Polish currency ordinarily was drab and in frayed condition, the paper money we received from America was considerably larger than ours and, emblazoned with golden eagles, appeared ever so much more impressive. It was tangible proof of all we imagined America to be. When American money was taken to the bank, we received the official rate of exchange; when it was put into the hands of Wolf Ofen, whose business (albeit illegal) it was to handle such matters, we received far more for our money. He was naturally always our first choice.

American money could make the difference, could enable some people to get by; it was the life preserver that kept many afloat. (Ten dollars a month would be sufficient to provide subsistence for a family.) Funds were sent not only by individuals, but by organized groups in America. This is a story in itself, similar, I'm sure, to what happened with other immigrant groups in America. No sooner do immigrants arrive than they begin organizing themselves for mutual support and for the benefit of those back in the old country. Committees are formed; money is collected and sent abroad to relieve distress among former friends and neighbors. Kolbuszowans in America, wherever they were—New York, Chicago, Cleveland, etc.—acknowledged such an obligation and managed to keep contributions coming our way: contributions, that is, in addition to the individual assistance sent to family members.

Some of the money sent from America was intended to assist families with the special preparations and expenses connected with various holidays. For example, money would arrive just before Passover so that those in need could buy matzoh and other necessities. Likewise funds went to meet other needs such as fuel for winter or to repair fire damage, fix the synagogue, or build a fence around the cemetery.

Also there were funds made available in the form of interest-free loans through the Free Loan Society to just about anyone who needed money to get through a particularly difficult time. Hundreds of loans (100 zlotys, 200 zlotys . . .) were made at one time or another to tailors, cobblers, carpenters, butchers, ped-dlers, farmers, laborers, and especially storekeepers. Once the money was repaid, it was lent out to others. The loans were ad-ministered in most proper fashion by a committee of the town's most reputable persons. Scrupulous records were kept of all trans-actions, copies of which were then forwarded to America; no loose accounting methods here. American money (local people also contributed funds) thus helped keep Kolbuszowa afloat, made it possible for us to carry on during the hard times that were so frequent.

Money aside, we were enchanted with anything American. So much was America a part of our thoughts, so central a feature of our hopes and dreams, that mere mention of the country's name was enough to spark enthusiasm and keen interest. How could I not but impress friends while playing this one game that involved shouting out the names of places? New York, Chicago, Cincinnati, Michigan—no one knew nearly as many American place names as I did. Quite an advantage I had, although whether I was right or wrong few really knew. My intense curiosity had led me to scrutinize an American atlas most thoroughly.*

American movies were much in demand. The twice-a-week Sa-turday and Sunday night offerings (the early show on Saturday attended mostly by Poles; the late show, with the Sabbath now over, having a predominantly Jewish crowd) attracted far more of an audience if the film was American. Made in America had a special, undeniable magic. Anything American attracted atten-tion, commanded an inflated price. Take the time my brother re-ceived suspenders from America, quite ordinary ones, hardly

---

*Certain candies that my father carried in the store outsold most others, no doubt because they carried American name: Florida candy, California candy, etc.

equal to those readily available around town. But because they were from America one of his friends begged to have them. Finally my brother gave in, receiving many times what they were worth, all because they had been produced in that far-off, fabulous place.

Uppermost was the America of the imagination, but along with it went some understanding of the realities. Our newspapers reported on developments there. We knew about the great stock market crash and the Depression. We learned about President Franklin Roosevelt—though many in town assumed that his name was in reality Franklin Rosenfeld, for that was the name of a prominent family in Kolbuszowa—and of his energetic efforts and New Deal proposals. We knew that all was not well with relations between blacks and whites, but in truth the sports news out of America held greater interest for us. Baseball and football we did not much relate to, but boxing—that was a different matter. We avidly followed the news and took notice of the big fights.

So closely connected did we feel to America that quite a few of us, especially the younger people, realized the importance of learning English. Because it wasn't offered in the schools you either taught yourself or took private lessons. We had "Charlie," whom my father hired to teach English to me and several of my friends. Kalman Kerenweiss was a scholarly young man who early on had developed a passion for America and proceeded to teach himself the English language.

His great goal in life was to live in America. To this end he wrote a letter to Eleanor Roosevelt, the wife of America's president, expressing his love for that country and his earnest desire to settle there. Remarkably enough, he received a response. This great woman had read his letter and had written back to him all the way to Poland. She would, she said, do what she could to help him fulfill his lifelong dream. You can well imagine the joy he felt on receiving the letter. He showed it to everyone; it was as if he was already on his way. That's why we called him "Charlie." It was, to our understanding, a typically American name, most fitting for Kalman, who would soon be heading off to the promised land. He rejoiced in the name.* Meanwhile he waited patiently for

*My father, on the other hand, always referred to him as "The Inpiniteev,"

something to happen and kept his spirits up by teaching English to us.* Charlie had one or two mostly torn English books and a few American newspapers; these were our texts. And in time we began to learn English, to understand it certainly, even to speak it, however haltingly. My sister Rachel made exceptional progress. In our letters to America she always included a sentence or two in English to show the recipients that the folks back in Poland were no slouches. (For further substantiation we usually included copies of all school report cards.) One way or another we continued with our English lessons as the war came and the terrible destruction began. It was just a matter of time, we thought, before we all would be safe in the land of the free.†

Clearly the most immediate source of information about America came from visitors, former townspeople who were back for a stay. All certainly appeared different from the way they had looked before they left. All were considerably more worldly; at least that's how they expected us to view them. Naturally we were hungry for information, and they were an obvious source. We gathered around eager to hear anything they had to say, putting question after question to them, trying to square our conceptions of the New World with their experiences.

It was, I know it now, a selective view that they presented, trying more to impress us than to describe things faithfully. We listened, mouths open, as they related how commonplace cars were over there. We had seen cars, but no one in Kolbuszowa owned one. To hear that cars filled the streets in American cities,

---

for he had one day poked his head in during our lesson and overheard Charlie explaining the English infinitive to us.

*Coming from a very poor family, Charlie relied heavily on the money paid him for the lessons. Just how desperate he was I did not realize until the day I learned why he walked about with his hands always crossed in front of his jacket, pressed to his sides. In an uncharacteristic moment of relaxation Charlie dropped his hands, and I got a look inside his jacket. All he wore underneath, in a desperate effort to maintain appearances, was the front portion of a white shirt and a frayed tie.

†Alas, Charlie never made it to America. Good fortune enabled him to survive a bout of typhus and to escape from the Germans into the woods. Then one day on a mission into a village to obtain food he was seized and killed by Polish peasants.

that was absolutely dazzling. And that some of our townspeople actually drove their own cars in America was utterly astonishing. In our region the few wealthy people with cars were almost always driven about by chauffeurs.

We listened to equally wondrous descriptions of American movie theaters. To be sure, we had a movie theater ourselves, but only on Saturday and Sunday nights did it show films. That in parts of America one saw theater after theater, huge palaces some of them, and that they were open every day, seemed truly fantastic. Imagine being able to see so many magical scenes on the screen whenever you wished! I myself had been overcome with delight watching Jeanette MacDonald and Nelson Eddy in "Rose Marie." That such entertainments abounded in America made it seem even more like a paradise.

Then there was Coney Island (actually "Tsoney Iceland" as we pronounced it), a great amusement center alongside a beach and an ocean, no less. The idea of ocean bathing was beyond our imagining. A small river on the outskirts of town was all we had. But why shouldn't America have its own ocean—it had everything else. Even exotic fruits and vegetables all year round; this probably was one of the most startling revelations. Strawberries and tropical fruit in winter! How could that be, we wondered, when supplies of such delights were always uncertain in Kolbuszowa, and certainly absent most of the year. Yet it was true, we were told. Indeed, in America it was no big deal—so much of everything was always available, and store shelves never empty.

I learned of another of America's delights when talk among the men turned, as it inevitably did, to the easy availability of prostitutes. On such occasions I was quickly ushered out of earshot, but usually not before overhearing some titillating tales of fleshpots and sexual favors.

But in all our conversations with visitors from America there was an overriding concern about making a living there. That was, after all, what made America so great an attraction, especially to those in our town who were less well off. Were there jobs? Could one find work easily? Was it possible to open up a business? Yes was the answer we received to all these questions. Jobs, good wages, business opportunities, savings, material possessions—it was, we were assured, all true. Success awaited you over there. Hard work, of course, was necessary, but always there were rewards.

Almost everyone who returned made even more of us want to go. How could it be otherwise? With our own eyes we could see what had happened to them. We all remembered them when . . . Now look. We didn't ask, nor did they tell us much, about the difficulties. Nothing about the sweatshops, the tenements, the discrimination, the hard times. And all we heard about was New York. Their America became our America. Kansas City, Chicago, Cleveland—they may just as well have been foreign lands. So we listened and we planned. Our time would come; of that we were sure.

At one time the trip to America had been a harrowing affair; certainly that had been so when the first residents of Kolbuszowa had gone in the 1890s. Now it aroused little anxiety; the chances of mishap, let alone disaster, were virtually nil. In ten days, maybe two weeks, the trip was over, the American adventure ready to unfold. Preparations to leave for America produced widespread excitement and emotions that were always bittersweet. The anticipation and the excitement loomed larger than the actual preparations. Almost always people turned to those who knew some English, hoping to acquire a few serviceable phrases. Usually they went out and bought some down pillows and quilts because rumor had it that such items were prohibitively costly in America. Two new suits or dresses and a comfortable, sturdy pair of shoes completed the preparations. Then, of course, there were the names and addresses of friends and relatives in America, slip after slip containing such information, put into their hands by townsfolk when they came to say goodbye. A messenger from the Old World bringing greetings to the new, except that many reckoned the slips would end up in the ocean. Once in America who would have time for these communications, for such niceties?

Everyone in town knew who was about to go and sensed the significance of the event. In a strange sense the emigrant's departure was an affirmation, for the community had long ago signaled its approval of such decisions. Most people understood how this outward flow actually made it possible for Kolbuszowa to carry on, how this release meant nourishment, how the emigrant's escape maintained the morale of those who were left behind. Still, those remaining envied those about to depart. Traveling light, taking little with them, fully expecting to start fresh in America, what good fortune! (Aside from necessities most took along little more than mementos to remind them of loved ones and of their former lives in Kolbuszowa.) When they were ready to leave, everyone who could get to their house—family, friends, townspeople—came to see them off. There was lots of crying and kissing and hugging, even though all understood that they were witnessing not a rupture, but merely a temporary separation.

The separation could well involve the immediate family itself. In quite a few instances that I knew of, it was the husband who left first by himself, the plan being for him to settle in America, find work, save money, and then send for the rest of the family to join him. Time and again it happened this way, though usually not overnight. Years might pass, many of them in fact, before a man was in a position to send for his family.

Some men lost themselves in America, their separation working to snap the ties that once joined the family together. Delays were followed by more delays, then excuses, then silence. What happened was no mystery. The man's head had been turned in America. In time the prospect of being reunited with his family from the Old World became less and less appealing. Compared to the women he saw in America his wife appeared old-fashioned, unattractive, unexciting. So he drifted off, leaving his family stranded in Kolbuszowa.

I recall the efforts often undertaken to search out such men and to persuade them to reconsider. I remember letters being sent to the Kolbuszowa *Landsmannschaft* [society] in New York urging people who might know the whereabouts of such men to talk with them, to bring them back to their senses, to remind them of their obligations. So far as I know, such efforts met with little success. The situation was especially tragic because not knowing what had happened to their husbands, these wives could not remarry.

Other stories, not much different, involved family members who had been expected to send for their brothers and sisters, to make all necessary preparations for their resettlement in America, but never managed to get around to it. It was hard for us back in Kolbuszowa to understand what was happening. Why had such arrangements so eagerly sought, such apparently sincere prior understandings, come to naught? Where was the sense of obligation? Did these men not realize how cruel a blow this was to people who lived for little more than the day they could leave for America?

I speak feelingly here because I myself knew such disappointment. By my teenage years, I had made up my mind to go to America if I could not get to Palestine. I wanted to go as eagerly as a deeply religious man longs for heaven. But what I wanted did not happen. In 1936 and again the following year I wrote to my brother in America asking him to send the affidavits that were necessary for me to enter the country. No response, no papers, no departure. Why, I still don't know. They never came.

Others waited, too, and were to experience bitter disappointment. The story of Noah Hutner, my best friend, comes to mind in this connection. One of ten children of a tavern owner, he was without much of a future in Kolbuszowa. Clearly America was the way out for him, and a most realistic prospect, too, since he had two uncles living there. In 1938 he applied for papers and permission to enter the United States. He waited and waited, and finally received word to call upon the American Consulate in Warsaw. "What will you do in America?" he was asked. "Work," he replied, in all innocence. "Then you cannot go" was the reply. Two days later he received from his uncles a signed affidavit with instructions to deliver it to the American Consulate. He was going to America, it stated, in order to study. Make sure you tell them you're going to America in order to attend school and not to work, the letter went on most emphatically. It was, of course, too late—by two days. At that point the war was almost upon us; Noah did not live to see it end.

Simply arriving in America did not guarantee that you would be admitted. Fail the health exam and you could be sent back.

What could be sadder? Consider all it took to leave, all the preparations, sacrifices, uncertainties, hopes—surmounting all this only to face final rejection when you were so close. A tragic story.

The story of Simchah Rubin is one of those. Simchah's difficulties began when he was drafted to fight in World War I. He did what many others had done to avoid serving with the regular army. He disabled himself by smearing his eyes with liquids from the eye of a person known to have trachoma. His success in this effort later proved his undoing. When he arrived at Ellis Island with his family in 1919, he was stopped, denied entry, and ultimately sent back. The rest of his family entered and remained, ultimately moving on and settling in Cleveland. They and Simchah were never to be reunited!

Stories involving children were even more poignant. Those with certain ailments, especially tuberculosis, were not let in. Mother and child were obliged to board ship for the return trip to Europe. That one opportunity, now dashed, was all most of them would ever have.*

The pain of separation was felt by all those back in Kolbuszowa who had seen friends and family members leave for America. A great gulf now existed, and a huge distance separated them. Had they arrived safely? How were they getting along? What were their lives like now? Were they still thinking about us? The answers to all these questions could only come through letters. If you believed people in Kolbuszowa, those in America never wrote enough, some not at all. Often it was painful to observe people waiting each day for the mail, sometimes right outside the post office hoping to encounter the postman before he went on his rounds, praying that this time a letter would come. Disappointment after disappointment.

Many a story and song spoke of this regrettable situation, "Children of Paper" being one of the better known. All this mother had left, according to the song, were her children's pictures sent from America (made of paper) hanging on the wall of her home.

---

*By the 1930s physical exams took place in Warsaw, so that medical disqualifications no longer happened in America at the last minute.

Another entitled "A Letter to the Mother" describes a mother in tears while urging those she loves and dearly misses to write to her. Of course everyone in America is too busy to write, too tired to write, too distracted to sit down and compose a letter. Some, of course, were illiterate and couldn't write, but that was no excuse. Everyone knew there were people who could write for them.

In time letters did come, ordinarily a month after they had been sent from America. You can well imagine with what excitement they were greeted. A holiday mood prevailed, everyone's spirits rose, all were eager to hear the latest news. The letter was read aloud, then reread many times over.* It wasn't so much what the letters contained. Although each bit of information—jobs, birthdays, celebrations, illnesses—was carefully digested, what mattered most was the fact that they had been written and contact renewed.† The correspondence might go on for years, sometimes at regular intervals, at other times infrequently, but so long as it continued both sides rejoiced in the connection, understood that a network of mutual support remained intact.

It happened now and then that a letter would arrive announcing a forthcoming visit. A relative in America was planning to return to Kolbuszowa for a reunion after years of separation, a coming together after it appeared as if the separation might be permanent, the bond severed. Boundless joy, incredible excitement, eager anticipation. One always hoped for such news, but who could be sure it would ever come to pass? So many difficulties existed. Even after word arrived uncertainties remained; nonetheless plans would go forward. Most importantly, word would go out and

---

*Letters from Uncle Shulim always followed a prescribed pattern that was perfectly symmetrical. On the first page were inquiries as to the well-being of each and every member of the family. Then followed an accounting of developments in minute detail. The letter concluded with yet another page, this time of regards from each and every family member and friend in America.

†Actually my father often became just as absorbed by news from America as he might be with developments in his own household. He fretted when news arrived that Frances, a niece who was already in her early thirties, had not yet found a husband. When he learned that a nephew was preparing to take the bar exam, he had the rabbi offer special prayers for his success. Sicknesses saddened him, and news of achievements never failed to lift his spirits.

spread quickly that a visitor from America could be expected in the near future. The visit represented an important step in the evolving relationship between one's place of origin and one's adopted country. A reaffirmation of one's European homeland, that it certainly was; but it also served as a personal vindication. Nourished on fresh soils, one had become a different person, had been transformed.

The visit involved lengthy preparations for both sides. To someone coming from America one must show that in Kolbuszowa, too, things had changed for the better. An effort had to be made to spruce up the old home, perhaps painting a room or two and buying new linens as a display of hospitality. Who knew when the visitor would return? Maybe never again, so distant and so costly was the journey. Besides, the visit would not be without tangible benefit to us. There would likely be gifts; money, too; maybe contributions in town as well.

The visitor also needed to prepare. The homecoming marked a pivotal stage in his new life. Sometimes, indeed often, many years had come and gone since he left for America—years of hard work, disappointments, some modest success. Always in the back of his mind was the thought, the hope, that he would one day return, not only because he dearly missed all he had once known but because he wished very much to show the wisdom of his decision to emigrate. He was now a better person for that decision— better off materially, happier, freer, more enlightened and progressive. Whatever the wounds, however many the scars he carried from his encounters in the New World, these he would not bare. Instead he would sing the praises of his adopted homeland, enumerate the wonders, demonstrate that it had changed him, made him a new man.

He would, certainly everyone hoped that he would, share some part of his good fortune with those left behind. Indeed, until he was prepared to do so there was no point in undertaking the visit. What good would it be to return to Poland and be unable to buy gifts, leave money, make contributions, in short prove that he now amounted to something? In order to be able to do all this in addition to paying for the trip and taking time off from work (the trip usually took two months, half travel, half visit), he would have had to put money aside, little by little, for a long, long time. But finally the time arrived, even if he had to borrow some of the money, and plans were put in motion.

Everyone in town knew the day, even the time, the visitor was expected. All who could be were on hand at the bus station or his family's house for his arrival. The mood was festive and would remain so even after the visitor settled in. The family, of course, would spend all available time talking, reminiscing, questioning, feasting, celebrating; but this was considered a community event as well, and all who wished to come were invited over, usually on a Saturday afternoon, to talk to the "newcomer" and look him over. Questions, questions, there was no end to them, nor did the visitor tire of answering them. He had center stage and usually made the most of it, presenting his version (who could contradict him?) of his new life.

America indeed was wondrous—the imagination took flight as one heard him describe places he had seen or heard of, the life he led, the opportunities available. All marveled at his free and frank discussions of politics, how casually he criticized officials and offered his opinions on public issues. Surely he was not the same person who had left Kolbuszowa years before. That much he wished to make clear, and especially the extent to which he had "modified" some of the more stringent religious practices he had once followed. All had abandoned the long black coat that men always wore in Kolbuszowa. Most had no beards and looked very different from those who had never plucked as much as a hair off their face.

I've already told you how daring my brother and his friends were when they returned for a visit, eating pork for one thing, smoking on the Sabbath (but not so that my father would see them), even appearing in public without hats. To be sure, they were trying to shock people with their "modern" ways, and to some extent they did. But almost everyone in town understood, and in fact many had warned, that such things were likely to happen to those who went off to America.

In preparing for the visit the family did its best to make things comfortable for the honored guest. The visitor, it was expected, would respond in kind, would contribute in tangible ways. Most did, beginning with gifts for family members—watches, pens, trinkets, a hat—modest gifts, perhaps, but all elevated beyond their mere market value by virtue of having been made in America. Beyond this came efforts to improve things for the family. If a roof needed fixing, repairs were under way within days after the visit began. Old furniture was conspicuously placed outside on the street, again in short order; all understood that it had been replaced with new pieces thanks to the generosity of the recent arrival. Family members went to cloth shops and seamstresses, there to be outfitted in finery paid for by—everyone knew whom.

At the community level, a generous contribution to the synagogue was expected. When as always contributions were solicited, it was time for the visitor to make his pledge, thereby demonstrating his abiding concern for the religious institutions of Kolbuszowa, the bedrock of its existence. I recollect that on one occasion when my brother was visiting, two other men had also returned to spend time with their families. Naturally all would be expected to make contributions; and quite obviously a competition would exist, for the one giving the largest amount would clearly establish himself as having made the greatest success in America. Now my brother planned to donate $25, an acceptable but not exceptional amount, and worried that this amount would be topped by the other two. My father also worried, and suggested that he contribute $75: such a sum surely would keep the competition at bay. My brother considered $75 somewhat too generous and instead pledged $50, itself a handsome amount. Since my brother was first, his generous pledge put pressure on the other two to increase theirs. And sure enough they did; all three parties contributed $50 each, no doubt more than each originally intended to give.

On occasion visits turned out to be more than exercises in nostalgia or celebrations of family solidarity. People came from America in search of marriage partners. What they had to offer—never mind who they were, what they were, or what they looked like—was America itself. Because they had become citizens (that was crucial), whoever they married would gain similar status. For many who had tried and failed to gain entry to America, especially in the 1930s, this was a decisive factor, important enough to overcome whatever other obstacles, or even personal preferences, might have argued against such a match.

For example, single women who returned to Kolbuszowa from America universally met with suspicion, even hostility, especially if they had originally emigrated by themselves. Rarely was such independence appreciated. Such women, it was suggested, had violated long-standing traditions about submissiveness, had doubtless behaved in ways unbecoming to females, had ventured down clearly immoral paths. It may be added that by and large these women were of less than average attractiveness. They were tainted—there was no question about it. Still, their coming back to Kolbuszowa in search of a husband tended to soften such attitudes, for after all it suggested a return to tradition, an apparent willingness to accept community standards.

My mother's cousin, a doctor who found it impossible to accumulate enough money to open an office, made such a marriage. One day there appeared a woman who had returned from America in search of a husband. At this point a matchmaker entered the picture and brought the two of them together. She was an American citizen; the prospects were too good to pass up. So they were married, and both went off to the United States.

It also happened that men returned to Kolbuszowa in search of wives. More often than not these were older men, usually widowers, who sought to attract younger women by virtue of their greatest possession—American citizenship. Ordinarily they looked to their own family, usually proposing marriages with distant cousins. By and large everyone seemed pleased with such arrangements, even though age differences exceeded normal expectations. In these circumstances a 40-year-old man and a girl 18 years old would be a fairly typical match.

Usually the bride was a poor girl, one whose dowry, if any, was insufficient to attract suitors. Her parents consented to such a match, even considered it a blessing, for not only would a dowry be unnecessary but they would likely receive money from the gentleman (and gifts from America once the couple returned there to live). All the bride's girlfriends envied her imminent escape from the poverty and dreariness that surrounded them. There was no indication that the young men of Kolbuszowa resented the departure of eligible females; after all, there were more young women than men in the town. No need to bemoan the loss, especially of those whose dowries, if present, were so paltry.

In Kolbuszowa there were perhaps ten families whose presence some might say testified to the enduring value of the ways of our town, though to others it might suggest instead that all was not well in America. I'm referring, of course, to people who had gone to America, lived there, and then decided for one reason or another to return to Kolbuszowa. There was, you should know, no shame or aura of failure attached to these people. Indeed they enjoyed something of a celebrity status back in our town. After all, they had been exposed to the ways of the wider world and so could interpret it to us when asked, or even without any prompting. Some clearly enjoyed their unique standing and by reason of their experience assumed that their comments on matters momentous and trivial would be taken as authoritative, even years after their return.*

People returned for any number of reasons. Some were elderly persons who from the first felt strangely out of place in America, who were not flexible enough to make the necessary adjustments. Better off back in Kolbuszowa, where the old familiar ways still prevailed. Take my Uncle Moshe Yosef Berle, for example. After spending a few years in America, he decided to return. He was a scholar, also a most rigid man who found little that attracted him there. Sewing buttons in a New York City factory was not how he wished to spend his life. Besides, he still had one son and two daughters living in Kolbuszowa, and their presence tempered the traumas of uprooting himself from New York. To be sure, he had

---

*One such person was Zeivil Einhorn, who "commuted" between America and Poland every few years. He achieved "success" in America in a most unusual manner: he became a professional beggar. Somehow he managed to tie up one leg to make it appear it had been amputated. So "handicapped," he attracted substantial contributions from passersby on New York's Lower East Side.

three other sons in America who stayed (two of them rabbis), resulting in yet another family that spanned the two worlds.

Some of the more religious people, as I have mentioned, were deeply disturbed at seeing just how easy it was in America to be lured away from Jewish orthodoxy, how great were the temptations. "Even the stones are *traif*" was an expression we often heard from them. Even though maintaining strict beliefs and rituals often involved considerable inconvenience,* they would themselves not succumb to the rampant secularism of America; but they worried about their children and concluded that for the sake of their souls it would be better to return home, where such matters were accorded greater attention.

Often more mundane considerations prompted decisions to return. Take Srulcie Blazer, who left with his wife for America in 1920 and started a family there that in time numbered four children. In 1928 his father-in-law, who owned a leather goods business in Kolbuszowa, died. What was to become of this business? After eight years in America Blazer was still struggling to make a living; if he returned, he could assume ownership of his father-in-law's business and thus be able to live more comfortably. His decision was to leave America and bring his entire family (including the four children who had been born there) back to Kolbuszowa.

So we had among us both those who had been exposed to new ways in America and reflected the new thinking, and people who appeared relatively unaffected by their sojourn in the New World.† Their return to Kolbuszowa was in a way a source of some comfort to us, since it suggested the continued value of our

---

*Though Uncle Shulim did send a photograph of a kosher butcher shop in New York City to assure us that such things existed there.

†Count among them one Josef R., who after two or three years in America returned to Kolbuszowa seemingly unaffected by his stay there. The only thing different about him was his tendency to employ one American word repeatedly in conversation. Everything was "fuck this" or "fuck that." For whatever reason, this was the only American expression that had caught on with him, so much so that it became our way of identifying him. As a friend of his son, I often found myself telling my parents quite innocently that I was going over to visit "with the Fuckers."

ways without ever seeming to tarnish the image of America! Nothing would ever do that. Maybe America wasn't for everyone, perhaps its ways were too new, even shocking, but still it represented everything that so many of us hoped for. It stood alluringly at the end of the road that led away from Kolbuszowa.

How proud we were as Poles of what we had contributed to America. The colonists, we were taught repeatedly, might not have won their independence had Pulaski and Kosciuszko not left for America and cast their lot with the patriots. The result was freedom for these one-time subjects of Great Britain and the promise of liberation one day for the rest of mankind. Later the sons and daughters of Poland left for America to add their strength, their labor, their numbers, to the building of a marvelously productive and bountiful society. America had fulfilled its promise and in our eyes had become incredibly rich, remarkably free, incomparably just, and all-powerful. It would not, we were sure, forget its debt to Poland; it would take notice of us and support us. As the 1930s wore on and the clouds of German militarism and Russian aggression loomed ominously on the horizon, we took comfort in our American connection. We could defy our enemies because America was our friend; we would emerge triumphant because America would be our protector.

Without the Messiah

Despite all that I've just said about America, it had a rival for our affections. In fact, as the years went on we looked elsewhere more and more, were attracted by another place with an intensity that even the "Golden Land" had not evoked in us. You could say that this was because entry into the United States became increasingly difficult during the 1930s, but that was not the whole story. We fell in love with the idea of Palestine, were swept away by the prospect of going to Palestine and establishing a Jewish homeland there. The land of Israel stirred within us emotions and dreams quite different from those associated with America. The promise of material well-being was the principal allure of the United States. But whereas America aroused our hungers, Palestine, as you will see, would come to stir our very souls.

To speak of an awakening interest in Palestine is not quite accurate. The land of Israel had always been in our thoughts and had an exclusive place in our hearts. It had ever been so. Palestine lay at the very core of Judaism, at the very center of our idea of peoplehood. There we had come to define ourselves as a special people, committed to a singular ideal and view of God. There we had enjoyed notable triumphs, produced outstanding leaders and sages, and gloried in the belief that our ways were in keeping with the will of an all-powerful, benevolent deity.

But we were destined, it seems, to serve other purposes, to be driven out of our land and to be sent wandering across the globe. Where other people might as a result have succumbed, blended in, even disappeared entirely, we, though suffering much, endured from century to century despite repeated misfortunes and malevolent adversaries. After all those years there remained the memory of Israel, maintained before us as a beacon, as a reminder of what had once been and could again be. No matter that Israel remained in the hands of others; by right it was still ours. Unaffected by the passage of time or by rival claims was our special relationship to that holy land. And one day, sooner or later, would come the time for our redemption, for our return. Our prayers would then be answered.

Wherever in the world there lived an observant Jew, "Eretz Israel" [the land of Israel] was on his lips and on his mind—and not by chance. Woven into the fabric of our faith, placed within the passages of our prayers, were repeated references to our days in the land of Canaan. Never were we allowed to forget that time; always we were reminded of the violent end to our rule and residence in the Holy Land, the almost total destruction by the Romans of the temple in Jerusalem, the central landmark of our religion. What remained standing was a single structure, the western wall of the temple, soon transformed into a sacred place, a powerful magnet for our faith, an emotionally wrenching reminder of how vicious and unrelenting were our enemies.

The destruction of the temple became for us a symbol of the Jewish condition, of the tragic course of so much of our history.* Even in my time some homes continued to mark this event in a very special way. Whenever the main room would be painted, a rectangular area on the eastern wall would be left undone, and on that space would be found the following words: "In remembrance of the destruction of the temple." Beyond that, ultra-orthodox

---

*There was, of course, Tisha B'av, when Jews recalled and mourned the destruction of the temple. (There had been two temples built in ancient Israel at different times. Both, however, were destroyed on the same date.) It was a sorrowful time indeed. As I have mentioned, people dressed in old, torn coats, no shoes were worn, and boxes were substituted for chairs. Meat could not be eaten, marriages were not to take place, and any display of happiness was considered inappropriate.

Jews were obligated each midnight to intone a lamentation recalling the temple's tragic history. I have a painting picturing that
scene, showing a Jew at prayer, the candle dripping, the clock at
twelve, tears coming down his face as he recalls the temple's end.
During one of the happiest moments of life, at the conclusion of
the marriage ceremony, there is a reminder. The service ends only
after a glass is broken, the fragments representing what had be-
fallen the temple.

The temple was no more, but still we hoped one day to return
to the land of our birth. When would that be? Easily answered:
when the Messiah would come. Of all the questions asked by our
faith, that one drew the most attention and probably the most
puzzling answers. We would wait for the Messiah, but also pray
earnestly for his coming and for our return to the land of Zion.*
This we did regularly in the course of our daily services, with special mention on the holidays of Yom Kippur and Passover, when
we prayed to be "next year in Jerusalem." For hundreds upon hundreds of years we had prayed, but without getting any closer to
Jerusalem or to Israel.

My father playfully suggested why our prayers had gone unanswered. It was not because of our misdeeds or the unworthiness
of the Jewish people. Indeed, were God to judge his people fairly,
surely they deserved to be reunited in the land of Israel. The problem, he said, was the wording of the repeated prayers, which succeeded only in delaying matters. When in late summer or early fall
people pray for "next year in Jerusalem," God prepares to grant
them their wish; but then in the spring during Passover he hears
once again a prayer for "next year in Jerusalem." What that does,
claimed my father, is continually postpone the blessed event. The
simple solution to the redemption of Israel, he assured everyone,
was to cut out one of the prayers, thus clearing the way for God
to respond!

*The return of the Jewish people most assuredly awaited the coming of the
Messiah, but individual Jews could take matters in their own hands. It was for
some a matter of the highest importance to die and be buried in Palestine, and
some were able to arrange for this to happen. I know of two instances before
World War I in which elderly Jews from Kolbuszowa managed to get to Palestine,
then died there.

It happened first in Russia before my day, and later spread to Poland. At first it was an idea, more of a dream perhaps. And as I grew to young manhood it became a stubborn reality, gaining in momentum, gathering support from all corners. Jews, it was declared, need not await the coming of the Messiah but could themselves take the initiative and fulfill the ancient promise of once more dwelling in the land of Zion. Living among the Gentiles, never easy, was now becoming intolerable. Why remain where we were unwanted, scapegoated, denied opportunities, obliged to dwell on the borders of economic life? How much better it would be to live in the Promised Land, rich in our history, to live free from the exactions of unfriendly regimes, free to give complete expression to the genius of our people. It was a compelling idea, and as the years passed more and more of the young people of Kolbuszowa gave themselves to it, prepared to join the wave building in eastern Europe that would wash ashore in the land of Palestine.

Support for Zionism ultimately would cut across the various groupings in Kolbuszowa and represent the will of nearly the entire Jewish community. But not at first. In general, socialists rejected the Zionist movement. The goal of the Jews should not be, they argued, to leave those countries in which they had lived for centuries. They had every right to equal citizenship there, plus the obligation to remain and advance the cause of economic and social justice.

Then, too, the more religious you were, the less Zionism appealed. The ultra-orthodox denied the possibility entirely. Longing for Zion, they said, was pointless so long as the Messiah had not returned; only his appearance could end the Diaspora and fulfill God's ancient promise to His people. Religious conservatives mistrusted Zionism and worried about how it would affect the fabric of religious commitment. Zionism, they believed, introduced a disruptive element, interfered with many of the obligations associated with Judaism. From Zionism the path to religious indifference appeared all too obvious and inevitable. A story was often told in Kolbuszowa about the town thief, a Jewish man who had repeatedly been convicted of crimes and sent away to prison. His mother, defending her son's reputation, would remind everyone, "At least a Zionist he was not."

Very religious Jews were probably right when they pointed to the corrosive possibilities of Zionism. Zionism did offer an alternative, an outlet, a challenge to the claustrophobic world of religion in which we lived in Kolbuszowa. Zionism represented a modern viewpoint that was not always in step with the traditional beliefs of the religious-minded. Young boys who were swept up by Zionism tended to relax, to be less rigorous in observing the rituals of their faith. They began to dress differently and assume a more independent attitude. And this was also true of the girls, who constituted at least half of those drawn to Zionism in Kolbuszowa. Surely for them it represented a form of release from an otherwise rigidly regimented life.

But Zionism was much more than a by-product of religious relaxation and gender segregation. It was a compelling answer to the many dilemmas and disappointments experienced by Jews throughout Europe. We had lived among Gentiles in their lands for centuries, but we were at best tolerated, rarely welcomed, too often taken to task for our supposed exclusivity and separateness. We were thrown off the land, often limited to occupations that brought us resentment, even envy. Had we made too much of the little allowed us? Zionism promised to remove Jews from exposed positions, to do away with the defensiveness forced on us, to let our many talents flourish in an environment that would support, not suppress, Jewish energy and activity. Zionism wished also to return Jews to the soil, to allow them to labor with their hands, to enjoy the exhilarating feeling of building a new society by harnessing the collective energies of a people who were thrilled at the prospect of rebuilding a land that once had flourished in their presence.

In Kolbuszowa it was impossible to overlook the growing influence of Zionism, the extent to which it was becoming an expression of almost the entire Jewish community. Most Jewish homes, for example, had one, sometimes two *pushkas* [collection boxes] devoted to Palestine. The most common was the box of the Jewish National Fund, which was used to purchase additional lands in Palestine for Jewish settlers. A fair number of homes also had a collection box for a yeshiva located in Tiberias, which had been founded by Mayer the Miracle Worker.

That there was a place in Palestine where students gathered to study the sacred texts was considered important enough to justify our support for this yeshiva. In fact my brother-in-law Reuben Weinstein served as collector for this institution, going from house to house emptying the *pushkas,* totaling their contents, and providing receipts for the money. Donors were usually rewarded by the yeshiva once a year, just before Passover, with a gift of dehydrated *haroset* [a concoction made of apples, nuts, and wine] sent from Israel. More substantial contributors could expect a prayer book with a distinctive olive wood cover. Coming from Palestine made these gifts special and most welcome.

Because Zionist organizations took root so easily in Kolbuszowa, all around us there arose a rich and varied chorus of voices in support of Palestine. There were adult groups and youth auxiliaries. There were organizations on the left like Hashomer, Gordonia, and Hitachtud and on the right groups like Betar, along with the general Zionists, the religious Mizrachi, and the orthodox Agudat Israel. The ultra-orthodox never came to accept Zionism. To this day they wait for the Messiah.

These many groups were free to organize and faced no opposition from the Polish authorities.* In fact our Polish neighbors seemed not at all displeased that so many Jews planned for a future outside the country. "You see, Jews don't consider themselves Poles after all"—such was the unspoken message we received. There were spoken declarations as well. All too often disputes with Poles led them to break off the argument with these bitter parting words: "Go to Palestine, Jew!"†

---

*In 1939, at a time when I had become leader of Hanoar Hazioni, a local middle-of-the-road Zionist group of about thirty young people, a Polish detective visited my father to inquire about my activities. With war clouds on the horizon, the Polish government had grown suspicious of any groups that had links outside the country.

†When I sent some money to my brother David in Palestine in 1937, the post office clerk took exception to the transfer of funds. "It won't be good for Poland," he muttered, "if all the Jews sent their money to Palestine."

For the young Jews of Kolbuszowa, joining any of the cluster of Zionist organizations was an exciting and exhilarating experience. It made them part of a nationwide, even international network of similar local organizations, each doing what it could to speed the exodus of Jews to the Holy Land. Regional and national representatives arrived regularly to keep local affiliates in touch with developments. When conventions were organized, people sensed that they were part of a growing movement. At the local get-togethers, some held almost daily, young people gathered and related to each other in ways previously unknown. There was socializing, of course; and often the Zionist organizations, either individually or together with others, put on plays, sometimes inserting comments that mocked the ultra-orthodox for their opposition to the Zionist program. But also serious attention was paid to the business at hand.

All this was by way of preparation for the day each of us would leave for Palestine. It was vital that everyone should be familiar with all aspects of Palestine, its geography, its people, its present conditions. It was essential that we learn Hebrew, the language spoken by Jews in Palestine. Hebrew was, of course, hardly unknown in Kolbuszowa, but it was the language of prayer, the language one used in most religious studies, rather than conversational Hebrew. So all Zionists took their Hebrew lessons, applying themselves fully, determined to be ready when the call came to leave.

It is impossible to exaggerate our enthusiasm for Palestine, the eagerness with which we absorbed any and all information about the land and its people. Zionist newspapers supplied us with a steady stream of pictures and stories. Especially eager to learn the songs of the country, we seized on each new melody as a precious addition to our inventory. How quickly we learned these songs, how rapidly they spread from group to group! From the songs themselves it was easy to tell how we felt about the land of Israel. Songs about the flowers, the fragrances, even the moon over Palestine, spoke to us of its beauty and of the love we had even for everyday elements there.

There were songs aplenty about the hard work and the very

simple, even crude living conditions, but this mattered little so long as it was in Palestine. Many songs spoke to us of the collective accomplishments of our people, the new roads, the growing settlements, the rising towns; none referred to the likelihood or even the value of individual achievement. To indicate how attached people were to the new land, there was a song about a mother writing her son in Palestine to return because his father has died, she is sick, and he is needed back home. The son responds by calling on his mother to come to him instead because Palestine is now his home and he can never leave it.

We had few illusions about conditions there. We knew that the work was hard and the rewards, at least at first, meager. We knew that the climate was altogether different from our own. The general hostility of the local Arab population was for us all too clear. The anti-Jewish riots of 1929 and again in 1936 dampened but could not for long diminish our enthusiasm. We were in it for the long run; slow progress, formidable obstacles, temporary setbacks—we would take all these in stride because Palestine meant so much to us.

Our emotional investment was almost without limits. In Palestine we would be free, Jews would be among Jews, our well-being would not depend on the tolerance and generosity of the Gentile majority. We would follow our talents and ambitions, not settle for occupations that others permitted us to enter. We would live our lives there unafraid, free from beatings, not hearing the chilling words "dirty Jew." We would mix our labor and sweat with the soil, revitalize a land grown arid and unproductive, build a vital and progressive society, a society fit for the return of the Jewish people so long scattered about the world. Noble objectives such as these could not fail to bring forth a high-minded idealism, stir up a tireless zeal, produce the kind of energy and dynamism rarely seen in our communities.

Zionism was no abstract philosophy. It called for the uprooting of Jews and their removal to Palestine. But the leadership was wise enough to realize that sending raw, unprepared recruits off to the new land would probably defeat the entire enterprise. Careful preparations were necessary; basic skills needed to be mastered and a close camaraderie developed. Much of this was accomplished by setting up *hachsharas* [training centers] throughout Poland, many of them farms rented from their owners. By this time relatively few Jews in Poland remained on the land as farmers. Yet in Palestine perhaps the majority could expect to enter agriculture and work the fields. Their efforts would not succeed unless Jews could recover long-lost agricultural skills. That was a primary purpose of these *hachsharas*. No less important was their contribution to producing a new breed of Jew equal to the formidable task that awaited him in Palestine.

After the training period ended, everything depended on the British, who governed Palestine under a mandate received at the end of World War I. It was Britain's practice to control the influx of Jews with a certificate system that granted entry to limited numbers each year. Certificates were distributed by the various Zionist organizations, with those in leadership positions ordinarily receiving priority.* With the certificate in hand it was just a matter of time before the long-held dream of resettling in Palestine would be a reality. For those who had prepared and were ready to leave but lacked a certificate, the disappointment was obvious. It was necessary now to be patient and remain hopeful that a certificate would not be long in coming.

Actually there was another way: one could marry a certificate holder. It became clear that sending unmarried persons to Palestine was not making full use of the certificates, since the British allowed a certificate to cover either an individual or a married couple. The many marriages that ensued were not instant marriages or marriages of convenience; rather they were fictitious affairs, authenticated by civil ceremonies but dissolved as soon as the couple arrived in Palestine. Still, this was a transparent subterfuge that worked well, rendering the certificate system less restrictive than intended.

---

*There was an alternative: a person could enter Palestine as a "capitalist" by proving he had 25,000 zlotys [about $5,000] in the bank. In Kolbuszowa we had only one such capitalist. In 1934 Zelig Rosenfeld, a carpenter, left for Palestine in this manner with his wife and sons. In Germany, by contrast, many Jews qualified on this basis.

One could also be smuggled into Palestine by Zionist organizations. There were risks, we knew, for we read of ships being intercepted and of Jews being detained; but without a certificate how long would it be before impatience set in and the desperate desire to get to Palestine overthrew all caution? In the end I would attempt to enter Palestine this way, but more about that later.

Kolbuszowa was represented among the early pioneers in Palestine. The procession first began in 1922 when three young people, two boys and one girl, left our town. How everyone envied them! How townspeople thrilled to the news contained in the letters they wrote back from there! Mostly their contents were shared with anyone curious to know of developments in Palestine, which included just about everyone. Not long afterward three members of the Leidner family, two sisters and a brother, also headed for Palestine.

As the 1930s wore on, the numbers preparing to leave and those actually departing continued to increase. Certainly my family had a part to play in this enterprise. My two youngest sisters joined Zionist organizations. When I was twelve and thirteen I too longed to do so, but my father would not have it, and at that point I was not yet ready to defy him. With my older brother David it was another story. He became a Zionist and prepared to go off for training. Although my parents did not try to stop him, they were less than pleased, my mother because she loved all her children and wanted them with her at all times, my father because he worried that David's devotion to Judaism would decline and because he very much needed his assistance in the store. But David was not to be dissuaded, and off he went to Cracow for his training. His preparation did not follow the typical pattern, for instead of working on a farm he was sent to a paper box factory, where he lived and worked together with a group of other Zionists. Upon completing his training David received a certificate, "married" another Zionist, and prepared to depart Kolbuszowa.

Strangely enough, the day he was to leave was also the day two others from our town, Shaya Dershowitz and Meyer Fliegelman—each from a different Zionist organization—also planned their departure. It was an event never to be repeated—three people leaving for Palestine from Kolbuszowa on the same day. And some day it was: a proud day for the Jews of Kolbuszowa, for by then (1933) most had come to see removal to Palestine, even if they themselves could not go, as the only reasonable hope for the future. They were eager to show their support for the effort by turning out at a farewell gathering.

Early on a Sunday morning the town's Jews gathered in the marketplace. The wagon that would take the three men to the railroad station was already loaded with their belongings. All these had been well wrapped courtesy of my brother Leibush, who as a measure of his support performed this valuable service for all those leaving for Palestine. Supplying sturdy sugar sacks made from linen, he packed their goods and then tied up the sacks in an expert, compact fashion, assuring their safe arrival.

Appearing at this festive sendoff was Hazamir, the Jewish band, which played the "Hatikvah" [Jewish national anthem] and all manner of other Jewish songs and melodies from the land of Israel. Hersch Gewirtz, one of the early Zionists in Kolbuszowa, delivered a speech reminding the audience that no longer could Jews afford to await the Messiah; these three pioneers, he said, were going to Palestine to build a Jewish state for everyone. There was much singing and clapping. Kolbuszowa was about to renew itself in the Promised Land; it was a glorious moment. Everyone then proceeded to march over to the post office, where the wagon of Mordechai Freifeld awaited. Amid cheers and tears they set out—destination Palestine.

Kolbuszowa would send a goodly number of its sons and daughters (I would say in equal numbers) off to Palestine in the 1930s. Before the decade was over, forty to fifty young people had left to build new lives and create a new country. Many more probably would have gone if more certificates had been available. Mostly those who went were the children of middle-level and well-to-do parents. That actually created problems, for some of them just weren't accustomed to the backbreaking labor and deprivations faced by most newcomers in Palestine. There was one instance that I know of when the youngest son of a rich man managed, through bribery, to get a certificate for Palestine. He had never performed much in the way of hard labor here, but discovered it would be necessary if he expected to get along there. It wasn't for him, he soon decided, and back he came—the only person from our town who ever returned after deciding to live in Palestine. (As noted earlier, this happened quite a few times with those who had left for America.) His return and his complaints about the harsh life in Palestine stirred up no small amount of resentment in town. People who knew how hard it was to obtain certificates criticized him for having wasted one.

There was another case, this one involving a well-to-do girl who settled in Palestine. According to her letters she had found a good office job; only later did we learn that she was working there as a maid. So what was the shame? Given her family background, to do household work was more than she could admit. But such considerations were unimportant in Palestine, where manual labor of any kind was acceptable and, of course, necessary. All labor there was noble, since we were doing it for ourselves, for the betterment of our people in our new land.

Whatever news people in town received from friends and relatives in Palestine usually was shared with everyone. We found out, for example, that our townspeople there had taken to meeting together and helping each other out as best they could. They sent along local newspapers and spoke glowingly of the new settlements, the growth of Tel Aviv, and the joy they felt, despite the very hard work, at being a part of something so exciting, an enterprise so noble. They wrote about the easy availability of such exotic fruits as grapes and oranges, but reminded us that potatoes, so much the staple in Poland, was not easily obtained there. There was no overlooking conflicts with the Arabs, though from their letters they seemed divided on this matter. Some advanced a policy of patience, passivity, and the avoidance of conflict; others advocated aggressive steps against the Arabs, retaliation for any and every attack on the Jews.

But it was not only on Arab policy that the Palestine Jews were divided. The Jews there, coming from many different parts of the world, were not, it seems, very comfortable with each other. Instead of blending easily into the new breed of Jew we had heard so much about, they had divided into groups, and the groups had come to regard each other with some suspicion. A basic division involved the Ashkenazi Jews from Europe and the Sephardic Jews, who came mostly from various Arab lands and from places like Greece and Bulgaria. Many of the Sephardic Jews spoke not Yiddish but Arabic, and some spoke Ladino (a mixture of Spanish, Arabic, and Hebrew). To the Ashkenazim the Jews of Algeria, Tunisia, Morocco, and Egypt seemed less like fellow religionists and more like strange and lesser beings.

But all was not harmonious among the Ashkenazim. The German Jews were a breed apart, living together in separate areas and generally speaking only German; they considered the Russian and Polish Jews, with few exceptions, to be rude and crude, certainly inferior to the Germans. On the other hand, there was a Russian Jewish elite, an idealistic intelligentsia who, we gathered, were most influential in the Jewish governing councils in Palestine. To a degree we were puzzled, saddened somewhat, by these divisions and antagonisms; but they scarcely diminished our enthusiasm or the support we were prepared to give to this ambitious collective enterprise of the Jewish people.

Unlike other family members who had left Kolbuszowa for distant places, David kept up a steady correspondence with us after he left. A letter from him arrived weekly, somehow almost always on a Friday, which gave us Saturday and Sunday to read and reread it and share the information it contained with others. In his letters we followed the slow but steady progress he was making in this far-off land. He had at first gone to work for a distant cousin, and then along with several others entered the construction business, having purchased a wagon and some mules to haul building materials. He enclosed photographs, in one wielding a pickaxe against the clear, brilliant sky of Palestine, in another keeping tight rein on a pack of mules—honest work for a noble purpose, the rebuilding of the land of Israel. Even more encouraging was his attitude. His spirit seemed to soar now that he was living there. He was happier, he said, than he had ever been before, and felt free for the first time in his life. Such enthusiasm had its intended effect on me and my sisters, making us even prouder to be Zionists.

You can well imagine how excited we were when we learned

that David planned to visit Kolbuszowa in 1937. Letters we had plenty of from Palestine, but rarely had people returned for a visit. Actually I can remember only one: Chana, the sister of Avram Leidner, who had left back in the 1920s. Her return, I remember, caused something of a stir around town because of her clothes, particularly the cap she wore and the blouse without sleeves. No girl of Kolbuszowa would let herself be seen clothed this way. I remember the other women watching her go by, remarking how "you can throw up just looking at her." Without doubt she had made an impression. So would my brother.

That he was the center of attention for the few weeks he was with us was beyond dispute. He could not be exclusively ours, but rather belonged to the whole town, carried with him their hopes, their sense of pride. He brought with him letters and re-gards from all those of Kolbuszowa now in Palestine. Everywhere he attracted people eager to ask him questions and listen to him. He was patient beyond belief and not the least reluctant to speak of his experiences; indeed sometimes, I think, he embellished his activities there. He addressed the many local Zionist organiza-tions in town, describing developments in Palestine, the founding and expansion of new communities, and the spread of *kibbutzim*. Most welcome were the new songs of the land that he sang before audiences eager to hear them and quick to adopt them. He at-tracted several matchmakers almost immediately, for surely here was a catch—good family, young, vigorous, established in a busi-ness, and able to provide anyone he married with a ticket out of Kolbuszowa. But he let it be known that a marriage had already been planned.*

One incident that occurred during his stay with us probably had a greater impact in fixing the image of Palestine in the minds of the Jews of Kolbuszowa than anything else he said or whatever else they had heard from others. Fortunately I was standing nearby when it happened, so a full accounting is possible. Before

*Actually one of the reasons he had returned was to "marry" the sister of a woman he knew in Palestine, enabling her to join her sister there. On arriving back in Palestine the two, by arrangement, divorced, and David later married the sister.

I tell you about it, I must tell you a related story about David that makes what he did this time even more understandable.

The first story takes us back to a hot summer day several years before. It was a Saturday afternoon, the Sabbath dinner had been completed, and people were sitting outside their homes in the marketplace, relaxing and doing their best to gain some relief from the heat. The favorite treat at such times had always been the icy water that was readily available from the deep town well located in the center of the marketplace. Accordingly many women had taken pitchers and basins and headed for the well, and many others eagerly awaited the cold water that they would soon bring back. So it might have been except for the fact that just as the women began gathering, two of the town's street cleaners attached their hose to the well and began drawing off water to fill the barrel they used to wash the streets.

Actually there was nothing particularly unsettling about this scene. Saturday was the day the streets in the marketplace were washed, and the street cleaners had always come to the well for their water. If you happened to arrive while they were filling the barrel, you simply waited till they were finished, maybe ten minutes at the most, and then proceeded to draw water for yourself. It was with that expectation that people gathered round the well this one hot Saturday afternoon, except that as the minutes went by it became clear that something else was happening. Sure enough, the barrel filled up in the usual time, but instead of detaching the hose the two street cleaners simply let it run and watched as the barrel overflowed, the water running off in all directions across the pavement. When asked why they were doing this, they laughed, nor did they respond to requests that they finish with their business and allow the many who had now gathered about the well to fill their containers. Clearly there was a confrontation in the making, except for the fact that none of the Jews were disposed to challenge the two. Jews rarely if ever asserted themselves; this was well understood and often commented on. Some of those who had waited at the well despaired of ever getting any water and started drifting away, and word spread across the marketplace about what was happening.

It's at this point that David heard the story and without hesitating decided to do something about it. Off he headed toward the well. When he got there the situation had not changed one bit: the two were still loitering about, the water continued to overflow, and the complaints of the Jews were still being ignored. David put the same question to them: Now that the barrel was full, why did they not detach the hose? Like the others he received no satisfactory response. Instead an argument ensued, and one of the two suddenly displayed a knife. Instead of leaving the matter there, my brother picked up an earthenware container and smashed it over the head of the one with the knife. He promptly collapsed in a heap, unconscious. Seeing this, the other one took off. David then detached the hose and invited those assembled to draw from the well.

You can well imagine the talk that went on after this. A Jew had not backed off, had actually confronted a Pole! It was positively exhilarating, although David's example did not in any way launch a trend in Kolbuszowa. Indeed repercussions were feared, but in fact nothing happened. The two street cleaners continued to draw water from the well prior to their Saturday cleanings, but it was noted that henceforth they did not linger a minute beyond the time necessary to fill the barrel.

That now prepares us for what happened during David's return visit from Palestine. Some background information must first be presented. Once a year the draft commission of the Polish government arrived in Kolbuszowa to register all the young men in the district and determine their military status. Young boys from surrounding villages would be summoned on particular days to Kolbuszowa and ordered to appear before the commission. For them it became a holiday, walking together into town, drinking, then horsing around in the streets before returning that same day.

But young, cocky peasants in high spirits often posed a danger for Jews. On their way to town if the boys encountered a Jew driving a wagon—heading off to a market, for example—it was more than likely that they would stop him, beat him up, and probably overturn his wagon before heading on. Whenever possible, Jews attempted to avoid such danger, and I played no small part in helping them do this. My father, you see, had an acquaintance who just happened to be the secretary of the draft commission. As a result I was able to get from him a schedule listing the villages to be summoned on particular days. This information proved most valuable. Many a Jew came to me to look it over so as to avoid certain roads where he might be attacked.

It so happened that during David's visit the draft commission arrived in Kolbuszowa to begin its work. The Jews in town shuddered as the high-spirited peasant boys came into town to perform their usual mischief, which generally involved breaking windows and harassing Jews. Sure enough, one such incident occurred in a barber shop in the marketplace when a group of Poles wandered in and started breaking things and threatening those around, who simply stood by and watched. David was standing nearby talking to a group of his friends about Palestine when he noticed the commotion. When he walked over to investigate, the situation was clear enough. Instead of waiting for the Poles to be done with the mischief and move on, he asked them to stop, which naturally had the effect of encouraging them to redouble their efforts. David's response was to pick up a chair and start swinging it in their direction, hitting several, as was his intention. At the same time he called upon some Jewish boys in the shop to help him. Surprisingly enough, heartened by his example, they joined in and succeeded in driving the Poles from the place.

Word of this dramatic confrontation and David's role in it spread rapidly through the town. My brother became a hero, a modern-day David overcoming the formidable Goliath. I was so proud of what he had done. That anyone else in the town would have reacted in this manner is most unlikely. For many the explanation was simple enough. Having gone to Palestine and lived there, David represented the new breed: no longer the timid, impassive Jew of the Diaspora who shied away from danger, but the proud and forceful Jew of Palestine prepared to defend what was his. David's combativeness sent a thrill through Kolbuszowa and convinced many that the Jewish cause would ultimately prevail in Palestine. His bold action served as the best advertisement Zionism ever enjoyed in town, not that the cause of Palestine was anything but popular. When David prepared to return at the end of his visit, there was no gathering in the marketplace, no bands to send him off. There was no doubt, however, that he had the approval of the entire community, that he had confirmed in dramatic fashion the value of a Jewish homeland.

By the late 1930s, I had come forth and declared myself a Zionist, having set aside the fear of my father's displeasure. I became active in a Zionist organization and become truly excited over the prospect of joining David in the land of Israel. But waiting for a certificate I knew would be uncertain and probably frustrating. I would do better to seize whatever opportunities were available at the moment. That, of course, meant being smuggled in past the British blockade. So be it. It would, I learned, cost 500 zlotys [$100] to proceed. At this point I was joined by a close friend, Yankel Shifman, who always had wanted to go. His problem was that he didn't have the money. So intense was his desire, however, that he convinced his mother to sell two candlesticks and two strings of pearls to raise the funds, which she agreed to do.

Gathering our money, we sent it off to the Zionist headquarters in Lvov, requesting immediate transportation to Palestine. You can't imagine how excited I was at the prospect of leaving for the Holy Land. For years I had already been living there in my mind, and I had come to know everything about it. "I'm going to heaven, I'm going home"—so I informed my friends. They must have believed me, for envy was written all over their faces. After we had sent the money, we received a response early in 1939. Be prepared, we were advised, and we were. Admittedly there was not much to be done by way of preparation, though I did gather some clothes together. Then in June another letter arrived, assuring us that we would receive information about the assigned plan and departure point "any day." We were as good as there. Rounds of farewells followed.

That we would be smuggled through successfully we had no doubt. But after the letter in June there were no others. Three months later the Germans invaded Poland. After that there could be no escape to Palestine.

The Isak Saleschütz family, Kolbuszowa, 1934, on the occasion of my brother Avrum's visit from America. I am in the front row, left. Next to me is Shulim (Leibush's son), my sister Rachel, and my sister Gela's daughter Shaindel. Al (Avrum) is in the middle row, left, and next to him my mother and father, Gela, and her husband, Ruben Weinstein. In the top row, left, is my sister Matel; next to her are Szaja David, my sister Malcia's husband; Malcia; then a picture of my brother David dubbed in (he was in Palestine at this time); Chancia, my brother Leibush's wife; Leibush; and my sister Leiba.

Kolbuszowa's coat of arms, dedicated in 1785. A Jew and a Pole shake hands between a Crusader's cross (above) and a Jewish star (below).

Mayor Osiniak, center, *with three municipal policemen and other unidentified residents of Kolbuszowa.* Courtesy of Yivo Institute.

Left to right: *Yossel Szemesz, a water carrier; his sister Rachel, always laughing, always in "love" with every boy in town; their aunt; and their cousin "Crazy" Meyer.* Courtesy of Yivo Institute.

Kolbuszowa's only hotel, located in the marketplace. Courtesy of Yivo Institute.

One corner of the marketplace. It was under this street lamp (one of the few in town) that political discussions were held. Courtesy of Yivo Institute.

Szymek, the municipal policeman, on patrol. Note wall advertisement for "Kalodont," a toothpaste. Courtesy of Yivo Institute.

Naftali Saleschütz, 1925.

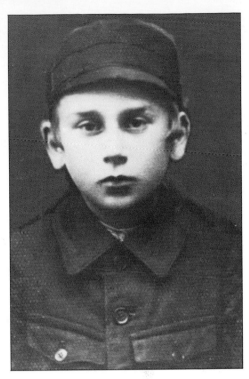

Naftali, 1929.

Naftali, 1937.

Naftali, 1939.

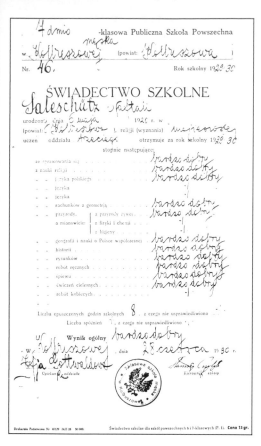

Report Card.
4th-grade Public School
       Boys
In Kolbuszowa   (County: Kolbuszowa)
No. 46   School Year 1929/30
SCHOOL REPORT CARD
Saleschütz   Naftali
Born on the 6th of May 1920
(County: Kolbuszowa), religion Jewish
Pupil of the third grade, receiving the report card
        for school year 1929/30
following grades:

Conduct		*very good*
Studies of religion		*very good*
"	" Polish language	*very good*
"	" math and geometry	*very good*
"	" natural science	*very good*
"	" geography and contemporary	
	Polish history	*very good*
"	" history	*very good*
"	" drawing	*very good*
"	" handicraft	*very good*
"	" music	*very good*
"	" gymnastics	*very good*

Number of missing (truancy) school hours 8,
     number of hours which were not excused -0-
Number of times arriving late (tardiness) -0-,
     which were not excused -0-
Average of all grades: *very good*
Kolbuszowa,   28th of June, 1930
Zofia Gottwaldowa   Stanislaw Przbyto
     Home Room Teacher   Principal

A melamed *and
his pupils.* Courtesy
of Yivo Institute.

Young men of Kolbuszowa standing in front of the synagogue. Courtesy of Yivo Institute.

The public school I attended. Courtesy of Yivo Institute.

My sisters standing in front of our store, 1935.

The famous well in the marketplace. Courtesy of Yivo Institute.

Lezer Nussbaum buying eggs from peasants on market day. Courtesy of Yivo Institute.

Peasant women shopping for ready-made dresses and skirts. Courtesy of Yivo Institute.

A village Jew arrives in town on market day with his produce. Courtesy of Yivo Institute.

Young girl leaving ritual slaughter with chickens. Courtesy of Yivo Institute.

Wagons crowd the area on market day. Courtesy of Yivo Institute.

In the market (separate from the main one) animals were bought, sold, and traded.
Courtesy of Yivo Institute.

Alter Horowitz, the Dzikiver Rebbe (with white beard), my father's spiritual leader, together with some followers, 1938.

Hazamir, Kolbuszowa's Jewish band, rehearsing. Courtesy of Yivo Institute.

At the Jewish cemetery. Avrum Polimer visits gravesite of a former rabbi of Kolbuszowa.

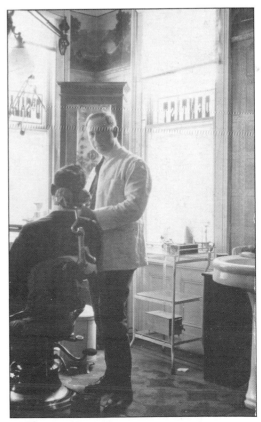

My uncle Max, the dentist, an American success story.

My brother David, a pioneer in Palestine.
This picture was taken in Tel Aviv in 1937.

My uncle Shulim and his wife, Esther, who
was the sister of the entertainer George
Burns. Shulim poses in front of a kosher
meat store to prove to my father that
kosher meat was available in America.

Rozia and Naftali, 1941.

Dr. Leon Anderman, 1930.

With my friends during the occupation, November 10, 1940. Front row, left to right: *Shmulek Weichselbaum, Noah Hutner, Meyer Orgel, and Kalman Kerenweiss ("Charlie"), our English teacher.* Second row, left to right: *Leon Gerstel, Naftali Saleschütz, and David Friedenrich. Note Star of David armbands.*

My nephew Henoch, left, and niece Blimcia in a picture I took on August 17, 1941, in the Kolbuszowa ghetto. Both were 3½ years old. Both were killed by the Germans in the Belzec death camp in July 1942.

Poles, Peasants, and Jews

U p to now I've spoken here and there about the relations between Jews and Poles in Kolbuszowa. A subject of such importance, however, deserves a closer look. For centuries we had lived together in Poland, had taken the measure of each other. What, then, was the result of all this contact? Where were matters during my years in Kolbuszowa?

Am I able to offer a fair picture? I would like to think so, but probably I'm deluding myself. My identification was clear. Never had I walked in another man's shoes or looked out on the scene as anyone other than myself. Certainly what I write cannot be separated from my experiences during World War II, when extreme conditions stripped away the restraints and conventions that had previously governed relations between Jews and Poles. But let me not offer excuses. In the end it is you who can judge the evidence and decide on my credibility as a witness.

In this small town of ours we lived together while we remained separate and apart. Practical necessities brought us into daily contact, but these encounters were specific and brief and rarely produced mutual understanding or respect. We needed each other, often complemented each other, and so there was reason for tolerance; but there was not much incentive for eliminating the barriers that separated us.

Poles dominated the government and administration of Kolbuszowa; Jews operated nearly all of the businesses. The Jews lived largely in and around the marketplace, the Poles in an area known as New Town. Most Poles were devout Catholics, and we Jews followed in the path of orthodox Judaism. Poles who were Catholic were automatically Poles; Poles who were Jewish were never referred to as anything but Jews. In look, in dress, in behavior, there was usually no mistaking the Pole and the Jew. Then, too, Poles all spoke Polish, Jews mostly Yiddish. Death brought a Pole to his final resting place in the Catholic cemetery in town. Jews were carried out of town to be buried in the Jewish cemetery.

Acquaintances among Poles and Jews were common, indeed nearly inevitable in a town the size of Kolbuszowa; but close friendships were practically nonexistent. Poles married Poles, and Jewish boys sought out Jewish girls. The one or two exceptions proved the point. Though my father had many Polish acquaintances from business, never were any invited to my sisters' weddings. Practically every Jew in town came, but not any Poles, nor was he ever invited to their celebrations. Organizations like the Scouts, the fire department, and the Kolbuszowa soccer team were exclusively Polish. No Jew in town had ever set foot in the Catholic church of Kolbuszowa; Catholic priests would not look at Jews, much less talk to them. Only on the rarest of occasions had a Pole been to the Jewish synagogue. Catholics celebrated their holidays throughout the year and Jews theirs, neither group much concerned with what the other was about.

On each side the separateness was seen as desirable. A coming together, a mixing—no one saw any need for it, any point to it. Best to let things stay the way they were. "We could be spoiled"— that's what Jews said would happen if we mixed with Poles. It could be threatening, could challenge the way it had always been. Certainly no Pole sought accommodation with us, made any effort to speak Yiddish or absorb any portion of our culture. Some Jews, not many, did attempt to move in the other direction. These were the modern men, professionals mostly, who wore their Judaism casually, if at all, and sought out friendships among the Poles. Dr. Leon Anderman was a notable example, at least until the Jewish crisis in Germany prompted a retreat.

Anderman and a few other men mingled almost exclusively with

Poles, were invited to their social gatherings, seemed to move among them with ease. But although they might not have noticed, even they were not really welcome. Poles had few kind words for traditional religious Jews, but they resented even more bitterly those who attempted to assimilate. These Jews were seen as threats, as people who, if they succeeded, would "penetrate" and "infiltrate," blur the line between Poles and Jews, a distinction considered absolutely vital to the maintenance of Polish peoplehood. There was a way, however, for these Jews to succeed in their efforts: conversion. The Jewish convert to Catholicism was more than just accepted into the fold. He was warmly welcomed, celebrated for his decision to reject his tradition and accept the Christian faith. Always Jews were stunned and shaken by such an event. Remember the impact that the conversion of Miriam G. had on her family and the community. Her name became synonymous with failure and tragedy.*

The ancient emblem of Kolbuszowa featured a handshake between a Pole and a Jew. It was not much noticed in my day, but it was intended once to symbolize the endless web of business and commercial connections that had always bound Poles and Jews. From the earth out beyond Kolbuszowa the Polish peasants brought forth food, while the Jews in town reached out across Poland for goods that they sold to the peasants. Each needed and depended on the other. Some peasants came to town almost every day of the week, but on Tuesday, market day, it was as if the entire countryside emptied into Kolbuszowa. Throughout the long day business was done, cash paid or produce exchanged for goods.

---

*[See pp. 189–90.] On the other hand, one of the supreme triumphs occurred when Dr. Marek Marienstraus, a recently arrived physician in Kolbuszowa, contemplated conversion to Catholicism so as to be qualified to assume the post of county doctor. The whole town knew that Marienstraus had visited the eminent and irascible lawyer Rabinovitz and asked him for advice. Rabinovitz, though not well-disposed toward the Jewish community, nonetheless dissuaded him from converting. Rabinovitz later had a heart attack and died the day the Germans invaded Poland, and some in town considered that God's reward to him. Surely, they agreed, Rabinovitz, a Jew, a lawyer, and a cripple, would almost immediately have been liquidated by the Germans. But because he had prevented a conversion, God watched over him, took him gently so as to spare Rabinovitz the pain he surely would have suffered at the hands of the invaders.

Poles almost always had their "Jew," a merchant or storekeeper whom they believed to be honest, whom they trusted. So long as that trust remained, the Jew could expect most of their business.

It is important to mention here the Jews who lived not in the larger towns but in the small villages among the peasants. They owned small stores and catered to the needs of their neighbors. It is probably true that between those village Jews and the peasants there existed, for a time, the strongest ties and the closest relationships that there were between the two groups. (Of interest here is the fact that town Jews tended to look down their noses at their brethren in the villages.) It is also true that the numbers of such Jews diminished throughout the 1920s and 1930s owing to a growing sense of isolation in the villages and increasing pressure placed on them to leave.*

After each market day Jewish middlemen spread out into the countryside, buying small amounts of farm produce that they sold to Jewish wholesalers in town. Poles with wagons and horses transported Jewish businessmen from town to town to buy goods and to sell their wares in the different marketplaces. In town Poles frequented Polish butchers and patronized Polish shoemakers, but most purchased from Jewish storekeepers, took their drinks in saloons with Jewish proprietors, and relied on Jewish lawyers, whom they acknowledged to be "clever." It was my father, for example, who supplied Catholic churches in our area with candles and other items used in various church ceremonies.

Economic ties created bonds that were long-lasting, if not deep, and were recognized as essential for the well-being of everyone in

---

*In the late 1930s, as noted earlier, peasants became better organized and grew more vocal and more active in defense of their interests. One result of this movement was the organization of peasant cooperatives and the introduction of boycotts against town merchants. To generate support for the peasant leaders' policies huge rallies were organized in the marketplace of Kolbuszowa, rallies attended by tens of thousands of peasants at a time. Jews in town worried greatly that the peasants would turn their wrath on them, especially as anti-Semitic sentiments spread throughout Poland in these years. What provided at least some small comfort to us was the fact that the leaders used my father's store as their headquarters on days when rallies were scheduled. Also they continued to purchase boycotted goods from my father for distribution to the peasants, making certain that these transactions were kept secret.

the region. But in business not everything went smoothly. There were complaints at times of overcharging, of all too frequent Jewish holidays when stores were closed, and of shoplifting and thefts by Poles.*

There were certain times when Poles and Jews came together in Kolbuszowa. When disaster hit, whether fire or flood, the relief committees were organized, both Poles and Jews did what they could to aid in the recovery. Jews (though they were not always welcome) participated in the celebration of Polish national holidays; a portion of the festivities took place in the synagogue, where the rabbi offered remarks on the occasion before an audience that included local Polish dignitaries. Always in the municipal government a Pole served as mayor and a Jew as deputy mayor. The municipal council was equally divided between the two. On the Kolbuszowa all-star soccer team were two Jews (from the town Gymnasium), probably the best two players on the squad.

In 1934 the town of Kolbuszowa responded in an unprecedented manner to the death of Jacob Eckstein. Eckstein, of course, was not an ordinary Jew. For many years, before his fortunes suffered at the close of World War I, he was thought to be the richest man in Kolbuszowa. More importantly, Eckstein had achieved prominence back in 1912: he had received a special commendation, a gold medal from Emperor Franz Josef, for contributing provisions to the Austro-Hungarian military during its maneuvers in

---

*We were no community of angels; no one group had a monopoly on mischief. Peasants colored their butter yellow, which drew a higher price, and added water to the butter to increase its weight. My father was especially fond of a story that to him indicated culpability on both sides. It involved a Jewish honey merchant who stopped to purchase honey from a peasant beekeeper. In order to keep track of how many measures of honey were delivered by the peasant, it was agreed that the merchant would place a penny on a handkerchief for each one, then pay a certain amount for each penny present. The peasant began bringing over the honey, and the merchant began placing his pennies. As they began to accumulate, however, the peasant was tempted, and soon enough he had placed several of them in his pocket. The merchant saw what was happening but said nothing, realizing that the missing pennies would be more than offset by the additional amount of honey he would not pay for. Who then was the thief, my father asked.

the region. He died on a Sunday in the middle of winter, and funeral plans came to a standstill when the way out to the Jewish cemetery became buried under deep snowdrifts. But the mayor came to the rescue by ordering fifty workers onto the road to clear a path to the cemetery. Out they came, and in relatively short order the burial procession was able to get under way. So eminent was Eckstein that no one thought it strange to see such extraordinary measures taken on behalf of the Jewish community.

In 1935 the death of Marshal Józef Piłsudski, the new nation's greatest hero, produced grief throughout the country. Towns across Poland staged funeral processions in memory of the fallen leader, and Kolbuszowa was no exception. What was unusual, however, was the specific invitation extended to the Jewish community to join in paying the town's respects to Piłsudski. Entering the procession were students of the Jewish schools; but it was even more of a sight to see my father marching along with scores of elderly orthodox Jews, a slow drumroll marking the beat. More surprising, all of them removed their hats in a show of respect. This affair was unique, the only one I can remember in which Jews and Poles participated as equal partners in an event of such national significance.

Sadly, the events I have just described were unusual. We Jews, despite having lived for centuries in Poland and contributed much to its development, understood that we enjoyed but a limited acceptance. We were not equal partners; we were at best tolerated by the Poles. I for one took this rejection very personally. Like my father I was a Polish patriot, spoke the language, enjoyed the literature, was proud of Poland's history. But that was of little concern to the Poles, who let me know in countless ways that I was not and would never be one of them. I was the killer of Christ, the "dirty Jew," the conniving Jew, the aggressive Jew, and later on, when Zionism awakened our interest in migrating to Palestine, the disloyal Jew. Jews could never be trusted.*

---

*I never understood, since Christ was a Jew, why the Jews never received the least credit from their Christian neighbors for having produced the "son of God." Around Easter every year a local society created a dramatization of Christ's

In my time all this became ever clearer once Poland became independent and was free to set its own policies and adopt its own style. Before World War I my part of Poland had been ruled by Austria-Hungary, and Jews looked upon those days as "the golden times" of Franz Josef, an era in which they enjoyed avenues to advancement in the universities, the professions, even the army, and freedom from anti-Semitic policies. After 1919 the atmosphere changed and restrictions increased. Jews, at least in Kolbuszowa, found themselves unable to alter the course of events and were disposed to let matters take their course.

We Jews tended to accept our place as second-class citizens; we tried to avoid giving offense or provoking an unfriendly Polish act. When Jews and Poles came together in an organization, the members of each group tended to keep to themselves. When it came time for discussion, the Jews never advanced their views forcefully; in fact mostly they kept quiet and allowed the Poles to take the lead. In the municipal government, a Pole always was mayor even though there were equal numbers of Jews and Poles in Kolbuszowa.* In a railroad car a Jew would not enter a compartment where Poles already were sitting, and would leave if it was made clear he was not welcome. Whatever form the abuse took the Jew was likely to accept it, to see it as the price of co-existence, to view it as confirming the need to stick to his own group and avoid involvement with the larger community.

To be a Jew in Kolbuszowa was to live with the knowledge that almost daily, at nearly every turn, one could encounter verbal, or worse, physical abuse. I have already spoken of the problem Jewish boys faced in public school; we were encouraged to sit in the back, singled out for ridicule, and physically assaulted, such as the time Mr. Wisniewski cut the *payes* of all the Jewish boys in the lower grades.

---

last days on earth that was performed in many of the Polish houses around town. Always present was Judas, dressed in the most unflattering and exaggerated manner as a Jew. Almost always Judas was attacked and beaten by members of the cast and the audience.

*There were probably a few more Jews in Kolbuszowa itself; but adjacent villages were incorporated into the municipality to avert the possibility of Jewish "rule" and assure a Polish majority.

Another incident involving Mr. Wisniewski goes to the heart of the matter. The occasion was the annual March 19 celebration of the nameday of St. Joseph, the patron saint of Marshal Piłsudski. A highlight of this day was always a show put on by certain public school students who were selected to participate. Oh, how much I wanted to be chosen, but it was almost unthinkable that Wisniewski, who produced the show, would allow a nine-year-old Hassidic Jew to perform during this most significant of national holidays. The show featured a special piece sung in honor of Piłsudski, a song that called for a sweet soprano voice. Many Polish boys auditioned for the part, but none was chosen. I stayed away, knowing I stood no chance. You can imagine my surprise when one day after class Mr. Wisniewski approached me.

"You will sing the Piłsudski tribute," he said. "Rehearsals are held three times a week after school." Quickly he turned away; no doubt he found my "victory" distasteful. I was astounded; it was too good to be true. Of course, my father thought otherwise. It was not fitting, he thought, for a Jewish boy to get involved in a Gentile holiday. Everyone else in the family, however, shared my joy.

For weeks we rehearsed after school. Mr. Wisniewski, who was to accompany me on the violin, was very polite and businesslike in his dealings with me. He confined his remarks to the music and my voice. I learned the words quickly and practiced the song diligently. There was little for him to criticize. Indeed he grew quite enthusiastic: "This will be the best part of the entire show," he assured me. The weeks of preparation were for me a joyful experience. It troubled me not in the least that I was the only Jewish boy scheduled to perform. Actually it made me feel superior to the others.

The night before the show I found sleep almost impossible. The next morning I awoke even earlier than usual, and at the synagogue prayed for God's blessings on my upcoming performance. My best Sabbath clothes were ready for me, including freshly polished shoes and a new shirt. My mother had cleaned my black velvet yarmulka with kerosene so that it gleamed with a bright luster. There could be no fault found with my appearance.

Too excited to stay at home, I headed over to the hall, which was decorated as I had never before seen it. White and red crepe paper, the national colors of Poland, covered the walls. Behind the stage hung a huge Polish eagle and alongside two large portraits: one of Ignacy Moscicki, President of Poland, and one of Józef Piłsudski, Marshal of Poland. Across the hall hung a large cross bearing Jesus.

The wait became unbearable for me as the audience began arriving at the conclusion of church services. The hall filled quickly, though very few Jews were there. The first two rows were reserved for the town's dignitaries. Finally the program began, and though I didn't think it possible, my heart began to race even faster. The speeches seemed like an eternity. All of us in the show were confined to a small dressing room next to the auditorium on the side of the stage. Mr. Wisniewski called each boy when it was his time to perform. Sweaty palms and stomach butterflies were the signal that my turn was drawing closer. I knew what I had to do, where on the stage I was supposed to stand, the direction I was to face. And then I heard my name called by Wisniewski, but as I started for my place he stopped me and directed me toward a partition standing out on the stage.

There was no time to question him, so I followed his instructions. What, I wondered, was happening. Why hadn't he told me about this? At the partition another teacher waited, then leaned over and said that this was where I would sing. I was in a daze. Why wasn't I allowed to go out in front of the audience? Had I done something wrong? Was there a problem with my appearance? My throat grew tight, my breath labored. They were ashamed of me, that's it; I was a Jew. I wasn't good enough to go on the stage in front of the audience. I began crying! I was only nine years old. Before I had time to think further and decide what to do, Wisniewski began to play, and almost automatically I began to sing, even as tears continued to well up in my eyes.

> Our beloved Pilsudski, Grandpa, as we called him.
> With his strong fist, he returned to us our dear Poland.
> We adore him everywhere, under a peasant's straw roof
>   and also in a factory . . .
> Let him live a long life, our dear leader.

All the time I was singing my confusion mounted. What could my mother and sisters be thinking as they sat there? What about the other people in the audience? I had no idea how well or badly I had sung or what happened during the rest of the show. When it finally was over, all my schoolmates rushed on stage to accept the applause. Only I remained in the small dressing room, my head bowed, overwhelmed by anger and a sense of injury. I had been betrayed by Wisniewski and the other teachers, my dignity stripped away. Never again, I vowed, would I trust them; never again would I feel I belonged in their world. Such was the burden of being a Jew.

I sat, my eyes downcast, until they all had left. When it was quiet I got up and walked slowly outside. My mother and sisters were there waiting. At first nobody said a word. Then my mother spoke: "Your song was the nicest part of the whole show. You sang out clear and loud." Her words made me despise them all the more.

With some care such humiliations could be avoided. But beatings were another matter. Throughout I have told you of the abuse and violence Jews faced at the hands of Poles. May 6, 1919, was a date no one in Kolbuszowa would ever forget, the day of the pogrom in which Jewish lives and property were taken in brutal fashion.* No more pogroms occurred, but physical bullying by Poles never ceased. At school Jewish boys could expect to be beaten up by their Polish classmates. In the evenings groups of Polish boys roamed the streets in the marketplace, forcing Jews to leave the sidewalk when they approached, stopping to thrash some now and then. When my friends and I played in certain areas of Kolbuszowa, we were always alert to the approach of Polish boys, who we knew would beat us up if we didn't leave when they arrived. Jews traveling the road to and from towns were never safe from groups of peasants who, for sport, would block and then overturn their wagons.

---

*[See pp. 23–24.] The Jews would not retaliate with violence of their own, but they were quick to inform the Poles of the contempt with which they regarded this anti-Semitic outburst. "What do you think this is, the 6th of May?"

At soccer games in town where the Jewish team faced the Polish squad, not only would the Polish players hit their Jewish opponents as hard as they could, but in the stands, among the spectators, Poles meted out the same kind of punishment to any Jews in attendance. When university students from the town were back home for vacation, it never failed that windows of Jewish businesses were broken. Always Poles were the aggressors, Jews the victims. With the notable exceptions that I have described [see pp. 134–35 and 236–40] Jews never fought back, and so the bullying by Poles went on from year to year until the Germans arrived to take over that job with unparalleled ferocity.*

Why were we treated so? What did we do to provoke such aggression? Were we at some level to blame? The abuse had become so much a part of our lives that we didn't stop to think about it or to ask these questions. We knew the usual explanations, of how the Catholic priests cultivated anti-Semitism among their devoted and loyal parishioners, of the age-old charges leveled at the Jews for killing Christ, and of the accusations that Jews enjoyed undue influence in the economy. There was nothing new in these accusations, nothing that had much to do with our situation in Kolbuszowa.

What I could see around me was something else. I could see Jews in long beards and black coats who looked different from the rest of the population and saw no reason to change that. I saw Jews whose forebears had lived in Poland for hundreds of years still speaking the Polish language poorly if at all. Still, if it is true that our people at times seemed distant and kept apart, when some had tried to cross over, had asked to be accepted, had they not been treated with contempt? Certainly some Jews had gained much in Poland, but had they not contributed out of proportion to their numbers and to the advantage of all?

In such discussions reason and reasons usually carried little

---

became the common way of rebuking Poles whom Jews saw as threatening and argumentative.

*Generally, as I have mentioned, Jewish girls were subjected to much less abuse. Indeed, there was a popular saying of the time that expressed this difference in attitude. "To hell with the Jew," it went, "but the Jewish girls we like."

weight. Few minds were open; emotions and long-standing prejudices prevailed, especially when anxious, unsettled times like the 1930s encouraged a search for scapegoats. Little surprise, then, that during the war far too many Poles were prepared to match the Germans in their unrelenting hatred and vicious treatment of my people.

I Never Tasted the Fruit

Certain exotic fruits rarely found their way to our table. That's why we considered it quite a treat one day in 1933 when my father ordered peaches—it was either from Czechoslovakia or Rumania—for the High Holy Days. They arrived and were judged an absolute delight, which is probably why I hit upon the idea of assuring a future supply for our family. I would plant the pits, I announced confidently, and in time we would have a stand of peach trees in our back yard. No one stopped me, but no one imagined there was the slightest possibility that it would come to anything. After all, no peach trees had ever been grown in our region. I was not in the slightest degree discouraged as I put the pits in the ground before the winter chills set in. Still, I'll admit I was surprised when the following spring there appeared a number of small plants, unmistakably the outcome of my bold experiment.

I made no effort to conceal my satisfaction and trumpeted my accomplishments far and wide. Still this was just the beginning; peach harvests lay well in the future. I lavished considerable care and attention on these young sprouts, making sure, for example, that in the frigid months of winter the roots were covered under a protective mantle of wood shavings. The years passed and several trees survived, growing taller, stronger, and fuller. Then in 1938 my labors were rewarded. One of the trees came of age and produced peaches—only three, mind you, and in no sense luscious-looking, but still I responded as if three were a bumper crop. But I would not taste them. Jewish law prescribed that the fruit of newly planted trees could not be eaten for the first three years.

Throughout the spring and summer of 1939 the trees grew nicely, and prospects for the fall seemed promising indeed. To my great delight a multitude of peaches appeared, one branch becoming so heavily laden that it broke. I learned of an ointment that could be used and applied it before I bound the cracked ends. Happily, they grew back together. But as the peaches ripened I became increasingly uneasy with the thought of having once again to abstain in accordance with Jewish law. Perhaps there was a way around it. With that hope in mind I approached my uncle "Rabbi" Saul, an acknowledged scholar, and asked him for an interpretation. A compassionate man, he understood my growing impatience. And he concluded that since leaves had appeared on the trees for over three years, it would be permissible to eat the fruit. You can well imagine how I watched and waited as summer turned to fall, the color of the peaches deepening, their skins softening. But one factor I hadn't counted on—the German invasion.

German troops occupied Kolbuszowa early in September and quickly became an established, threatening part of our existence. Whatever they needed, whatever struck their fancy, the Germans simply took. We were helpless; we could not oppose them. As luck would have it, the Germans discovered my peach trees; they entered my back yard and unceremoniously picked off every single peach. I was crushed. If there was any consolation, it was that the trees themselves remained standing. Maybe next year, I thought, but with all that was happening in Kolbuszowa who could tell?

Seemingly in defiance of all the ugliness and violence that descended on our town, the trees seemed ready to yield their biggest harvest ever in the summer of 1940. But once again I suffered a cruel fate. This time members of the German police discovered the trees, and even though the peaches had not yet ripened, plucked them all off. It was in vain that I begged them to wait, assured them that in a short time they could feast on luscious, ripe fruit.

Still the trees remained, determined, it seemed, to bring forth their fruit whatever the circumstances, to remain productive amid the destruction all around. In 1941 we were denied any hope of peaches; in June of that year the Germans forced us from our home and herded us into the ghetto. No longer could I care for my precious trees. The following year saw me confined in a labor camp, though still in Kolbuszowa. When that time of the year came, I passed by my old house. Sure enough, the trees were once again heavy with fruit, but my house was now occupied by strangers. I had no chance; I dared not enter. That was the last time I ever saw the trees I had nurtured years before with such care and high hopes. Years of waiting, years of hungering, had come to naught. I never tasted the fruit.

The Germans would in time strip us of everything, eventually even of our lives. We had no illusions when, over the inevitable static of one of the few radios in town, we heard that German troops had crossed the border into Poland. It was a war we knew we could not win. Even in Kolbuszowa that was plain to see, so clumsy was the mobilization, almost a joke. Whom did the Polish government call up and whom did they accept? World War I veterans, older men; not the young reservists, who would surely have given a better account of themselves. The younger soldiers, it was explained, were not needed immediately; they would be called up in time. But the real explanation was probably the one I got when, Polish patriot that I was, I appeared at the recruiting center, eager to enlist. "We don't have uniforms for our regular army," the recruiting officer laughed. "Where are we going to find one for you?" So here I was having failed to leave Poland for America or Palestine, unable to fight for my country, simply forced to stand by and watch as the invading Germans brought us to our knees.

The traffic through Kolbuszowa told the story. At first there was the rush of troops to the front, originally in trucks, then in wagons, on horseback, many on foot. But not long afterward the flow reversed; the army was in retreat. At first orderly, the retreat turned increasingly chaotic; units were dispersed, and soon everyone was on his own. Then came the looting, almost always of Jewish stores in town. The reason: "It is the duty of every patriotic

Pole to clean out Jewish stores," a Polish officer declared, "so that merchandise does not fall into the hands of the enemy."

And every day more refugees passing through, mostly Jews from the west, especially from Katowice, Cracow, and Tarnow, fleeing the German advance. Should we do the same, many in town asked them. Probably not, they answered, for by the time we were on the way we'd be overtaken by the Germans, Poland would have surrendered, and what would be the benefit? We listened to them—a grave error, it turned out. Had we fled eastward, into Russian-occupied territory, many more of us would have survived.

The war was just one week old when the first German tank, accompanied by a motorcycle, appeared in Kolbuszowa. Polish soldiers opened fire, killing the motorcyclist, forcing the tank to pull back. The following day the Germans returned in force. We hid in our cellars, listening with growing apprehension to the crack of bullets and the muffled explosions. In about two hours it was all over. Then we heard shouts: "Everyone outside! Everyone outside!" As we came out of our houses into the marketplace, German tanks and soldiers were everywhere. So were dead bodies, Poles and Germans alike, along with scores of dead horses. We were all ordered to raise our hands and keep them over our heads. We were to begin marching, they shouted. As we moved, a sea of upraised hands heading for the edge of town, the soldiers were already busy plundering our homes, piling up their booty outside on the sidewalks. In this manner did the German occupation begin.

No one doubted that the Germans would enter Kolbuszowa; still, it was a severe shock when they did. Then came a more crushing blow. Because of the death of some sixty-five Germans in the battle for Kolbuszowa, all of us, it was announced, would be burned alive. By the hundreds we cried, hugged, said our brief prayers, prepared for death. All through the night we waited, hands upraised, then into the next day. Still nothing happened. Even our guards grew noticeably bored. The order was revoked! You can imagine how we reacted to hearing this, having stood so close to the edge of death. The immense relief we felt was quickly tempered by the realization that we were still at the complete mercy of the Germans, a chilling prospect.

The Germans would be cruel and unrelenting taskmasters; that was made clear immediately, in unmistakable fashion.* The initial looting had been relatively mild, but it would continue without letup; each new contingent of soldiers sent to Kolbuszowa, each new commandant or group of high officials who arrived, did not hesitate to requisition and confiscate whatever they wished from our homes. Individual soldiers were also on the prowl. There was, for example, a police sergeant by the name of Schmucker who terrorized the town right from the start. Tall and powerfully built, he patrolled the streets accompanied by a German shepherd dog. At night he was his most menacing, knocking randomly at any door, thrashing anyone he encountered, and helping himself to whatever he wished inside.

Nothing served to restrain the Germans in their behavior toward us. Indeed, they exceeded all existing bounds of viciousness, so certain were they that we were a subhuman species, undeserving of the slightest mercy, having by our actions and attitudes, even our appearance, brought this destruction down on ourselves.† They toyed with us, humiliated us at every turn, tortured us and killed us without the slightest remorse. What was the provocation, you may wish to know? Nothing more than that we were Jews. That fact alone was sufficient to send our conquerors into a rage, so completely had they cast us out beyond the borders of acceptable society.

The local police force, which we called the "blue police" because they wore blue uniforms, were mostly young *Volksdeutschen* [eth-

---

*We learned that at the same time the Germans had entered Kolbuszowa they captured Mielec, a neighboring town. There they had driven a large number of Jews into the local synagogue, locked all the doors, and burned the building to the ground, killing everyone inside. Was this indicative of German intentions and plans for us? No, we said. It had happened while the fighting still raged. It was an act of war, we explained, that would not recur now that the Germans were victorious.

†Aside from the usual propaganda about Jewish guilt originating from the killing of Christ, the Germans charged us with being at the same time rapacious, bloodsucking capitalists and insidious, atheistic revolutionary communists.

nic Germans] from eastern Europe, people notorious for their hatred of Jews. Any Jew, they decreed, who passed a policeman had to take off his hat and greet him. But whenever an old Jew would do so, the policeman would spit in his face, grab him by his coat lapels, slap his face, and shout, "You cursed Jew, why do you greet me? Am I your friend?" But it was no better if the same Jew, later seeing another policeman, this time refrained from greeting him and taking off his hat. He received the same treatment, then was reprimanded: "How long does it take for you to learn that when you meet a policeman you must take off your hat and greet him?" We soon understood that our best hope on spotting a policeman on the street was to head off quickly in another direction.

At the beginning, however, we had precious little time out on the streets, thanks to a strict German curfew. We were allowed out only between 10:00 in the morning and noon, and then between 4:00 and 6:00 in the afternoon. These hours were strictly enforced; violators were dragged into the police station and fined. Under the curfew, life as we knew it no longer was possible.

Other humiliations followed. First we were forbidden to use the sidewalks; then it was decreed that outside our houses we were obliged to wear white armbands bearing a blue Star of David. We were responsible for producing these armbands and seeing to it that they were worn wrapped around the arm. A great variety of bands appeared, some embroidered in elaborate fashion. Intended as a symbol of our shame and degradation, they were transformed by some of us into something quite different. "Take good care of these armbands," I heard my mother tell a neighbor one time. "When the war is over and the Germans are beaten, we will edge these bands with gold thread and wear them on every Jewish holiday."

The Germans were not our only tormentors. All too eagerly did members of the local Polish population add to our burdens. The limited social relations between Poles and Jews built up over the years ceased abruptly. German questions about the whereabouts of all Jews in Kolbuszowa were easily resolved when Poles volunteered to point out each and every one of us. Debts owed to

Jewish storekeepers were forgotten, requests for payment ignored. Soon the Germans announced that Poles would be permitted to take over Jewish businesses in town simply by walking in, offering token payments, and ousting existing owners. At first most hesitated to do so, fearful perhaps of disrupting existing relationships, maybe uncertain about their ability to carry on the business; but only long-time Polish residents of Kolbuszowa had such doubts. Once the war began, there was an influx of Poles from other regions, and these newcomers, without any local ties, were less hesitant about stepping forward and claiming our businesses. Once they did, it was not long before local residents followed suit.

Were the Poles then selected out for favored treatment by the Germans? Let me not forget to mention that the Germans quickly rounded up those they thought might stir up opposition and serve as potential leaders. So Polish priests, teachers, university students, and officers in the reserves were seized and jailed. Many of them simply disappeared and were never heard from again. This accomplished, however, the Germans eased up on the Poles in and around Kolbuszowa, indeed favored them, certainly when compared to the Jews. Some were given administrative posts; nothing was said when German soldiers took up with Polish girls. And when it was time to press people into service for heavy, dirty labor, almost always it was the Jews; the Poles were usually spared.

A typical dirty job was given us in the days following the German occupation. Along many of the streets in town were the bodies of Poles killed in the fighting, along with scores of dead horses, their carcasses lying about everywhere. The Jews were ordered to rid the town of the dead horses, a task for which the Germans often selected the most frail or the most prominent citizens, beating them severely when they were unable to perform rapidly enough. Let me assure you, moving dead, decaying, heavy horses around was no simple task. Neither was digging pits large enough to accommodate all the carcasses. While the Poles looked on, this is what we were obliged to do. It was two months before we finished our work, which also included collecting unexploded shells.*

*All the Polish troops killed in the battle for Kolbuszowa had been buried

The Germans next selected certain Jews to be the street cleaners of our town, making certain that leading Jews, especially ultra-religious Jews with long beards, were assigned the more degrading tasks. There was Akiva Schmidt, for example, forced to carry heavy loads of water on his back for washing the streets. To humiliate us, to break our spirit—that was the German design.

It would be misleading to say we were abandoned by all the Poles. Some connections remained. Our store stayed open; we still did business with many of our regular Polish customers. A good many suppliers across Poland continued as before to send us goods and maintained a business-as-usual attitude. Expecting the worst when the war broke out, we, as well as others, hid as much merchandise as we could and also distributed goods among Polish acquaintances and storekeepers for safekeeping. Some of them, it is true, later denied accepting our merchandise and refused to return any of it. But others proved thoroughly trustworthy and honest; when called on, they returned what had been given to them. This was critical to the survival of some of us.

Few Poles, however, seemed aware of or were willing to talk of our mutual victimization; most preferred to accept the brutalization of the Jews as something separate from their own fate. That's what made the following conversation I had on one occasion so unusual. It was with a Polish woman, a widow named Kotulova, who owned a small grocery store and who for years had bought from us. "If only the Poles would realize that the Germans are no less our enemies than yours," she observed, shaking her head, "we would all be much better off. We would join your people and we would fight together. But the Germans are very clever. They succeeded in turning us against the Jews and getting us to help them destroy your people; then, when they are finished with

---

together in a mass grave in the Catholic church cemetery. The fact that Jewish soldiers had been so interred was deeply offensive to many of us. When Berish Bilfeld and Leib Lampel told the Germans of our distress, the authorities agreed that we could, if we wished, remove the Jewish dead to our cemetery. For two weeks that is precisely what we did, checking every body for identification (ID cards often indicated which soldiers were Jewish, as did circumcision). Altogether we reburied about fifty Jewish soldiers in the Jewish cemetery outside of town.

you, they will turn on us. They will kill many of us, and those that are left will be their slaves. But our people don't want to see this, so we all have to suffer. May God have mercy on us all." Sad to say, Kotulova's understanding of the situation was prophetic. Even later on in the war when Polish resistance forces in our area rose in some strength against the Germans, too many times they struck against the Jews as well. They saw no reason to join with us to fight the common, hated enemy.

Enemies there were also within our own ranks—not many, mind you, but with nearly everyone else against us betrayal by fellow Jews was all the more devastating. To call them "fellow" Jews is a bit misleading. Two of them were not originally from Kolbuszowa, and the third, though a longtime resident, had always been a disreputable and marginal character. Actually he had had some business dealings with my father going back to World War I, but there had been a falling out. That he developed a most unsavory reputation in town is barely surprising. What he did time and again was to serve as a witness in court for anyone for a price. You paid and you could then be certain that his testimony would support your case.

Would not such a man try to take advantage of the situation with the Germans in control? Naturally the Germans were willing to listen to him, interested in whatever information he might have to pass on. And when we saw him speaking to German police and going in and out of military headquarters, we understood that he enjoyed a privileged position. Naturally he was not shy about playing it to his advantage. He would look the other way, he said, when Jews violated German instructions—for a price. When, for example, the ritual slaughterers in defiance of orders continued to provide kosher meat to Jews in town, they had first to satisfy this man's demands for fear he would report their activities to the authorities.

When bribes had to be given to German officials he served willingly as an intermediary, taking a portion of the money as his "share." He warned of upcoming raids on our houses and seizures of property and persons, but suggested how, for a sum of money, all might be averted. We paid him, suspecting that most of the time no such raids were planned, that such talk was merely a device to line his own pockets. But who could be sure? What if we were wrong? So we paid off and, when he was gone, cursed him as if he were the devil himself.

He did, however, perform a major service for the town of Kolbuszowa, or so it seemed at the time. Only later would it be viewed in an altogether different light. The Germans gave the order that all Jews living within fifty kilometers of the River San, the border between the German- and Russian-occupied sections of Poland, must leave their homes and head east across the border.* We had five days in which to move, with hostages taken to assure our compliance. When word arrived, many of us began packing up our belongings. Some, including my family, had already traveled as far as Sokolow, a nearby town, fully expecting to head toward the San.

It's at this point that the informer went to work, handing out as bribes some 50,000 zlotys that he had been given by Jews hoping to avert the evacuation. This money helped convince a number of local authorities that a recalculation was in order, and it was decided that because portions of Kolbuszowa lay beyond the fifty-

---

*The Germans preferred at first that the "Jewish problem" just disappear, that Jews simply leave those areas under their control. The planned expulsion was but one example of such intentions. In this connection I should also mention certain notices placed in newspapers after the Germans arrived offering us the opportunity to leave for America so long as we had relatives there and could provide supporting documents. We were instructed to register by corresponding with a Berlin address and to forward a nominal amount of money for processing our request. It seemed to us legitimate, and so I and my sister Rachel and my sweetheart, Rozia, all registered. We sent our forms off to Berlin, responded to subsequent requests for further information, obtained registration numbers, and fully expected to receive clearance at any point. But then nothing happened. Naturally we waited and wondered, but eventually we gave up hope.

Later on I learned of exchange programs conducted by the Germans that allowed Jews under their control to leave in exchange for Germans living in other parts of the world, for example in Palestine or in South America, who wished to be repatriated. I even know of a woman and her two children from Rzeszow who were let out in return for Germans living in Palestine who wished to return home. (She agreed to carry a letter for me to my brother David in Palestine.) I also understand that the Germans later used such promises of exchange to flush out Jews who were in hiding. In time, of course, the Germans chose to remove the Jews in quite another manner.

kilometer limit the town was exempt from the order. There was much rejoicing over the reversal, and most Jews already on their way (my family included) turned back and returned to their homes. Others chose to continue on their journey to the Russian side. Who could know that many of them, unlike nearly everyone else who chose to stay in Kolbuszowa, would survive the war?

Regarding a second informer in town, Shmul Czolik, no one was likely to be surprised at his actions. Czolik was one of those itinerants who traveled from town to town begging. Kolbuszowa happened to be on his route, and in the years before the war we saw him about from time to time. It so happened that he met and married a girl from Kolbuszowa. Yet he remained a professional beggar, now supporting himself and his wife with the money given him. But Czolik's fortunes improved noticeably when the Germans came to town; however it happened, we soon discovered that he enjoyed close contacts with them. He wore no Jewish armband, and we could see him entering and leaving police headquarters on a regular basis. What a change for Czolik now, from a person who was barely tolerated to one who was suddenly courted, treated with respect. I noticed it even in the way my father spoke to him.

Czolik was a threat, and he knew it full well. With his access to the Germans, something practically no one else had, he enjoyed the upper hand. Often he arrived with confidential information, he said, about how the Germans were about to seize a certain person or confiscate a business. But he usually assured people that "something can be done." No one misunderstood his meaning. Money put into Czolik's hands usually meant an end to that "threat." He would then return and assure the intended victims, "It's settled." I don't know how many times he spoke of imminent "threats," but few dared question his inside information. That he terrorized the town for a time is certainly no understatement.

Then there was Pearlman, a thoroughly contemptible creature who also joined the ranks of the informers in town. Like Czolik, Pearlman came from some other place, but unlike him he dressed most stylishly and spoke only German; though Jewish, he identified his fortunes with those of the Germans. Many a time the story was told of how Pearlman exulted in public when the Germans conquered France: "Good news! We took Paris without firing a shot!"

The success enjoyed by all three informers was fortunately cut short when they overstepped boundaries and their bribe-taking and bribe-giving was uncovered by the Gestapo. Now the Gestapo could be fiendishly cruel, but it also could be rigidly moral when it uncovered what it saw as corrupting influences. Each of the three was at some point caught in a compromising position. Their past services to the Germans counted for little, could not save them from being executed. Their deaths freed us from a form of terror we had come to despise; but with all the other horrors about, their elimination brought no dramatic change in our condition.

The Germans sought to take our possessions, humble us, humiliate us, break our spirits, but they also came to recognize our value to them as workers.* There were the basic town services around Kolbuszowa that were needed, official headquarters and officers' quarters that had to be maintained, new structures and facilities that needed to be built and new roads constructed. The Germans established a daily quota of two hundred workers out of a total of about a thousand Jews who could do any work at all. Few volunteered, so the Germans were obliged to round up a daily work force. This produced a terribly disruptive situation, with the police and soldiers daily breaking into homes and Jews scrambling madly to get out of their way and hide. Often the hunt for workers went on for hours. The fear of being dragged out for forced labor was with us constantly. When finally the work force had been gathered, we were given pails and brooms, ordered to shoulder the brooms like rifles, then marched off to a place of work. Men and women, bearded patriarchs and young children, marched to-

---

*Though apparently it took time for this to sink in. For example, shortly after the Germans arrived, I and others from Kolbuszowa were taken away to a prison camp a good distance from the town, where we spent each day breaking up rocks and moving the debris from one location to another. This was just aimless labor, none of it productive. Fortunately security there was lax, and almost all the people from Kolbuszowa managed to escape eventually and find their way back to town and to their families.

gether; often they were ordered to sing Jewish songs while they paraded through the town. At the labor site the work was hard and beatings were frequent. Few were spared.

I wished to avoid the uncertainties of the daily roundup, and so appeared at a registration conducted by German officials for males between the ages of twelve and sixty. We were ordered to march around in a hall under the watchful eye of those in charge until they had selected those they considered suited. I was young (twenty), strong, and in good health, and so was picked. For several months I worked helping to build garages for the Wehrmacht, and also was engaged in some road construction. Having a "permanent" job like this was preferable to attempting to dodge the German manhunt every day. That is why many Jews volunteered for road work despite the hard labor involved.

Roads were being built in our area by Schtikel, a German company that was authorized to recruit Jewish workers. Each day their trucks picked up about a hundred workers in the marketplace and drove them out to the construction sites. Those who worked for Schtikel not only were freed from the daily terror of the roundup, but also received some food and a token payment. It was also an opportunity to get out of Kolbuszowa and a chance to mingle with peasants in the countryside, who were in a position to buy or exchange goods and to sell food.

My next job came in the fall of 1940. It was one that nearly ended my stay here on earth. As before, there was a registration at which numbers of the able-bodied gathered. We waited hours this time before the inspectors arrived. Then a group of SS* men led by an officer named Schmidt stormed into the building and immediately shut all the doors and windows. Amid curses and blows from their whips we were ordered to line up and await inspection in an adjoining room. When my turn came I was shoved in the back with a rifle butt and sent flying across the room. Everything went black. When I regained consciousness I was on my feet, being held up by two SS men while a third was slapping my face and telling me to wake up. Then I saw Schmidt sitting behind a desk.

*Schutzstaffel, an elite army unit.—RS

"Is anything wrong?" Schmidt asked.

"I am bleeding," I answered, immediately wondering whether I had said the wrong thing.

"So I see, so I see," he said in a pleasant voice. Taking out a clean handkerchief and handing it to me, he said, "Here, use this. Go ahead, don't be afraid."

I took the handkerchief and dabbed my forehead with it. Schmidt got up and walked around the desk in front of me. "Get down on your knees," he ordered. Three SS men were flanking me, watching my moves. I did as I was told.

"Now, shine my boots with this," he said, pointing to the blood-soaked handkerchief. Over and over I had to wipe my wound and apply my blood to his boots.

"That will do," he said at last. Turning to his men he added, "Put him on the list."

The list was the names of the men who were to be taken that day to Pustkow. I found myself on a truck, sitting next to my friend Noah. We arrived at the camp in the evening. Early the next day we were awakened and taken into an empty barracks, where our heads were shaven; we were then ordered outside to a central square and told to line up in four rows. In the center of the square was a gallows, a new rope hanging from the upper beam, a wide noose on its end. We stood there without making a sound, silently wondering what would happen next.

Schmidt finally appeared and had his assistant take the roll. Next Schmidt pointed to a man at the end of the second row and had him step out. He ordered a second man to do the same. The second man was then told to put a noose around the neck of the first. The man obeyed. "Proceed with the hanging," he then told him.

An air of grim unreality attended the entire procedure. A random, wanton murder was being performed before our very eyes, and we felt helpless to do a thing about it. No one, not even the man being hanged, uttered a sound or even made a gesture as they played out the macabre script. We were like robots. Surrounded by a heavy guard with machine guns, we could do nothing but stand and watch. The rope jerked, a gurgling sound came forth,

and before long a limp body dangled in midair. All day long, as
we worked in the forest felling trees, I saw that body in front of
my eyes.

When we returned from work, the terrible scene was repeated.
This time the man picked to do the hanging refused to do it. He
was a young man from Tarnow, with dark, defiant eyes. He stood
next to the gallows and refused to budge. Schmidt's face was con-
torted with rage.

"Get moving, you dirty pig!" he bellowed, the veins in his neck
bulging. The man remained glued to the spot.

"Take him away," Schmidt ordered his assistants.

Two SS men took him by the arms and dragged him away. As
they went past Schmidt, he called upon them to stop; with a sudden jerk he pulled out a knife and plunged it into the man's neck,
then quickly drew it out. The two SS men then resumed dragging
the victim, leaving a trail of blood along the way.

And so it went each day at the Pustkow concentration camp.
Each morning and evening the same hanging ritual, each day random killings by Schmidt, who would often shoot haphazardly into
a work party as it left for work in the morning. He once boasted
with pride that he could not sit down to breakfast in the morning
unless he had first killed at least one Jew.

We were all, it became obvious, condemned men; sooner or
later our turn would come. The only uncertainty was the method
of our execution. But a week later the first man escaped. He disappeared while we were working in the woods and was never
found. Taking heart from this, many of us planned our own escape. The next day, however, while marching to work, Schmidt as
usual fired his pistol into our ranks. This time a bullet hit my right
hand, went through the flesh, but luckily without touching a
bone. I tied the wound with a rag to stem the bleeding, and went
to work. During the day my fellow inmates did their best to help
me out, sparing me from the most strenuous work. I realized I
would not be able to hold an axe in my hand for some time, and
sooner or later the SS men watching over us would realize that I
was wounded and finish me off.

With the help of a man from Tarnow named Izio Kleinhandler,

a cousin of Rozia who had a position of some authority in the camp, I was able to transfer to another labor detail. Each morning we left the camp by truck to install telephone poles along the roads in the direction of Tarnow. It was hard work, but because there was no close supervision I was able to avoid using my right hand. I was also able to exchange valuables for food with peasants we encountered while performing our work. Truckloads of new prisoners were arriving daily in the camp, and the Germans, for the moment at least, were somewhat lax in guarding the Jewish laborers. Accordingly more and more of the contingent from Kolbuszowa were managing to escape.

Just when I was making my final plans for escape I injured my back lifting a telephone pole. I felt something snap; then I collapsed and couldn't get up. With the help of friends I managed to get to the truck and back to camp. One of the inmates, a Jewish physician, diagnosed my problem as a slipped disk. It would take a long time to heal, he told me; I would need to wear a support for my back. "You must run away," he insisted. With lame workers the Germans had little patience.

The next day, with great difficulty, and with the help of friends, I went back to work. Along with a man from nearby Dembica, who was also planning to escape, I abandoned my work post, set out for Dembica, and hid there. After a few days, still hardly able to straighten my back, I made it back to Kolbuszowa.*

Compared to Pustkow, Kolbuszowa was a paradise, thanks in large part to the heroic efforts of Dr. Leon Anderman, a physician who had practiced in Kolbuszowa before the war. He was an assimilated Jew, one who had never set foot in a synagogue and had never been associated with any of the Jewish institutions in our town. He was a Polish patriot who had served with distinction in the Polish Army, and for that reason was highly regarded by the

---

*Pustkow, it later turned out, in addition to being a notorious labor camp, was also the place where the Germans began their experiments with the V-1 and V-2 rockets. In an area so thickly forested, it was a simple matter to hide this operation; moreover, most of the work was performed in deep underground chambers. Work groups sent into these chambers always were killed after a certain time, then replaced, so as to ensure that the experiments remained secret.

leaders of the Polish community. Tall, broad-shouldered, dark, with strong features and an open, honest face, Dr. Anderman belonged to that unusual breed of human beings who, like the prophets of Israel, proclaimed high moral principles and subordinated their personal interests to what they knew to be the just and right cause.

About a year before the war broke out, Dr. Anderman somehow sensed the coming crisis. Terrible times were in store for his fellow Jews, he believed, and he became concerned about their fate. He could easily have run away, but he chose to stay in Kolbuszowa and cast his lot with us. In 1938, when German Jews were forced across the border into Poland, the Jewish community throughout Poland organized relief committees to help the refugees. Dr. Anderman joined the committee in Kolbuszowa. In this connection he made his first appearance ever in our synagogue. There I heard him deliver an impassioned appeal for funds for the hapless refugees. I liked him from the moment I first saw him.

In every Jewish community in Poland, large or small, the Germans appointed a Jewish Council, or *Judenrat,* shortly after they arrived. The Council was a puppet government that enabled the Germans to get what they wanted from the Jewish population with minimum effort. More often than not the Germans chose the less honorable and more pliable elements of the Jewish community for the Council, weak men on whose collaboration they could depend. In 1940 when the Germans came to considering potential members for the local Council, Januszewski, the Polish mayor of Kolbuszowa, prepared a list for them. The Germans then agreed to make these appointments. But Jews throughout Kolbuszowa took exception to these men and made strong efforts to have the composition of the Council changed. In the end the Germans agreed, recognizing that the new candidates put forth carried more weight in the community than those selected by the mayor.

After some discussion, the community leaders decided that the most suitable person for the office of president of the Jewish Council was Dr. Anderman. A delegation called upon him with the offer, which he at first refused. He would be no German stooge, he explained. But when it was pointed out that the Germans would no doubt appoint the mayor's unwelcome choices if he declined, he accepted. Anderman selected twelve Council members, among them my brother Leibush and my brother-in-law Szaja David, then took over as the first president of the Council.

Dr. Anderman's administration brought a measure of stability and confidence to the Jewish community. The task of providing workers was put in his hands. No longer would we be the victims of random kidnappings at any odd hour. The Council organized a system whereby each Jew took turns working for the Germans. Thus a settled, orderly plan produced a dramatic change in mood in Kolbuszowa.

Dr. Anderman's manner of dealing with the Germans was no less than awe-inspiring. Where other Jews stood in fear and trembling, almost incoherent, before their overlords, he was cool and composed. One time the Germans asked him for a hundred workers to chop down trees. There was no way, he replied, to get so many axes. The Germans made it clear, however, that if he did not comply, the whole community would suffer the consequences. When the SS officer in charge returned to Kolbuszowa, Dr. Anderman presented him with a hundred men, mostly teen-age boys.

"Here are your men," the doctor reported in his typically unperturbed manner, "but I am afraid they cannot do the work."

"Why not?" the German snapped.

"Because they have no axes, and without axes you can't chop down trees."

"Is that so?" the German replied in mock surprise. "Then let me remind you, Herr Doktor, that in the German Reich, under Hitler, everything is possible."

"I am sorry," Dr. Anderman rejoined. "You are asking me to do something I can't do."

The German was furious. "And what would you do," he shouted, "if I ordered all these Jews to be hanged?"

"Nothing, I suppose. Your hangman's the one who will have a great deal to do."

The German walked away in a huff without saying a word. Later he ordered the group to disperse, and he left town. For twenty-four hours the community lived in fear and dread. The doctor, it was felt, had gone too far this time; we would all have to pay a high price. The following day a German truck came roaring into the marketplace. Dr. Anderman was immediately summoned by the police. When he arrived, he was told that the Landsrat had sent him a supply of axes for his workers. That evening, in all the Jewish homes in Kolbuszowa, and even in the surrounding villages, a toast was offered in honor of our brave doctor.

Again and again Anderman took the lead, showed us what we must do. On the day the Germans issued an order forbidding the Jews to use the sidewalks, Dr. Anderman promptly went out and walked in the street, a message to Jews to obey the order strictly. He did the same when we were forced to wear an armband with the Star of David. He walked with his head lifted, making a point of showing that he was proud to wear the emblem of the Jewish people.

On one occasion four Gestapo men came to Kolbuszowa and demanded from Dr. Anderman a list of the richest Jews in the town. Dr. Anderman informed them, "There are no rich Jews in this town." He was pressed to give a few names nevertheless. He then wrote something on a piece of paper and handed it to the Gestapo man, saying, "Yes, there is one rich Jew in Kolbuszowa, and here is his name." When the officer in charge unfolded the paper, he found Dr. Anderman's name on it. Without saying a word, the four men got into their car and drove off. Another time a truck with SS officers came to the Jewish Council and asked Dr. Anderman to point out some Jewish homes where they could obtain good furniture for their headquarters. He took them to the poorest Jewish homes, where they could find only the most dilapidated, broken pieces. This was the best he could do, he told them, since Kolbuszowa had always been a poor Jewish community. Next he took them to his own house to prove that he was the only Jew in the town with enough money to buy new furniture. They went away empty-handed.

Returning home after my escape from Pustkow, I offered to assist Dr. Anderman in the free clinic he had opened. He agreed to teach me to wash and dress wounds, administer medications, and perform other tasks normally undertaken by a doctor's assistant. At the same time I did what I could to keep the family business going, traveling to other towns for goods as I had done before the war and taking advantage of our many peasant contacts to obtain additional supplies. After the initial shock of the German occupation and the brutalization that followed, we recovered and adjusted to the new conditions. Life was by no means normal— we were all forced to make do with much less, even those who had had little to begin with—but for many it became manageable, especially with the measure of stability brought about by Dr. Anderman and the Jewish Council. It was even possible at first to hope that we could wait out the war in this way.

Also giving us a measure of hope and some sense of control was the efficacy of bribes. Nearly all the German authorities accepted them; our task was to direct the bribe to the proper person, someone we hoped might then cooperate, although some simply pocketed the money and did nothing. Bribes worked best in gaining the release of people who had been jailed. Opportunities were greater in the early days of the occupation. In those days all of us still had money, and with families intact, funds could be raised when a member found himself in trouble with the authorities.

Bribery apart, here and there contacts were established between Jews and Germans. Not all the Germans were vicious, unapproachable beasts. My brother Leibush, for example, remained on friendly terms with a German commandant who each time he returned from Germany brought items for my brother to sell for a share in the profits. Then there was Lazar Spielman, a refugee from Germany, who prepared official reports for a certain German policeman who could not write German well. But such connections were few, and they in no way altered the overall picture. Most Germans had been taught or trained to despise us absolutely, to consider us subhuman, to subject us to the grossest of humiliations, and to snuff out our lives for any reason whatsoever. Lazar Spielman's policeman, for example, let it be known in an offhand comment that he was sure at some point he'd kill me. On one occasion I tried to broach the subject with him as casually and as playfully as possible. "Would you do harm to me?" I asked him. "Why not? You're a Jew."

Wartime conditions, together with the many troops in the area,* ushered in a new economy that brought benefits to the enterprising. Some took to manufacturing soap, and a brisk business developed in imitation tea produced from roots. Homemade liquor also proved popular and profitable. Many businessmen had managed to hide substantial amounts of goods from the Germans; when prices soared, they were able to sell these goods most profitably. As I mentioned, many of our suppliers continued to ship their products to our store. Those products, together with the goods I acquired from my travels, kept our business going.

The Jews generally defied the authorities by continuing to hold religious services. It was just a matter of avoiding detection. The Germans saw to it that many of us were put to work on Saturdays and that special projects were scheduled on Jewish holidays. Still, many were able to maintain Jewish observances and attend clandestine services on a regular basis. But others, myself included, saw the new conditions as an opportunity to set aside, if not eliminate, certain religious observances we considered onerous. Before the war such behavior might have brought down on our heads the wrath of our families and neighbors, but under the occupation the "relaxation" could be excused. My friend Noah Hutner, once a most observant Jew, explained it to me this way: "When the war is over and I am still alive, I will become an observant Jew again. Right now I follow just one *mitzvah* [commandment]: "And thou shalt choose life." My friends and I did what we could. We met together as often as possible and attempted to keep our spirits up, assuring each other that the dark days would pass and speculating about how we might kill Germans if we got the chance. Rozia and I drew very close in these days; the barriers that had once sepa-

---

*This was before the German invasion of Russia in June 1941. Often when I rode my bicycle from Kolbuszowa to Rzeszow I passed through forests in which enormous amounts of military supplies were stored just off the road. The thick cover of trees made this a perfect location for stockpiled supplies.

rated us and kept me silent were easily ignored. We held each other and prayed that there might be better times ahead for us.

Despite a certain stability locally, the overall situation had worsened. Our hopes for a German defeat were dashed by developments on the battlefield. The German Army, to judge from newspaper accounts, was everywhere on the move, the Allies faltering on all fronts. Our darkest moments came when we realized that the Germans might actually win the war.

One day Dr. Anderman told me he had heard from a reliable source that the Germans were about to send a Gestapo chief to our town, from which he would administer the region. This was bad news because each new top official always felt it necessary to demonstrate just how tough he could be on the Jews, and because the person picked for the job was one of the most infamous Gestapo men in our area. His name was Twardon. The authorities in Rzeszow were debating whether to send him here or to nearby Strzyzow. Dr. Anderman remarked with a bitter chuckle that he had gone to Rzeszow to bribe German officials to send Twardon to Strzyzow, only to encounter an emissary from Strzyzow who hoped his bribes would steer Twardon to Kolbuszowa. In the end the choice was left to Twardon, who, as luck would have it, chose Kolbuszowa.

The following week Herr Landscommissar Twardon arrived in our town. He immediately summoned all the members of our Jewish Council and those of some neighboring small towns. My brother Leibush, who attended the meeting, described what happened. Twardon he described as evil personified. He was half German, half Polish, and combined the worst traits of both nationalities. He was in his mid-thirties, short and fat like a barrel on legs, with a bulldog face, two small, piercing eyes, a shiny, clean-shaven scalp, and a grating, shrill voice. First he announced to all assembled that unlike other Germans, he meant business; everything would have to click. Then most ominously he observed that Jewish lives meant nothing to him.

Without wasting any time, he issued his first decree; all the Jews of Majdan had to evacuate the town within twenty-four hours and move to Rzeszow, where some hovels had been prepared for them. That day he dispatched a contingent of Sonderdienst* to round them up. About 80 percent of Majdan was Jewish. It was not long before we saw a caravan of horse-drawn wagons full of Jews going through the main thoroughfare of Kolbuszowa on the way to Rzeszow. It was a ghastly picture: hundreds of Jews evicted without notice, heaped like garbage on high wooden wagons, children screaming and crying, women fainting, men with eyes full of despair, old men mumbling their prayers.

I was home with my mother, inside our house, when the caravan came through the marketplace. The wagons had halted to regroup. My mother and I went outside and stared at the woeful scene. Her eyes filled with tears, and I heard her murmur to herself, "Those poor souls, they have no food and no clothes. They will die of hunger and cold in a few days. We must do something to help."

She went back to the house and returned with a basket of bread. I offered to carry the basket for her, but she insisted on doing it herself. I followed behind her as she walked over to the wagons. Just then a Sonderdienst man with a riding crop approached my mother, demanding to know what she was doing. She pointed to the bread and then to the wagons. The man's face turned crimson. He lashed at the basket with his whip, striking my mother's knuckles and forcing her to drop the basket. My mother drew back and looked in anguish at me over her shoulder. I had clenched my fist and was about to pounce on the man, but my mother placed herself between us, clutched my arm, and whispered to me not to do anything foolish. At that moment it took more courage to do nothing than to do something; my mother, of course, was right.

It was just a matter of time before what happened to the Jews of Majdan would happen to us. Almost everyone agreed that this was so. We were beginning to understand the larger pattern. Jews from small towns like Majdan were being sent to larger towns like Rzeszow, where they were concentrated in one area with little or no means of subsistence. All those expelled Jews of Majdan soon died of hunger and cold. Those few who had gone into hiding

*Forces auxiliary to the SS, consisting of ethnic Germans.—RS

were turned in by local peasants and shot. Majdan thus became one of the first localities in Poland to become *Judenrein* [empty of Jews]. Twardon's accomplishments were cited in German newspapers and he received a citation from Himmler himself. Twardon's action, it later became clear, was part of the master plan to confine Jews in ghettos and from there ship them off to the death camps.

Twardon had promised Dr. Anderman that the Kolbuszowa Jews would not be sent away. We heard this with great relief; doom was forestalled, hope was not yet lost. But our relief was short-lived. His promise was not forty-eight hours old when, in the middle of the day, two army trucks arrived in the marketplace. Some hundred SS men jumped out and rounded up the Jews who lived in the immediate area. Everyone had to turn over his keys. Twardon, who personally supervised the operation, declared that all Jewish homes around the market were now the property of the German government. Our home was among them. My entire family was taken to the marketplace along with the other Jews who lived in the area. At the last moment, as the Germans were coming into our house, I ran out through the back door and hid at Rozia's house. Later in the afternoon I found out from a Polish neighbor that the evicted Jews had been loaded on wagons and were being taken to Rzeszow.

The road to Rzeszow passed by Rozia's house. We waited in the house for the caravan to pass by. An hour later the wagons appeared, escorted by armed SS men. We could make out the people in the wagons, the unmistakable pain and fear in their eyes. Respectable Jewish citizens were suddenly transformed into destitute prisoners being driven to an unknown fate. On the last wagon I saw my entire family, huddled together, silent and forlorn. Even the little ones were quiet. I had every intention of jumping out of our hiding place to join them, but Rozia held me back. "Don't be a fool, Naftali. You can't do any good by joining them." Instead Rozia went outside and signaled, letting them know that I was safe.

As the wagons disappeared behind the hill I began to cry. I seldom cried, but this time there was no holding back. I lay on the floor, face down, and wept until my bones ached. After I was too tired to go on crying, I got up and trudged back to town in the dark. I reached our house and let myself in through a door in the roof. I knew it would be the last time I could enter my house, so I proceeded to pack up all the valuables I could carry away with me, including all the money and jewelry that my father had hidden in several places in the house. All this the Germans would not get.

Twardon, it was now clear, had planned to establish a ghetto in Kolbuszowa from the beginning. The evacuation of the Jews from the market area was part of the plan. In their place the Germans now planned to house another 1,100 Jews there. When Twardon made this plan known to the Jewish Council, Dr. Anderman responded that as a physician he could not allow it because of the extreme hazard of epidemic; indeed, the whole idea was simply not feasible. Realizing that Dr. Anderman was right, Twardon devised a way to make things fit. Without any forewarning he proceeded to round up several hundred more Jews from the market area and send them away. Now the ghetto plan was feasible!

The order was given for all Jews to move into the ghetto within forty-eight hours. The ghetto in Kolbuszowa consisted of a few meandering alleys, densely populated with Jews of little means, on which were situated the old synagogue, the Beth Hamidrash, the public bathhouse, and a few other Jewish institutions. Into these cramped quarters an additional seven or eight hundred Jews were forced to crowd.

Moving to the ghetto was no simple matter. Everyone wanted to relocate as quickly as possible, fearing that those who lagged behind would not find a place to live. No means of transportation were available. Jews were not allowed to enlist the aid of Polish peasants, so old and young were forced to carry their possessions on their backs. The alleyways leading to the ghetto and inside it became so choked with people that it took hours to go back and forth. Men and women were seen carrying old beds, cupboards, trunks full of cloths, blankets and pillows wrapped in bedsheets. Everywhere goose feathers poured out of down pillows and featherbeds and filled the air like snow.

The transfer of belongings that had taken generations to acquire was done in such haste that the scene produced a mix of tragic and comic overtones. The poverty of most of the Jews was inescapably evident. But everything that could be carried was taken into the ghetto. The old schoolteacher was lugging his school bench, the only tool of his trade left to him; Basheh, the lady baker, was dragging boards for making bagels; Naftali Nessel and his sons carried between them a heavy stand for splitting logs. People were seen carrying pails for drawing water, crates full of coal, broken mirrors, rusty ovens, old wagon wheels. Everything imaginable was brought in, with no one taking the time to figure where all those things were going to be kept. In reality most items had to be left in the street, where they cluttered the way until they fell apart or in some cases were put to use as fuel.

By Saturday night all the Jews were packed within the ghetto walls. In every house in the ghetto, including the synagogue and the Beth Hamidrash, several Jewish families were thrown together. Altercations and squabbles were inevitable. Dr. Anderman and the councilmen tried their best to settle these disputes and establish some order. But clearly Dr. Anderman was discouraged, realizing Twardon would probably not stop here.

"We are in trouble," he told my brother Leibush, "because Twardon lied to us twice, once when he sent the people to Rzeszow and the second time when he ordered us into the ghetto. If someone lies to me twice, I won't believe him the third time. Now I have to deal not only with a murderer and a sadist, but a liar as well."

During the day Twardon came to the ghetto. He saw Dr. Anderman and the councilmen scurrying about trying to put a roof over everyone's head and rearranging quarters in an effort to please as many people as possible. Twardon stopped Dr. Anderman and inquired if he had picked an apartment for himself, since, as the Council's president, he rated a choice place. Dr. Anderman replied that he would choose an apartment for himself only when all the others had a place to live. Twardon walked away without a word.

Later the same day Twardon returned to the ghetto with some

of his henchmen and arrested twenty-six Jews, including nearly all the councilmen. Everyone looked to Dr. Anderman to arrange their release, but the following day he himself was arrested. The community mourned deeply the loss of their leader, a man who had been like a father to them and who had fought so bravely in their behalf. They were left frightened and helpless. A delegation from the Polish community actually went to Twardon to request Dr. Anderman's release, testifying about how honest and trustworthy a person he was, respected by Jews and Poles alike. "This is precisely why I had him arrested," Twardon replied. "He's too honest for my liking."

Dr. Anderman was later sent to Auschwitz. He never returned.

The creation of the ghetto in Kolbuszowa marked a critical turning point. Life, though hardly normal before, now turned markedly bitter; the struggle for survival became sharper, its outcome far from certain. The crowding at times reached intolerable proportions, food supplies were sharply curtailed, and the overall level of brutality rose. We were being squeezed mercilessly. It soon became difficult or impossible to think of anything much beyond day-to-day survival.

Still, my family and I managed. Well-placed bribes had succeeded in getting them back from Rzeszow, and together my mother, my father, my two single sisters, and I occupied one room in the house of my brother Leibush in the ghetto. A new Jewish Council had been appointed—consisting of men with hardly the stature of their predecessors, but still conscientious men, not stooges—and had called on me to travel, as I always had, outside Kolbuszowa to acquire food supplies that would then be allocated to the ghetto's residents. This gave me the chance to transact a little business on my own and kept my family from the suffering that afflicted so many others.*

---

*Unlike the ghettos that were established elsewhere, especially in the large cities, ours was not completely cut off from the outside world. The side of town facing the river was open, and the homes of many Poles stood close by the ghetto quarters. As a result some trade, some circulation of goods, continued, though the Poles, recognizing our predicament and our desperation, made us pay dearly for what they supplied us. I should not forget to mention the day a "miracle"

By the spring of 1942, with the ghetto already about eight months old, the situation in Kolbuszowa had become desperate. The stench of death was everywhere. People were dying of starvation; others were being shot for grasping for a morsel of bread. The chief executioner was Twardon himself, always on the lookout for someone he could himself kill. A week before Passover, he shot Itchele Trompeter, one of the best-liked young men in our town. Itchele had married a girl from Rzeszow, and had gone to live there shortly before the war. He used to commute to Kolbuszowa, to see his parents, who helped him out with food. One day he was going home with some food when Twardon spotted him. He stopped the wagon to see if Itchele had smuggled anything forbidden. He found a pound of butter, shot Itchele on the spot, and ordered the wagon driver to take his body back to Kolbuszowa. That night the entire ghetto cried.

On Passover Eve four Gestapo men went to the neighboring town of Glogow and dragged the four most distinguished leaders of the Jewish community from their homes. All four were old men with gray beards. The Germans tortured them all day in public, making them crawl and lick their boots, humiliating them in countless ways. One German set fire to the rabbi's beard, and another took pictures of him lighting his cigarette from the fire. Toward evening the four Jews were ordered to climb telephone poles. After struggling for a time they were shot, one by one.

Passover, the Festival of Freedom, was not celebrated in Kolbuszowa that year. No matzohs were baked; no one recited the story of the exodus of Jewish slaves from Egypt. Worse, Hitler

---

package arrived for us in the ghetto! It was from Turkey, and it left us totally puzzled. Who could have sent it? Inside was a dazzling, incredible assortment of items worth their weight in gold: Swiss cheese, salami, chocolates, olive oil, coffee. We treasured each one, divided it up with extreme care. After the war I learned that it had been sent by my brother in America. (It cost him $15.) He did not send any more, he said, never having received any acknowledgment or indication that it had been delivered. In the ghetto we still received letters from America up until Pearl Harbor. They were cut open and most likely reviewed by a censor. We also sent letters to America, trying in as many ways as we could to tell people there what was happening to us in a manner that would not arouse the suspicion of authorities in Poland, who we knew would not let incriminating correspondence get through.

was approaching his fifty-third birthday and rumors had it that the Nazi Party had promised him a birthday present—half a million dead Jews. Each town had to deliver its quota of victims. One German policeman in our town—we called him "Morris"—dedicated himself to the task, cutting a notch in his rifle stock each time he killed a Jew. His ambition was to have fifty-three notches in time for Hitler's birthday, and he did not fall short. The rifle with the fifty-three notches he sent directly to Hitler. In return he received a medal and a letter of commendation praising him for his devotion to a noble cause.

Every day new demands were made, each more severe than the day before. Furs, Persian carpets, jewelry, and gold had to be furnished on short notice. Pashek Rapaport, the new president of the Council, was made personally responsible by Twardon for seeing to it that these demands were met. The townspeople would groan and complain, but in their hearts they knew that Pashek had no choice. If the demands were not met, Pashek and his councilmen would be shot along with many others.

The day after Passover Pashek summoned fifteen of the community leaders, my father included, to inform them that Twardon considered it a personal embarrassment to have so many Jews with long beards in the town; all beards must now be shaved off. To a pious Jew like my father, shaving was a violation of Biblical law. In his entire life my father had not cut off even one hair of his beard. When the barber came to our house, he sat at the table, mute and somber, his face pale and sagging. After the barber left, my father remained silent a long time. "Now I have felt the taste of death," he muttered as he got up from the table.

That my father's lifelong faith in God was shaken is clear. Some part of his confusion was revealed when he questioned one of the most respected scholars of our town, a cousin and close friend of my father whom we knew as "Rabbi" Saul. He was a man of great learning and could easily have qualified as a rabbi, but he was too modest to want the title and preferred to remain a layman, using his wisdom and erudition for heaven's sake rather than worldly honors.

"Tell me, Saul," my father began. "I consider you a *tsadik* [a learned and righteous man]. Granted, we cannot question the Almighty, His ways are kept from us, but we still have to ask ourselves what is going to become of us, what is going to become of our people. The sword has been unsheathed, yes, and many will die. But if the Germans kill all of us, and none remain alive, what will become of the Holy Torah, the Holy Sabbath, and all the Commandments? Will they die, too—is that possible?"

We looked at my father in amazement; we had never heard him question the ways of the Almighty, even by inference. Nor could we imagine what "Rabbi" Saul's reaction would be. "Rabbi" Saul cleared his throat to speak. He looked sadly at my father, who looked away from him—sorry, I think, that he had spoken as he had.

"You are right to ask these questions, Itche," "Rabbi" Saul began. "Without the Torah the world cannot exist. The Torah can exist without the world, but the world cannot exist without the Torah. Now the Holy One, blessed be He, wants the world to exist, as He told Noah, and He will not permit the destruction of His people Israel, as He promised Jacob. 'A thousand may fall on your right, and ten thousand on your left, but you will not be harmed.' Unfortunately, evil is powerful, and many of us will fall. But in the end evil will lose. The Germans, may they burn in hell, are already spread too thin. They will lose this war; the only question is how soon. In the meantime they will kill many of us, but they will not be able to kill the Torah, no matter how hard they try. The Torah is the word of God and is stronger than any human power.

"The real question is not whether we will survive as a people; we will. The real question is how will the Gentiles be able to expiate their guilt for what they are doing: not only the Germans, but the Poles, the Ukrainians, and all other nations that helped and stood idly by while we bled. And how will those of us who survived be able to live in the same world with people so full of guilt? For as long as the guilt weighs on them, we will suffer, too. And so it will go on for a long time after we are gone."

About three weeks after Passover, while our family was having lunch at Leibush's house, there was a sudden pounding on the door. We knew it was the Germans. We also knew they were after the men, so we quickly bolted the door on the inside while the men ran out through the back door. There was an outhouse in the back yard, and Matil told my father to hide there; she would put a padlock on the outside, hoping to create the impression that no one was inside. Leibush and I went to a neighbor's house across the yard and hid in the attic. From there we could view the street and the back yard. Two Gestapo men had been at the front door. Unable to force it open, one of them went around several houses, then entered the back yard through a gate.

By now we could hear shooting and screaming coming from other parts of the ghetto; a raid was on. My sister Matil came into the back yard again. Thinking my father would be safer somewhere else, she unlocked the outhouse. But just at this moment the Gestapo man who had come around the back saw them and ordered them to stop. My father, asked for his name, mumbled out a different one. By this time the other Gestapo man had forced the door and entered the yard dragging Israel Hofert, a neighbor, by his sleeve. He asked Israel to identify my father, which he did. Both drew their guns and started to push my father into a shed that was used to store firewood. My sister Matil screamed, and threw herself between my father and the Germans. Then Rachel came out of the house, pleading with them to spare his life. They made no reply.

I was paralyzed. I wanted to shout, but I couldn't. I wanted to get up, but I couldn't. I looked on as if in a trance. I saw Racnel trying to wrest the gun out of the hand of one of the Germans; he struck her over the head and she fell. Matil tried to seize the other man's gun; the first man struck her, too. While this man was struggling with my sisters, the other was shoving my father into the shed, out of view.

I heard two shots. They were the loudest sounds I had ever heard in my life. Even to this day they continue to ring in my ears.

After the shots I heard screaming and shouting, then my father's voice. The two bullets had wounded him, but he was still alive. "Pigs! Executioners!" he screamed. Then, "Nekuma! Nekuma! Nemt nekuma!" [Revenge! Revenge! Take revenge!]. Then he called out the prayer of the Jew in his last moments: "Hear, oh Israel, the Lord is our God, the Lord is one." Five more shots rang out, then silence.

I had to go down. Leibush warned me not to, but I insisted. At the shed I saw my father, lying in a pool of blood. His right arm was almost severed from his body. The women and children of the family were there, caressing him, their tears falling on his body. My little niece Blimcia, with her curly blonde hair and blue eyes, was crying, not sure what the commotion was about. I stood there consumed with shame for having been so helpless, for seeing my father murdered, unable to save him and not even trying.

Three days after the slaughter the same six Gestapo men appeared in Kolbuszowa, prompting a renewed panic. But this time their intention was not to murder but to extort. They came with a list of special items to be provided, including furs, silk stockings, leather gloves, wool fabric, canaries, and other luxury items that could no more be found in the ghetto than at the North Pole. Well-to-do Poles could provide them, but for these items the Jewish Council paid dearly. Included in the list of demands was compensation for expenses incurred during the recent slaughter, including even the cost of the bullets! By nightfall everything was paid for and delivered, and further bloodshed averted.

It was only a momentary respite. The Germans were playing with us. Like condemned men we awaited execution, not knowing exactly when it would come. I wanted to live, for my father's sake and for my own sake, but mostly I wanted to be present when the tables were turned, when the arrogant, "all-powerful" Germans would be defeated, humbled.

The Council, fearing that all who remained might be deported at any time, attempted to avert what was in effect a death sentence. If people in the ghetto performed vital services for the Germans, it reasoned, they would be less likely to be deported to the death camps. So the entire ghetto was mobilized, and a cooperative workshop was set up in the synagogue. All the local trades were represented, including cobblery, bookbinding, tailoring, and tin-smithing; there was also a workshop to produce lingerie. Jancze Rapaport, a brother of the Council's president, was put in charge of the entire program. All available sewing machines were collected, and anyone with the slightest ability was put to work. And so men and women, young and old, pedaled or hammered away all day, making clothes and boots for the Germans, promised nothing but ever hoping to survive. At first this strategy seemed to have the desired effect. After a special committee came from the German district office in Rzeszow to inspect the workshops, it announced that the workers and their families could remain in Kolbuszowa. Indeed, an employment office with a German director opened at the Town Hall, and my sister Rachel was selected by the Jewish Council to be his secretary.

Then in June 1942 the Council was summoned by Dr. Ehaus, the chief German administrator of our district, to come to Rzeszow for an important meeting. Eight other councils in our area were similarly summoned. At the appointed time Dr. Ehaus walked in briskly. Without asking anyone to sit down, he started to speak.

"Good morning, Jews. I am pleased to inform you that you Jews are dirty and full of lice, and that you have been spreading contagious diseases throughout this district. Therefore I have decided to levy a special tax on you, which comes to the following amounts: Rzeszow, 1 million zlotys; Sokolow, 400,000; Blazowa, 260,000; Glogow, 260,000; Strzyzow, 360,000; Tyczyn, 200,000; Czudec, 200,000; and Kolbuszowa, 360,000."

The funds had to be raised in one week. The councilmen were to assemble at the same place with the money in hand. Should any community not fulfill its quota, a proportional number of its councilmen would be shot. Pashek knew what it would take to raise such a sumn, but he was convinced that Ehaus meant what he said. After much quarreling and complaining, the Jews in Kolbuszowa were forced to sell more of their remaining possessions, and the full amount was raised.

Leibush was present when the money was delivered and told me what took place. Kolbuszowa was the only community that raised its full quota. Rzeszow, for example, was 25 percent short, and Ehaus ordered 25 percent of its councilmen to step aside. The same procedure was followed for the other communities. Then all of the condemned men were led to the back yard of the district building, lined up against the wall, and shot.

When this had been done, Ehaus went back to the room where the surviving councilmen were assembled and read a new decree. All taxes that any Jew owed to the government, for the twenty-eight years from 1914 to the present, must now be paid in full. If the debtors were deceased, or had no means of paying, the Jewish Council would become responsible for the money. Again just a week was allowed, and the same punishment was prescribed for failure.

Pashek estimated that the full amount would come to about 200,000 zlotys. He gathered those Jews who still had merchandise hidden away and black marketeers able to raise respectable sums of money, and ordered them to produce half that amount. For the other half he would turn to the rest of the Jews in the ghetto, most of whom were nearly destitute.

Pashek's estimate was far off the mark. The manager of the local tax office dug out musty ledgers, covered with decades of dust, from the Town Hall cellar. They listed taxes going back beyond memory. A detailed itemization was prepared showing taxes owed by Jews who had been dead a quarter of a century; by Jews who had emigrated years ago; by Jews who had fought with the Austrian Army alongside the Germans during World War I and had been killed in action.

In the end the total amounted to almost 900,000 zlotys, which had to be raised within a week. Pashek exhorted the Jews to make this one last desperate sacrifice. It was, he assured them, the final test. If we passed this test, we could hope to survive the war. It was a staggering amount, but if everyone did his utmost, it could be raised. Few believed him; most understood we were buying time. After threats and a few beatings the full amount was raised, and the councilmen returned to Rzeszow, their quota met. The scene there was much as it had been the previous week. Wherever the quota had not been met, a proportional number of councilmen were shot.

Then Ehaus delivered the worst decree of all: within three days, all the Jews in the district had to leave their homes and resettle in the ghetto in Rzeszow. We did not know it at the time, but Rzeszow was the last stop on the way to the death camps. Barely able to catch our breath from raising over a million zlotys, we now had to start packing for the trek to Rzeszow. Like the Israelites at the time of Moses we were to leave in haste, but unlike them we had no Promised Land. A year earlier our moving into the ghetto had produced a pathetic scene. Now it was worse still. We were going into the unknown, torn away from all that was familiar and to that degree comforting. The sick and the elderly despaired of surviving the change, even the trip itself. When I went to say goodbye to my old Hebrew school teacher, Chaimche Birnbaum, who was a cripple, he told me, "Don't wish me a good trip, Naftali, for I know I will be among the first to die today."

My family decided that all except me would leave for Rzeszow on the first day of deportation and do their best to get settled there, and that I would wait for the third day. In the interval I would take whatever possessions they were forced to leave behind to certain friendly Poles for safekeeping in the event we came back.

Most of the Jews left that first day. The police opened the ghetto gates, shouting "Faster! Faster!" By afternoon the wagons had been loaded, not with people, but with their possessions. The people, regardless of age or health, had to walk on the right side; German and Polish police walked on the left. Occasionally a German policeman would allow a child or an old person to ride for a time on the wagons, but not the Polish police. They were determined to exceed their German masters in severity toward the Jews. The next day the wagons returned to evacuate most of the remaining population. The ghetto gates remained open; thousands of peasants descended on the houses, removing the last sticks of furniture and whatever else they could find. To give this looting an air of legitimacy, the Germans had posted the head of the Jewish police at the gate, where he collected a pittance from each peasant for what he took.

I spent the night in the ghetto, sleeping in the same house with the few men who had waited until the last day of the evacuation to leave. In the morning I packed my knapsack with provisions for the hike to Rzeszow. Before leaving, I took a stroll around the empty ghetto. It looked like a ghost town. Broken windows, gaping doors, feathers flying through the air with every gust of wind, clouds of dust stirred up—only the ghosts of the many who had lived for generations in these old, tumbledown quarters remained. I walked down the path to the synagogue, which my father and his father and his father's father had trodden nearly every day of their lives. The ground was packed tight and hard as a rock, as firm as their abiding faith in their maker. Why had this happened? I looked toward the old synagogue, but no answer came. There was not much time to meditate. The wagons were lining up, and we were hurried along. Guarded by German and Polish police, we marched to Rzeszow.

The ghetto there was far worse than we had encountered before. Thousands of Jews from surrounding towns and villages had been crammed into the already crowded ghetto; there was no possibility of finding living quarters for all of them. Those like my family who had relatives in town somehow managed a few square feet for themselves. Others remained in the streets, entire families camping on the sidewalks and in the narrow alleys, packed so close together that it was impossible to cross the street without stepping on someone. Lost children roamed about looking for their parents; desperate mothers cried out for their offspring. Everywhere I turned I saw eyes filled with exhaustion and despair.

After much searching, I found my family, now living in the cellar of a relative named Spitz. Everyone was sitting around, dazed and in despair. I tried to cheer them up by mentioning the valuable merchandise I had left with friendly Poles, but nothing dispelled the gloom. Yet what we had experienced was not nearly as disastrous as events in other communities. In Sokolow, for example, Twardon, dead drunk, announced he was going to kill thirty Jews. The Jewish police brought him thirty sick and elderly Jews who were already near death. Twardon personally shot them; after each execution he washed his hands, downed some more vodka, and kept shrieking, "Blood, more blood! Give me Jewish blood!" Then he turned on two women and killed them, and after them two teen-aged girls. When he was through, forty-nine corpses lay on the ground.

We were all exhausted. After a meager meal we went to sleep. The next day we heard that Twardon was in Rzeszow looking for a hundred able-bodied men to return to Kolbuszowa to demolish all the buildings in the ghetto. Pashek was to draw up the list. Not too many were willing to go and risk leaving their wives and children alone. Most of the volunteers were single. Leibush and I decided to go back, hoping to use our contacts there to obtain food to help feed our family. My sisters accompanied us to the place of assembly, everyone suspecting that this was not an ordinary farewell. Nothing was said, but all wondered: Would we ever see each other again?

We marched during the night, each with a knapsack on his back. In the morning we reached Kolbuszowa, where we were quartered on the synagogue compound, or—as it became known—the Kolbuszowa Labor Camp.

While we were busy destroying the houses of the former ghetto, the SS and special "death squads" were busy in Rzeszow destroying our families, sending some off to the death camp at Belzec, killing the rest with machine gun fire in a specially prepared area outside of town. Shortly before my family was taken away, my mother sent a letter to Leibush and me. Never will I forget those words. "I don't know what will become of us. We will, it seems, share the fate of the whole community. But you, Naftali, are young and strong, and your duty is to live. Don't let orphanhood break your spirit. Stay alive, and when the war is over, let the world know what the Germans did, what kind of murderers they are!"

Our families were gone. Many of us wished we had stayed with them. After we finished razing the ghetto we expected Twardon would probably dispose of us, too. But we were young, the instinct of living took over, and we threw ourselves into our work. We had been there two days when Twardon appeared. He lined us up against the synagogue, counted us, and lectured us briefly. If we did our work, we would have nothing to worry about. But if we tried to escape, ten men would be hanged for each one who escaped. He appointed Yankel Lampel, who had served as a sergeant in the Austrian Army, as our drill commandant. He gave Yankel a hat that the Jewish police used to wear, and a toy pistol to carry. He was ordered to line us up every morning for a brief drill, then to march us to our place of work. In the evening, our work completed, we had to march back, shouldering our spades like rifles. Yankel did as he was ordered. Twardon in fact became quite pleased with us: we were his private little army. This he found amusing.

One by one the ghetto houses came down. Hundreds of years of Jewish life were being destroyed; what had been passed on from father to son and from mother to daughter was reduced to rubble. From the attics we tossed out cradles in which our great-grand-parents had slept from the time they were born until they became toddlers, and which had then been handed down through the gen-erations in each family. We came across items attesting to the pov-erty of the Jews who had lived there, people so poor that nothing was ever thrown away. Kneading troughs, dented brass tubs, washboards, old rusty buckets, moldy barrels, broken crates, clus-ters of branches used in the steam baths, decrepit wrought-iron stoves—old junk, yes, but also an extension of ourselves. As each item crashed to the ground, throwing up clouds of dust, our hearts wept.

The most heartbreaking thing of all was the destruction of the holy books. Even for someone like myself, hardly pious, it was terrible to see those old volumes—which had been accumulated over centuries, for torn or worn books were never discarded but were stored in the attic of the synagogue—desecrated, tossed aside like junk. Because of the shortage of paper during the war, the Poles had helped themselves to many of these books: using the pages for wrapping paper, converting the parchment on which the Torah was written into slippers and shopping bags. Once when I stopped at an inn, I was shocked to see a Jewish book in a wash-room serving as toilet paper. It was a volume of *Mesillat Yesharim* [The Path of the Upright], by the eighteenth-century mystic Moses Hayyim Luzzatto, a book I had once studied and revered as one of the finest books I knew on Jewish ethics.

After we tossed everything we could out of the houses, we be-gan taking apart the walls, the roof beams, the shingles, and all other structures. We came across coins and other valuables hidden by the inhabitants in the hope of returning one day. Some of us took these; others refused, fearful of being caught and shot. From the accumulated trash, items were sorted and put in separate piles. There were piles for brass, paper, lead, and so on.

The house next to the synagogue was used as a warehouse to store this material. In one of the rooms books had been placed. One day I entered this room accompanied by an SS man. Hundreds of books were stacked on either side of a narrow aisle. Located at the end of the aisle was a high window, through which a shaft of sunlight penetrated into the darkness, illuminating the motes of dust in the air and forming a square of light on the floor next to me. Could this shaft of light be the pillar of fire that the Lord sent before the Israelites to lead them in the desert?

The German must have had a similar thought. He placed himself in the square of light, looked up at the window, and shouted, "Jehovah, Jehovah, where are you?"

Silence.

"Jehovah, Jehovah, why do you not help your children?"

Silence.

"You see," the German said, looking at me with his bloodshot eyes, "your Jehovah is too old. He is so old he has become completely deaf, and he can't hear a thing."

He spat on the floor and walked out. I was certain that God was in the shaft of light and would punish that murderer. But nothing happened.

By fall, when the razing of the ghetto in Kolbuszowa was completed, the Germans employed us in other odd jobs, many along the river. But with fewer and fewer such projects left for us, our elimination seemed to be just a matter of time. How else explain the fact that the wood collected from the demolished houses was made available only to the German and Polish population? None of it was put aside for us.

For hour after hour we discussed the choices open to us. Henrik Mund and Yossl Rapaport, who were directly responsible to the Germans for our actions, counseled against any action. The Germans, they argued, would certainly foil any escape attempts, and torture and death would follow. Better to die painlessly, they advised. Leibush and I insisted that an escape attempt could succeed. The forest, where other Jews were known to be, would shelter us. In time we might join the underground, fight the Germans, and avenge ourselves.

Opinions were evenly divided, and the more we debated, the more obvious it was that they would remain so. Those who opposed escaping had their reasons. Some were not in good health, others were no longer young; some did not have the stamina, others lacked the courage. Some spoke no Polish; others were afraid that their appearance would betray them. The decision to try to escape or not usually turned on whether a person knew a friendly Pole who would be willing to hide him. Escaping in itself was no problem, since we were not guarded. The problem was finding a place to hide.

I now remembered Kotulova, the Polish widow woman whom I had visited just before I left Kolbuszowa to stay with my family in Rzeszow, and with whom I had left some belongings and merchandise. Her house was right behind the fence that surrounded the ghetto. I resolved to see her at once. After nightfall I left the camp without telling anyone, not even my brother. I climbed over the fence and knocked on Kotulova's door.

"Pani Kotulova, I have to run away. I need false papers, and I may need a place to hide."

"I will help you," she said.

"Where can I get papers?"

"I'll have to talk to the priest."

"Do I know him?"

"You should. Monsignor Dunajecki has been our parish priest for nearly twenty years."

"Yes, I know of the Monsignor."

"He has all the birth records of the parish, and he may be able to give you the birth certificate of someone who died during the war."

"I had a friend in grade school, about my age, who was killed at the front in 1939. His name is Tadeusz Jadach. Maybe I could use his birth certificate."

"I'll see what I can do. Come back tomorrow night."

"Thank you, thank you for everything. God bless you."

When I returned the next evening, Kotulova gave me something more precious than gold: the birth certificate of Tadeusz Jadach, a Roman Catholic Pole. With that paper I could start a new life; with that paper I might survive the war. I put my arms around the ample frame of my saving angel, and hugged her until she protested she couldn't breathe.

"I will be indebted to you as long as I live," I told her.

"You would have done the same for me," she said.

"Just one more thing, my brother Leibush; I need a certificate for him. Could you possibly get one for him, too?"

"I'll talk to the Monsignor."

The next day I had a birth certificate for Leibush: Ludwig Kunefal. As she handed it to me, she mentioned that the Monsignor wanted to meet Leibush and me. A few days later we went to her house to meet the Monsignor. When we saw him, neither of us knew what to do or say; we had never in our lives spoken to a priest, and we were overwhelmed by the man's appearance. He was tall and majestic-looking, with an inscrutable face. We stood there embarrassed, but he quickly realized our discomfort and extended his hand to us in greeting.

"I am Proboszcz Dunajecki," he said in a warm, disarming voice. "I am pleased to meet both of you."

We shook his hand, after which our hostess invited us to share some food she had prepared for us. Soon we were immersed in lively conversation.

"I would like to suggest something," Father Dunajecki said after we had been chatting a while. "You, Tadeusz, you speak Polish like a Pole. But Leibush's Polish is a dead giveaway. I would suggest that Leibush not use the certificate that I have made available to him. You don't have to decide now, but think about it."

We told him we would reconsider. As it turned out, we realized that the Monsignor was correct; we never used that certificate.

With Leibush in the other room talking to Kotulova, the Monsignor and I began to talk. The priest grew pensive.

"You know, Tadeusz," he said, "I have been a priest here in Kolbuszowa for nearly twenty years, and I have never gotten to know a single Jew. I have never had any dealings with any Jewish organizations, and I have never had the slightest idea what was going on in the Jewish community. I have never even met your rabbi. Now, in view of what's happened to the Jews here, I deeply regret not having made the effort to know your people better. What's most upsetting to me is the thought that I could have saved scores of Jewish children by placing them among my parishioners; it would have been an easy thing to do. But no one said anything to me, and I myself have been remiss in neglecting what was going on under my very nose. I can't tell you how sorry I am."

I could tell he was really sincere. I didn't know how to respond. He was blaming himself, but who really was to blame? As we were about to leave, he shook our hands and wished us luck. Then he made the sign of the cross over us and bade us goodbye.

We spent the next two weeks urging the men in our camp to prepare to escape. Repeatedly Mund threatened to turn us in to the Germans, but we ignored him. Time was running out; why sit by idly and await destruction? We were determined to go, no matter how many or how few joined us. And then one day it happened. According to a contact, the Polish police planned to surround the camp later that night and remove us all. Whether we were to be executed or taken to a concentration camp he did not know. I had no reason to doubt his word.

Back at camp this new information convinced fifty-five men that it was time to escape. It was November 18, 1942, and winter was setting in. Each man packed a knapsack with warm clothes, food, and other necessities. An almost unbearable tension filled the air. We were going into the unknown, either to start a new life or to be caught and promptly shot. How, I wondered, had the children of Israel felt on the night they fled Egypt?

One by one the men left. I kept counting them, and with each departure I felt more encouraged. The plan was working. I decided to be the last to leave. We had agreed that in a few weeks all those who had escaped would try to establish contact and join together in the forest.

I had prepared a knapsack to take with me, filled with food, medicine, clothes, money, jewelry, and most precious of all, a diary my sister Rachel had kept from the day the war began. As soon as Leibush left, I decided to take the knapsack to Kotulova's house and then come back. It would be comforting, I thought, to know that my possessions were safe, and I would not be encumbered by the knapsack when it was my turn to leave. I threw the knapsack over the fence, jumped over, and ran up to Kotulova's house. I asked her if I could leave it in her attic, explaining that this was the night we were escaping.

At about 3:00 in the morning, two lookouts informed us that Polish police were surrounding the area. But by this time, I and Leiser Spielman, who was to escape with me, were the only ones prepared to leave who were still left. We waved goodbye, and exited at the far end of the synagogue. From this point we had to cross a street, then dash to a warehouse. As we crossed we were stopped by two Polish policemen, one of whom I knew.

"What's going on?" I asked him.

"You can't go anywhere," he said. "You're surrounded by German police on the other side of the street."

"We have to go, anyway."

"You can't."

"Why not?"

"We're not supposed to let you."

"In that case, just look the other way and pretend you never saw us, and we'll be out of your way."

He wasn't sure what to do, and looked to his companion questioningly. I grabbed Leiser's arm and we made a dash for the warehouse. Once inside, we walked to the opposite end, and peered through a window. The street was full of German policemen, one of them with two dogs. A searchlight scoured the street from one end to the other.

"We have to run across the street to the outhouse over there," I told Leiser. "We have to go one at a time."

"You go first," said Leiser.

"*You* go first," I replied. I figured that if I were shot he would not be able to make it, since he knew no Polish and had nowhere to go.

"No, you go first," Leiser insisted.

"Very well," I said. "I'll go first."

I let myself out the window and crawled across the street to the other side. When I reached the outhouse I heard shots, but I could not stop to look around. I got into the outhouse and waited there about ten minutes. Leiser never came. I could hear shouting in German, barking, shooting; then the noise receded into the distance. When the sounds seemed far enough away, I bolted from the outhouse to the ghetto fence, jumped over, and ran to Kotulova's attic, where I dropped to the floor exhausted.

For years before the war I had tried to leave Kolbuszowa. Now I had escaped and, for the moment at least, saved my life. Never would I return.

A Jewish Boyhood in Poland: Remembering Kolbuszowa was composed in 11/13 Galliard on a Merganthaler Linotron 202 by Brevis Press; printed by sheet-fed offset on 60-pound, acid-free Glatfelter Natural, and Smyth-sewn and bound over binder's boards in IGC Arrestox by Braun-Brumfield, Inc.; with dust jackets printed in 2 colors and laminated by Braun-Brumfield, Inc.; designed by Kachergis Book Design of Pittsboro, North Carolina; and published by Syracuse University Press, Syracuse, New York 13244-5160.